THE COMPLETE
AMERICAN REVOLUTION
ROAD TRIP GUIDE

ALSO BY MICHAEL WEEKS

*The Complete Civil War Road Trip Guide:
More Than 500 Sites from Gettysburg to Vicksburg*

THE COMPLETE
AMERICAN REVOLUTION
ROAD TRIP GUIDE

*More Than 500 Sites from
Lexington to Yorktown*

Michael Weeks

Countryman Press

*An Imprint of W. W. Norton & Company
Independent Publishers Since 1923*

Copyright © 2026 by Michael Weeks

All rights reserved
Printed in the United States of America
First Edition

For information about permission to reproduce selections
from this book, write to Permissions, Countryman Press,
500 Fifth Avenue, New York, NY 10110

For information about special discounts for bulk purchases,
please contact W. W. Norton Special Sales at
specialsales@wwnorton.com or 800-233-4830

Manufacturing by Lakeside Book Company
Production manager: Devon Zahn

Countryman Press
www.countrymanpress.com

An imprint of W. W. Norton & Company, Inc.
500 Fifth Avenue, New York, NY 10110
www.wwnorton.com

Authorized EU representative: EAS, Mustamäe tee 50, 10621 Tallinn, Estonia

978-1-68268-299-9

10 9 8 7 6 5 4 3 2 1

*To my wife, Charlotte,
for her unending love and support
and
to all those fighting
to preserve America's history*

CONTENTS

Introduction	ix
How to Use This Book	xi
Important Things to Remember When Visiting Revolutionary War Sites	xviii

PART 1. ORIGINS: THE REVOLUTION IN THE NORTH — 1

1. The Head of the Serpent: Boston and the New England Colonies	3
2. The Fourteenth Colony: Quebec	93
3. Routes of Invasion: Upper New York, Vermont, and New Hampshire	137

PART 2. FORGING A NEW NATION: THE MIDDLE COLONIES — 197

4. Retreat and Redemption: New York and New Jersey	199
5. Capital of America: Philadelphia	285

PART 3. THE FINAL BLOW: THE REVOLUTION IN THE SOUTH — 345

6. A New Strategy: Georgia and South Carolina	347
7. War and Remembrance: North Carolina, Virginia, and Washington, DC	423

PART 4. THE SHOT HEARD 'ROUND THE WORLD: THE WIDE-RANGING WAR — 489

   8. The American Revolution on the Frontier — 491
   9. The World War — 517

Acknowledgments — 543
Bibliography — 545
Index — 549

INTRODUCTION

THERE'S NO BETTER WAY to learn than through experience. It's easy to read about the American Revolution—there have been thousands of books dedicated to its battles, its personalities, its politics, and its impact on history. But none of these books (including this one) can take the place of seeing the landscape, walking the paths, and communing with the ghosts of the people who made this war a defining moment in world history. Anyone can read about the encampment at Valley Forge. But when you stand there, looking at what little shelter they had, imagining a harsh winter with no food, you not only better understand the scenes that played out on these hallowed grounds, but you also begin to ask the really important questions. How did they do it? Why? Using all your senses to experience history brings the facts together and helps them sink in. It involves you wholly, and you learn in a way that no book, no photograph, and no map can teach.

This book will help you get to those places where you can experience the Revolutionary War in a way that no history book can. It takes you to all the most important sites of the war—whether remnants of the war still exist or not—and helps you understand why they remain important. It will help you learn more by seeing and feeling, and hopefully it will deepen your understanding and inspire you to see more. When you're ready for that, this book will help you get to those places, too.

This book is going to give you guidance on what to see. It lays out the best ways to see the most critical sites of the war. But it doesn't stop at the Saratogas and Yorktowns. It visits the places that might not be so legendary today, but were just as important—places like Quebec, Brandywine, and Kings Mountain.

In addition to the battlefields, action took place in hundreds of other sites and places. In some cases, only a sign or roadside memorial remains. In others, there's no memorial at all. But that doesn't mean that it's not worth visiting. Some of these places exist in absolutely unspoiled country, and with a little information, you can re-create the entire scene in your mind without distractions or interruptions. Yes, some of them are now under water or have become parking lots for shopping centers. But if you're interested in a certain general's battles or following a campaign, you might want to see every place on the map. This book will help you get there and know what to expect when you arrive.

It also explains why you might want to see these places, and why they're important, without presenting a lengthy history lesson. How much you want from your experience is your decision. Some people drive to the edge of the Grand Canyon, look in awe for five minutes, and are satisfied. Others will feel like they're missing out if they don't learn the name of every rock formation, study the geology, hike down to the bottom, and camp for three days. You'll learn enough to get there, know what you're seeing, and why it matters. What you do from there is up to you.

A final note: One of the reasons that I wrote this book is to increase visitation at *all* the sites, large and small. The more awareness there is about them, the more likely they'll receive funding for improvements and the creation of new visitor experiences. When you go, let people know why you came. Stay and have a bite to eat, talk to some locals, and show them that preserving history in their backyard brings dollars into the local economy. If you live in one of the locations noted in this book, but little to nothing exists to indicate the history that took place there, I hope that you will be inspired to raise your voice, tell your community, and join or start the preservation efforts. There's still much work to be done.

HOW TO USE THIS BOOK

WHERE TO BEGIN

Lots of essential guides to the American Revolution focus on one particular site, providing great detail, while others cover a small area or region. This book is different. The chapters are organized into recommended tours, all of which can be done in a weekend or a long weekend (three to four days). The tours will take you to the most important sites of the war. How much time you spend at these sites is up to you. You can pick which to see and which to skip. This book aims to give you all the options so you can tailor your trip(s) to exactly what you want.

BEFORE YOU GO: PLANNING YOUR TRIPS

There are a couple of resources online that can add a lot to your experiences.

- *Journal of the American Revolution*'s "The 100 Best American Revolution Books of All Time"—This resource is a curated catalog compiled by the Journal of the American Revolution, and it provides the best information sources you can find on the Revolutionary War. The catalog is split into five broad categories—all-in-one histories, the origins of the revolution, people, politics, and conflict and war—and within each of those categories you are sure to find a title that has what you're looking for. Need more information about the Stamp Act or Paul Revere's ride? How about women in the Revolution, or Native Americans? What about the United States Navy? This catalog has you covered. You can find it online at www.allthingsliberty.com/2017/03/100-best-american-revolution-books-time.

- *Report to Congress on the Historic Preservation of Revolutionary War and War of 1812 Sites in the United States*—This 2007 official report, commissioned by Congress, is a sobering assessment of the great danger facing the integrity of our nation's history. It is a government document, and you have a right to a copy of it. The entire report is accessible online through the National Park Service, www.nps.gov.

Each chapter of this book begins with mini-biographies of people who feature prominently in it. Knowing the personalities involved and relating to them as actual human beings makes history much more interesting than just reciting cold, hard facts from events of 250 years ago. So take time to look up a little bit of extra information on these folks, even if it's just a quick peek on Wikipedia.

As for the sites themselves, I have tried to provide the most up-to-date internet and contact information for each. But site details often change, particularly open days and hours. Always double-check before you go.

GETTING TO THE SITES

The classic gas station road map is a thing of the past. The modern road tripper is most likely to refer to the mapping app on their phone. With this in mind I have given locations for each site that are as precise as possible, including GPS coordinates for those so inclined to use them. If an exact address is available, it is provided, but be aware that the mailing address used for a facility is sometimes very far away from the actual site.

Often markers or locations are found at or near intersections, also easily entered into a GPS app.

Of course, you can get countless apps for those same phones to help you find food and lodging along the way, and some apps (such as Tripadvisor or Yelp) will even help you determine if you've found a hidden gem or if you should move on to the next stop down the line.

THE HISTORIC SITES

Hundreds of military actions occurred during the American Revolution, ranging from skirmishes to bloodbaths. Still more sites are significant for political or social reasons. However, as cities and towns grow, the sites of these actions are gradually being obscured by progress. Recognizing this, Congress passed the Revolutionary War and War of 1812 Historic Preservation Study Act of 1996, which created a commission tasked with reviewing each of these historic sites, evaluating the condition of the sites, determining which ones were the most important to the outcome of the respective war, and cataloging the state of preservation of each site. With the help of the National Park Service, state historical societies, local groups, and hundreds of volunteers, the commission created a list of 476 Revolutionary War battlefields and associated properties that were deemed "principal sites" and prioritized them according to their impact on the course of the war, as well as the need for preserving them.

The list of 476 Revolutionary War sites is divided into three classes:

- Class A (117 sites)—a military or naval action having a vital objective or result that shaped the strategy, direction, outcome, or perception of the war, or a site associated with government or citizen actions that had a direct influence on social, political, economic, diplomatic, or military activities and policies during the war

- Class B (135 sites)—a military or naval action having a significant influence on a campaign, or a site that helped shape social, political, economic, diplomatic, or military activities and policies during the war

- Class C (224 sites)—a military or naval action that influenced the strategy, direction, or outcome of a campaign; or a site that had a limited influence on social, political, economic, diplomatic, or military activities and policies during the war

As for visiting sites, the road trips described in this book mostly focus on Class A and sometimes Class B destinations. The sites are organized into three main regions, which match the parts in the book: the north, the middle colonies, and the war in the south. There's also a fourth part that looks at sites outside the original thirteen colonies and Canada. Each part is organized into chapters that examine the war in manageable pieces that can be seen in a weekend or a long weekend road trip.

If you take all seven tours described in this book, you'll see almost all the Class A sites and many others, as well. But this book still will help you get to all 476 sites—and then some. These tours hit all the major sites of the war, as well as other sites that might not have been as important strategically but are perhaps very well interpreted or shouldn't be missed for some other reason.

If you do take all seven tours, you'll be at the head of the class as far as knowledge of the American Revolution is concerned.

OTHER REVOLUTIONARY WAR SITES

Think the American Revolution was just a bunch of battles? Think again. It was full of people, stories, and events having nothing to do with combat that are better than the best fiction. Visiting only the battlefields won't teach you the whole story. This book will help you learn about the people involved: See where citizens met to debate and protest issues of the day, where Native Americans gathered to debate how to respond to the war, and where the Founding Fathers worked—and played—as they forged a new nation.

You will also see sites that can help you understand the period. Some of these are museums, while others are living history sites, where you can use all your senses to put yourself back in that time. Some sites described in this book were essential to war efforts (for example, the ironworks of Pennsylvania and Maryland). Others are sites with such strange, touching, and wonderful stories that they simply cannot be left out (such as Fort Mose in St. Augustine, Florida). A number of them also tell stories of slavery, the legacy of which continues to shape our history to this day.

WHERE TO STAY

There are two prevailing philosophies to the road trip. One is to throw your map out the window and go where the road leads you, hopefully winding up at your final destination, eventually. The other is to plan out every detail, knowing exactly what you're going to see, how long it's going to take to get from point A to point B, and where you're going to stop for the night.

Most people fall somewhere in the middle of that spectrum, so you will be given just a little guidance about where you can bed down for the night. You will be presented with some great options for lodging, in case you're the type to plan ahead, and especially if you plan on staying in one place for a while. Some of these can greatly enhance your experience; for instance, if you are studying the sites in the Boston area for a few days, staying at an old colonial-era home can add a lot to your visit.

If you're not the B&B type and simply like to drop and sleep wherever you finish sightseeing, you're covered there, too. Usually the tours follow major interstates and highways, and there are plenty of hotels and motels that will suit just about anybody. But some of the places described in this book are *way* off the beaten path, and you might not have a lot of options. If you do plan to stray from the interstates and visit sites that are a little more isolated, this book will let you know if you have to plan ahead.

Of course, another great option, if you're so inclined, is camping. Many of the battlefields are located near national parks, national forests, state recreational facilities, or other great places to pitch a tent or sleep in a lodge. It can be a cheap and very fun way to hit the road.

A NOTE ON NUMBERS, NAMES, AND TERMS

As you read through this guide, you may note some apparent inconsistencies, or wonder what some terms mean or how they are used. One essential term for military historians that is commonly misunderstood is "casualties." Casualties, or losses, suffered in battle are often assumed to mean the number of persons killed, but the term actually includes those killed, wounded, missing, captured, or otherwise "lost" to a force during a battle. For instance, if an army suffered 500 casualties during a battle, perhaps 50 men were killed, 150 were injured, and 300 were captured by the enemy. Other military terms or expressions of the time may seem somewhat mysterious (after all, the Revolutionary War was two and a half centuries ago), but I have tried to keep these (such as "abatis") to a minimum.

Another difference you might notice is in town names. Over time, many towns that now end in the suffix "-town" (for example, Yorktown, Virginia) were originally known differently (it was then known as York, Virginia). There are several cases of this when it comes to names of towns, rivers, and other points of interest. In general, in historical passages I use the spelling of the town that was used during the era, but if I am referring to present-day names and addresses, I use the modern names or spelling.

Finally, when it comes to sites in and around what was the American frontier at the time, what we recognize today as the boundaries of the original thirteen colonies often do not apply. For instance, much of what is now Kentucky, Ohio, Indiana, and Illinois was configured as part of Virginia, and even some of that was disputed with Pennsylvania. In fact, disputes between the colonies regarding borders were common; the entire state of Vermont, as we know it today, was one such area, claimed by both New York and New Hampshire.

Other foreign powers still had a presence on the North American continent, and after the French and Indian War ended in 1763, their possessions were shuffled among England, France, and Spain, leading to colonies in Louisiana (which was, confusingly, Spanish during the Revolution) and East and West Florida (both of which were British). I have tried to make this all clear where I can; just remember that during the

American Revolution, the border situation outside of the heavily populated areas was often disputed and somewhat fluid and does not always match what we see today.

HOW *NOT* TO USE THIS BOOK

This is a guidebook. Use it as a guide. You can even use it as a checklist, of sorts. But *please*, don't rely solely on this book to tell you exactly where to go. When you visit these places, discover them, appreciate them for the gifts that they are, learn the deep lessons that they teach, and then decide for yourself what is important to experience next. If you stick to that guideline, you will want to see more than anyone could ever outline in any book.

IMPORTANT THINGS TO REMEMBER WHEN VISITING REVOLUTIONARY WAR SITES

- Many of these sites are on private property. If you would like to see a site that is on private property, and contact information is available, be sure to ask before you go *trespassing* through somebody's yard. If you don't know, stay out, or take pictures from the roadside.

- Many of the sites in this book that are staffed are done so only seasonally and either reduce their hours in the off-season or close entirely. Other smaller sites (for example, town and county museums) may be open only one day a week or month throughout the year. If you want to be sure a site will be open when you get there, and it's not part of the National Park Service, be sure to call ahead and confirm their hours. (There's also a good chance that someone at the site will be able to meet you by appointment on those closed days; these folks tend to be very eager to share their history.)

- All of these sites, including those overseen by the National Park Service, are desperately short of funding, not only to keep their site open, but to heighten the experience for the visitor and, with some luck, acquire and restore surrounding land that is currently privately owned. Often the sites that are staffed depend on volunteers. So when you visit, be sure to add a little to the donation box, even if the site is free, and sign the guest book so that when the time comes to ask for funding, they can demonstrate that the site is bringing people like you in to support not only the site but also the local economy.

- If you go through rural areas, make sure your vehicle is in good working order. You don't want to break down where your phone doesn't get reception. Always plan for the worst. Keep an emergency road kit with you and make sure it includes first-aid supplies. Some locations described in this book are accessible only by dirt or gravel roads that are not always well maintained. If you have *any* doubt that your vehicle can't handle going up the mountainside or on a muddy road, don't try it.

- As you go through these tours, you will see some very different parts of the country, each with its unique flavors, customs, and cultures. You may even come to some areas where you feel a little out of place, as if you don't belong. Although you should always follow your better judgment, do not be afraid to approach the locals and ask for directions, about the town, or where a good place to eat might be. They are usually just as friendly as you are and will almost always be as eager to help as you would be if they visited your neck of the woods. In fact, you will find that most people are proud of the history that surrounds them and will happily share what they know. These conversations will probably be the highlights of your trip.

- Good shoes, water, sunscreen, and insect repellent: Keep these items with you, and you'll be able to enjoy every site.

PART 1

ORIGINS: THE REVOLUTION IN THE NORTH

1

The Head of the Serpent: Boston and the New England Colonies

OVERVIEW

In the minds of King George III and many in the British Parliament, the trouble all began in Massachusetts. No matter that the people and even the legislatures of the other American colonies largely supported the Massachusetts colony in standing up for its rights, or that those colonies were, for the most part, equally affected by Parliament's actions. The trouble lay in Massachusetts, particularly in Boston, and bringing Boston under control would allow the king's loyal subjects throughout the colonies to enjoy his protection peacefully once again.

These "troubles" dated to 1763, the end of the Seven Years' War, known more commonly in America as the French and Indian War. The war had cost the English government an exorbitant amount of money, and the British decided to raise revenue by laying taxes on the colonies. Americans thought they had already done their fair share—they had helped to win the war too, after all, in proportions greater even than the English—and resisted with vehemence. The problem was not the taxation itself; in fact, Americans were, even this early in their existence, the wealthiest people in the world. It was that Parliament had chosen to lay the taxes on not only just a select portion of her English subjects, but

Opposite: The site of the Boston Massacre is marked inconspicuously along the Freedom Trail.

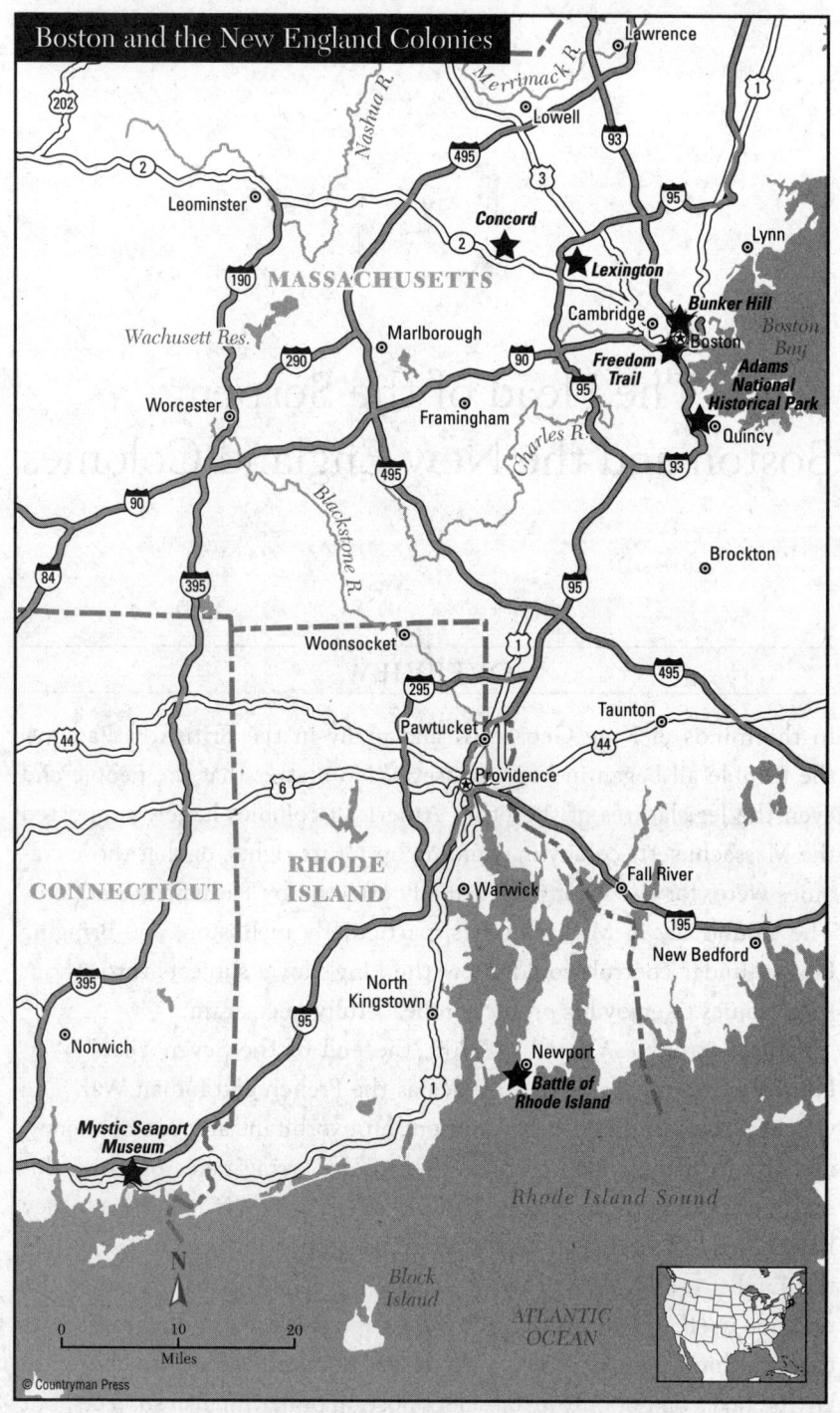

ones that also had no representation within the governing body. In a land that jealously guarded her liberty, this was tyranny.

The first of these levies, the Sugar Act, came into effect in 1764. Predictably, the strongest resistance came from Boston. It would be a mistake to think that resistance did not originate in other colonies; indeed, it was these revenue acts that first caused the colonies to work together as one. But those known to Parliament as the worst of the rabble-rousers—and in the eyes of some, traitors—were names like Samuel Adams, James Otis, and John Hancock, all Bostonians.

Other revenue acts followed, some repealed due to the shocking resistance in America. Revenue collectors for the 1765 Stamp Act resigned from their posts under threat of violence. When taxes on other goods came into effect, Americans retaliated with nonimportation agreements, refusing to use the newly taxed items. Colonial legislatures met to denounce the measures and appeal to the king's mercy for relief from Parliament's actions. But the king sided with Parliament on each issue, impressing on the Americans that they belonged to Britain. New taxes and duties came into effect, and Parliament dissolved legislative bodies that protested. With each action, Americans saw their precious liberty dissolving like sugar in a hot cup of tea.

Eventually, additional British troops were sent to Boston to enforce the acts, further antagonizing the citizens. The agitation led to the Boston Massacre in 1770, when a small group of soldiers being abused by a mob fired into the crowd, killing five. When Parliament attempted to force British tea into American markets, Bostonians responded by sneaking onto three ships holding the tea and dumping their precious cargo—approximately $3 million in today's money—into the harbor. The Boston Tea Party of 1773 was the last straw. Parliament passed what became known as the Intolerable Acts in 1774, closing the port of Boston and asserting more direct control over the governance of Massachusetts.

All these actions served to further unify the colonies, which had heretofore been largely independent and even, at times, at odds with each other. Few wanted to separate from the mother country; the British were the most freedom-loving people in the world. But the colonists, British subjects by right, felt they were being treated as less. Ultimately, the colonies formed a Congress that met in Philadelphia in 1774. Within each colony, committees of safety and militias arose to prevent further trampling of their liberties. For leadership, Americans looked to Massachusetts, just as Parliament had.

The smoldering powder keg of war finally detonated in Lexington and Concord, just outside Boston, in April 1775. The first large-scale battle of the war took place at Bunker Hill, across Boston Harbor from the city. The first great American success of the Revolution came with the British evacuation of Boston in early 1776.

All of New England plays a part in the American Revolution: its people, its ways of life, and particularly its ties to the sea. The focus of this chapter is Boston and the Freedom Trail, but the chapter also looks at one of the largest, most forgotten battles in Newport, Rhode Island; explores seafaring life in Mystic, Connecticut; and observes how the region's Puritan roots and religious oppression sowed the seeds of war. But as King George III knew, long before the war had started, the American Revolution began in Boston.

PEOPLE TO KNOW

SAMUEL ADAMS—If one man embodies the word "Patriot," along with all the American tradition and symbolism that comes with that word, it is undoubtedly Samuel Adams. A New England Puritan from modest stock who rose to fame on both sides of the Atlantic, Sam Adams, though somewhat less famous than other Founding Fathers, had as much impact on the direction of American politics as anyone in the colonies.

Born in 1722, Adams attended Harvard and then tried several occupations—lawyer, brewer, tax collector—before finding his true calling: politics. Being politically active was a hallmark of good citizenship in New England, but Adams soon stepped to the front of the pack as a leader. Adams and his fellow "radicals" immediately saw danger in the passage of the Sugar and Stamp Acts, and his organization of the opposition to those acts and those that followed made his name known throughout the colonies and in the British Parliament. When the Tea Act came in 1773, Adams unified Bostonians and the rest of the colonies in opposition. When war finally came and the British were under siege in Boston, it is telling that amnesty was offered to all Americans who would show loyalty to the king, with two exceptions: John Hancock and Sam Adams. Adams represented Massachusetts in the Continental Congress and signed the Declaration of Independence and would later be elected governor before his death in 1803. He is buried in the Old Granary Burying Ground, along Boston's Freedom Trail, in the company of his fellow Patriots, John Hancock and Paul Revere.

JOHN HANCOCK—Possibly better known for his impressive signature than for his accomplishments, John Hancock is one of our least-known Founding Fathers. Just like his contemporaries in Boston, though, Hancock played a critical part in early resistance to the crown.

John Hancock was born in 1737. From an early age, Hancock was raised by his uncle, one of Boston's most prominent shippers, and was eventually made a partner. John inherited the firm in 1764, instantly making him possibly the wealthiest man in New England. Within a year the Stamp and Sugar Acts were passed, and Hancock sided with the colonists, but it was in 1768 that events pushed him over the edge. Trying to make a point, British customs officials in Boston seized several ships in Boston Harbor, including one belonging to Hancock. From that point on he was a devoted Patriot, and the trial resulting from the seizure of his ship won him national attention. Hancock was elected to the Second Continental Congress and was soon made president of the Continental Congress, a position he held from 1775 to 1777. This, of course, included the period when the Declaration of Independence was signed; legend has it that Hancock signed his name large enough so that King George III would easily recognize Hancock as a "traitor." Hancock spent the remainder of his life in public service—helping to create a constitution for Massachusetts, serving as its first governor, and fighting for ratification of the United States Constitution. Hancock was still serving as governor when he died in 1793; he is buried in the Old Granary Burying Ground in Boston.

PAUL REVERE—The Paul Revere that most people know is something of a mythical figure, the midnight rider who alerted the minutemen that "the British are coming!" (which, of course, he would never have said; after all, everyone in Massachusetts, including Paul Revere, was

British at the time). The real Paul Revere is a much more compelling figure and was one of the most well-respected activists in the Sons of Liberty, a group of Americans committed to defending colonial rights, in colonial Boston.

The son of an immigrant, Paul Revere was born in 1735, the third of 13 children. Before going off to fight in the French and Indian War, Paul learned the silversmithing trade from his father. Revere branched out, becoming an engraver and an outspoken leader of tradesmen in the city. He became deeply involved in the Sons of Liberty Patriot movement, and his depiction of the Boston Massacre in a political cartoon, though somewhat inaccurate, had great influence both at home and abroad. Revere became an official rider for the Patriot movement, serving as courier between the Continental Congress and the Massachusetts Provincial Congress. And it was Revere who rode to Concord, two days before the British troops came out, to warn that the munitions stored there were in danger of being seized. While he was not the only rider on the night the British Regulars did come out, he was certainly the most well-known, and it is a small miracle that the British, who captured him that night, released him soon afterward. Revere would go on to military command, resulting in a severe and embarrassing loss at Penobscot Bay in Maine. Paul Revere would continue as one of the best silversmiths in America through to his death in 1818. Henry Wadsworth Longfellow would ensure that Paul Revere's midnight ride would never be forgotten, but it is for so much more that we should remember this brave American hero.

JOHN AND ABIGAIL ADAMS—By most accounts, John Adams was a squat, moody man who had difficulty working with people. And by most accounts, his wife, Abigail, was a lovely, kind person who garnered attention and respect, a tall order for a woman in the 18th century. What is without doubt is that these two people, opposites in so many ways, were deeply in love, and for over 25 years were possibly the premier power couple in American politics.

John Adams, born in 1735 and a Harvard graduate, was at the forefront of the Boston resistance movements. He established his honesty and faith in the law when he defended both John Hancock in a high-profile customs matter and the British soldiers accused in the Boston Massacre. By this time he had married Abigail, born in 1744. Adams went on to represent Massachusetts in the Continental Congress and served on the committee that forged the Declaration of Independence, which he signed. After working tirelessly to unite the colonies in the cause of the Revolution, Adams left for France and the Netherlands to serve a critical role as ambassador (taking his son John Quincy with him, and giving him a crash course in diplomacy that would make his political career, as well). His time in Paris was followed by the first US ambassadorship to Great Britain, after which he came home to become George Washington's vice president and finally spend significant time with his wife, Abigail, after his considerable foreign service. Adams went on to become the second president of the United States, and though his term was troubled, he was able to keep America out of the French Revolution, a significant achievement. After 1800, the Adamses remained in the spotlight, raising John Quincy to become America's sixth president. Abigail died in 1818, and John followed on July 4, 1826—the 50th anniversary of the Declaration of Independence, as well as the same day Thomas Jefferson passed away. The letters between John and Abigail are exceptional reading, demonstrating love, patriotism, intellect, wonder, and remarkable humanity. John, Abigail, John Quincy, and his wife and First Lady Louisa, are all buried in a common crypt in Quincy, Massachusetts.

THINGS TO KNOW

History is in every corner of New England. Whether you're interested in Native American history, the early colonial period, pilgrims, witch trials, religious intolerance—it's all here. While this itinerary necessarily focuses on the Revolutionary period, try to make some time to explore any of those other interests, too, as well as the great cities of Boston, Newport, and Providence. And if natural beauty is your thing, you can always go during leaf-peeping season, when the fall colors set the landscape afire; you can either stay on the path described here or take a quick jump north into the mountains of Vermont or New Hampshire.

THE TRIP

This entire road trip is arranged as a circle, beginning and ending in Boston (though you could begin anywhere you'd like). Many of the sites are in and around greater Boston, but it would be a mistake not to venture farther afield. For those who don't live in the area and aren't used to driving very short distances across states, the short travel times between these locations will surprise you. Be sure not to skip Rhode Island and Connecticut, both rich in their history of the American Revolution.

Pay attention to traffic. Much of the travel will follow interstate highways, but some sites may require going on smaller highways. For Cape Cod in particular, *always* check traffic conditions. There's one road in and out, and while it's beautiful, it may be worth avoiding if your schedule doesn't allow time for it. But don't let slow backroads stop you. Driving New England will take you through picture-perfect towns and scenery. Stop in as many as you can for a good meal or just to enjoy the quiet.

THE CAN'T-MISS SITES

Boston and the Freedom Trail
The old city of Boston has remained remarkably intact. Always compact, even after more than two centuries of growth, the core of the city is easily walkable. The best and easiest way to experience old Boston is on foot via the Freedom Trail.

Though the trail is maintained by Boston National Historical Park, many of the sites along the way are privately owned and operated. The sites will take you from the colonial period just before the war all the way through the Battle of Bunker Hill, and except for the site of the Boston Tea Party, all the familiar locations of the American Revolution are covered. You'll want to set aside ample time for the trail; it is 2.5 miles long and involves a few slight hills, and you're going to want to stop a lot to explore things off the trail or to get a bite to eat.

The Freedom Trail begins in Boston Common, and following it is easy: just follow the red brick line in the walkway. You can find information about the Freedom Trail at www.nps.gov/bost or by calling Boston National Historical Park at 617-242-5601.

Boston Common is the starting point for the popular Freedom Trail.

Off the Freedom Trail are two critical pieces of Boston's story, the Boston Tea Party and the Siege of Boston. While you will find information about both at the trail's museums and visitor centers, there are places to visit that will put you on the spot and interpret what happened in those critical years at the beginning of the American Revolution.

In 1773, Parliament ratified the Tea Act, which restricted the price and trade of tea to only the English East India Company. Although no direct tax was applied, New Englanders were cut out of the trade, which went to appointed agents. This was interpreted as yet another sign of oppression levied by Parliament, and there was soon a nonimportation agreement throughout the colonies. In some locations, the tea was loaded into warehouses but never sold; other cities never let the tea ships into port. In Boston, however, three tea ships docked and were not allowed to leave until they had unloaded their cargo.

On December 16, 1773, after appeals to the governor of Massachusetts went unheeded, Bostonians met at Old South Meeting House and

SITE DETAILS

Boston Common—A natural beginning for the Freedom Trail, Boston Common has been part of the city's landscape since 1634. A "commonage" shared by the populace, the common was community property and was used as such—as a park, pasture, training ground for militia, and for public events. Today's Boston Common has lost some of these elements, but it is still very much the people's park, and the tradition of using the Common to espouse one's views (particularly in the Speaker's Corner, at Tremont and Park Street) is alive and well. Along and within Boston Common, you'll also find some magnificent artwork, as well as the Massachusetts State House. The Freedom Trail begins at the address provided here, where you'll also find a Boston welcome center. *Boston Common—beginning of Freedom Trail, 139 Tremont St., Boston, MA 02118. GPS: 42.355399, -71.063653. Open daily.*

Old South Meeting House—The largest and most important meeting house in the city during the colonial and Revolutionary periods, the Old South Meeting House, built in 1729, was ground zero for all of Boston's major resistance activities. Every year, an emotional commemoration of the Boston Massacre is held here, generally to a standing-room-only crowd. And on December 16, 1773, it was here at the Old South Meeting House that Samuel Adams invited 5,000 people to head for Griffin's Wharf to initiate the Boston Tea Party. Though the British would use the building as a stable during their occupation of the city, the Old South Meeting House remains a venerated symbol of the public demonstration of liberty. You can view exhibits or take a cell phone tour of the building, and if you get the chance, try to be there in December for the reenactment of the Tea Party, which begins at the Old South Meeting House with rebellious speeches and ends at the Boston Tea Party Ships and Museum. Your ticket is also good for admission to the Old State House. *Old South Meeting House, 310 Washington St., Boston, MA 02108; 617-482-6439; www.revolutionaryspaces.org. GPS: 42.357036, -71.058513. Open daily.*

Massachusetts Colonial State House—Once the center of government for Massachusetts, the Old State House still bears the crests and symbols of imperial times. They are replacements, though; the originals were torn off by a jubilant crowd after the Declaration of Independence was read from the building's balcony in 1776. The oldest public building in Boston, the Old State House now serves as an outstanding museum, operated by the Bostonian Society, with permanent and rotating exhibits examining Boston's history during the colonial period. You'll find John Hancock's coat, tea from the Boston Tea Party, and Paul Revere's famous woodcut of the Boston Massacre among the museum's treasures. Admission covers both the Old State House and Old South Meeting House, and guided tours are available. *Old State House, 206 Washington St., Boston, MA 02109; 617-720-1713; www.revolutionaryspaces.org. GPS: 42.358744, -71.057349. Open daily.*

Boston Massacre Site—In early 1770, the rising tension between the king's soldiers stationed in Boston and the citizenry was coming to a head. It erupted on March 5, when an unruly mob pelted a small group of soldiers with rocks, snowballs, and other objects, and the soldiers felt threatened enough to fire into the crowd. Five people were killed in what we know today as the Boston Massacre, and though the action may have been provoked (only two of the soldiers, defended by none other than John Adams, were found guilty), the image of British soldiers "massacring" the citizens they had supposedly been sent to protect shocked Americans and Britons alike. Today the site of the Boston Massacre is commemorated with a modest sidewalk memorial. If you have time, inquire at the Massachusetts Colonial State House or Old South Meeting House about their excellent guided tour, Massacre and Memory. *Boston Massacre Site and Memorial, at the intersection of State St. and Devonshire St., Boston, MA 02109. GPS: 42.358773, -71.057163. Accessible daily.*

Faneuil Hall—Now double the size of its colonial-era construction, Faneuil Hall has become a symbol of freedom through speech. Many of the Patriots' town meetings and rallies were held here, and a statue of Samuel Adams, noted as the most influential and gifted of the Patriot speakers, stands just outside. Faneuil Hall is still a place where landmark speeches are held, and you can visit the second-floor hall, which also hosts park ranger programs. On the ground floor, you will find the primary visitor center for Boston National Historical Park. *Faneuil Hall, 1 Faneuil Hall Square, Boston, MA 02109. GPS: 42.360015, -71.056467. Open daily.*

continued on next page

Paul Revere House—The oldest house in Boston, the Paul Revere House will give you a glimpse into both the amazing life of this Patriot—which involved a lot more than just that famous midnight ride—as well as the times he lived in. Nestled in what was even then a residential area, the old house distinctly stands out from its neighbors. Tours of the house are available, and the complex includes two other homes and a museum encircling a courtyard. *Paul Revere House, 19 North Square, Boston, MA 02113; 617-523-2338; www.paulreverehouse.org. GPS: 42.363646, -71.053784. Open daily, April through December; closed Mondays, January through March.*

Old North Church—"One if by land, two if by sea." The famous lantern signal given from the steeple of Old North Church, as immortalized in Longfellow's famous poem, is as well-known as Paul Revere's midnight ride itself. It was here that two men, under Revere's instructions, lit two lanterns to signal militia leaders across Boston Harbor that British Regulars were headed for the countryside by boat. Instantly, a network of messengers spread word from town to town, turning out the minutemen to meet the redcoats. Today you can take a tour of Old North Church that includes a short presentation that tells the story of that fateful night. The tour also goes up the old steeple, and though the climb is a bit steep, it's a once-in-a-lifetime experience. Be aware that the church is still active, so there are no tours on Sunday mornings, though you're more than welcome to worship with the parish. *Old North Church, 193 Salem St., Boston, MA 02113; 617-858-8231; www.oldnorth.com. GPS: 42.366420, -71.054664. Open daily.*

heard speech after speech rallying the Patriots and denouncing the Tea Act, Parliament, and the governor. The last words, spoken by Samuel Adams, were a signal: "This meeting can do nothing more to save the country." The meeting then abruptly adjourned. To this day, parts of what happened next remain secret; what is known is that over 100 men, crudely disguised as Native Americans, boarded the three tea ships and dumped the entire cargo into Boston Harbor as thousands—including some British soldiers and officers—watched. The impact of destroying

Top: Samuel Adams, John Hancock, and Paul Revere are among those at rest at the Old Granary Burying Ground along the Freedom Trail.
Bottom: The Massachusetts Colonial State House was once the seat of government in Boston.

A statue of Founding Father Samuel Adams stands outside Faneuil Hall.

£9,000 worth of tea (about $3 million in today's money) was enormous, but the impact felt around the world was even greater. The king, shocked, ordered Boston Harbor closed as punishment for this open defiance of his law. And the colonies, already well into the process of unification, rallied around the oppressed city of Boston.

In April 1775, fighting finally broke out in Lexington and Concord, and the English army was forced to hole up in the city of Boston. While the Patriot army around them grew and the British looked for a way out of their besieged state, they eyed two pieces of high ground that would give them the advantage. One of these was Bunker Hill, and the English assault of that position in June 1775 resulted in a very costly victory for the king's troops. The other location, south of the city proper, was Dorchester Heights.

The debacle at Bunker Hill led to the resignation of British General Thomas Gage and the appointment of General William Howe as commander of the king's army in America. Howe did not want a repeat

SITE DETAILS

Boston Tea Party Ships & Museum—Near the spot of the original Boston Tea Party are the Boston Tea Party Ships & Museum. (Griffin's Wharf, where the tea ships docked, is now dry land.) A guided experience, the tour begins with a small "town meeting" with your tour group, after which you proceed to one of the two ships in the harbor to board and explore. Children, to the delight of everyone watching, are encouraged to throw bundles of tea into Boston Harbor. The tour continues to showcase the maritime life of Boston, much of which is interactive and kid friendly. The final part of the tour is heavily multimedia while showcasing some wonderful artifacts of the original Tea Party. If possible, reserve your tickets in advance; depending on the time of year, you may have to wait for your tour time or may even be shut out. *Boston Tea Party Ships & Museum, 306 Congress St., Boston, MA 02210; 866-955-0667; www.bostonteapartyship.com. GPS: 42.352124, -71.051405. Open daily.*

of Bunker Hill, so Dorchester Heights remained virtually undefended. The British eventually planned an assault, but a fierce storm delayed the movement. And it was shortly after this attempt that an American triumph, bloodless but decisive, occurred.

After George Washington took control of forming the Continental Army, he appointed Henry Knox colonel of artillery. Despite almost all of Knox's military knowledge being gleaned from the books in his bookshop and conversations with British officers, his leadership earned Washington's respect. Knox conceived a plan that would retrieve the artillery from the captured Forts Ticonderoga and Crown Point in New York and bring them to Boston. Though the transport of some 60 or more cannon 300 miles over the mountains took months, the payoff proved worth the effort.

On the night of March 4, 1776, with an artillery bombardment distracting the British, American troops entrenched and fortified Dorchester Heights in the darkness, then placed Knox's newly brought artillery

Children can throw bundles of "tea" into Boston Harbor at the Boston Tea Party Ships & Museum.

atop it. The British awoke to find the city completely under the American guns. Howe even remarked that the Americans had done more in one night than his troops could do in three months. Seeing that his position in Boston was now untenable, Howe, under a flag of truce, arranged to evacuate Boston, sparing the town from destruction in exchange for not being bombarded. The British sailed out on March 17, never to return. The American artillery on Dorchester Heights, without firing a shot, had given the Americans a major victory.

Lexington and Concord

On September 1, 1774, British soldiers seized colonial gunpowder stored at the Provincial Powder House northwest of Boston. Over the following months the government would make several other attempts to confiscate the colonials' powder, and though violence was avoided, each instance brought the situation closer to conflict. These "powder alarms" led the

SITE DETAILS

Dorchester Heights—The surprising spectacle of American artillery atop Dorchester Heights ultimately won Boston for the Americans. A public park with memorials and interpretation sits atop the heights today. The slope is steep, and it is now thickly surrounded by houses on narrow streets, so you may need to circle a bit to find a parking spot, particularly one close to the top. Once you've gotten there, however, the open view of the city is worth it. You will still find artillery guarding the city, as well as a monument to Knox's achievement. *Dorchester Heights, intersection of Telegraph St. and Thomas Park, Boston, MA 02127. GPS: 42.332865, -71.045761. Accessible daily.*

A view toward downtown Boston from Dorchester Heights.

JOIN, OR DIE

In 1754, English colonists in America were rightfully worried about defending themselves against the Native American populations to the west. Threatened by English encroachment on their land and encouraged by the French, these populations were conducting numerous raids on the frontier and were beginning to take a frightful toll on the colonists. A movement was started to unite the seldom-cooperative colonies into a common defense, including a Congress at Albany to discuss the issue. It was the first time the colonies had united for—well, just about anything.

Philadelphian printer Benjamin Franklin, already well known, captured his opinion in a political cartoon. Franklin's creation featured a rattlesnake cut into pieces, each piece representing one or more of the colonies; at the head of the snake was New England. Underneath the snake were the simple words, "Join, or Die." The message was clear: If the colonies insisted on maintaining their separation, they would all fall.

Patriots, determined to protect their remaining caches, to devise a system that would allow for a quick response. This defense network, the minutemen, would be put into action when the situation came to a head on April 19, 1775, at Lexington and Concord.

When the British left Boston for Concord on the night of April 18, the local Sons of Liberty, the tightly knit Patriot group, initially thought that their target was not gunpowder but Samuel Adams and John Hancock, who had been staying in Lexington. In actuality, it was indeed gunpowder, ammunition, and weapons that the British were after. These munitions weren't in Lexington but in Concord, just a bit farther down the road. Nevertheless, the newly devised alarm system was triggered.

Twenty years later, Franklin's cartoon was given new life, with the same meaning but a much different purpose. The snake still represented the necessity of the colonies uniting. This time, however, the cause was a common defense not against Native Americans, but their shared mother country of England. As it turned out, the initial British plan for quashing dissent in the colonies involved pacifying the troublesome New England colonies—cutting off the head of the snake, as it were. Instead, "Join, or Die" became a rallying cry for the newly united colonies that would go on to become the United States of America.

Patriot Paul Revere initiated the alarm. Revere was quietly rowed across the Charles River to a waiting horse while another rider, Joseph Dawes, took an alternate route. Two lanterns were hung in the steeple of Old North Church to notify fellow Sons of Liberty across the countryside that the British were advancing by sea, not across the narrow strip of land along Boston Neck. Revere and Dawes rode along crying that the British Regulars were turning out; this in turn sent up to 30 other riders on their way to the surrounding towns. By 2:00 AM, word had reached as far as New Hampshire, a remarkable feat of rapid communication for the day that could only have worked with the careful plan that the Sons of Liberty had devised. And as soon as word arrived, men began to march for Lexington.

Lexington Green, where first blood was drawn in the American Revolution.

Revere arrived in Lexington to rouse Hancock and Adams and persuade them to ride for safety. Once done, he and Dawes united and picked up a third rider, Samuel Prescott, a known Patriot on his way back home from visiting his sweetheart. Soon after, the three encountered a British patrol. Revere was captured, while Dawes and Prescott escaped; Prescott would ride on to alert the town of Concord. (Astoundingly, even though Revere told the British exactly who he was and what he was doing, he was released several hours later.)

Meanwhile, the British marched along the Lexington Road, bound for Concord, hearing bells and gunfire in the distance. They arrived at Lexington Green at dawn and found 60 to 70 local militia members. The British ordered the militia to disperse, and the militia slowly began to do so, when someone—it is still not known from which side—fired a shot. It was enough to provoke the nervous British soldiers, who leveled their muskets and fired. When they were done, eight Patriots had been killed, with another 10 wounded, most of the fighting occurring in front of their own families. The British, releasing a cheer, went on their way to Concord, leaving the bleeding men on Lexington Green.

Word of what happened in Lexington reached Concord quickly. The defenders, already receiving reinforcements from other militia that were passing through to Lexington, gathered on high ground just past the town on the west side of North Bridge. For several hours, they watched as the British searched for the munitions they had come to seize. (They had already been removed from the farm of Colonel James Barrett weeks before.) A standstill between the frustrated soldiers and the wary militia eventually developed at the bridge. The British fired a confused first shot, then a few scattered shots, followed by one volley that finally hit home. As the first men fell at Concord, the Patriot militia leveled a more effective fire that killed three and wounded nine. The shocked British soldiers, already in confusion and stunned that this American rabble would dare approach them in military order, broke and ran.

Over the next 12 to 14 hours, the British soldiers marched through a devastating gauntlet of fire. Having marched 20 miles overnight from

Concord Bridge, scene of the critical standoff between the British and the minutemen.

SITE DETAILS

Minute Man National Historical Park—Minute Man National Historical Park has two visitor centers. The best place to begin is the Minute Man Visitor Center, where a film will take you back to the events of April 18–19, 1775. Among other exhibits, you will find an interesting recap of the archaeological investigation of Parker's Revenge, where the British made their way back through Lexington and encountered fierce resistance. Once done, you can walk a short part of the original road that the redcoats used and can visit Parker's Revenge, one of the many sites where a heavy firefight occurred. (If you're up for a peaceful, safe, and historic hike, you can walk more than 10 miles of the Lexington Road and discover all sorts of surprises, such as the site where Paul Revere was captured.) After you're done exploring here, you can head to the North Bridge Visitor Center, which highlights the action that occurred at Concord, including a scale model of the action. This visitor center is in an old mansion, and as you leave through the lovely gardens you will see the muster ground of the Concord militia with a short path to the famous bridge itself. Frequent ranger programs bring the action of "the shot heard 'round the world" to life. There's a lot to explore nearby, including the town of Lexington, where you'll find several monuments. But the bridge is the main attraction here, and you may find yourself lingering for a while soaking in the moment. *Minute Man National Historical Park—Minute Man Visitor Center, On Route 2A 0.2 mile east of Mill St., Lincoln, MA 01773; GPS: 42.448830, -71.273307. Open daily, January through October. Minute Man National Historical Park—North Bridge Visitor Center, 174 Liberty St., Concord, MA 01742; GPS: 42.471316, -71.352511. 978-369-6993; www.nps.gov/mima. Open daily.*

Colonel James Barrett Farm—Much of the Barrett Farm, including the original farmhouse, is now owned by Minute Man National Historical Park. The Barrett Farm was the original target of the British raid, though the munitions stored there were long gone; Barrett was also the leader of the local militia that confronted the British Regulars at North Bridge. The house is only occasionally open to the public for special events, but grand restoration efforts are underway that may change this in the future. *Colonel James Barrett Farmhouse, 448 Barrett's Mill Rd., Concord, MA 01742; www.nps.gov/mima/learn/history*

culture/colonel-james-barrett-house.htm. GPS: 42.473016, -71.380416. Open only by appointment or special event; refer to website.

Hancock-Clarke House—It was in the wee hours of the morning of April 19, 1775, that Paul Revere rode up to the elegant home of Reverend Jonas Clarke, burst past a guard, and awoke the sleeping John Hancock and Samuel Adams. It took some convincing to get them to leave for safety (Hancock was determined to fight). Guided tours of the home are given on the hour, and guides will tell you the story of that night as well as the home's family connections to Hancock. Some original pieces remain, including the table where Hancock, Adams, and Clarke took tea the evening before; continuing excavation and other projects within the home continue to reveal surprises. Note, too, that a combination ticket can be bought for the Hancock-Clarke House, Buckman Tavern, and Munroe Tavern, and it is highly recommended, as all three are exceptional visits offering different perspectives on the battle. *Hancock-Clarke House, 36 Hancock St., Lexington, MA 02420; 781-861-0928; www.lexingtonhistory.org. GPS: 42.453634, -71.228519. Open daily, May through September, Sat.–Sun., April and October.*

Buckman Tavern—Standing right across from Lexington Green, Buckman Tavern is the location where the local militia gathered and waited as the redcoats marched toward them. The tavern contains the best museum in Lexington, explaining the battle while also displaying some exceptional artifacts, such as John Hancock's waistcoat and Patriot Captain Reverend Jonas Clarke's diary, open to the day of the battle. Rotating exhibits are also shown and help bring the past's events into a modern context. Finally, you'll tour the tavern and experience what the minutemen would have been doing before and after the fight; the tour is self-paced with an audio guide. Visiting Buckman Tavern is also a good opportunity to explore Lexington Green, so take time to walk around and view the many monuments to the events of that fateful day. *Buckman Tavern, 1 Bedford St., Lexington, MA 02420; 781-862-5598; www.lexingtonhistory.org. GPS: 42.449281, -71.229804. Open daily, March through November, Sat.–Sun., December through February.*

Munroe Tavern—A bit outside of Lexington, Munroe Tavern was used by the retreating British as a field hospital and headquarters for the relief force.

continued on next page

Recently renovated, the tavern presents the British side of the events of April 19, 1775. It's about the only place where you will hear the details of what the common British soldier—who didn't even know their mission when they left Boston—had to do to survive the gauntlet of fire they passed through on their retreat. The tavern was also visited by Washington in 1789. *Munroe Tavern, 1332 Massachusetts Ave., Lexington, MA 02420; 781-862-0295; www.lexingtonhistory.org. GPS: 42.441434, -71.216228. Open daily, May through September, Sat.–Sun., April and October.*

Jason Russell House—As the British retreated back down the Lexington Road and got closer to Boston, the fighting became even more fierce and personal. The Jason Russell House presents a simple home at the center of some of the bloodiest fighting of the battle. Russell himself, a Patriot sympathizer, was killed defending his home, which was looted, and bullet holes still pockmark the inside of the house. A small museum is also attached that serves the Arlington Historical Society. *Jason Russell House, 7 Jason St., Arlington, MA 02476; 781-648-4300; www.arlington historical.org. GPS: 42.416148, -71.158527. Open Sat.–Sun., May through mid-October.*

Boston to Concord with no rest, they now had to return down the same narrow road with American minutemen forming and firing under the cover of fences, trees, and rocks. Though British reinforcements would arrive in the afternoon, the retreat continued well into the night until the exhausted soldiers staggered into Boston. By the time it was all over, 73 British Regulars had been killed and over 200 wounded.

The running Battles of Lexington and Concord, "the shot heard 'round the world," as Longfellow put it, was a watershed moment in world history. The best troops in the world had been bested by common militia. Colonists of the world's most powerful empire had defied their king in the name of liberty and would go on to form a republic that would forever change everything. The American Revolution had begun.

Top: The farm of Colonel James Barrett was the target of the British raid on Concord, Massachusetts.
Bottom: You can see where the Lexington militia waited for the British to approach at Buckman Tavern.

Bunker Hill

Following Lexington and Concord, the British army, with no feasible land route of the city, was essentially under siege in Boston. At that time, Boston was connected to the mainland only by a narrow strip of land known as Boston Neck, a natural choke point that kept the troops bottled up. (The city has grown through the filling of the harbor, obliterating Boston Neck.) Movement by water was not much easier. Boston Harbor was enclosed, and any action would need to be carefully coordinated and done in secret to prevent the Patriots from intercepting the British soldiers where they landed. The British army was surrounded.

Still, there was hope for the British. The damage the Patriots inflicted had been severe and embarrassing, to be sure, but many were still convinced that local militia, when faced with the mightiest army in the world, would turn and run, or at least make a very poor showing. Plans were soon underway to break out of the stalemate and bring the Patriots to battle.

Colonel William Prescott, commander of the American forces at Bunker Hill.

Two points of high ground commanded the British position in Boston: Dorchester Heights, to the south, and Bunker Hill, to the north across the harbor in Charlestown. The British had been planning to seize Bunker Hill until, to their surprise, the Americans struck first. On the evening of June 16, 1775, militia from Massachusetts and Connecticut under command of Colonel William Prescott advanced to the smaller but adjacent Breed's Hill and built a strong redoubt at the top. By the time the sun was up on June 17, the Patriots had already begun to extend their earthworks, including a fortified rail fence along the Mystic River to the northeast.

The stunned British prepared to assault the position at once. General Thomas Gage, commander of all British forces in North America, began an immediate but largely ineffective artillery bombardment of the Americans as British troops prepared to cross the water by boat in an amphibious assault. The Americans kept digging, strengthening their position and preparing to receive the enemy.

At approximately 3:00 PM, British infantry led by General William Howe advanced in two groups, one focused on the American redoubt and the other headed for the rail fence to their right. The soldiers began to take sniper fire from Charlestown, causing Gage to order its bombardment. As the town was engulfed in flames, the British kept advancing, with the American line holding its fire. As legend has it, Prescott had commanded his 2,500 men not to fire "until you see the whites of their eyes," and the Patriots did just that, releasing their first volley at near point-blank range. The redcoat line, stopped in its tracks, retreated down the hill with heavy losses.

Howe regathered his troops and made a second assault, but again the British were forced back down the hill. At this point, though, the Patriots were beginning to run low on ammunition, a constant problem early in the American army's existence. When the third wave of British soldiers came, the Americans held their ground briefly but were ultimately forced out of their entrenchments and off the battlefield.

By 5:00 PM, the British held the critical high ground of Bunker Hill, but both sides seemed to know who really won the battle. The Americans had lost between 400 and 600, either dead or wounded, while the British had suffered over 1,000 casualties, nearly half their men involved, including a disproportionate number of key officers. American General Nathanael Greene remarked that he hoped "to sell them another hill at the same price," and across the ocean in Parliament, ministers knew that more "victories" like Bunker Hill would ruin the army. King George III agreed, and by October, Thomas Gage was replaced with William Howe as commander of the king's forces in America. There was no turning back now, no reconciliation between England and the colonies. A major battle had now been fought, and the British army would be focused on crushing the American rebellion.

Adams National Historic Park

When compared with some of the astonishing homes of our other Founding Fathers—Washington's Mount Vernon, Jefferson's Monticello, even John Hancock's now-gone mansion in Boston—the Adamses' homes are remarkably modest. This is due in part to their Puritan, New England environment, but also happens to closely reflect the personalities and life stories of John and Abigail Adams.

Three of the homes that John Adams owned are preserved at Adams National Historic Park.

SITE DETAILS

Boston National Historical Park (Bunker Hill Unit)—The 221-foot-tall Bunker Hill monument was completed in 1842. Visitors can still climb to the top to get a bird's eye view of Boston and the harbor. If you walk around the hill, you will find statues of Colonel Prescott and Dr. Joseph Warren, who fought heroically but was killed in the battle, as well as markers in the ground showing exactly where the American redoubt and entrenchments were placed. Along with a small building housing exhibits at the base of the monument, the visitor center across the street helps visitors learn all about the lead-up to the battle as well as every moment of the action. There is a narrated light map program that demonstrates the battle and troop movements, as well as a miniature copy of a cyclorama (a 360-degree panoramic painting) of the Battle of Bunker Hill. The construction of the monument is also detailed. Tours of the battlefield are also given regularly, along with other programs; check the website for details. *Boston National Historical Park—Bunker Hill, Monument Square, Charlestown, MA 02129; 617-242-5601; www.nps.gov/bost. GPS: 42.375707, -71.061380. Open daily.*

John Adams was born in a modest house in Braintree, Massachusetts, the son of a deacon. He soon inherited his father's interest in public affairs, graduated from Harvard, and passed the bar. Shortly after this he met Abigail Smith, a young woman of exceptional intelligence and learning. The two were married in 1764, and after moving into a newly built farmhouse near his birthplace, their first son, John Quincy, was born.

In 1765, with the coming of the Stamp Act, the Adamses' political activity ramped up. Keeping their home in Braintree, Adams became heavily involved in the Boston political scene, and soon both John and Abigail—a perfect political couple—were well known around Boston and beyond. This would eventually lead to John's increased absence, as his growing practice and then his involvement in the Continental Con-

ABIGAIL ADAMS BIRTHPLACE

Martha Washington was our first first lady, and Dolly Madison was the fourth; both were remarkable women. But if there was a First Lady of the American Revolution, one would be hard pressed to find a woman more suitable for the position than Abigail Adams. From the insightful correspondence she kept with her husband to her constant remonstrances to him to remember "the ladies" as the new country was built, the passionate relationships she had with her two greatest loves—John Adams and liberty—has forged Abigail Adams a well-earned place in Americans' hearts.

The Abigail Adams (née Smith) Birthplace was Abigail's home for two decades before her marriage to John Adams. It is maintained by the Abigail Adams Historical Society, dedicated to maintaining her memory. Though it is open only on some Sundays and special occasions, just seeing the outside of the small home is worth the side trip. *Abigail Adams Birthplace, 180 Norton St. North, Weymouth, MA 02191; www.abigailadamsbirthplace.com. GPS: 42.232357, -70.945689. Open select Sundays; see website for details.*

gress required frequent travel. They soon both grew adept at writing letters to each other, letters that are now an American treasure, both for capturing the thought of the times as well as their personal nature.

Throughout the Revolution, though John traveled extensively to Europe on diplomatic missions, the farmhouse in Braintree remained the Adamses' home. This residency changed in 1788, when they bought the Vassall-Borland House in Braintree. Elegant and more spacious and with plenty of room to grow, the family maintained ties to the house far after the deaths of both John and Abigail.

The modest birthplace of Abigail Adams.

The impact of the Adams family on the formation of the United States of America is enormous. John was a thought leader in Congress, understanding well the need for unification of the colonies. He was on the committee to draft the Declaration of Independence, is often considered father of the United States Navy, was our first vice president and became our second president. Abigail, a perfect counterbalance to his temperament, was not only an influential First Lady and mother to another president, but her thoughts, opinions, and intelligence highly influenced John's thinking, not to mention greatly enhanced his social reputation. And throughout over 50 years of influencing American political thought, the center of the Adamses' world remained Braintree, Massachusetts.

Mystic Seaport Museum
To understand the culture and people of New England, one needs to understand the sea. From the time the *Mayflower* landed in 1621 to the present day, the mariner's way of life is strongly interwoven into

SITE DETAILS

Adams National Historical Park—Adams National Historical Park preserves all three of the homes that John Adams inhabited in Quincy, formerly Braintree, Massachusetts. The home he was born in and the farmhouse he built for Abigail are next to each other, and although both are large, especially for their time, they are modest both inside and out. The Old House, as they called the Vassall-Borland House, is considerably larger and, while not exactly ornate, is still a beautiful home with extensive gardens and outbuildings. (The library, in particular—the work of grandson and famous historian Charles Francis Adams and essentially the first presidential library—is outstanding.) The homes can be seen only through a guided tour of all three; transportation is provided between the houses and the starting point at the visitor center. Just down the street from the visitor center and not to be missed is the family crypt at United First Parish Church, where the two presidents and their first ladies lay at rest. *Adams National Historical Park, 1250 Hancock St., Quincy, MA 02169; 617-770-1175; www.nps.gov/adam. GPS: 42.251928, -71.003657. Homes open for tours May through November; grounds open daily.*

the fabric of New England. And since understanding New England is so critical to knowing how the American Revolution came about, it becomes necessary to know the sea as well. There are few better places to gain that understanding than the Mystic Seaport Museum in Mystic, Connecticut.

Encompassing much more than maritime history, the Mystic Seaport Museum provides a thorough understanding of the seafaring life. There is history, to be sure; you will find exhibits about everything from the Viking era to modern shipbuilding and navigation. But you will also find more practical exhibits. Ever wonder how sailors could navigate by the stars? There's a planetarium for that. Walking through the museum's living history town, you will find a sutler's shop, a ropemaking factory, a cooper's

The preserved maritime village at the Mystic Seaport Museum.

shop, and a blacksmith's shop that forges ship's parts. You'll also walk by the homes of the families whose lives depend on the sea. Whether you're interested in the merchant marine, whaling, fishing, or pleasure craft, you will find a vast amount of information. You can also take a cruise around the Mystic River, either under sail or by a powered vessel.

The central point of the museum, however, is the waterfront. Not only will you find the many trades required to keep the ships afloat, but you will also find the ships themselves, beautiful tall-masted vessels that are still seaworthy. Tours of the ships are given regularly.

Scattered between all this activity are numerous interactive exhibits that demonstrate the practical elements of sailing: wind and water demonstrations that reveal water dynamics, physics lessons using ship loading equipment and machines, instructions in how to read signal flags—there is plenty to keep you busy. Almost all these exhibits are kid-friendly, though adults will find it hard to resist trying them, too.

SITE DETAILS

Mystic Seaport Museum—If you visit the Mystic Seaport Museum, don't expect to be able to do an hour in-and-out visit. The museum is a large, sprawling facility and is packed with activities. It would be wise to take a look at the museum's website and decide which activities you'd like to see, then note the times for them, as some of them don't occur throughout the entire day. If you don't feel like planning ahead, that's okay, too; there will always be something interesting going on. Some suggested itineraries are provided online, if you need a little help, and you'll find lots to do just wandering around. There are also plenty of restaurants around the 19-acre complex, from quick bites to fine dining. Finally, if you'd like to mix up your visit, admission to the Mystic Aquarium can be purchased as a combo ticket. *Mystic Seaport Museum, 75 Greenmanville Ave., Mystic, CT 06355; 860-572-0711; www.mysticseaport.org. GPS: 41.363409, -71.962908. Open daily, but hours for museum and seaport vary seasonally.*

And if the kids (or parents) need a break, there are locations throughout the park that are less intense and simply give kids a place to play games, do puzzles, sing songs, and otherwise relax.

Finally, there is the shipyard. Not just an exhibit, the shipyard is used by both the Mystic Seaport Museum and others to refit their ships and keep them seaworthy. You will be able to see for yourself how a keel is laid, why different types of wood are used for different parts of the ship, and how sails are rigged. These are not small projects, either: One recent ongoing project at the shipyard was to create a seaworthy, life-sized reproduction of the *Mayflower*.

It's a full day's adventure, to be sure, but learning about the oceangoing life at the Mystic Seaport Museum will do much to aid your understanding of colonial America's dependence on the sea and how it led to our war for independence.

Battle of Rhode Island

The British occupation of Newport, Rhode Island, and the subsequent American effort to retake it often appears only as small blips on the timeline of the American Revolution. In truth, both events were significant, though for different reasons.

Interestingly, one who argued against the importance of Newport was British General Henry Clinton, who was tasked by General William Howe to take it November 1776. Clinton thought it somewhat of a backwater assignment, as the rest of the army had the more glorious task of chasing George Washington's Continental Army through New Jersey. What Newport provided, however, was critically important: a deep, ice-free winter port for British ships. Clinton took the city virtually unopposed, and the British added another major coup to their list.

During their time in Newport, the British established several encampments around the city on Aquidneck Island (aka Rhode Island) and built strong entrenchments to solidify their position. Clinton eventually passed command to General Robert Pigot, who further solidified the Newport garrison with 6,000 men. On the ground, Newport was incredibly strong; set on Aquidneck Island, it is attached to the mainland only by a narrow neck of land. By sea, there was even less to worry about, as the weak Continental Navy did not have the resources to mount or support any sort of assault.

Then came the French. In late 1777, with the great American victory at Saratoga, a Franco-American alliance became possible. After several months of preparations, a French fleet under the Admiral comte d'Estaing arrived in July 1778 with 15 ships and 4,000 troops. An agreement was made to coordinate land forces and conduct an attack on Newport, retaking the city and providing d'Estaing with a safe harbor. Washington sent troops to gather north of Newport under General John Sullivan, while the French would assault from the west. The Americans included many local Rhode Island men, including the 1st Rhode Island Regiment, a mostly Black unit of freemen and slaves who had gained their freedom with their enlistment. Clinton, then in charge of all British forces on the continent, received word of the mounting pressure on Rhode Island and sent British ships and 5,000 men.

On August 9, just as the entire operation was about to come to a head, comte d'Estaing received word that the British ships, under the command of Admiral Richard Howe, had arrived just off the harbor. Even as American troops were marching down the east side of the island, the French loaded their soldiers back aboard the ship and went to greet Howe.

On the brink of battle, nature intervened. A terrible storm swept through the area, damaging French and British ships alike to the extent that attack was no longer an option for either fleet. Howe sailed back to New York for repairs, while d'Estaing limped for Boston Harbor. The first joint operation between the Americans and the French had ended in inglorious failure.

Sullivan's isolated and unsupported American troops, continuing to prepare for battle, were suddenly in grave danger of being cut off and captured whole. Sullivan, at the south end of Aquidneck Island, began to move north on August 28. With the British on their heels, the Americans turned and constructed a defensive line on high ground 7 miles north of Newport, utilizing two hills for defense, Turkey Hill on the east and Quaker Hill on the west, with Butts Hill to the north serving as a reserve.

British assaults on the American line began early on August 29. Though Sullivan continued his retreat, the American line held strong, with the 1st Rhode Island Regiment repulsing three attacks by Hessians, mercenaries employed by the British, with great force. Just as oppressive as the combat was the heat, and it was reported by both armies that a number of men died of sunstroke. As the day went on, the British weakened the outnumbered Americans, who slowly fell back and withdrew off Aquidneck Island under cover of darkness. The British remained in control of the island until abandoning Newport and Rhode Island in October 1779.

The Americans had suffered a loss, but the greater toll was taken on the Franco-American alliance. The Americans were furious by what they saw as being deserted by the French, while Admiral d'Estaing was greatly insulted by the implication of cowardice. Though Washington was among those incensed by what happened, he saw the greater implications of a rift and worked hard to smooth things over, as did the Marquis de Lafayette, who was in Newport but followed the French fleet to Boston to try to control the damage.

REVOLUTIONARY NEWPORT

In addition to the battle that occurred here, Newport has plenty of other things to offer in terms of Revolutionary history. Most of the locations described here are in the old city of Newport and are easily walkable. Many of the homes are owned by the Newport Restoration Foundation, which rents them to steward-tenants in an effort to preserve them; though not all of these can be toured, any excuse for a walk around old Newport is a good one.

HUNTER HOUSE—One thing that Newport is famous for is its collection of Gilded Age mansions—the magnificent homes of Rockefellers and Vanderbilts abound here. That collection includes the notably older but still impressive 1748 Hunter House. Newport has always been a center of opulence, and that extended to the home of Colonel Joseph Wanton, a deputy governor of colonial Rhode Island. After Wanton, a Loyalist, was forced to flee at the outbreak of the war, the home became the headquarters of the commander of the French Naval Fleet in the Americas, the Admiral de Ternay. The home was purchased by future Senator William Hunter after the war, where it gets its name.

Hunter House can be toured individually, but it is also part of the collection of mansions maintained by the Preservation Society of Newport County, and you can buy a combination ticket that includes some of those other famous mansions. But Hunter House is impressive on its own, nestled just outside downtown on the waterfront. Timed tickets are available at any of the tour homes, at ticket centers throughout Newport, and online. *Hunter House, 54 Washington St., Newport, RI 02840; 401-847-1000; www.newportmansions.org. GPS: 41.492514, -71.321041. Open daily from mid-May to mid-October.*

continued on next page

MUSEUM OF NEWPORT HISTORY AT THE BRICK MARKET—The 1762 Brick Market building, at the heart of Newport's market district and just off Long Wharf, is an excellent place to start a walking tour of Newport. Several guided tours of the city start from here, including some focused on the Revolution and the colonial period; check with the museum for dates and times. While the lower floor is mostly dedicated to a gift shop, the upper floor contains exhibits on Newport's history, from precolonial times to the present. Just outside, you will also find an interpretive sign (one of many in the city) about the French presence in Newport during the Revolution. *Museum of Newport History at the Brick Market, 127 Thames St., Newport, RI 02840; 401-841-8770; www.newporthistory.org/museum-shop. GPS: 41.489890, -71.315424. Open daily.*

OLIVER HAZARD PERRY HOUSE—Built in 1750 by the Buliod family, the house was bought by famed Admiral Oliver Hazard Perry shortly after the War of 1812. The house was used as headquarters of the quartermaster during the occupation of the French army. Today the house is the property of the Newport Restoration Foundation. *Oliver Hazard Perry House, 29 Tuoro St., Newport, RI 02840; www.newportrestoration.org. GPS: 41.489746, -71.314421. Private property.*

RHODE ISLAND COLONIAL STATE HOUSE—Completed in 1739, the Newport Rhode Island Colony House remained in the service of the state through 1901. During the British occupation, it was used as a barracks, while the French used the large building as a hospital. Today the building, still property of the state, is maintained by the Newport Historical Society, which provides tours on a limited basis; call to check the schedule.

Rhode Island Colonial State House, Washington Square, Newport, RI 02840; 401-841-8770; www.newporthistory.org/properties/the-colony-house. GPS: 41.490370, -71.313054. Tours given at specified times; call for details.

TOURO SYNAGOGUE—The Colony of Rhode Island and Providence Plantations has always been noted for its religious tolerance. The first record of a Jewish presence in Newport goes all the way back to 1658 and the Spanish Inquisition, with Touro Synagogue dating to 1763, the oldest in the nation. During the British occupation, the large building was used as a hospital and meeting house for British soldiers. Touro Synagogue has since become an international symbol of religious freedom, as George Washington, working to garner support for the Bill of Rights, wrote to the congregation of the nation's commitment to protecting religious freedom. Today the synagogue is open for tours and hosts a small museum, and in front of the building is lovely Patriot's Park, dedicated to America's early Jewish Patriots, which contains monuments and interpretative signs. *Touro Synagogue, 85 Touro St., Newport, RI 02840; 401-847-4794; www.tourosynagogue.org. GPS: 41.489410, -71.311986. Open Sun.–Fri., May through October, Sun. only November through April.*

CLARKE STREET MEETING HOUSE—Clarke Street Meeting House, so obviously a church from the outside, is privately owned today. The meeting house was built in 1735; during the British occupation it was used both as a barracks and a hospital. *Clarke Street Meeting House, 15 Clarke St., Newport, RI 02840. GPS: 41.489282, -71.313630. Private property.*

continued on next page

VERNON HOUSE—The Newport Restoration Foundation maintains a number of historic homes, but the Vernon House stands out as a gem. When the French arrived in 1780, owner William Vernon offered his home to the French commander, comte de Rochambeau, to use as his headquarters. It was here that the Marquis de Lafayette, on behalf of General Washington, met with Rochambeau and his staff to plan the movements of 1780 and 1781 that ultimately ended the Revolutionary War. Like other properties of the Newport Restoration Foundation, the Vernon House is private property, but several plaques are on the home noting its significance. *Vernon House, 46 Clarke St., Newport, RI 02840. GPS: 41.488482, -71.313353. Private property.*

LUCAS-JOHNSTON HOUSE—The Lucas-Johnston House, built in 1713, is notable for its colonial connection. Augustus Johnston was attorney general of the colony of Rhode Island and, when the Stamp Act came around, was appointed as stamp master. Johnston was hounded and harassed until, after first hiding here in his basement and then fleeing, he was forced to resign his commission. The home was also occupied by several French officers during their stay in Newport during the war. Today it is private property; a sign notes its significance on the outside. *Lucas-Johnston House, 40 Division St., Newport, RI 02840. GPS: 41.488274, -71.312285. Private property.*

JOHN BANNISTER HOUSE—The John Bannister House was the headquarters of General Richard Prescott during the British occupation of Newport. Prescott, however, did not like his new quarters and decided to move to a farm just outside the city; it proved to be a poor decision, as he was captured from the much less secure farmhouse. The Bannister House is currently under a much-needed renovation, but will likely remain in private hands. *John Bannister House, 56 Pelham St., Newport, RI 02840. GPS: 41.486067, -71.312840. Private property.*

CAPT. JOHN MAWDSLEY HOUSE—The Mawdsley House (also known as the Bull-Mawdsley House for its builder) is one of the oldest houses in Newport, built in 1677. When the French arrived, second-in-command General Francois Jean de Chastellux chose Mawdsley House as his residence. Besides his military service, Chastellux was a writer, and his famous *Travels in North America* was mostly written here. Today the house is privately owned. *Capt. John Mawdsley House, 228 Spring St., Newport, RI 02840. GPS: 41.484787, -71.312862. Private property.*

JOHN TILLINGHAST HOUSE—The John Tillinghast House dates to 1758. Tillinghast continued to occupy the house until the French arrived, when it was used by several high-ranking officers. In addition, American General Nathanael Greene lived in the home shortly after the war, hosting the Marquis de Lafayette, Baron von Steuben, Thaddeus Koszciusko, and other notable comrades in arms. *John Tillinghast House, 142 Mill St., Newport, RI 02840. GPS: 41.486099, -71.309701. Private property.*

Top: Touro Synagogue in Newport, a symbol of America's commitment to religious freedom.
Bottom: Overton Farm, site of the John Bannister House, is where British General Richard Prescott was captured.

Even with this inauspicious start, the Franco-American alliance would provide ultimate victory. When the French army came in 1780, they made their American headquarters at Newport. A statue stands where the French commander, comte de Rochambeau, made his landing, and many buildings in downtown Newport were used by French officers. Newport may not be in the spotlight when it comes to the American Revolution, but its place in that history is assured, and when you add the numerous other great things Newport has to offer, it stands out as a premier historical destination.

OTHER SITES IN NEW ENGLAND

JOSHUA LORING HOUSE—A large country mansion when built in 1760, the Joshua Loring House was left empty when Loring, a Tory, fled to the relative safety of nearby Boston. The house was used as a hospital during the Battle of Bunker Hill, and the mansion's outbuildings were used to help supply the Continental Army headquartered at Cambridge. The home was also used as a headquarters by General Nathanael Greene.

The house is in excellent condition today and is open for tours on most Sundays, while the grounds are always open (except during special events; the beautiful home is often rented out for weddings and other occasions). The tour focuses on the colonial and Revolutionary periods as well as afterward, when the Greenough Family owned the house, which they did for over 140 years. *Loring-Greenough House, 12 South St., Jamaica Plain, MA 02130; 617-524-3158; www.loring-greenough.org. GPS: 42.309662, -71.115417. Grounds open daily; house open for tours by reservation.*

ROXBURY HIGH FORT—Part of the defenses bottling up the British army, Roxbury High Fort was a strong earthwork on high ground. Built by the American army in June 1775, the same month as Bunker Hill, High Fort was the preeminent work on the Roxbury Line, the primary fortification of the southern wing of the siege of Boston.

The site of Roxbury High Fort is a public park. Although the earthworks are gone, the outline of the old works is clearly demarcated on the ground as a sidewalk. Not only is the rocky area picturesque, you will

A public park in Boston preserves the site of Roxbury High Fort.

also have a nice view of the city, demonstrating why this position was such a critical one. Monuments and interpretive signs help explain the fort's importance. (Like Dorchester Heights, if you don't feel like climbing, try to park near the top; the hill can be steep in parts.) *Roxbury High Fort—Highland Park, intersection of Fort Ave. and Beech Glen St., Boston, MA 02119. GPS: 42.324414, -71.094740. Open daily.*

SHIRLEY-EUSTIS HOUSE—William Shirley, two-time Royal Governor of the colony of Massachusetts and commander of British forces in North America during the French and Indian War, built this home in the Boston countryside in 1747. The home was occupied by another governor after the war, William Eustis, and had such distinguished visitors as Lafayette, John Quincy Adams, Aaron Burr, Henry Clay, and Daniel

Webster. During the Revolution, though, the large home served a much more practical purpose as a barracks for American troops during the siege of Boston.

One of only a handful of still-existing colonial governors' mansions, the Shirley-Eustis House is as renowned for its architecture as for its history. That history doesn't take a back seat, however; the home and its surrounding grounds are constantly under study. The grounds around the mansion are well-kept, including the carriage house, and are always open, but try to get a tour if you can arrange it. *Shirley-Eustis House, 33 Shirley St., Boston, MA 02119; 617-442-2275; www.shirleyeustishouse.org. GPS: 42.323549, -71.072113. House open for tours Tues.–Fri. and summer Saturdays and by appointment; grounds open daily.*

FORT INDEPENDENCE—Perhaps the strongest fortification in Boston Harbor, Fort Independence, previously known as Castle William, was a significant defensive deterrent to would-be attackers. The British were able to retain control of Castle William during the siege of Boston but largely destroyed it during their evacuation in 1776. What was left was then repurposed as Fort Independence.

The site of Fort Independence remained fortified until 1960, when it was turned into Castle Island State Park. A large, sprawling park, there is plenty of interpretation, though little is left from the Revolutionary era. A visit to the site will make it obvious why there was a fortification here. Note that this is a significant recreation area for the locals, too, so be prepared for a little traffic if you visit on a nice summer weekend. *Fort Independence—Castle Island State Park, 2010 Day Blvd., Boston, MA 02127; 617-727-5290; www.mass.gov/locations/castle-island-pleasure-bay-m-street-beach-and-carson-beach. GPS: 42.338798, -71.015326. Open daily.*

BOSTON LIGHT—Today's Boston Light is at the site of America's oldest lighthouse, first put into action in 1716. It was this lighthouse that was still active during the Revolution, and which the British shut down during the closing of the Port of Boston. Though the lighthouse withstood several American attacks in 1775, it was ultimately replaced in 1783 with the lighthouse that stands today.

SITE DETAILS

Beavertail Lighthouse—Preserved within Beavertail State Park, the existing Beavertail Lighthouse is not the original. The base of the lighthouse which stood during the Revolution was uncovered by a hurricane in 1938. The lighthouse was only the third in the Americas and was critical for ships entering the safety of Narragansett Bay. The British, knowing this, destroyed the light during their evacuation in 1779. Today, a museum sits at the base of the existing lighthouse, and you will find not only a detailed history of the lighthouse but also exhibits on natural history and marine biology, not to mention magnificent views of the bay and the Atlantic shore. *Beavertail Lighthouse and Museum, on Beavertail Road at south end of Conanicut Island, Jamestown, RI 02853; 401-423-3270; www.beavertaillight.org. GPS: 41.449637, -71.399414. Area accessible daily; museum open daily during summer months and weekends in May and September.*

Conanicut Battery—This battery was initially built by the colonists of Rhode Island, who removed the artillery before the British invaded in 1776. The battery was improved and modified by the British, and though it fired on the French fleet during their 1778 appearance, it saw little action. The battery was also used by the French after the British evacuated. When you stand in the battery itself, you can easily see why it was placed here. Atop a commanding rise known as Prospect Hill, the battery had a clear field of fire of the critical West Passage through Narragansett Bay. The land is preserved today as a public park, and the earthworks still stand prominently, just a short walk down an easy path from the parking area. *Conanicut Battery, on Battery Lane 0.2 mile west of Beavertail Rd., Jamestown, RI 02853. GPS: 41.481607, -71.392307. Open daily.*

Fort Adams—An earthwork was first constructed at the site of the existing Fort Adams in 1776 by the Rhode Island colonists. Like Conanicut Battery, Fort Adams was taken when the British invaded, then subsequently manned by the French when they came to Newport. The existing Fort Adams was the third fortification built here, and there are no remnants of the original. Still, a visit to Fort Adams State Park, site of the famous Newport Jazz

Festival, is worth the trouble, either to visit the fort itself or to enjoy the open seaside park. *Fort Adams State Park, 90 Fort Adams Dr., Newport, RI 02840; 401-841-0707; www.riparks.ri.gov/parks/fort-adams-state-park. GPS: 41.468141, -71.340051. Park open daily; tours of fort available daily April through December and March weekends.*

Rochambeau Monument—The commander of French forces in America, Jean-Baptiste Donatien de Vimeur, comte de Rochambeau, is one of the American Revolution's unsung heroes. Rochambeau would later command with Washington at Yorktown, but it was here in Newport that he and five French regiments first landed on American shores. In King Park, along the shore just east of Fort Adams, a statue of Rochambeau (a replica of one that stands in Paris) as well as a large monument chronicles his accomplishments in America. The monument recently underwent a major restoration sponsored by the Alliance Francaise of Newport. *King Park—Rochambeau Monument, 125 Wellington Ave., Newport, RI 02840. GPS: 41.476232, -71.321258. Open daily.*

Fort Hamilton—Fort Hamilton, on Rose Island, was an ideal spot for a fortification guarding the middle passage of Narragansett Bay. Not known as Fort Hamilton until after the war, the earthworks were manned by the colonists, British, and French. Those earthworks now lie beneath the existing fortifications, but there is plenty of interpretation, as well as guided tours of the fort, which will help you navigate Narragansett Bay during the war. The island is only accessible by ferry during the spring and summer, so plan ahead if you'd like to go; you can also get a good view of Rose Island from afar at Fort Adams State Park. *Fort Hamilton, Rose Island; Jamestown Newport Ferry leaves from Fort Adams, Ann St. Pier, and Perotti Park in Newport, RI 02840; 401-847-4242; www.roseisland.org. GPS: 41.495800, -71.341657. Island accessible by ferry weekends from Memorial Day through early October.*

North Battery—The North Battery lies just north of the city of Newport. It was initially constructed by Patriots, but was later greatly modified by the British, as it was one of the primary land batteries near the city. When the British left in 1779, they mostly destroyed the earthwork, but the Americans and French repaired it. It was later replaced with a more modern struc-

continued on next page

ture that lasted through the 19th century. Today nothing remains of North Battery, though there is a public park at the site with a small memorial to Rhode Island's Patriots and a great view of the waterfront. *North Battery, or Battery Park, intersection of Washington St. and Battery St., Newport, RI 02840. GPS: 41.496808, -71.321680. Open daily.*

Green End Fortifications—The Green End Fortifications, originally a British work, was turned and rebuilt during the French occupation by French and American soldiers to protect against a British attempt to retake the city. Overlooking the Green End Valley, it is the most impressive and easily accessible of the remaining earthworks around Newport, though there is little interpretation. The property, a public park, is owned and maintained by the Newport Historical Society. *Green End Fortifications, on Vernon Rd., 0.1 mile east of intersection with Boulevard, Middletown, RI 02842; 401-841-8770; www.newporthistory.org/properties/green-end-fort. GPS: 41.504051, -71.293729. Accessible daily.*

Miantonomi Fortifications—Miantonomi Hill, a commanding height, was the seat of power of a local Indian tribe long before it was used by the Patriots. In 1776, Americans built a signal tower atop the hill, along with fortifications, and the remains of these works can still be seen along the ground. The area atop the hill also contains a memorial tower to World War I veterans, rising an additional 78 feet above the 150-foot-tall hill. The climb to the top can be difficult to find, as much of it is overgrown, but if you stay on the path you will come to an unmistakable clearing at the tower. You can park along Hillside Avenue and find one of several ways up the hill. *Miantonomi Memorial Park, street parking on Hillside Ave. near Kennedy St., Newport, RI 02840. GPS: 41.511503, -71.308675. Open daily.*

Heritage Park—The small area set aside at Heritage Park is one of only a few critical areas that has been preserved from the Battle of Rhode Island. Situated in the center of the British line of August 29, 1778, Heritage Park has a short trail and some interpretive signs to help explain the landscape, the battle, and the story of Rhode Island in the American Revolution. The park is almost entirely open ground and is easy to navigate. There is a small parking area for visitors. *Heritage Park, parking on Capillary Way or Highpoint Ave. just north of Hedly St., Portsmouth, RI 02871. GPS: 41.594454, -71.263381. Open daily.*

Patriots Park—Patriots Park is the best-interpreted location that remains of the Rhode Island battlefield. Though the park is small, the impressive monument to the 1st Rhode Island Regiment is not to be missed. The memorial commemorates Bloody Run, where Black slaves and freemen fighting alongside their white fellow soldiers repulsed multiple British assaults. The large, beautiful granite work was erected in 2005 and contains a history of the 1st Rhode Island, a retelling of the battle, and a list of the men in the regiment. If you go—and you should go if you want a good understanding of the battle—be aware that navigating to the park is somewhat challenging. It is located on the left side of a curving ramp, and it comes up quickly when you're driving, so slow down to avoid missing it but be sure to also get out of traffic quickly. *Patriots Park, on northbound West Main Rd. immediately after split with RI 24, Portsmouth, RI 02871. GPS: 41.601494, -71.258107. Open daily.*

Lehigh Hill—Lehigh Hill, one of the critical Patriot defensive positions, contains a wonderful overlook of not only the middle passage of Narragansett Bay but of the Rhode Island battlefield as well. Serving as the right side of the American line and protecting the right flank of the Patriot forces, Lehigh Hill saw significant action, with the Patriots repulsing several attacks here. Like at Heritage Park, there is a small parking area as well as several interpretive signs. *Lehigh Hill, 169 East Main Rd., Portsmouth, RI 02871. GPS: 41.611245, -71.260162. Open daily.*

Butts Hill Fort—The initial American position during the Battle of Rhode Island, standing just behind and between Turkey and Quaker Hills, Butts Hill Fort is the most intact remaining work involved in the Battle of Rhode Island. Though there is little interpretation here, a memorial is there that explains the fortifications and that memorializes the action. The location is a bit off the beaten path, as compared to the other preserved locations, but it is also the most peaceful. *Butts Hill Fort, intersection of Fort St. and Butts St., Portsmouth, RI 02871. GPS: 41.615384, -71.250243. Open daily.*

Fort Barton—Fort Barton was an American work long before the Battle of Rhode Island, as the Patriots bided their time waiting for the right opportu-

continued on next page

nity to make their move. When that time came and went with the French fleet, Fort Barton was the rallying point where the Americans gathered after leaving Aquidneck Island the night of the battle. The site and some of the earthworks of Fort Barton have been well preserved and are now part of a public park. The park contains interpretation as well as an observation tower that allows you to see across the East Passage of Narragansett Bay all the way to Aquidneck Island. The hill and the tower are a bit of a steep climb, but the park and the view are worth the effort. *Fort Barton, 360 Highland Rd., Tiverton, RI 02878. GPS: 41.625100, -71.207499. Open daily.*

Only the base of the original Beavertail Lighthouse remains today.

Top: Conanicut Battery, overlooking Narragansett Bay at Newport.
Bottom: The massive Green End Fortifications in Newport, Rhode Island.

Boston Harbor Islands National and State Park oversees the management of all the harbor's many small islands, teeming with wildlife and history. Opportunities abound for harbor cruises, hikes, and camping. There are cruises that focus on the lighthouses and their histories, including Boston Light. If you come during the offseason, or just don't have time for the cruise, your best view of Boston Light and the harbor is from the southside town of Hull. *Boston Harbor Islands National and State Park, 66 Long Wharf North, Boston, MA 02110; 617-227-4321; www.bostonharborislands .org. GPS: 42.359800, -71.050728. Ferries run regularly; see website for tour hours. Boston Light viewpoint, intersection of Fitzpatrick Way and Nantasket Ave., Hull, MA 02045. GPS: 42.307077, -70.893738. Accessible daily.*

NANTASKET ROAD—On May 17, 1776, only two months after the British had evacuated Boston, the American privateer *Franklin* captured a British ship laden with much-needed gunpowder. The British fleet, however, was still anchored just outside Boston Harbor and viewed the action. The American captain grounded his ship and unloaded the precious cargo, but two days later, the British approached the still-grounded ship and tried to board her. The *Franklin*'s much greater firepower was enough to keep the British away, with light casualties.

The Battle of Nantasket Road happened around Deer Island, now connected to the mainland. A good place to view where the action happened is Coughlin Park, though no interpretation of the battle exists. *Nantasket Road—Coughlin Park, intersection of Bay View Ave. and Grand View Ave., Winthrop, MA 02152. GPS: 42.362072, -70.974922. Site accessible daily.*

FORT STRONG—Camp Hill, which had stood on Noddle's Island east of Charlestown, was consistently used as a site for fortifications until the hill itself was cut down in 1833. During the Revolution, the fortification at Camp Hill, known as Fort Strong, had a commanding view of the eastern portion of Boston Harbor.

Nothing remains of Fort Strong today, and Noddle's Island has been filled in and is part of East Boston. Brophy Park is in the general area where the fort stood, but no interpretation exists. *Fort Strong—Brophy Park, near intersection of Webster St. and Lamson St., Boston, MA 02128. GPS: 42.365285, -71.033625. Park open daily.*

FORT PUTNAM—Fort Putnam, originally built on what was known as Lechmere's Point, was part of the Boston siege line for the Patriots. It was constructed just south of what became Camp Putnam, named after General Israel Putnam, the pugnacious and somewhat famous commander from Massachusetts.

Fort Putnam has been built over and is part of the East Cambridge neighborhood. The Putnam School Building, now apartments, sits on the site; a concrete monument has been affixed to one side of the old building. *Fort Putnam, intersection of Otis St. and Sciarappa St., Cambridge, MA 02141. GPS: 42.370484, -71.081785. Site accessible daily.*

OLD CAMBRIDGE AND CAMBRIDGE COMMON ENCAMPMENT—As the men who would ultimately become the Continental Army gathered before Boston, Cambridge became the natural muster point, and Cambridge Common became the center of the Patriots' encampment. The surrounding buildings of Harvard were also used as barracks. The common was used to train the eager but green soldiers, and when Washington arrived, Cambridge continued as the army's headquarters.

Whether you're interested in the American Revolution, want to tour Harvard, or would just like to see a great neighborhood, Cambridge is a wonderful visit. Unique shops and restaurants abound, and Harvard is still the center of life here, but plenty is left from the Revolution. On Cambridge Common, you will find many memorials, pieces of art, and interpretive signs that paint a good picture of the still-wide-open common during the army's encampment. Around the common, a short walk in any direction will take you into Cambridge's old streets and houses, many of which are marked with historic signs. *Cambridge Common, intersection of Garden St. and Mason St., Cambridge, MA 02138. GPS: 42.376372, -71.121332. Accessible daily.*

REVEREND APTHORP HOUSE—The home of Reverend East Apthorp, a staunch Tory, was abandoned when the British became bottled up in Boston in 1775, and the large home became a barracks for American soldiers during the siege. Later, in 1777 after the Battle of Saratoga, none other than British commander General John Burgoyne and his staff were confined in the house until they were exchanged as prisoners.

One of several monuments at the site of the Cambridge Common Encampment.

Today the house belongs to Harvard University and is used as a dean's residence. Just outside the home, though, there is a small memorial recognizing Burgoyne's short stay here. *Reverend Apthorp House, on Linden St. just north of Bow St., Cambridge, MA 02138. GPS: 42.372116, -71.117441. Private property; memorial on west side of home.*

WILLIAM BRATTLE HOUSE—In 1727, British General William Brattle built a large house in Cambridge. Brattle stayed in the home until he and his family were forced to leave in 1774 after informing British General Thomas Gage that towns were withdrawing their gunpowder from the Provincial Powder House. The Brattle House became the headquarters of American Quartermaster General Thomas Mifflin during the siege of Boston.

The Brattle House is private property today, serving as the Cambridge Center for Adult Education. A small sign explains the building's significance on the white picket fence in front of the house. *William Brattle House, 42 Brattle St., Cambridge, MA 02138. GPS: 42.373747, -71.121499. Private property.*

LONGFELLOW HOUSE–WASHINGTON'S HEADQUARTERS NATIONAL HISTORIC SITE—George Washington took command of the disorganized, ramshackle Continental Army in Cambridge and would spend nine months with them here. It is difficult to underestimate how much this time influenced his command of the army. It was in Cambridge that he disciplined both the army, so that it could function, and himself, so that he could command such a diverse group of individuals, many of whom did not think like him at all. But Washington used this time to his advantage, forging a fighting force that would ultimately defeat the most powerful empire in the world.

The house Washington chose was one of the finest in Cambridge and is now the Longfellow House–Washington's Headquarters National Historic Site. To be sure, this is Longfellow's home, and much of the tour is focused on his fascinating life and work. But it quickly becomes evident that Longfellow, too, knew the importance of this house, and he obviously cherished the fact that Washington's influence hangs so heavily. There are full, 50-minute house tours as well as 30-minute "express tours," along with interpretation of the garden and the neighborhood. Get here early, if you can, to assure a good tour time. *Longfellow House–Washington's Headquarters National Historic Site, 105 Brattle St., Cambridge, MA 02138; 617-876-4491; www.nps.gov/long. GPS: 42.376604, -71.126622. Open for tours Wed.–Sun., May through October; grounds open daily.*

EDMUND FOWLE HOUSE—When the British shut down the Massachusetts Congress, a Provincial Congress was organized that met outside of Boston in Watertown. After the war broke out, the large home of Edmund Fowle was used for committee meetings of the Congress and was eventually the headquarters of the executive branch as well, all through the British occupation of Boston and for some time afterward. It was in this house that the first treaty between the United States and a foreign power (in this case, the Mi'kmaq and St. John's First Nations) was signed, on July 19, 1776.

The Edmund Fowle House is the headquarters of the Historical Society of Watertown. The house is open for tours one day per month and by appointment. *Edmund Fowle House, 28 Marshall St., Watertown,*

MA 02472; 617-923-6067; www.historicalsocietyofwatertownma.org. GPS: 42.368618, -71.180107. *Open for tours on third Sundays of the month and by appointment.*

ISAAC ROYALL HOUSE—It is sometimes difficult to remember that the entire United States of America, and not just the South, was a slaveholding nation. The Isaac Royall House was home to the largest slave-owning family in Massachusetts. When the Revolution broke out, the Royall family fled for England, and the home was used by General John Stark of New Hampshire during the siege of Boston.

Not only does the Royall House still stand, but so do the slave quarters, the only existing such building in the northern United States. Tours are given of the home and slave quarters, and the stories of both the Royall family and the slaves that made their opulent lifestyle possible are related. Archaeological digs on the property continue to unearth new discoveries, and a museum in the slave quarters building showcases the findings. This is one of New England's truly unique sites, and its tale is well told. *Royall House and Slave Quarters, 15 George St., Medford, MA 02155; 781-396-9032; www.royallhouse.org. GPS: 42.412049, -71.111737. Open Sat. and Sun. mid-May through October.*

PROVINCIAL POWDER HOUSE—An old windmill on a hill, 6 miles northwest of Boston, was eventually turned into a gunpowder storage house for several towns and, eventually, the colony of Massachusetts. Over the summer of 1774, the towns began to withdraw their powder, leaving only the Massachusetts stores. On September 1, 1774, General Thomas Gage, newly named military governor of Massachusetts, sent 260 men to seize the rest of the gunpowder. The detachment was unopposed in taking the 250 or so half-barrels of powder, but the populace was shocked and enraged. As word spread, the man who informed Gage that the powder was being withdrawn—William Brattle—was driven out of his home in Cambridge. More important, the Sons of Liberty devised a speedy communications network that would prevent such a thing from happening again. The next several times a "powder alarm" occurred, the British Regulars were beat to the powder by minutemen and backed down—that is, until they attempted to seize the powder in Concord.

Before Lexington and Concord, British troops confiscated gunpowder belonging to the colony of Massachusetts here at the Provincial Powder House.

The Provincial Powder House still stands in modern-day Nathan Tufts Park. Though one can't enter the powder house, it's compact enough that you can look through the grated door and windows and see inside. There is usually plenty of street parking around the park. *Provincial Powder House—Nathan Tufts Park, on Powder House Square at intersection of Broadway and College Ave., Somerville, MA 02144. GPS: 42.399833, -71.116310. Accessible daily.*

WESTON TOWN COMMON—Like many other towns in the area, Weston, Massachusetts, responded to the call when the minutemen were summoned in the early hours of April 19, 1775. Captain Samuel Lamson gathered 103 men on the Weston Town Common and headed for Lexington, where they joined the other Patriots and hit the line of British Regulars making their way back to Boston.

The Weston Town Common is still exactly that. There is a public park where you will find a boulder with a memorial plaque to Weston's minutemen. *Weston Town Common, intersection of Boston Post Rd. and Church St., Weston, MA 02493. GPS: 42.368433, -71.298451. Open daily.*

CAPTAIN JOHN MOORE HOUSE AND FITCH TAVERN—Bedford, Massachusetts, had one of the many militias to respond to the march of the British Regulars on April 19, 1775. The center of most town life in colonial New England was the tavern, and in Bedford when riders came from Lexington to spread word of the British attack it was to the taverns they went. Some of Bedford's minutemen met at Fitch Tavern for a cold, quick breakfast before marching. Along their path (denoted by small markers through the town of Bedford) is the home of Captain John Moore and his slave, Cambridge. The militia, which included Cambridge, rallied at the home before heading for Concord.

Both the 1710 Fitch Tavern and the Captain John Moore House, built in 1680, are private homes in Bedford today. A small wooden plaque on the outside of each notes its significance. *Captain John Moore House, 191 Concord Rd., Bedford, MA 01730. GPS: 42.486085, -71.296495. Fitch Tavern, 12 Great Rd., Bedford, MA 01730. GPS: 42.493519, -71.282905. Private property.*

BILLERICA TOWN COMMON—The town common served many purposes for their respective communities—gathering place, pasture, and military training ground. The militia company of Billerica, Massachusetts, gathered here early on the morning of April 19, 1775, and headed for Concord, arriving in time to assist the Concord militia in firing "the shot heard 'round the world" and pursuing the British soldiers.

The Billerica Town Common is still there and hasn't changed much. Though there are no memorials to the minutemen, you will find some plaques noting Billerica's long history and the founding of the first meeting house in 1660, several years after the town was founded. *Billerica Town Common, intersection of Boston Rd. and Cummings St., Billerica, MA 01821. GPS: 42.558510, -71.269017. Open daily.*

PARKER TAVERN—Ephraim Parker was the owner of the local tavern in Reading, Massachusetts, during the Revolution and through to his death in 1804. Parker served as a minuteman, fighting at Lexington and Concord. What puts Parker Tavern on the map, however, is the service Parker rendered after the battle. Parker Tavern was the holding place for British colonel and prisoner of war Archibald Campbell, captured in Boston in 1776. A valuable officer, Campbell stayed at the tavern until 1778 when he was exchanged for none other than Ethan Allen.

Dating to 1694, Parker Tavern is the oldest home in Reading. Today it is home to the Reading Antiquarian Society. The society provides tours of the home on Sundays for part of the year as well as by appointment. *Parker Tavern, 103 Washington St., Reading, MA 01867; www.friendsof parkertavern.com. GPS: 42.520728, -71.106847. Open Sun., May through October and by appointment.*

MARBLEHEAD AND FORT SEWALL—In the lead-up to the Revolution and for long after, citizens all over New England would participate in town hall meetings, open forums allowing all to speak their minds freely. Marblehead, Massachusetts, was typical, with its town house dating back to 1727. Fierce and inspiring debates were held here and all over the country regarding the acts of Parliament. Marblehead, particularly affected because of its reliance on the sea, eventually raised one of the most well-regarded regiments in the Continental Army. The Marblehead Regiment, almost all seamen, were responsible for the army's overnight escape from Long Island by boat as well as rowing Washington and his army across the Delaware River on the eve of the Battle of Trenton. Marblehead was also home to an ocean battery that came to be known as Fort Sewall after the Revolutionary War. Originally erected in 1742, it was refitted and improved in 1775 by a vote of the town, then manned by women and the elderly, as most of the men had joined the regiment.

The Marblehead Town House is still in use as the town hall after all these years; during normal business hours, you may be able to peek inside. (The Marblehead Police Museum is also in the basement.) It underwent a major renovation in 2013. Fort Sewall still guards Marblehead Harbor, though it is no longer used for defense and is instead a nicely interpreted public park. You will find several memorials to the Marblehead Regiment here, as well as signs telling the story of Fort Sewall and its most famous moment, when it protected "Old Ironsides," the USS *Constitu-*

Fort Sewall at Marblehead, Massachusetts.

tion, as she raced for cover from two British ships during the War of 1812. The signs provide a nice evolution of the fort, and the views from the park are lovely. One note: Parking is a little tight around Fort Sewall, but follow the posted signs and you'll be fine. *Marblehead Town House, 1727 Town House Square, GPS: 42.505307, -70.849646; Fort Sewall, intersection of Front St. and Fort Sewall Lane, GPS: 42.508399, -70.842812; both in Marblehead, MA 01945. Town House open during business hours; Fort Sewall open daily.*

SALEM—Salem, Massachusetts, was a critical port, and two fortifications existed here during the Revolution, though neither saw action. Fort Number Two, later known as Fort Pickering, was the southern fortification, sited on Winter Island; the fort had been in use to some extent since the 17th century and remained in active service until 1972. Fort Lee, more inland, was another such fort, a large and impressive earthwork that easily towered above the surrounding land.

After years of neglect, Fort Pickering was recently cleaned up and made safe for public use. It lies within Winter Island Park, and not only can you visit the old fortification, but you can also camp on the site, and a public beach is available in the park as well. There are historical markers to help you interpret the fort's history as well as a scenic overlook; most of the brick and stone are left from the Civil War era. As for Fort Lee, it is remarkably intact and can be visited—but take care doing it, as the area is entirely overgrown. A group called the Friends of Fort Lee is working to keep the site clean, as best they can, and hopefully this unique resource will soon be more accessible. *Fort Pickering—Winter Island Park, 50 Winter Island Rd., GPS: 42.527100, -70.867195; Fort Lee, west of intersection of Fort Ave. and Memorial Dr., GPS: 42.532194, -70.874300; Salem, MA 01970. Open daily.*

BEVERLY—Situated across the harbor from Salem, Beverly contained several wharves, one of which, Glover's Wharf, outfitted the schooner *Hannah* on the orders of General Washington, making it the first armed vessel of the newly united colonies. Beverly served as a naval base in 1775 and 1776, but by far the most important and profitable enterprise in Beverly at the time was privateering. Privateering, in loose terms, is legalized, government-sanctioned piracy; British vessels (merchant or naval) captured by privateers were taken to a prize court and had their contents auctioned, with part of the money going to the government and part going to the men aboard the capturing vessel. Privateering became so profitable that it became difficult for the United States Navy to recruit sailors and shipbuilders because men could make far more money through privateering. Men such as Colonel John Glover, William Bartlett, and John Cabot, each of whom had a wharf in Beverly, made small fortunes outfitting and equipping privateers to prey on British vessels.

Neither Bartlett's Wharf nor Glover's Wharf remains; the water on which they were once located has been filled in, and the land is now occupied by condominiums. But you can still visit the site, and there is a nice boardwalk with an interpretive sign from which you can picture the scene. Glover's Wharf would have been to your right, Bartlett's Wharf to your left. To really get a handle on privateering during the Revolution, visit the John Cabot House, one of the properties of Historic

Beverly. The home itself is a treat, but there is an exceptional museum that explains privateering—what it was and how it worked—and contains interesting artifacts and great exhibits on Beverly's Revolutionary past. You can also pick up a brochure for The Privateer Trail, a short tour through Beverly that will take you to several historic points related to Beverly's maritime history. *Bartlett's and Glover's Wharves, view from walkway along Water St., 0.1 mile east of Cabot St., Beverly, MA 01915. GPS: 42.541118, -70.881410. Accessible daily. John Cabot House and Visitor Center, 117 Cabot St., Beverly, MA 01915; 978-922-1186; www.historic beverly.net. GPS: 42.545884, -70.879908. Open Wed.–Sat.*

GLOUCESTER—The British ship HMS *Falcon* had been raiding American shore towns for food to feed the British army trapped in Boston. On August 8, 1775, the soldiers of the *Falcon*, after capturing one American schooner and chasing another into Gloucester Harbor, intended to land, collect stores, and burn the town. However, while the ship's men rowed toward the second schooner, they were attacked by artillery and musketry onshore. The small British boats were trapped, and not only were the men captured, but the British also sent the first schooner back to shore. Later that year, on November 29, 1775, the United States Navy schooner *Lee*, operating off Cape Ann, saw the British ordnance brig *Nancy* headed for Boston to resupply the besieged British. The British did not recognize the *Lee* at first, and she was able to approach the *Nancy*, whose seamen thought she was a pilot ship. The *Lee* did not reveal her intentions until the last minute. The *Nancy* was captured, along with her large stores of arms and ammunition.

Stage Fort Park has been the site of fortifications in Gloucester since the 17th century, and there is some interpretation about the raid in the park. The action occurred right offshore in the harbor, as did the capture of the *Nancy*. *Gloucester—Stage Fort Park, 24 Hough Ave., Gloucester, MA 01930. GPS: 42.603539, -70.679842. Open daily.*

BRADFORD MEETING HOUSE—On June 20, 1776, only 10 days after a motion to consider independence was raised in the Continental Congress, the town council of Bradford, Massachusetts, gathered to consider the motion themselves. Acting independently of their state representatives, the council formed a committee, which quickly resolved to authorize and encourage the Congress in Philadelphia to sever ties with the mother country.

Bradford is now part of Haverhill, Massachusetts, but the Bradford Meeting House still exists. It is not the same building, but it is in the same location, and portions of the original foundation were likely used in the existing structure. There is no interpretation at the site. *Bradford Meeting House Site, 10 Church St., Haverhill, MA 01835. GPS: 42.767068, -71.076062. Site accessible daily.*

NEWBURYPORT—Like Beverly, Newburyport was a significant privateering center, and was also one of the earliest. Nathaniel Tracy, an outfitter in Newburyport, had one of the first such shops in the nation. Offin Boardman, who had his own wharf in Newburyport, was one of the more bold and clever privateers; once, approaching a British warship looking for directions to Boston, Boardman tricked the captain into thinking he would be landing in Boston. He guided the captain into the Newburyport harbor, tied up the ship at his own wharf, and captured the vessel.

Newburyport is an attractive port town and is very tourist friendly, with lots of shops, restaurants, and activities along the water. Boardman's wharf, now filled in, was along this waterfront; Tracy's outfitter shop would have been near State and Temple Streets. The Custom House Maritime Museum, one of the premier maritime museums in New England, contains information on both and contains many wonderful stories about Newburyport's maritime history. *Custom House Maritime Museum, 25 Water St., Newburyport, MA 01950; 978-462-8681; www.customhousemaritimemuseum.org. GPS: 42.811857, -70.868279. Open Thurs.–Sun.*

EXETER—The town of Exeter provided conspicuous service to the independence movement in America. It was home to the New Hampshire Provincial Congress, which met in the Exeter Town House and adopted the first state constitution of any of the colonies. The state treasury was held in the Ladd-Gilman House, one of the earliest and most impressive mansions in town; it also happens to be the birthplace of Nicholas

Gilman, Jr., signer of the United States Constitution. Exeter's jail also chipped in; with New York jails filled to the brim, Exeter held several Tory prisoners from that colony during the war. Finally, Exeter's Powder House protected not only the local militia's gunpowder but also some captured from the British fort at New Castle; some of this gunpowder was rushed to Charlestown for the Battle of Bunker Hill.

Exeter's American Independence Museum includes both the Ladd-Gilman House and the Folsom Tavern. The buildings are like museums themselves, but there is plenty to see inside including an original Purple Heart awarded by George Washington himself. The Exeter jail and Exeter Town House are both gone, but Town House Common memorializes the site of the latter as well as the town's Revolutionary history. The square is a public park and contains some interpretation and memorials. The Exeter Powder House is still in its original location; a short walk on a gravel trail along the shore of a pond will take you to there, where interpretation and memorials will help you understand the importance of this remote but critical cache. There is also a sign that outlines a walking tour through the town. *American Independence Museum at Ladd-Gilman House, 1 Governor's Lane, Exeter, NH 03833; 603-772-2622; www.independencemuseum.org. GPS: 42.981809, -70.949661. Open Tues.–Sat., May through November. Exeter Town House Common, intersection of Front St. and Court St., Exeter, NH 03833. GPS: 42.980367, -70.947032. Exeter Jail location, intersection of High St. and Chestnut St., Exeter, NH 03833. GPS: 42.981061, -70.943659. Exeter Powder House, parking end of Jady Hill Ave. west of Chestnut St., Exeter, NH 03833. GPS: 42.985097, -70.947302. Sites accessible daily.*

WILLIAM PITT TAVERN—Stavers' Tavern in Portsmouth, like most taverns, was a gathering place for social life and debate, and John Stavers had the additional attraction of having space for meetings of the local Freemasons. However, Stavers, whose loyalties are still not clear, had used the sign of the Earl of Halifax to distinguish his tavern. On January 29, 1777, the fiercely Patriot locals tried to chop the sign down, leading to a scuffle and the jailing of a number of suspected Loyalists, including Stavers. Ultimately, Stavers did what a prudent businessman would do, he renamed his establishment the William Pitt Tavern, after the Englishman who had been so outspoken for American liberties in the British Parliament.

William Pitt Tavern is part of the sprawling Strawbery Banke Museum complex. A wonderful collection of 39 historic buildings, most of which are original, Strawbery Banke's living history programs cover the colonial era through World War II. While some houses can be toured at your leisure, others serve as museum spaces with both established and rotating exhibits. Your admission will get you access to all 10 acres of the museum. The tavern has been restored largely to its 18th-century appearance on the ground floor, while the upper floors are still used for the local Masons, just as John Stavers had intended when he built the building in 1766. If you come during the offseason, you won't be able to enter the tavern, but the property is on the edge of the Strawberry Banke Museum, and you can still see it from the outside. You will find an interpretive sign across the street. *William Pitt Tavern—Strawbery Banke Museum, 14 Hancock St., Portsmouth, NH 03802;605-433-1100; www .strawberybanke.org. GPS: 43.075112, -70.753086. Open daily. Tavern is located at 416 Court St.; GPS: 43.076578, -70.754084.*

NEW HAMPSHIRE COLONIAL STATE HOUSE—New Hampshire, formerly part of Massachusetts, was made its own separate colony in 1741 by King George II. The old colony house, which was eventually also used as the New Hampshire State House after the war, saw a lot of history—protests of the Stamp Act, the first public reading of the Declaration of Independence in New Hampshire, the celebration of the end of the Revolutionary War, and a visit from President George Washington after the Constitution was ratified. The state house remained in use until 1836, when most of the building was torn down and the rest refurbished.

The New Hampshire Colonial State House still exists, but it is not standing. It was dismantled and kept in storage. Hope remains that someday this old state house can be partially rebuilt, even if not in its original location. Its former location is marked by a monument and historical markers in downtown Portsmouth. *New Hampshire State House Site, intersection of Pleasant St. and Daniel St., Portsmouth, NH 03801. GPS: 43.076933, -70.757721. Site accessible daily.*

Strawbery Banke, a living history museum in Portsmouth, New Hampshire.

GOVERNOR JOHN WENTWORTH HOUSE—John Wentworth was the last royal governor of New Hampshire. Wentworth had accomplished much in the colony, including the establishment of Dartmouth College, and stayed here at his Portsmouth home through the beginning of the war. However, in June 1775, Wentworth made it clear where his loyalties lay when he housed a prominent royalist. A mob formed and threatened to destroy the house before the man was given up for trial, and Wentworth and his family left that night.

Today the Wentworth home is a senior living community and is not available for tours. Outside of a few additions, though, the mansion has not changed much, and there is a sign outside with a history of the home, Wentworth's life, and the night of the riots that drove his family out. *Governor John Wentworth House, 346 Pleasant St., Portsmouth, NH 03801. GPS: 43.073767, -70.752780. Private property.*

FORT CONSTITUTION—After the British seized the gunpowder and munitions at the Provincial Powder House outside Boston in September 1774, a network of communication was established to warn of similar events. The day came on December 13, 1774, when Paul Revere, after a long ride through a harsh winter day, pulled into Portsmouth, New Hampshire, with information that British Regulars would be marching there to take possession of the arms and ammunition at Fort William and Mary, just outside the town. The next day, 400 of Portsmouth's militiamen marched on the fort and approached it by sea, much to the distress of the six British soldiers garrisoning the post. New Hampshire Royal Governor John Wentworth sent for assistance, but the fort was easily overrun and the six soldiers taken prisoner. As the fort's contents were distributed throughout New England, further warnings carried on, and the next morning over 1,000 Patriots were at Portsmouth, hauling away additional artillery and other stores. The Portsmouth Alarm served as a successful test of the communications network created by the Sons of Liberty; it would prove extraordinarily effective at Lexington and Concord four months later.

Fort Constitution, as it was renamed after the war, is now a state historic site in what is now New Castle. The grounds are open to the public for recreational purposes, and though you will find features that show the fort's use through World War II, there is plenty of interpretation about the Portsmouth Alarm. The signs around the fort recognize the action here in 1774 as the first victory of the American Revolution—a point that's hard to argue. A neat place to climb around and explore as well as take in Portsmouth Harbor and its historic lighthouse, Fort Constitution also makes a great picnic site if you're looking for a stop. *Fort Constitution State Historic Site, 25 Wentworth Rd., New Castle, NH 03854; 603-271-3556; www.nhstateparks.org/visit/historic-sites/fort-constitution-historic-site. GPS: 43.071159, -70.710150. Open daily.*

NEW HAVEN AND BLACK ROCK FORT / FORT NATHAN HALE—By 1779, after the French entered the war, the British strategy for subduing the rebellious colonies had shifted to the south, with the additional priority of holding on to New York City. There was still the problem of the Continental Army's presence near New York, and it was decided to try to lure it into action. On July 5, 1779, a British force led by General William Tryon, a former governor of both New York and North Carolina, landed at New Haven, Connecticut, with the intention of raiding and

A monument to the American defenders at New Haven.

then burning the town. The British targeted Black Rock Fort, on the east side of New Haven Harbor, as well as the western shore. After taking the fort, the British met heavy resistance at Beacon Hill and to the west. They were able to do a significant amount of damage, however, and went on to raid and burn other towns on the Connecticut shore. Ultimately, Tryon's campaign was a failure, as both the Americans and British protested his destructive acts.

Several sites in New Haven commemorate Tryon's Raid. Black Rock Fort, later known as Fort Nathan Hale, has been preserved and is open for visitation; though used all the way through the Civil War, the earthworks are in the same location, and interpretive signs are around the site. A self-guided tour brochure is available when the visitor center is closed. In a nearby public park is Beacon Hill, where locals lit a signal to warn the countryside of the British attack and where the Patriots later resisted. Take care in visiting this site, as the fort is somewhat overgrown. On the west side of the harbor in Defender's Park is an impressive

The moat surrounding Black Rock Fort.

memorial to the citizens of New Haven at the point where they turned back the British wave. *Fort Nathan Hale / Black Rock Fort, 36 Woodward Ave., New Haven, CT 06512; www.fort-nathan-hale.org. GPS: 41.270070, -72.900982. Site accessible daily; visitor center open Memorial Day through Labor Day. Beacon Hill—Fort Wooster Park, intersection of Beacon Ave. and Clarendon St., New Haven, CT 06512. GPS: 41.282806, -72.892743. Open daily. Defender's Park, intersection of Columbus Ave. and Davenport Ave., New Haven, CT 06519. GPS: 41.297697, -72.947294. Open daily.*

JOSEPH WEBB HOUSE—A small suburban street in Wethersfield, Connecticut, is just outside Hartford, which holds a remarkable amount of Revolutionary history. One home belonged to Silas Deane, member of the Continental Congress and the negotiator who, along with Benjamin Franklin and Arthur Lee, brought France squarely to the side of the Americans for the duration of the war. His neighbor, Joseph Webb, had one of the finest houses in Wethersfield, and when General George Washington needed a temporary site for five days in May 1781, the Webbs happily offered. Why Wethersfield? It was halfway between Washington's headquarters at New Windsor, New York, and the headquarters of comte de Rochambeau, head of the French army in America, at Newport, Rhode Island. On May 22, 1781, Rochambeau arrived, and he and Washington met to discuss a joint strategy. Although tentative plans had the armies meeting to the west of New York City, it also allowed for a contingency; that contingency led to the Yorktown Campaign, the siege that would ultimately end the Revolutionary War.

The Joseph Webb and Silas Deane homes have been meticulously restored and are available for tours, as are several other sites around Wethersfield. They are part of the Webb Deane Stevens Museum, owned and maintained by the National Society of the Colonial Society of Dames of America in the State of Connecticut. One admission will get you into all the homes. Although the tour of the Webb home obviously focuses on the Washington-Rochambeau meeting, there are plenty of interesting stories about the Webbs, too, and the parlor in which it is thought the two generals met holds two curious murals painted in 1916 by artist Wallace Nutting showing the meeting as well as the surrender at Yorktown. The Deane House, a lovely home in its own right, presents the controversial Deane in a fair and fact-based way that sidesteps his alleged treacheries. *Webb Deane Stevens Museum, 211 Main St., Wethersfield, CT 06109; 860-529-0612; www.wdsmuseum.org. GPS: 41.712033, -72.652972. Open daily May through October; weekends April and November; by appointment only January through March.*

WEST HARTFORD CANTONMENT—For a short time in November 1778, the Continental Army camped in West Hartford, Connecticut. That short time left a big imprint: Approximately 860 acres were utilized, and over 200 stone fireplaces were built. The site is preserved as the Continental Army Hospital State Monument, though it is difficult to visit; there are no facilities or trails at this time. Hopefully, some interpretation and the opportunity to experience the site will be installed in the future. *Eltham's Landing, north of Albany Ave. between Hartford Reservoir No. 6 and Ferncliff Dr., West Hartford, CT 06107. GPS: 41.794574, -72.778526. Site inaccessible.*

Loyalists and American deserters were kept at Old New-Gate Prison & Copper Mine in East Granby, Massachusetts.

OLD NEW-GATE PRISON & COPPER MINE—In 1773, the colony of Connecticut came up with what, at the time, seemed like a novel and even progressive way to treat prisoners: put them to work. The location chosen was a copper mine in the town of Simsbury, and the prisoners were forced into underground mining. After the war began, the prison also began to house British Loyalists and deserters from the Continental Army. The conditions were atrocious; prisoners were forced to both work and sleep in the damp, cold mine, and escape attempts were common (and often successful). The prison was closed after the prisoners burned down buildings three times during escape attempts, but it was reopened by the state after the war and remained in use for several decades, with additional buildings and prisoners' quarters erected.

Old New-Gate Prison & Copper Mine has been preserved as a state museum. Though many of the buildings are now in ruins, the high prison walls make it easy to picture the scene. A small museum and a lot of interpretation is on this small site, and guides are available to answer your questions. The mountaintop view from the site is picturesque, but it is the view underground that you will remember. Paved walkways will take you through the mining tunnels and help you get a sense of the harsh conditions prisoners faced. (Be sure to bring proper shoes, as well as a jacket; it's a cool 55 degrees down there.) *Old New-Gate Prison & Copper Mine, 115 Newgate Rd., East Granby, CT 06026; 860-653-3563; www.portal.ct.gov/DECD/Content/Historic-Preservation/04_State_Museums/Old-Newgate-Prison-and-Copper-Mine. GPS: 41.963094, -72.745257. Open Thurs.–Mon., May through October.*

STAFFORD HOLLOW FURNACES—In 1779, the mostly rural community of Stafford Hollow, Connecticut was transformed into an industrial center. A local man named John Phelps saw promise in the local bogs—specifically, the "bog iron" in it. Phelps built a furnace that eventually grew into a promising local enterprise and went to work producing artillery and cannonballs for the Americans.

Stafford Hollow is a historic district today, but not much is left of the furnaces. However, one can easily find the dam that forms the critical millpond around which the town developed; just look under the Leonard Road Bridge, and you'll find the original dam that turned Furnace Brook into Riverside Pond. There is no interpretation about the furnaces in town. *Stafford Hollow Furnaces—Mill Dam, underneath bridge on Leonard Rd. just south of intersection with Old Monson Rd., Stafford Springs, CT 06076. GPS: 41.985569, -72.290207. Site accessible daily.*

NATHAN HALE HOMESTEAD—Few Connecticut legends loom larger than Nathan Hale. Captured as a spy, the 21-year-old Hale, standing on the gallows, spoke his now immortal last words: "I only regret that I have but one life to lose for my country." Though there is some tarnish on the legend—the inexperienced Hale should never have been sent on his failed mission, and it is possible that he did not utter those inspiring words—Hale is worthy of remembrance nonetheless. In the end, it's enough to realize that the young schoolteacher volunteered for a dangerous mission and indeed gave his life for his country, making the ultimate sacrifice.

The Nathan Hale Homestead is the site where Hale grew up, as did his seven brothers—six of whom served the American army, and three of whom died for its cause. The site is a remembrance of all of them as well as the sacrifices made for liberty by countless families like theirs. The grounds are open throughout the year but try to visit for a tour of the home; it will give you the best background on the Hale family's devotion. The home is remarkably intact, and other period buildings are on site that provide plenty of fun and worthwhile activities for kids. The Hale Homestead has plenty of modern facilities as well and is open for other special events throughout the year; check the website if you plan to visit on an off-day, there's a good chance you'll get lucky. *Nathan Hale Homestead, 2299 South St., Coventry, CT 06238; 860-742-6917; www.ctlandmarks.org/nathan-hale-homestead. GPS: 41.764436, -72.345738. Tours available Fri.–Sun., May through October; grounds open daily.*

REVOLUTIONARY WAR OFFICE—Before and during the Revolutionary War, colonial and local organizations formed Committees of Safety, or Councils of Safety, organizations whose purpose was primarily to see to public safety and defense. These councils and committees arranged everything from training soldiers to the logistics operations needed to get them supplies and transport. Connecticut, which remarkably kept British colonial Governor Jonathan Trumbull in office from 1769 through and beyond the war until 1784, had one of the most impressive records of any of the Committees of Safety, with much of the credit going to Trumbull, a former merchant. Connecticut was soon known as the Provision State, working hard to supply not only its own needs but also those of George Washington's Continental Army. Just down the street from Trumbull's home was his store where he met with many of the army's leaders including Washington; the store became headquarters for Connecticut's Council of Safety and was known as the War Office.

The Revolutionary War Office still stands and is available for tours. Maintained by the Connecticut Sons of the American Revolution, you can visit the original building (though moved from its original location) and learn about both Trumbull and the long strides Connecticut made in supporting the Revolution. Trumbull's home, though it is not open for tours, is still just down the street. There is a maxim among history buffs that "amateurs study strategy, professionals study logistics"; if you ever wanted to learn more about that surprisingly fascinating aspect of the American Revolution, this is the place. *Revolutionary War Office, 149 West Town St., Lebanon, CT 06249; 860-334-2858; www.sarconnecticut .org/historic-sites/trumbull-war-office. GPS: 41.637620, -72.215832. Open Fri.–Sun., June through August, Sat.–Sun. in September.*

HUNTINGTON HOMESTEAD MUSEUM—In 1731, Samuel Huntington, one of 10 children, was born into a prosperous and well-established Connecticut family. The young Samuel would learn much from his family, eventually going into law practice and then launching an impressive political career. Elected to the Continental Congress, Huntington would sign the Declaration of Independence and become its president from 1779 to 1781. Huntington would go on to replace the venerable John Trumbull as governor of Connecticut in 1785, an office he would hold until his death in 1796.

The Huntington Homestead is the birthplace of Samuel Huntington. Built for his father in 1723, Huntington remained here for almost 30 years before striking out on his own and initiating his remarkable career. The home seen today is an expansion of the original; tours are limited but provide a good overview of this little-known Founding Father's life. Continuing exploration of the house and the grounds continues to reveal much about the site's history. Huntington Homestead is also a stop on the Washington-Rochambeau Revolutionary Route, as the French army marched past the home on their way to rendezvous with the Americans before the Yorktown Campaign. *Huntington Homestead, 36 Huntington Rd., Scotland, CT 06264; 860-423-1547; www.huntingtonhomestead.org. GPS: 41.698589, -72.085400. Open first Saturday of each month, May through October.*

NEW LONDON AND FORT GRISWOLD—New London Harbor, at the mouth of the Thames River, was a hotbed for American privateering. British General Henry Clinton was ready to put a stop to it and sent none other than turncoat Benedict Arnold on a mission to destroy supplies and, possibly, New London itself. On September 6, 1781, Arnold's men landed on both shores of the river; the eastern column moved toward lightly held Fort Trumbull while the western contingent headed for Fort Griswold atop Groton Heights. Fort Trumbull was almost immediately abandoned, with the men moving to the much more defensible Fort

The entrance to Fort Griswold in Groton, Connecticut.

Griswold. The British attacked Fort Griswold on three sides and overwhelmed the defenders after 45 minutes. It is from this point that the details are difficult to discern. The American commander, Colonel William Ledyard, attempted to surrender, but he was allegedly killed with his own sword after he turned it over. Before long, the surrender turned into a massacre, with the angry British soldiers, who had lost two of their commanders, bayoneting many of the Americans on the spot. In all, 145 of the 175 defenders of Fort Griswold were killed or mortally wounded. Arnold would go on to capture New London and its many supplies; the town was also burned, which Arnold said was an accident but which many Americans said was intentional.

Both Fort Trumbull and Fort Griswold are state parks today. Fort Trumbull State Park and Museum, now a massive stone fortification, is virtually unrecognizable from its appearance during the Revolution, but there is a museum that covers the fort's evolution, and one can easily view Fort Griswold across the harbor from the fort's grounds. Fort

Griswold Battlefield State Park, where the massacre at Groton Heights occurred, has been restored to its wartime appearance. There are plenty of interpretive signs that tell the story of the battle and the massacre, as well as the history of the massive stone obelisk erected in 1830. A stone marks the spot where Ledyard was slain, and the steep hilltop fortification contains a viewing platform, a covered way to still-preserved forward trenches, and a small museum. Finally, if you feel like a short cruise, a water taxi will take you between Fort Trumbull and Fort Griswold. *Fort Trumbull State Park, 90 Walbach St., New London, CT 06320; 860-444-7591; www.portal.ct.gov/DEEP/State-Parks/Parks/Fort-Trumbull -State-Park. GPS: 41.343620, -72.094806. Open Sat.–Sun., Memorial Day to Labor Day. Fort Griswold Battlefield State Park, intersection of Monument St. and Smith St., Groton, CT 06340; 860-444-7591; www.portal.ct .gov/DEEP/State-Parks/Parks/Fort-Griswold-Battlefield-State-Park. GPS: 41.354736, -72.080167. Grounds open daily; visitor center open Wed.– Sun., Memorial Day to Labor Day.*

BLOCK ISLAND—On April 5, 1776, a squadron of the fledgling Continental Navy ran into the British frigate HMS *Glasgow* in the waters between Long Island and Block Island, off the Rhode Island coast and just east of Long Island Sound. The Americans engaged, but although they damaged the ship, *Glasgow* was able to escape and fight another day, much to the chagrin of Congress, who launched an investigation that resulted in the dismissal of a few of the captains involved.

The Block Island Ferry runs from three locations: Narragansett and Newport, Rhode Island, and Fall River, Massachusetts. It's a lovely island to visit and taking the trip via ferry is probably the best way to see the actual battleground itself—the ocean. Check the website for specific departure times from each location; the information from the nearest point, Narragansett, is provided here. On a clear day, you can also see Block Island from several points along the Rhode Island and Connecticut shores, as well as from Montauk on Long Island. *Block Island Ferry, 304 Great Island Rd., Narragansett, RI 02882; 866-783-7996; www.blockislandferry.com. GPS: 41.379205, -71.510276. Check website for schedule.*

POPLAR POINT—Poplar Point, overlooking the upper part of the West Passage of Narragansett Bay, held a small contingent of artillery to guard Wickford Harbor. Though not as large as Newport, Wickford was an important port town, and it managed to escape the war without having been attacked.

At the existing Poplar Point Lighthouse, a marker tells of the arming of Poplar Point by the locals. The lighthouse itself postdates the revolution. *Poplar Point, on Poplar Ave. 0.1 mile east of Armington St., North Kingstown, RI 02852. GPS: 41.570863, -71.439443. Signs accessible daily.*

GENERAL JAMES MITCHELL VARNUM HOUSE—From the outbreak of the Revolutionary War, James Mitchell Varnum was at the forefront of the military action, and he quickly rose through the ranks to become a brigadier general and one of Washington's trusted lieutenants. Varnum was a radical in one important sense: He openly advocated for an armed regiment of Black soldiers. Though Washington was skeptical at first, Varnum got his wish and formed what became the 1st Rhode Island Regiment, a largely African American unit. The regiment distinguished itself for its valor at the Battle of Rhode Island, impressing the value of Black soldiers on both sides of the battle line.

Today, General Varnum's house in East Greenwich, Rhode Island, is maintained by the Varnum Continentals, a group dedicated to encouraging American patriotism. Built for Varnum in 1773, the home contains several of his original pieces, including his writing desk, and contains items not only from his life but other periods of American history as well. Tours are limited to the summer, so be sure to check for times. *General James Mitchell Varnum House Museum, 57 Peirce St., East Greenwich, RI 02818; 401-884-1776; www.varnumcontinentals.org. GPS: 41.662141, -71.451201. Open for tours in summer; check website for days.*

NATHANAEL GREENE HOMESTEAD—Nathanael Greene, named a general first in Rhode Island's provincial forces and shortly after in the Continental Army, had been raised by his father to be an ironmaster, and in 1770 he chose to build a forge here in Coventry, Rhode Island. Despite some initial setbacks, the forge maintained as a maker of anchors and chains. Greene was living here when he married his lovely and popular wife, Catharine. The Greene family was generous to its community, and the home they built here was soon known as Spell Hall, with Nathanael—who had no formal education—providing a teacher for local children. Caty, as she was called, proved equally generous, opening the home to recovering veterans, several of whom died in the home. During the war, Greene personally assumed some of the debts his military forces took on; ultimately, he was forced to turn the property over to his brother in 1785, and he and Caty moved to Savannah, Georgia, where he died the next year at the young age of 44. The homestead remained in the family until 1915.

Greene's legacy of humble Quaker turned war hero is well told here at the Nathanael Greene Homestead, maintained as a historic site since 1919, shortly after the family sold it. There is no better place to understand Greene's remarkable beginnings and to see how sheer will forged him into one of America's great generals. The Greene home, Spell Hall, is in excellent condition and can be toured, and there are also several monuments and other interpretive signs on the grounds. Efforts to expand the property's use are progressing, with plans to build a period-style barn in the works. *Nathanael Greene Homestead, 50 Taft St., Coventry, RI 02816; www.nathanaelgreenehomestead.org. GPS: 41.694188, -71.544296. Open for tours Fri.–Mon., April through October.*

WATERMAN TAVERN AND ENCAMPMENT—Comte de Rochambeau's French army, on its way to unite with Washington's Continentals, stopped for the night in the area around Waterman Tavern and camped. The officers stayed in the comfort of the tavern itself, but not for long; the army was on the move the next day.

The former Waterman Tavern is now a private home. There is a small boulder in front of the home noting its importance, as well as a small sign near the door, but please respect the rights of the owners. *Waterman Tavern, on Maple Valley Road at intersection with Chaplin Dr., Coventry, RI 02816. GPS: 41.719330, -71.659533. Private property.*

HOPE FURNACE—Like other forges in the area, the Hope Furnace was pressed into the service of the Continental Army, making artillery for

Washington's men. The furnace, located in the village of Scituate, was one of several industrial works throughout town.

Scituate's history has been nicely preserved through a community project taken up by the local school of North Scituate. The school has planted QR codes throughout the town with which you can download historic information. The sign for Hope Furnace is in front of the Hope Library, where you'll also find a monument that preserves one of the actual cannons produced at Hope Furnace and that serves as a memorial to all of Hope's Patriots through the centuries. The furnace itself, at least the portions above ground, are no longer to be found. *Hope Furnace Memorial—Hope Library, 374 N Rd., Hope, RI 02831. GPS: 41.736507, -71.563727. Site accessible daily.*

GASPEE AFFAIR—Before the Boston Tea Party, there was the *Gaspee* Affair. HMS *Gaspee* was a revenue cutter, a small ship designed for enforcing the British Parliament's taxation acts as well as intercepting

Gaspee Point Overlook on Narragansett Bay, Warwick, Rhode Island.

smuggling ships. The acts were particularly unpopular in Rhode Island's port communities, and *Gaspee* had become infamous among the locals for its aggressive actions. Late on June 9, 1772, the ship ran aground just off Namquit Point, and her captain decided to wait for high tide before attempting to get off. The citizens of Rhode Island, sensing an opportunity, were not willing to wait that long. A contingent of men from Providence rowed out to HMS *Gaspee*, took her crew captive, and burned her to the waterline. A ship of his majesty's navy being destroyed by citizens did not sit well with the British government, and the men were charged with treason. Ultimately, though, protests throughout the colonies, jurisdictional issues, and other complications prevented the men from ever being brought to trial. It was a major act of rebellion that not only encouraged further acts of resistance but also proved that when it came to the perceived injustices of Parliament, the American colonies were united. Before long, Namquit Point took on the name of Gaspee Point in remembrance.

Warwick has erected an overlook of Gaspee Point that holds an interpretive sign and a memorial boulder commemorating the event. It is usually kept up nicely, with wooden benches and some local gardening, though occasionally the view of the water is obscured by the surrounding vegetation. Even with this, it's the best place to view where the Patriots took their revolutionary action. Note that there is no parking at the site, and traffic can be heavy, so find parking in the local neighborhood and take care crossing the road. *Gaspee Point Overlook, on Narragansett Ave. across from intersection with Carrie Brown Ave., Warwick, RI 02888. GPS: 41.748731, -71.384606. Site accessible daily.*

ROGER WILLIAMS NATIONAL MEMORIAL—To fully understand New England's high regard for liberty, one must study its history of tolerance. In the beginning, the settlers of the Massachusetts Bay colonies were seeking religious freedom, but they also had little tolerance for faiths outside Puritanism. Enter radical Roger Williams, who challenged these ideas, believing that freedom of religion was as important as all other liberties. Eventually his ideas caught up with him, and he was forced to leave in 1635. Rather than be deported, though, Williams fled west, eventually leaving the jurisdiction of Plymouth colony and, thanks to the again-radical good relations he had forged with the Native American population, was allowed to settle, with his followers, in what he dubbed Providence. The new settlement—not bound by any charters from the king—provided an equal amount of land for each household, equal voting rights, and complete freedom of thought, including religious worship. Williams would eventually secure a royal charter for the Colony of Rhode Island and Providence Plantations; his ideas of tolerance and the separation of church and state spread and ultimately became founding principles of the United States of America.

Roger Williams National Memorial is a celebration and examination of diversity and religious tolerance. At the beautiful park along the Moshassuck River, you will find memorials and gardens dedicated to several notables who have contributed to Rhode Island's well-earned reputation as a world pioneer in this area. Taking center stage, though, is the monument to Williams, as well as the spring that led him to found Providence here. The visitor center is exceptional, showing a film about Williams's legacy and featuring several exhibits showcasing not only how radical these ideas were in the 17th century but also relating them to issues of today. *Roger Williams National Memorial, visitor center at 282 North Main St., Providence, RI 02903; 401-521-7266; www.nps.gov/rowi. GPS: 41.831363, -71.410769. Grounds open daily; visitor center open Wed.–Sat., January through March; open daily April through December.*

BRISTOL WATERFRONT—By the time of the Revolutionary War, Bristol, Rhode Island, was a leading commercial port and center of the slave trade. As such, it became a target for the British. On October 7, 1775, a group of 10 British ships shelled the town, demanding provisions; much damage was done, but a compromise was reached before the town was destroyed. They returned on May 25, 1778, however, burning 16 houses and a church. Bristol soon recovered and resumed her place as a major shipping center.

Almost all colonial Bristol is gone, but you can still walk along the waterfront for a view of Narragansett Bay, from which the British shelled the town. Some interpretive signs are here, but nothing related to the Revolution. If you'd like more detail, you can visit the museum of the Bristol Historical & Preservation Society, where you'll find a few artifacts from the British bombardment. *Bristol Waterfront, access at Independence Park, intersection of Thames St. and Franklin St., GPS: 41.673489, -71.278984; Bristol Historical & Preservation Society Museum, 48 Court St., Bristol, RI 02809; 401-253-7223; www.bhpsri.org. GPS: 41.669689, -71.275156. Waterfront accessible daily; museum open Wed.–Fri. and summer Saturdays.*

MOUNT HOPE FARM—In 1744, Mount Hope Farm, just outside Bristol, Rhode Island, came into the possession of Isaac Royall, a member of one of New England's wealthiest families and possibly its largest slaveholder. Royall built a mansion the next year, and the family leased the property for farming in 1762. When the Revolutionary War came, the Royall family was forced to flee, and Mount Hope Farm became the property of the new state of Rhode Island. The home was used as headquarters by Generals John Stark and John Sullivan, and the grounds around the home were used as an encampment. After the war, the home was sold to General Nathan Miller, who subsequently sold it to William Bradford, a future deputy governor of Rhode Island and champion of the United States Constitution.

Mount Hope Farm is open for tours today, and the mansion that Royall built is still standing. The above is just a snippet of the history you'll find here. The land was previously the seat of the great Native American Chief Massasoit's Wampanoag tribe. Massasoit was succeeded by his sons, Wamsutta and Metacomet; Metacomet, who would legally change his name to Philip, allied other tribes against the colonists and instigated King Philip's War, during which he was killed near the Mount Hope property. There's plenty to see and do here—the site is still a working farm, and kids will love the interactions with the animals. Better yet, get the full treatment and stay at the farm; it also serves as an outstanding bed and breakfast in a beautiful setting overlooking Mount Hope Bay. *Mount Hope Farm, 250 Metacom Ave., Bristol, RI 02809; 401-254-1745; www.mounthopefarm.org. GPS: 41.669900, -71.257895. Open daily.*

PORTSMOUTH FRIENDS MEETINGHOUSE AND PARSONAGE—The Revolutionary War put Quakers in a difficult position. Generally, they made a point of not committing to either side of the conflict, and certainly not fighting on one side or the other. As a result, they gained the enmity of both. The Portsmouth Friends Meeting House, one of the first in the Americas, represents one of the many Quaker communities that suffered. The Meeting House was built between 1699 and 1702 and had a well-established following until the British arrived in 1776, when both shipping and the population dried up. The meetinghouse itself was used as a barracks and ammunition magazine by the British and Hessians, and its location near the crest of Quaker Hill put it squarely in the line of fire during the Battle of Rhode Island, though it suffered little damage.

The Portsmouth Friends Meetinghouse and Parsonage is still in active service. It is not open for public tours, but the property can be visited. There is a cemetery onsite that may hold some veterans of the Revolution. There is also a small memorial in the median of the roadway across from the church that contains a British cannon used during the Battle of Rhode Island. *Portsmouth Friends Meetinghouse and Parsonage, 11 Middle Rd., Portsmouth, RI 02871. GPS: 41.590536, -71.254016. Site accessible daily.*

OVERING FARM / PRESCOTT FARM—Nicholas Overing had a fine farm north of Newport, and when the British occupied the city in 1776, General Richard Prescott, who disliked his location in the city, chose to make his headquarters at the Overing House. On July 10, 1777, a daring night raid was led by American Lieutenant Colonel William Barton. His men landed near the house, overpowered the single guard stationed there, and captured Prescott. The incident proved embarrassing for the British but profitable for the Americans; Prescott would be exchanged for a man who was, at the time, one of America's most respected generals—Charles Lee.

Today Overing Farm is better known as Prescott Farm. The property is carefully maintained by the Newport Restoration Foundation. The site contains several period buildings, gardens, and orchards, and even a windmill. The grounds are free to roam, and interpretive programs are held regularly. Though the Overing House itself is privately owned, it is easily viewed from the property, and there are interpretive signs that tell the story of Prescott's capture. *Prescott Farm, 2009 West Main Rd., Middletown, RI 02842; 401-846-4152; www.newportrestoration.org/nrf -property-spotlight-prescott-farm/. GPS: 41.553410, -71.290994. Open daily.*

TIVERTON FOUR CORNERS—When the British occupied Aquidneck Island, many of the Patriot locals who did not want to stick around relocated just off the island to the town of Tiverton. Tiverton's Four Corners was the center of community life and soon hosted a large refugee population. As American forces prepared for the invasion of Rhode Island, the Marquis de Lafayette took his headquarters here at Tiverton, just north of the Four Corners.

Though many of the homes don't date to the colonial period, the Chace-Cory House, from 1730, now serves as the Tiverton Historical Society Museum. Several outbuildings are also on the property, and you'll find information on Tiverton's diverse history. If you can't visit during the museum's limited open hours, it's only a few extra steps to the Four Corners, where you'll find some interpretation of the town's history. *Tiverton Four Corners—Chace-Cory Museum, 3908 Main Rd., Tiverton, RI 02878; www.tivertonhistorical.org/chace-cory-house. GPS: 41.570448, -71.187494. Open Sun., June through August and by appointment.*

WESTPORT POINT—Westport Point in Massachusetts saw its first wharf as early as 1740. Though it would later be known as a major whaling town, during the Revolutionary War the well-protected Westport Point was a natural center for privateering.

Though the whaling industry has disappeared, Westport remains tied to the sea. A drive down the point, now a historic district, contains many historical homes, several of which are from the colonial period. There is some interpretation at the marina at the end of the point, as well as a memorial to those Westport mariners who were lost at sea. *Westport Point Historic District, on Main Rd. south to end of point, Westport Point, MA 02791. GPS: 41.516582, -71.071298. Site accessible daily.*

NEW BEDFORD / FAIR HAVEN / FORT PHOENIX—The British fight against privateering, which had made a measurable dent in their shipping to and from the colonies, was a never-ending battle. In September 1778, after the British had solidified their base in Newport, an expedition under General Charles Grey raided towns along the Massachusetts coast to deter further privateering. On September 5, Grey approached Buzzard's Bay, leading to the port towns of Fairhaven and New Bedford.

Artillery is displayed at the site of Fort Phoenix outside New Bedford Harbor.

The first target was the small fortress at Fair Haven protecting the harbor. Manned by only 34 men, the fort was quickly overwhelmed and destroyed. Grey's troops went on to destroy New Bedford as well, devastating its local economy. It was not long before signs of life reappeared, though; the fort was rebuilt and named Fort Phoenix, and New Bedford would go on to have a notable future as a whaling port.

Fort Phoenix State Reservation preserves the fort, which remained active through the 1870s, and it is in excellent shape today. There is plenty of interpretation, and besides having the fort to explore and climb around, there is an excellent beach that is part of the park, making it a great stop for the kids. As for New Bedford, most of the history that you'll find is contained within New Bedford Whaling National Historical Park. There are also a few interpretive signs around the city that relate to its Revolutionary past. One of these is outside the former shop of Leonard Jarvis, a prominent outfitter of privateers and spy ships whose shop was burned by the British. Also, the New Bedford Common

Burying Ground, somewhat inconspicuous along the city's wharves, is said to contain both Continental and British sailors from a naval battle that occurred just outside the harbor. *Fort Phoenix State Reservation, entrance to fort area at Fort St. and Beacon St., Fairhaven, MA 02719; 508-992-4524; www.mass.gov/locations/fort-phoenix-state-reservation. GPS: 41.624604, -70.900528. Open daily. Jarvis outfitter shop site, southeast corner of intersection of Union St. and Water St., New Bedford, MA 02740. GPS: 41.634486, -70.922666. Site accessible daily. New Bedford Common Burying Ground, intersection of Griffin Ct. and 2nd St., New Bedford, MA 02740. GPS: 41.627992, -70.922972. Sites accessible daily.*

MARTHA'S VINEYARD—After raiding New Bedford and Fair Haven, General Charles Grey's force moved on to target privateering originating out of Martha's Vineyard. Entering Vineyard Haven Harbor on September 10, 1778, Grey's troops went on a six-day spree, raiding the island's towns and gathering food and supplies, leaving the inhabitants with little. Grey also made it a point to destroy their boats and related industries, a devastating blow to a place so dependent on the sea.

The recently opened Martha's Vineyard Museum showcases a comprehensive history of the island, including the colonial and Revolutionary periods. There's something for everyone here, including enough interactive exhibits to keep kids busy. The museum also overlooks Vineyard Haven, center of British operations during Grey's raid. *Martha's Vineyard Museum, 151 Lagoon Pond Rd., Vineyard Haven, MA 02568; 508-627-4441 www.mvmuseum.org. GPS: 41.449521, -70.598708. Open Tues.–Sun.*

LAFAYETTE-DURFEE HOUSE—Colonel Joseph Durfee, an officer in the Continental Army, returned home to Fall River, Massachusetts, to find that it had been receiving frequent harassment from British forces. Durfee raised his own units and organized a regular watch for the town. This proved wise, for on May 25, 1778, the British approached under darkness. Not responding to a sentinel's calls, a British landing party of 150 men were fired upon and forced to retreat from the small port. Durfee served under the Marquis de Lafayette, who would become a frequent visitor.

The Lafayette-Durfee House just underwent a major rehabilitation and is now a living history center. For now, it is only open for special events, but those events are frequent, so check the website to see what's coming up. *Lafayette-Durfee House, 94 Cherry St., Fall River, MA 02722; 774-322-1598; www.lafayettedurfeehouse.org. GPS: 41.705846, -71.157091. Open for special events and by appointment; see website for details.*

COLONEL GILBERT HOUSE—Loyalist Thomas Gilbert owned a home in Assonet, Massachusetts, a Loyalist hotbed. Gilbert was the overseer of a cache of guns, ammunition, and other supplies, which he kept in his home. On April 9, 1775, as many as 2,000 militia appeared at the Gilbert House to demand that he turn over the cache; he did so without a shot being fired. This event, occurring only nine days before the battle at Lexington and Concord, could have been a valuable lesson for the British; Patriot forces had been able to quickly gather 2,000 men and conduct a secret raid on short notice.

The Colonel Gilbert House, located in what is now Freetown, is still privately owned today. There is a plaque on a boulder outside the home that commemorates the house's significance. *Colonel Gilbert House, 1 Elm St., Freetown, MA 02702. GPS: 41.795175, -71.067564. Private property.*

HMS *SOMERSET* SHIPWRECK—HMS *Somerset*, a powerful 64-gun ship of the line in the mighty British Navy, had seen her share of duty, particularly in the Seven Years' War and the American Revolution. It was under *Somerset*'s guns that Paul Revere was silently rowed across the Charles River to his waiting horse, and she lent artillery support during the British assault on Bunker Hill. But in 1778, off Cape Cod, a storm got the best of her, and she was wrecked just offshore with the loss of 21 men. Within months, winter storms pushed her up onto the beach, and before long she was buried under the shifting sands (and likely plundered a bit by the locals).

In 2010, for only the third time since she was lost, the world got a glimpse of HMS *Somerset*'s hull when the sands along Cape Cod National Seashore shifted just enough to expose it. Protected by international law and still the property of the British Navy, she was permitted to remain

The remains of HMS *Somerset* are buried in the sands at Cape Cod National Seashore.

in place and was quickly covered up again; perhaps the elements will allow her to be viewed once again within our lifetimes. In the meantime, you can learn more about the *Somerset* at Cape Cod's Province Lands Visitor Center, where you will not only hear her story but see a few artifacts. You can also walk the sands above where she is buried. *HMS Somerset—Cape Cod National Seashore, Province Lands Visitor Center, 171 Race Point Road, Provincetown, MA 02657; 508-255-3421; www.nps.gov/caco. GPS: 42.073124, -70.204894. Seashore open daily; visitor center open May through October.*

EASTON FURNACE—Easton Furnace, one of several foundries in the area, produced artillery before and during the Revolutionary War. It is not certain, but it is possible that one of the cannon forged at Easton fired the first artillery round of the war.

Little remains of Easton Furnace outside of its mill pond. There is a small marker noting its founding in 1752 and its contribution to America. *Easton Furnace marker, intersection of Foundry St. and Poquanticut Ave., South Easton, MA 02375. GPS: 42.024468, -71.130899. Site accessible daily.*

STOUGHTONHAM FURNACE—Stoughtonham Furnace was one of several foundries in southeast Massachusetts that tried to meet the many demands of the Continental Army. Stoughtonham was a significant producer of cannon and shot for the fledgling army from 1775 through the end of the war.

Nothing remains of the Stoughtonham Furnace, though its original site and mill pond are preserved. Part of the area is public parkland and is accessible, but there are no historical markers interpreting the furnace. *Stoughtonham Furnace site, area south of Gavins Pond Rd. and west of Grape Shot Rd., Sharon, MA 02067. GPS: 42.083879, -71.209471. Signs accessible daily.*

WHERE TO STAY IN NEW ENGLAND

As you travel from one location to another in Massachusetts, Connecticut, Rhode Island, and southern New Hampshire, you should have no problem finding plenty of lodging that will suit your needs. The many interstate highways host a multitude of hotels and motels. You will also find plenty of restaurants.

New England's compact size also holds some great cities. It's difficult to see everything in and around Boston in one day, so you'll probably want to consider staying in or near downtown. Newport, Rhode Island, also has plenty to offer besides Revolutionary War history, and if you're looking for opulence, you're in the right place.

Your travels through New England will also bring you through plenty of small towns, and many of them have great things to offer in the way of bed and breakfasts and great, locally sourced food in their cozy restaurants. And, of course, you'll be surrounded by some of the best, freshest seafood in the world, so eat up!

2

The Fourteenth Colony: Quebec

OVERVIEW

In North America, the newest jewel in the crown of the British Empire was the colony of Quebec. A solely French possession since its founding by explorer Samuel de Champlain in 1608, Quebec had come into the king's dominion in 1763 as a result of the French and Indian War. Its inhabitants did not have an easy transition to British government after generations of French settlement, and there was strong speculation in both England and America that, given the chance, they would be more than eager to shake off their newfound rulers, either to join their rebellious neighbors to the south or to return to the protection of their mother country, France.

In truth, things were more complicated. For one, the British governor of Quebec, Guy Carleton, had been fair and tolerant to his new charges, taking the important step to reassure the inhabitants that they could keep their Roman Catholic faith. Then there was France itself. Despite the blood that was spilled to keep Quebec, other colonial possessions in the Caribbean had become much more profitable, and the prospect of the Canadian colony returning to the fold was not as attractive an option

Opposite: A stone monument marks the site of Fort Saint-Jean, a critical fortification between Montreal and Lake Champlain.

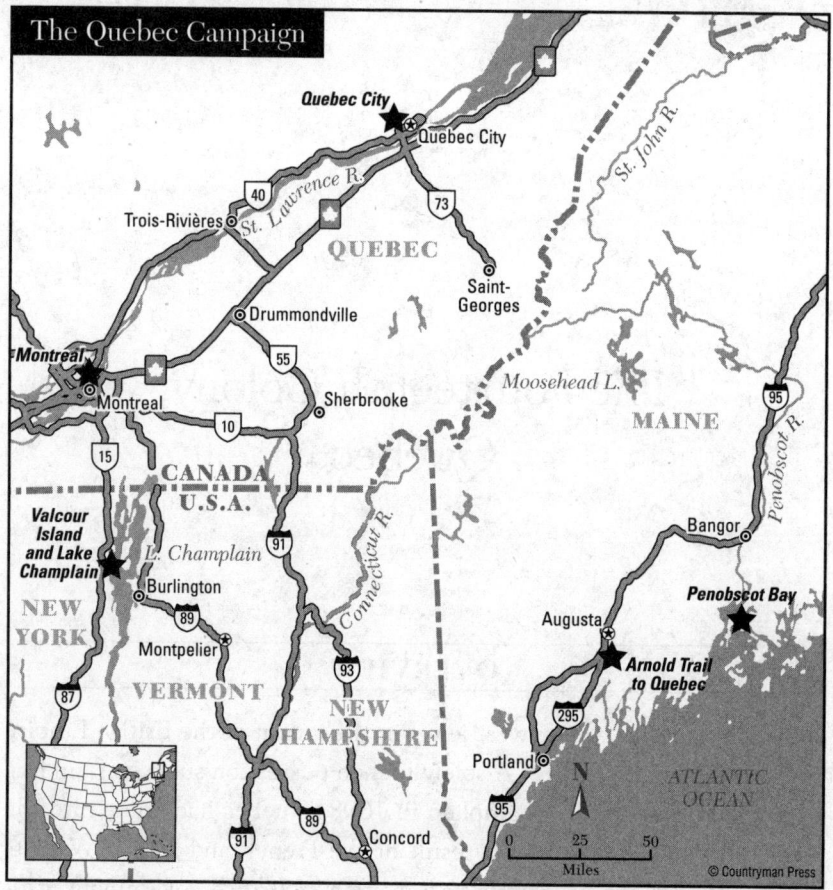

as it may have seemed on the surface. And as for the Quebecois, though the spirit of increased independence had taken hold in Canada, the will to fight for that independence did not exist.

Still, many in America, both in the Continental Congress and the Continental Army, saw Canada as either an opportunity or a looming threat. Should Quebec remain in British hands, an invasion south through the Hudson Valley, splitting the troublesome New England colonies from the rest of America, would always be a possibility. So, when one of America's most promising officers came forward with a plan to conquer Quebec before it could be reinforced by the British, it was embraced by George Washington and by Congress.

That brave officer was none other than Benedict Arnold. Though his name would eventually be permanently linked with the word "traitor," Arnold had shown bravery, imagination, and an ability to get things done. His mission to capture Fort Ticonderoga in May 1775 had been enormously successful (Ethan Allen co-led the assault), and the action would provide the artillery that forced the British to evacuate Boston in March 1776. Therefore, in 1775, when Arnold presented his plan for what seemed a well-considered two-pronged assault of Quebec, a land seemingly ripe for the picking, it was quickly approved.

Since Arnold had not yet earned his general's stars, overall command of the invasion of Canada went to General Philip Schuyler. Schuyler was to lead a force north from Fort Ticonderoga up Lake Champlain to capture Montreal, then down the Saint Lawrence River toward Quebec City. Arnold would have the more arduous task of leading a group of men from the east through Maine. Arnold and Schuyler would then join forces and complete the conquest of Quebec.

Arnold's 1775 winter trek through the Maine wilderness proved an incredible feat, but things did not go as planned in Quebec. Schuyler would leave his part of the mission to a subordinate, General Richard Montgomery, who occupied Montreal but was killed before the gates of Quebec City. Arnold was also seriously wounded in the action. It would not be long before the Americans withdrew from Canada entirely.

The American invasion of Canada was nothing short of a disaster, and unbelievably, it could have been much worse, were it not for the almost superhuman efforts of that future traitor, Benedict Arnold, at the Battle of Valcour Island.

This chapter focuses on the Quebec expedition and its aftermath, as well as another fantastic American failure at Penobscot Bay, Maine, involving another famous American, Paul Revere. Though these events are largely forgotten by Americans today, they had a tremendous impact on the events that followed in America's Revolutionary War.

PEOPLE TO KNOW

BENEDICT ARNOLD—Almost every American knows who Benedict Arnold was, at least in the simplest sense. It is difficult to hear his name without attaching the word "traitor," and for good reason. But the story is much more complicated and fascinating than that. Even before the American Revolution began, Arnold was an ardent Patriot, and he quickly proved himself one of the Continental Army's best commanders. Yet somehow, in a span of just a few years, his personal shortcomings were cause enough for this most talented and dependable of officers to betray his country.

Born into a prominent family in Connecticut, Arnold made a fortune as a shipping merchant. Thirty-four years old when war broke out, he was a physically dominating and ambitious man, a born warrior, and he eagerly joined the cause of liberty. Raising money and men in Connecticut, Arnold made his mark early, showing bravery and imagination in his successful capture of Fort Ticonderoga, leading an expedition through the Maine wilderness to conquer Quebec, and providing enough resistance with his tiny, outgunned navy on Lake Champlain to fatally delay the British Northern Campaign of 1776. Arnold was wounded at Quebec City, and he would suffer another more serious wound at Saratoga, where he demonstrated conspicuous courage and leadership in the great American victory. Despite these gargantuan efforts and successes, Arnold felt overlooked, and perhaps rightfully so. He was passed over for promotion several times (unlike other generals who were better politicians and visited Congress often) due to both his lengthy absence in the field and the poor relationships he had formed with several influential officers. He would be carefully but aggressively coaxed to the British side, with the promise of cash and a command of his own. Arnold began actively working to betray his fellow Americans, and after he was given command of the critical fort at West Point, he made plans to hand the post to the British. Arnold's plot was discovered before the deed could be done, but he escaped to British lines; though he did get his British command, his time as a British officer was covered with the cloud of his betrayal among his new compatriots. After the war, Arnold moved to Canada and then London, where he died in 1801.

DANIEL MORGAN—Unlike Benedict Arnold, Daniel Morgan is known to far too few Americans. Morgan was more than a great leader; in many ways he was larger than life, seemingly stepping out of a frontier storybook to make a significant mark on the outcome of the American Revolution. Though he has faded into relative obscurity as compared to his peers, those peers, in his time, almost unanimously viewed Daniel Morgan with tremendous admiration and respect.

Originally from New Jersey, Morgan went to the rough, unsettled Virginia frontier on his own at age 17. An immense man, tall and over 200 pounds, Morgan earned respect not only from his physical stature and dominance but from a keen intellect and a natural ability to lead. He was also known for being a no-nonsense man, and during the French and Indian War, this would lead to trouble. Serving the British army as a teamster, Morgan was struck by a British officer, and Morgan struck back, a very serious offense. Morgan was arrested and sentenced to receive 500 lashes in public; he survived (most men would not have), and forever harbored a keen hatred for the British, long before the American Revolution began. When the war did come, he organized a rifle company and marched over 600 miles to join in the siege of Boston. Morgan's riflemen struck a bizarre appearance in Cambridge, Massachusetts, appearing in their customary buckskin and carrying Virginia rifles, a weapon that would come to be greatly feared by the British rank and file, especially when in the hands of Morgan's men. Marching with Benedict Arnold through Maine only to be captured at Quebec and released soon afterward, Morgan's company would perform with skill and valor during the Saratoga Campaign in 1777, with Morgan himself showing great leadership during the Battle of Saratoga. After the American victory, as British commander General John Burgoyne was introduced to his captors, he notably showed Morgan immense respect, saying, "Sir, you command the finest regiment in the world!" Becoming physically limited (and, like Arnold, passed over for several much-deserved commands), Morgan would retire from the Continental Army, only to return in 1780 when the American cause in the south appeared to be at the failing point. Morgan's tremendous victory as commander at the Battle of Cowpens cemented his reputation as a tactician and greatly contributed to the British surrender at Yorktown. After the war, Morgan would serve in Congress, dying in his hometown of Winchester, Virginia, in 1802.

THINGS TO KNOW

Though other chapters in this book profile locations outside the country, this is the only tour that takes you outside the United States. That shouldn't complicate things very much, but you will need a valid passport. And although you'll be visiting Canada, our friendly neighbor to the north, be aware that this is Quebec, and they remain closely tied to their French heritage—including their language. Don't let that stop you; signs are generally in both French and English, and if you do happen to run into the unlikely situation where language becomes a barrier, chances are that someone will be around who can help translate, or you can always turn to Google Translate or a similar tool.

You may also want to check your cell phone plan before you cross the border. Most plans have easy ways to accommodate international roaming and/or calling, but you may need to notify your provider or take other steps to arrange the right service. This can be especially true if you're relying on your phone as a navigation tool; you can eat up a surprising number of megabytes using your mapping program. The last thing you want after your relaxing vacation is cell phone bill shock.

THE TRIP

The tour in this chapter covers more miles than any other in the book, and it's also the most remote. Don't let that be a deterrent; it may be exactly what makes this tour one of the most enjoyable. If you take the time to make some simple preparations, you are really going to enjoy this one.

Make sure you note the information above about foreign travel and at the end of the chapter regarding lodging. Other than that, this is one of those trips where occasionally going off the beaten path can be richly rewarding. You'll drive through beautiful wilderness in Maine, have a little taste of Europe in Quebec, and find great food and great people in the small towns and cities all along the way.

THE CAN'T-MISS SITES

Penobscot Bay

The Penobscot Bay Expedition was one of the worst losses ever suffered by the United States Navy. Let that sink in for a moment, particularly if, like most Americans, you've never heard of it. But it's true: From the early losses against the British during the War of 1812, through the ironclads of the Civil War, the great battleships of the Spanish-American War and World War I, the emergence of the aircraft carrier in World War II, all the way to the present day, when accounted for by the number of ships lost in combat, the Battle of Penobscot Bay on the coast of present-day Maine ranks near the top of the list of the worst naval disasters in American history.

By 1779, the war had begun to shift south to Georgia and the Carolinas. The British needed a secure base from which to launch northern operations along the coast, as well as a safe place to relocate Loyalists. Maine, a northern wilderness that was still technically part of the Massa-

The Penobscot River opens into the bay along the coast of Maine.

chusetts colony, seemed like a low-risk venture for the British Navy, and the protective harbor at Penobscot Bay seemed like a good fit. So, when three British ships appeared in the isolated bay on June 17 and landed 800 troops on a small peninsula near the present-day town of Castine, it came as a surprise, particularly to the local inhabitants.

Reaction was swift. Word of the British landing—and of the chaos they were causing in seizing local livestock and other stores—reached Boston quickly, and forces were immediately gathered to counter the threat. Within a few weeks, a joint land-sea operation had been formulated. One thousand militia were placed under the command of American General Solomon Lovell, with none other than Paul Revere who was made a lieutenant colonel of artillery. For the naval force, 40 vessels, ranging from a 32-gun frigate to transport ships for an amphibious assault, were placed under the command of Commodore Dudley Saltonstall. The fleet arrived at Penobscot Bay on July 25.

Knowing that their invasion and occupation of the American shore would garner a response, the British, led by General Francis McLean, had fortified their position. Their land defenses were centered on a strong work called Fort George, built on high, commanding ground on the Castine Peninsula. Outward from the fort, artillery positions and accompanying earthworks were built to counter any invasion, and additional works were built on the surrounding islands. By the time the Americans arrived, all of these—particularly Fort George—were very strong works. Added to these were the artillery of the three ships that had brought the British there in the first place, each of them mounting 18 guns.

Patriot landings on the outer islands began on July 26 and reached the Castine Peninsula on July 28, with the guns of the American ships adding to the onslaught. The land forces began to make their way toward Fort George with the intention of besieging it. After some tough fighting, the Americans began to gain ground and pushed the British back toward Fort George, but a night assault on the fort failed, and both armies settled into siege warfare for about two weeks. On August 11, the British launched a counterattack that, although ultimately unsuccessful, raised considerable doubt among the Patriot militia. The American commanders, at a loss, began to consult, then argue, about what to do next. Unfortunately, much of what would ultimately happen had already been decided for them.

Before the Americans arrived, British intelligence had caught word that American naval forces would be moving toward Penobscot Bay, and they therefore sent seven large warships to aid the defenders. On August 13, those ships—led by a 64-gun ship of the line—appeared at the mouth of Penobscot Bay. Commodore Saltonstall, in a move that would eventually see him court-martialed and drummed out of the American Navy, refused to engage the enemy. Seeing no need to wait, the Royal Navy entered Penobscot Bay.

It was no contest. Even though Saltonstall's 40 ships greatly outnumbered his foe, there was no question that the British held the advantage in size and number of guns. Numerous American vessels were quickly sunk or captured; those that were not, retreated up the Penobscot River as far as they could, where most were eventually grounded and then burned by their crews to avoid capture. A small number of these ships managed to evacuate a portion of the Americans from the peninsula, but approximately half of the force was captured. The rest would eventually make their way back to Boston in pieces, a shattered army.

In terms of loss of life, the Battle of Penobscot Bay was relatively light. The Americans lost 35 men killed and 30 wounded, while the British suffered 16 killed and 35 wounded. The Americans did lose 500 men captured, however, and the vast majority of those 40 ships, a loss that a fledgling naval force could ill afford. It was an overwhelming victory for the British, who would hold their position in Penobscot Bay until the end of the war, not to be challenged again.

The Arnold Trail to Quebec

Benedict Arnold was a man without a mission. A wealthy citizen of Connecticut, he had raised a unit to join the Patriot army forming outside Boston. Not seeing enough action there and too restless to sit through a siege, he developed a plan to capture British-held Forts Ticonderoga and Crown Point, both located at the southern end of Lake Champlain. Though that mission was a triumph, he could only watch as bureaucracy and politics handed Ethan Allen and his Green Mountain Boys most of the credit. Having accomplished what he could with limited resources,

SITE DETAILS

Penobscot Marine Museum—On the northern end of Penobscot Bay is a gem of a site called the Penobscot Marine Museum. Spreading itself over several small buildings within the town of Searsport, which dates back to 1815, the museum complex brings together history, science, storytelling, and a lot of hands-on fun. There is a full exhibit on the Battle of Penobscot Bay in the Merithew House, including an interactive 3D map and plenty of artifacts; you'll even find portions raised from the shipwreck of the privateer brigantine *Defence,* one of the American ships scuttled in the river. Other buildings focus on the bay's more prominent mariners, including those lost at sea, and more thorough examinations of a typical mariner's life in their own original homes. If sailboat racing is your interest, there are boats and exhibits here for that; if you've ever wondered about the life of a lobster fisherman, or wanted to know about Maine's fisheries, there are exhibits for those, too. Many of the activities are centered on kids, from trying to raise an actual sail on a mast to building their own boat and operating it in the museum's pond, but this is truly an all-ages experience. *Penobscot Marine Museum, 40 East Main St., Searsport, ME 04974; 800-268-8030; www.penobscotmarinemuseum.org. GPS: 44.458821, -68.925076. Open Thurs.–Sat., Memorial Day through June and open daily, July through third weekend in October.*

Penobscot River Overlook—On the drive out to the Castine Peninsula, you will wind around the northern end of Penobscot Bay and eventually cross the Penobscot River, a great gorge reaching south to the sea. Just before you cross the impressive Penobscot Narrows Bridge, there is a roadside overlook that provides a beautiful view of the river and the northern end of the bay. It was just below you that the fleeing remnants of the American fleet grounded and destroyed their boats, and you will be elevated enough to see quite a bit of the 40-mile-long Penobscot Bay. If you really want a grand view and you have the time, you can stop at the Penobscot Narrows Bridge Observatory, the tallest public bridge observatory in the world; picnic areas are there, along with plenty of information about the river and the building of the bridge. *Penobscot River and Penobscot Narrows Bridge Overlook, on northbound side of Maine Highway 3, 0.2 mile north of Switzer Spring Rd., Prospect, ME 04891. GPS: 44.557212, -68.807849. Open daily.*

Fort George—Fort George, reoccupied by the British during the War of 1812, is in remarkably good shape. Though only a small fragment of an original building remains, the earthworks are mostly unchanged since the Revolutionary era, and it is a testament to the strength of the fort. Surrounding growth (both of the town and plant life) now obscures the view to Penobscot Bay and the American positions, but the sheer size of the fort will give you an idea of how imposing the work would have been to the American attackers. (Oddly, the best gauges of its size are the baseball diamond situated in one corner of the fortress and the overlook from the east rampart onto an adjacent golf course.) The fort contains an interpretive sign describing both the land and sea aspects of the Battle of Penobscot Bay, and there is a small stone marking the dates the site was occupied by the British. Finally, a short drive down the street will take you to the several markers denoting where the American lines were, though the ground itself is not open to the public. *Fort George, intersection of Battle Avenue and Wadsworth Cove Rd., Castine, ME 04421. GPS: 44.390519, -68.804834. Open daily. Battle Avenue marker, on Battle Avenue 0.1 mile west of Fort George parking area, GPS: 44.388585, -68.806160; Second Line of American Intrenchments marker, on Battle Avenue 0.5 mile west of Fort George parking area, GPS: 44.386499, -68.810795. Signs accessible daily.*

British earthworks at Fort George in Castine, Maine.

Arnold made his way back to the still-motionless Continental Army. But even before he stepped into George Washington's headquarters at Cambridge, Massachusetts, Arnold already had a plan to keep himself, and the American cause, moving forward: the invasion of Canada.

To the north, the British Province of Quebec was seemingly ripe for the picking. Only 12 years before, Quebec had been French territory, and its inhabitants did not become stalwart British citizens overnight. Over 150 years of ties to France, a different language, and an overwhelmingly Roman Catholic populace that was actively repressed in other parts of the British Empire kept the Quebecois distanced from their new mother country. It seemed only natural to many Americans that French Canadians would rally to the cause of liberty, if for no other reason than a chance to stick it to the British.

There was also a practical reason to invade Quebec. Both the Americans and the British recognized the importance of the Saint Lawrence River separating the American colonies from Canada. Com-

The Colburn House marks the beginning of the Arnold Trail to Quebec.

mercially, the river provided direct access to the significant trading centers of Quebec City and Montreal. More important, should the British elect to invade from the north, the Saint Lawrence River provided easy access for a large army to push south from Montreal to Lake Champlain and the Hudson River Valley, ultimately arriving at New York City and splitting the American colonies in two. But for now, there was no army in Quebec; most of the province's troops had been sent to Boston. American possession of Quebec and the Saint Lawrence River would seal off one of the most practical avenues of invasion available to the British.

American plans to conquer Quebec had begun before Benedict Arnold arrived at Cambridge in August 1775. In fact, Washington had already given command of the expedition to General Philip Schuyler, who would proceed north from Fort Ticonderoga to Montreal. But he was also excited to hear Arnold's firsthand reports that the region around Lake Champlain would support the American effort, and he

SITE DETAILS

Colburn House State Historic Site—The Major Reuben Colburn House dates to 1765. Now a state historic site, Colburn had a major part in organizing the Arnold expedition, and his home served as the muster point for the 1,100 Patriots who dared to go on this dangerous mission. This was Arnold's headquarters before the expedition left for Quebec, and Colburn, who also traveled with the party, was responsible for building and repairing the bateaux that played such an important part. Today the house and its outbuildings are open for only special events, but interpretive signs and monuments are on the property that tell the story of Arnold's mission. *Colburn House State Historic Site, 33 Arnold Rd., Pittston, ME 04345; 207-624-6080; www.maine.gov/dacf/parks. GPS: 44.198204, -69.753658. Grounds open daily; house open only during special events.*

Old Fort Western—Old Fort Western was part of a system of forts along the Kennebec River dating to 1754 and was a trading post as early as 1628. Unlike many sites like it, the main feature of Old Fort Western, its large garrison building, is *not* a reproduction, and your guided tour of the fort will take you through it, including the office that Arnold used. Other parts of the fort, such as the stockade wall and blockhouse, have been restored to the period. Inside the fort, you will also find reproductions of the bateaux used

---

was impressed with the drive and creativity of the 34-year-old colonel. Washington would soon endorse a plan presented by Arnold that, on the face of it, was brilliant. Using a little-known route through the Maine wilderness up the Kennebec and Chaudière Rivers, Arnold would lead 1,100 men north to the gates of Quebec City, surprising British forces and virtually ensuring Schuyler's success.

Preparations began immediately. Reuben Colburn, a boatbuilder living on the Kennebec River, was put to work building 200 bateaux, heavy wooden boats capable of carrying up to seven men and their supplies. What few maps and other pieces of intelligence existed were gathered,

by the Arnold expedition, and living history exhibits are always going on while the fort is open. Old Fort Western is the founding site of what would become the city of Augusta, you'll have a nice view of the modern city from the park alongside the fort's Kennebec River landing. *Old Fort Western, 16 Cony St., Augusta, ME 04330; 207-626-2385; www.augustamaine.gov/old_fort_western. GPS: 44.316517, -69.770613. Open daily July and August, Fri.–Mon., June, September, and October.*

Arnold Trail to Quebec—The Arnold Expedition Historical Society has devoted itself to the preservation and study of the march, and they have created the Arnold Trail to commemorate it. Making their headquarters at the Colburn House State Historic Site, this dedicated group has gone so far as to conduct a reenactment of the entire march to Quebec. For those looking for a bit less of a challenge, the society has preserved and interpreted several critical parts of the original path, and they are committed to maintaining the trail so that others can experience at least part of the army's extraordinary journey. Members of the society also have access to a campsite at the Middle Pond of the Great Carrying Place. Finally, if you'd like to pick and choose selected sites to visit, you can find the entire trail marked out on Google Maps via the society's website. *Arnold Trail to Quebec—Arnold Expedition Historical Society, headquarters at 33 Arnold Rd., Pittston, ME 04345; www.arnoldsmarch.com. See website for location and accessibility of trail sites.*

and men familiar with life in the wilderness were recruited. Three battalions were formed, two of Continental Army volunteers and one of frontiersmen from Pennsylvania and Virginia. This last battalion, commanded by Captain Daniel Morgan, stood in marked contrast to the British Regulars, not only carrying different weaponry—usually consisting of tomahawks and the legendary Pennsylvania long rifle—but even in dress, often wearing buckskin and other exotic clothing. Arnold's army would be built from men of special character. No one realized how necessary that character would be on this expedition.

Traveling north along the Atlantic coast by ship, Arnold's soldiers found their way up the Kennebec River to Reuben Colburn's homestead in late September. It may have occurred to many that the harsh northern winter was already approaching, but the trip to Quebec was expected to be completed in a relatively short time. After several days gathering men and supplies at Colburn's, Arnold moved upriver to Fort Western in present-day Augusta, Maine. From Fort Western, Arnold wrote Washington and estimated the journey to his endpoint at Chaudière Pond (also known as Lake Mégantic) at 20 days and 180 miles. He would soon find out both these estimates were less than half the actual number, and that the wilderness his men were about to enter was more unforgiving than he could have imagined.

The expedition left Fort Western on September 25. Almost immediately, the bateaux, which had been built quickly, poorly, and of green wood, were found to be leaky. The Kennebec River, thought to be easily navigable, was quite the opposite, often requiring the men to either haul the heavy boats to shore and carry them or to wade through the swift water pulling them by rope. Under these extreme conditions, the

The reconstructed Fort Western in Augusta, Maine.

bateaux further deteriorated, many becoming useless along the way and ruining the food and supplies they carried.

On October 11, the expedition reached a point known to the local Abenaki tribe as the Great Carrying Place. This overland route bypassing the falls of the Kennebec is 12 miles long, with its elevation varying by over 1,000 feet. The men needed to cross the Great Carrying Place five times—once with the bateaux, then back and forth to retrieve the party's food, then back and forth for a final trip carrying military supplies. To boot, the ground, already swampy in parts and beginning to ice over, was even more wet and muddy from unceasing rain, the soldiers sinking as they carried their great weight. So many became weak because of their exertions, poor diet, and sickness that a hospital was built for those who could not go on. A storehouse was also built to secure supplies in the increasingly likely event that the entire expedition would need to turn back.

Arnold reached the endpoint of the Great Carrying Place—the upper branch of the Kennebec, also known as the Dead River—only to find that his lead division was almost out of food. He sent word to his rear division, led by Colonel Roger Enos who was carrying the army's reserves, to come up and resupply the rest of the force. However, realizing the precarious situation, Enos sent forward only two barrels of flour and the news that he and his entire division of 450 men, nearly half of Arnold's remaining force, would turn around and head back to Fort Western with the army's provisions. (Roger Enos would be court-martialed upon his return to Cambridge for leaving the expedition without orders, but with all the men he had abandoned still in Quebec and unable to testify against him, he was acquitted.)

With nothing left to do but push on, Benedict Arnold's ragged, starving army crawled through the wilderness. Among the articles consumed as food were leather moccasins, candles, and what tiny amounts of flour remained, thickened with water and campfire ash. Many fell out of march and died from their exertions, while their comrades, unable to do anything else, trudged past in pity, hoping that they would not suffer the same fate.

On November 3, 1775, the lead division finally reached the first of the villages on the Chaudière River—French villages, the Quebecois.

The Americans were greeted with kindness, charity, and care by both the inhabitants and the local Native Americans, some of whom agreed to join in the invasion of Quebec City. Over the next few days, the survivors of this incredible journey floated into the villages, where most would regain their strength, thankful that they had completed the trek. Their rest was not long; advance units of the army began to move toward Quebec City on November 6, reaching it only two days later. They arrived with much less than half their force, and that half much depleted from exposure, hunger, and fatigue. But their accomplishment remains one of the most impressive military marches in history.

Quebec City

Guy Carleton, governor of Quebec, already knew through gathered intelligence that an American force was moving toward Quebec City through the Maine wilderness. Even before his arrival from Montreal, the citizens of Quebec City—the majority of whom might support the Americans, at least if it appeared that they would emerge victorious—were instructed to come to its defense. But for the most part, *Les Habitants*, the early French citizens of Quebec, who had little to gain from getting into a fight with or for either side, simply waited to see what would happen.

The Americans were first seen on the south bank of the Saint Lawrence River on November 8, 1775, but it would be some time before they were ready to assault the great city. Besides needing time to recover from their expedition, their first glimpse of Quebec City, founded where the Saint Charles River enters the Saint Lawrence, must have been daunting. Quebec then consisted, as it does today, of two distinct parts, a lower and an upper town. While Basse-Ville, or Lower Town, lies along the shore and is easily accessible, Haute-Ville, or Upper Town, sits atop 300-foot cliffs with few easy routes of access, particularly for an invading army. Even more imposing than the cliffs is what sits atop them, the Citadel of Quebec. The key point of a large defensive system, the citadel and its surrounding walls are more akin to a European castle than any other fortress built on the American continent, with tall, thick stone walls and only a few carefully placed but easily defended gates into the city.

Both sides knew that despite its strength, Quebec could be conquered. In fact, a victory here over the defending French in 1759, largely

The beautiful lower town of Quebec, scene of the American assault.

fought to the west of the city on an expanse known as the Plains of Abraham, was the battle that decided the fate of North America for the British during the French and Indian War. Hoping to duplicate this success, Benedict Arnold led his force across the Saint Lawrence River in the darkness on November 13, 1775, and arrived at the Plains of Abraham, scaling ladders at the ready. But when a third of his force had to be left behind because of poor weather, the Americans decided against an assault and instead tried to goad the British out of the fortress and onto the open land. Governor Guy Carleton, however, had been one of the attackers of Quebec in 1759, and was not about to repeat the French army's fatal mistake. The British remained safely inside their walls, and the American offensive became a siege.

Over the next month and a half, conditions rapidly changed. The British, who had only 1,000 men on the day that the Americans crossed the river, would be quietly reinforced to almost double that strength. Carleton immediately put those extra hands to work, and the British

SITE DETAILS

Pres-De-Ville Barricade Site—Two large plaques high on the city walls, one in English and one in French, mark the location of the Pres-de-ville Barricade, where American general Richard Montgomery met his fate and his force sealed that of the American conquest of Quebec. The plaques are not difficult to find, but they are located along a busy road and can be difficult to read if you're speeding by in your car. The walk from Lower Town is about 0.25 mile each way; should you choose to drive instead, there is some room on the opposite side of the road to pull over and view the markers—just use caution and approach from the west, which will eliminate any need for you to perform a U-turn in a dangerous spot. *Pres-De-Ville Barricade Site, on Boulevard Champlain 0.3 mile south of Rue des Traversiers, Quebec, QC G1K 4H9. GPS: 46.806793, -71.204351. Accessible daily.*

Sault-au-Matelot Barricade Site—Similar to the large plaques at the site of the Pres-de-Ville Barricade, markers have also been placed at the location of the Sault-au-Matelot Barricade, where the Americans made their final determined stand before being forced to surrender. There is also an interpretive plaque placed by the Historic Sites and Monuments Board of Canada briefly telling the story of the siege of Quebec and the American assault. Much more accessible than the Pres-De-Ville site, the Sault-au-Matelot Barricade markers are in the heart of Lower Town and are an easy walk from the charming historic area. *Sault-au-Matelot Barricade Site, markers and interpretive plaque at intersection of Rue de la Barricade and Rue de Sault-au-Matelot, Quebec, QC G1K 4A6. GPS: 46.815529, -71.203361. Accessible daily.*

defenses improved in strength and readiness. For the Americans, General Richard Montgomery, who had moved up Lake Champlain and captured Montreal in November, brought 300 additional men on December 1. Even before Montgomery arrived and took command, however, American strength was waning. Smallpox had ravaged much of the American

Montgomery House Site—Following the Battle of Quebec, the body of American general Richard Montgomery was brought inside the walls of Quebec and prepared for a proper burial at the home of citizen Jean Caubert. Though the house is no longer there, the Maison du Général, a small boutique hotel, stands on the site, and a plaque on the side of the building relates its significance. *Montgomery House Site (Maison du Général), 72 rue St. Louis, Quebec, QC G1R 3Z3. GPS: 46.810739, -71.209150. Accessible daily.*

American Soldiers' Burial Site and Montgomery Burial Place—General Richard Montgomery, along with 13 of his men, were buried within the walls of Quebec near the Saint Louis Gate. Though Montgomery's body was removed from a cemetery to New York City in 1818, the other American soldiers, who had been placed in a mass grave, were not rediscovered until 1891. Their burial place is now marked by a large stone memorial and several plaques. There is also a large interpretive sign describing the attack and the commemoration of the site. *American Soldiers' Burial Site and Montgomery Burial Place, on Côte de la Citadelle just south of Rue Saint Louis, Quebec, QC G1R 3R2. GPS: 46.809013, -71.210957. Accessible daily.*

Musée du Fort—Located in the heart of Upper Town near the Place d'Armes, the Musée du Fort shows a 30-minute active diorama presentation depicting Quebec City's storied military history, including detailed retellings of the critical battle on the Plains of Abraham in 1759 and the American assault in 1775. Presentations alternate between English and French versions. The Musée du Fort also has several exhibits and artifacts highlighting Quebec's history. *Musée du Fort, 10 rue Sainte-Anne, Haute-Ville, Quebec, QC G1R 4S7; 418-692-2175; www.museedufort.com/en. GPS: 46.813023, -71.205211. Open Fri.–Sun., June and August, and Tues.–Sun. in July.*

force. Though the defenders of Quebec were forced to reduce rations, they could wait out the siege within the comfort of the city walls, while the Americans, though resupplied by Montgomery, were forced to contend with the elements or find shelter in scattered buildings west of the city. Perhaps most important for the Americans, winter had arrived, and the situation was only going to get worse. Though Montgomery's arrival and charismatic leadership helped, morale was deteriorating.

The siege made little progress. Montgomery and Arnold realized that they could not maintain it under the current circumstances, and the additional issue of expiring enlistment periods for many of the men only increased urgency. The commanders planned an assault, a do-or-die attempt to conquer Quebec City. The first attempts were scheduled for shortly before Christmas, but each was cancelled due to poor weather, or to good weather that would insufficiently mask their approach, or to an abundance of moonlight that would expose the attack. Finally, on December 30, conditions promised to be favorable, and the assault was planned for the following morning. Rather than scaling the city walls, however, Montgomery and Arnold devised a new plan that, though risky, promised great reward if successful.

The American plan of attack did include two direct assaults on the western defensive wall, but these would be diversions. The main assault would attack Lower Town from two sides, Montgomery leading one group from the west, along the Saint Lawrence River, and Arnold leading a larger group from the north along the Saint Charles River. The attackers would need to advance undetected for as long as possible under the guns of Quebec's defenses, then break through barricades that had been constructed in Lower Town. If all went according to plan, Montgomery and Arnold would join forces in Lower Town, then breach the British defenses at the lightly guarded passage into Upper Town.

Shortly before daylight on December 31, 1775, in a blinding snowstorm, the attack began. Almost from the beginning, fortune fell on the side of the defenders. The diversionary attacks were not effective, leaving British troops to move where needed and alerting everyone within the walls of Quebec that something larger was afoot. Both Montgomery's and Arnold's attacks were discovered quickly, and Arnold himself soon fell with a bullet through the leg, taking him out of the fight. Montgomery would fare worse. Almost all the Canadian defenders in his path fled or surrendered without firing a shot, and he and his men reached the first barricade quickly. But one man—a drunken British sailor pressed into artillery service—vowed to fire at least one shot before retreating. That fateful blast instantly killed five Americans, including Montgomery and his two most senior officers. Suddenly having no leadership and no momentum, the western arm of the American attack, unaware that there were no obstacles to their front, turned and headed for the rear.

Benedict Arnold's force, now led by the determined Captain Daniel Morgan, pressed on through Lower Town. Though they faced greater resistance, Morgan's men captured the first barricade, then advanced to the second. For a time, it seemed certain that Morgan's men would take this obstacle too, but the timely arrival of reinforcements, as well as a detachment of British soldiers suddenly attacking from their rear, brought the fighting to a fierce crescendo. After waiting in vain for three hours for Montgomery to appear from beyond the British barricade, Morgan and his men, surrounded, finally surrendered.

The American conquest of Canada was now a lost cause. Though General Richard Montgomery's well-executed plan had captured the British forts north of Lake Champlain and the city of Montreal, and Benedict Arnold's men had accomplished an incredible feat with their journey through the Maine wilderness, the combined American force had been shattered. They would begin their retreat almost immediately, with the faint hope of recovering enough to try again in the spring. What they could not know was that British strategy had shifted, and that plans were underway to bring not just reinforcements but an entire army to Quebec, with the goal of crushing the Americans and bringing their rebellion to an end.

Montreal
As Benedict Arnold's force approached Quebec City, General Richard Montgomery, who had taken command of Philip Schuyler's force in the field, moved his way up Lake Champlain and then further north, eventually placing the British garrison at Fort Saint-Jean under siege. The fort held out for almost seven weeks but eventually fell on November 3, 1775. This critical strongpoint was the final obstacle between the Continental Army and the city of Montreal.

Guy Carleton, governor of Quebec, had known for some time of the American threat south of Montreal and decided that his presence was more critical there. What he found upon his arrival from Quebec City was not encouraging. Despite easily turning back an unauthorized and badly planned attack on September 25 by Ethan Allen and 100 Green Mountain Boys, resulting in the Battle of Longue-Pointe and Allen's capture, the city was poorly defended, and many of the Canadian militia had deserted upon hearing that the Americans were coming. Just as the Americans would find when they asked men to die for their cause, few of the Quebecois rallied to the British colors. When Fort Saint-Jean fell, the rate of desertion only increased. Seeing that there was little he could do, Carleton evacuated what troops and ships he could gather and began to make his way back to Quebec City.

Montgomery wasted no time. After wrapping up the surrender of Fort Saint-Jean, the Americans immediately began to move northwest to Montreal. In less than a week, on November 11, American troops crossed the Saint Lawrence River and occupied Montreal virtually unopposed. The British ships heading downriver to Quebec City had a close call, and part of the fleet was captured as they attempted to get underway. Remarkably, Guy Carleton himself was on one of these ships, but after taking on a disguise, he was able to walk out of the hands of the Ameri-

Château Ramezay is now a museum in Montreal.

cans and make his way to Quebec City to prepare for the attack he knew would come.

In Montreal, General Richard Montgomery received a hero's welcome. As seen time and time again in the history of occupying armies, the Americans were treated as though they had liberated the citizens of Montreal from their oppressive leaders. Montgomery read a proclamation to the people of Montreal, declaring that his army had come with the hope that all of Canada would rally to the cause of liberty and join them in their fight. The response was enthusiastic. It was also temporary.

Montgomery established a military government in Montreal, then requested that a delegation from the Continental Congress waste no time in coming to solidify the American position in Canada. He then left to link up with Benedict Arnold before Quebec City, leaving General David Wooster and a small number of troops in command of the city.

Wooster's government of Montreal was not popular with the locals. Several of his actions—imprisonment of suspected Loyalist citizens, seizure of arms, and a noticeable prejudice against the predominant Catholic faith—lessened Canadian enthusiasm for the American cause. This erosion of support greatly quickened when the inhabitants of Montreal heard about the important British victory at Quebec City.

By the time the American Congressional delegation—consisting of Benjamin Franklin, Samuel Chase, and Charles Carroll—reached Montreal, bringing Canada into the American Union was a lost cause. It was an arduous journey, especially for the aged Franklin, and though they stayed in Montreal for almost a month, the writing was already on the wall, and they turned around and left for America. Two months later, on June 14, 1776, it was the Americans who evacuated Montreal in a hurry, heading south toward Lake Champlain with a British army now led by General John Burgoyne close behind them. The invasion of Quebec had ended; now the only question remaining was whether the Americans could escape.

Valcour Island and Lake Champlain

The first wave of British relief forces sailed for Quebec in March 1776, followed by a much larger second wave of 10,000 men, half British Regulars and half Hessian mercenaries, in April. Sailing with this second wave

> ## SITE DETAILS
>
> **Chateâu Ramezay**—The Chateâu Ramezay, built in 1705, has always been a strong symbol of power in Montreal. When General Richard Montgomery arrived in Montreal with the American army, it was a natural choice for his headquarters, and the Chateâu soon became the center of military government. Montgomery, of course, would soon leave for Quebec City, but the Chateâu Ramezay remained headquarters for Generals David Wooster and then Benedict Arnold. When the American Congressmen arrived in Montreal, though they did not lodge here, Chateâu Ramezay is where all the government's business was conducted. Chateâu Ramezay is now a museum with excellent exhibits and living history tours, and though much of Old Montreal still stands, visiting the Chateâu is the most direct link you will find to the American occupation. There is a room in the museum dedicated to the American invasion, highlighting both military and political aspects. In addition, the building, lovingly restored and with some of the original gardens, is a treat. Finally, little remains of the original city walls that stood in 1775, but if you'd like to see a portion, go behind the courthouse across the street, where you'll find a few remnants with a bit of interpretation. *Chateâu Ramezay, 280 Notre Dame St. East, Montreal, QC H2Y 1C5; 514-861-3708; www.chateauramezay.qc.ca/en. GPS: 45.508820, -73.553367. Open daily.*

was British General John Burgoyne, a proven leader hand-selected by the new British secretary of state to the American colonies, Lord George Germain. Burgoyne and Germain shared a vision: This new British army would not just protect and regain Quebec but would also take the fight back into America, pushing south from Montreal through Lake Champlain and eventually all the way to Albany, New York.

American reinforcements were also on their way to Quebec. Ten additional regiments were earmarked by Congress for General Philip Schuyler, still in overall command of the campaign for Canada. However, winter weather delayed their transport until May 7, 1776. Unknown to

Schuyler, the American forces still in front of Quebec City had learned only two days before that the arrival of British reinforcements was imminent, and they began to retreat up the Saint Lawrence River toward Montreal. With the British right behind them, Montreal was evacuated as well, with the Americans racing for Lake Champlain.

For as large a lake as it is, Lake Champlain was notably lacking in boats, not surprising given its wilderness location. But the war and the strategic value of the lake suddenly made the need for watercraft paramount. The British had been building ships at Fort Saint-Jean in 1775, but all three were captured by the Americans; the Americans had also confiscated a schooner from Philip Skene, the former royal governor of New York, bringing their small but dominating fleet to four gunboats. Needing smaller boats to transport men and supplies, Schuyler had constructed boatbuilding facilities at Lake George, at the south end of Lake Champlain, and had almost 100 bateaux by the end of 1775. Schuyler's large fleet of bateaux, as well as the handful of available ships, were able to quickly ferry the retreating Continental Army south to their new

The Battle of Valcour monument, with Valcour Island in the distance.

home base at Fort Ticonderoga, putting over 100 miles between them and the temporarily boatless British by July 2, 1776.

It was here that the race for naval superiority on Lake Champlain began. While continuing to build bateaux at Lake George, the Americans also took advantage of other facilities confiscated from Philip Skene—sawmills, forges, and other craft operations in his namesake town of Skenesborough. Now under the supervision of Benedict Arnold, an experienced merchant seaman, the Americans could build gondolas, 50 feet long with a single sail but relying heavily on oars, and capable of mounting three large cannons as well as swivel guns and other small artillery. Galleys were also built—longer than the gondolas, with round bottoms, better sailing capability, and capacity for more cannons. With operations continuing nonstop, the first gondola was launched on June 27, 1776, and the second only two days later; construction on the next three began immediately. The boats were then floated to Fort Ticonderoga, where they were made ready for service with what little material they could gather. Despite a serious lack of experienced shipwrights and proper supplies, a small American inland navy was quickly taking shape.

Though the British had many ships on the Saint Lawrence River, they could generally not be moved south up the rapids of the Richelieu River. Exceptions were made, however. One ship and three schooners were partially disassembled and moved 12 miles overland to Fort Saint-Jean in a remarkable feat of manpower and engineering; the largest of these, the *Inflexible*, was a triple-masted, 180-ton monster and would be the largest vessel on Lake Champlain. And once the British regained Fort Saint-Jean, shipbuilding began in earnest. Contrary to the Americans' lack of experience, the Royal Navy possessed abundant expertise when it came to watercraft. Preconstructed boats from England were assembled and new boats were built from scratch, taking advantage of the region's rich forests and commandeering other plentiful material, such as sails, from the ships on the Saint Lawrence. One of these new boats, christened *Thunderer*, was a radeau, 90 feet long and 33 feet wide with a flat bottom, a square bow, and capable of mounting 12 large guns. Though the British had had a late start, they were quickly catching up and would soon overtake the American operations in both production and quality.

The British also held a decisive advantage in the ability to sail. The

Americans—trying to recruit experienced sailors but unable to entice them to come to Lake Champlain—were forced to rely on soldiers to operate their vessels. The British, of course, had an overabundance of sailors at the ready. Though both trained their naval forces in how to operate the new boats and navigate the lake, for the British it was merely an adjustment, while for the Americans it was an entirely new skill.

The American fleet made its first coordinated sail with 10 boats on August 24. Arnold was in command, initially using the schooner *Royal Savage* as his flagship but later moving to the galley *Congress*. Small encounters occurred here and there, mostly with British troops onshore, but Arnold knew that eventually the British fleet, which would surely be stronger than his when ready, would come looking for him. He chose Valcour Island, near the western shore of Lake Champlain, as the place to make a stand. The fleet anchored in Valcour Bay between the island and the shore on September 24, 1776, and over the next few weeks several recently completed row galleys joined them, bringing their strength to 15 boats.

On October 9, the British fleet sailed south from their base at Isle aux Noix. The naval force they had assembled over the summer and early fall was astounding. *Inflexible*, reassembled and mounting 18 guns, served as the flagship, leading four large ships and approximately 20 gunboats, plus additional supply boats, for a total of 89 guns on 34 vessels. The British advantage in power was also significant. Though the American fleet carried 78 guns, the much larger British guns gave them an advantage of almost two to one.

On October 11, 1776, the Americans, sheltered and hidden by Valcour Island, spotted the British flotilla moving quickly toward them. Arnold formed his boats into a line of battle, sending out a handful of ships to lure the British into Valcour Bay. It proved to be an ideal place for the Americans. Though the *Royal Savage* took considerable damage and ran aground, the other American boats held their places. And while the smaller British gunboats were able to turn into Valcour Bay, the larger, more heavily armed ships were carried by the southerly wind that had taken them down the lake, unable to join the action.

The fight in Valcour Bay was a slugfest. As the large British ships attempted to make their way into the battle, the boats in the bay tore into each other with fury for two hours. When the British schooner *Carleton* finally made its way into the fray, it was met with similar effect, inflicting but also taking heavy damage, so much so that she had to be towed to safety. The fight continued until the British gunboats withdrew at sundown.

The small American fleet had lost only two vessels, *Royal Savage* (burned by the British that night) and the gondola *Philadelphia*. (*Philadelphia*, raised from the deep, can now be seen in the Smithsonian Museum of American History.) The rest of the boats had been badly damaged but were still intact. However, the Americans were not out of danger. The British were now between them and their home base of Fort Ticonderoga. Arnold made the decision to retreat overnight, quietly making their way around the British fleet undetected. The British awoke the next day ready to fight but without an opponent.

The chase was now on. With their sailing ships intact, the British quickly began to close the distance to the American boats, many of which, with their small sails shot to pieces, were powered by men rowing into a south wind. After stopping briefly to make what repairs they could, the Americans made their best effort to reach the safety of Fort Crown Point at the south end of Lake Champlain. But one by one, the boats began to sink. Their flight continued through the night of October 12 and into the next morning. The British did capture one row galley, the *Washington*, before reaching the last of the shattered American fleet. But the Americans would not give up without a fight. A two-and-a-half hour running battle occurred, Arnold's flagship *Congress* in the lead. Finally, rather than surrender, the Americans entered Ferris Bay (now called Arnold Bay), ran their ships aground, and set them afire.

The Americans had lost the Battle of Valcour Island. Only four tattered boats made it back to Fort Crown Point, which was quickly abandoned and burned, and most of Arnold's navy was forced to return to Fort Ticonderoga on foot. However, the consequences of the American resistance were immense. Guy Carleton—still in overall command of the British force, rather than the more aggressive John Burgoyne—had been surprised at the ferocity of the American fighting spirit. Furthermore, conquering massive Fort Ticonderoga, even with his much larger army, seemed improbable without a lengthy siege, and it was far too late in the season to do that. So, to the surprise of the Americans, Carleton turned around and returned to Canada on November 2, 1776. The plan to push down the Hudson Valley and split America in two would have to wait for next year's campaign, a campaign that, for the British, would end in inconceivable disaster. There would be other raids in the Champlain Valley—notably one by Christopher Carleton, nephew of the governor, in 1778—but they would all be after the great American victory at Saratoga.

OTHER SITES IN QUEBEC AND THE NORTHEAST

FALMOUTH—As the British army remained pent up in Boston, the British Navy did its best to supply them and carry out their own missions. One of these was to sail to nearby port towns that had shown any signs of rebellion and enforce the king's authority—by destroying them, if necessary. On October 17, 1778, a small flotilla of British ships anchored just outside of Falmouth, Maine, and sent an emissary telling the townspeople that they had two hours to evacuate. After some negotiation, the citizens were told that the town would be spared if they would take an oath of allegiance to King George III. They decided to evacuate after all, and the next morning, October 18, the guns opened on Falmouth, turning it to ashes. Word quickly spread across the colonies, but with its opposite intended effect, casting the British as ruthless oppressors, and George Washington sent his opposing command a stern letter protesting the Navy's actions.

The harbor where the British anchored and from which they conducted their bombardment is about the only thing left in Falmouth that commemorates this piece of its history, and even some of that has since been filled in. You can get a good view of the harbor from the pier at Falmouth Town Landing. *Falmouth Town Landing, on Town Landing Rd. just east of Ayers Ct., Falmouth, ME 04105. GPS: 43.732650, -70.204904. Accessible daily.*

FORT FOSTER—After a brief encounter with a British ship in June 1775, the Patriot citizens of Machias, Maine, decided to build fortifications to protect the town. One of the results was Fort Foster, a large earthwork

SITE DETAILS

Valcour Island—Located 1 mile off the New York shore of Lake Champlain, Valcour Island is accessible by boat and provides great opportunities for camping and hiking. If your primary interest is the naval battle, though, you don't necessarily need to visit the island. The main scene of the engagement is to the west and southwest of the island, meaning that you can easily see the battle area and the island from the mainland. A couple of historic markers are in the area, one of them right on the shoreline, that commemorate the battle that did so much to gain American independence. Note that if you're coming from the Vermont side of the lake, there are several frequent ferry routes across; you can also drive across the bridge on US 2 to South Hero Island, then take the short ride to Cumberland Head on the New York side. *Historical highway marker—Battle of Valcour, on US 9 just north of intersection with Lapham Mills Rd., Peru, NY 12972. GPS: 44.605499, -73.440695. Battle of Valcour monument, on US 9 0.3 mile south of intersection with Lapham Mills Rd., Peru, NY 12972. GPS: 44.600238, -73.438373. Sites accessible daily.*

Lake Champlain Navy Memorial—In many respects a small inland sea that stretches through two countries, it is no surprise that Lake Champlain has been the scene of a few noteworthy events in American maritime history. Besides the Battle of Valcour Island and the several campaigns up and down the lake that preceded it during the American Revolution, Lake Champlain was also the site of the Battle of Plattsburgh Bay, an American victory over the British Navy that no less than Winston Churchill called the most decisive engagement of the War of 1812. The Lake Champlain region continues to serve in a military capacity, and a Navy Reserve Center occupied the Lake Champlain shoreline in Burlington, Vermont, until 1995. On that site now is the Lake Champlain Navy Memorial, a dignified tribute to the area's many contributions to the United States Navy, Marine Corps, Coast Guard, and Merchant Marine. The centerpiece of the memorial is the compelling statue of the *Lone Sailor,* the original of which stands at the US Navy Memorial in Washington, DC. Around the sailor are several granite monuments telling the story of Lake Champlain's naval history, including the critical Battle of Valcour Island. Adjacent to the excellent Leahy Center for Lake Champlain, an aquarium and museum complex, getting to the Navy Memorial is a quick, easy stroll that you will long remember. *Lake Champlain Navy Memorial, 3 College St., Burlington, VT 05401. GPS: 44.475952, -73.221573. Site accessible daily.*

Lake Champlain Maritime Museum—In the town of Vergennes, Vermont, about 20 miles north of Crown Point by water, is the Lake Champlain Maritime Museum. The complex is a wonderful combination of history museum, research facility, school, advocacy center, and art studio, and is totally free. For the history buff, there is plenty of information and artifacts, from the Native Americans who first plied the lake all the way through to modern shipwrecks. And though you'll find mentions of the Battle of Valcour Island scattered throughout the 15-building complex, the Key to Liberty exhibit, a study of the Revolutionary War in the Champlain Valley, is devoted to the battle and its aftermath. The exhibit tells the story through film, scale models of the ships involved, interactive exhibits showing how the boats operated, boat frames, cannons, and other artifacts dragged up from the bottom of the lake, and the extraordinary results of an ongoing underwater archaeological expedition that has mapped out the battlefields at Valcour Island and other locations on the lake. Even with all this, perhaps the most memorable piece in the collection is the full-size replica of the gunboat *Philadelphia* floating in the North Harbor, allowing visitors to imagine the cramped, harsh conditions faced by the makeshift Continental Navy. It is difficult to list everything the museum offers—boatbuilding, sailing, painting and sculpture classes, racing—so reserve at least a few hours or more in order to properly experience it. *Lake Champlain Maritime Museum, 4472 Basin Harbor Rd., Vergennes, VT 05491; 802-475-2022; www.lcmm.org. GPS: 44.197152, -73.356390. Open daily, May to mid-October.*

Top: The statue of the *Lone Sailor* looks out over Lake Champlain in Burlington, Vermont.
Bottom: The reconstructed *Philadelphia* at her berth at the Lake Champlain Maritime Museum.

up to 6 feet high on a peninsula known as The Rim. The town's foresight proved wise. On August 13, 1777, four British ships appeared outside the town with the intention of raiding it. Fort Foster and other defenses on the river slowed the British, and though the naval forces landed the next morning, they found Fort Foster abandoned. Concluding that additional attempts on the town would be fruitless, the British sailed away, Fort Foster having deterred the raiders.

Fort Foster is still in good condition, but it takes a little work to get there. The road that once led to the site is now used only for hiking or other recreation, and cars and other motor vehicles are not allowed. The road itself is wide and well-maintained, however, and if you do make the effort, you will have a splendid view of the Machias River and its islands. The trail is out and back—you'll have to walk out the same way you came in—so make sure you plan for a good day's hike and look for a map online. The fort is overgrown, partly by timber and partly by blueberries, but it should be easy to spot. *Fort Foster, Sunrise trailhead on Rim Rd. 0.3 mile south of Holmes Way, then hike 0.1 mile to gravel road, turn right, then head east 0.2 mile, East Machias, ME 04630. GPS: 44.717001, -67.403942. Accessible daily.*

FORT MACHIAS/FORT O'BRIEN—On June 12, 1775, a naval engagement between a sloop commanded by Captain Jeremiah O'Brien and a small British tender provoked the locals of Machias to build fortifications below town on the Machias River. One of these was a small battery on the west bank of the river, opposite Fort Foster. First named Fort Machias, the battery grew into a larger outpost and was soon renamed after Captain O'Brien. Though the site saw no further action during the Revolution, the naval battle, which occurred about 2 miles offshore, was the first battle between an American ship and that of a foreign power, making the waters in front of Fort O'Brien one of the birthplaces of the United States Navy.

Fort O'Brien State Historic Site is under the care of Cobscook State Park. There is plenty left of the earthworks, though some of these date to the Civil War. A large interpretive sign tells of the action around Machias during the American Revolution, including the naval battle, as well as the fort's continuing history through the 1920s. There are also signs around the site marking various parts of the fort over the years. Note that if the gate is closed, visitors are allowed to park there and walk in; it's only a short stroll. *Fort O'Brien State Historic Site, on Port Rd. 0.4 mile south of Old County Rd., Machiasport, ME 04655; 207-726-4412; www.maine.gov/dacf/parks. GPS: 44.689222, -67.398153. Open daily.*

TROIS-RIVIÈRES—After the death of General Richard Montgomery and the wounding of now-General Benedict Arnold at Quebec City, General John Thomas took command of American forces. Within a week of his arrival in front of Quebec on May 1, 1776, Thomas learned that British reinforcements were on their way and decided to move his troops upriver to a more defensible position at Trois-Rivières, or Three Rivers, ending the siege of Quebec City. Thomas soon realized that the torturous campaign, as well as a smallpox epidemic, would doom his force, and he ordered the men left at Trois-Rivières to fall back toward Montreal. However, Thomas himself fell victim to the smallpox, and his successors, first General William Thompson and then General John Sullivan, decided to send 2,500 men back to surprise the British troops who had occupied their previous position. What they did not know was that British and Hessian reinforcements—12,000 troops—were now waiting for them at Trois-Rivières. When the Americans attacked on June 7, 1776, they found not only the British army but the British Navy blasting away at their vastly outnumbered force. Though they advanced to within 80 yards of the British lines, the Americans were soon in a disorganized retreat toward Montreal, with the British hot on their heels.

The Battle of Trois-Rivières National Historic Site of Canada consists of a stone marker memorializing the action. The marker stands on a very busy road in Trois-Rivières; one can park across the one-way street, but cross with great caution, as oncoming traffic is semi-hidden and tends to speed. *Battle of Trois-Rivières National Historic Site of Canada, 983 Boulevard des Forges, Trois-Rivières, QC G8Z 1T7; www.pc.gc.ca. GPS: 46.343988, -72.551878. Accessible daily.*

THE CEDARS—When American forces occupied Montreal, a small post was established 50 miles to the west at the Cedars, along the Saint Lawrence River, to guard against an approach from that direction. On May 19, 1776, a force of 300 British Regulars, Canadians, and Native Americans under Captain George Forster surrounded the American garrison there and forced them to surrender the next day, then did the same a day later to an American column on their way to support the post. The British and their captives were pursued and caught by Benedict Arnold and 100 men, but instead of giving battle, Forster, not wanting to drag the prisoners through the wilderness but also wary of leaving them with the Native Americans, proposed an exchange of prisoners. Arnold, knowing that the Americans' time in Quebec was limited, agreed to the terms.

Battle of the Cedars National Historic Site of Canada is a very small plot of land with a stone memorial. It stands along an isolated highway, so if you decide to visit be sure to pull safely off the road. The battle occurred in the fields north of the monument. *Battle of the Cedars National Historic Site of Canada, on Chemin du Fleuve 0.7 mile east of Rue Daoust, Les Cèdres, QC J7T 1L3; www.pc.gc.ca. GPS: 45.309891, -74.035293. Accessible daily.*

LONGUEUIL—With Fort Saint-Jean under siege to the south and the Americans on the verge of capturing Montreal, Governor Guy Carleton sent a relief force across the Saint Lawrence River, landing at the settlement of Longueuil on October 30, 1775. Waiting for them at Longueuil were the famous Green Mountain Boys, led by Seth Warner following Ethan Allen's capture the month before. The Vermonters never allowed the British force to advance farther than the river shore. After artillery was brought up to add to the American fire, the British relief column boarded their bateaux and returned to Montreal.

Fort Longueuil National Historic Site of Canada consists only of a plaque, but it is on the site of the former fort at Longueuil, which stood under the present cathedral. The plaque only briefly mentions the American occupation in 1775 and does not mention the battle that occurred nearby along the river. There is an additional interpretive sign across the street that provides more detail about the fort, showing drawings and dimensions to give you an idea of what the scene may have looked like; it is difficult to picture, however, as Longueuil is now in the center of town, and the sign is in French only. *Fort Longueuil National Historic*

Site of Canada, intersection of Rue Sainte-Charles Est and Rue Charlotte, Longueuil, QC J4H 1J3; www.pc.gc.ca. GPS: 45.540431, -73.508136. Site accessible daily.

FORT CHAMBLY—General Richard Montgomery's advance north from Lake Champlain to Montreal besieged Fort Saint-Jean. Not far beyond it was Fort Chambly, a masonry fortification at the falls of the Richelieu River. Reflecting the initial local support for the army that was on top at the time, a force of 300 Canadians and 50 Americans began a siege of Fort Chambly on October 15, 1775, in parallel with the American siege at Fort Saint-Jean. Fort Chambly only garrisoned 100 officers and men and their families, and the American artillery pounding away at the walls of the fort served to shorten the siege. The British surrendered on October 18, providing Montgomery's army with much-needed supplies and a big morale boost as they continued the work at Fort Saint-Jean. The following year, however, activities at Fort Chambly were quite different. A council of war at the fort among American generals Arnold, Wooster,

Fort Chambly has stood at the falls of the Richelieu River since 1711.

Thompson, Thomas, and Sullivan was conducted on May 30, shortly after which Thomas died of smallpox and word was received of the rout at Trois-Rivières. Within a couple of weeks, the Americans would evacuate Fort Chambly, burning the garrison building and almost all the stores present, leaving nothing for the pursuing British army.

Fort Chambly National Historic Site preserves the stone fortification built by the French in 1711. This strategic site alongside the falls of the Richelieu was recognized by Samuel Champlain as early as 1611, and there was a military presence here through 1869, so Chambly has many interesting stories to tell. Virtually all the interior of the fort has been turned into exhibit space, showcasing the building of the four fortifications erected on the site, the history of the French, British, Americans, and Iroquois who played such major parts in its legacy, and the modern archaeological excavations that have revealed so much. (Note that because there is so much history, you won't find much about the American occupation, but the guides are always happy to answer your questions.) The exhibits are all modern, interesting, and interactive, and are designed to appeal to all ages. Living history activities and tours are also frequent, so check the schedule before you go. *Fort Chambly, 2 Rue de Richelieu, Chambly, QC J3L 2B9; 450-658-1585; www.pc.gc.ca/en/lhn-nhs/qc/fortchambly. GPS: 45.449369, -73.276963. Open daily, mid-June through August, and Wed.–Sun., mid-May through mid-October.*

FORT SAINT-JEAN—Sited above the rapids of the Richelieu River, Fort Saint-Jean was the key British fortification between Lake Champlain and Montreal. More than just a military post, the fort also had boat-building facilities, and when the American force preparing for the invasion of Canada learned that a British schooner was being built there to threaten Forts Crown Point and Ticonderoga, the capture of the fort became critical. The Americans first approached the fort from Isle aux Noix on September 6, 1775, but turned back after seeing the fort's abundant artillery. After further planning, the Americans besieged the fort on September 17, traveling down the river by boat and cutting off access to the British posts at Fort Chambly and Montreal. The British resisted with their artillery, but soon American guns arrived to hasten the siege along. Forty-five days passed before the British surrendered on November 2, 1775, with the Americans capturing not only numerous pieces of artillery but the all-important British schooner, along with another that was almost completed. A year later, the Americans retreating from Canada would remember how easy it was to cut off the fort and decided to abandon it, taking what they could carry and burning the rest. Fort Saint-Jean was still burning when the British reoccupied it on July 18, 1776, but they quickly resumed building gunboats for the purpose of reoccupying Lake Champlain.

Royal Military College Saint-Jean now occupies the site of old Fort Saint-Jean, but the history of the site has not been forgotten. The Fort Saint-Jean Museum contains plenty of information about both the American siege of 1775 and the British activities after their reoccupation in 1776. You may also walk the campus, and the North Redoubt built by the British in 1775 is still here. You will also see a relief of the original French and the later British fortifications. South of the college, you will find the Battle of September 6, 1775, National Historic Site of Canada, a stone monument and plaque commemorating the small action that occurred during the initial American advance toward the fort. *Fort Saint-Jean Museum, 15 Rue Jacques-Cartier North, Saint-Jean-sur-Richelieu, QC J3B 8R8; 450-358-6500 ext. 5769; www.mfsj.ca/. GPS: 45.280071, -73.256726. Museum open Wed.–Sun., May through August, and by appointment. Battle of September 6, 1775, National Historic Site of Canada, on Rue Jacques-Cartier South just north of Rue Brais, Saint-Jean-sur-Richelieu, QC J3B 8R8. GPS: 45.280069, -73.256726. Site accessible daily.*

ISLE AUX NOIX—The American army moving north from Lake Champlain descended the Richelieu River to Isle aux Noix, approximately 15 miles south of British Fort Saint-Jean, on September 5, 1775. Isle aux Noix would serve as the launching point for the capture of Fort Saint-Jean, and the island would eventually become a fortified American camp and hospital for the duration of the American occupation of Canada. During the American retreat, the island was quickly recognized as a poor defensive position and was hastily abandoned. The British would occupy the island shortly thereafter, eventually building fortifications and establishing a presence that would last until 1870.

Fort Lennox, a British fortification erected on Isle aux Noix well after the American Revolution, is a National Historic Site of Canada. Though the exhibits focus on this period, you will have access to the entire island during your visit, and there is plenty of other interpretation here. Visiting the island will require a ferry ride, and if you don't feel like crossing, you can always stop at the visitor center at the ferry landing. You'll have a good view of the island, and there is some interpretation along the shore, including about the American occupation and British reoccupation. *Isle aux Noix—Fort Lennox, ferry landing at 1 61e Ave., Saint-Paul-de-l'Île-aux-Noix, QC J0J 1G0; 888-773-8888; www.pc.gc.ca/en/lhn-nhs/qc/lennox. GPS: 45.126897, -73.270895. Riverside accessible daily; check website for access to fort.*

ETHAN ALLEN HOMESTEAD AND MONUMENT—Ethan Allen, the larger-than-life leader of the partisan Green Mountain Boys, remains a controversial figure. To this day, perhaps as much as any figure of the Revolution, it is difficult to separate fact from fiction. What cannot be

The humble Ethan Allen Homestead in Burlington, Vermont.

disputed is that Allen was a stalwart defender of Vermont and the rights of those who called themselves its citizens before, during, and after the Revolution. In the latter years of his full life, Allen settled here near Burlington in 1787, taking up farming while remaining active politically. He died at his homestead only two years later in 1789, too soon to see Vermont become America's 14th state in 1791.

The Ethan Allen Homestead and Monument preserves the farmhouse and part of the land where Allen spent his last years. The museum presents a full picture of Allen's life and the archaeology that has revealed so much about his final home and small farm, but to appreciate the site you'll want to take the tour of the Allen cottage. You'll see that even being the legend he was, maintaining a home in what was then the edge of the wilderness took a great deal of hard work and humility, even for a man as concerned about his reputation and legacy as Ethan Allen. Tours are given by costumed guides, and there are plenty of other living history demonstrations and events throughout the year, including presentations and meetings of the native Abenaki tribe that is so much a part of Vermont's history. The site also contains walking trails and other amenities that make it a great place to settle in and enjoy the visit. *Ethan Allen Homestead and Monument, 1 Ethan Allen Homestead, Burlington, VT, 05408; 802-865 4556; www.ethanallenhomestead.org. GPS: 44.502643, -73.230121. Open daily May through October; check website for other dates.*

WHERE TO STAY IN QUEBEC AND THE NORTHEAST

While Maine, Quebec, and the Lake Champlain area all have some fantastic options for food and lodging, it is highly recommended that you do at least a little bit of planning for this trip. Depending on where you are and the time of year, last-minute places to stay may be very difficult to find.

In Maine, all the major cities and several points along the interstates have a good number of chain hotels. However, because the entire state is a recreation paradise, its proximity to Boston means that finding a last-minute available room during the summer or on a weekend, particularly at a reasonable price, can be near impossible. You could find yourself making some long late-night drives searching for a hotel, ending up far from your desired destination. One option is to make hotel reservations well ahead of time; while it may feel limiting, you will be far more relaxed. You could also take advantage of the wilderness around you and reserve time at a more remote location such as a lodge, cottage, or even a campground. You won't be far from one of America's true treasures, Acadia National Park, and mixing your history road trip with Maine's abundant and extraordinary natural beauty is sure to be rewarding.

Quebec City and Montreal present similar problems, but for different reasons. The drive between the two cities will not present many hotel or food options, and if you don't speak French, the farther you get from the cities, the more difficulties you may have. The good news is that both Montreal and Quebec City are wonderful cities that contain plenty of options, and they're less than three hours apart.

Burlington, Vermont, is less than a two-hour drive south from Montreal. Though it's a small city by population, it's also a college town and the focal point for many visiting Lake Champlain. Its waterfront location, easy transition from urban life to untouched nature, and youthful but full-of-tradition vibe have great appeal. Its popularity means you'll find lots of hotel and restaurant options. Don't forget to top some pancakes with pure Vermont maple syrup, and to reserve time to visit a Vermont culinary landmark, the Ben & Jerry's ice cream factory, located just a short drive outside the city limits in Waterbury.

3

Routes of Invasion: Upper New York, Vermont, and New Hampshire

OVERVIEW

During the winter of 1776–1777, the British worked to come up with a grand strategy for ending the war in America. Part of this strategy centered on control of the Hudson River. By controlling the Hudson from Montreal all the way to New York City, the British would have a solid barrier separating the New England colonies from the rest of America. Not only would the British have a much smaller area to subdue, but the other colonies would also be prevented from aiding the rebellion in New England.

The strategy that would ultimately be approved by Lord George Germain, secretary of state for the colonies, and King George III would be one presented by General John Burgoyne. Burgoyne, who had brought relief to Quebec in 1776, proposed that a large army composed of British troops and Hessians move south over Lake Champlain all the way to Albany, New York. General William Howe, whose army was currently in possession of New York City, would march north to meet them. Finally, a diversionary force under Lieutenant Colonel Barry St. Leger would land at Fort Ontario, along the Saint Lawrence River in western New

Opposite: A plaque is embedded in the rock face at the site of Fort Anne.

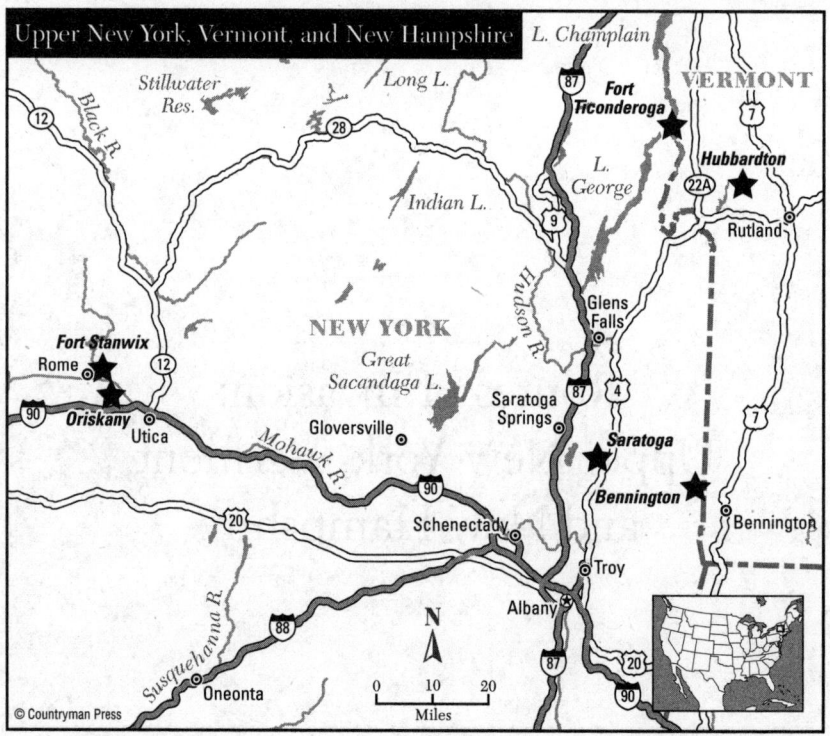

York, and march east through the Mohawk River Valley until reaching Albany. The Northern Army would be led by Burgoyne himself.

The Americans at Fort Ticonderoga, at the south end of Lake Champlain and the northernmost point held in the Hudson Valley, were not surprised when the British finally made their move in July 1777. They had been preparing for a British assault on the fort since the previous fall. What they were not prepared for, however, was the speed with which the British would take the fort. It was a matter of only a few days before the Americans abandoned the fort and began quickly moving south, with the British in hot pursuit.

Over the next few months the British pushed southward, cutting their way through the New York wilderness. The tedious work through short stretches of rough terrain was exhausting, and the farther they moved, the more difficult it became to maintain their supply line to the north. On top of that, their slow pace allowed the Americans to regroup and reinforce.

The western British movement under St. Leger went even worse. Although they surrounded Fort Stanwix in the Mohawk Valley, their siege was broken up following a major battle at Oriskany, the approach of a relief force, and some creative stratagems by the Americans. St. Leger turned back, never able to approach Albany. Burgoyne also held out hope that help would come from Howe in New York City, but a combination of poor communication and lack of cooperation led Howe to make barely any effort to save his counterpart.

Becoming increasingly desperate, Burgoyne nevertheless decided to push on, but a severe British defeat at Bennington caused irreparable losses. Americans continued to pour into the northern army, limiting British movements. The campaign finally stalled out at Saratoga, where two major battles sealed the fate of Burgoyne's army, and they surrendered to the Americans.

The repercussions of the American victory at Saratoga were immense. For the British to lose an entire army to the ragtag American Patriots was an unthinkable blow, and the American triumph proved to doubters everywhere that they could win this war. The most important to receive that message was the country of France, which was now able to come forward and declare openly their alliance with the colonists, providing badly needed soldiers, sailors, and supplies.

This chapter will take you through the Hudson and Mohawk River Valleys following the critical Saratoga Campaign of 1777. It will also take you to the wilderness that was New York during the colonial period, all the way to the frontier.

PEOPLE TO KNOW

HORATIO GATES—If Horatio Gates were remembered solely for his great victory at Saratoga, perhaps he would be a household name today. Unfortunately, his legacy is complicated by a few other incidents that make his place in the American Revolution, at best, a subject of debate.

Gates was an Englishman and an officer in the British army who retired to Virginia with the help of his then-friend George Washington. When the Revolution came around, Gates sided with the colonists and received a generalship in the Continental Army. (Some surmise that Gates, ambitious to a fault, did not support the cause as much as he saw an opportunity to advance his station.) Gates performed well at the beginning of the war and was eventually promoted to command the Northern Department in a messy and confusing move by Congress to replace the existing commander, Philip Schuyler, in 1777. His victory at Saratoga (which his detractors credit to Benedict Arnold and Schuyler more than him) put him on the map, but it proved to be his climax. Smelling further advancement, Gates became caught up in the Conway Cabal scandal, in which several officers in the army and a few members of Congress attempted to replace Washington with Gates. Gates eventually came to a working understanding with Washington, and he was given a command in the new seat of war, the Southern Department, in 1780. Soon after, however, his force was routed at Camden, and he fled, leaving his command behind. Though cleared of misconduct a few years later, Gates never held an important command again. He died in 1806.

JOHN BURGOYNE—One of several intriguing characters among the British command, John Burgoyne showed much promise as an officer. However, his surrender at Saratoga will forever be what he will be remembered for.

Burgoyne became an officer of the British army at the age of 18 but soon became sidetracked when he eloped with the daughter of the Earl of Derby. After being estranged and living in France for several years, Burgoyne returned to the army and rose through the ranks quickly. He served in several small campaigns in continental Europe, showing insight and originality in command and earning the nickname Gentleman Johnny from his troops for his kind treatment of them. Burgoyne entered the American Revolution during the siege of Boston in 1775, where his primary contributions were the authorship of a play spoofing the situation and of several letters disparaging the generalship of Thomas Gage. Burgoyne returned to action in 1776 when he repelled the American invasion of Canada, then returned to England where he concocted his plan to take the Hudson River Valley and end the war. But Burgoyne's relative inexperience in higher command led to the collapse and capture of his army at Saratoga, though he was able to return to England on parole. He went on to serve as commander in chief in Ireland, and he was able to write a number of plays, achieving a small degree of success. Burgoyne died suddenly in 1792 and is buried in Westminster Abbey.

THINGS TO KNOW

Almost all the sites described in this chapter have something there to mark their importance, whether it's a full-fledged historical site or just a plaque on a boulder. For those sites that are not very substantial, you can find further information at a few key sites. The museums at Fort Ticonderoga, Saratoga National Historical Park, and Fort Stanwix National Memorial contain a wealth of information about the Saratoga Campaign. If you are more interested in the raids that occurred in the Mohawk Valley, then the Fort Plain Museum and Historical Park and the Old Stone Fort are your best bets. For a Native American perspective, the Skä-noñh Great Law of Peace Center and the Shako:wi Cultural Center are excellent. If you have any questions at all, the staff at these sites will be glad to help you out.

THE TRIP

There are two main legs for this trip, one through the Hudson River Valley and another through the Mohawk River Valley and beyond. It's suggested that you do the Hudson River portion first, moving south from Fort Ticonderoga toward Albany, roughly following the path of the American and British armies as they moved toward the great clash at Saratoga. In the Mohawk Valley, the order you visit the sites isn't quite as important. It's worth noting that most sites are not far off the beaten path, so let yourself explore a bit—you'll find it very rewarding.

THE CAN'T-MISS SITES

Fort Ticonderoga
Before the American Revolution, Fort Ticonderoga had earned the nickname Gibraltar of the North. Built by the French as Fort Carillon in 1755, the imposing stone fort holds a commanding position at the southern end of Lake Champlain. In 1758, during the French and Indian War, the British unwisely and unsuccessfully attacked the fort, the failure cementing

Part of the massive fortifications at Fort Ticonderoga.

its reputation of impregnability. But by the time the American Revolution came about, Fort Ti, as it was often called, had slipped into decay and was held only by a skeleton crew of about 50 British soldiers.

Shortly after the fight at Lexington and Concord, Benedict Arnold, who had arrived in Cambridge with a band of men to join the Continental Army, came up with a plan to capture Forts Ticonderoga and Crown Point. At the same time, another group—the Green Mountain Boys, led by Ethan Allen—had also received authorization to take the forts. The two forces met and, after some haggling about who was in charge, agreed to cooperate. In the early hours of May 10, 1775, the Americans caught the small British garrison, who had not even heard that hostilities had broken out, completely by surprise and captured Fort Ticonderoga without firing a shot. Fort Crown Point, which had an even smaller garrison of nine men, was taken the next day.

The capture of Fort Ticonderoga proved to be a significant morale boost to the American cause. In addition, the 60 cannons at Fort Ticonderoga, badly needed by the Americans, would be moved to Boston by General Henry Knox. That artillery, when mounted on Dorchester Heights south of the city, was instrumental in forcing the British to evacuate.

Once the Americans had possession of Fort Ticonderoga, they quickly came to the realization that while it was certainly a key strategic position, it was not without its shortcomings. For one, the fort, designed by the French to protect against British incursions from the south, was now facing the wrong way, since any British attack would come from the north. Then there was the condition of the fort; no longer needed by the British after the French and Indian War, it was largely an afterthought, as most of the other forts in the Hudson Valley were. The Americans would need to make significant improvements for the fort to once again be defensible.

With the invasion of Canada, the fort became a key location on the supply line to the Northern Army, and its garrison slowly began to build under the guidance of General Philip Schuyler. Engineers began to rehabilitate the works around the fort, improving its defenses. The British delay resulting from the Battle of Valcour Island in 1776 bought the Americans even more time, and by the spring of 1777 Fort Ticonderoga was once again becoming a strong fortification.

The new American defenses did not just consist of the fort itself. Earthworks were constructed outside the fort to the north. To the southeast, just across the water, rose Mount Independence, which held a commanding position over Fort Ticonderoga. The Americans fortified the mountain and added artillery, making it easily defensible. A bridge was also built over Lake Champlain connecting the fort with Mount Independence, securing a line of communication. An additional point to the west, Mount Hope, was also set up as an outpost. The Americans also considered fortifying a third high point, Mount Defiance, to the southwest of the fort. From this point, artillery could command both Fort Ticonderoga and Mount Independence; however, the hill was deemed too steep to pull cannons to the top, and Mount Defiance was left undefended. This proved to be a fatal mistake.

In June 1777, command of Fort Ticonderoga and its 2,500 men passed to General Arthur St. Clair. Though he arrived at a time of great uncertainty about British plans, he would not have long to wait. On June 20, a British army of 8,000 men under the command of General John Burgoyne began moving south on Lake Champlain. The force was composed of British soldiers, who moved down the west side of the lake under Brigadier General Simon Fraser, and Hessians, under the command of Major General Friedrich Adolph Baron von Riedesel and moving down the east side. Also part of Burgoyne's force were about 800 Indians of various tribes. Confirming the size of the approaching British army on June 30, St. Clair consolidated his forces, abandoning Mount Hope and preparing his men for an attack.

On July 4, as the British took their positions around Fort Ticonderoga, Fraser noted the superior position of Mount Defiance. He sent British engineers to inspect the position and they confirmed that though it would be a difficult undertaking, they could get artillery to the top. By the next day, the British had cannons atop Mount Defiance and began building a battery. It was immediately evident to both sides that neither Fort Ticonderoga nor Mount Independence could be held.

St. Clair knew that giving up a position as important as Fort Ticonderoga would likely end his military career, but he was presented with no other option. That night, July 5, the American position was evacuated as quietly as possible. Boats were filled with critical supplies for transport to the town of Skenesborough and the men gathered on the south side of Mount Independence. By daybreak on July 6, the main American column was hurrying southeast from Fort Ticonderoga on the road to Hubbardton.

A view of Fort Ticonderoga from the commanding position at Mount Defiance.

SITE DETAILS

Fort Ticonderoga—Visiting Fort Ticonderoga today is a full experience. One can easily spend hours wandering around the fort, but so many activities are going on during a typical day that you'll want to take advantage of at least some of them. There are living history exhibits and costumed interpreters throughout the site, and the fort boasts the largest 18th-century artillery collection in North America. Several museum exhibits, some permanent and some rotating, tell the fort's history and explain what life was like here during its heyday. A guided cruise on Lake Champlain is also offered, and a restaurant is on site. The grounds around the fort offer a chance to hike through history as well, and you can walk the French earthworks from the 1758 French and Indian War battle or take a climb up Mount Defiance. If you come to Fort Ticonderoga, plan for a full day, as the experience and the surrounding scenery are superb. *Fort Ticonderoga, 102 Fort Ti Rd., Ticonderoga, NY 12883; 518-585-2821; www.fortticonderoga.com. GPS: 43.848810, -73.402690. Open Tues.–Sun., May through October, and for special programs November through April.*

Mount Independence State Historic Site—Mount Independence State Historic Site preserves what's left of the fortification atop Mount Independence. Archaeological excavations have revealed the locations of some of the original campgrounds, buildings, and roads, and 6 miles of trails will take you through what's been found as well as provide great views of the surrounding area. The visitor center has an orientation film and excellent exhibits, including pieces of the Great Bridge that connected Mount Independence to Fort Ticonderoga across the lake. *Mount Independence State Historic Site, 497 Mount Independence Rd., Orwell, VT 05760; 802-948-2000; www.historicsites.vermont.gov/mount-independence. GPS: 43.818242, -73.384423. Open daily, Memorial Day through mid-October.*

Mount Defiance—The British position on Mount Defiance is owned and maintained by Fort Ticonderoga, and your admission to the fort will get you into the site. A short drive through town and up the mountain will provide you with a stunning view of lower Lake Champlain, Fort Ticonderoga, and Mount Independence. Tours of the site are also given each afternoon. *Mount Defiance, 72 Defiance St., Ticonderoga, NY 12883. GPS: 43.8319920, -73.406422. Open Tues.–Sun., May through October, and for special programs November through April.*

Top: The visitor center at Mount Independence State Historic Site.
Bottom: The untouched battlefield at Hubbardton.

Hubbardton

General Arthur St. Clair and the American force evacuated Fort Ticonderoga early on the morning of July 6, 1777. The men were strung out on a single road heading south and east, headed for Skenesborough to gather the supplies they had sent off by boat. Behind the main force was a rear guard led by Colonel Ebenezer Francis. Their task was straightforward but difficult: Protect the rear of the column if and when the British pursuit caught up.

That pursuit was not long in coming. Daylight revealed that Fort Ticonderoga had been completely abandoned, and Brigadier General Simon Fraser quickly organized a column to chase the Americans down. His 850 men were soon followed by 180 Hessians under Major General Friedrich Adolph Baron von Riedesel.

The day was extremely hot, and both armies struggled to keep the pace. The main body of the Americans managed to travel approximately 30 miles to Castle Town, in what is now Vermont. Francis halted with the rear guard 6 miles behind them at the small hamlet of Hubbardton, where he was joined by the Green Mountain Boys under Seth Warner (who took command) and a New Hampshire regiment. The group of approximately 1,200 men, exhausted from the day's march, camped for the night at the small farm of the Selleck family.

The British, only a few miles behind, got an early start the next morning, July 7, leaving the Hessians behind. At approximately 7:00 AM, after four hours of marching, they came upon the first elements of the rear guard and immediately opened fire, sending forward a regiment. Though initially surprised, the Americans were able to form a long line behind a stone wall and deliver a countervolley that stopped the British in their tracks. The two sides slugged it out ferociously, with the British bringing up more troops on their right. The Americans fell back to successive strong positions first on a slight rise and then behind a log fence east of the Castle Town Road, standing strong in the face of the British fire.

After about an hour and a half, the Americans noticed that the British left was in a weak position and began to move forward to envelop it. But just as the opportunity presented itself, the Hessians under Riedesel, hurrying to the sound of the guns, appeared in the vulnerable spot and advanced straight toward them. For a short time, they held, but the push by the Hessians was irresistible. Francis was killed, and the American line broke, with most of the men scrambling up a steep slope to the east to escape.

The British had won the Battle of Hubbardton, losing 60 killed and 168 wounded. However, the Americans had more than held their own, suffering 41 killed, 96 wounded, and 200 taken prisoner. More important, the critical rear guard action served to stop the British pursuit. The stand at Hubbardton served notice to many on the British side that the Americans could be a formidable fighting force and were not just the peasant rabble that many made them out to be.

Bennington

As he consolidated what was left of the American army, General Philip Schuyler did his best to make sure that the British would have a tough time of things. There were only a few routes through the wilderness that the British could use, and Schuyler dedicated men to making those routes as difficult to traverse as possible. Felling trees across the roads and tearing up already delicate roadbeds, the Americans made conditions miserable for the British, slowing their movement to a crawl. Schuyler also effectively followed a scorched-earth policy, assuring that the British could not procure any food, animals, wagons, or other supplies from the countryside. American efforts were so effective that the British were forced to rely almost entirely on what they had brought with them from England.

After weeks of hacking their way through the wilderness, the British army finally reached Fort Edward and the Hudson River. Already the British supply chain was showing signs of strain, and the soldiers were forced to reduce rations. In addition, each location captured had to be garrisoned with troops, reducing the strength of the force at hand. General Burgoyne was beginning to see that he had a major problem on his hands and decided to halt the army until he could relocate his supply base from Skenesborough to Fort Edward. In the meantime, though, word had reached the British that rebel supplies were being held in the town of Bennington, not far away in the disputed New Hampshire Grants

SITE DETAILS

Hubbardton Battlefield State Historic Site—Hubbardton looms large in Vermont history, and the battlefield there is among the most well-preserved Revolutionary War sites you'll find. Besides boasting one of the earliest battlefield monuments in the United States, Hubbardton Battlefield State Historic Site has a short grass trail with interpretive signs that will take you through the battlefield. The land surrounding the field is still farmland and looks very much like it did at the time of the fight, and it's easy to make out the rises and other features that played a part in the battle. The visitor center is excellent, with exhibits, a video, and an interactive map that explains the events of the day. *Hubbardton Battlefield State Historic Site, 5696 Monument Hill Rd., Hubbardton, VT 05735; 802-273-2282; www.historicsites.vermont.gov/hubbardton-battlefield. GPS: 43.695609, -73.138248. Open Wed.–Sun., Memorial Day through mid-October.*

---

territory that would later become Vermont. Burgoyne directed a corps of Hessians, Tories, and Indians, almost 1,200 strong and commanded by Lieutenant Colonel Friedrich Baum to move toward Bennington, attempt to recruit locals to the cause, and seize the supplies.

At about the same time, a force of 1,800 New Hampshire militia was also headed for Bennington. They had been recruited and were led by John Stark, a man who had already earned a reputation as a fighter and had been made a general by the state. Stark was moving to the relief of the American army when an advance party ran into Baum's force just west of Bennington. Only a brief skirmish ensued, but it was enough to make each party aware of the other. A cautious Baum advanced to within 5 miles of Bennington and set up a strong defensive position, building two redoubts atop high ground and defending a bridge crossing the Walloomsac River. Baum also sent word back to Fort Edward that he needed reinforcements.

Over the next two days, many of the locals passed through the Brit-

Interpretive markers and signs at Bennington Battlefield State Historic Site.

ish camp as they constructed their defenses. In the view of the Hessians, these were Tories who were coming over to support the British. In reality, many of them were only there to spy on Baum's force and relay the details of the encampment back to Stark, who had moved to within a mile of the position. Stark came up with a complicated plan of attack, with one party attacking the main redoubt from the north, one attacking the same redoubt from the south, and one party advancing directly west toward the second redoubt. All three attacks would occur simultaneously.

At 3:00 PM on the afternoon of August 16, 1777, the militia advanced under the cover of the woods. Surprisingly, the Hessians saw many of the Americans moving through the woods but thought they were friendly; only when they opened fire did the Hessians realize that they were under attack. The fighting at the first redoubt was desperate and became hand to hand. At the sound of the guns, Stark shouted to his men, "There are the redcoats and they are ours, or Molly Stark sleeps a widow tonight!" before leading them against the second redoubt, which was manned mostly by Loyalists and was easily routed. The Hessians were pushed off the hill they had fortified and made a determined stand in a small meadow, but after Baum fell mortally wounded, the defenders gave way, with the Americans pursuing them and capturing many of them.

The fighting was not finished yet, however. Baum's request for reinforcements two days earlier had been granted, and a relief party led by Lieutenant Colonel Heinrich Breymann was on its way and had heard the gunfire. Breymann had moved very slowly toward Baum's force and could have easily joined him before the fighting occurred. As it was, though, he appeared just in time to surprise the now-exhausted Americans. Before the Hessians could advance, though, another American force appeared on the field—Seth Warner's Green Mountain Boys, who had been marching to join Stark's force after recovering from their defeat at Hubbardton. Warner quickly arranged his 300 men and charged Breymann's position. The Hessians turned and ran, again with many of them captured.

All told, the expedition to Bennington had not only gained nothing in terms of acquiring supplies but had cost the British army 200 men killed and another 700 captured, with only 30 Americans killed and 40 wounded. In addition, many of the Loyalists who had been with the British left, as did most of the Indians, who no longer saw Burgoyne's efforts as those of a clear-cut winner. The Battle of Bennington was a severe blow to British efforts to capture Albany, and things would only get worse for them.

Saratoga

As the summer of 1777 came to a close, it was becoming evident to both armies that the British situation was becoming dire. The loss at Bennington left the British army with less than 6,000 men, two-thirds of what he had started with. General Burgoyne was left with only two clear choices: push forward to Albany, as intended, and hope to join the other British forces in the area or retreat to Canada before winter set in, abandoning the campaign. Honor dictated that he risk all and continue

SITE DETAILS

Bennington Battlefield State Historic Site—The core of the Bennington battlefield is now preserved as a New York state historic site. The main interpretive area is atop the hill at the site of the main Hessian redoubt, the center of the hardest of the fighting. Several interpretive signs tell what happened on the battlefield, and you'll also find a few monuments to Stark and his men. *Bennington Battlefield State Historic Site, 5231 Route 67, Walloomsac, NY 12090; 518-860-9094; www.parks.ny.gov/historic-sites/benningtonbattlefield. GPS: 42.933758, -73.304878. Open May through Veterans Day.*

Bennington Battle Monument—Standing at 306 feet tall, the Bennington Battle Monument is the second tallest unreinforced masonry building in the world, second only to the Washington Monument. You can take an elevator to the top for a fantastic view; signs will help you interpret what you're looking at, including the battlefield itself, just across the border in New York. You'll also find plenty of interpretation of the battle, the Saratoga Campaign, and the monument itself inside. Outside is a nice open green space that makes a great place for a picnic. *Bennington Battle Monument, 15 Monument Cir., Bennington, VT 05201; 802-447-0550; www.benningtonbattlemonument.com. GPS: 42.889146, -73.216343. Open Memorial Day through October.*

to head south, so after a brief period of consolidating men and supplies Burgoyne crossed from the west bank of the Hudson to the east, putting him on a collision course with the American army.

That American army, by contrast, was rapidly growing. Pleas for help from Philip Schuyler, as well as the horrifying murder of settler Jane McCrea by Native Americans, who were serving the British, had attracted patriots from Massachusetts, Connecticut, New York, Pennsylvania, New Jersey, and Virginia. Now numbering over 7,000, the American army for the first time held a numerical advantage. Other changes came, too: Schuyler, who had done well in keeping his force intact but who also had many enemies in Congress, was replaced by General Horatio Gates. Gates was popular with the soldiers, unlike Schuyler, and he turned his men to the north to face the British.

The Americans took a strong position along the west bank of the Hudson at Bemis Heights, a plateau that allowed them to see any oncoming British movements. The position covered the only road to Albany, meaning that the British would either have to go through the American encampment or cut through the wilderness and find a way around them. The Americans fortified the heights with strong entrenchments, under the direction of Polish engineer Thaddeus Kościuszko, and continually improved their position for a week before the British crossed the Hudson on September 13. Gates established his headquarters within the fortified position and waited for the British to arrive.

One particular American was not content with waiting. Benedict Arnold, now a major general, had been given command of the left wing of the army, while Benjamin Lincoln commanded the right. Arnold argued that the British could outflank the American position from the

Artillery overlooking the field at Saratoga National Historical Park.

west, forcing them from their strong ground. Further, that would put the British in open fields, where they excelled at fighting, rather than forcing them to move through the thick woods and ravines that surrounded the land north of Bemis Heights. Arnold pressed his case with Gates and was finally given permission to advance with 2,000 men on the army's left flank, including the crack Virginia riflemen commanded by Daniel Morgan and light infantry under Major Henry Dearborn.

At the same time, Burgoyne, not knowing the exact position of the Americans, decided to venture out of his camp to the north. He divided the army into three wings. The Hessians under Baron von Riedesel were on the left, cautiously pressing down the river road with 3,000 troops. In the center were another 1,700 soldiers under Brigadier General James Hamilton. On the right were 3,000 men under Brigadier General Simon Fraser. Burgoyne himself moved with Hamilton's force as the army felt its way south.

It was September 19 when the two forces unknowingly began to move toward each other. After a heavy morning fog, the British moved as best they could through the terrain. Arnold's force, smaller and more capable of moving quickly through the woods, made better time and reached a clearing at John Freeman's farm in the early afternoon. Arriving just after them was the picket line marching in advance of the British center. Morgan's sharpshooters took careful aim and opened fire, driving the British into a hurried retreat. After a short lull in the fighting, during which both sides were reinforced, the struggle resumed, with both sides alternately losing then regaining control of Freeman's farm. Finally, late in the afternoon, the Hessians under Riedesel moved from the river road to the battlefield, seizing the initiative and pushing the Americans off the field just as darkness fell.

The Battle of Freeman's Farm was a British victory, technically, since they held the field when the fighting was over. But both sides knew that it was the Americans who had won the fight. The British had lost 160 killed, 364 wounded, and 42 captured or missing, almost 600 casualties that they could not afford. The Americans had lost fewer than half that. In addition, the American position at Bemis was still secure and the British still could not move toward Albany on the river road. Perhaps most important, the Americans had stood toe to toe on the battlefield with the best of the British army and demonstrated that they could fight.

The triumph was not without drama on the American side. General Gates, who had never ventured out of his headquarters during the battle, sent the details of the day in a report to Congress. Curiously, he did not mention Benedict Arnold, who had both fought bravely and led conspicuously. Whether it was out of jealousy, as many believe, or was done simply because he disliked him, Arnold was enraged.

Two days after the Battle of Freeman's Farm, Burgoyne received word that British forces in New York City, who he had counted on to join him in Albany, were making plans for a movement up the Hudson River. Overjoyed at the possibility of another 2,000 men joining him, Burgoyne decided to hold his position and dig in. The British position was fortified with several large earthworks constructed in advance of the line. In the meantime, however, rations were dwindling, and the weather was beginning to turn colder. No word of the expected reinforcements arrived from the south, so a desperate Burgoyne called a council of war and discussed the army's options. After ruling out a retreat to Canada and an all-out attack, it was decided that the British would advance with a force of about 2,000 men, determine the strength of the Americans, and prepare for a larger assault the next day with the entire army.

On October 7, Burgoyne's reconnaissance force, again split into three groups, ventured out of the British camp. This time, the right was commanded by General Fraser, with the Hessians under Riedesel in the center and the left under Major John Acland. Early in the afternoon, the force entered a wheat field and rested while the British generals stopped to try to view the American lines.

At the American headquarters, word quickly arrived that the British were moving. Generals Arnold and Lincoln advised Gates to send a sizeable force to meet the British. Gates hesitated, and when Arnold replied to him sharply, the situation between the two came to a head. Gates removed Arnold, his most effective general, from command. Morgan and Dearborn were sent around the British right and another brigade commanded by General Enoch Poor around the British left, moving silently into place such that they could then attack simultaneously while a third brigade under General Ebenezer Learned could press the center.

At 3:00 PM, the attack began, completely surprising the British. Both flanks folded quickly, exposing the center. Incredibly, Learned's brigade was accompanied by Benedict Arnold, who could not remain out of the fight. By all accounts Arnold fought like a man possessed. Before long the entire British reconnaissance force was streaming rearward, headed either for the British camp or for a redoubt commanded by Major Alexander Balcarres that had been built on Freeman's farm. The Americans pressed on and assaulted this redoubt, though they were initially pushed back; not wanting to lose momentum, Arnold changed direction and attacked a second redoubt under Lieutenant Colonel Heinrich Breymann. Breymann's redoubt, attacked from the rear, soon fell, though Arnold was shot in the same leg that was wounded at Quebec. The Balcarres redoubt could no longer hold and also fell, and the entire right side of the British line collapsed. By the time nightfall ended the fighting, the British had lost 278 killed, 331 wounded, and 285 captured for a total of 894 casualties. The Americans had only 30 killed and approximately 100 wounded. This time, the American victory was unmistakable.

The British began a retreat for Canada the next evening, but the exhausted soldiers did not make it very far. The army was practically out of food and morale was at a terrible low. Within days the Americans had surrounded them. Burgoyne opened talks to surrender his army. After several days of back and forth, the surrender was signed on October 16, 1777. The surrender had massive repercussions; besides the stunning defeat and blow to the British crown's pride, the victory at Saratoga was the major victory the French needed in order to officially enter the war on the side of the Americans.

Fort Stanwix
Though the main effort of General John Burgoyne's Campaign of 1777 centered on the Hudson Valley, there was another critical component to its design. Largely a diversion, a force of 875 British Regulars and Tory militia was to land at Fort Ontario, move east through the Mohawk Valley, and ultimately link up with Burgoyne at Albany so as to add to his numbers. The movement, commanded by Lieutenant Colonel

> ## SITE DETAILS
>
> **Saratoga National Historical Park**—This historical park includes virtually all the sites where the battles took place, as well as much of the area of both encampments. The visitor center contains a film and light map presentation, as well as exhibits on the battle and the events surrounding it. The tour road through the park is the simplest way to see each location, including Bemis Heights, Freeman's farm, and the defenses built by the British and Americans, but you'll find plenty of trails that will take you through each site. Perhaps the best way to tour the park is by hiring a licensed Saratoga Battlefield Guide; for a very reasonable fee, you'll have an intimate private tour of the park with a vetted, certified expert. To the north of the battlefield in satellite units are the surrender site, with its own interpretation, and the 1877 memorial, a 155-foot stone obelisk that you can climb. Also part of the park is the Philip Schuyler house, and a visit to it is a great way to better understand not only life on a large northern plantation but also learn about Schuyler himself. *Saratoga National Historical Park, 648 Route 32, Stillwater, NY 12170; 518-670-2985; www.nps.gov/sara. GPS: 43.013841, -73.651152. Open daily, March through November; open weekends, December through February.*

Barry St. Leger, was designed to pull critical American strength from the Hudson Valley as well as provide a muster point for the Tories of the Mohawk Valley.

The Mohawk Valley, sparsely populated mostly with homesteads and farming communities, provided few obstacles to an invading force. The exception was Fort Stanwix. The fort had been built in 1758 at a critical point along the Oneida Carrying Place, a portage along the route from the Mohawk River to Wood Creek and, beyond, the Great Lakes. It had been the site of the Treaty of Fort Stanwix between the Native Americans and the British in 1768.

Realizing its importance, the Americans had been working hard to improve the fort. Stanwix had been designed for protection from frontier

Outside the walls at Fort Stanwix National Monument.

raiding parties, and in May 1777 work began to transform the works to be able to withstand a siege. By the time the British arrived, Fort Stanwix (now also known as Fort Schuyler) was a formidable bastion, garrisoned with 700 soldiers commanded by Colonel Peter Gansevoort.

The British Regulars, under the command of Lieutenant Colonel Barry St. Leger, landed at Fort Ontario and on July 26, 1777, moved nearly undetected toward Fort Stanwix. They were soon joined by 1,000 Iroquois under Chief Joseph Brant. The Americans were alerted to the approaching army with little notice, and St. Leger's force began surrounding the fort on August 3. Though runners were able to escape and send word to Fort Dayton that the British had arrived, the Americans were largely outnumbered, and a demand for surrender soon came. Gansevoort refused the surrender, buying time and hoping that his messengers would be able to summon enough men to assist the fort.

Because Fort Stanwix was far too strong a position to take by assault, St. Leger began siege operations to force the Americans out. While the

British dug trenches and crept closer to the fort, both armies engaged in a long-range duel, sniping at each other and picking off men as opportunities presented themselves. Other demands for surrender came, but all were refused, primarily for two reasons. First, the Americans held a strong position, and they held out hope that a relief party would soon arrive. Second, the men inside the fort knew all too well that if they surrendered, there was the possibility that they would be left to the devices of the Iroquois, and most would rather die fighting than face the brutal, vicious torture that could be their fate.

Word finally reached the garrison of Fort Stanwix on August 6 that a relief party, 800 men of the Tryon County Militia, was indeed approaching. Unfortunately for them, word of their imminent arrival also reached the Iroquois, and the party was ambushed at Oriskany, resulting in a severe defeat for the militia and forcing them to turn back. However, the Americans at the fort were able to take advantage of the situation. An attack party was able to leave the fort and raid the encampment of the Indians while all the warriors were at Oriskany. The raid not only helped the Americans gather critical food and supplies but also severely embarrassed the Iroquois, damaging the relationship with their British counterparts. Between the raid and the losses suffered at Oriskany, the Indian willingness to stay through the siege—a method of warfare extremely foreign to their nature—was beginning to waver.

General Philip Schuyler, still in command in the Hudson Valley, heard about the defeat at Oriskany and, on August 13, arranged for another relief party to be sent to the fort, this one commanded by now-General Benedict Arnold. Arnold's force left Stillwater the next day and headed west through the Mohawk Valley. Though he had a sizeable force of 1,000 men, Arnold faced a problem: He could not approach Stanwix on the single road to the fort without running the same risk of ambush that the militia had. While he prepared to move, however, an extraordinary opportunity presented itself.

A group of Tories had been captured while attempting to recruit for St. Leger near Fort Dayton. Among those captured was a man named Hon Yost Schuyler. It was well known that Schuyler suffered from mental deficiencies; remarkably, though, the Iroquois regarded him as something of a savant and held his word in very high regard. He had been sentenced to death because of his activities, but a deal was struck between Arnold and those pleading for mercy on his behalf. After shooting his coat full of holes, the Americans sent Schuyler west to the British at Fort Stanwix to tell the Indians that Arnold was approaching with a relief force of thousands of men.

The creative ruse exceeded all expectations. Once the Iroquois heard Han Yost Schuyler's tales, they lost all willingness to remain at Fort Stanwix and almost immediately abandoned the British. St. Leger, whose force had been suddenly and severely reduced, was now in danger of being outnumbered. In addition, he now had too few men to effectively invest the fort without the siege becoming impossibly long. The British withdrew from their encampment and headed back west to Fort Ontario, leaving Fort Stanwix behind. Arnold's party arrived shortly after, relieving the garrison.

The consequences of the failed siege at Fort Stanwix were significant for Burgoyne's invasion. Not only did the British lose a significant number of troops that would have potentially bolstered their force, they also left open a potential source of invasion in their rear should they venture past Albany. In addition, most of the Americans who were at Fort Stanwix now headed east to join the Northern army in defending the Hudson Valley. This failed diversion would contribute heavily to the pending American victory at Saratoga.

Oriskany
Word of the siege at Fort Stanwix soon traveled up the Mohawk Valley, and it was not long before a relief effort was underway. A call for militia went out, requesting that all able-bodied men gather at Fort Dayton to march west to Stanwix and assist the beleaguered garrison as best they could. At the muster point 850 men soon arrived to fall in under the command of Nicholas Herkimer, a well-known and respected veteran of the French and Indian War as well as friend to the local Native American tribes.

Though the Patriot militia gathered quickly, the Mohawk intelligence network was even speedier. As men made their way into Fort Dayton, the keen-eyed Molly Brant was watching closely. Brant was the sister of Chief Joseph Brant and had been married to the now-deceased William Johnson, perhaps the most prominent pioneer in the Mohawk Valley.

SITE DETAILS

Fort Stanwix National Monument—One of the best historical sites in the Mohawk Valley, Fort Stanwix National Monument provides the visitor with a unique experience. Though the fort you see today is a reconstruction, it sits on the site of the original. Seeing the size of Fort Stanwix comes as somewhat of a revelation, and it becomes obvious just what a significant position this was. The interior of the fort is impressive as well, with many of the rooms providing further interpretation about life inside the stockade. The excellent visitor center, opened in 2006, presents not only the history of Fort Stanwix but sheds light on the choices the people of the Mohawk Valley had to make during the Revolution. Living history programs and special events are common, too, and the rangers here provide excellent additional interpretation. *Fort Stanwix National Monument, 112 East Park St., Rome, NY 13440; 315-338-7730; www.nps.gov/fost. GPS: 43.210617, -75.457274. Grounds open daily; visitor center and fort open seasonally—check website for hours.*

Molly took careful count of the forces passing by and relayed this information through runners to her brother, who was taking part in the siege at Fort Stanwix. Joseph Brant, knowing the information was reliable, gathered 800 of his Mohawk allies, along with a group of Tory militia, from the siege party and moved east to meet Herkimer's force.

Brant and his Mohawks knew the valley well. Aware that the militia would be using the only road available to them, Brant selected an ambush point near Oriskany Creek, approximately 6 miles east of Fort Stanwix. The site was a small but steep, densely wooded plateau in the road, with deep ravines to the east and west. The ravines would serve as an ideal hiding spot for Brant's forces. They would wait until the Patriots were past the first ravine and atop the plateau, then would attack them from front and rear, trapping them. The attack would commence upon Brant's signal.

The Oriskany Battlefield monument.

On August 6, 1777, a blisteringly hot day, Herkimer's men approached the plateau and passed the first ravine. Brant's warriors had been in place since early in the day, and they were ready for the fight—in fact, perhaps a bit too ready. When the advance guard of the column approached the second ravine, they lunged forward to get a drink from the creek at the bottom of the ravine. The Mohawks posted nearby could not resist, and rather than wait for Brant's signal, they opened fire. While the fire was effective, it also signaled the entire column of the ambush before the rear had crossed the second ravine. Herkimer's force was able to form quickly and deliver a devastating counterfire, allowing the men to fall to defensive positions within the trees of the plateau.

The fighting at Oriskany, conducted at close quarters, was exceptionally brutal. Much of the fighting was hand to hand, with the combatants

SITE DETAILS

Oriskany Battlefield State Historic Site—The center of the Oriskany battlefield is preserved today as a state historic site. A large monument sits atop the hill where the Americans made their last stand, and it is easy to see the undulating landscape and picture the fight that occurred here. Interpretive signs allow you to visit any time and still appreciate what happened, though the hours of the visitor center are somewhat limited. *Oriskany Battlefield State Historic Site, 7801 NY 69, Oriskany, NY 13424; 315-655-3200; www.parks.ny.gov/historic-sites/oriskanybattlefield/details.aspx. GPS: 43.174210, -75.367218. Grounds open daily; visitor center open Wed.–Sun., Memorial Day through Labor Day.*

often having little time to reload their muskets before the enemy was upon them. Herkimer was seriously wounded, but amazingly sat against a tree and directed the battle, smoking his pipe while guiding the action. For the next two hours, men butchered each other until a summer storm came through and paused the battle. Both sides used it as an opportunity to regroup and reform, and when the storm passed an hour later, the combat resumed. The militia gathered itself in a strong position atop the plateau, and Brant, realizing that further attacks would be fruitless, withdrew his warriors and headed back to Fort Stanwix, but not before Herkimer had been killed in one last devastating charge. Brant's mission had been accomplished, however. Herkimer's relief column had taken far too much damage to continue to Stanwix, and the survivors were forced to return to Fort Dayton.

The fighting at Oriskany lasted for five hours. The results for both sides were devastating but were especially so for the Patriots. The militia had lost approximately 500 men killed, with another 200 or so wounded. The British side had lost fewer men, but still a significant 250 killed. In both sheer number of casualties and in percentage of killed and wounded, Oriskany was by far the bloodiest battle of the entire Revolutionary War.

OTHER SITES IN THE CHAMPLAIN, HUDSON, AND MOHAWK VALLEYS

CROWN POINT—Only one day after their capture of Fort Ticonderoga, part of the colonial force led by Benedict Arnold and Ethan Allen moved north to take possession of the British fort at Crown Point, a choke point at the southern end of Lake Champlain. On May 11, 1775, led by Seth Warner, the Green Mountain Boys of Vermont occupied the fort with little difficulty, given the virtual abandonment of the post by the British after a fire had largely destroyed it two years earlier. The Americans took possession of 111 cannon here, 29 of which went with Henry Knox to aid in the siege of Boston. Though the capture of Forts Ticonderoga and Crown Point were great morale-boosters for the Americans, in truth, both the condition of Fort Crown Point and its location made it much less defensible than mighty Fort Ticonderoga. When the British invaded from Canada in 1776, Fort Crown Point was abandoned and given back without a fight.

Ruins of the barracks at Crown Point State Historic Site.

The events of the early American Revolution are some of the later ones in the long history of Fort Crown Point. The French built a strong stone fortification here in 1734 named Fort St. Frederick, which they destroyed in a spectacular explosion as the British approached in 1759 during the French and Indian War. The British, rather than rebuild from the ruins, constructed a massive earth and stone fortification near the French one. Crown Point State Historic Site now carefully preserves and interprets what is left of both forts. A self-guided walking tour through the grounds will take you through both sets of ruins; though there isn't much left of the man-made portions of the forts, there is enough to interpret, and the earthen walls of the British fort, over 20 feet high, are still in excellent shape. The grounds are open daily but check the fort's website for times and try to visit when the museum is open. There is a small theater with an excellent audiovisual presentation, and the exhibits, models, and artifacts will give you a good idea of the importance of the site and what life was like here. *Crown Point State Historic Site, 21 Grandview Drive, Crown Point, NY 12928; 518-597-4666; www.parks.ny .gov/historic-sites/34/details.aspx. GPS: 44.024638, -73.424979. Grounds open daily; museum open Wed.–Mon., May through October.*

SKENESBOROUGH—Considering its remote location, the town of Skenesborough saw quite a bit of action during the American Revolution. Its first primary role was as a pass-through for the Continental Army on its way to and from Fort Ticonderoga. Before too long, Skenesborough became an industrial center, supplying the American garrison at Fort Ticonderoga with what little they could fashion out of the surrounding wilderness. Eventually, boat-building operations began at Skenesborough for the fleet that would patrol and defend Lake Champlain under Benedict Arnold, and for this reason, the small hamlet today proclaims itself as the birthplace of the now-mighty United States Navy. During the evacuation of Fort Ticonderoga, boats were loaded with supplies and sent to Skenesborough to keep them out of enemy hands, but the British arrived only hours behind and destroyed or confiscated almost all of them on July 7, 1777. General John Burgoyne would keep his headquarters here until July 24, when the British army would finally move south toward Fort Anne.

The small harbor at Skenesborough, one of the birthplaces of the United States Navy.

Skenesborough is now known as Whitehall. Taking a walk along the Champlain Canal, adjacent to Skenesborough Drive, will take you to several historic markers and interpretive signs describing Skenesborough's naval legacy, plus monuments proudly proclaiming Skenesborough as the birthplace of the United States Navy. Though not associated with the American Revolution, perhaps your most extraordinary find will be the hull of the USS *Ticonderoga*, American flagship during the War of 1812's Battle of Plattsburgh, raised from the bottom of Lake Champlain in 1958. A bit farther down the road, you will come to the site of Skenesborough Harbor, where the British destroyed the last of the Lake Champlain fleet in 1777. (Don't be surprised if you see a few signs and sights related to Bigfoot, too. Whitehall is New York's Sasquatch capital, with many sightings over the years; it is the town's official animal and is protected by law, and there is an annual festival in its name.) *Interpretive sign—Birthplace of the United States Navy, along Champlain Canal adjacent to Skenesborough Museum, Skenesborough Dr., GPS: 43.553908,*

-73.402426. Historical marker and monument—Birthplace of the United States Navy, in park at intersection of Skenesborough Dr. and Saunders St., GPS: 43.555081, -73.402335. Skenesborough Harbor, historical marker near intersection of Main St. and Clinton St., GPS: 43.557399, -73.401433. Whitehall, NY 12887. Sites accessible daily.

FORT ANNE—Fort Anne was one of the formerly French and British forts along the Hudson Valley that had been commandeered by the Americans. After the fall of Fort Ticonderoga, however, most of the Americans evacuated toward Fort Edward, leaving only a small group behind to keep an eye on the enemy. On July 8, 1777, the day after the British occupation of Skenesborough, a scouting party approached Fort Anne and ran into the Americans, who put up a tough fight and drove the redcoats back. The British retreated back to Skenesborough, while the Americans went south to rejoin the main army.

All that remains of Fort Anne today are a few historical markers scattered around town, as well as the remains of the old fort well. An interpretive panel near the battlefield tells about the fort and the battle. There is also a large bronze plaque at the site of the fighting, but it is along a very busy road, and your safest bet will be to see it while driving by rather than stopping. *New York Historical marker—Old Powder House, on Ann St. just east of Mountain View Rd., Ft. Ann, NY 12827. GPS: 43.414535, -73.493402. New York Historical marker—Old Well, intersection of George St. and Charles St., Ft. Ann, NY 12827. GPS: 43.416516, -73.487276. Fort Ann Interpretive Plaza, intersection of US Highway 4 and Crandall Ln., Ft. Ann, NY 12827. GPS: 43.419227, -73.486703. Battle Hill Marker, on US Highway 4 0.5 mile north of Crandall Ln., Ft. Ann, NY 12827. GPS: 43.424328, -73.482023. Signs accessible daily.*

FORT GEORGE—Fort George stood at the southern end of Lake George, the long, thin lake that leads from the Hudson River to Lake Champlain. The Americans took possession of the fort in 1775 but destroyed and abandoned it to the British when General John Burgoyne's invading army approached in 1777. Burgoyne used the Lake George water route to haul heavy equipment such as artillery south to meet the Americans, moving from the landing here to meet the rest of the army at Fort Edward.

Lake George Battlefield Park is mostly dedicated to the major events of the French and Indian War that occurred here at Fort George and its predecessor, Fort William Henry, but portions of the park are devoted to telling the story of the American Revolution. You'll find the ruins of the fort as well as plenty of recreation, including camping. The park opened a new visitor center and museum in 2022, and it is expanding to tell the many stories about this history-rich site. Aside from the historic site, Lake George is a beautiful place with lots of tourist attractions, making it a good stop for the whole family. *Lake George Battlefield Park, 34 Fort George Rd., Lake George, NY 12845; www.lakegeorgebattlefield.org. GPS: 43.418387, -73.706331. Site accessible daily; visitor center open Memorial Day through Labor Day.*

MILITARY ROAD FROM FORT EDWARD TO LAKE GEORGE—The primary connection between the Hudson River and Lake George, this military road was constructed in 1755 just in time to serve as a critical artery during the French and Indian War. The road retained its importance during the Revolution, as thousands of American troops moved through the area. During the British invasion in 1777 the road was used to move heavy equipment and supplies from points north to Fort Edward. During the invasion, a young American woman, Jane McCrea, was killed by Indians belonging to Burgoyne's British army. Though it was only one of many similar incidents at the time, McCrea's murder shocked Americans and British alike, serving to galvanize anti-British sentiment and inspiring many young men to join the effort to stop the invasion.

Most of the military road is easy to travel today as US Highway 9. There are several historic markers and monuments along the way, not only to mark the military road but also important points along the way, such as the site where McCrea was killed. *Old Military Road Historic Marker, intersection of Broadway and McCrea St., Fort Edward, NY 12828. GPS: 43.272151, -73.588188. Jane McCrea Murder Site, on Broadway 0.1 mile north of intersection with McCrea St., Fort Edward, NY 12828. GPS: 43.272493, -73.586607. Jane McCrea Memorial, intersection of Broadway and Case St., Fort Edward, NY 12828. GPS: 43.273416, -73.586614. Half Way Brook, on US Highway 9 0.1 mile north of Glenwood Ave., Queens-*

bury, NY 12804. GPS: 43.326072, -73.664201. *Old Military Road Historic Marker, on US Highway 9 0.1 mile north of Highway 149, Queensbury, NY 12804. GPS: 43.370868, -73.697948. Sites accessible daily.*

FORT EDWARD AND PATRICK SMYTH HOUSE—The Fort Edward that stood during the French and Indian War had fallen into disrepair, so in 1772, the fort's remnants were reused to build a grand home and tavern for local Patrick Smyth. When the American Revolution rolled around, the Fort Edward site was still a significant one, and the Smyth house was a natural place for a headquarters. The home was used by General Philip Schuyler and General Benedict Arnold when the Americans were in residence, as well as by General John Burgoyne during the extended stay of the British army.

The original Fort Edward exists today only as a set of historic markers outlining the old site, but the Patrick Smyth house, now known as the Old Fort House, is now a museum. The museum covers the house's interesting history through the Revolution and beyond; notably, when serving as a boarding house, it was the home of Solomon Northup, author of *Twelve Years a Slave*. Consisting of the house, several buildings, and a garden, this local museum is worth a stop. *Old Fort House, 29 Broadway, Fort Edward, NY 12828; 518-747-9600; www.oldforthousemuseum.com. GPS: 43.261659, -73.580825. Signs accessible daily; museum open June through mid-October.*

LANDLORD FAY'S / GREEN MOUNTAIN TAVERN—The Green Mountain Tavern, as it was originally known, was built in 1767 in Bennington. It soon became home of the Green Mountain Boys, the rowdy militia who defended the rights of Vermonters and disputed New York claims to the area. Also known as Landlord Fay's Tavern, it was here that the group met before their successful capture of Fort Ticonderoga in 1775.

The tavern is long gone, burned down in 1871. You will find a monument there to the Catamount Tavern, another of its names; the monument is a large wildcat, or catamount, atop a granite base. *Catamount Tavern Monument, on Monument Ave. just north of Main St., Bennington, VT 05201. GPS: 42.884871, -73.213422. Site accessible daily.*

FORT SALEM—In 1776, a small church that was under construction was repurposed as a depot and barracks for the local Patriot militia. Christened Fort Salem, the building was subsequently captured and burned by the British in 1777.

The site is home now to the Fort Salem Theater. The building you see today is the third iteration of the original church, which suffered several other fires after the war. A historic marker is also at the site. *Fort Salem, 11 East Broadway, Salem, NY 12865; 518-854-9200; www.fortsalemtheater.com. GPS: 43.172686, -73.326209. Site accessible daily.*

ELIJAH WEST'S TAVERN—The Hampshire Land Grants, that piece of land that we now call Vermont, had been a subject of dispute between the colonies of New Hampshire and New York for years. Many of those who settled here, however, had their own ideas, wanting to form their own colony or, perhaps, an independent republic. After several attempts, a delegation meeting at Elijah West's tavern in Windsor came together and named the new state Vermont (meaning "green mountain" in French).

Elijah West's tavern at Old Constitution House State Historic Site.

Thus, the Republic of Vermont was born, and it would remain independent until it became America's 14th State in 1791.

Elijah West's tavern is now known as the Old Constitution House State Historic Site. Tours of the site are available and tell the story of Vermont's birth as well as that of a typical 18th-century tavern. The room where the delegates met and made their historic decision is still set up as it was then, and there are exhibits and maps that clearly explain the sometimes-complicated history of the Republic and later State of Vermont. *Old Constitution House State Historic Site, 16 North Main St., Windsor, VT 05089; 802-672-3773; www.historicsites.vermont.gov/constitution-house. GPS: 43.484272, -72.385480. Open Sat.–Sun., Memorial Day weekend through mid-October.*

CROWN POINT ROAD—In 1759, after a string of significant victories in the French and Indian War, British General Jeffrey Amherst halted at Crown Point to prepare for the defense of the region around Ticonderoga. Though the end of the North American portion of the war was on the horizon with the British capture of Quebec, Amherst planned to establish Crown Point as a stronghold. Needing a more direct supply line to the eastern seaboard, he ordered a road to be built across the Vermont country eastward to the Fort at No. 4. A party led by Captain John Stark cut the road through the wilderness, finishing with a length of just over 77 miles. Though no longer needed for the war, the military road helped settle the Vermont region and became a critical passage through the Vermont wilderness. When the Revolutionary War came, it was the Americans, many of whom had built the road, who took advantage of it. The road's original construction included a branch to Fort Ticonderoga, and with the improvements made during the interwar years, the Crown Point Military Road became a critical American artery for both men and material.

The Crown Point Road Association, in an obvious labor of love, has done an amazing job of tracking down and marking the Crown Point Road along its length. They have produced a guidebook and website that enable a tourist to hike or drive the length of it using the original path wherever possible. Markers have been placed along the length of the road and have been carefully documented and pictured in the association's guide; two of the markers even date back to the road's origin in 1759–1760. (Hunt for these two, #18 and #22, in the town of Weathersfield, if you can; the rewarding feeling of finding these two remarkable pieces of history is something you won't forget.) *Crown Point Road Association, www.crownpointroad.org. Origin at Crown Point State Historic Site, 21 Grandview Drive, Crown Point, NY 12928; GPS: 44.024638, -73.424979. Terminus at the Fort at No. 4, 267 Springfield Rd., Charlestown, NH 03603; GPS: 43.255089, -72.428530. Open daily; see guidebook on website for precise location of road and markers.*

FORT AT NO. 4—Once one of Great Britain's most remote outposts in New England, Plantation No. 4 was established in 1740. The growing settlement soon realized the need to fend for itself when it came to defense, and a fort was built, consisting of an enclosed square of homes surrounded by a stockade wall. The plantation and fort became occasional targets for local Native American tribes when conflicts flared up, and British troops were quartered there during the French and Indian War. It was during this war that John Stark, destined to become an American general and one of New Hampshire's true heroes, was tasked with building the Crown Point Military Road, creating an easily passable route from critical Crown Point to Plantation No. 4, by this time better known as Charlestown, New Hampshire. In 1777, during the American Revolution, Stark would return to muster his men at No. 4 and make their way to Bennington, scoring a crucial American victory that contributed mightily to the coming British surrender at Saratoga.

The reconstructed Fort at No. 4 is staffed by dedicated volunteers. Though not in the precise location of the original fort, the reproduction is historically accurate, and living history exhibits and demonstrations portray the frontier life of the colonial period in Vermont. The reconstructed buildings, particularly the fort's hall, are impressive in their construction and size, reflecting Plantation No. 4's importance. Frequent festivals and special programs are also held to highlight the period's history, and there is a museum on site to help with interpretation. *The Fort at No. 4, 267 Springfield Rd., Charlestown, NH 03603; 603 826-5700; www.fortat4.org. GPS: 43.255089, -72.428530. Open Wed.–Sun., May through October.*

The interior grounds of the re-created Fort at No. 4 in Charlestown, New Hampshire.

WYMAN TAVERN—Several days after the fighting at Lexington and Concord, on August 22, 1775, a group of 29 men from the distant New Hampshire town of Keene gathered at the tavern of Captain Isaac Wyman and mustered in. These men then made their way southeast to join the Patriot army growing around Boston.

Wyman Tavern has some other great history associated with it, too. In 1770, a group of trustees met in the parlor to found Dartmouth College. Later, the building was used as the Keene Academy, with future Secretary of the Treasury and Chief Justice of the United States Supreme Court Salmon Chase as one of its pupils. Tours of the home are somewhat limited, so plan ahead if you'd like to visit. *Wyman Tavern, 349 Main St., Keene, NH 03431; 603-352-1895; www.hsccnh.org. Open Thurs.–Sat., June through August and by appointment September and October.*

SCHUYLER FLATTS—A large flatland along the Hudson River near Albany, used for several decades as a trading post, soon housed one of the mansions and plantations of the Schuyler family, already on its way to being one of New York's most prominent families. American General Philip Schuyler stayed at what became known as Schuyler Flatts as he planned the invasion of Canada in 1775. The large, flat land proved to be an ideal muster ground for American troops, and it became particularly important as Patriots flocked toward the American army that would eventually triumph at Saratoga.

Schuyler Flatts Cultural Park preserves the site, including the location of the old mansion and the grounds where the Patriots mustered. The park contains an easy, short loop pathway with interpretive signs that include some of the site's other interesting history. Though the Schuyler Mansion unfortunately burned down in 1962, you can still stand on the original ground—the home's foundation is clearly and accurately marked in stone, courtesy of the still-ongoing archaeological investigations done over the years. *Schuyler Flatts Cultural Park, 595 Broadway, Watervliet, NY 12189; 518-783-2760; www.colonie.org/departments/parksandrec/parks/#schuylerflatts. GPS: 42.706509, -73.710891. Open daily.*

FORT SCHLOSSER—Sitting above Niagara Falls, Fort Schlosser was constructed during the French and Indian War near the site of a recently burned French fortification. The original French fort was designed to guard the upper (southern) landing of the Niagara Portage Road, a bypass of the falls that enabled supplies to move more freely to and from western settlements along the Great Lakes. British engineers moved the upper portage landing upstream to take advantage of less turbulent currents, and Fort Schlosser protected the new landing location. The British continued to occupy Fort Schlosser through the Revolutionary War, and though they eventually left after the American victory, they would recapture the post during the War of 1812.

There is a scenic overlook, the Upper Niagara Intake Observation Area, that preserves the site of Fort Schlosser and overlooks the Niagara River. Several interpretive signs are here that describe Fort Schlosser in detail, and though they are focused on the period of the French and Indian War, they will give you a good idea of the fort's importance and what the area was like during its occupation. *Upper Niagara Intake Observation Area, entrance ramp to parking area on Eastbound Niagara Scenic*

Parkway 1.8 miles east of John Daly Blvd., Niagara Falls, NY 14304. GPS: 43.077533, -79.015587. Site accessible daily.

NIAGARA PORTAGE ROAD—Stretching 7 miles between the Upper Niagara River and the end of the Niagara Gorge, the Niagara Portage Road was a vital transportation path around Niagara Falls since long before Europeans arrived in the area. Control of the road meant control of the falls and, to a great extent, the Great Lakes beyond them. Once the road fell into the hands of the British after the French and Indian War, the road was improved and moved slightly. When the American Revolution began, the importance of the road required that critical British resources be dedicated to its protection, even though the Americans never attempted to capture it.

Many of the area's existing streets and highways follow the path of the original Niagara Portage Road. Its original location at the Upper Landing, when under French control, is marked by the Old Stone Chimney, the only remaining remnant of the original French fort guarding the landing (though it has been moved several times). The site contains interpretive signs describing both the fort and the portage. From there, you can follow Portage Road through the town of Niagara Falls, then keep going onto New York Route 104 all the way to the Lower Landing site at Lewiston. You will find several historic markers, monuments, and interpretive signs along the way. *Old Stone Chimney, entrance ramp to parking area on Eastbound Niagara Scenic Parkway 0.3 mile east of John Daly Blvd., Niagara Falls, NY 14304. GPS: 43.079277, -79.045041. Historic marker—Portage Road, just west of intersection of Buffalo Ave. and Portage Rd., Niagara Falls, NY 14303. GPS: 43.083065, -79.041137. Monument—Historic Falls Portage Under Four Nations, intersection of Portage Rd. and Falls St., Niagara Falls, NY 14303. GPS: 43.087050, -79.042337. Interpretive sign—Portage Road, on Portage Rd. 0.1 mile north of Walnut Ave. outside Niagara Arts & Cultural Center, Niagara Falls, NY 14301. GPS: 43.094119, -79.047887. Sites accessible daily.*

LEWISTON PORTAGE LANDING—Now the town of Lewiston, New York, the Lower Landing of the Niagara Portage Road sits at the end of Niagara Gorge, formed by the rapid (in geological terms) erosion of the rock underneath Niagara Falls, now miles upstream of its original location here. The last easily navigable water before reaching the foot of the falls, the Lower Landing would see travelers and supplies put ashore to travel the Niagara Portage Road for 7 miles, bypassing the tumultuous rapids of the gorge and the falls themselves. Critical property for the British, the Lower Landing, as well as the Portage Road and the Upper Landing kept British soldiers dedicated to its defense for the duration of the American Revolution.

The site of the Lewiston Portage Landing is now the Artpark, a riverside public park and arts and entertainment facility in Lewiston. There is an interpretive sign in the parking lot that tells the story of the Lower Landing. *Lewiston Portage Landing, located in the southwest corner of the Artpark parking lot, entrance on South 4th St. 0.1 mile south of Tuscarora St., Lewiston, NY 14092. GPS: 43.166351, -79.046140. Site accessible daily.*

FORT NIAGARA—The British post at Fort Niagara guarded the Niagara Portage Road and was therefore the door that controlled access to the Great Lakes. The first post here was founded by French explorer La Salle in 1678 before he made his way down the Mississippi River; the British would capture the fort during the French and Indian War and would hold it until 1796, well after the American Revolution was over. They would recapture it during the War of 1812, only to return it two years later. Still, as comparatively isolated as the outpost was, it played an active part in the American Revolution. Besides guarding the Niagara Portage, Fort Niagara became an important refugee center for Loyalists fleeing the colonies for Canada. Loyalist militia units were formed from these refugees, and these units, in concert with the Iroquois, conducted devastating raids from Fort Niagara, including the massacres in the Cherry Valley of New York and Wyoming Valley of Pennsylvania. While these raids did more to enrage the American populace than produce significant military results, they did threaten the farms feeding the Continental Army. The Americans countered with the Clinton-Sullivan Campaign of 1779 and other punitive expeditions, destroying Iroquois villages, food, and winter stores. It was now the Iroquois who sought shelter with their allies at Fort Niagara, but with British supplies already stretched thin, little relief was available, and hundreds died of starvation in the camps surrounding the fort.

The parade ground at Old Fort Niagara State Historic Site.

Old Fort Niagara State Historic Site is operated by the Old Fort Niagara Association. The massive fort is in excellent condition, and the remaining original elements thoroughly tell the history of the site. The visitor center contains an excellent museum, and a short walk will take you through the earthworks and brickwork into the extensive fortifications. Here you will find pieces of varied history throughout; a French crest here, a British coat of arms there, each marking different periods and pieces of the life of the fort. Several buildings contain additional exhibit space, and you will find large maps, models, and other interpretation, all up to date and well kept. Perhaps the most impressive piece is the Castle, a 1726 building remaining from the French fortification that holds barracks, the old chapel, officer's quarters, and a grand dining hall. There is also a monument to the Rush-Bagot Treaty that limited American and British naval power on the Great Lakes. On a clear day, from the site, you can see all the way across Lake Ontario to the Toronto skyline. *Old Fort Niagara State Historic Site, entrance near intersection of*

New York State Route 18F and Robert Moses Parkway, Youngstown, NY 14174; 716 745-7611; www.parks.ny.gov/historic-sites/31/details.aspx and www.oldfortniagara.org. GPS: 43.264720, -79.052332. Open daily.

FORT ONTARIO—Built at the mouth of the Oswego River on the southeast shore of Lake Ontario, Fort Ontario traded hands several times over the course of the French and Indian War. When the British planned the campaign of 1777, intending to take possession of New York's Hudson Valley, Fort Ontario was an obvious launching point for the army approaching from the west under the command of General Barry St. Leger. When St. Leger's expedition was stopped at Fort Stanwix and forced to turn back, Fort Ontario was abandoned, and an American force destroyed it the following year. The British would return several years later to rebuild the fort, which saw further action during the War of 1812 and again traded hands several times. Though abandoned and reoccupied several times, Fort Ontario remained in use through World War II.

Fort Ontario has changed a lot over the years, and all its varied con-

Fort Ontario overlooks Lake Ontario at the mouth of the Oswego River.

structions, uses, and occupations are described at Fort Ontario State Historic Site. The fort you'll see today represents its mid-1800s' appearance, and exhibits within and outside its buildings fully describe the fort's history. The museum is notably well-done, with short, modern videos and multimedia presentations and a nice collection of artifacts. (An exhibit about Fort Ontario's use as a refugee shelter for victims of the Holocaust is particularly poignant.) The grounds are extensive, and you could spend quite a bit of time exploring the outer works, artillery emplacements, monuments, and the fort cemetery, all thoroughly interpreted and with a scenic view of Lake Ontario in the background. *Fort Ontario State Historic Site, 1 East 4th St., Oswego, NY 13126; 315-343-4711; www.parks.ny.gov/historic-sites/20/details.aspx and www.historicfortontario.com. GPS: 43.463432, -76.507027. Open Wed.–Sun., mid-May through June and September through mid-October; open daily July and August.*

FORT HALDIMAND AND BRITISH NAVY YARD—On its way to Fort Ontario as part of the campaign of 1777, British General Barry St. Leger's force landed on Deer Island, a transfer point between the Saint Lawrence River and Lake Ontario, to prepare for the expedition. After St. Leger's defeat, the region was virtually devoid of British troops, and in 1778 a decision was made to fortify the island, now named Carleton Island after Guy Carleton, an army general and the governor of Quebec. In a very short time, Fort Haldimand and Carleton Island became critical to the British possession of Lake Ontario; what had been a small merchant post soon boasted a shipbuilding facility and naval yard, a garrison of troops, and commercial operations to support the British presence. The boom lasted only through the American Revolution, however, and shortly after the war ended the island was quickly depopulated, only to be used sporadically over the years for military and then private use.

A handful of ruins are left from Fort Haldimand and the British presence here, but the island is now conservation land maintained by the Thousand Islands Land Trust. The island can only be visited with their permission, but the trust does occasionally sponsor guided trips to the island. If you're not able to arrange a trip to the island, you can still view the site of the fort from a distance. The town of Cape Vincent maintains several parks along the Saint Lawrence River, one of which contains interpretation regarding the fort—more, in fact, than you'd find on the island itself. The St. Lawrence River Historical Foundation also maintains a great website about Fort Haldimand's history and its state today, and projects to interpret the site are continuing. *Thousand Islands Land Trust, www.tilandtrust.org. Contact for tours. Fort Haldimand Viewpoint, park entrance at intersection of Broadway St. and Centre St., Cape Vincent, NY 13618; www.forthaldimand.com. GPS: 44.132138, -76.324633. Site accessible daily.*

NEWTOWN—After massacres in the Wyoming Valley of Pennsylvania and at Cherry Valley, New York, in 1778, George Washington decided on a punitive expedition that would hopefully neutralize the Iroquois threat to the frontier. The ultimate goal of the expedition was to destroy Native American villages and crops, forcing the Iroquois to be a burden to the British at Fort Niagara. Command of the expedition was given to General John Sullivan, and his command moved toward the Chemung River

The viewing platform at Newtown Battlefield State Park.

Valley. After a small action at New Chemung on August 13, more troops arrived under General James Clinton, and the Colonials, now 4,000 strong, headed along the Chemung River toward an awaiting force of about 600 led by British Major John Butler and Chief Joseph Brant. On August 29, 1779, Sullivan advanced against the enemy breastworks and was able to surround them, forcing the British and Indians back. The victory freed Sullivan's men to set about destroying the native villages. Washington achieved his desired result, as Native American raids on the frontier were severely curtailed. Although Newtown was its only significant engagement, the Sullivan-Clinton Campaign was the largest of 1779 for the Patriots.

Newtown Battlefield State Park preserves a portion of the battlefield. You'll find a large monument to the battle as well as a scenic overlook that will give you a wonderful view of the Chemung Valley and the rest of the battlefield. The park also has camping and a number of hiking trails. In addition to the park, the Chemung County Historical Society has created a driving tour of the battlefield that starts and ends at the county museum. The tour brochure, available online, does a great job of telling the tale of the Newtown action and pointing out the remaining features of the landscape. *Newtown Battlefield State Park, 2346 County Route 60, Elmira, NY 14901; 607-732-6067; www.parks.ny.gov/parks/ newtownbattlefield. GPS: 42.050848, -76.746806. Open daily. Chemung County Historical Society, 415 E. Water St., Elmira, NY 14901; 607-734- 4167; www.chemungvalleymuseum.org/special-tours. GPS: 42.088391, -76.800466. Open Mon.–Sat.*

ONONDAGA CREEK—Onondaga, for centuries the political and spiritual center of the Iroquois Confederacy, was the target of the Americans' first coordinated punitive action against the Iroquois after the massacres at Wyoming Valley and Cherry Valley. In April 1779, 558 men led by Colonel Goose Van Schaick left Fort Stanwix and headed west for Onondaga. Early on the morning of April 21, Van Schaick's men surprised the village, killing 12 and taking 34 captives without suffering any casualties. Much more devastating to the Iroquois, however, was the complete destruction of the town. Included in this destruction was the sacred Long House of the Iroquois, a devastating symbolic loss not just to the Onondaga but to the entire Iroquois Confederacy. The survivors of the raid, destitute and homeless, made their way toward Fort Niagara to seek assistance from the British.

A plaque in Onondaga Park marked the site of the village and Van Schaick's attack, but the plaque's theft was so common that an unofficial decision has been made not to replace it. (It may be just as well; the text on the original marker, though scant, is embarrassingly misleading.) The stone slab on which it had been mounted still stands, for the moment, and the park still roughly marks the site of the village. Another marker south of the park depicts where Van Schaick's expedition crossed Onondaga Creek to move on to other targets. To really learn about Onondaga and its important place in Iroquois culture, visit the Skä-noñh—Great Law of Peace Center. Located on the northern shore of Lake Onondaga, the extensive and modern museum presents the story of the Iroquois, from their origins through the present, from the viewpoint of the Onon-

The Skä-noñh—Great Law of Peace Center in Liverpool, New York, displays a re-created Jesuit missionary village.

daga and their role as keeper of the Central Fire. In addition to these permanent exhibits, frequently updated temporary exhibits spotlight issues affecting Native Americans today. Behind the museum is a reproduction of Sainte Marie de Gannentaha, a French Jesuit mission built on the lake in 1656. *Historic Marker—Site of Van Schaick Expedition's attack, Onondaga Park, on west side of Onondaga Ave. 0.1 mile north of Centennial Dr., Syracuse, NY 13207. GPS: 43.027217, -76.162978. Accessible daily. Historic Marker—Col. Van Schaick crossing, intersection of W. Colvin Rd. and Onondaga Creek Pkwy., Syracuse, NY 13207. GPS: 43.023251, -76.155353. Accessible daily. Skä-noñh—Great Law of Peace Center, 6680 Onondaga Lake Pkwy, Liverpool, NY 13088; 315-453-6767; www.skanonhcenter.org. GPS: 43.096445, -76.200527. Open Wed.–Sun.*

ONEIDA CASTLE—The Oneida village of Kanowarohare, also known as Oneida Castle, was founded a century before the Revolution, and a stockade was built for the village at the outset of the French and Indian War. It would eventually become the Oneida Nation's most important village, and as such it was a primary target for the Iroquois allies of the British, particularly Mohawk leader Joseph Brant. In 1780, Brant led a raid through the Mohawk Valley, reaching Oneida Castle on July 25. Brant's men spent two days thoroughly destroying the now-abandoned village and its stockade before continuing their raid.

A handful of historical markers and sites related to the Oneida are in and around present-day Oneida Castle. However, the hands-down must-see site regarding the Oneida and the American Revolution is the Shako:wi Cultural Center. The center tells the history of the Oneida from its origins through the present day, showcasing priceless artifacts using modern, concise exhibits and interpretation. The Oneida are understandably proud of their status as America's first ally, and you'll find plenty about that here; staff are also on hand to answer any questions. The center is also very active, with frequent public education programs and lectures; check the website for these events before you go. *Shako:wi Cultural Center, 5 Territory Rd., Oneida, NY 13421; 315-829-8801; www.oneidaindiannation.com/shakowiculturalcenter. GPS: 43.039430, -75.622346. Open Mon., Wed., and Fri., plus Sat. seasonally.*

THE ONEIDA—AMERICA'S FIRST ALLIES

The mighty Iroquois Confederacy consisted of six nations that had been banded together for centuries. One of these nations was the Oneida, a largely peaceful tribe but one that could be as fierce as any other when required. By the time the American Revolution began, the Oneida had been greatly influenced by an American missionary, developing many ties to colonial religion and especially Boston. The other Iroquois nations, however, decided to keep their alliance with the British. This resulted in a devastating split within the Iroquois, but also resulted in the formation of the American colonies' first alliance in their war for independence.

The Oneida served the Patriot cause with passion. They helped defend the frontier in the New York wilderness, working as scouts, spies, and guides, as well as warriors, often fighting their former Iroquois brethren. They fought fiercely alongside the militia at the Battle of Oriskany. A small band of 50 Oneida even joined the American encampment at Valley Forge during the winter of 1777–1778, participating in the Battle of Barren Hill northeast of Philadelphia.

Though their efforts were recognized with gratitude by General George Washington and Congress, the Oneida suffered greatly. Their villages were destroyed at the hands of the Loyalists and Iroquois during the wilderness war, resulting in severe hardship. Congress authorized some restitution after the war, but the Oneida were forced to try to reestablish themselves among an increasing white population. It was not long before their way of life began to vanish, and many of them left New York for Wisconsin or Ontario. Still, the Oneida contribution to the American Revolution holds a place of great pride today.

STEUBEN MEMORIAL STATE HISTORIC SITE—After the American Revolution had ended, General Friedrich Wilhelm, Baron von Steuben, was awarded 16,000 acres in the Mohawk Valley and New York citizenship in 1786. Initially spending only summers here, debt and a disappointing and delayed pension from Congress forced Steuben to move here permanently in 1790. Though he had planned a grand estate, Steuben died in 1794 in the cabin he had built on the land. At his request, he was buried in an unmarked grave in his military cloak; however, after construction of a road threatened this site, his body was relocated in 1804 and memorialized. In 1930, the bicentennial of Steuben's birth, the state of New York permanently protected the site.

Steuben Memorial State Historic Site preserves the core of Steuben's land grant. The cabin is a reproduction, but it houses interpretive space that shows the history of the land and Steuben's plans for it. The site is comanaged by the state and Fort Stanwix National Monument, and though staff is not always available, there are plenty of interpretive

The final resting place of the Baron von Steuben at Steuben Memorial State Historic Site in Remsen, New York.

signs that will help you enjoy the site without the help of a park ranger. The most striking area is the Sacred Grove, site of Steuben's final resting place. An easy, short walk from the parking area, the grove is a peaceful, secluded space, an ideal place to reflect on his accomplishments. The grove contains several memorials and tributes; the most impressive, of course, marks the Steuben's burial site. Though it bears only his name, its simplicity and gravity suitably convey his standing. *Steuben Memorial State Historic Site, 9941 Starr Hill Road, Remsen, NY 13438; 315-655-3200; www.parks.ny.gov/historic-sites/2/details.aspx. GPS: 43.335292, -75.232916. Open Memorial Day through Labor Day; contact site for details.*

WEST CANADA CREEK—After their October 1781 raid was checked at the Battle of Johnstown, the British, led by Major John Ross and the infamous Captain Walter Butler, attempted to flee to Fort Ontario. They were pursued by American Colonel Marinus Willett and a force over 500 strong, as well as 60 Oneida scouts who were eager to avenge their losses during the war. On October 30, Willett's party began to snipe at the tail end of the British column, now in full flight. Though the Americans never fully caught them, there was one very significant British casualty—Butler, who was found shot, tomahawked, and scalped.

As West Canada Creek was a running fight through the wilderness, not all its locations are known. There is a historic marker, and while it's a little off the beaten path, you will be rewarded with a beautiful view of Black Creek as it feeds off its reservoir. *West Canada Creek Historic Marker, on Black Creek Rd. 0.5 mile north of intersection with Stanley Rd., Norway, NY 13324. GPS: 43.253351, -74.928366. Site accessible daily.*

GERMAN FLATTS—On September 17, 1778, a raiding party of 450 Tories and Mohawks under Chief Joseph Brant entered the German Flatts settlement in the Mohawk Valley. Though the inhabitants had been warned and had fled to Fort Dayton and Fort Herkimer for safety, over 120 buildings were burnt to the ground, leaving over 1,000 settlers without shelter or food just before the winter.

Fort Herkimer, which sat within German Flatts, is memorialized at and around Fort Herkimer Church, which is one of the few buildings to survive the raid. Also memorialized here is Nicholas Herkimer, who was born within the fort. *Fort Herkimer Church, 55 State Route 5S, Herkimer, NY 13350. GPS: 43.017737, -74.954891. Sign accessible daily.*

FORT DAYTON—Built in 1776, Fort Dayton was meant to protect the Mohawk Valley against a possible British invasion from Canada. It was here that the Tryon County Militia, summoned to relieve the siege at Fort Stanwix, gathered early in August of 1777, only to be ambushed and largely destroyed at the Battle of Oriskany on August 6. Fort Dayton was also the site of several negotiations between the Iroquois and Philip Schuyler.

Though the fort is now gone, there are several plaques throughout the town of Herkimer indicating where the fort was located, as well as some of the events that occurred here. Perhaps the most notable memorial, however, is the statue of Nicholas Herkimer, the admired leader of the Tryon County Militia who was mortally wounded at Oriskany. You'll find the statue in Myers Park, along with several other historical markers. *General Herkimer Monument, Myers Park, North Bellinger St., Herkimer,*

Nicholas Herkimer monument, Herkimer, New York.

NY 13350. GPS: 43.025338, -74.989703. *Historic Marker—Revolution in the Mohawk Valley: Fort Dayton, Herkimer County Historical Society, 406 North Main St., Herkimer, NY 13350. GPS: 43.029351, -74.989664. Signs accessible daily.*

SCHOHARIE MIDDLE FORT—In October of 1780, Colonel Sir John Johnson led the largest of the British raiding parties into the Schoharie and Mohawk Valleys, intent on causing as much destruction as possible. On October 17, his force of 800 Tories and Indians reached the Schoharie Middle Fort of the Schoharie Valley, which held about 350 men. Johnson kept the militia holed up in the fort while the rest of his men burned local houses and farms. Johnson then asked for the fort's surrender but was refused, and the raiders moved on to the Schoharie Lower Fort.

The site of the Schoharie Middle Fort is marked by a boulder with a plaque. The boulder sits in front of a church. More information on the fight can be found at the Old Stone Fort, site of the Schoharie Lower Fort. *Historical marker—Middle Fort, 178 River St., Middleburgh, NY 12122. GPS: 42.605313, -74.337551. Accessible daily.*

SCHOHARIE LOWER FORT—After attacking the Schoharie Middle Fort earlier in the day, on October 17, 1780, Colonel Sir John Johnson moved on to the Schoharie Lower Fort. Though only holding 170 men, the stone work within a stockade was too strong to overcome, so Johnson, after some cursory firing, largely bypassed the fort. There were no casualties, and Johnson continued his destruction of the area.

The Schoharie Lower Fort is preserved today as the Old Stone Fort Museum Complex. The strong stone building is in remarkably good shape, despite a still-existing hole in the side from a British cannonball. The interior contains an excellent museum with exhibits on the raid and a nice collection of artifacts. *Historical highway markers—Old Stone Fort Museum, 145 Fort Rd., Schoharie, NY 12157; 518-295-7192; www.theoldstonefort.org. GPS: 42.677102, -74.301601. Open weekends and Mon., May through October, and Tues. and Fri., June through September*

STONE ARABIA—On October 19, 1780, Colonel Sir John Johnson's British raiding party approached the settlement of Stone Arabia. Colonel

The Old Stone Fort, also known as the Schoharie Lower Fort.

John Brown was ordered to attack the British, but expected reinforcements never arrived, and he and his militia found themselves badly outnumbered. Brown and most of the 40 men with him were killed, and Stone Arabia was burned.

An interpretive sign at Stone Arabia Church briefly tells about the battle. The church that you see was rebuilt after the raid; the battle occurred in the fields to the south. *Historic Marker—Battle of Stone Arabia, Stone Arabia Church, 5371 Ephratah Rd., Fort Plain, NY 13339. GPS: 42.942589, -74.555980. Sign accessible daily.*

FORT KLOCK AND KLOCK'S FIELD—Johannes Klock built a fortified house in the Mohawk Valley in 1750, and it served as a fortification throughout the French and Indian War and the American Revolution. On October 19, 1780, after the destruction of the Stone Arabia settlement, Colonel Sir John Johnson's British raiding party approached the fort and were confronted by American militia on Klock's farmland. As daylight waned, the British withdrew, with no clear victor emerging. The British then moved back to their base, ending the raid.

Fort Klock still stands and is now a living history site, and events are frequent during the site's open season. You can tour the house and see up close just how strong a work it is, and guides will show you the unique elements of the home that allowed it to double as a fortification. The Battle of Klock's Field occurred in the fields just to the west of the historic site. *Fort Klock, 7203 Route 5 Street, Johnsville, NY 13452; 518-568-7779; www.fortklockrestoration.org. GPS: 42.985924, -74.648259. Tours available Fri.–Mon., mid-May through Columbus Day, variably; contact site for more details.*

PALATINE CHURCH—Palatine Church was built in 1770 on land donated by the Nellis family, who would fall to the Loyalist side during the American Revolution. When the British raided the area in 1780, Palatine Church was one of the few buildings spared, though the family had by this time fled to Canada.

The Old Palatine Church is still there and is in use but welcomes visitors. There is a historical marker outside, and inside the church you will find a rare 13-star American flag from the Revolutionary era, discovered when the church underwent renovations in 1870. *Old Palatine Church, Route 5 and Palatine Church Road, Fort Plain, NY 13339; www.oldpalatinechurch.org. GPS: 42.969221, -74.628539. Accessible daily.*

CANAJOHARIE DISTRICT—A large raiding party of 600 British Regulars, local Tories, and Indians approached the Canajoharie District settlement along the Mohawk River and burned it to the ground. The villagers fled to the safety of nearby Fort Plain, whose garrison (which included most of the men from the settlement) was away on a mission to Fort Stanwix. In desperation, the women put on the uniforms they found in the fort and fooled the raiders, who thought that the fort was fully manned.

Fort Plain Museum and Historical Park preserves the site of the original fort. Though nothing remains of the fort, interpretive signs will help you orient yourself. You will also have a great view of the Mohawk Valley. The museum has excellent exhibits about not only the Canajoharie Raid but all the major and minor battles and sites in the valley, as well

Interpretive signs and a view of the Mohawk Valley at Fort Plain Museum and Historical Park.

as the forts of the era. *Fort Plain Museum and Historical Park, 389 Canal St., Fort Plain, NY 13339; 518-993-2527; www.fortplainmuseum.org. GPS: 42.940771, -74.629221. Open seasonally; call or check website for hours.*

JOHNSTOWN—In October of 1781, 700 British and Indian raiders under Major John Ross and Walter Butler penetrated the Mohawk Valley on a surprise raid, causing what damage they could. Ross eventually settled on Johnstown as a target, with the intention of setting up a headquarters at Johnson Hall. Colonel Marinus Willett quickly organized a force of 400 to oppose them, and they collided at Johnstown on October 25. The fight was heavy, with both sides racking up casualties quickly, but eventually the Americans gained the upper hand after a timely flanking maneuver. The British were forced to flee with the Americans in pursuit, leading to the fight at West Canada Creek. Johnstown was one of the last large engagements of the Revolutionary War, coming several days after Washington's surrender at Yorktown.

The battlefield at Johnstown is marked by several historic markers and interpretive signs, including a large memorial boulder with a plaque on it commemorating the fight. The battle largely occurred along what is today Johnson Avenue. *Memorial Boulder and Interpretive Sign—Battle of Johnstown, Southeast corner of intersection of Johnson Ave. and O'Neil Ave., Johnstown, NY 12095. GPS: 43.022185, -74.380875. Site accessible daily.*

JOHNSON HALL—Sir William Johnson, the largest landowner in the Mohawk Valley, was singularly influential in the development of the valley and in relations with the local Native American tribes. A hero of the French and Indian War, Johnson negotiated treaties and kept a steady peace between the Iroquois nation and British settlers that lasted until the Revolution broke out. Molly Brant, older sister of Chief Joseph Brant and a significant leader of the Mohawk herself, was Johnson's consort, and they had eight children together. In 1763, Johnson built Johnson Hall, a large Georgian home with two blockhouses that became a center

The mansion and block house at Johnson Hall State Historic Site.

of valley life for the Mohawk. Johnson died in 1774, just before the Revolution, and his family remained loyal to the British, eventually relocating in Canada.

Johnson Hall State Historic Site preserves the home and a portion of the once-sprawling estate. The home is in excellent condition and can be viewed as a guided tour, while the blockhouses (one original, one rebuilt) contain museum exhibits explaining the significance of Johnson in the Mohawk Valley. The grounds make for an inviting stroll, with markers showing where other buildings once stood. *Johnson Hall State Historic Site, 139 Hall Avenue, Johnstown, NY 12095; 518-762-8712; www.parks.ny.gov/historic-sites/10/details.aspx. GPS: 43.015756, -74.383600. Open for tours Wed.–Sun., mid-May through mid-October; contact site for details.*

CHERRY VALLEY AND FORT ALDEN—A large force of 800 British Regulars, Tories, and Indians, led by Captain Walter Butler and Chief Joseph Brant, approached the prosperous community of Cherry Valley, New York, with the intent of raiding the village and procuring supplies. The town contained a stronghold named Fort Alden and was garrisoned with local militia. On the morning of November 11, 1778, one part of Butler's force attacked the fort while the Indians raided the surrounding farms. Colonel Alden, whose headquarters was outside the fort, was killed, along with a small group of other soldiers. Most of those killed, however, were noncombatants (including some Loyalists) whose homes and farms were attacked. The Cherry Valley Massacre endures as one of the most infamous events of the American Revolution.

The Cherry Valley Museum, run by the Cherry Valley Historical Association, does an excellent job of explaining the massacre. A diorama with interactive lights helps you orient yourself to the valley and provides a timeline of events, and the museum houses a nice collection of artifacts. The site of Fort Alden is now the Cherry Valley Cemetery, where there is a large memorial to the victims of the massacre. There are also historical markers at the sites where Colonel Alden and Lieutenant Wormuth were killed. *Cherry Valley Museum, 49 Main St., Cherry Valley, NY 13320; 607-264-3098; www.cherryvalleyny.com/museum.htm. GPS: 42.797432, -74.751125. Open Memorial Day to mid-Oct. Cherry Valley Historic Cemetery (Site of Fort Alden), 20 Alden St., Cherry Valley, NY*

A marker denotes the site at Cherry Valley where Lieutenant Martinus Wormuth was killed.

13320. GPS: 42.794223, -74.756344. Open daily. Col. Alden Monument, on Alden St. north of intersection with Fish and Game Road, Cherry Valley, NY 13320. GPS: 42.791513, -74.758645. Site accessible daily. Lieut. Wormuth Monument, on Van Derwerker Rd. 0.1 mile north of intersection with Salt Springville Rd., Cherry Valley, NY 13320. GPS: 42.826646, -74.736775. Site accessible daily.

SHARON SPRINGS—In response to several raids and ambushes occurring early in July 1781, a party of New York militia led by Colonel Marinus Willett caught up to a large group of Tories and Iroquois who had just destroyed the village of Currytown, massacring many. The Tories had chosen their campground near Sharon Springs poorly, being surrounded by swampland on three sides, and Willett, though outnumbered more than two to one, planned a clever attack. The ruse began early on July 10, quickly pulling the raiders into an ambush that left them surrounded. The New Yorkers moved through the camp quickly, avenging many of the deaths at Currytown and giving the Tories no quarter. Though a number escaped, Willett's successful attack raised spirits among Patriots in the Mohawk Valley and helped swell the ranks of the state militia.

A historical highway marker denotes the site of the Sharon Springs fight, while another marks the site of the Tory camp just to the east. Both are on a busy highway, and though you should have ample room to pull over, take care in doing so. *Historical highway marker—Sharon Battle, on US Route 20 eastbound 0.1 mile west of intersection with Gilberts Corners Rd., Sharon Springs, NY 13459. GPS: 42.780045, -74.588042. Historical highway marker—Camp of Cedar Swamp, on US Route 20 westbound 0.3 mile west of intersection with Gilberts Corners Rd., Sharon Springs, NY 13459. GPS: 42.781717, -74.592729. Signs accessible daily.*

WHERE TO STAY IN UPPER NEW YORK

Though the area may seem a bit remote, there is no shortage of lodging to be found in the Hudson Valley. Most of the chain hotels are along the Interstate 87 corridor, with the number increasing as you get closer to Albany, and you'll find plenty of options for bed and breakfasts off the beaten path. Albany, the largest city in the region, also provides a large variety when it comes to dining choices and other amenities.

Along the Mohawk Valley, things are a bit farther in between, but you'll still have plenty of options at the two bookends of Albany and Syracuse. There are also options between the two along Interstate 90. The two cities are only about two hours apart, so if you plan ahead you can find a home base in the middle and never be too far away from any of the sites.

PART 2

FORGING A NEW NATION: THE MIDDLE COLONIES

4

Retreat and Redemption: New York and New Jersey

OVERVIEW

After the British evacuated Boston in March 1776, it was evident to both sides what the next target would be. Even as the ships were still sailing out of Boston Harbor, George Washington sent troops to New York City to begin to fortify the city and guard against an invasion there. New York was not the hotbed of dissent that Boston and Virginia were, nor was it the largest city in the colonies (that was Philadelphia). But its importance as a commercial center, its large natural harbor, and its position at the mouth of the Hudson River made New York City an obvious location from which the British could regain control of the American colonies.

The British saw an additional advantage to possessing New York. Many in the court of George III, Parliament, and even in the colonies thought that New York City was, at its heart, a Loyalist town, ready to reject the rebellious Continental Congress and support the crown. The British thought this Loyalist sentiment to be especially strong on Long Island, at this time still a largely rural area. The British army, in particular, suspected that taking control of the area would allow those loyal subjects to take up arms and fight for their king.

After first heading to Halifax to drop off refugees from Boston and

Opposite: A monument to the American soldiers who defended Danbury, Connecticut.

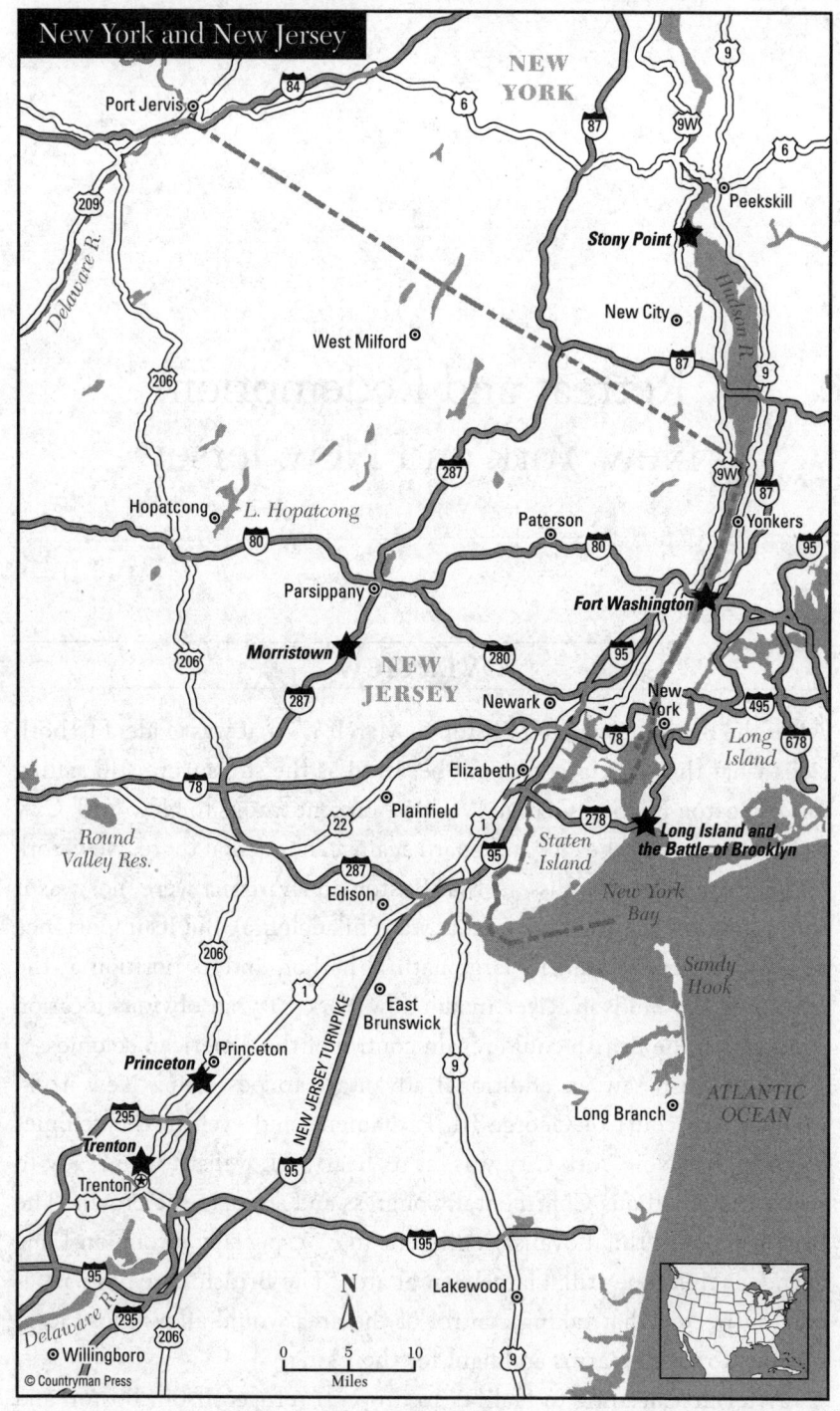

refit, British vessels began to arrive in late June 1776. Over the next two months, as George Washington and the Americans watched with trepidation from Manhattan, more and more ships arrived with troops and supplies, filling the harbor with masts as far as the eye could see. The Americans continued to strengthen their position, fortifying Manhattan, Governors Island, and Brooklyn and preparing for the invasion that they knew was coming.

On August 22, 1776, British boats began ferrying soldiers and artillery to Long Island. The string of defeats and retreats that followed almost ended the American Revolution altogether. Washington's army was driven off Long Island to Manhattan, where they were eventually pushed northward all the way to White Plains. Shortly afterward, the British took the last remaining outpost on Manhattan, Fort Washington, followed by Fort Lee on the opposite side of the Hudson. The Americans were then driven southward through New Jersey, fleeing for their very survival until the British finally went into winter quarters.

The Continental Army, however, was not yet finished. On Christmas Day, 1776, the Americans crossed the Delaware River in the dead of night and launched a surprise attack on the garrison at Trenton, New Jersey, completely routing the Hessian soldiers stationed there. Before the British could react, Washington raced north and surprised them again at Princeton, gaining another astounding victory. This electrifying turn of events proved to everyone on both sides of the fight that a British victory was anything but a foregone conclusion.

New York City remained in British control throughout the Revolutionary War, with the American army always close by waiting for an opportunity. In this chapter are descriptions of many sites along the lower Hudson River, including the location of a surprising American victory at Stony Point. We will also explore the trying winter encampments at Morristown as well as other sites throughout New Jersey, also known as the crossroads of the Revolution.

As Thomas Paine fled through New Jersey with Washington's army, he famously wrote that these were the times that tried men's souls. Despite their trials and tribulations, however, that army emerged stronger than anyone could have imagined. Exploring the sites detailed in this chapter will help you understand the desperate situation the Continental

Army faced in 1776 as well as the courage they had to summon to continue the fight.

PEOPLE TO KNOW

GEORGE WASHINGTON—George Washington, Father of his country and America's first president, has always seemed to be more myth than legend. While there is something to that, there is in truth quite a lot about Washington that makes him perhaps the most remarkable American ever to have lived.

Washington was born a fourth-generation American in 1732 in Virginia. His childhood was somewhat uneventful, and his formal education stopped at the age of 15, though his elder brother kept him on a program of self-study. Washington was a farmer and surveyor but eventually found his place in the military. He was appointed to his first command by the governor of Virginia in 1753. In 1755, Washington served as an aide during an expedition against the French at Fort Duquesne at modern-day Pittsburgh. The expedition ended in disaster, and its leader, British General Edward Braddock, was killed, but Washington organized a skilled retreat, demonstrating great courage and leadership. Braddock's failed mission sparked the French and Indian War, and at age 23 Washington was given command of all Virginia militia; over the ensuing four years, he gained valuable experience and earned considerable fame and respect. He married widow Martha Dandridge in 1759 and made his home at the family estate at Mount Vernon and continued as a planter for the next 15 years. A noted supporter of American rights, Washington was named to the First and Second Continental Congress, and when war broke out in 1775, he was unanimously selected by the Congress to be the Continental Army's commander in chief. He spent the next eight years shepherding the Americans to victory, after which time, instead of demanding or using the army to be made king, he simply retired to Mount Vernon, to the astonishment of everyone in the Old World. A few short years later, however, he was pulled out of his retirement to lead the country again, this time as presiding officer at the Constitutional Convention, and then president of the United States of America under that new constitution once it was ratified. He served for two terms, setting many precedents and establishing the traditions under which the government would work—not the least of which was his leaving the presidency in 1797, when he again could have tried to serve for the rest of his life. Washington died in 1799. Though he did bear the black mark of being a slaveowner—as did most of America's Founding Fathers—George Washington was certainly a giant among the men of his time.

WILLIAM HOWE—General William Howe was one of the British army's most respected officers when the American Revolution came about, and he was commander in chief of the forces in America for three years of the war. His legacy, though, is one of inaction, and he remains a puzzle to historians to this day.

Howe was born into the aristocracy in 1729 and entered the military, as did his two brothers, George (killed at Ticonderoga during the French and Indian War) and Richard (an admiral in the British Navy). During the French and Indian War, Howe played a conspicuous part in the great victory at Quebec, leading his light infantry onto the Plains of Abraham, and went on to earn a stellar record through the rest of that conflict. He then went on to serve in Parliament, where he became a staunch supporter of the American cause and even said that he would never accept a command against them. (It is said that he and his brother Richard were eternally grateful for a monument to their brother George placed at Westminster Abbey by the Colony of Massachusetts.) However, Howe did eventually take that command, arriving in Boston in May 1775. Howe took over the position of commander in chief officially in April 1776 and led the army through their campaigns to capture New York and Philadelphia. Throughout those campaigns, however, many noted that Howe was notably lax in following up his successes and not taking advantage of his victories. Some have speculated that Howe was indeed too sympathetic to the Americans, or that he was too distracted by his mistress in America, frequent parties, and a gambling problem. Howe was relieved at his request in 1778 and replaced by General Henry Clinton. Howe went on to other commands and remained in the military until 1803, dying in 1814.

THINGS TO KNOW

At first glance, there isn't much left of the historic sites in this chapter. The New York City metropolitan area is the most densely populated region in the United States, and it has grown and changed almost beyond recognition in the past 250 years. But with a little knowledge, patience, and imagination, what remains of the American Revolution today can still be experienced, even in Manhattan. You will be surprised at just how much there is to see.

It is important to realize that because of the congestion in this part of the country, traveling from one point to another can be challenging and frustrating, at times. Anticipate at least some traffic at all times of the day and remember that New York City is made up of islands—there are only so many ways to get where you're going, and everyone is using those same routes. Planning will go a long way but expect the unexpected.

THE TRIP

This trip begins in New York City, followed by a quick detour up the Hudson River before finishing in central New Jersey. Because of the challenges of getting around New York, you would probably do well to base yourself in or very near the city for the first part of the trip. Don't let those challenges discourage you, though; there is so much history to see here that you could easily spend several days exploring these sites (along with the many other treasures New York City holds).

Though many of the sites along the Hudson River are not as well known, many of them are in a remarkable state of preservation, and they hold some great stories. The Hudson Valley also makes for a beautiful drive, so be sure not to skimp on your time here—there's plenty to see and do. Northern and central New Jersey, likewise, contain numerous sites, and some of them are quite remarkable, so don't hesitate to stray off the beaten path.

THE CAN'T-MISS SITES

Long Island and the Battle of Brooklyn

In June 1776, rumors reached New York City that the British fleet had left Halifax, with New York City as its destination. The first 12 ships appeared in the lower part of New York Harbor on June 25, one of them with Sir William Howe aboard. General Howe had been appointed the new commander in chief for America, taking over for General Thomas Gage after his humiliation at Boston. Within a week, the rest of the 130-ship fleet arrived at New York, and on July 2, Howe's ships landed at Staten Island, taking it over as a staging ground in preparation for the invasion of New York. Another 44 ships arrived on August 1, the remnants of a command that had just assaulted Charleston, South Carolina, and failed, followed by another 22 ships a few days later, and another flotilla of over 100 ships a week after that. All in all, the invasion force consisted of 24,000 soldiers and 10,000 sailors, with 30 warships and over 400 transport ships under the command of Admiral Richard Howe,

The Verrazano-Narrows Bridge stretches over New York Harbor at Denyse's Ferry.

the general's brother, who was also given the mission of peace commissioner to the colonies. It was, by far, the largest invasion force that had ever been seen in North America.

While the Americans were awed by the British display of power, they did not stop working on their defenses. Every street in Manhattan was barricaded. Artillery was posted on Governors Island. And in Brooklyn, which at that time was the countryside, the Americans built a fortified line on Brooklyn Heights that guarded against an attack from both the East River and from the Long Island side. Soldiers also occupied Gowanus Heights, a ridge of hilltops through which four major roads passed. Three of the four passes were heavily occupied and fortified. The fourth, farthest to the east and 4 miles away from the fortified line, was Jamaica Pass. It was left untouched.

On August 22, the British unleashed their invasion. At 9:00 AM, a signal gun was fired and the boats began making their way to Long Island, dropping off the soldiers with efficiency at Denyse's Ferry, the southwest tip of Brooklyn. Except for a few light skirmishes, the landing went largely uncontested, and Howe's army arrived safely. The British quickly moved to occupy the towns on the south side of the Gowanus Heights and carefully pushed up to the American positions. George Washington, who had been hearing conflicting rumors about where the British might land, eventually moved the bulk of his army to Brooklyn as well. The Americans were far outnumbered—approximately 20,000 British troops to 8,000 Continentals—but their position was strong, and Washington was willing to fight.

After several days of inaction, on the evening of August 26, the British made their move. General Henry Clinton, who had come up with the plan, led a contingent of 4,000 men on a night march to the north and east, far beyond the American position. The soldiers moved in silence completely around the American left flank until they reached Jamaica Pass. At 2:00 AM on August 27, to their astonishment, they found it completely unoccupied, save for five American cavalrymen. They seized the pass and marched through it, then waited for another 6,000 men under Howe, who arrived two hours later.

At about the same time, a firefight erupted on the American right

The Harbor Defense Museum in Brooklyn.

flank at Martense Lane Pass, with the British taking the upper hand and taking the pass. This advance was met quickly by a force of 2,000 Americans under General William Alexander, Lord Stirling, with the Americans holding their ground and trading blow after blow with the British.

By 9:00 AM, the 10,000 British soldiers under Clinton and Howe were well in the rear of the American position, largely undetected. As they advanced, the outflanked American positions on the Gowanus Heights were abandoned one by one, with the men racing for the safety of the fortified line behind them. The last group standing was Stirling's men. He kept 250 men to hold as long as he could and sent the rest across the swampy Gowanus Creek for the safety of the line. Though Stirling and his command were captured, his heroic actions saved many more men.

It was the largest battle of the Revolutionary War, and it was decisive. British casualties amounted to 61 killed, 267 wounded, and 31 captured.

SITE DETAILS

Denyse's Ferry and Harbor Defense Museum—The base of the Verrazzano-Narrows Bridge is the former location of Denyse's Ferry, where the British landed on Long Island. You can overlook the area of the landing from John Paul Jones Park or Shore Road Park, which contains a couple of interpretive signs. But perhaps the better visit is to the Harbor Defense Museum on the grounds of Fort Hamilton, south of the bridge. The museum presents a lot of information and artifacts from the landing and the Battle of Brooklyn and will give you a good idea about the changes in New York's defenses over the years. Additional interpretive signs are also on the grounds outside the museum. Note that Fort Hamilton is an active army base, so you'll need to check in at the Visitor Control Center first. *Harbor Defense Museum, 230 Sheridan Loop, Brooklyn, NY 11252; 718-630-4349; history.army.mil/museums/IMCOM/fortHamilton/index.html. GPS: 40.610447, -74.031776. Open Tues.–Fri. Shore Road Park—Interpretive Signs, on Belt Pkwy. just north of 4th Ave., Brooklyn, NY 11209. GPS: 40.611128, -74.036683. Accessible daily.*

Old Stone House—The best place to learn about the Battle of Brooklyn is the Old Stone House at Washington Park. The house dates to 1699, though it's been rebuilt over time. It was here that General William Alexander and a Maryland regiment of 400 men held against 2,000 British soldiers under Lord Charles Cornwallis. The house contains an excellent museum, with plenty of kid-friendly activities and interactive displays. The Old Stone House also organizes tours of the Battle of Brooklyn and has a downloadable walking guide that will take you through the battle. This site is an excellent resource and a pleasure to visit. *The Old Stone House, 336 3rd St., Brooklyn, NY 11215; 718-768-3195; www.theoldstonehouse.org. GPS: 40.672954, -73.984489. Open Fri.–Sun. and by appointment.*

Lefferts Homestead and Battle Pass—Flatbush Pass, later known as Battle Pass, was one of the sites of American defense that was outflanked by Clinton's march on the American left. Located within today's Prospect Park, there are several markers denoting the pass, as well as the Dongan Oak, which once served as a landmark but was cut down to serve as a barrier before the battle. You'll also find the Lefferts House nearby; relocated six blocks from its original location, it still sits on the Lefferts Homestead. (The original home was burned down during the battle; the existing home dates to 1783.) The home is now an interpretive center, and there is some discussion of the Battle of Brooklyn here. *Historic Markers—Battle Pass, Dongan Oak, and Line of Defense, in Prospect Park on East Dr. north of Prospect Park Zoo, Brooklyn, NY 11238. GPS: 40.666117, -73.966554. Accessible daily. Lefferts House, in Prospect Park just off Flatbush Ave. south of Prospect Park Zoo, Brooklyn, NY 11238. GPS: 40.664260, -73.964156. Call for hours.*

The Evergreens Cemetery—It was at Howard's Inn that the British flanking maneuver moved with no resistance to crumble the American line. Howard's Inn was located in what is now The Evergreens Cemetery, and a marker is there denoting the inn as well as the little-known Rockaway Footpath that the British used. *The Evergreens Cemetery, entrance on Bushwick Ave. at Conway St., Brooklyn, NY 11207. GPS: 40.681436, -73.902517. Open daily.*

Green-Wood Cemetery—The area around Green-Wood Cemetery is near the site of the first fighting at the Battle of Brooklyn. Within the cemetery you'll find Battle Hill, scene of some of the battle's most ferocious fighting as the Americans under Stirling made a stand here. On the hill, you'll also find the Altar to Liberty, featuring a statue of Minerva with her arm outstretched to the Statue of Liberty in the distance. Memorials and interpretive signs are present for both Battle Hill and the Altar to Liberty. *Green-Wood Cemetery, entrance on 5th Avenue at 25th St., Brooklyn, NY 11215. GPS: 40.657223, -73.989525. Open daily.*

Other Points of Interest—Cobble Hill Fort, also known as Ponkiesburg Fort, is where Washington watched the Battle of Brooklyn, and it is marked by a large bronze plaque on the side of a building. The evacuation of the American troops occurred at the Fulton Ferry Landing, right underneath where the Brooklyn Bridge is today; there is a boulder with a plaque on the site. *Plaque—Ponkiesburg Fortification, on southwest corner of intersection of Atlantic Ave. and Court St., Brooklyn, NY 11201. GPS: 40.689511, -73.992503. Plaque—Brookland Ferry Landing, at Fulton Ferry Landing near intersection of Furman St. and Old Fulton St., Brooklyn, NY 11201. GPS: 40.703161, -73.994899. Sites accessible daily.*

The Americans lost only about 200 killed or wounded, but had 800 men captured—men they could not afford to lose. What's more, the British still anticipated bagging the rest of the American force within the fortified lines. They chose to be patient, initiating siege warfare tactics that would allow them to assault the American line.

It was not to be. On the evening of August 29, under the cover of a thick fog, Washington's army silently slipped across the East River, one small boat at a time. The boats were skillfully manned by two Massachusetts regiments composed of mariners and fishermen, moving back and forth from one shore to another and back throughout the night. When daylight broke, the British were surprised to find not a single soul left in the American works. Washington's withdrawal from Brooklyn is still regarded as one of the most skillful retreats in military history.

The Altar to Liberty at Green-Wood Cemetery in Brooklyn.

THE BATTLES FOR NEW YORK CITY

Between the Battle of Brooklyn and the Battle of Fort Washington, several engagements took place that decided the fate of New York City during the Revolution. Most of these took place on and around Manhattan, and although the battlefield landscape is gone, in most cases the terrain or some memorials remain.

EAST RIVER—The *Turtle*, a small, one-person submersible, was invented by a Connecticut engineer named David Bushnell and offered to the American army. On the night of September 6, 1776, the *Turtle*, armed with a torpedo containing 130 pounds of gunpowder, slipped into New York Harbor and made its way toward HMS *Eagle*, the flagship of Admiral Richard Howe. The pilot of the *Turtle*, Ezra Lee, was able to get below the *Eagle* but could not fasten its torpedo onto the hull. It was the first use of a combat submarine in history.

There are many places from which you can view the East River, but Lee himself got back to land at Whitehall Slip, now the location of the Staten Island Ferry Whitehall Terminal. If you're curious about the *Turtle*, you can find a life-size working replica of the boat at the Connecticut River Museum in Essex, Connecticut. *Turtle landing site, 4 Whitehall St., New York, NY 10004. GPS: 40.701139, -74.012468. Site accessible daily. Connecticut River Museum, 67 Main St., Essex, CT 06426; 860-767-8269; www.ctrivermuseum.org. GPS: 41.351357, -72.384904. Open Tues.–Sun.*

KIP'S BAY—British General William Howe, looking for a way onto Manhattan, eventually settled on the landing site of Kip's

continued on next page

Bay, a small, deep harbor in the East River well north of what was then the city. On the morning of September 15, 1776, British soldiers piled into boats hidden across the river in Brooklyn and crossed the East River. Though Americans were stationed at Kip's Bay to watch for such a landing, the overpowering cannonade from the British Navy and the waves of redcoats coming ashore sent them to flight, despite their officers' attempts to restrain them. The Americans raced north on Manhattan until reinforcements finally stopped the British advance and allowed American soldiers in New York City at the south end of the island to escape to the north.

Kip's Bay has been filled in and is no longer recognizable. A historical marker is located at the site of the British landing, on the waterfront just south of the East 34th Street Ferry. A few blocks inland from the former site of the bay is a monument to Mary Lindley Murray; legend has it that when General Howe took Murray's home as his headquarters during the landing, she and her daughters entertained just well enough so that the American army could escape. Another marker at Bryant Park (formerly known as Reservoir Square) notes that the American troops retreated through this site, now a lovely space adjacent to the New York Public Library; it was near here that Washington himself tried his hand at corralling his fleeing soldiers, to no avail. Finally, at the north end of Central Park is McGowan's Pass, where the Americans made a last stand during the battle, and where the British set up their defensive line. A monument and several interpretive signs are located atop and around a hill that overlooked the pass, where the British built a redoubt. *Historical marker—E 34th Street, on waterfront just south of East 34th Street Ferry Stop, New York, NY 10016. GPS: 40.743680, -73.971309. Sign accessible daily. Historical Plaque—Mary Lindley Murray, in south median of Park Ave. at intersection with 37th St., New York,*

NY 10016. GPS: 40.748944, -73.980003. Sign accessible daily. Historical marker—Reservoir Square, south/southeast corner of Bryant Park near 40th St., New York, NY 10018. GPS: 40.753200, -73.983388. Site accessible daily. Monument—McGown's Pass and interpretive sign—Fort Clinton: On Top of Manhattan, in Central Park just west of intersection of 5th Ave. and E. 107th St., New York, NY 10029. GPS: 40.795305, -73.952156. Sites accessible daily.

HARLEM HEIGHTS—After the debacle at Kip's Bay, the Americans settled on a line that crossed Manhattan at Harlem Heights, while the British formed opposite them to the south. The next day, September 16, 1776, an American scouting party ventured south and engaged the British, triggering a larger action along the entire line. This day, the Americans fought bravely, pushing the British soldiers back and keeping the upper hand throughout the two-hour fight. Though neither army changed their positions, the Americans had clearly won the battle, providing a much-needed boost to their morale.

Washington made his headquarters during this period at the deserted home of British Colonel Roger Morris, which once had a sweeping view of Manhattan. Now known as the Morris-Jumel Mansion, the home is Manhattan's oldest surviving residence and is open for tours. You can still make out the heights along which the Americans formed their line at the Trinity Church Cemetery and Mausoleum, and there is a plaque marking its importance. Six blocks south, you can find another marker at the American first line of defense. On the actual Harlem Heights battlefield, a marker is at ground level, just south of General Grant National Memorial in Riverside Park, as well as another on the campus of Columbia University at Mathematics Hall. *Morris-Jumel Man-*

continued on next page

sion, 65 Jumel Terrace, New York, NY 10032; 212-923-8008; www.morrisjumel.org. GPS: 37.676144, -77.310921. GPS: 40.834555, -73.938896. Open Tues.–Sun.; check website for tour hours. Historical Plaque, NW corner of intersection of Broadway and W 153rd St., New York, NY 10032. GPS: 40.831653, -73.946922. Site accessible daily. Historical marker—The First Line of Defence, in median north of intersection of Broadway and 147th St., New York, NY 10031. GPS: 40.827879, -73.949415. Site accessible daily. Historical marker—Battle of Harlem Heights, in triangle of grass between north and southbound lanes of Riverside Dr., New York, NY 10027. GPS: 40.812082, -73.963686. Historical marker—Battle of Harlem Heights, on Broadway 0.1 mile north of 116th St., New York, NY 10027. GPS: 40.808909, -73.962991. Site accessible daily.

MONTRESOR'S ISLAND—Faulty intelligence gathered from two British deserters led to a raid on British-held Montresor's Island on the night of September 22, 1776. The raid was hastily planned and poorly executed, and the small British garrison on the island was alerted well before the Americans made their landing. The result was that the Americans barely made it to shore, but still suffered 14 casualties.

Montresor's Island—owned by British Captain John Montresor before and during the war—is known as Randall's Island today. There is no interpretation of the little-known raid on the island today, though you can visit, as it's home to a number of recreational opportunities. *Randall's Island Park, 20 Randall's Island Park, New York, NY 10035. GPS: 40.793353, -73.922460. Accessible daily.*

PELL'S POINT—After several weeks of inaction, British General William Howe finally made a move to dislodge the Americans from their position on the island of Manhattan. British soldiers landed at Throg's Neck in the Bronx on October 12, 1776, attempting to outflank the American position and possibly trap them on the island. The landing point, however, provided little cover for them, and a small group of American soldiers, along with the strategic dismantling of some bridges, was enough to prevent them from moving inland. Howe then shifted slightly east and made another landing at Pell's Point in Pelham Bay on October 18, and though a single brigade under the command of Colonel John Glover provided a fierce resistance, the British were able to gain their foothold. The results of the fighting at Pell's Point clearly favored the Americans, who lost 8 killed and 13 wounded, as opposed to no less than 200 and possibly up to 800 casualties for the British. But Howe's move had forced its objective, as the Americans had already begun to retreat north to White Plains, leaving only Fort Washington on Manhattan Island in their control.

The site from which Glover's men cut down the British from behind stone walls is along Rodman's Neck Road within Pelham Bay Park in the Bronx. Some parts of those walls are still visible, and they lead to the famous Split Rock (now also known as Glover's Rock), which itself has an interesting history. There is not a lot of interpretation here, but it is a nice, quiet place and serves as New York City's largest park. *Pelham Bay Park, intersection of Middletown Rd. and Stadium Ave., New York, NY 10465. GPS: 40.865132, -73.803053. Site accessible daily.*

WHITE PLAINS—Washington's army settled on a set of hills east of White Plains, New York, facing the Bronx River, then had several weeks to solidify their defenses as the British stalled. On October 28, 1776, British General Howe finally moved toward

continued on next page

the American position with 14,000 men. After pushing a skirmishing party back, the first attack occurred at a height called Chatterton's Hill, where the Americans stopped a frontal assault from a body of Hessians before British grenadiers crossed the Bronx River and pushed up the hill. Though they met a withering fire, they were able to force the Americans into a retreat. Again, the British held the ground at the end of the fight, but again, they paid a high price for it, losing 200 casualties to the Americans' 175. Though there were several artillery duels over the next few days, the British went no farther.

The battlefield at White Plains contains several preserved parcels of land as well as a few monuments. The most significant of these sites is Battle of White Plains Park, located at the crest of Chatterton's Hill. The park contains excellent interpretive signage that tells the story of the battle, and though the views of the surrounding battlefield are now obstructed, there's still enough left for one to figure out what happened there. Another good site for interpretation, though open less frequently, is the Jacob Purdy House, which served as Washington's headquarters both during this period and in 1778. There is also the Battle of White Plains Heritage Trail, which identifies 12 locations pertinent to the battle throughout the town and is your best way to experience the complete battlefield. *Battle of White Plains Park, 76 Battle Ave., White Plains, NY 10606. GPS: 41.030187, -73.780072. Site accessible daily. Jacob Purdy House, Jacob Purdy Park, 60 Park Avenue, White Plains, NY 10603; 914-328-1776. GPS: 41.037114, -73.773240. Open by appointment; call for hours. Battle of White Plains Heritage Trail, www.sites.google.com/site/troopxwp/white-plains-heritage-trail. Sites accessible daily.*

Top: A memorial at McGowan's Pass in Central Park, critical point of the Battle of Kip's Bay. *Bottom*: A boulder marks the site of an American redoubt that saw action during the Battle of Harlem Heights.

Top: Glover's Rock at Pelham Bay Park, site of the Battle of Pell's Point.
Bottom: Battle of White Plains Park is one of several battlefield sites throughout White Plains, New York.

Fort Washington

After the fight at White Plains, British General William Howe moved quickly to control the territory around New York City. Moving south, Howe left the Americans in their fortified lines and occupied the crossing from the Bronx into Manhattan at Kingsbridge. General George Washington surmised that the British were getting ready for a move into New Jersey to strike at Philadelphia but knew that before leaving the area Howe would attempt to take the American stronghold at Fort Washington, at the north end of Manhattan Island.

Though many among Washington's staff thought that Fort Washington should be abandoned, General Nathanael Greene, one of Washington's most valued lieutenants, thought otherwise. Greene was confident that the fort was strong enough and had enough stores to last until at least December. Washington was doubtful, but at this stage of the Revolution was relying on councils of war (that is, the majority opinions of his generals and staff) to make decisions. To boot, Greene was at Fort Washington and knew the conditions better than Washington could. So, after much persuasion, Washington decided that the Americans would hold the fort.

Fort Washington and its accompanying defenses held 2,800 Americans. Aside from the main fort, there were lines facing south (the original Harlem lines), east, and north, as well as a redoubt just north of the fort. The only easy way to approach the fort was from the south, where a gradual slope led into the works. To the west of the pentagon-shaped fortification was a high cliff that dropped to the Hudson River. Though a large earthwork, the fort contained no barracks or powder magazines.

On the morning of November 16, 1776, a day after demanding Fort Washington's surrender, British troops began their assault. Two thousand British soldiers under General Hugh Percy approached the fort from the south, coming up first against the American lines at Harlem. A force of Hessians, 8,000 strong and under the command of General Wilhelm von Knyphausen, marched south from Kingsbridge with the objective of storming the redoubt and then advancing on the fort. Later that morning, British troop ships landed at two locations on the Harlem

Bennett Park, on the northwest side of Manhattan, marks the site of Fort Washington.

River, between Manhattan and the Bronx, with 3,000 troops under the command of General Charles Cornwallis to attack from the east.

The first action occurred at 7:00 AM from the north and south. Percy easily broke through the American lines at Harlem, pressing them back into Fort Washington. After some confusion and a slight delay, the Hessians began the grueling climb up the steep hill toward the redoubt. The fighting here was fierce, but Knyphausen managed to keep advancing and took the outer work after a two-hour slugfest, sending those Americans also into the main fort. As the last Americans from the south were making their way into Fort Washington, the Hessians appeared from the north to attack them, pinning down the defenders. With many of the Americans trapped within and outside of the works, Knyphausen asked for and received the fort's surrender.

As was the case in many of the battles for New York, the British suffered more killed and wounded than the Americans—approximately

SITE DETAILS

Fort Washington—Bennett Park on the northern end of Manhattan is where Fort Washington was located. There is a memorial to the Americans who fought here, and the location of the fort is outlined in the pavement with some commemorative words. There is also a marker denoting the highest point in Manhattan, which is why the fort was built here in the first place. *Fort Washington—Bennett Park, intersection of West 183rd St. and Fort Washington Ave., New York, NY 10083. GPS: 40.852910, -73.937721. Accessible daily.*

Fort Tryon—The outer work to the north of Fort Washington that was taken by the Hessians was renamed Fort Tryon after the British took possession. Nothing remains of the fort today, but a walk through Fort Tryon Park will give you a good idea of the difficult terrain on which the fight occurred. There is a memorial to the soldiers who fought here, as well as one to Margaret Corbin; Corbin was assisting her husband, an artillerist, when he was killed, and Margaret took over his post. *Fort Tryon, near Margaret Corbin Dr. just south of intersection with Fort Tryon Place, New York, NY 10040. GPS: 40.861798, -73.932741. Margaret Corbin Memorial, Margaret Corbin Circle, New York, NY 10040. GPS: 40.859425, -73.933975. Accessible daily.*

78 killed and 374 wounded (mostly Hessian) to the Americans' 59 killed and 96 wounded. But the 2,830 Americans who surrendered, including 230 officers, was a staggering blow, along with the loss of Manhattan. In addition, Fort Lee, directly across the Hudson River, was now untenable and had to be abandoned quickly, with a loss of massive amounts of irreplaceable stores and ammunition, including 146 pieces of artillery. The British now had firm control over New York City, while the Continental Army was sent into a desperate race across New Jersey with their pursuers not far behind.

Stony Point

In 1779, after a period of inaction, the British army was holed up in New York City, with the Americans warily watching them from their surrounding positions. The most important of these was the Hudson Highlands, the mountains surrounding the Hudson River. Both armies knew that the river was a critical point strategically, and even though the British were in firm control of its mouth, the rest of the river belonged to the Americans.

Also still part of the British grand strategy, at least in the mind of General Henry Clinton, now commander of British forces in North America, was that the war could be won in one decisive battle. For years, though, General George Washington was successful in avoiding that battle. Clinton decided to try luring Washington out one more time, and on May 31, 1779, seized control of Stony Point, a short but commanding peninsula of land jutting out from the west bank of the Hudson. Stony Point was also one side of the critical Kings Ferry crossing, further stressing its importance.

The rough terrain at Stony Point Battlefield State Historic Site.

Washington was not about to give Clinton the general engagement that he wanted. However, he was not about to let the move go unanswered. Washington gathered a crack brigade of Continental light infantry and selected General "Mad" Anthony Wayne to lead the assault.

The move on Stony Point had to be carefully planned. The fortifications that the British had built were atop a steep, rocky outcropping. The point could only be approached easily from the west; the Hudson River and low, swampy ground surrounded the rest of the peninsula. There was an exception, however; with some care, the edges of the peninsula could be traversed at low tide. Assaulting the point would still be a significant challenge, but with the element of surprise—by attacking at night—it could just work.

At about noon on July 15, 1779, 1,350 Americans marched south from Fort Montgomery and went on a roundabout march to Stony Point. Reaching a point just to the west at about 8:00 PM, the force split into three groups. The main attack, 700 men strong, would come from the south, and would be led by Wayne personally. Another, smaller group would approach from the north. The third group would cause a diversion from directly west of the point—the only direction from which the British might expect an attack. In the front of Wayne's column were 150 men with axes and other tools to remove obstructions for the assaulting force. Perhaps most critically, the assault would ensue using bayonets only, lest a misfire signal to the British that the attack was coming.

The assault began at 12:30 AM on July 17. It wasn't long before a British picket discovered the Americans and fired a warning shot, alerting the 625-man British garrison to their presence. By this time, though, the Americans were on the move and on their way up the steep hill. The British tried to use artillery to blunt the assault, but because of the placement of the guns and the high elevation, they could not be pointed down to an effective angle. As the Americans made their way to the top, the remainder of the garrison attempted to flee west, where they ran into the diversion force.

The attack was over in less than 30 minutes. The Americans had captured Stony Point with great skill and efficiency, suffering 15 killed and 83 wounded. For the British, the loss was much more significant: 20 killed, 74 wounded, and 530 captured or missing, as well as losing a

> ## SITE DETAILS
>
> **Stony Point Battlefield State Historic Site**—Many of the original British fortifications can still be viewed at Stony Point Battlefield State Historic Site. Even the drive up to the top of the point will give you an excellent idea about just how formidable an obstacle Stony Point was. When you get to the top, you will be able to access the excellent museum and can walk the surprisingly large area, where there are plenty of interpretive signs and monuments for you to see. The area within and surrounding the park is quite beautiful, too, and it's a peaceful place, providing nice views of the Hudson River. Living history programs are frequent, so check before you go to see if you can catch one. *Stony Point Battlefield State Historic Site, 44 Battlefield Rd., Stony Point, NY 10980; 845-786-2521; www.parks.ny.gov/historic-sites/stonypoint battlefield/details.aspx. GPS: 41.241062, -73.976570. Open Wed.–Sat.*

number of pieces of artillery. Though it was a decisive victory, it was a fairly meaningless one, from a strategic standpoint; the Americans abandoned the point in only a couple of days. But the successful covert attack against the vaunted British was a morale-boosting victory for the Americans. Stony Point was the last significant battle of the American Revolution in the northern colonies.

Trenton
The fall of Forts Washington and Lee forced the Continental Army into retreat across New Jersey, with the British not far behind. The Americans headed southwest toward Philadelphia, with General George Washington anticipating that the British would make an attempt to capture the city. The army moved quickly, shedding men as they went because of expiring enlistments and desertions. The chase ended on December 8, 1776, when the British reached the Delaware River at Trenton, only to find the Americans on the other side; Washington had ordered that every boat in the area be destroyed, leaving the British stranded.

By this time, the British commander, General William Howe, had already concluded that the time was right to end his campaign for the year. Winter was fast approaching, and conditions were only going to worsen for a massive army moving through the field. Howe left General Charles Cornwallis in charge of the pursuing force and put the rest of his army into winter quarters in New York City and northern New Jersey. Cornwallis established a string of lightly manned outposts in Hackensack, Brunswick, Kingston, Princeton, Trenton, Bordentown, and Burlington, then joined the rest of the army in waiting out the winter. Howe left for Manhattan on December 15, confident in his plans.

Washington was not finished. He knew that the morale of his army and his country were at perhaps its lowest point. Despite his diminished force and despite the odds, he needed a victory, and quickly. And in Howe's inaction, he saw an opportunity.

From his position across from Trenton, Washington could see the occupying force, approximately 1,400 Hessian troops under Colonel Johann Gottlieb Rall. The Americans would have a large number of

The Delaware River at Washington Crossing Historic Park in Pennsylvania.

enlistments expiring near the end of the year, but they had temporarily been reinforced, mostly by Pennsylvania volunteers, and Washington could count on having about 10,000 men at his disposal. Even with those numbers, attacking a defensive position would be extremely difficult, especially across a river and in the winter. But the situation was desperate and required a bold stroke.

For the next two weeks, the Americans planned their attack. The army would be divided into three units. The main force, led by Washington himself, would attack the outpost at Trenton directly from the north and west. A smaller unit would approach from the south to prevent any escape by the Hessian forces in that direction. A third group would feign an attack on the outpost at Burlington, causing a diversion and preventing Trenton from being reinforced. Boats were gathered to ferry the men across the Delaware River as quickly as possible. The utmost secrecy was held, with only a small handful of people knowing about the attack. Finally, Washington chose the morning of December 26, the day after Christmas, for the assault, hoping that the Hessians would still be recovering from their Christmas celebrations.

The Americans set out across the icy Delaware River on Christmas evening, 1776, at McConkey's Ferry, 9 miles northwest of Trenton. The weather that night, heavy snow and sleet, was both a complication and a blessing; while it made conditions extremely difficult, it also helped preserve the element of surprise. Still, Washington's force, hoping to complete the crossing by midnight, took an extra three hours. That was a better result than the other two arms of the attack, which were unable to get into their positions at all. The main force split into two columns and began the long, cold march to Trenton, unaware that they would be unsupported.

The two columns both arrived at Trenton at approximately 8:00 AM on December 26. General Nathanael Greene's men approached from the north, with General Henry Knox setting his two artillery pieces to fire directly down Trenton's two main avenues, Queen Street and King Street. As the Hessians jumped into action to meet them from the south, General John Sullivan approached from the west, firing into their flank. The fighting quickly became house to house and hand to hand. The Americans, though, with surprise and a numerical advantage on their side, pushed the Hessians south through the town. Rall, the Hessian commander, attempted to rally his men in an orchard east of the town, but in the process he was mortally wounded. After about an hour and a half of fighting, the last of the Hessians surrendered.

With the victory at Trenton, Washington had pulled off one of the most audacious victories in history. The Americans had captured 918 Hessians, with another 40 killed and 66 wounded, while losing only 4 killed and 8 wounded. The attack had been a master stroke. However, Washington wasn't done.

Upon receiving word of the attack, Cornwallis, who had been in Brunswick, quickly organized 8,000 men and moved on the Americans at Trenton. After leaving a rear guard at Princeton, on January 2, 1777, the British met the Americans again at Trenton, this time at the south end of town on Assunpink Creek. The Americans took a strong position on the south bank of the creek, and with darkness coming, Cornwallis planned to attack them there in the morning. The next day, however, the British woke to find that their enemy had disappeared.

The Americans were not done yet.

A memorial outside the Old Barracks at Trenton, New Jersey.

SITE DETAILS

Washington Crossing Historic Park—On the Pennsylvania side of the Delaware River is Washington Crossing Historic Park, preserving the land where the Continental Army assembled and loaded themselves into Durham boats to cross the river and march to Trenton. The visitor center has an outstanding museum, as well as an exact, life-size replica of the famous painting of *Washington Crossing the Delaware* by Emanuel Leutze. Every year, the park conducts a well-attended reenactment of the crossing that shouldn't be missed if you can catch it. There is a historic village on site that includes the McConkey's Ferry Inn that witnessed the crossing. In addition, the park is caretaker of the Thompson-Neely House, which served as a hospital during the campaign; one of the patients here was future president James Monroe, who was wounded at the Battle of Trenton. *Washington Crossing Historic Park, 1112 River Rd., Washington Crossing, PA 18977; 215-493-4076; www.washingtoncrossingpark.org. GPS: 40.295127, -74.872061. Open daily.*

Washington Crossing State Park—The New Jersey side of Washington's crossing is preserved as Washington's Crossing State Park. The park features an excellent visitor center with a nice collection of artifacts and an orientation film about the crossing as well as the Battle of Trenton and the Battle of Princeton. There is also the Johnson Ferry House, which dates to 1740 and may have been used by Washington's staff during the crossing. The park also has numerous opportunities for outdoor activities, including camping, fishing, and hunting. A nature center is also onsite. *Washington Crossing State Park, 355 Washington Crossing-Pennington Rd., Titusville, NJ 08560; 609-737-0623; nj.gov/dep/parksandforests/parks/washingtoncrossingstatepark.html. GPS: 40.304933, -74.856894. Open daily.*

Trenton Battle Monument Historic Site—The Trenton Battle Monument is a large column standing 148 feet tall. Dedicated in 1893, it marks the spot where General Henry Knox placed his artillery at the head of Queen and King Streets (now known as Broad and Warren Streets, respectively). The monument has statues of Washington and others, as well as bas-reliefs of the battle and the crossing of the Delaware. *Trenton Battle Monument Historic Site, 348 North Warren St., Trenton, NJ 08638; 609-737-0623; nj.gov/dep/parksandforests/historic/trentonbattlemonument.html. GPS: 40.225687, -74.764801. Accessible daily.*

Old Barracks Museum—The barracks in Trenton were built in 1758 during the French and Indian War by the colony of New Jersey. During the American Revolution the barracks were used by both the British and the Americans, including the Hessian troops who fought in the Battle of Trenton. Today the Old Barracks Museum tells the story of the building and the armies who used it. Guided tours will take you through much of the building, and there are a number of other exhibits you can see before and after. Special events are frequent, so check in before you go. *Old Barracks Museum, 101 Barrack St., Trenton, NJ 08608; 609-396-1776; www.barracks.org. GPS: 40.219853, -74.768249. Open Wed.–Sat.*

Mill Hill Park—Mill Hill Park is the site of the Battle of Assunpink Creek, also known as the Second Battle of Trenton. There are interpretive signs and maps at the park that explain the battle and all of the features you can still distinguish today. There is also a monument to Washington at the site. Walking across the footbridge over the creek will take you to the American positions. *Mill Hill Park, intersection of South Broad St. and East Front St., Trenton, NJ 08608. GPS: 40.218896, -74.764008. Accessible daily.*

WHO WERE THE HESSIANS?

In 1776, the British could not raise a sufficient number of soldiers to carry out the war in America. The crown decided to go with a tried-and-true method of building armies in the Old World: hiring mercenaries. Mercenaries, in those days, were subjects of their rulers pressed into military service to fight for another country, with the arrangement that the ruler would receive money for that service.

George III initially asked Russia for assistance, but he was rebuffed after France and Prussia intervened. He then approached the rulers of the German states, among whom he had many close relatives. The first to agree to provide mercenaries for the Revolutionary War was Landgrave Friedrich II of Hesse-Cassel, and so these mercenaries were often collectively called Hessians. In fact, more than a third of the troops who fought as mercenaries on the British side were not actually Hessian but instead hailed from places like Hanau, Brunswick, Anspach-Bayreuth, Anhalt-Zerbst, and Waldeck. In all, 30,000 soldiers served as mercenaries for the British. Less than half would return to their homes; though a good number of them were killed in battle or died of disease, many also deserted or were captured and went on to make a new life in America.

Princeton

When General Cornwallis postponed his attack at Trenton on the evening of January 2, 1777, he was certain that the Americans had nowhere to escape. But there was one direction they could go that he did not count on. Washington directed his men to tie rags to their wagon wheels to dampen the noise of their passage, and prepare to retreat. He left 400 soldiers to tend to the campfires and make a little bit of noise, giving the illusion that the army was staying put. At 1:00 AM, January 3, the Continental Army silently slipped east and then north, past Cornwallis's left flank and into the heart of British-held New Jersey, heading directly for the British outpost at Princeton.

Cornwallis had left a 1,200-man rear guard at Princeton under Lieutenant Colonel Charles Mawhood, but had just issued orders for those men to join him at Princeton. Mawhood's command was heading in that direction at 8:00 AM on January 3 when they saw what must have seemed an illusion: an American brigade under the command of General Hugh Mercer. Mercer had been sent by Washington to block Mawhood's possible escape to Trenton, not anticipating that he would already be on the move. The Americans immediately went on the attack, and the two forces collided just southwest of Princeton near the crossing at Stony Creek.

The Americans, who were exhausted after marching throughout the night and largely consisted of inexperienced militia, did not fare well

The Thomas Clarke House, where American General Hugh Mercer died after the Battle of Princeton.

at first. Mawhood was able to get his troops into a line and ordered a bayonet charge that surprised and scattered the Continentals, mortally wounding Mercer. But just as the Americans were beginning to retreat, General George Washington, the rest of his army behind him, raced onto the battlefield. Washington rode among the men and rallied them, urging them to stand their ground and fight the much smaller British force.

Soon, the rest of the Americans came up and began to form, enveloping both sides of the British line. Mawhood saw that he was outnumbered and in a dangerous position. Out of desperation, he ordered another bayonet charge that broke through the Americans. Many of the British soldiers who did make it through were able to flee, making their way toward Trenton, but after a short chase a number of them were captured. Washington then turned his attention to the town of Princeton, where Mawhood had left a small contingent who had barricaded themselves in Nassau Hall at the College of New Jersey (now Princeton University). After Captain Alexander Hamilton fired a couple of cannonballs at the building, however, the stranded British soldiers surrendered.

The Battle of Princeton lasted only two hours. Though the British casualty numbers—28 killed, 58 wounded, and 187 captured—were much smaller than at Trenton, it was another astounding American victory. Casualties for the Continental Army were 23 killed and 20 wounded.

Following the battle, Cornwallis, worried about his supply base, headed for Brunswick, and the British pulled back many of their forces in New Jersey toward New York City. The Americans, exhausted but riding the wave of victory, finally went into winter camp, not across the Delaware but in Middletown, New Jersey.

The twin victories at Trenton and Princeton, only nine days apart, sent shock waves throughout the colonies and Great Britain. The American cause that only a short time ago seemed lost now had tremendous momentum. On both sides of the Atlantic, it was sensed that this was a great turning point in the American Revolution, and it was.

Morristown

Over the course of a war, there are occurrences besides battles and generals that determine whether one side or another will emerge victorious. Undoubtedly, for the Americans, suffering through the winter

SITE DETAILS

Princeton Battlefield State Park—Much of the Princeton battlefield is still intact and is preserved at Princeton Battlefield State Park. The park is small and easily walkable, with interpretive signs and monuments describing the events leading up to the battle and the prominent points of the battlefield. You'll also find a descendant of the Mercer Oak, the tree under which General Mercer lay after he was mortally wounded; the original tree collapsed in 2000. There is also a mass grave of 15 American and 21 British soldiers, all unknown, who were buried nearby. The Thomas Clarke House, which witnessed the battle and is where Mercer died, is also part of the park and is open for tours. *Princeton Battlefield State Park, 500 Mercer Rd., Princeton, NJ 08540; 609-921-0074; nj.gov/dep/parks andforests/parks/princetonbattlefieldstatepark.html. GPS: 40.330801, -74.676853. Park open daily; Clarke house open Wed.–Sun.*

Princeton Battle Monument Historic Site—Just off the Princeton University campus is the Princeton Battle Monument, dedicated in 1902. The striking monument depicts Washington and the death of General Mercer. There are also several other small monuments and interpretive signs at the site. *Princeton Battle Monument Historic Site, 55 Stockton St., Princeton, NJ 08540; 609-921-0074; nj.gov/dep/parksandforests/historic/princetonbattle monument.html. GPS: 40.347931, -74.665955. Accessible daily.*

Nassau Hall—On the Princeton University campus is Nassau Hall, the first building on the College of New Jersey campus. It has suffered several fires and is not exactly the same in appearance, though it is close. There is a memorial plaque on the outside of the building, but please do not enter unless you have official business or are on a campus tour. *Nassau Hall, on Nassau St. near intersection with Elm Dr., Princeton, NJ 08542. GPS: 40.348837, -74.659381. Accessible daily.*

encampment at Morristown in the winter of 1779–1780 was one of these events.

Morristown was an ideal spot for the Americans to make their winter camp. Only about 30 miles from New York City, it was close enough to keep a wary eye on British movements but far enough to prevent any kind of surprise attack. The Watchung Mountains provided a formidable natural barrier between the two armies, giving the Continental Army security and control over any movements toward them. The local road network allowed quick movement in any direction. The resources required for a large cantonment (a camp with more permanent structures)—particularly wood and water—were in abundance. Finally, the local inhabitants were extremely supportive of the cause. There was a lot to like about Morristown.

The Continental Army spent two winters here. The first winter was 1776–1777, after the Battle of Trenton and the Battle of Princeton. General George Washington needed a secure base for his army that was still, to some degree, threatening to the British positions in New Jersey,

Site of Fort Nonsense, Morristown National Historical Park.

so immediately after the victory at Princeton the Continentals moved to Morristown. Washington's unassailable location in the middle of the state further forced the British to withdraw toward New York City. In addition, from here, the Americans could still disrupt British logistics, and they spent much of the first half of 1777 harassing British efforts to gather food and supplies in what became known as the Forage War. The army stayed in Morristown until late May, when they moved to Middlebrook, inching closer to British lines.

After the American victory at Monmouth in the summer of 1778, the British withdrew into New York City, and for the next two years large engagements between the two armies in the north were limited. For the winter of 1779–1780, Washington again chose Morristown for his cantonment. This time, his army was much larger, over 10,000 men. Washington made his headquarters at the mansion of Theodosia Ford, the widow of a New Jersey militia colonel. Washington, his wife Martha, his five staff members (including Alexander Hamilton), and their 18 servants and slaves all stayed in the mansion, with Ford and her four children moving into another part of the house.

No one could have anticipated the winter of 1779 to 1780, which came to be known as the Hard Winter. It is highly possible that it was the worst winter ever recorded in the northeastern United States. Temperatures were below freezing for long stretches. Snowfall was prevalent, with one blizzard in early January dropping over 6 feet of snow on the encampment. Roads were so impassable at times that supplies could not be gotten to the camp, and at one point, according to soldiers' accounts, there was no food for four entire days; men resorted to eating tree bark or boiling the leather of their shoes out of desperation, and it was not uncommon for them to steal from the local inhabitants. The suffering of the troops through this winter was beyond comprehension.

That is not to say that the soldiers were not disgruntled. On May 25, 1780, things came to a head when two regiments of Connecticut troops mutinied over the lack of food, as well as a pay dispute. Though the mutiny was quickly put down, the poor conditions that the troops had to live through was a constant worry to Washington and his staff, with the threat of further mutinies always hanging over the camp.

The Hard Winter proved to be one of the Continental Army's harsh-

SITE DETAILS

Morristown National Historical Park—Much of the Morristown cantonment is preserved as Morristown National Historical Park. The park contains two primary units, each with its own visitor center. Begin your visit at the Ford Mansion Visitor Center to watch an orientation video and view the exhibits, then take the guided tour of the home where Washington stayed during his time here. When you've finished, head to Jockey Hollow, where you can learn more about the terrible winter of 1778–1779 and see a reconstructed soldiers' hut and view the encampment. There is a driving tour of the large encampment area, with plenty of interpretive signs to help you visualize what the encampment was like. Finally, you can stop at Fort Nonsense, a redoubt built to command Morristown in case of an attack. There is plenty to see at Morristown, so be sure to set aside ample time. *Morristown National Historical Park, 30 Washington Place, Morristown, NJ 07960; 973-539-2016; www.nps.gov/morr. GPS: 40.797158, -74.466022. Grounds open daily; visitor centers open Wed.–Sun. during summer months and Thurs.–Sun. rest of year.*

Jacob Arnold House—During the first winter encampment at Morristown, Washington took his headquarters at the Jacob Arnold Tavern. The tavern no longer stands, but there is a historic marker on the site. *Historical*

est tests, but through the incredible perseverance of the soldiers, they endured. It is a testament to them that they were able to survive such conditions with the army intact and struggle on to victory.

OTHER SITES IN NEW YORK AND NEW JERSEY

SAG HARBOR VILLAGE—The pretty whaling town of Sag Harbor, with its safe waters and strategic location and safe waters, became an early British post on Long Island after its occupation. That's not to say it never saw action—it was the subject of an American raid on May 23, 1777—

marker—*Arnold Tavern, on Morristown Green at North Park Pl., Morristown, NJ 07960. GPS: 40.797316, -74.481685. Accessible daily.*

Ogden Farm—Jonathan Ogden established his farm just before the Revolutionary War. During the winter of 1779–1780, it is thought that General Henry Knox made his headquarters at the Ogden farmhouse. The house today is part of the Fosterfields Living Historical Farm, a park in Morris County. You can tour the working farm, including the house, though there is not much interpretation of the Revolutionary War period. *Fosterfields Living Historical Farm, 73 Kahdena Rd., Morristown, NJ 07960; 973-326-7645; www.morrisparks.net/parks_trails/fosterfields-living-historical-farm. GPS: 40.802864, -74.505066. Open Wed.–Sat. April through June and Wed.–Sun., July through October.*

Schuyler-Hamilton House—Also known as the Dr. Jabez Campfield House, this home was used as a headquarters for Washington's doctor during the 1779–1780 encampment. The doctor's niece, Elizabeth Schuyler, joined him that winter, and met her future husband, Alexander Hamilton, in the home. The house still stands and is home to the local chapter of the Daughters of the American Revolution; there is a historical marker in front of the house, and it is open for tours. *Schuyler-Hamilton House, 5 Olyphant Pl., Morristown, NJ 07960. GPS: 40.796375, -74.472727. Open Sun.*

but its importance in the Revolution has to do with service as a British stronghold and port of entry.

There are historical markers around Sag Harbor that detail its varied history, but the best place to start, if possible, is the Sag Harbor Historical Society. The society operates a museum, open summer weekends and by appointment, that will tell you all you need to know about the town's wartime history. *Sag Harbor Historical Museum, 174 Main St., Sag Harbor, NY 11963; 631-725-5092; www.sagharborhistorical.org. GPS: 40.998690, -72.296347. Open weekends late May–Columbus Day and by appointment.*

WILLIAM FLOYD ESTATE—William Floyd, born into a large estate on Long Island, was a community leader from the outset. Despite his lack of a formal education. Floyd's outspoken ways in Patriot-sympathizing Suffolk County earned him a seat in the Continental Congress. It also earned him the enmity of the British, who commandeered his home and estate as a barracks in 1776. Floyd bravely stayed the course, signing the Declaration of Independence and remaining with the Congress until 1777. He returned home in 1783 to find his estate stripped bare and much abused. Floyd went on to serve in the first United States Congress and as a major general in the New York state militia.

What is now known as the William Floyd Estate remained in the Floyd family from its purchase in 1718 until 1976, when it was donated to the National Park Service. Today, the estate is preserved as part of Fire Island National Seashore. Visitors can tour the Old Mastic House, built with six rooms in the 1720s but greatly expanded over the years. The remaining grounds, over 600 acres, contain 12 outbuildings and tell the changing story of the land, from its development using slave labor to its late use as a recreational haven. The grounds also contain the family cemetery and several hiking trails. *William Floyd Estate, Fire Island National Seashore, entrance on Park Dr. just south of intersection with Washington Dr., Mastic Beach, NY 11951; 631-399-2030; www.nps.gov/fiis/planyourvisit/williamfloydestate.htm. GPS: 40.770490, -72.834633. Open Fri.–Mon., Memorial Day to Veterans Day.*

FORT ST. GEORGE—As the British occupation of Long Island spread, St. George's Manor, on a strategic neck of land, was fortified and named Fort St. George. It became a supply depot, and was soon the target of a raid behind enemy lines. On November 23, 1780, a small American force raided the manor and quickly captured it, destroying the supplies. The fort was quickly reoccupied by the British.

St. George Manor is operated as a historic home today. Information about the battle can also be found here. The hours can be hit-and-miss, so be sure to call ahead. The entrance can be a bit difficult to find off the main road, so keep your eyes open for it. *St. George Manor, entrance on west side of William Floyd Parkway at intersection with Neighborhood*

Road, Shirley, NY 11967; 631-281-5034. GPS: 40.758596, -72.872237. Open Thurs.–Sun., May through October.

FORT SALONGA—British-occupied Long Island saw a number of fortifications built, including Fort Salonga overlooking Long Island Sound. Early in the morning of October 3, 1779, after crossing the sound, a group of 100 American raiders attacked the fort and burned much of it. The Americans took a number of prisoners, with only one wounded; that man, Sergeant Elijah Churchill, became one of the first Americans to receive the Badge of Military Merit, created by George Washington himself. The award is known today as the Purple Heart.

There are some remaining vestiges of Fort Salonga, but they are on private property and inaccessible. Though removed a bit from the site of the fort, there is also a historic marker telling the story of the fort. *Historical marker—Battle of Fort Slongo, east of intersection of Route 25A and Bread and Cheese Hollow Rd., Northport, NY 11768. GPS: 40.912417, -73.299925. Sign accessible daily.*

FORT GOLGOTHA AND BURIAL HILL CEMETERY—Burial Hill Cemetery was established in the mid-17th century in Huntington, New York, on Long Island. In 1782, occupying British troops tore down the local church and built a fortress within the cemetery, leveling the hill. A large number of gravestones were removed and used as parts of the fort, including its ovens, which would bake bread with the inscriptions of the tombstones on them. This insult to the town was largely thought to be solely out of spite; it would be only four months before the British evacuated Long Island completely.

Fort Golgotha was torn down shortly after the British left. Though it saw no action, the indignity suffered by the town was never forgotten. You can still visit the cemetery, which contains several historical markers noting the incident. *Burial Hill Cemetery, intersection of Main St. and Nassau Rd., Huntington, NY 11743. GPS: 40.872046, -73.424063. Open daily.*

RAYNHAM HALL—In 1740, Samuel Townsend purchased a large estate in Oyster Bay, New York. Townsend was well known for his patriotic

A memorial plaque in Burial Hill Cemetery marks the site of Fort Golgotha.

views, which stood out among his mostly Tory neighbors on Long Island. After the fall of New York City, the Townsend home was taken over as headquarters for the Queen's Rangers, led by Lieutenant Colonel Robert Graves Simcoe, who, while in the home, would author America's first valentine, to Samuel's daughter Sarah. Samuel's son, Robert, who was heavily involved in his father's shipping business, was recruited by George Washington as part of an intelligence network that came to be known as the Culper Spy Ring. The intelligence Robert provided from his observations and connections at the docks of Manhattan proved invaluable to the Americans during the entire occupation of New York City. Robert's extraordinary service to the Continental Army would not be known until 1930, when handwriting analysis identified him as the famous Culper Junior.

Raynham Hall, in downtown Oyster Bay, is open for tours. The staff knows all the good stories that you would expect to be associated with a spy ring, though the tour also focuses on how the home has changed over the years, including being used as a tea room. If you're interested in the Culper Spy Ring, a fan of the show *Turn: Washington's Spies*, or ever wanted to try out some invisible ink for yourself, this is the place. *Raynham Hall Museum, 20 West Main St., Oyster Bay, NY 11771; 516-922-6808; www.raynhamhallmuseum.org. GPS: 40.872298, -73.531624. Open Tues.–Sun.*

ST. JAMES CHURCH—Once the British had settled into Long Island, St. James Church, whose parishioners were split on the idea of independence, became the local Anglican church for the who's-who of the British army. Generals Howe, Clinton, and Cornwallis all worshipped here, as did the future king of the United Kingdom, George IV.

St. James Church is still an active parish, and though the congregation has moved to a newer building, the original church still stands and is still used. The original building dates to 1735, and it is generally not open to tours, but there is some interpretive signage outside. *St. James Church, 8407 Broadway, Elmhurst, NY 11373. GPS: 40.739676, -73.878016. Site accessible daily.*

PRISON SHIP MARTYRS' MONUMENT—Once the British gained control of New York and its harbor, it began the then-common practice of converting vessels that were not fully capable of serving the Royal Navy into prison ships. The conditions on these ships, overcrowded and unsanitary, were horrendous for the soldiers and political prisoners they housed. Estimates of the lives lost on the New York City prison ships, particularly the *Jersey*, range from 8,000 to 11,500 souls.

Formerly the site of American Fort Putnam and now Fort Greene Park, the Prison Ship Martyrs' Monument extends 143 feet atop the park's already considerable hill. The monument marks the burial spot of those thousands of prisoners, moved here in 1873 after first being interred at the Brooklyn Navy Yard. After a major restoration in 2008, the tall column and the copper ornamentation that tops it is striking. Near the monument is a small interpretive center that tells the stories of both the prison ships and the monument, and there is also a small redoubt here to represent Fort Putnam. *Prison Ship Martyrs' Monument, intersection of Myrtle Ave. and St. Edwards St., Brooklyn, NY 11205; 718-*

The Prison Ship Martyrs' Monument, burial site of thousands of American prisoners of war.

722-3218; www.nycgovparks.org/parks/fort-greene-park. GPS: 40.691800, -73.975539. Site accessible daily.

GOVERNORS ISLAND—American efforts to protect New York City from a British attack included the defense of the East River. General Israel Putnam recognized that mounting artillery on Governors Island, which splits the mouth of the river in two, would likely prevent any British warships from entering from the south. On April 8, 1776, Putnam seized the island, building earthworks and mounting cannons trained on the passage past Brooklyn. Though Governors Island did not witness any fighting, its strategic location ensured that a military presence would remain; in fact, it was the longest continually operated military post in the entire United States, serving from 1799 until the Coast Guard left in 1997.

Today Governors Island serves as a bucolic playground for New Yorkers looking to escape the city for a little while. Easily accessible by ferry from either Manhattan or Brooklyn, the island contains over 100 acres of fields and gardens for hiking, biking, public art, and all sorts of other recreational activities. The island's history is not forgotten, either; remnants of the former military activity remain, including Fort Jay and Castle William, part of Governors Island National Monument. Though both fortifications postdate the Revolution, there is plenty of interpretation at both locations. The island also has several restaurants and concessions, as well as walking tours; you can sign up for those on the website. *Governors Island, ferry access from Battery Maritime Building, 10 South Street, Manhattan (daily), Pier 6 in Brooklyn Bridge Park (weekends, Memorial Day through Labor Day), and Red Hook / Atlantic Basin, intersection of Pioneer St. and Conover St., (weekends, Memorial Day through Labor Day), New York, NY 10004; www.govisland.com. GPS: 40.701354, -74.011897. Open daily.*

FRAUNCES TAVERN—The original Fraunces Tavern dates to 1712 and has served a variety of functions over the years. It began as a private residence but was bought by Samuel Fraunces in 1762 and turned into

Today, Governors Island is an easy retreat from the hustle and bustle of New York City.

a tavern. In 1775, the tavern became the home of the New York Provincial Congress as they chose their delegates to the Second Continental Congress. In 1776, the tavern hosted George Washington, among others, before the British occupied New York City, after which it was used by British generals. The tavern's most famous moment was in 1783, when George Washington said a very emotional goodbye to the officers who had served him throughout the Revolutionary War. The tavern would go on to host offices for the United States' first government, including the Department of the Treasury and the Department of Foreign Affairs.

Fraunces Tavern today, which features both a museum and a restaurant, is operated by the Sons of Revolution in the State of New York. The museum is excellent and is a great way to learn about the American Revolution in New York City. Featuring unique historic exhibits, an outstanding art collection, and lots of activities for children, the crown jewel of the museum is the Long Room, which witnessed most of these historical gatherings, including Washington's famous address. Make the time to explore this one, then have a drink in the tavern to round out your visit. *Fraunces*

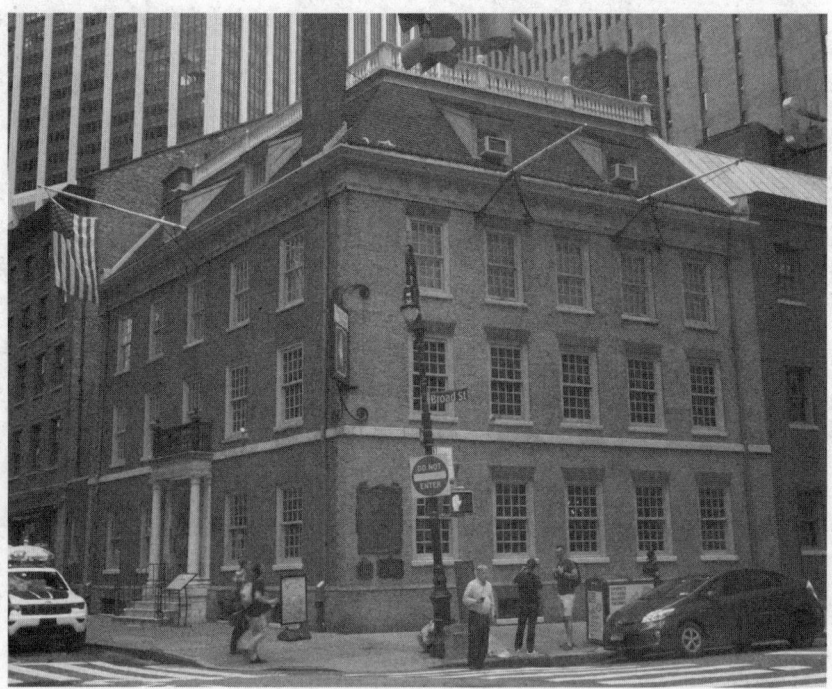

Fraunces Tavern in lower Manhattan.

Tavern Museum, 54 Pearl St., New York, NY 10004; 212-425-1778; www
.frauncestavernmuseum.org. GPS: 40.703493, -74.011364. Open daily.

BOWLING GREEN—Bowling Green is New York City's oldest public park. In 1770 a statue of King George III was raised on the spot, with iron fencing installed around the statue in 1771. On July 9, 1776, shortly after a public reading of the Declaration of Independence, the statue was torn down by enthused citizens and, among other things, melted down to make ammunition.

The fencing surrounding the statue remains here, even though it still shows the damage sustained when the statue was toppled. Today a fountain and garden sit in the park, and the northern part of the park is the site of the famous *Charging Bull* statue representing nearby Wall Street. *Bowling Green, Broadway and Whitehall St., New York, NY 10005; www .nycgovparks.org/parks/bowling-green. GPS: 40.704896, -74.013670. Park accessible daily.*

TRINITY CHURCH CEMETERY—With a congregation dating back to 1697, Trinity Church is the oldest parish in New York City. Still an active congregation, the church building has been built and rebuilt several times over the years, one of the times being after the great fire that engulfed Manhattan in 1776.

The churchyard cemetery contains several great names of the Revolution, but the one that stands above all others is undoubtedly Alexander Hamilton, buried here after being mortally wounded in his famous duel with Aaron Burr. But a stroll around the cemetery will reveal surprises such as the burial site of a second signer of the Constitution (William Livingston); a signer of the Declaration of Independence (Francis Lewis); the Hero of Saratoga (Horatio Gates); Continental Army General William Alexander, Lord Stirling; super-merchant John Jacob Astor; and steamboat pioneer Robert Fulton, among others. *Trinity Church, Broadway at Wall St., New York, NY 10004; 212-602-0800; www.trinity churchnyc.org. GPS: 40.707865, -74.011690. Open daily.*

FEDERAL HALL—Federal Hall memorializes the site where George Washington took the oath of office and became our first president, as

Federal Hall, on Wall Street in Manhattan, is where George Washington became America's first president.

well as where America's first Congress met under the new constitution. It is not the original building (the current building is a custom house from 1842), but its Federal style and dominance in the middle of Wall Street—not to mention the statue of Washington on the front steps—make it clear that something very special happened here.

Now a National Park Service site, the interior of Federal Hall has undergone a recent revamp of its excellent exhibits. Also on display are the Bible on which Washington took the oath of office and part of the original portico where he stood is on display in the rotunda. Guided tours of the site and its importance are also available. The building itself is magnificent; even if you don't have a lot of time, it's worth popping in for a visit. *Federal Hall National Memorial, 26 Wall St., New York, NY 10005; 212-825-6990; www.nps.gov/feha. GPS: 40.707141, -74.010467. Open Mon.–Fri.*

RIVINGTON'S PRINT SHOP—James Rivington, the enterprising man who would eventually produce America's first daily newspaper, remains something of a mystery. Rivington attempted to produce an even-sided newspaper in 1773, *Rivington's New-York Gazetteer*. This didn't sit well with many of the locals, and his print shop at the foot of Wall Street was destroyed in November 1775. Rivington fled to London, only to return after the British took control of the city to produce a starkly Loyalist paper. Despite all appearances, however, Rivington had secretly been working with the Continental Army's intelligence service, which had to protect him from vengeful Patriots reentering the city after the British evacuation.

Rivington has a street in Manhattan named after him, but there are no markers commemorating his actions or his print shop. With the changing of the Manhattan waterline, his shop would have been on Wall Street near where it meets Pearl Street. You can find more information on Rivington and his activities at Fraunces Tavern. *Rivington's Print Shop, intersection of Wall St. and Pearl St., New York, NY 10005. GPS: 40.705586, -74.007964. Accessible daily.*

AFRICAN BURIAL GROUND NATIONAL MONUMENT—Historical memory in the United States often strictly associates slavery with the Southern states, but the ugly history of our "peculiar institution" incorporates all corners of the nation. Partial emancipation began in New York State only in 1799, 23 years after the Declaration of Independence. And it was only until just before that time that African Americans—free and enslaved—were buried at their own separate graveyard in Manhattan, the 6-acre "Negroes Buriel Ground." In use from the 1630s to 1795, it is estimated that over 15,000 African men, women, and children were interred in the cemetery while it was used.

Discovered only during the construction of a new building in 1991, that graveyard, now the African Burial Ground National Monument, preserves a small portion of this ground that was once thought forever lost. Above ground is a striking memorial to those buried here and lost elsewhere as part of the American slave trade. Entering the memorial will take you below ground, where more interpretation on the burial site and slavery in New York and the colonies can be found. There aren't many quiet corners of Manhattan, but the silence at this one is deafening. *African Burial Ground National Monument, intersection of Broadway and*

Duane St., New York, NY 10007; 212-637-2019; www.nps.gov/afbg. GPS: 40.714550, -74.004348. Open Tues.–Sat.

WASHINGTON SQUARE—During the Revolution, Washington Square would have sat well north of Manhattan. Today, it's one of New York's most recognizable landmarks. A large and popular city park, Washington Square is home to a large fountain, several monuments, a couple of dog parks, and other facilities. But it is the giant Washington Square Arch, a triumphal arch that harkens back to ancient Rome, that captures the imagination. Built in 1892, the massive work is 74 feet high, 57 feet wide, and 30 feet thick. Of course, one thing separates this arch from its many predecessors: rather than celebrating military victory, this one celebrates the victory of liberty, and its inscription calls on us to strive for the highest aspirations of humanity. *Washington Square Park, intersection of 5th Ave. and Washington Square North, New York, NY 10011; www.nycgov parks.org/parks/washington-square-park. GPS: 40.730836, -73.997469. Accessible daily.*

HAMILTON GRANGE NATIONAL MEMORIAL—One of America's most controversial Founding Fathers, there is no question that he was also one of the most brilliant and most fascinating. Of course, the popularity of the smash hit play *Hamilton* has ensured that interest about the guy on the ten dollar bill is soaring and promises to for some time. Hamilton was born on the Caribbean island of Nevis but came to America at age 17 and quickly established himself in New York City. When the Revolution came around, Hamilton clawed his way up from militia member to George Washington's staff, establishing his bravery on the battlefield on the way. After the war, Hamilton became indispensable in the effort for a new constitution, followed by a stint as secretary of the treasury where he did much to build the nation's economy. Through all this, though, the first home he would ever own, Hamilton Grange, was not completed until 1802 on his large estate in northern Manhattan. Intimately involved in its creation, Hamilton would live here for only two years before being killed in his famous duel with Vice President Aaron Burr.

Moved twice but now extensively restored and on Hamilton's original estate, Hamilton Grange is open for tours. The home tells the story

Hamilton Grange, home of Alexander Hamilton, is now a National Memorial.

of Hamilton and his family and brings a remarkable insight to the man and his achievements. The beautiful grounds, part of a larger New York City park, nicely frame the large home atop its steep hill. Tours can be booked in advance; while waiting, a film and exhibits on Hamilton's life are available. There are also short periods when the home is open for self-guided tours on a first-come-first-served basis. You will want to plan ahead for Hamilton Grange; due to the small group size allowed in the home, frequently visiting school groups, and Hamilton's current popularity, like the play, this is sometimes a tough ticket to get. *Hamilton Grange National Memorial, 414 West 141st St., New York, NY 10031; 646-548-2310; www.nps.gov/hagr. GPS: 40.821328, -73.947258. Open Wed.–Sun.; call ahead to reserve tours.*

PHILIPSE MANOR HALL—Frederick Philipse I, a Dutch carpenter, traveled to New Netherland, on the US East Coast, and made a fortune in trade and in real estate, becoming the wealthiest man in the colony. In approximately 1686, Philipse built a home, the centerpiece of a much larger estate that stayed in the family through the British takeover of the colony. By the time the estate was passed to Frederick Philipse III in 1751, it had reached 52,000 acres and 32 enslaved persons. However, Frederick was a Loyalist, and after being placed under arrest by General Washington for much of 1776, he took an oath not to aid the British. He soon broke that oath, warning a British outpost before a raid, and he and his family fled for the relative safety of New York City in 1777 rather than face a death sentence for treason. The family was forced to emigrate to England in 1783 when the war ended.

Philipse Manor Hall State Historic Site preserves what's left of the original estate. The site presents the history of not only the Philipse family but also the Native Americans who first settled the land as well as the slaves who toiled here. The house contains a museum as well as a self-guided tour through the original rooms. The art collection is particularly impressive, as are the displays and exhibits about the hidden and changing architecture of the house over the years through renovation,

Philipse Manor Hall State Historic Site in Yonkers, New York.

restoration, and preservation. *Philipse Manor Hall State Historic Site, 29 Warburton Ave., Yonkers, NY 10701; 914-965-4027; www.philipsemanorhall.com. GPS: 40.935461, -73.899528. Open Wed.–Sun.*

ODELL HOUSE—Early in 1781, French forces, having moved from their base at Newport, Rhode Island, to join with the American Continental Army, made camp near the Americans north of New York. The French commander, Jean-Baptiste Donatien de Vimeur, comte de Rochambeau, took his headquarters at the home of the widow Sarah Bates during their encampment from July 6 to August 18. George Washington was a frequent visitor during this time as the two commanders planned a strategy for retaking New York City. However, when they received word that the French fleet would be sailing to Virginia, that strategy shifted south, and the two armies marched to Yorktown, where they would ultimately defeat the British and win the war.

Exciting things are happening at the former Bates home, now known as the Odell House. After years of neglect, the house is being renovated by the Friends of Odell House Rochambeau Headquarters with the goal of housing a museum. The opening of the museum is being timed for 2026. The site itself is still worth visiting, however, as there are several interpretive signs around the house that explain its significance. *Odell House Rochambeau Headquarters, 425 Ridge Rd., Hartsdale, NY 10530; www.odellrochambeau.org. GPS: 41.019320, -73.816908. Site accessible daily.*

FORT STAMFORD—In August 1781, as the Continental Army prepared to move south to Yorktown, Connecticut Governor John Trumbull erected several fortifications to guard against British excursions from New York City. One of these was Fort Stamford, a four-sided earthwork that could hold up to 700 men. Completed in December of that year, the fort never saw any action.

What remains of Fort Stamford is now part of a public park. The outline of the fort is readily visible, and there are interpretive signs around the site that tell the story of the fort. There is also a lovely public garden adjacent to the park. *Fort Stamford, 900 Westover Rd., Stamford, CT 06811. GPS: 41.085006, -73.577694. Open daily.*

DANBURY—On the evening of April 25, 1777, 2,000 British raiders under the command of General William Tryon (a former governor of New York and Virginia) landed on the beach near today's Westport and advanced toward a known rebel supply depot at Danbury. Arriving the next day, the soldiers set fire to 19 houses and 22 barns, along with numerous other supplies found there. Three of the town's citizens were killed; one citizen, though, 16-year-old Sybil Ludington, rode 30 miles to alert the Connecticut militia that the raid was underway. After their plunder was complete, the British headed back for their boats, but not before a heavy firefight at the town of Ridgefield.

Danbury has several markers and monuments commemorating the raid, including a statue of Sybil Ludington. Two of the markers are in the town green, where the three men died in defense of the town. You can also visit the Danbury Museum and Historical Society for more information. *Historical markers—Danbury and Raid on Danbury, in Elmwood Park at intersection of Main St. and Wooster St., Danbury, CT 06810. GPS: 41.390398, -73.448122. Site accessible daily. Sybil Ludington Statue, outside of Danbury Public Library, 170 Main St., Danbury, CT 06810. GPS: 41.393106, -73.451515. Site accessible daily. Danbury Museum and Historical Society, 43 Main St., Danbury, CT 06810; 203-743-5200; www.danburymuseum.org. GPS: 41.388460, -73.446513. Open Wed.–Sun.*

RIDGEFIELD AND COMPO HILL AND KEELER TAVERN—The Connecticut militia, under the command of Generals David Wooster, Benedict Arnold, and Gold Selleck Silliman, mustered in time to harass the British raiding party that had just burned much of Danbury. On April 27, 1777, the 700 men of the militia split into two groups, with those under Wooster attacking the British column's rear guard while Arnold and Silliman blocked their path back to their landing site. Wooster hit the British first, but he was mortally wounded in the fight; Arnold and Silliman put up stiff resistance as the British made their way through the heart of Ridgefield, but were eventually forced to fall back to superior numbers. On their way back to shore, the British let out their anger by firing on Keeler Tavern, a local gathering site known to be owned by a Patriot. The next day, Arnold posted an artillery battery atop Compo Hill, near the beach where the British had landed, but the raiders were able to outmaneuver the position and return to their boats.

The best place to learn about the battle at Ridgefield is at Keeler Tavern Museum. This building survived its scrape with the British and still stands today. The museum details not only the Revolutionary War period but also all of the tavern's owners from its inception in 1713. There are also historical markers scattered throughout the town of Ridgefield that mark important sites, including the site where Wooster fell. The battle itself raged along what is now Main Street. Near Compo Hill, there is a statue of a minuteman and a plaque dedicated to those who fought there, and on the beach is another monument commemorating the action. *Keeler Tavern Museum, 152 Main St., Ridgefield, CT 06877; 203-438-5485; www.keelertavernmuseum.org. GPS: 41.273595, -73.497034. Open Thurs.–Sun., March through December. Historical marker—Place Where Wooster Fell, on North Salem Rd. at intersection with Tackora Trail, Ridgefield, CT 06877. GPS: 41.305503, -73.509035. Site accessible daily. Minuteman Statue and Historical marker, intersection of Compo Rd. South and Compo Beach Rd., Westport, CT 06880. GPS: 41.111325, -73.355245. Site accessible daily. Compo Beach Memorial, on Compo Beach just south of parking lot, Westport, CT 06880. GPS: 41.103045, -73.353375. Site accessible daily.*

CAMP READING CANTONMENT—In the winter of 1778–1779, General Israel Putnam decided to make winter camp for his division at Redding, Connecticut. This position was chosen as it could support the fortress at West Point as well as protect the supply depot at Danbury in the event of another raid. The soldiers of Putnam's division were in desperate need of clothing and other supplies, and on December 30, 1778, began to mutiny. But Putnam, always persuasive, managed to get the men back to their log huts before any harm was done. The encampment lasted until late May 1779, with all the units departing for duty in the Hudson Highlands.

The cantonment at Redding is now preserved as Putnam Memorial State Park. The park contains a 1-mile interpretive trail that you can walk or drive. Throughout the trail are monuments and interpretive signs that explain what camp life was like and help interpret the remaining features, such as the collapsed stone chimneys (firebacks) that mark where the soldiers' huts stood. The park also has a very nice museum, as well as plenty of recreational activities such as camping, fishing, and hiking. *Putnam Memorial State Park, 499 Black Rock Turnpike, Redding, CT 06896; 203-938-2357; www.putnampark.org. GPS: 41.337016, -73.378404. Open Thurs.–Mon.; visitor center open summer months through Veterans Day.*

NORTH SALEM TOWN HALL—In early 1782, after the Patriot victory at Yorktown, the French army marched back to New England. They stopped to camp for some time in North Salem, New York, and comte de Rochambeau and his officers stayed in the former Delancey house, which had been abandoned by its Tory owner. The building also served as a jail during the Revolution.

North Salem Town Hall (also known as Delancey Hall) is still used as a building for the town government. The interior of the building can't be visited, but there are a couple of interpretive signs outside the building. *North Salem Town Hall, 266 Titicus Rd., North Salem, NY 10560. GPS: 41.329008, -73.597961. Private property; interpretive signs accessible daily.*

JOSEPH PURDY HOMESTEAD—In those areas of Westchester County, north of New York City, that were not occupied by an army, it was not uncommon for local residents to fall victim to partisans operating in the area. Those partisans known as "cowboys" fell to the Tory side, stealing livestock and supplies to support the British, while "skinners" were revolutionaries. Joseph Purdy, owner of a large homestead, decided to try to put a stop to the activity, laying a trap for a local cowboy who was stealing cattle for the British army. Purdy hung the man from the large oak tree in front of his house but let him go before he was killed as a warning to other partisans in the area.

Today the Purdy house is known as Purdy's Farmer & the Fish, a fine dining establishment in what is now North Salem. The restaurant is open for lunch and dinner, but there is no interpretation at the site. The oak tree, though, still stands in front of the house. *Purdy's Farmer & the Fish, 100 Titicus Rd., North Salem, NY 10560; 914-617-8380; www.farmerandthefish.com. GPS: 41.328141, -73.655702. Open daily.*

JOHN JAY HOMESTEAD STATE HISTORIC SITE—Among our nation's Founding Fathers, few had as many highlight achievements as John Jay of New York. Among many other accomplishments, Jay served as president of the Second Continental Congress, helped to negotiate the Treaty of Paris that ended the American Revolution, coauthored the bedrock Federalist Papers with Alexander Hamilton and James Madison, and was America's first chief justice of the Supreme Court. In 1800, Jay began building Bedford House, an elaborate home on a 750-acre estate. Shortly after, however, his beloved wife Sarah died, and Jay quietly lived out the rest of his life with his children in the home.

Newly renovated, Bedford House is the centerpiece of John Jay Homestead State Historic Site. The house can be seen on a guided tour, and the outbuildings and visitor center provide many exhibits on Jay and his family, as well as his many accomplishments. The site also takes a good look at Jay's relationship with slavery; while owning slaves himself, Jay denounced the practice, and several members of his family went on to become abolitionists. The grounds themselves, which are open daily, contain several wonderful gardens and are worth the visit by themselves. *John Jay Homestead State Historic Site, 400 Jay St., Katonah, NY 10536; 914-232-5651; www.johnjayhomestead.org. GPS: 41.250549, -73.659356. Grounds open daily; house and visitor center open seasonally—check website.*

BEDFORD GREEN—Bedford, New York, between enemy lines, was often the target of partisans and other raiding parties. On July 11, 1779, British raiders came to the town hoping to capture soldiers and supplies, but after being disappointed on both counts, burned the town. In 1781, French commander comte de Rochambeau camped here on his way to rendezvous with George Washington; his soldiers mustered on the village green.

Bedford Green is a bit smaller than it was originally, but it still sits in the town center of Bedford. All the buildings surrounding it postdate the American Revolution. There is no interpretation on the green, but you may be able to gather some information about the raid at the adjacent Bedford Historical Society. *Bedford Green, intersection of Old Post Rd.*

and Pound Ridge Rd., Bedford, NY 10506; www.bedfordhistoricalsociety.org. GPS: 41.202876, -73.643393. Accessible daily.

ST. MARK'S CEMETERY—After the Battle of White Plains, the wounded of both armies were treated in whatever buildings could suit the purpose. One of these was St. George's Church and Cemetery (now known as St. Mark's) in Mount Kisco, New York, and some of the dead from that battle are buried here. Washington's army also passed through the area on their way to cross the Hudson River at Peekskill.

The former church once stood within what is now St. Mark's Cemetery. There is a memorial plaque in the cemetery that describes its history. *Historical marker—St. George's Church, intersection of East Main St. and St. Mark's Pl., Mount Kisco, NY 10549. GPS: 41.194484, -73.725475. Site accessible daily.*

CHAPPAQUA MEETING HOUSE—Chappaqua Meeting House was built in 1753 to serve the local Quaker community. In 1776, the meeting house served as a hospital after the Battle of White Plains.

The meeting house is still used today by the Society of Friends. Though it is not open for tours, there is a wooden plaque on the home noting its historic nature. *Chappaqua Meeting House, 420 Quaker Rd., Chappaqua, NY 10514. GPS: 41.173188, -73.777058. Site accessible daily.*

YOUNG'S HOUSE—The house of Joseph Young served as an outer post of the American lines north of New York City. On February 3, 2024, a British raiding party of 600 men attacked the outpost on the morning of February 3, 1780, and in a short but heavy firefight overwhelmed the small number defending the house. Over 70 Americans were taken prisoner while a small number were killed and wounded.

On the grounds is a memorial plaque that purports to mark the graves of both Continental and British soldiers killed at Young's House; it is possible that the marker may have been moved, but it still indicates the general area of the fight. The marker is in a very heavy traffic area, so if you decide to view it up close, use extra caution. *Historical marker— Young's Corners, on north side of Grasslands Rd. just west of intersec-*

tion with Sprain Brook Parkway, Mount Pleasant, NY. GPS: 41.074444, -73.802732. Site accessible daily.

VERPLANCK'S POINT AND KING'S FERRY—King's Ferry, at Verplanck's Point on the Hudson River, was a critical crossing point for both armies. The area south of the point was mostly in dispute, so American forces frequently used the crossing in their movements. General Henry Clinton landed at Verplanck's Point in 1777 in preparation for taking Forts Montgomery and Clinton to assist General John Burgoyne during his ill-fated Saratoga Campaign. American General Anthony Wayne attacked the post at Stony Point just across the river in a surprise attack. And in 1781, the American and French armies both crossed here on their way to Yorktown, Virginia, to end the war.

Cortlandt Waterfront Park at Verplanck's Point today is in the vicinity of the King's Ferry landing. The park contains wonderful views of the Hudson River and Stony Point and contains a dock and some short walking paths. There are a number of interpretive signs in the park that explain the ferry's significance in the war. *Cortlandt Waterfront Park, intersection of Broadway and Riverview Ave., Verplanck, NY 10596. GPS: 41.249102, -73.963821. Site accessible daily.*

FISHKILL SUPPLY DEPOT—In October 1776, as the British consolidated their control of New York City, General Washington worked to establish logistics around the area. A sprawling supply depot was created near the town of Fishkill, close enough to support the army but far enough north to keep it out of reach of British incursions. The Fishkill supply depot lasted the duration of the war and was one of the Continental Army's largest bases.

A few vestiges of the Fishkill Supply Depot remain in the area. One of these is the Van Wyck Homestead, which served as headquarters for the depot and was visited by Washington, Alexander Hamilton, and the Marquis de Lafayette, among others. The homestead is open for guided tours occasionally, but you can take a self-guided tour of the grounds at any time. Just down the street is a burial site with several memorials; this has been the center of a preservation fight in recent years, as the land around it is slated for development. Finally, there are historical markers at the site of an artillery battery at the depot's perimeter. Fishkill's First Dutch Reformed Church, which served as a prison, and Trinity Church, a hospital site, were also tied to the depot; both are still active congregations, so be respectful. *Van Wyck Homestead Museum, 504 US Route 9, Fishkill, NY 12524; 845-896-9560; www.fishkillhistoricalsociety .org. GPS: 41.522319, -73.889084. Grounds open daily for self-guided tours; home open for tours Sat.–Sun., June through October. Fishkill Supply Depot Burial Ground, intersection of US Route 9 and Van Wyck Lake Rd., Fishkill, NY 12524. GPS: 41.519307, -73.888306. Site accessible daily. Battery Site, on US Route 9 0.1 mile north of Carol Ln., Fishkill, NY 12524. GPS: 41.494293, -73.900339. Site accessible daily. First Dutch Reformed Church, 1153 Main St., Fishkill, NY 12524. GPS: 41.535835, -73.899634. Site accessible daily. Trinity Church, 5 Elm St., Fishkill, NY 12524. GPS: 41.535188, -73.897604. Site accessible daily.*

JOHN BRINCKERHOFF HOUSE—John Brinckerhoff was lucky enough to make the acquaintance of General George Washington when he was at the Fishkill Supply Depot, and the two struck up a friendship. Brinckerhoff hosted Washington several times on his visits to the depot.

The Brinckerhoff House is privately owned today. You may only view it from the roadside; it is on Lomala Road just south of its intersection with Broadway. There is a historical marker near the home. *John Brinckerhoff House marker, intersection of Lomala Rd. and US Route 82, Hopewell Junction, NY 12533. GPS: 41.557691, -73.850983. Marker accessible daily; house is private property.*

KINGSTON AND ABRAHAM VAN GAASBEEK/SENATE HOUSE—In 1777, with the British threatening to invade Albany and already in occupation of New York City, the newly created senate of New York convened for the first time in the town of Kingston. They used the home of Abraham Van Gaasbeek, a local merchant, and made the most of what they had in the relatively small house. The senate met here in September and October, then fled before the British raided Kingston and burned much of the town on October 16.

Senate House State Historic Site preserves the Van Gaasbeek House.

The Van Gaasbeek House hosted the New York State Senate in 1777.

Guided tours of the home tell the story of the house and the meeting of the senate, and present a nice picture of life during the period. There is also an excellent museum on site that presents artifacts and artwork, and also provides information on the burning of Kingston. If you decide to take a short walk through this lovely town, look for several buildings in the Stockade District, identified with plaques, that were only partially burned during the raid and survive to this day. *Senate House State Historic Site, 296 Fair St., Kingston, NY 12401; 845-338-2786; www.parks.ny.gov/historic-sites/senatehouse/details.aspx. GPS: 41.935143, -74.018608. Grounds open daily; house and museum open Wed.–Sun., mid-April through October.*

GOMEZ-ECKER MILL HOUSE—Founded in 1714 for trading, the Gomez House is the oldest existing Jewish home in North America. The property was sold to Wolfert Ecker just before the Revolutionary War. Ecker was a prominent Patriot and held meetings for local Whigs in the house; there is even an escape route hidden by bookshelves from the library to the woods outside.

The Gomez-Ecker Mill House is still in excellent shape today and is situated on lovely grounds. The grounds contain the home, an outbuilding thought to be slave quarters, and an adjacent dam and mill on a nearby creek. The house is occasionally open for tours and is administered by the Gomez Foundation. *Gomez-Ecker Mill House, 11 Mill House Rd., Marlboro, NY 12542; 845-236-3126; www.gomez.org. GPS: 41.586560, -73.981591. Site accessible daily; home open for tours Sat.*

WEST POINT FORTIFICATIONS—General George Washington considered West Point, with its commanding position along the Hudson River, the most strategically important location in America. Holding it would prevent the British from controlling the Hudson and thereby dividing America in two. To accomplish this, the Americans, led by Polish engineer Thaddeus Kosciuszko, built a set of strong fortifications and stretched a 65-ton chain across the river to prevent British ships from passing through. Though West Point saw no action during the war, it was at the center of its most scandalous event. Benedict Arnold was placed in command of the fortress in 1779 but had made a treasonous arrangement with the British to deliver the post to them without a fight. Luckily for the Americans, Arnold's plot was discovered just in time, preventing the fall of West Point. Today, serving as home to the United States Military Academy, West Point is the United States Army's longest continually held installation.

Because it is an active military base, visiting West Point (unless you have official business or are visiting a cadet) can be done only as part of a guided tour. These tours are outstanding, and they do discuss West Point's role in the Revolution, but they do not usually take visitors to the Revolutionary War fortifications. Private group tours of these sites can be arranged through West Point Tours. The West Point Museum, just behind the visitor center, is also worth visiting, so if you're there for the tour, set aside a little additional time. Note that tour reservations must be made online. *United States Military Academy, West Point Tours, 2107 New South Post Rd., Highland Falls, NY 10928; 845-938-2638; www.west pointtours.com. GPS: 41.372721, -73.963753. Open daily.*

FORTS CLINTON AND MONTGOMERY—Near the end of the Saratoga Campaign, British General John Burgoyne was becoming desperate for

THE NEW WINDSOR CANTONMENT

In the last winter of the war, the Continental Army chose New Windsor, near Newburgh, for their winter quarters. The position offered the ability to keep an eye on the British in New York City while still avoiding a larger engagement that could disrupt the peace talks that were ongoing in France. The army arrived at the cantonment (a camp with more permanent structures) in October 1782 and left in October 1783.

During this time, some of the army's senior officers circulated what became known as the Newburgh Addresses, which espoused a plan to threaten Congress with force over a series of pay disputes. Washington gathered the officers at the building in the cantonment known as Temple Hall to encourage them to abandon the plan. During his remarks, Washington tried to read a letter from a member of Congress, but the print was too hard to read; he took out his glasses, saying "Gentlemen, you will permit me to put on my spectacles, for I have grown not only gray, but almost blind in the service of my country." That reminder to his officers of the sacrifices he had made, as well as the love and respect they had for him, led to an emotional abandonment of the entire plot.

There are a number of historic sites across the Newburgh area that preserve parts of the cantonment, and several of them are excellent places to visit.

NEW WINDSOR CANTONMENT—The New Windsor Cantonment preserves a good portion of the Continental Army's camp. An original log soldier's hut remains, perhaps the only one of its kind. There is also a reconstruction of Temple Hall, where Washington gave his famous remarks on the Newburgh Addresses. The

continued on next page

visitor center is outstanding and gives a good picture of life in the cantonment. Adjoining the visitor center is the National Purple Heart Hall of Honor, which tells the story of the award—created as the Badge of Merit by Washington right here at New Windsor. *New Windsor Cantonment State Historic Site, 374 Temple Hill Rd., New Windsor, NY 12553; 845-562-7141; www.parks.ny.gov/historic-sites/ newwindsor/details.aspx. GPS: 41.470700, -74.060900. Closed Mon.*

HASBROUCK HOUSE—George Washington took his headquarters at the home of John and Tryntje Hasbrouck, just outside the New Windsor Cantonment. The home is now preserved as Washington's Headquarters State Historic Site. He was here from April 1782 to August 1783, his longest stay at any headquarters site. The home is open for guided tours year-round, and the museum features artifacts from Washington's time. After you have completed your tour, you can walk outside to climb the Tower of Victory, a commemorative work that provides an amazing view of the Hudson River. *Washington's Headquarters State Historic Site, 84 Liberty St., Newburgh, NY 12551; 845-562-1195; www.parks .ny.gov/historic-sites/washingtonsheadquarters/details.aspx. GPS: 41.497120, -74.009140. Open Wed.–Sun., mid-April through October; Fri.–Sat., November through mid-April.*

JOHN ELLISON HOUSE—Henry Knox, one of Washington's most reliable generals, took the John Ellison House for his headquarters several times during the Revolution. Knox commanded the Continental Army's artillery arm and was very competent, even though he had little military experience and learned much of what he knew before the war by reading the books he sold in his Boston bookstore. During the winter of 1782–1783, the home was used as headquarters for General Horatio Gates, commander of the cantonment; it was one of Gates's aides who authored the Newburgh Addresses. The home is available for tours during the summer and contains excellent interpretation of the home, the cantonment, and the addresses. *Knox's Headquarters State Historic Site, 289 Forge Hill Rd., Vails Gate, NY 12584; 845-562-7141; www.parks.ny .gov/historic-sites/knoxheadquarters/details.aspx. GPS: 41.455513, -74.048882. Open Wed.–Sun., Memorial Day through Labor Day.*

EDMONSTON HOUSE—The James Edmonston House was used as a headquarters by Continental Generals Arthur St. Clair and Horatio Gates during the winter of 1782–1783. The site was also used as a medical center and a storage facility. Also on the grounds is a preserved part of the soldiers' cantonment. The house is open for tours on Sundays during the summer. *Edmonston House, 1042 State Highway 94, Vails Gate, NY 12553; 845-926-6290. GPS: 41.453340, -74.061596. Open Sun., July through September.*

NEWBURGH DOCKS—The Newburgh docks were a critical logistical for the cantonment. In addition, the ferry ran between Newburgh and the Fishkill Supply Depot, and provided an important link between the New England and southern states. The docks are no longer present; the part of the Hudson River where they once stood has since been filled in, and the site of the docks is now approximately 100 feet in from the riverbank. The general area of the docks is part of the East End Historic District. *Newburgh docks site, 1 Washington St., Newburgh, NY 12550. GPS: 41.498026, -74.005524. Site accessible daily.*

Top: A memorial to Washington and his army at New Windsor Cantonment State Historic Site.
Bottom: The Tower of Victory at Hasbrouck House, Washington's Headquarters State Historic Site.

assistance from some other quarter. General Henry Clinton, who had few options as acting commander in New York City, moved up the Hudson River to attack Forts Clinton and Montgomery, hoping to draw strength from the American force at Saratoga and relieve Burgoyne. The two forts were separated by a creek and held a commanding position on the Hudson. On October 6, 1777, Clinton's force attacked simultaneously in two columns, with 900 men assaulting Fort Montgomery and another 1,200 moving against Fort Clinton. The Americans were outnumbered with only 600 men to face them, and though the fighting was intense, it was relatively short. More than half the American force was killed, wounded, or captured, and 67 pieces of artillery were lost. However, the effect of the battle was not what the British had hoped; the action provided no help to Burgoyne, who fought the decisive battle at Saratoga the next day. The British abandoned Forts Clinton and Montgomery less than three weeks later, destroying them both before they left.

The sites at Forts Clinton and Montgomery are preserved as part of the state park system, and because they are so close together you can

The rocky landscape at Fort Montgomery State Historic Site.

walk from one to the other via a footbridge. Fort Montgomery State Historic Site contains a good portion of the original works and outbuildings and has an excellent museum. Bear Mountain State Park has reconstructed one of the redoubts of Fort Clinton, and a historical museum is there on the site of the original fortification. Both parks are in a beautiful setting and offer sweeping views of the Hudson River. Bear Mountain State Park also has plenty of opportunities for fishing, hiking, and swimming, so if you're traveling with the family, this might be a good place to stop and enjoy what they have to offer. *Fort Montgomery State Historic Site, 690 Route 9W, Fort Montgomery, NY 10922; 845-446-2134; www.parks.ny.gov/historic-sites/fortmontgomery/details.aspx. GPS: 41.324532, -73.988701. Open Wed.–Sun. Bear Mountain State Park, entrance at Seven Lakes Drive at intersection with Route 9W, Bear Mountain, NY 10911; 845-786-2701; www.parks.ny.gov/parks/bearmountain. GPS: 41.312977, -73.989003. Open daily.*

MABIE'S TAVERN—Mabie's Tavern, operated by brothers Casparus and Yoast Mabie, was a regular meeting place for Patriots in the days leading up to the American Revolution. In 1780, British Major John Andre was caught in civilian clothes behind enemy lines and carrying papers with him that implicated American General Benedict Arnold in the betrayal that would have given West Point to the British. By the rules of war, Andre was considered a spy and sentenced to death by hanging; he was mourned on both sides as a gentleman and a fine officer. It was here at Mabie's Tavern that Andre was kept during his trial and leading up to his execution.

Mabie's Tavern today is The Old '76 House, a fine-dining establishment in Tappan, and you can visit and have a meal here to see the quarters where Andre was kept. Only a few blocks away, in the middle of a residential neighborhood, you can also view a memorial to Andre's death at the site where he was hanged and buried; his remains were sent back to England in 1821 for burial in Westminster Abbey. *The Old '76 House, 110 Main St., Tappan, NY 10983; 845-359-5476; www.76house.com. GPS: 41.021740, -73.947858. Open daily. Major John Andre Monument, on Andre Hill just south of Old Tappan Rd., Tappan, NY 10983. GPS: 41.021314, -73.954839. Site accessible daily.*

DEWINT HOUSE—The house of Johann DeWint served as General George Washington's headquarters on two memorable occasions, in 1780 and in 1783. It was here that Washington stayed during the trial of Major John Andre and where he approved his death sentence as a spy for plotting with Benedict Arnold to hand over the fort at West Point. At the end of the Revolutionary War, Washington entertained Sir Guy Carleton, the commander in chief of the British forces, as they arranged for the evacuation of New York City and subsequent occupation by the Americans.

The DeWint House is open to visitors most days and is furnished as it was when Washington took his headquarters here. There is also an excellent visitor center onsite that contains artifacts found during archaeological work on the site and contains excellent information about the Arnold plot. *DeWint House, 20 Livingston Ave., Tappan, NY 10983; 845-359-1359. GPS: 41.019043, -73.945327. Closed Mon.*

Near the DeWint House, a marker denotes the site where British Major John Andre was hanged as a spy.

RINGWOOD MANOR AND IRON WORKS—Robert Erskine was selected to lead the Ringwood Iron Works, part of the larger Longwood Iron Works, in 1771. Erskine was openly sympathetic to the American cause and was appointed geographer of the Continental Army in 1777, all the while producing iron goods to help the cause. Among his products was the 65-ton chain stretched across the Hudson River at West Point. Erskine hosted George Washington and Alexander Hamilton, among others, at his home before he died in 1780.

The version of Ringwood Manor that you see today, part of Ringwood State Park, is a later construction than the one used by Robert Erskine, but the park encompasses some of the area of the former iron furnaces. Plenty of other activities besides touring the historic home are also available, such as fishing, hiking, and boating. For a better perspective on the iron industry, you can visit Long Pond Ironworks State Park, which also operated for the Continental Army; a museum is on site, and tours of the ruins of the works are offered by the Friends of Long Pond Ironworks. *Ringwood State Park, 1304 Sloatsburg Rd., Ringwood, NJ 07456; 973-962-7031; nj.gov/dep/parksandforests/parks/ringwoodstatepark.html. GPS: 41.138854, -74.253559. Open daily. Long Wood Ironworks State Park, 1334 Greenwood Lake Turnpike, Hewitt, NJ 07421; 973-962-7031; nj.gov/dep/parksandforests/parks/longpondironworksstatepark.html. Park open daily; museum open Sat.–Sun. and by appointment.*

OLD TAPPAN—On September 28, 1778, George Baylor's 3rd Continental Light Dragoons, an American regiment, camped for the night near Old Tappan, New Jersey. Officers retired to local homes while the 104 soldiers found shelter in local barns. Tipped off by a local resident, British soldiers under the command of General Charles "No Flint" Grey surrounded the barns. Grey had earned that nickname after the Paoli Massacre, in which his soldiers removed the flint from their guns to prevent their firing, relying entirely on the bayonet. Grey's men did the same here in New Jersey, and just as at Paoli, it was widely reported that the Americans tried to surrender but were given no mercy. Sixteen Americans were killed, with another 34, including Baylor himself, captured. Baylor's Massacre, though a defeat, proved to be a rallying cry for American forces from then on.

In 1967, an archaeological dig discovered the remains of six victims of the Baylor Massacre. The soldiers were reburied with honors in a memorial park in present-day River Vale. The site contains plenty of interpretation as well as several memorials and the solemn gravesite. *Baylor Massacre Burial Site, 486 Rivervale Rd., River Vale, NJ 07675. GPS: 41.013325, -74.008637. Open daily.*

STEUBEN HOUSE—New Bridge was one of the few crossings of the Hackensack River south of the American position in New York City, so when the Americans were forced to abandon Fort Lee and head south through New Jersey, the bridge became a critical crossing. The Americans did reach the bridge first and spent four days in this area, finally driven away after a firefight around the bridge. Adjacent to the bridge was the home of Jan Zabriskie, who ran a mill on the river; Zabriskie was a Loyalist and had to evacuate to New York City after his home was confiscated by the state. The state then gave the home to American General Baron von Steuben after the war, who used the home for several years before selling it back to the Zabriskies in 1788.

The Steuben House and New Bridge are part of a larger historical park at New Bridge Landing. The home is open for tours only during special events; however, the grounds are open every day, and you can go to the Bergen County Historical Society's Website to download a self-guiding tour. The site is also in the process of raising funds for a new visitor center, so stay tuned. *Steuben House at Historic New Bridge Landing, 1209 Main St., River Edge, NJ 07661; 201-487-1739; www.bergencounty history.org/discover-hnbl. GPS: 40.913682, -74.030582. Grounds open daily; home open for tours only for special events—see website for details.*

FORT LEE—After the fall of Fort Washington on the Manhattan side, the usefulness of its corresponding fort on the New Jersey side, Fort Lee, was questionable. When the British landed just north of the fort on November 20, 1776, with the intention of taking it, the Americans hastily abandoned the post, leaving critical supplies and numerous pieces of artillery. The Americans mostly escaped, but just barely, and were sent into a monthlong retreat across New Jersey. It was an embarrassing and devastating loss for the Continental Army.

Artillery overlooking the Hudson River at Fort Lee Historic Park.

Fort Lee Historic Park preserves the site of Fort Lee. While the vast majority of the works there are reconstructed, it is enough to provide a good visual of what the fort looked like. There is also a museum on site that tells all about the situation in New York and the evacuation of Fort Lee. The park itself is large and quite lovely, and there is a lot to see, including a tremendous view of Upper Manhattan and the George Washington Bridge. *Fort Lee Historic Park, entrance at intersection of Bruce Reynolds Blvd. and Hudson Terrace, Fort Lee, NJ 07024; 201-461-1776; www.palisadesparks.org/fort-lee. GPS: 40.852553, -73.964027. Grounds open daily, museum open Wed.–Sun.*

PLAINS OF WEEHAWKEN—Alexander Hamilton, America's first secretary of the treasury, and Aaron Burr, vice president of the United States, were bitter enemies. They came into conflict numerous times over major political events, but things finally came to a head when Burr accused Hamilton of insulting him. Burr challenged Hamilton to a duel, and

Hamilton accepted. The two were rowed across the Hudson River early in the morning on July 11, 1804, to a known dueling ground at Weehawken, New Jersey. There is much about the duel that can only be speculated—even the seconds, or those assisting the duelers, had their eyes averted at the time of the shooting. But we do know that Burr mortally wounded Hamilton, shooting him in the abdomen. It remains to this day one of the most scandalous events in American history.

You can visit the site of the duel, though its exact location is not known. A public park preserves the grounds, and you will find a memorial to Hamilton here, as well as the boulder he allegedly rested his head on after being shot. Note that the park is on a narrow street that is sometimes difficult to navigate, so use caution when parking. *Weehawken Dueling Grounds, on Hamilton Ave. just south of intersection with JFK Blvd. East, Weehawken, NJ 07086. GPS: 40.770225, -74.016978. Open daily.*

The memorial to Hamilton overlooks Manhattan and the Hudson River.

PAULUS HOOK—In a surprise night attack similar to the action at Stony Point, New York, a month earlier, American Major Henry "Light-Horse Harry" Lee led 300 men on a raid at the British outpost at Paulus Hook, New Jersey, just across the Hudson River from Manhattan. At 4:00 AM on August 19, 1779, the Americans stormed the fortress, and again they met with overwhelming success, capturing 150 prisoners in only half an hour. Lee's men abandoned the fort immediately, hastening their prisoners back to their own lines.

In the middle of the Paulus Hook neighborhood of Jersey City is a stone obelisk and a historical marker memorializing the battle. The site of the fort is no longer recognizable. *Paulus Hook Memorial, intersection of Grand St. and Washington St., Jersey City, NJ 07302. GPS: 40.715247, -74.037651. Site accessible daily.*

FORT WADSWORTH—In 1779, British engineers built an artillery battery on the bluffs on the Staten Island side of the Narrows, the tight ship channel between that point and Long Island. Fortifying the Narrows guaranteed that any enemy ship trying to enter New York Harbor would face a gauntlet of fire. When the Revolutionary War ended in 1783, the Americans took over the fortifications. Over the years, the batteries were improved and expanded. The entire complex was named Fort Wadsworth during the Civil War and remained an active military installation until 1994, when it was given to the National Park Service.

Fort Wadsworth is now part of Gateway National Recreation Area. There is a walking trail that will take you around the batteries that have been built, and the views of New York Harbor are outstanding. None of the original British fortifications remain; however, the visitor center at the fort provides an excellent overview about the fort and seacoast defenses, including the colonial and Revolutionary War periods. The exhibits are interactive, including a walk-through display of the various artillery positions, and there are dioramas and models of the British fortifications. This one is a hidden gem—if you ever wanted to know about the defenses of New York Harbor, this is the place to go. *Fort Wadsworth, on New York Ave. just north of intersection with Tompkins St., Staten Island, NY 10305; 718-354-4606; www.nps.gov/gate. GPS: 40.603464, -74.058108. Grounds open daily; visitor center open Fri.–Mon.*

The visitor center at Fort Wadsworth, Gateway National Recreation Area.

CHURCH OF ST. ANDREW—When the British landed on Staten Island before their invasion of Long Island, they established a hospital and headquarters at the Church of St. Andrew near Richmondtown, an early center for Loyalist sentiment. On October 17, 1776, General Hugh Mercer led a raid on the spot, taking about 20 prisoners. Another action occurred here on August 8, 1777, when British soldiers hid inside the church and took fire from the Americans, who destroyed all the church's windows.

The Church of St. Andrew is still an active parish. The church suffered fires in 1867 and 1872, but the stone foundation and portions of the exterior walls are from the colonial period. Several memorial plaques are on the outside of the church that note its significance. *Church of St. Andrew, 40 Old Mill Rd., Staten Island, NY 10306. GPS: 40.573175, -74.147453. Site accessible daily.*

BENTLEY / CONFERENCE HOUSE—Lord Admiral Richard Howe had a dual mission when he came to America in 1776. The first was as admiral of the British fleet in North America, and the second was as a peace commissioner to the colonies in the hope of finding some common ground. After he sent word of his intentions to the Continental Congress, Congress authorized a small contingent to meet him. On September 11, 1776, Benjamin Franklin (who had been well-acquainted with Howe in London), John Adams, and Edward Rutledge met with Howe at Bentley Manor, the estate of the Billopp family in then-occupied Staten Island. The commissioners met for only a few hours, and little common ground was found; the Declaration of Independence had already been signed, and the British would not accept anything less than a formal recognition of Parliament's supremacy. The conference would be the last before the British recognized American independence in 1783.

Today the Conference House is open for weekend tours during summer hours. Located in Conference House Park on the western side of Staten Island, the home has been restored to the period of the conference and is in excellent shape. *Conference House, 7455 Hylan Blvd., Staten Island, NY 10307; 718-984-6046; www.conferencehouse.org. GPS: 40.503450, -74.252382. Open Sat.–Sun., April through October.*

SPRINGFIELD AND ELIZABETHTOWN—In 1780, the British made a last push toward the Continental Army's position in the Watchung Mountains at Morristown. On June 6, they crossed from Staten Island to Elizabethtown (now Elizabeth), and the next day met American General Lord Stirling in a series of actions throughout Elizabethtown and Springfield known as the Battle of Connecticut Farms. Much of Elizabethtown was burned as the British were forced back. On June 23, another push was made into Springfield, but again the Americans, heavily outnumbered, were able to blunt the assault. The British pulled back into Staten Island the next day.

A number of historical markers memorialize the action at Elizabethtown, Springfield, and Connecticut Farms. A minuteman statue with a historical plaque tells about the action in Elizabethtown, and one street in particular has a number of markers dedicated to the buildings the British burned. Several markers within Union and Springfield describe the locations of the action in detail, referencing modern streets and bridges. It takes some effort to picture the battle, but there's a lot here if you look

A peace conference between the Americans and British occurred at the Bentley House.

for it. *Elizabethtown Marker, in traffic square at intersection of Elizabeth Ave. and High St., Elizabeth, NJ 07201. GPS: 40.658516, -74.202612. Burning of Elizabethtown markers, on Broad St. between Elizabeth Ave. and Dickinson St., Elizabeth, NJ 07201. GPS: 40.662511, -74.215014. Historical marker— American Troops Withdraw, intersection of Elmwood Ave. and Caldwell Ave., Union, NJ 07083. GPS: 40.696346, -74.278314. Historical Plaque— Jersey Militia and Continental Army, intersection of Washington Ave. and Morris Ave., Springfield, NJ 07081. GPS: 40.707794, -74.302282. Historical marker—Battle of Springfield, intersection of Morris Ave. and Maple Ave., Springfield, NJ 07081. GPS: 40.710037, -74.306810. Minuteman Monument—Springfield, First Presbyterian Church, 37 Church Mall, Springfield, NJ 07081. GPS: 40.711107, -74.310415. All markers accessible daily.*

RALSTON GRISTMILL—While the Continental Army was encamped at Morristown in 1779–1780, the army had to procure food and supplies largely from the local inhabitants. The gristmill of Jonathan Logan (subsequently purchased by his son-in-law, John Ralston) supplied Washington's army with food during the winter encampments.

The gristmill, as well as a number of buildings in the area, are now part of the Ralston Historic District. The mill itself still stands, but it was converted into a private home in the 1940s and is private property today. Visit the website of the Mendham Township Historic Preservation Committee to find out more about the property. *Ralston gristmill, intersection of US-24 and Roxiticus Rd., Mendham Township, NJ 07945; historicmendhamtwp.com. Private property.*

MIDDLEBROOK CANTONMENT AND WALLACE HOUSE—In late May 1777, after spending most of the winter at Morristown, the Continental Army shifted its cantonment slightly east to Middlebrook in order to keep a closer eye on British movements. They remained here until British General William Howe moved on Philadelphia in July. Two years later, during the winter of 1778–1779, the army established a cantonment at Middletown, secure in the natural defenses of the Watchung Mountains. During this time, Washington established his headquarters at the home of John Wallace while the soldiers built log huts for their winter quarters.

A portion of the cantonment at Middlebrook is preserved as a public park, with several interpretive signs that tell the story of the encampment, as well as the 13-star American flag, which may have first been flown with the Continental Army at Middlebrook. In addition, Washington's headquarters, the Wallace House, is still standing and is open for tours. You can also tour the Old Dutch Parsonage while there, which was the home of the first president of Queens College, later known as Rutgers University. *Middlebrook Encampment, on Middlebrook Rd. just west of intersection with Cedar Crest Rd., Bound Brook, NJ 08805. GPS: 40.579141, -74.537307. Accessible daily. Wallace House and Old Dutch Parsonage, 71 Somerset St., Somerville, NJ 08876; www.wallacehouseassociation.org. GPS: 40.569687, -74.622564. Visit website and contact site for tours.*

PLUCKEMIN ARTILLERY CANTONMENT AND JACOBUS VANDERVEER HOUSE—While most of the Continental Army was encamped at Middlebrook in the winter of 1778–1779, the artillery arm of the army established their cantonment at nearby Pluckemin. During this time, the soldiers underwent extensive training in the use of artillery, as their commander, General Henry Knox, had proposed to Congress years before. Knox established his headquarters at the nearby home of Jacobus Vanderveer.

The Jacobus Vanderveer House is still standing and is open for tours by appointment. It is the only structure left from the cantonment. The grounds around the house are generally where the cantonment was located. *Jacobus Vanderveer House, 3055 River Rd., Bedminster, NJ 07921; 908-397-3377; jvanderveerhouse.org. GPS: 40.666816, -74.644819. Grounds accessible daily; house tours available by appointment.*

PISCATAWAY—On May 10, 1777, a small force of Americans attacked a British garrison at Piscataway. The Americans were turned back severely, with the British chasing them for several miles back to their camp.

The most likely area of the battle at Piscataway is now an industrial plant. There is no interpretation at the site, and the exact location of the fight is unknown. *Piscataway, along River Rd. south of Overbrook Rd., Piscataway, NJ 08854. No site.*

NEW BRUNSWICK—After the British ventured out from Staten Island in June 1777, General George Washington wanted to check them, stopping any possible advance toward Philadelphia. On June 22, 1777, a force of Americans under General Nathanael Greene advanced on the town of New Brunswick, a known British outpost through which the army had recently moved, with the objective of capturing the bridge over the Raritan River. The British, who were already withdrawing when the battle took place, were driven off, and the Americans captured the town and the bridge with little loss.

Although many historical markers are located throughout New Brunswick that tell about the town's time during the American Revolution, none of them discuss this battle. A marker is on the campus of Rutgers University where the British had built a redoubt during their occupation of the town. *Historical marker—On This High Ground, on walking path in front of 15 Seminary Place between East and West Wings of Academic Buildings, New Brunswick, NJ 08901. GPS: 40.501933, -74.448021. Accessible daily.*

METUCHEN MEETING HOUSE (OAK TREE) AND SAMPTOWN—Shortly after moving the Continental Army from Morristown to Middlebrook, George Washington noticed increased British activity that indicated they were first moving toward the Delaware River, then back to Staten Island. It was a ruse; British General William Howe was trying to lure the Americans out of their stronghold in the Watchung Mountains and into a general engagement. The ruse worked, as Washington sent several American units out from the mountains into the low country. On June 26, 1777, Howe turned his army around and approached the Americans from two directions, hoping to cut them off from the mountains. The plan unraveled when American pickets detected one of the British movements, resulting in the Oak Tree Engagement. Washington quickly pulled the Americans back while a few select units held the British back at Metuchen Meeting House and Samptown. The Continental Army's escape became known as the Battle of the Short Hills.

Though much of the scenery has changed, there is some great interpretation of these battles. Start at Oak Tree Pond Historic Park, where there are interpretive signs that explain how the battle started in this area, along with a map of the battle using modern roads. After that, head to the Old Colonial Cemetery of Metuchen, site of the Metuchen Meeting House, which was in the thick of the fight; there is also an interpretive sign here, and a memorial to the Americans who died in the battle. Finally, a monument to the Battle of the Short Hills is at the entrance to a golf course that has great interpretation and a map. *Oak Tree Pond Historic Park, 1165 New Dover Rd., Edison, NJ 08820. GPS: 40.575948, -74.375820. Old Colonial Cemetery of Metuchen, intersection of Main St. and Woodbridge Ave., Metuchen, NJ 08840. GPS: 40.540287, -74.360723. Monument—Battle of the Short Hills, at entrance to Ash Brook Golf Course near intersection of Raritan Rd. and Ashbrook Dr., Scotch Plains, NJ 07076. GPS: 40.611380, -74.373619. All markers accessible daily.*

RAHWAY (SPANKTOWN)—On February 23, 1777, a British foraging incursion into what is now Rahway ran into an ambush. It was a lopsided fight, with the Americans taking relatively light casualties compared to as many as 100 for the British.

The Merchants and Drovers Tavern in Rahway serves as a local history museum and has some information about the Spanktown fight, as well as other actions in the area. The battle mostly occurred along St. George's Avenue between the Rahway River and Robinson's Branch. *Merchants and Drovers Tavern, 1632 St. George's Ave., Rahway, NJ 07065. Open Tues., Thurs., and Fri., with some Saturdays and Sundays.*

BLUE MOUNTAIN VALLEY—The vessel *Blue Mountain Valley* was hired in late 1775 as a supply ship to take food and other necessities from the British Isles to the besieged British army in Boston. On her way she went off course and ended up off Sandy Hook at the southern end of New York Harbor and was looking for assistance. Patriots outside of New York had been looking for just such opportunities as this. Having discovered the wayward boat several days earlier, members of the local Committee of Safety made a plan to take her, and they did just that on January 23, 1776, capturing her without a shot. She was towed to Elizabethtown and had her valuable cargo unloaded as prize money. The British raided the dock where the empty ship was moored on March 27 and burned her.

There's nothing left of the *Blue Mountain Valley*, but you can view the waters where she was taken, about 40 miles offshore near the Sandy Hook Lighthouse. The same lighthouse is still operational and is part of the Sandy Hook Unit of Gateway National Recreation Area. Besides the lighthouse, Sandy Hook contains beautiful beaches, wildlife, and plenty of outdoor activities. *Gateway National Recreation Area—Sandy Hook, 128 South Hartshorne Dr., Highlands, NJ 07732; 718-354-4606; www.nps .gov/gate. GPS: 40.398124, -73.976372. Open daily.*

ROCKINGHAM STATE HISTORIC SITE—In 1783, while Congress was meeting in Princeton, New Jersey, George Washington took his headquarters at the mansion of John Berrien in Kingston, New Jersey. It turned out to be the last headquarters that he occupied. Washington was here when America found out that the Treaty of Paris had been signed, ending the American Revolution, and it was here that he wrote his farewell address to the Continental Army.

The mansion, later renamed Rockingham, has been moved several times but is still intact and can be visited at Rockingham State Historic Site. The home, which has been restored to the time of Washington's occupation, is open for guided tours. *Rockingham State Historic Site, 84 Laurel Ave., Kingston, NJ 08528; 609-683-7132; www.rockingham.net. GPS: 40.384147, -74.618775. Grounds open daily; see website to reserve tour times.*

BOGART'S TAVERN—As the British Parliament began to oppress American colonists, different locations often created Committees of Safety to organize resistance to those acts. Most of these types of organizations met at their local tavern. One of these committees was in Bucks County, Pennsylvania. Bogart's Tavern, which had been operating since 1763, began to house these meetings. In 1776, General Nathanael Greene made his headquarters at the tavern; it was from here that the general ordered boats for the crossing of the Delaware prior to the attack on Trenton.

Bogart's Tavern is no longer a tavern. At present the building is up for sale, and local groups are hoping for a restoration. Referring to it as the Nathanael Greene Inn, the historical markers and signs outside the building explain its significance. *Bogart's Tavern, intersection of York Rd. and Durham Rd., Buckingham, PA 18912. GPS: 40.323566, -75.060395. Private property.*

DURHAM VILLAGE MILL AND FURNACE—In 1727, Durham Furnace became one of many iron-making ventures in the area. To transport their goods down the Delaware River to Philadelphia, Robert Durham created the Durham boat, a large, flat-bottomed vessel that could carry great weight. During the Revolutionary War, the furnace made cannonballs and other iron goods for the Continental Army. When Washington crossed the Delaware with his army on Christmas in 1776, it was the Durham boat that was used to transport the troops across the icy river.

Remnants of the Durham Furnace are still present and are easy to spot. The recently spruced-up flour mill sits on the foundation of the original furnace, and an entrance to one of the former mines is still visible—now providing a habitat for several species of bats. There is also a full-scale reconstruction of a Durham boat that you can inspect up close. Several interpretive signs are present that explain everything you'll find here. *Durham Village Mill and Furnace, 955 Durham Rd., Riegelsville, PA 18077. GPS: 40.576321, -75.223961. Accessible daily.*

NEWTOWN—During the period after the Battle of Trenton, the town of Newtown, Pennsylvania served the Continental Army as both a temporary prison and a headquarters. Hessian prisoners were kept in the Presbyterian Meeting House, and George Washington used both the Keith House and the Harris House as a headquarters before and after the battle, respectively. The Justice House was the headquarters for General Lord Stirling, who was responsible for watching the river crossings at Trenton for signs of a British advance. The Brick Hotel housed officers and men before and after the Battle of Trenton and the Battle of Princeton, and later saw negotiations between the British and Americans for prisoner exchange. The hotel also saw a Loyalist uprising during the British occupation of Philadelphia in 1777.

The Newtown Historic Association has placed interpretive signs in front of many of the town's historic buildings and has organized several self-guided walking tours, including one focused on Revolutionary War sites; you can download the tour at their website. The Harris House no longer stands, and the Keith House and Justice House are private residences, but you can still stay at the Brick Hotel and can view several of the other buildings. A good place to start is the Presbyterian Meeting House, which is no longer used for worship but still belongs to the parish. *New-*

The peaceful Durham Village in Riegelsville, Pennsylvania.

town Revolutionary Walking Tour, download at www.newtownhistoric.org. Presbyterian Meeting House, 76 North Sycamore St., Newtown, PA 18940. GPS: 40.232071, -74.938108. Brick Hotel, 1 Washington Ave., Newtown, PA 18940. GPS: 40.229413, -74.936525. Interpretive signs accessible daily.

WYOMING VALLEY—British Loyalists, alongside their Native American allies, conducted several raids into the frontier areas of New York and Pennsylvania in 1778. John Butler and a force of over 500 entered Pennsylvania's Wyoming Valley in July, sending the inhabitants into fortifications built around the settlements. On July 3, after refusing to surrender, the local militia marched out of Forty Fort and faced the British force, but outflanked and outnumbered, the Americans were quickly routed. After the battle, there were numerous reports of atrocities, leading to the battle being known as the Wyoming Massacre. One such legend concerns the Seneca leader Esther "Queen Esther" Montour, who reportedly killed 13 men on one large rock.

A number of monuments and historic markers tell the story of the battle at Wyoming, but the best place to start is the Luzerne County Historical Society Museum, where there are a number of exhibits about the fight and plenty of artifacts. The Wyoming Monument, a large obelisk built over a mass grave of those killed in the battle, lists both those killed and the survivors. Two historic plaques are in the town of Exeter that describe the location of the battlefield, and another that preserves Queen Esther's Rock. Finally, the locations of the fortifications around the settlement—Pittston Fort, Jenkins' Fort, Forty Fort, and Wilkes-Barre Fort—all have some historical interpretation. *Luzerne County Historical Society Museum, 69 Rear South Franklin St., Wilkes-Barre, PA 18701; 570-823-6244; luzernehistory.org. GPS: 41.245980, -75.885016. Open Sat. and by appointment. Wyoming Monument, intersection of Wyoming Ave. and Susquehanna Ave., Wyoming, PA 18644. GPS: 41.305689, -75.844812. Historical Plaque—Battle of Wyoming, intersection of Wyoming Ave. and Valley St., Exeter, PA 18643. GPS: 41.321135, -75.817845. Historical Plaque—Battlefield of Wyoming, intersection of Wyoming Ave. and 4th St., Wyoming, PA 18644. GPS: 41.315161, -75.832471. Queen Esther's Rock, on Susquehanna Ave. just west of East 7th St., Wyoming, PA 18644. GPS:*

41.308174, -75.832103. Pittston Fort, intersection of North Main St. and Parsonage St., Pittston, PA 18640. GPS: 41.329510, -75.787523. Jenkins' Fort, intersection of Wyoming Ave. and Susquehanna Ave., West Pittston, PA 18643. GPS: 41.327773, -75.792930. Forty Fort, intersection of River St. and Fort St., Forty Fort, PA 18704. GPS: 41.278877, -75.872113. Wilkes-Barre Fort, in Public Square Park at intersection of North Main St. and West Market St., Wilkes-Barre, PA 18701. GPS: 41.246299, -75.881908. All sites other than museum accessible daily.

WHERE TO STAY IN THE NEW YORK METROPOLITAN AREA

The area around New York City and northern New Jersey offer numerous options for lodging, and you won't have any trouble finding a place to stay. The rich history of the area provides many opportunities for bed and breakfasts in older homes, but few of them have direct ties to the Revolutionary War.

5

Capital of America: Philadelphia

OVERVIEW

Geographically, this chapter covers less area than any other in this book. From a military standpoint, too, it really only covers one campaign over the course of less than a year, though there were certainly some major battles fought here. But from a political standpoint, the sites noted in this chapter are critically important to understanding how the United States of America was formed. It was here in Philadelphia that the 13 British colonies came together and declared their independence, creating a new nation unlike any other in the history of the world.

Philadelphia was the second largest city in the entire British Empire, trailing only London. It was the center of manufacturing in America. It was a thoroughly modern city, more advanced in many respects than even the largest cities in Europe. So once it was decided that the American colonies would need to unite to address the seemingly unjust acts issued by Parliament, Philadelphia was the natural place for them to meet, hosting the First Continental Congress in 1774 and the Second Continental Congress from 1775 through the end of the Revolutionary War.

As the center of government for the rebellious colonies, Philadelphia also became a military target. In 1777, the British commander of

Opposite: The mass grave at the Paoli battlefield.

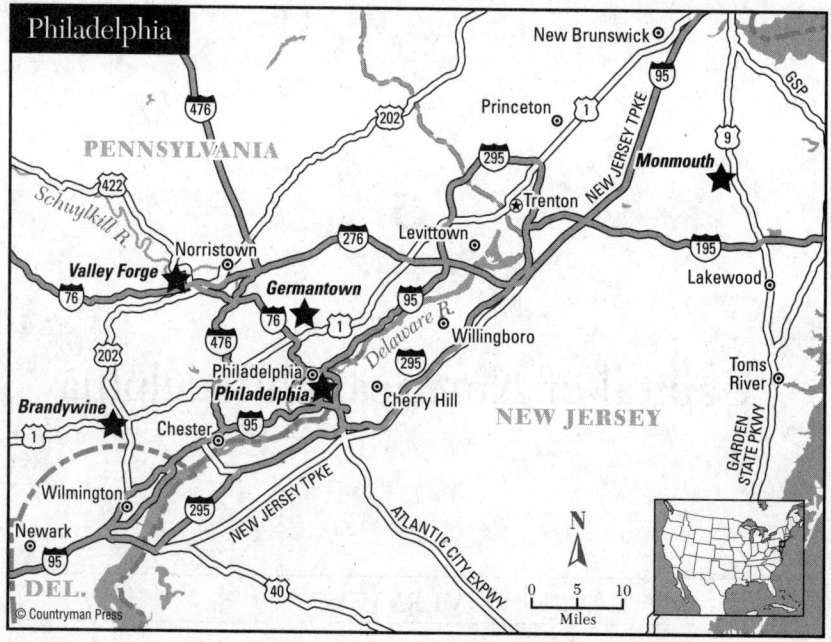

all armed forces in America, General William Howe, loaded most of his army at New York on boats and shipped them up the Delaware Bay, intent on capturing the city. Moving from the south, Howe's forces won a significant victory at the Battle of Brandywine on September 11, 1777, driving the Americans from the field and delivering another devastating blow. Following the battle, the British outmaneuvered the Continental Army and took possession of Philadelphia on September 26, 1777, putting Congress to flight.

The Americans did not go quietly. American General George Washington, hoping to spring one more surprise before winter put an end to the fighting, learned that the British encampment at Germantown was lightly guarded. The Americans launched a major surprise attack on October 4, 1777, and initially gained a good deal of ground, sending the British troops running. But errors in generalship and a complicated battle plan slowed and then stopped the Americans' progress, and the British came roaring back, taking advantage of American confusion and sending them fleeing to the north.

Though Howe had achieved his objective, the capture and possession of Philadelphia was, in the end, more trouble than it was worth. Congress simply reconvened in York, Pennsylvania, and essentially operated just as they had before. During the British occupation, much of the city fell quiet; many homes were simply abandoned, hundreds of shops had been closed, and most men of military age were already gone. The British also faced supply problems, particularly until the fall of American Forts Mifflin and Mercer on the Delaware River, which then allowed British ships to reach the city. The British army nonetheless still had to forage the countryside for food and other goods. In traditional European warfare, the capture of a capital meant a major victory and often the end of a war; here in America, it achieved very little. By the time Howe resigned his command over that winter, the British realized their mistake and evacuated Philadelphia, giving it back to the Americans.

There was another major development over the winter of 1777–1778. Washington had selected good ground northwest of Philadelphia at Valley Forge for his winter encampment. During their time here, the soldiers went through tremendous hardships, lacking even the simplest supplies such as food and clothing, and suffering terrible illness. But not only did the Continental Army survive these trying times, they came out the other side a harder, more capable force. The army took the opportunity to give the soldiers something that had been lacking since the beginning: training and discipline, instilled through repeated drilling. The winter at Valley Forge has become a symbol of the American spirit and marked a major turning point of the American Revolution.

The Americans would soon get the chance to show their stuff. When the British evacuated Philadelphia on June 18, 1778, Washington sent his army in pursuit, catching up with them at a small farming town called Monmouth Court House. The battle here was one of the longest and fiercest of the war, and though it ended in a tactical draw, the Americans demonstrated that the training they underwent at Valley Forge had paid off, as they had withstood repeated British assaults without breaking, as they had in the past. The war would soon shift to the southern colonies, and the new Continental Army was up to the task.

This chapter will take you through the incredible history in and around Philadelphia, including our nation's founding and early years, as well as the critical Philadelphia Campaign.

PEOPLE TO KNOW

BENJAMIN FRANKLIN—Few people have ever achieved even a portion of what Benjamin Franklin did during his lifetime, and few were as celebrated. Sometimes referred to as the First American, Franklin was a scientist, inventor, scholar, author, and statesman even before the American Revolution came about. But it was his achievements during this period that cemented his place in history.

Franklin was born in Boston in 1706. Making his way to Philadelphia at the age of 17 with barely a penny to his name, within six years he had become part owner of a newspaper. Only two years later, he began editing the famous *Poor Richard's Almanack*, which he continued to do for 25 years. Among other achievements, Franklin subsequently founded the American Philosophical Society, the Philadelphia Free Library, the University of Pennsylvania, and the city's first hospital and fire company. At the same time, he was conducting scientific experiments, including his famous work with electricity, and inventing items such as the Franklin stove, bifocals, and musical instruments. During all of this, Franklin served in various government positions, and was the American agent for not only the colony of Pennsylvania but also for Georgia and Massachusetts as well. Traveling to London for these positions, Franklin returned to America in May 1775, just after hostilities had broken out in Massachusetts. He was immediately chosen as a delegate to the Continental Congress and made his mark, moderating debates and serving on the committee for the Declaration of Independence. Franklin was chosen in late 1776 to be one of three commissioners to France to negotiate an alliance; already famous, he was received with celebrations and honors. Franklin's work in France was instrumental in forging a treaty with America's most important ally, and he remained in France until 1785, helping to negotiate the Treaty of Paris that ended the Revolutionary War. Shortly after his return, Franklin served at the Constitutional Convention in 1787, proving a moderating voice to the intense debates. Franklin died in Philadelphia in 1790.

THOMAS JEFFERSON—For several reasons, Thomas Jefferson remains one of the most controversial figures among our Founding Fathers. His towering role in the American Revolution, however, is indisputable.

Thomas Jefferson was born in 1743 into a prominent Virginia family. He was given a classical education and became a lawyer under the tutelage of George Wythe. Elected to the House of Burgesses in 1769, Jefferson served tirelessly until he was appointed to the Second Continental Congress in 1775. Though he was not known as a speaker, it was obvious that he had a talent for writing, and this reputation led to his selection to write the Declaration of Independence. In June 1779 he became governor of Virginia but did not perform his duties well, losing the confidence of the populace. He essentially retired until the death of his wife in 1782, after which time he was reelected to Congress, and then went to Paris to become minister to France. During all this time, Jefferson continued to pursue scientific study, particularly in agriculture and natural sciences, for which he became internationally famous. After the United States Constitution was ratified, Jefferson became the country's first secretary of state under Washington, then vice president under John Adams before defeating him in the contentious election of 1800. Jefferson served two terms as president, during which time he authorized the game-changing Louisiana Purchase and arranged the Lewis and Clark expedition. After his presidency, he retired into private life, carrying on a famous correspondence with fellow revolutionary John Adams and dying just hours before him on July 4, 1826, the 50th anniversary of the Declaration of Independence. In recent years, Jefferson's reputation as a man who took a slave as his companion has brought much into question about his character and achievements, helping to spur a national conversation on how we view the heroes of early America. But in his time, it cannot be denied that Thomas Jefferson was a giant among men.

MARQUIS DE LAFAYETTE—Much beloved in America, the Marquis de Lafayette's heroism and enthusiasm made him an emblem for the cause of liberty throughout the world. More than anyone else, Lafayette symbolizes the large part that foreign assistance played in the American Revolution.

Lafayette was born into a military family in 1757, but was orphaned at an early age. He joined the army at age 13, and although he married into a very prominent family at 16, he was soon looking for adventure.

The American fight for independence caught his fancy, and with the promise of a generalship from American commissioner Silas Deane, he set sail for America at age 19. Lafayette was only one among a number of foreign officers seeking glory and a command in America, but his offer to forego a salary and serve as a volunteer made him stand out from the crowd, and he was commissioned a general on July 31, 1777. He immediately made an impression on George Washington, who would come to see Lafayette as the son he never had. Lafayette performed well at Brandywine and was wounded, then served with distinction in the Monmouth Campaign. He was also a critical go-between when the French arrived, helping to smooth misunderstandings and arrange cooperation. Lafayette served in Virginia in a prelude to the surrender and was present at Yorktown with his command. Lafayette's adventures didn't stop there; he assisted Thomas Jefferson in his overseas duties as minister to France, commanded the French national guard, and saved the king's family during the French Revolution, which forced him to flee in 1792. He was subsequently imprisoned for the next five years by the Prussians until being freed by Napoleon. In 1824–1825, after years of retirement, Lafayette was invited by President James Monroe, another of Washington's officers, to revisit the United States, and his celebrated tour of the country during those years was met everywhere by enthusiastic crowds. Lafayette returned to France and died there in 1834.

THINGS TO KNOW

Many of the sites in this chapter are well preserved as parts of parks, while absolutely nothing remains of others. But the resources available to you for your travels in this region are plentiful, and you can find information on even the smallest sites and battlefields. The staff at Independence National Historical Park and Valley Forge National Historical Park know the events described in this chapter inside and out, especially as these sites are all relatively close to each other in terms of location and when the historic events took place in them. If you have any questions at all, they will be glad to help you out.

THE TRIP

The major sites for this trip are all within a short drive of Philadelphia. If you choose to see some of the smaller sites, you will venture a little farther into Maryland and New Jersey, but not much. Lodging and restaurants are plentiful in Philadelphia, so your best bet is probably to set up there and use it as a base for all of your exploring. If you go during the summer, though, be sure to plan ahead and make hotel reservations; Philly sees a lot of tourist traffic, and rooms can be snatched up quickly.

If you do venture south, Baltimore and Wilmington are other options that are very close by. Some of the farther drives may take you into western Pennsylvania, as well; Lancaster and York are great places to visit and will be your best stops.

THE CAN'T-MISS SITES

Philadelphia

No city looms larger in America's early history than Philadelphia. Both the birthplace of the American experiment and America's de facto capital during the Revolution, the city played an outsized part in the formation of the new nation. Philadelphia is where Americans from all the colonies came together as one to boldly separate from the crown and strike a new course that would set the rest of the world on fire.

As a result of what many colonists considered an assault on their freedom, America's Founding Fathers first gathered at Carpenter's Hall in Philadelphia in September and October 1774, convening what would be known as the First Continental Congress. The body, which contained delegates from every colony except for Georgia, decided that they would unite in their boycotts of British goods as well as compose a list of grievances to King George III. Agreeing to reconvene the following year, the congress held out hope that the ties of America and Great Britain, though strained, would be maintained.

However, before they could meet again, war broke out at Lexington and Concord outside of Boston on April 19, 1775. Meeting on May 10, 1775 at the Pennsylvania State House (now known as Indepen-

The iconic Independence Hall in Philadelphia.

dence Hall), the Second Continental Congress would remain in session through the end of the Revolutionary War. It was this body that served as a government for the American colonies, organizing an army, creating alliances, and uniting the people in a common cause.

The most revolutionary act of the Second Continental Congress came over a year after the conflict broke out. In June 1776, delegate Richard Henry Lee of Virginia introduced a resolution that "these united colonies are and of right ought to be free and independent states." Congress formed a committee of five—John Adams, Richard Sherman, Benjamin Franklin, Robert Livingston, and Thomas Jefferson—to draft a document laying out the argument for their abandonment of the British government. The committee decided to hand the pen to Jefferson, and his Declaration of Independence became a blueprint for governments the world over. After several days of debates and revisions, the Declaration of Independence was approved early in the morning of July 4, 1776, a day Americans still celebrate with pride.

Congress continued its work in Philadelphia until September 1777. In a bold move, British General William Howe moved most of his army from New York and landed his troops in Maryland with his eyes on Philadelphia. After the Continental Army lost the Battle of Brandywine, Congress evacuated first to Lancaster, Pennsylvania, then to York. They remained there as the British occupied Philadelphia from September 26, 1777, through June 18, 1778. During their stay, the Pennsylvania State House served as a prison, among other things. Congress reoccupied the building upon their return to Philadelphia and stayed there through most of the rest of the Revolutionary War.

During Congress's time in York, the Articles of Confederation, which established the American government, was ratified. However, it was soon realized that the articles were too weak, and that a stronger, more centralized government would be needed if the states were going to stay together as a new nation. On May 25, delegates met again in Philadelphia to amend the Articles of Confederation, and it was soon determined that a complete overhaul was needed. What they came up

The Liberty Bell is enshrined just outside Independence Hall.

with was a masterwork of balancing governmental power with personal liberty. The Constitution of the United States was the world's first and is the foundation for our national government. The delegates signed the document on September 17, a date commemorated as Constitution Day.

The new government was not quite done with Philadelphia. It was resolved that the city would serve as America's first capital under its new constitution until a new capital could be decided upon. Congress sat in the west wing of the Pennsylvania State House, now known as Congress Hall, while the Supreme Court adjourned in what was then the Philadelphia City Hall. President George Washington's quarters, the first White House, was at the corner of 6th and Market Streets. It was here in Philadelphia that many of the traditions that are still held in government today were formed.

Today, Philadelphia is still one of America's largest and most vibrant cities, and there is plenty to see and do here. Many of the buildings and sites that the Founding Fathers used can still be visited, and just walking around the Old City neighborhood will reveal treasures galore.

Brandywine

In terms of casualties, the battle at Brandywine was one of the largest of the Revolutionary War. It also covered the most ground, and it was the first true set-piece battle between the Continental Army and the British. Most important, the American loss at Brandywine allowed the British to occupy Philadelphia. What Brandywine was not, however, was the decisive battle that the British had thought would end the American Revolution.

British Commander in Chief William Howe finally moved his forces out of northern New Jersey on June 8, 1777. The move was shrouded in secrecy, and General George Washington was at a loss as to where the British were going. Rumors abounded, and their possible destinations ranged from Boston to the Caribbean. A period of close observation by watchmen positioned along the Atlantic Coast saw the British approach Delaware Bay but then turn around, indicating that a move on Philadelphia was just a feint. But after almost two months—a gruelingly long time to be aboard ship, especially for such a short journey—the British reappeared in Chesapeake Bay and made their way north to the head of the Elk River in Maryland, just a short distance from Delaware and the capital at Philadelphia.

Washington, who had waited anxiously for information, finally sent his army south to Delaware in a hurry. The Americans made their camp in Wilmington and sent out small parties to watch the British and gather intelligence as Howe's force moved north. There was some skirmishing, including an action at Cooch's Bridge south of Wilmington, but the British steadily pushed their way toward Philadelphia. The Americans abandoned their encampment in Wilmington and took up a strong position across the Pennsylvania state line along Brandywine Creek. The army centered its position on Chadds Ford, directly in line of the British march, and posted detachments along other fords of the creek for several miles.

The British were able to gather intelligence on the American position easily, and Howe quickly came up with a strategy for forcing the Americans out of their position. The British army, only a few miles to the west, would indeed approach the Americans at Chadds Ford with 5,000 men

Part of the rolling battlefield at Brandywine in Pennsylvania.

SITE DETAILS

Independence National Historical Park—Much of what has come to symbolize the birth of America in Philadelphia has been preserved as part of Independence National Historical Park, including many of the listings provided here. In addition to icons such as Independence Hall and the Liberty Bell, the park lays out the foundations of what the early city looked like using existing buildings, reproductions, and preserved archaeological works. A good place to start is the visitor center, where you can find information on any of the area's many historic sites and plan your visit; park rangers are all over the neighborhood to help you as you walk from one site to another. There's a lot to see, and the park is very popular (especially in the summer), so set aside at least a couple of days if you can. *Independence National Historical Park Visitor Center, intersection of Market St. and 6th St., Philadelphia, PA 19106; 215-965-2305; www.nps.gov/inde. GPS: 39.950817, -75.150207. Open daily.*

Independence Hall—The centerpiece of Philadelphia's historical sites is Independence Hall. Built as the Pennsylvania State House in 1732, the building went on to host the Second Continental Congress, which signed the Declaration of Independence here in 1776. After the Revolutionary War, the building was the site of the Constitutional Convention, which met in 1787 to ratify the Constitution of the United States. Independence Hall also served as the country's first capitol building, with the first Supreme Court and first few congresses meeting in the building's wings. You can tour the building, but most of the year you will need a timed ticket. It is highly recommended that you obtain your ticket in advance through the Independence National Historical Park website; if you don't, you can get one at the visitor center. The tour is short, only about 20 minutes, but you will get chills up your spine as you realize the history that occurred in the room in which you're standing. *Independence Hall, on Chestnut St. between 5th St. and 6th St.; Philadelphia, PA 19106. GPS: 39.949087, -75.150025. Open daily; obtain tickets in advance through Independence National Historical Park website.*

Liberty Bell—The Liberty Bell was inscribed with the motto "Proclaim liberty throughout all the land unto all the inhabitants thereof" when it was cast in 1751. However, it didn't become an American symbol until the 1830s, shortly before it developed its famous crack. (It was abolitionists who made the bell's message an emblem of their movement, and only later did it come to encompass American freedom.) You can get up close to the Liberty Bell at the Liberty Bell Center, where you can review exhibits about the bell's history before you view it. While you're waiting in line, you can also take in the foundation of America's first White House—the ruins of George Washington's home while he served as president of the United States here in Philadelphia. The line for the Liberty Bell can get a little long, but it generally moves pretty fast, so don't let it scare you off—it's worth the wait. *Liberty Bell, entrance near 6th St. and Market St., Philadelphia, PA 19106. GPS: 39.950339, -75.150132. Open daily.*

Carpenters' Hall—Before the Second Continental Congress met in Independence Hall, the First Continental Congress gathered in Carpenters' Hall, just a short walk away. The building is open to visitors today, and you'll see artifacts, exhibits, and models relating the history of the congress and the building. It's a gorgeous building, built in 1771, and there's a lot to appreciate. *Carpenters' Hall, 320 Chestnut St., Philadelphia, PA 19106; 215-925-0167; www.carpentershall.org. GPS: 39.948283, -75.147158. Open Tues.–Fri. most of year; closed Tues. in January and February.*

Franklin Court—Franklin Court, which once housed Benjamin Franklin's home, is now the home of the Benjamin Franklin Museum. The museum contains fascinating exhibits about Franklin's life and legacy, and you are sure to learn something new here about the legendary American's influence on the world. Franklin's print shop is also here and can be toured. Though the home is now gone, viewing pits in the ground reveal archaeological remnants of the house, and its outline is framed in white beams so that you can visualize it. *Franklin Court, on Market St. between 3rd St. and 4th St., Philadelphia, PA 19106. GPS: 39.950186, -75.146511. Franklin Court and Museum open daily; Print Shop open Thurs.–Mon.*

Graff House—When Thomas Jefferson was tasked with writing the Declaration of Independence, he was living at the Graff House on the corner of Market Street and 7th Street. The home was later demolished, but a faithful

continued on next page

reproduction was built in 1975 for the bicentennial of the American Revolution and called Declaration House. Though the house is now closed, there is plenty of interpretation on the outside; check the Independence National Historical Park website to see if the house might be open again. *Declaration House, 700 Market St., Philadelphia, PA 19106. GPS: 39.950863, -75.152222. House closed to visitors; signs accessible daily.*

City Tavern—Built in 1773, the original City Tavern was a popular gathering place for members of both the First and Second Continental Congress and was the site of debate as well as social recreation, even the occasional ball. The tavern was torn down in the middle of the 19th century but was reconstructed in 1975 for the bicentennial. Until recently, City Tavern hosted a fine dining restaurant and served both traditional and more modern food and drink; the National Park Service is hoping to reestablish restaurant service here as soon as they can find a tenant. In the meantime, you can see the building on 2nd Street from the outside. *City Tavern, intersection of 2nd St. and Walnut St., Philadelphia, PA 19106. GPS: 39.947082, -75.144394. See Independence National Historical Park website (www.nps.gov/inde) for information.*

Museum of the American Revolution—The Museum of the American Revolution is one of Philadelphia's newer attractions as well as one of its finest. The exhibits are comprehensive, thoroughly exploring the reasons why America chose to separate from Great Britain, the Revolutionary War, and the impact the American Revolution had on the rest of the world. Each of the artifacts are presented to tell a unique story, and there are bound to be things here that you haven't seen before. The museum also covers diverse viewpoints such as soldiers of both sides, women, enslaved persons, and Native Americans. There are also plenty of interactive exhibits, including a section of the museum just for kids. If there was ever a single place to learn all about the American Revolution, this is it. *Museum of the American Revolution, 101 South 3rd St., Philadelphia, PA 19106; 877-740-1776; www.amrevmuseum.org. GPS: 39.948557, -75.145937. Open daily.*

National Constitution Center—Across the mall from Independence Hall, the National Constitution Center is a center for thought on the US Constitution. It is also a great museum, focused on the origins and development of the Constitution, the Constitutional Convention of 1787, the different amendments, and how the Constitution is interpreted today. Before you view the excellent exhibits and artifacts, be sure to watch "Freedom Rising," a short live performance that neatly capsizes just what the constitution means to America. On your way out, stop by the Signers' Hall, where you can spend time with 42 life-size statues of the men who participated in the Constitutional Convention. *National Constitution Center, 525 Arch St., Philadelphia, PA 19106; 215-409-6600; constitutioncenter.org. GPS: 39.953048, -75.149097. Open Wed.–Sun.*

Betsy Ross House—Did Betsy Ross sew the first American flag? We may never know for certain, but you can explore both the real woman and the legend at the Betsy Ross House. Audio tours will guide you through the humble home, and you can view artifacts from Ross's life as you tour what may have been the birthplace of the flag. Costumed interpreters are also available to answer your questions and provide an idea of what life was like in the late 18th century. You'll also find the grave of Betsy Ross and her third husband at the site. *Betsy Ross House, 239 Arch St., Philadelphia, PA 19106; 215-629-4026; historicphiladelphia.org. GPS: 39.952139, -75.144672. Open daily, March through November, and Wed.–Mon. rest of year.*

Christ Church—Founded as a condition of William Penn's original charter for the Pennsylvania colony, Christ Church dates to 1695. The church was the center of worship for many members of the First and Second Continental Congress and was the church of choice for both President George Washington and Vice President John Adams when Philadelphia served as the nation's capital. The church building dates to 1744, and its steeple made Christ Church the tallest structure in North America for an astounding 56 years. You can view the interior of the church on a self-guided tour or, if you wish, attend a service—it's still an active parish. *Christ Church, 20 North American St., Philadelphia, PA 19106; 215-922-1695; christchurchphila.org. GPS: 39.950663, -75.143567. Open daily.*

Christ Church Burial Ground—Benjamin Franklin, one of our most revered and fascinating Founding Fathers, grew up in Boston but made his life in Philadelphia, and it is here at Christ Church Burial Ground that he is laid to rest. It's a humble grave, but easy to pick out, as people tend to leave

continued on next page

their pennies on it in tribute. Four other signers of the Declaration of Independence are here, too, as well as other leaders and victims of the yellow fever epidemic that terrorized the city shortly after the Revolutionary War. *Christ Church Burial Ground, Intersection of Arch St. and 5th St., Philadelphia, PA 19106; 215-922-1695; christchurchphila.org/burial-grounds. GPS: 39.952482, -75.147971. Open daily, March through December.*

Thaddeus Kosciuszko National Memorial—Thaddeus Kosciuszko was a Polish engineer who came to fight in the American Revolution. Kosciuszko designed the defenses of the Delaware River at Philadelphia, assisted at the Battle of Saratoga, and served under General Nathanael Greene in the southern campaigns. After the American Revolution, he went on to fight for Poland's independence; he then returned to America after being freed from a Russian prison. It is here at the home preserved by Thaddeus Kosciuszko National Memorial that Kosciuszko spent his second life in America, visiting old friends and receiving dignitaries. The home contains plenty of interpretive material about his life and his time here in Philadelphia, as well as his far-reaching efforts to free slaves and work for independence for all. The site is generally only open on weekends, so plan ahead. *Thaddeus Kosciuszko National Memorial, intersection of 3rd St. and Pine St., Philadelphia, PA 19106; 215-965-2305; www.nps.gov/thko. GPS: 39.943367, -75.147316. Open Sat.–Sun.*

Tomb of the Unknown Soldier of the Revolution and Walnut Street Prison—Washington Square in Philadelphia was used as a potter's field for decades before the

under Hessian General Wilhelm von Knyphausen. However, the bulk of the army, 8,000 soldiers under General Charles Cornwallis, would undertake an early morning march and move north, making a wide swing to the left and moving past the American right. The strategy was essentially a repeat of the Battle of Long Island, where the Continental Army would theoretically be caught in a pincer movement, stuck between two large forces attaching from different directions.

The action began early at Chadds Ford on September 11, 1777. Two

American Revolution. After the British occupied the city, however, the field came into heavy use as a burial ground for Americans who died in the terrible conditions at the Walnut Street Prison. The prison no longer stands—a historical marker is at the location—but those still buried in Washington Square are remembered by the Tomb of the Unknown Soldier of the Revolution. Dedicated in 1957, the solemn memorial holds the body of a single American buried in the square with a nearby statue of George Washington. It's a simple memorial but a memorable one. *Tomb of the Unknown Soldier of the Revolution, Washington Square, south of Walnut St. between 6th St. and 7th St., Philadelphia, PA 19106. GPS: 39.947145, -75.153028. Historical marker—Walnut Street Prison, intersection of Walnut St. and 6th St., Philadelphia, PA 19106. GPS: 39.947564, -75.151089. Sites accessible daily.*

Benjamin Franklin National Memorial—In the rotunda of the Franklin Institute, Philadelphia's premier science and industrial museum, is the Benjamin Franklin National Memorial. The impressive 20-foot marble sculpture was finished in 1938 for the institute and designated a national monument in 1972. The statue's setting, a beautiful dome reminiscent of the Roman Pantheon, is also remarkable. The memorial can be visited for free any day the institute is open, but be sure to set aside some time for the incredibly interesting and fun museum, too. *Benjamin Franklin National Memorial, 222 North 20th St., Philadelphia, PA 19103; 215-448-1200; www.nps.gov/inde. GPS: 39.958136, -75.172480. Open daily.*

American divisions under Generals Nathanael Greene and Anthony Wayne were posted east of the crossing, with smaller detachments west of the ford. The British eventually forced all the Americans to the east side of the creek, but Knyphausen played his part very well, occupying the Americans at the ford and distracting them from other parts of the battlefield. Washington thought that the entire British army was advancing here, and it would be several hours before reports of Cornwallis's march floated in to American headquarters.

Top: The outstanding Museum of the American Revolution in Philadelphia.
Bottom: The rotunda at the National Constitution Center in Philadelphia.

SITE DETAILS

Brandywine Battlefield—Brandywine Battlefield preserves many of the key areas of the battle. The battlefield is large, and the best way to experience it is through a driving tour, which you can obtain from the visitor center. The visitor center itself is worth the visit; you can view artifacts from the battle, and there is an orientation film that will help you interpret what you'll see. Other satellite portions of the park preserve key areas, including Birmingham Hill, and those areas contain plenty of interpretation to help you understand what you're looking at. Preservation efforts continue here, and you can bet that other key areas of the battlefield will be protected in the future. *Brandywine Battlefield, 1491 Baltimore Pike, Chadds Ford, PA 19317; 610-459-3342; www.brandywinebattlefield.org. GPS: 39.874706, -75.576285. Park open Tues.–Sat.; visitor center open Fri.–Sat.*

At about 2:30 PM, Cornwallis crossed the Brandywine at Jefferis Ford, far to the right of the Continental line. By this time, Washington had suspected the British movement, and he sent two divisions under Generals Adam Stephens and William Alexander, Lord Stirling, to meet them. The two units were to take a position on Birmingham Hill, over 3 miles from Chadds Ford. After confirming the British position, General John Sullivan's division was sent to join them.

For a number of reasons, including a lack of knowledge about the area and the terrain, Sullivan's division was unable to join with the other two. The Americans took an isolated position well forward and to the left of Stirling and Stephens. When Cornwallis sent his forces forward along the entire position at about 4:00 PM, the two divisions on Birmingham Hill were able to hold their ground, but Sullivan, outflanked and outnumbered, was not. Once the Americans on that side of the line fell, the other two divisions on Birmingham Hill were also outflanked. The line finally broke after an hour and a half, with the entire Continental Army forced into a general retreat.

Top: The Tomb of the Unknown Soldier of the Revolution in Washington Square, Philadelphia.
Bottom: The Benjamin Franklin National Memorial stands within the Franklin Institute in Philadelphia.

While the Continental Army raced to the nearby town of Chester, Pennsylvania, to gather and regroup, the British attempted to pursue them. However, after a long march taken under a very hot day and intense fighting, they were in no condition to move much farther, and darkness was quickly enveloping the field. The Americans formed one last position at Dilworthtown, where an ambush put a stop to the battle.

The Americans had suffered a severe defeat, losing 200 killed, 500 wounded, and 400 captured. British losses were 89 killed, 488 wounded, and 6 missing, only about half the American total. However, Howe was not able to deliver the devastating victory that he had hoped would crush the Continental Army and end the American Revolution. Washington was able to extract his forces and soon maneuvered freely in the field. While Howe was able to occupy Philadelphia on September 26, the American army had escaped again.

Germantown

Following the Battle of Brandywine, the consensus among the British was that the Continental Army was spent. It was true that General William Howe had not destroyed the American fighting force, but almost everybody thought that the Americans had taken such a severe beating that they would be inoperable for some time. Howe took advantage of the American defeats at Brandywine and Paoli by occupying Philadelphia on September 26, 1777, believing that he would be more than secure. Although there were still obstacles to overcome—Forts Mifflin and Mercer blocked British shipping on the Delaware River, and the American army still lingered off to the northwest—Howe had achieved his campaign objective by capturing the American capital.

General George Washington, on the other hand, was looking for opportunities. The American army may have been beaten, but they were far from being finished. They were still mobile, and winter was still months away. So upon gathering intelligence that the British encampment at Germantown, northwest of Philadelphia, was lightly guarded and that no entrenchments had been built, Washington decided to pounce. He would try to repeat his phenomenal success at Trenton a year before and launch a surprise attack.

Again with the utmost secrecy, Washington and his generals quickly

The Chew House was at the center of the fighting during the Battle of Germantown.

planned the assault. The entire army would be used against the British camp in Germantown. The army would march at night and spring the attack at daybreak, relying on surprise to carry the day. The Americans would move in four columns. On the far left, Maryland militia under General William Smallwood would attempt to get into the rear of the British, while on the right General John Armstrong would pin down the Hessians positioned along the Schuylkill River. The two columns in the middle would make the brunt of the assault. On the center left, General Nathanael Greene would lead the attack on the British right, with Generals John Sullivan, Thomas Conway, and Anthony Wayne focused on the British center. The plan depended on significant coordination and timing among the four separate elements, which would have no communication with each other until the battle had begun.

The attack began at 4:00 AM on October 4, 1777, in a thick fog. General Wayne's Pennsylvania veterans were the first to push forward. These men were survivors of the recent "massacre" at Paoli, and they took

SITE DETAILS

Cliveden—The Benjamin Chew mansion, Cliveden, still bears the marks of the Battle of Germantown. You can take an excellent guided tour of the mansion and the grounds and learn the story of the Chew family and the assault on the home. The mansion's carriage house also serves as a visitor center, where you will find more information on the battle. The grounds of Cliveden, too, are impressive, a green oasis in now-congested Germantown; in fact, Cliveden is now a certified arboretum and even contains at least one tree that was witness to the battle. *Cliveden, 6401 Germantown Ave., Philadelphia, PA 19144; 215-848-1777; cliveden.org. GPS: 40.048227, -75.181590. Open Thurs.–Sun.*

Battle of Germantown Monument—A large monument to the Battle of Germantown is in Vernon Park, at what would have been the farthest point reached by the Americans during the battle. The monument contains a simple inscription and a map of the battlefield. *Battle of Germantown Monument, Vernon Park, on Germantown Ave. between West Rittenhouse St. and East Chelten Ave., Philadelphia, PA 19144. GPS: 40.036308, -75.175858. Accessible daily.*

Battle of Germantown Marker: American Right—A marker denotes where Armstrong's men met the Hessians at Germantown, which was on the right of the American line. The marker is in Blue Bell Park at the head of a trail; it's easy to find but a difficult place to park, so plan on walking a little bit to reach it. *Battle of Germantown Marker—American Right, Blue Bell Park, at trailhead on Lincoln Dr. 0.2 mile east of Henry Ave., Philadelphia, PA 19144. GPS: 40.027574, -75.192742. Accessible daily.*

the opportunity to avenge themselves. The British in this sector were quickly overwhelmed, and once they realized that the Americans were taking no prisoners, they began to flee for the rear. Wayne continued to drive them, even though General Greene's force—which had been held up—was nowhere to be seen for the moment.

As the rest of the British army fled, however, one British regiment—

the 40th Regiment of Foot—instead quickly occupied a stone mansion known as Cliveden, owned by Pennsylvania Justice Benjamin Chew. The mansion was made of heavy stone, and the regiment quickly made a strong defensive position out of it. Wayne's division pushed past the mansion, but a decision had to be made about what to do with this now-isolated British unit. Most of Washington's generals and staff thought that they could be kept in the mansion, and that the attack could continue; however, General Henry Knox, one of Washington's most trusted generals, made a strong argument that they could not leave any British elements in their rear. The fateful decision was made, therefore, to assault Cliveden and drive the British out.

The Americans made repeated assaults with infantry and even artillery against the building's massive stone facade, and they suffered extremely high casualties in their attempts to storm Cliveden, knock it down, and even set it on fire. All was to no avail. Although the British regiment also suffered a number of casualties, they were willing to hold out rather than surrender to the Americans, and kept on defending their nearly impenetrable fortress.

When General Greene's force finally arrived on the field, they stopped near Cliveden. Wayne's men were already far ahead but realized that they needed to coordinate with the rest of the army, and so they turned around and marched back toward the sound of the guns at Cliveden. Tragically, Greene's men mistook them for British soldiers in the fog and fired on them, causing devastating losses. The obvious confusion in the American lines as well as the delay at Cliveden provided the British enough time to regroup and counterattack, driving the Americans back the way they came. The Americans spent the rest of the day in retreat until the British stopped pursuing them late in the day.

The Americans had suffered a serious defeat, with 152 killed, 521 wounded, and 400 captured compared to the British losses of 71 killed and 450 wounded and 14 captured. Washington's battle plan was far too complicated to keep the separate elements of the army working as one. However, the spirit of the American soldiers after Germantown was very different than after their defeat at Brandywine. This time, there was a sense that they had fought a good battle against the vaunted British army, and that only some bad luck had cost them a victory.

Valley Forge

On December 19, 1777, after the British army withdrew back into Philadelphia, the Continental Army marched into Valley Forge for their winter encampment. The six months they spent here were trying, to be sure, but they were also formative. It was at Valley Forge that the United States Army grew into the effective fighting force that would win the Revolutionary War.

In late 1777, Washington needed a location for the Continental Army that served several purposes. The position needed to be near enough to the British at Philadelphia to keep an eye on them, but not too close, lest it be vulnerable to a surprise attack. At the same time, the army still needed to be able to protect Congress, then meeting in York, Pennsylvania. Also needing protection were the critical and numerous iron works in the area, which were supplying the army with much-needed armaments. In addition to these needs, Washington needed sufficient space to properly train his army, which had shown a lack of discipline on and off the battlefield. Valley Forge, with plentiful water and lumber and in an easily defensible position, met each of these needs.

Once the army arrived at Valley Forge, they began to build their winter quarters. Housing 12,000 men as well as hundreds of camp followers meant the construction of thousands of small huts, each sheltering six men. Though crude, the huts, each constructed to the same specifications and containing a small hearth, provided some semblance of protection from the cold of the winter. Washington, meanwhile, established his headquarters at the home of Isaac Potts. Defensive positions, including five redoubts, were also built around the camp.

Though no battles were fought here, the Continental Army faced numerous challenges during their time at Valley Forge. One of the main problems, as it was during much of the war, was a lack of supplies. Food was scarce, and many in the surrounding countryside were hesitant to take the American scrip that was offered in exchange for foodstuffs. (In fact, some in the area chose to supply the British instead, receiving the more valuable English currency.) Clothing and shoes were also badly needed by the soldiers. To make things worse, the wet, muddy winter conditions made it more difficult to transport supplies to the soldiery.

Finally, sickness decimated the army, with 2,000 soldiers dying over the course of the winter.

Washington did what he could to address the army's needs, but he knew that he needed the support of Congress to make a real impact. Pleading for action and imploring them for assistance, Washington was finally visited by a congressional delegation, who saw firsthand the army's condition and their troubles. As a result, additional resources were promised to the army. General Nathanael Greene, at Washington's suggestion, was made quartermaster general, and Greene overhauled the entire supply chain, finding efficiencies and getting supplies to where they were needed most, increasing the morale of the troops.

Despite these improvements, the most striking change in the army was yet to come. On February 23, 1778, a Prussian, Friedrich Wilhelm, Baron von Steuben, arrived at Valley Forge to oversee the army's training. To this point, any training the soldiers received had been provided by their states, which meant that nobody was trained the same way. Baron von Steuben created a single system of drill based on his knowledge of

Reconstructed soldiers' huts at Valley Forge National Historical Park.

SITE DETAILS

Valley Forge National Historical Park—The site of the winter encampment has been preserved at Valley Forge National Historical Park. Begin your tour at the excellent visitor center, where you can watch a film about the encampment and its importance, as well as view a number of exhibits. From here, you have several options for touring the site, including a self-driving tour, renting a bicycle, or taking a guided, 90-minute trolley ride through the camp. Highlights of the park include the reconstructed soldiers' huts, the impressive memorial arch, the redoubts, and the parade ground, where you'll also find a statue of Baron von Steuben. You can also tour Washington's headquarters, for which you'll need to plan ahead, since its hours are restricted for parts of the year. The park is large, not to mention very peaceful, so be sure to set aside enough time to see everything and still enjoy the bucolic Pennsylvania countryside. *Valley Forge National Historical Park, 1400 North Outer Line Dr., King of Prussia, PA 19406; 610-783-1000; www.nps.gov/vafo. GPS: 40.100596, -75.421141. Open daily.*

European armies and began teaching the Americans. Things were difficult at first; von Steuben spoke no English, and he was often frustrated by the Americans' curious tendency to ask "why?" when given a command. But his persistence created a discipline in the Continental Army that was notably lacking prior to his instruction. Baron von Steuben created a manual for his soldiers called the Blue Book, and parts of this manual are still in use by the United States Army today.

By the time the Continental Army was ready to move again, it had been completely transformed. The discipline instilled by its drilling and the perseverance it showed in surviving through the winter had paid off. So when the British evacuated Philadelphia in June 1778 and began to march for New York City, Washington seized the opportunity for his new army to show their mettle. They would get their chance at a remote location in New Jersey known as Monmouth Court House.

Monmouth

By October 1777, British General William Howe had had enough. Even though he had led the army to great victories in America and captured New York City and Philadelphia, he still faced significant criticism both within his army and back home in Great Britain. In addition, his repeated requests for more resources had been denied. Feeling a lack of support, and perhaps not fully committed to the task, Howe decided to resign command of the armed forces in America, and in April 1778 he received word that his resignation had been accepted. His successor was one of his chief critics and a man who he had been at odds with since they came to America, General Henry Clinton.

Clinton had been left in charge of the British garrison at New York City. By the time he arrived at Philadelphia, a new strategy had been selected for the war in America. The war would shift south, where it was thought more support for the king could be found. Philadelphia, which on its face was a major coup but in reality provided very little gain, would be evacuated and left to the Americans. Clinton immediately began to make plans to leave the city and get his troops safely back to New York, marching across New Jersey rather than moving by sea as they had come.

The Americans began to hear rumors of the British departure from their encampment while at Valley Forge in May 1778 and prepared for a major movement. On June 18, 1778, the British marched out of Philadelphia, and the next day, the Continental Army left Valley Forge and headed for New Jersey. The British moved in a somewhat leisurely fashion, moving east instead of north in fear that the northern American army under Horatio Gates was pursuing them. Washington guessed this course correctly and put the Americans on a parallel track to the north, bringing them within striking distance quickly.

While the Americans harassed the British column in a series of small skirmishes, Washington intended to do more: He wanted to bring on a major engagement. He knew that the British army would be vulnerable, strung out along a line of march on a single road rather than prepared for an attack. When it became clear that the British would be marching through Monmouth, New Jersey, Washington, who had already sent a small force to harass the British, decided to strike a more significant blow.

Increasing the manpower to 5,000 troops, this unit would attack the rear guard of the British column while they were in motion. Washington initially gave command to the Marquis de Lafayette, but General Charles Lee, who had been captured by the British in 1776 but had recently been returned to the Americans in an exchange, begged for the role. Washington relented, despite Lee's clearly stated opinion that the Americans were not good enough to stand toe to toe with the British army.

The British arrived at Monmouth Court House on June 26 and halted temporarily, with most of the army taking up their march again at daybreak on June 28, 1778. The rear guard of 1,500 men was left in Monmouth, and significantly, Generals Clinton and Cornwallis remained with them. They were completely unaware that Lee's force, with the rest of the Continental Army close behind, was anywhere near. At 9:00 AM, Lee's men made their attack, with General Anthony Wayne's division making the initial assault. Unfortunately for the Americans, Lee had not planned well for the attack, though he had been cautioned by Washington to do so carefully. The Americans went ahead in a piecemeal, unco-

The visitor center at the beautifully preserved Monmouth Battlefield State Park in New Jersey.

ordinated fashion, and Lee, rather than taking command of the situation, continued to issue confusing orders. After several hours of fighting, with no leadership to guide them, the Americans began to retreat in an uncoordinated fashion. Clinton ordered Cornwallis to retrieve his own forces from the marching column and bring them to the field, with the intention of crushing this impudent American force.

As the Americans pulled back with the British on their heels, Washington arrived on the battlefield. Shocked, he immediately found Lee and demanded to know what was happening and why. Lee was taken aback and repeated his opinion that the Americans were not ready to stand up to the British in a general engagement. Washington, furious that his orders were not obeyed, sharply reprimanded Lee, then immediately set himself to the task of rallying his troops.

Creating a new defensive line, Washington gathered the fleeing Americans together and ordered his artillery up, posting them on high ground known as Combs Hill. Two lines of infantry were formed, one at a hedgerow as a delaying action and the rest of the army behind them. As the British went forward, they soon began to feel the weight of the Continental artillery and brought up their own guns. Meeting the first line, the British, suddenly encountering fierce resistance from the Americans, pushed hard against the delaying line. The fighting was fierce and often hand to hand as the two sides battled, with the British eventually collapsing this line and moving forward, only to find the entire American army waiting for them. The battle went on for hours, and the heavy bombardment, as well as the extremely hot day, took numerous casualties. Finally, the British, outnumbered and exhausted, pulled back and followed the rest of their column. The Americans, equally spent, were unable to pursue them.

It is generally agreed that the casualty numbers for both sides are probably low. Officially, the British lost 147 killed and 170 wounded, with another 60 soldiers dying of heat stroke. For the Americans, 72 were killed, 161 wounded, and 130 missing, with 37 also dying from the heat. Tactically, the battle was a draw, though the Americans held the field at the end of the day. The real victory for the Americans, however, was the discipline that they had shown on the field. With the intense training they had received while at Valley Forge showing its worth, the Americans had rallied after a disastrous opening to the fight and stood

> ## SITE DETAILS
>
> **Monmouth Battlefield State Park**—Monmouth Battlefield State Park preserves one of the most complete battlefields of the American Revolution. The land has been restored to something like its wartime appearance and is still actively farmed, just as it was in 1778. The visitor center will help orient you with exhibits and a fiber-optic map presentation, and its commanding position atop Combs Hill gives you a great view of the battlefield. You can explore the area by car or by taking one of the self-guided hiking tours found at the visitor center, and the Friends of Monmouth Battlefield offer guided tours monthly. Hiking the battlefield is especially rewarding, as the preserved landscape offers plenty of great opportunities to interact with nature. *Monmouth Battlefield State Park, 20 State Route 33, Manalapan, NJ 07726; 732-462-9616; nj.gov/dep/parksandforests/parks/monmouthbattlefieldstatepark.html. GPS: 40.256246, -74.320782. Grounds open daily; visitor center open Wed.–Sun.*

before the British army, giving as good as they were getting. It was the longest battle of the war and one of its fiercest, and the Americans had more than held their own.

Following the battle, the British reached New York City on July 5. General Charles Lee, who had disgraced himself on the field, defended his actions, and eventually demanded a court-martial to clear his name; instead, the court found him guilty as charged on all counts, and his military career was over. The change in British strategy meant that the fighting would shift south, and Monmouth would be the last major battle in the north during the Revolutionary War. The fighting was far from over.

OTHER SITES IN THE PHILADELPHIA AREA

FORT MERCER—Although the British occupied the city of Philadelphia, they did not have control of the Delaware River. The Patriots had placed obstructions in the river, the Pennsylvania Navy had several gunboats present, and the Continental Army still occupied two fortifications—Fort Mifflin, south of Philadelphia on the Pennsylvania side of the river, and Fort Mercer, just across from it on the New Jersey side. Desperately needing to break this blockade to get their ships and supplies to Philadelphia, it was decided that a Hessian attack would be made on Fort Mercer. On October 22, 1777, in what is also known as the Battle of Red Bank, Colonel Carl von Donop led the assault on the earthen fortification with 2,000 men against the Patriots' 600. The Hessians attacked in three columns but were repulsed heavily on all fronts, and Donop was mortally wounded in the action. The Americans held the fort until November 20, when it was finally abandoned.

Red Bank Battlefield Park protects what is left of Fort Mercer, with paved pathways through the old earthworks along with plenty of interpretation about the Hessian attack. Also on site is a mass grave for the Hessian attackers, as well as pieces of the chevaux defenses raised from the river. The 1748 Whitall House, witness to the battle and the home

Earthworks remain at Red Bank Battlefield Park, site of Fort Mercer.

where Donop died, is also here and serves as a museum. The park offers plenty of tours and other interpretive programs year-round. *Red Bank Battlefield Park, 100 Hessian Ave., National Park, NJ 08063; 856-853-5120; gloucestercountynj.gov/671/Red-Bank-Battlefield. GPS: 39.869149, -75.189761. Open daily.*

FORT MIFFLIN—The assault of Fort Mifflin began on September 26, 1777, the same day that the British army occupied the city. Over the following weeks, the British tried in vain to pound the fort into submission, marveling at the occupants' ability to withstand the terrible bombardment. On October 11, a British group stationed on nearby Province and Carpenter's Islands even managed to be captured by the American garrison. The constant artillery barrage did take a toll, however, and as the British batteries grew more powerful, one by one, Fort Mifflin's guns were knocked out of commission. The British prepared to assault the fort, but just before they could do it, the survivors evacuated the fort on November 15, 1777, leaving the American flag flying. The fort never surrendered.

The swampy ground outside of Fort Mifflin, south of Philadelphia.

Now in the shadow of Philadelphia International Airport, Fort Mifflin still stands sentinel along the Delaware. Though little remains of the fort's buildings, the earthworks and casemates that form the surviving fort's walls are still intact and offer a grand view of the river. The casemates contain exhibits related to the Revolution and the fort's history, including a grand scale model of the river defenses used during the British bombardment. *Fort Mifflin, 6400 Hog Island Rd., Philadelphia, PA 19153; 215-685-4167; fortmifflin.us. GPS: 39.876480, -75.212102. Open Wed.–Sun., March through mid-December; for other times of year, call for appointment.*

BENJAMIN COOPER HOUSE AND COOPER'S FERRY—Cooper's Ferry, the primary route of travel from Philadelphia across the Delaware River to New Jersey, began in operation in 1688, and the Cooper family operated the ferry continuously for many years. During the Revolution, the ferry was critically important to both sides, particularly as the armies maneuvered around Philadelphia in 1777–1778. Perhaps the most important date associated with Cooper's Ferry is June 18, 1778, when the British army began their evacuation of Philadelphia and started the long march to New York.

The Benjamin Cooper House still stands, but barely. The home survived a fire on Thanksgiving Day 2012, and though it has garnered the interest of preservationists, it is still in poor condition and cannot be visited. The site is surrounded by chain link fencing, but one can see the home well from the street. A historic marker also sits at the former ferry site. *Benjamin Cooper House, on Erie St. at intersection with Point St., Camden, NJ 08102. GPS: 39.956207, -75.124726. Currently private property. Cooper's Ferry marker, intersection of Cooper St. and Front St., Camden, NJ 08102. GPS: 39.947933, -75.126024. Accessible daily.*

HILLMAN HOSPITAL HOUSE—The Hillman Hospital House, also known as the Gabreil Daveis Tavern, was once thought to have served as a hospital after the Battle of Red Bank. While it turns out that this was probably not accurate, the house did serve as a meeting place for local Patriots.

The Hillman Hospital House is occasionally open for tours. You can contact the Gloucester Township Historic and Scenic Preservation Committee for information. *Hillman Hospital House, 500 3rd Ave., Glendora, NJ 08029; www.facebook.com/glotwphistory. GPS: 39.837625, -75.060956. Call for hours.*

INDIAN KING TAVERN AND HADDONFIELD—In January 1777, the newly organized government of New Jersey began meeting in Haddonfield at the Indian King Tavern. The legislature met here through September 1777, and during that time formed many of the laws that would shape the new state as it transitioned from being a subservient colony. As temporary capital and a crossroads, Haddonfield became an important center for the Patriot movement. In addition, Hessian troops on their way to the Battle of Red Bank in 1777 camped in the town.

The Friends of the Indian King Tavern provide excellent tours of the original tavern house. The tavern has been restored to the period of the meeting of the legislature, and you can see the rooms where they met as well as the tavern downstairs. The tour not only tells the story of the formation of New Jersey but also the importance of taverns in the lives of the townspeople at the time. Best of all, the tour is absolutely free. There are also a few other sites from the Revolutionary era within a short walk that have historic markers, including the guard house where Loyalists were kept before their trials in the tavern, Greenfield Hall (which serves as the home of the Haddonfield Historical Society), and the site of the Friends Meeting House. *Indian King Tavern, 233 Kings Highway East, Haddonfield, NJ 08033; 856-429-6792; indiankingfriends.org. GPS: 39.898932, -75.030299. Open Wed.–Sun. Guard House, 258-260 Kings Highway East, Haddonfield, NJ 08033. Private property. Greenfield Hall, 343 Kings Highway East, Haddonfield, NJ 08033. Open occasionally for tours. Friends Meeting House, 15 Haddon Ave., Haddonfield, NJ 08033. Private property.*

THOMAS SMITH HOUSE—During the British army's movement from Philadelphia to New York, General Henry Clinton used the house of Thomas Smith as his headquarters on the night of June 19, 1778. Clinton coordinated the massive march from here prior to the Battle of Monmouth.

The Thomas Smith House is still standing today but is privately owned. It is on the National Register of Historic Places. *Thomas Smith House, 1645 Hainsport-Mount Laurel Rd., Mount Laurel, NJ 08054. Private property.*

MOUNT HOLLY—After the fall of Forts Washington and Lee in late 1776, the British extended their reach into New Jersey, mostly with Hessian mercenaries. The contingent at the post in Bordentown, led by Colonel Kurt von Donop, left Bordentown to pursue reported American militia in the area. Though the militia group was much smaller than they had surmised, it was enough to provoke the Hessians into a fight at Mount Holly, New Jersey on December 23, 1776. The Americans, after being driven away from a strategic bridge, took a position at Iron Works Hill. Donop posted his men and artillery on Mount Holly, and the two sides exchanged artillery fire for the rest of the day. The next day, the Hessians planned to attack the Americans, but they had left during the night. Though the action was relatively small, the consequences were not, as Donop's Hessians were no longer in a position to support the post at Trenton, which Washington famously attacked and defeated three days later.

There is a memorial at Iron Works Hill, where the Patriots had their position, and there are plans to put interpretive signs here in the near future. There is also a historical highway marker at the scene, as well as one at Mount Holly. *Historic Marker—Battle of Iron Works Hill (at Iron Works Hill), on Pine St. just north of intersection with Shreve St., Mount Holly, NJ 08060. GPS: 39.988578, -74.784501. Historic Marker—Battle of Iron Works Hill (at Mount Holly), intersection of High St. and Evergreen St., Mount Holly, NJ 08060. GPS: 40.002598, -74.792569. Signs accessible daily.*

HANCOCK HOUSE—The winter of 1777–1778 found both armies foraging for food. In March 1778, British troops led by General Charles Mawhood went in search of forage in southern New Jersey but encountered significant resistance from the Salem County Militia. On March 21, 1778, Mawhood's men, having been given orders to "spare no one," did just that when they attacked the home of Judge William Hancock. After a short firefight, the British soldiers did their worst, forcing their way into the home and using only their bayonets as they slaughtered the

The Hancock House in New Jersey was the site of a bloody action in 1778.

men, both militia and civilians. Ten were killed, including Hancock, and five were wounded.

Hancock House State Historic Site preserves the 1734 home, which is in fine condition. The excellent tours of the house take you through the restored home, including the attic, where it is suspected that a number of the deaths occurred, and you will learn about the Hancock family over the years as well. The grounds also contain a number of memorials and interpretive signs. This is a small site and a little out of the way, but the story here is unique and well worth your time. *Hancock House State Historic Site, 3 Front St., Hancocks Bridge, NJ 08038; 856-935-4373; nj.gov/dep/parksandforests/historic/hancockhouse.html. GPS: 39.507610, -75.460105. Open Wed.–Sun.*

WILMINGTON AND BRANDYWINE VILLAGE—As it became apparent that the British army would be moving on Philadelphia via Chesapeake Bay, George Washington moved his army south to Wilmington,

Delaware to put his forces directly in their path. In late August 1777, entrenchments were dug, and the Americans established an encampment, which they occupied until they moved to Brandywine Creek on September 9. The adjacent village of Brandywine was also occupied; the village contained several mills, and Washington ordered them destroyed before the British arrived. Following the battle at Brandywine, the British occupied Wilmington, establishing a hospital there and using the town to transport prisoners to their ships. The Americans returned to Wilmington in December to keep an eye on British movements as they occupied Philadelphia.

One of the earthworks built by the Continental Army is still intact and is indicated by a historical marker. There is another historical marker in Brandywine Park that indicates the location of the encampment. The former village of Brandywine also contains a couple of historic properties, including the Joseph Tatnall house; the home was used as headquarters by General Anthony Wayne, who was tasked with building the earthworks. *Historical marker—Washington's Earthworks, on Newport Rd. 0.1 mile north of intersection with Kiamensi Rd., Wilmington, DE 19804. GPS: 39.725225, -75.628441. Historical marker—Encampment of Continental Troops 1777, intersection of Lovering Ave. and Hancock St., Wilmington, DE 19806. GPS: 39.756795, -75.555875. Joseph Tatnall House, on Business Route 13 between 18th and 19th Sts., Wilmington, DE 19802. GPS: 39.751290, -75.543108. Signs accessible daily; house is private property.*

FIRST STATE NATIONAL HISTORICAL PARK—Outside of its original Lenape population, Delaware was first settled by the Dutch, then the Swedish, and shortly afterward taken over by the English. Because of these quick but substantial changes, Delaware developed into a very diverse state in terms of its people, its religion, and its traditions. In June 1776, Delaware declared its independence from the crown—and from the state of Pennsylvania, the colony to which it technically belonged. After the American Revolution, in 1787, Delaware was the first to ratify the new constitution, becoming America's first state.

All this history and more is celebrated at First State National Historical Park in Delaware. The park has six units scattered throughout the state, each of them telling a different story of Delaware's past. The New

Castle Court House Museum, dating back to 1732, is where the assembly took their vote for independence. Many other interesting events took place here over the years, too. You can tour the courthouse and see where the assembly met, and the tour of New Castle around the green is very enlightening. The John Dickinson Plantation is also worth visiting; Dickinson wrote the influential "Letters from a Pennsylvania Farmer" in response to the Townshend Acts that imposed taxes on the colonies, and though he could not bring himself to sign the Declaration of Independence, he did sign the US Constitution 11 years later. The plantation describes Dickinson's life here as well as the lives of the enslaved people who worked here. The park's other units are interesting as well, so try to see them all if you can. *First State National Historical Park—New Castle Court House Museum, 211 Delaware St., New Castle, DE 19720; 302-323-4453; www.nps.gov/frst. GPS: 39.659736, -75.563766. Open Wed.–Mon. First State National Historical Park—John Dickinson Plantation, 340 Kits Hummock Rd., Dover, DE 19901; 302-739-3277; www.nps.gov/frst.*

A statue of William Penn at the New Castle, Delaware unit of First State National Historical Park.

GPS: 39.104482, -75.449692. Grounds open Tues.–Sat.; tours of mansion Thurs.–Sat.

HALE-BYRNES HOUSE—As the British approached Philadelphia, the Continental Army watched and tracked their movements. On September 6, 1777, Washington held a council of war at the Hale-Byrnes House. Many of Washington's lieutenants and aides, including the Marquis de Lafayette, Anthony Wayne, Nathanael Greene, and John Sullivan were present as the Americans came up with a defensive strategy.

The Hale-Byrnes House is in great shape, and you can visit it, though it is not open very often. Check the website for times, as special events at the house are frequent. *Hale-Byrnes House, 606 Stanton-Christiana Rd., Newark, DE 19713; 302-543-5723; halebyrnes.org. GPS: 39.701275, -75.650677. Open first Wed. of each month and for special events.*

CHRISTIANA—When the British landed in Maryland, Washington tried to keep close to them in order to anticipate their movements. Christiana, Delaware was home to a major intersection, so for some time the town was his headquarters and a critical supply base for the Continental Army.

Several of the original buildings of old Christiana are still standing, but all are privately owned and not open for visitation. All are within a short walk of each other, so by finding a convenient parking spot you can walk past the homes. However, there is no interpretation at the site. *Christiana Buildings, 2 Old King's Highway, 1 South Old Baltimore Pike, 29 South Old Baltimore Pike, 1 East Main St., Christiana, DE 19711. Private property.*

COOCH'S BRIDGE—American infantry who had been harassing the invading British army set up an ambush for them on September 3, 1777, along the Old Cooch's Bridge Road in Delaware. A running fight erupted, with the Americans being pushed slowly back for a half mile until they got to Cooch's Bridge, where they briefly held before withdrawing. Each side suffered approximately 30 to 40 casualties. The British encamped on the ground for five days, then marched toward Newark.

Portions of the Cooch's Bridge Battlefield have been preserved, and there is a good interpretation station that will help you get your bearings. Once you've done that, you can either walk or drive to several memorials

Interpretive markers at the Cooch's Bridge Battlefield in Delaware.

and historic markers that point out the key areas of the fight. (Be careful if you walk; traffic moves swiftly through the area.) *Cooch's Bridge Battlefield, just south of intersection of South Old Baltimore Pike and Dayett Mill Rd., Newark, DE 19702; friendsofcoochsbridge.org. GPS: 39.641122, -75.732308. Battle of Cooch's Bridge Memorial, intersection of South Old Baltimore Pike and Old Cooch's Bridge Rd., Newark, DE 19702. GPS: 39.639875, -75.736716. Sites accessible daily.*

PRINCIPIO FURNACE—The Principio Iron Works, established in 1720, built the first blast furnace and refinery in Maryland. One of the first in the country, it also became one of the largest. The company was founded in London, so when the American Revolution broke out, they no longer had control of the facilities. However, the furnace was used to make iron and cannon balls for the Continental Army. The furnace went on to make cannons for the American military through the War of 1812, when it was burned by the British; the furnace operated sporadically after that until World War I.

The Principio Furnace Foundation has preserved much of the site of the original iron works, but as of now it is still off limits to visitors. Some elements of the works are still left standing, and hopefully these will someday be made available to the public. Private tours of the grounds are available; you can also view the office building (circa 1820) as well as a historic marker and an interpretive sign. *Principio Iron Works, on Philadelphia Rd. 0.1 mile east of Jackson Station Rd., Perryville, MD 21903; 410-642-9213. GPS: 39.577136, -76.033368. Signs accessible daily; grounds are private property.*

JERUSALEM MILL—Jerusalem Mill was founded in 1772 as Lee's Merchant Mill and supplied flour and became part of a larger Quaker village along the banks of Little Gunpowder Creek. The village contained a cooperage, which was also referred to on occasion as the gun shop, since it may have produced weapons for the war effort.

Historic Jerusalem Mill Village is now part of Gunpowder Falls State Park and serves as its visitor center. The mill is still intact, as are a number of other historic buildings on the property. The village is a living history center when it is open, with interpretation of life in the village from its founding through the 1950s; the site even operates a blacksmith school. If you can't visit when it's open, you can still tour the grounds and take a walk through this very peaceful site. *Historic Jerusalem Mill Village, 2813 Jerusalem Rd., Kingsville, MD 21087; 410-877-3560; jerusalemmill.org. GPS: 39.462313, -76.390941. Grounds open daily; visitor center open Sat.–Sun. and most weekdays.*

NORTHAMPTON IRON WORKS—Colonel Charles Ridgely, who purchased the Northampton tract in Maryland in 1745, began an iron operation on the land with his sons in 1761. The works were fully integrated, including the mining of ore and limestone, making of charcoal for the blast furnace, and the casting of pig iron. The family's furnaces produced cannons and cannonballs for the Continental Army during the Revolutionary War, which brought the family great wealth and led to the estate's expansion. After the war, the Ridgelys built Hampton mansion, a huge house that may have been the largest in the new United States.

The furnaces stopped producing iron in 1829, when the plantation transitioned primarily to farming.

The grounds of the ironworks are now public land, though much of it is beneath the waters of Loch Raven Reservoir. You can hike through the area, and a historic marker is near one of the trailheads. To learn about the Ridgely family and their empire, you can visit the exceptional Hampton National Historical Site. The Hampton mansion has been restored and can be viewed as a guided tour, and you can also visit an extensive array of outbuildings, the farm, and the family's beautiful garden. The site focuses on interpreting not only the Ridgelys but also all of the people who worked for them, from the enslaved to indentured servants, so you will get a complete picture of what life was like on the plantation. *Hampton National Historic Site, 535 Hampton Ln., Towson, MD 21286; 410-962-4290; www.nps.gov/hamp. GPS: 39.416138, -76.590005. Grounds open daily; visitor center open Thurs.–Sun. Historical marker—*

The mansion at Northampton, centerpiece of Hampton National Historic Site.

Northampton Furnace, intersection of Dulaney Valley Rd. and Chapelwood Ln., Timonium, MD 21093. GPS: 39.441220, -76.596829. Accessible daily.

POOLES ISLAND—In the middle of the upper Chesapeake Bay, Pooles Island is an isolated spot that was used over the years as a plantation. During the American Revolution, owner John Bordley operated a gunpowder factory and raised cattle, with both going to support the needs of the Continental Army.

Pooles Island can and should be viewed only from a safe distance. The island was used for many years as a bombing range and unexploded ordnance litters the island. Several good vantage points of the island can be found, with perhaps the most convenient being Miami Beach Park in Middle River. This could also be your excuse to get close to Chesapeake Bay to grab some beach time and excellent seafood at one of the many local spots. *Poole's Island, view from Miami Beach Park, 4001 Bay Dr., Middle River, MD, 21220. GPS: 39.307057, -76.369814. Open daily.*

FELLS POINT SHIPYARDS—Founded in 1726 and then annexed into Baltimore shortly before the American Revolution, Fells Point once served as a mighty shipbuilding center for the colonies, with 12 shipyards to its name. During the American Revolution, Fells Point came to specialize in lightning-fast boats that could serve as blockade runners. It also served as a center for privateering and was an essential port for the Patriot cause.

Fells Point is a great place to spend a day or two. There is an excellent online walking tour, available through Fells Point Main Street, that will let your phone be your guide using QR codes on posted interpretive signs. Be sure to wander a bit, too, as there are a lot of fun things to see and do here. *Fell's Point , intersection of South Ann St. and Thames St., Baltimore, MD 21231; fellspointmainstreet.org. GPS: 39.281958, -76.5911888. Accessible daily.*

BALTIMORE AMERICAN NEWSPAPER OFFICE—The *Maryland Journal, and Baltimore Advertiser*, a predecessor of the *Baltimore American* newspaper, began publication in 1773. Its views were entirely pro-American, reflecting the views of its editor, Mary Katherine Goddard. When the Continental Congress relocated to Baltimore in 1776, she became its official printer, and on January 18, 1777, made history when she produced the first printings of the Declaration of Independence, with the names of those who had signed the document included.

The spirit of the intrepid *Baltimore American* lives on, though the newspaper and its colonial-era building are gone. Now housing offices and a 7-Eleven, the newspaper's final headquarters building was built on the site of the original, and it still proudly bears the standard of the *Baltimore American* and showcases its founding in 1773. Though no interpretation is here regarding the printing of the Declaration of Independence, it's still a grand old building. *Baltimore American Newspaper Office, 231 East Baltimore St., Baltimore, MD 21202. GPS: 39.289655, -76.611184. Accessible daily.*

BALTIMORE WASHINGTON MONUMENT—In 1815, the cornerstone for America's first monument to George Washington was laid in Baltimore. Designed by Robert Mills, the monument is a tall column, 178 feet high, with a grand statue of Washington at the top. The column contains a staircase allowing visitors to climb to the top to get a view of Mount Vernon Square, which was redesigned by Frederick Law Olmsted in the 1870s. The monument led to Baltimore being nicknamed the Monumental City.

Visitors to the Washington Monument today can still climb the steps to the top, and there is a free visitor center in the base of the monument. The center contains an interactive museum explaining the history of the monument as well as original artwork in the form of plaques and busts. The monument recently underwent a massive restoration, making this site much more than just the monument—definitely worth your time. *Washington Monument, 699 Washington Place, Baltimore, MD 21201; 410-962-5070; mountvernonplace.org. GPS: 39.297675, -76.615687. Monument accessible daily; visitor center open Wed.–Sun.*

BELVOIR—Belvoir was a large tobacco plantation in the Maryland countryside belonging to the widow of John Ross. In 1781, the French army, on their way to Yorktown, camped at Belvoir September 16 and 17, with comte de Rochambeau staying in the home. One of the Rosses also married a surgeon in Washington's army who removed a bullet from the leg

The impressive Washington Monument in Baltimore, Maryland.

of the Marquis de Lafayette; when Lafayette came back to the United States in 1824, he visited the surgeon here at Belvoir. The family is also related to the Keys, and Francis Scott Key, composer of "The Star-Spangled Banner," also stayed here.

A historical marker is outside of Belvoir attesting to its history. The home itself is private property. *Historical marker—Belvoir, on Generals Highway 0.2 mile northwest of Belvoir Farms Rd., Crownsville, MD 21032. GPS: 39.018756, -76.583711. Sign accessible daily; mansion is private property.*

MARYLAND STATE HOUSE—The oldest state house in the nation, the Maryland State House was completed in 1779. From November 1784 to August 1784, the Maryland State House hosted Congress in what was then the Senate chamber. It was here at Annapolis that George Washington came before Congress to resign his commission in the United States Army on December 23, 1783. The Treaty of Paris, which ended the Revolutionary War, was also ratified while Congress was in session here. The building also hosted the Annapolis Convention in 1786, which called for a radical restructuring of the government and led to the Constitutional Convention.

The Maryland State House is still in use today. It's a beautiful building and is filled with artwork and statues that represent the historical events that happened here. There is plenty of interpretation, too, so you won't feel lost on your tour. The Maryland State House is right in downtown Annapolis, and there are plenty of great shops and restaurants around, so plan on staying a bit longer to take advantage of them. *Maryland State House, 100 State Circle, Annapolis, MD 21401; 410-260-6418; statehouse.maryland.gov. GPS: 38.979095, -76.491382. Open daily.*

UNITED STATES NAVAL ACADEMY MUSEUM—After decades of effort, the United States Naval Academy was founded in 1845 at Annapolis. Since its founding, the academy has turned out trained and educated officers to serve aboard the vessels of the US Navy.

The Maryland State House, still in use, is where George Washington resigned his commission in the United States Army.

The academy postdates the American Revolution, but the development of America's naval forces begins with the Revolutionary War. In fact, one of the most revered places on the campus is the chapel, where the body of John Paul Jones, naval hero of the Revolution, is kept in an elaborate and impressive crypt. You can view the crypt, as well as historic artifacts related to Jones's life and naval career. The US Naval Academy Museum holds fascinating exhibits on the birth of the navy, as well as marine life, naval warfare, and just what it takes to be a seaman, both in the past and today. The museum's special exhibits are also usually impressive. You may also tour the campus at Annapolis for free, but you will want to take one of the guided tours offered at the visitor center. The tours are led by expert volunteers and leave the visitor center frequently. *United States Naval Academy, enter at Gate 1, intersection of King George St. and Randall St., Annapolis, MD 21402; 410-293-5261; www.usna.edu/visit. GPS: 38.978650, -76.484991. Open daily.*

FRENCH SOLDIERS AND SAILORS MONUMENT—On the campus of St. John's College in Annapolis is a monument to French soldiers who were buried nearby during the American Revolution. Dedicated in 1911, the monument features a bas-relief of Liberty and an inscription from the Sons of Liberty, who commissioned the monument. The monument is in a large field and a little bit out of the way, making it a good spot to reflect a little bit on the sacrifices French men made for American liberty. *French Soldiers and Sailors Monument, near soccer fields between St. Johns St. and King George St. along College Creek, Annapolis, MD 21401. GPS: 38.984044, -76.493511. Accessible daily.*

HESSIAN BARRACKS—The state of Maryland constructed a new set of barracks for their troops in 1777. The troops, though, were out in service, so when a large number of Hessian soldiers were captured during the Saratoga Campaign, what became known as the Hessian Barracks was used to house the prisoners. Additional Hessian prisoners came in 1781 after the surrender at Yorktown.

The Hessian Barracks still stand today and are part of the campus of the Maryland School for the Deaf, of which the barracks were the institute's first building. The building cannot be entered at this time, though there is some interest in restoring the interior. Plenty of markers and interpretive signs are outside the building, however, and it still retains its original character. *Hessian Barracks, 101 Clarke Place, Frederick, MD 21705. GPS: 39.408870, -77.409690. Accessible daily.*

WASHINGTON MONUMENT MARYLAND STATE PARK—The residents of Boonesboro, Maryland, decided to celebrate July 4, 1827, by constructing a monument to George Washington on nearby South Mountain. Remarkably, they completed half of it that day, and over time it has been repaired and restored several times. The tower also served as a signal station and observation point during the Civil War.

Restored to its original appearance, you can still view the Washington Monument. Just as impressive as the monument is the view, as you can see for miles from your vantage point atop the mountain. There is a visitor center here as well, with information on both the monument and the Civil War Battle of South Mountain, which raged around you in 1862 just a few days before the Battle of Antietam. Note that there is a bit of

Washington Monument State Park in Boonesboro, Maryland.

a climb from the visitor center to the monument, but it's worth it—it's part of the Appalachian Trail, too, if you need to check that off your bucket list. *Washington Monument State Park, 6620 Zittlestown Rd., Middletown, MD 21769; 301-791-4767; dnr.maryland.gov/publiclands/Pages/western/washington.aspx. GPS: 39.498922, -77.623629. Open daily.*

FORT FREDERICK—Fort Frederick, a substantial stone fortification, was built by the colony of Maryland in 1756 to protect frontier settlers during the French and Indian War. During the American Revolution, the fort's strong works and remote location made it an ideal location to house British prisoners of war after the surrender at Saratoga and again after the surrender at Yorktown. The fort was also used during the Civil War due to its proximity to the Chesapeake and Ohio Canal.

Fort Frederick State Park is your best place to learn about what an American prison camp was like during the Revolutionary War. The fort has been restored to its 1758 appearance, and although most of the interpretation focuses on its use during the French and Indian War, there's plenty about its time as a prison. Living history programs occur every weekend, and in addition to all the interpretation you'll find in the fort's barracks, there is also an excellent visitor center. The park also features camping, hiking, canoeing, and other outdoor activities. It's a little out of the way but worth the trip. *Fort Frederick State Park, 11100 Fort Frederick Rd., Big Pool, MD 21711; 301-842-2155; dnr.maryland.gov/publiclands/Pages/western/fortfrederick.aspx. GPS: 39.610212, -78.004593. Grounds open daily; barracks and visitor center open Thurs.–Mon. Memorial Day to Labor Day and weekends in spring and fall.*

YORK COURTHOUSE—When Philadelphia was threatened by the British invasion in 1777, the Continental Congress fled first to Lancaster and then York, Pennsylvania, to continue its work. Congress met here from November 1777 to June 1778, and during that time in Lancaster tended to some critical business. The Articles of Confederation, which formed America's first government, was adopted on November 15, 1777. Congress also established America's alliance with France while in Lancaster, securing vital support and recognition for the new United States. Congress returned to Philadelphia after the British evacuated the city in June 1778.

The reconstructed York courthouse (built in 1976 for the bicentennial) is the centerpiece of the York County History Center's Colonial Complex. The building is not in its original location (which is outlined in the intersection of Market and George Streets in red brick), but it is a faithful reproduction of the original. Guided tours are available of the courthouse and the other buildings in the complex, which include the 1741 Golden Plough Tavern and the General Gates House, where Horatio Gates took his headquarters while Congress was in session; it was here that Gates and others were involved in a plot to supplant Washington as commander in chief of the Continental Army and replace him with Gates. The complex also has an excellent museum that focuses on York's history. *York County History Center, 157 West Market St., York, PA 17403; 717-848-1587; www.yorkhistorycenter.org. GPS: 37.297745, -77.409701. Open Tues.–Sat.*

CAMP SECURITY—In 1781, additional prison facilities were required to house British prisoners from the surrender at Saratoga. Camp Security, just east of York, Pennsylvania, provided a secure, remote location. Prisoners were housed in log huts within a large stockade. Additional prisoners were added after the surrender at Yorktown, and the camp stayed operational through the end of the war in 1783.

There is a historical marker pertaining to Camp Security, but it is almost a mile away from the original site. There is an effort underway by the Friends of Camp Security to preserve some of the original site, which is still in mostly untouched condition and has been the subject of several archaeological surveys. You can walk some of the grounds at Camp Security Park. *Camp Security Park, intersection of Locust Grove Rd. and Eastern Blvd., York, PA 17402; www.campsecurity.org. GPS: 39.980721, -76.644893. Historical marker, intersection of Market St. and Cinema Dr., York, PA 17402. GPS: 39.983862, -76.648370. Sites accessible daily.*

LANCASTER COUNTY COURTHOUSE—When Congress fled the British invasion of Pennsylvania in 1777, they first settled on Lancaster, Pennsylvania, to resume their session. At the time, Lancaster was America's largest inland city, which some thought made it a possible target of the

British, so Congress met here for only one day in the Lancaster Courthouse before moving on to York.

The Lancaster Courthouse burned down in 1784. On the site, there is a memorial to those who fought in America's wars, including the Revolution; on the memorial is an inscription that this was the site where Congress met in 1777. *Soldiers and Sailors Monument (Lancaster County Courthouse), Penn Square at intersection of King St. and Queen St., Lancaster, PA 17603. GPS: 40.038015, -76.305658. Accessible daily.*

EPHRATA CLOISTER—The Ephrata Cloister was founded in 1732 as a monastic retreat. The cloister became famous for its calligraphy, a capella music featuring four-part harmony, and its printing. After the Battle of Brandywine, the cloister, true to its mission, served as a hospital for 260 sick and wounded from the Continental Army. Though Ephrata Cloister

The beautiful grounds at Ephrata Cloister, a hospital site for the Continental Army in Pennsylvania.

began to decline soon after its founder's passing, the settlement lasted until 1934.

Ephrata Cloister is now run by the Pennsylvania Historical and Museum Commission. You can visit the cloister and tour many of the buildings, learning about the lifestyles of the inhabitants. The visitor center has a great museum and talks a little bit about the care given to the troops in the winter of 1777–1778. The buildings where the soldiers were housed are now gone, but archaeological digs have pinpointed their location, and you can still visit the site where they were. You can also visit the common grave and large monument where the 57 men who died are buried. Walking around the cloister today is still a peaceful experience, and it's a unique place to visit. *Historic Ephrata Cloister, 632 West Main St., Ephrata, PA 17522; 717-733-6600; ephratacloister.org. GPS: 40.184475, -76.186300. Open Wed.–Sun. during summer; check website for hours other times of year.*

STRODE'S MILL—Strode's Mill in West Chester, Pennsylvania, which dates back to 1721, was on the British line of march as they made their way to the Battle of Brandywine, and the army paused here to organize their lines of attack. They did not destroy the mill, however, even though it was supplying food to the Continental Army. The mill continued to operate after the battle and kept supplying the Continentals during the encampment at Valley Forge.

Strode's Mill is still standing, and while it is a private business today, it is at the center of a preservation effort. Plans focus on restoration of the area and possibly the construction of a visitor center to highlight the 300 years of history at this intersection. This is one to keep an eye on. *Strode's Mill, 1000 Lenape Rd., West Chester, PA 19382; www.friendsof strodesmill.com. GPS: 39.928964, -75.617334. Private property.*

DILWORTHTOWN INN—Dilworthtown was the site of the final actions of the Battle of Brandywine. After the battle, the British occupied the town, including the inn, and did some pillaging of the village structures.

The Dilworthtown Inn was a fine dining establishment for many years, but recently closed. Efforts to revive it are ongoing, however, and the hope is that the inn will soon welcome visitors once again. In the

PENNSYLVANIA'S IRON INDUSTRY

The ironmaking industry in South Central Pennsylvania helped propel America into the Industrial Revolution. It also supplied the Continental Army with some of its most vital resources. Though these sites are no longer producing iron, some of them are still remarkably intact and make for a great visit.

If you would like to learn about these sites and more, one great way to do it is through an Iron and Steel Tour through the Iron & Steel Heritage Partnership. The group offers both guided and self-guided tours through what remains of the industry. *Iron & Steel Heritage; ironandsteelheritage.org.*

CORNWALL FURNACE—Peter and Samuel Grubb opened a blast furnace in Cornwall, Pennsylvania, in 1742, where the resources of wood for charcoal and water were in abundance. During the American Revolution, the furnace produced shot, shell, and 42 cannons for the Continental Army. The furnace remained operational until 1883.

The Cornwall Iron Furnace, now administered by the Pennsylvania Historical and Museum Commission, is proud of its status as one of the most complete charcoal-fueled ironmaking sites in the world. Much of the original complex is still intact and spreads over several acres. You can take a guided tour of the sites, and the museum in the visitor center is excellent, explaining not only the history of the furnace but also the finer points of producing iron. *Cornwall Iron Furnace, 94 Rexmont Rd., Cornwall, PA 17016; 717-272-9711; cornwallironfurnace.org. GPS: 40.271546, -76.406668. Open Fri.–Sun.*

HOPEWELL VILLAGE AND FURNACE—A relatively new furnace when the American Revolution came about, Hopewell Furnace began producing iron in 1771. Hopewell's owner, Mark Bird, was an ardent Patriot, participating in committees and serving in the militia. Hopewell produced 115 guns for the Continental Navy, the first of its kind in America, in addition to shot and shell.

Hopewell Furnace National Historic Site explores the ironmaking trade from its founding in 1771 to its close in 1883. The site captures the entire Hopewell village, including all of its ironmaking facilities as well as the Ironmaster's Mansion, which was also the business center of the furnace, and tenant housing. The site also has all the ancillary buildings Hopewell required at the time, including a barn, schoolhouse, and church. The visitor center features a film outlining Hopewell's history and the process and importance of making iron. The site is mostly self-guided, but plenty of staff are still there to help answer your questions. The site also has hiking trails that link to other trail networks. *Hopewell Furnace National Historic Site, 2 Mark Bird Lane, Elverson, PA 19520; 610-582-8773; www.nps.gov/hofu. GPS: 40.206965, -75.773943. Open Wed.–Sun.*

WARWICK FURNACE—Built by widow Anna Nutt per her late husband's wishes in 1737, Warwick Furnace supplied cannon, shot, and other supplies to the Continental Army and to the Pennsylvania Committee of Safety.

A good portion of the original grounds of Warwick Furnace has been preserved by the French and Pickering Creeks Conservation Trust, including portions of the old furnace. In addition to occasional tours of the grounds, the group hosts an annual French Creek Iron Tour bicycle ride to aid their efforts. If you can't catch a tour or the bike ride, you can still see the remnants of the furnace, and interpretive signs are available. *Warwick Furnace,*

continued on next page

> *intersection of Valley Rd. and Warwick Furnace Rd., Warwick Township, PA 19343; frenchandpickering.org. GPS: 40.149840, -75.739152. Site accessible daily.*
>
> **COVENTRY FORGE**—Coventry Forge, the first iron site in Chester County, was an ironmaking center from its founding in 1717 through the next century. Coventry supplied munitions for the Continental Army in conjunction with Warwick Furnace.
>
> Some of the remnants of Coventry Forge can still be seen. Warwick County Park preserves several of the charcoal hearths along its hiking trails, and interpretive signs are along the way as well. The Coventryville Historic District also has some original buildings, though these are all private property. *Warwick Park, 191 County Park Rd., Pottstown, PA 19465. GPS: 40.167654, -75.724015. Open daily.*

meantime, you can view the inn from the outside. *Dilworthtown Inn, 1390 Old Wilmington Pike, West Chester, PA 19382; www.historicdilworthtown.com. GPS: 39.899912, -75.567402. View from outside.*

PAOLI—A week after the Battle of Brandywine, American General Anthony Wayne was in the rear of the British army searching for a way to strike with his 1,500 men. The British knew of his presence, however, and they decided to strike first. On the night of September 20, 1777, a force of 5,000 British soldiers under General Charles Grey marched to Wayne's camp, with the men ordered to remove the flints from their guns and rely on attacking with the bayonet in order to preserve secrecy and induce panic. At 1:00 AM on September 21, the attack began, with the British pushing past American pickets and falling on the camp. The Americans could not organize an effective resistance in the darkness, and the attack turned into what became known as the Paoli Massacre. The Americans fled, losing 53 killed,

The ruins of Warwick Furnace in Pennsylvania.

100 wounded, and 71 captured, while the British only lost 4 killed and 7 wounded. General Grey was thereafter known by the ominous nickname No Flint.

Paoli Battlefield Historical Park preserves much of the battlefield, and it appears much the same as it did in 1777. The large, quiet tract is surrounded by a walking trail with plenty of interpretive signs that tell about the battle and its legacy. There is also a memorial, erected in 1817 where the 53 killed in the battle lie; it is believed to be the second-oldest war memorial in the United States. Lots of great information about the battle and the park are also on the website of the Paoli Battlefield Preservation Fund. *Paoli Battlefield Historical Park, on Wayne Ave. near intersection with West 1st Ave., Malvern, PA 19355; pbpfinc.org. GPS: 40.029624, -75.518392. Open daily.*

PETER WENTZ HOMESTEAD—Peter Wentz and his wife Rosanna settled their farmstead in 1744. Before and after the Battle of German-

A trail on the battlefield at Paoli in Malvern, Pennsylvania.

town in 1777, General George Washington chose the Wentz house to use as headquarters for the Continental Army. The army was here when it learned of the great victory at Saratoga, prompting great celebration.

The Wentz home and farm have been restored to their 1777 appearance. Interpretation includes Washington's time here at the home, as well as the history of the family and the enslaved persons who worked at the farm. The site is maintained as an 18th-century working farmstead and includes animals that you would have expected to see at that time. Tours of the house and a small visitor center help you interpret the homestead, and there are frequent living history programs. *Peter Wentz Farmstead 2030 Shearer Rd., Lansdale, PA 19446; 610-584-5104; peterwentzfarmsteadsociety1.org. GPS: 40.200678, -75.337980. Open Tues.–Sun.*

DAWESFIELD—After the British withdrew from Germantown in 1777, the Continental Army moved toward Philadelphia and briefly established an encampment around the Dawesfield estate, the home of James

Morris. The army stayed here for two weeks while Washington established his headquarters at the Dawes mansion.

Dawesfield is still very much intact but is a private home today. It is not open to the public. *Dawesfield, 565 Lewis Lane, Ambler, PA 19002. Private property.*

WHITEMARSH (CHESTNUT HILL)—On November 2, 1777, the Continental Army established a defensive position on a ridgeline northwest of Philadelphia near the Whitemarsh estate. The strong position faced the city and consisted of three hills, allowing them to see any assault forming against them. Washington made his headquarters in the nearby George Emlen House. In early December 1777, British General William Howe decided to test the position and moved most of his army toward the American position. After several days of skirmishing on December 5–7, the British withdrew back into Philadelphia. Shortly afterward, Washington moved the American army to Valley Forge for the winter.

Fort Washington State Park preserves the site of two of the primary hills that held the American defenses. While there is no interpretation at the Militia Hill Unit, where the Pennsylvania Militia was encamped, the hill now known as Fort Hill has a partially reconstructed redoubt and some interpretive signage. The park also has camping, hiking, and other outdoor recreational activities. A memorial to the battle is also near the redoubt. The Emlen House is private property today; there is a historic marker near the home. *Fort Washington State Park—Fort Hill, entrance on South Bethlehem Pike 0.5 mile north of Route 73, Fort Washington, PA 19034; 215-591-5250; dcnr.pa.gov/StateParks/FindAPark/Fort WashingtonStatePark/Pages/default.aspx. GPS: 40.129796, -75.217125. Open daily. Fort Washington State Park—Militia Hill, entrance on Militia Hill Rd. 0.1 mile southwest of East Skippack Pike, Fort Washington, PA 19034. GPS: 40.124283, -75.222876. Open daily. Monument—American Redoubt, on South Bethlehem Pike 0.1 mile south of Fort Hill Dr., Fort Washington, PA 19034. GPS: 40.131311, -75.216101. Monument accessible daily. Historic Marker—Whitemarsh, on Pennsylvania Ave. 0.1 mile south of Emlen Way, Fort Washington, PA 19034. GPS: 40.124180, -75.192336. Marker accessible daily; home is private property.*

BARREN HILL—In late May 1778, the Americans learned of British plans to evacuate Philadelphia, and Washington decided to send out an expedition to cover the encampment at Valley Forge while harassing British foraging expeditions. The Marquis de Lafayette led 2,200 men, including 50 Oneida warriors, to a strong position at Barren Hill midway between Valley Forge and Philadelphia. Alerted to this plan, the British sent 7,000 men up the Ridge and Germantown Roads to cut off Lafayette's route of retreat and capture him. On the morning of May 20, 1778, the Americans realized that they were about to be caught in a trap. Lafayette, however, had been very careful in choosing his position, and had planned a retreat route along a concealed road. The discipline that the troops had gained during their training at Valley Forge, along with Lafayette's leadership, played a huge part in the Americans' ability to extract themselves with minimal losses.

A historical marker is on Barren Hill at St. Peter's Church, and though it is not the building that stood at the time of the battle, the cemetery where the soldiers gathered to hear Lafayette's instructions is still here. Another historical marker is down Ridge Road where the Americans conducted a delaying action. *Historical marker—St. Peter's Church, intersection of Church Rd. and Park Ave., Lafayette Hill, PA 19444. GPS: 40.082870, -75.250905. Historical marker—Lafayette, intersection of Ridge Pike and Barren Hill Rd., Lafayette Hill, PA 19444. GPS: 40.078356, -75.249836. Signs accessible daily.*

WHERE TO STAY IN THE PHILADELPHIA AREA

Philadelphia offers numerous options for lodging, and you won't have any trouble finding a place to stay. The rich history of the area provides many opportunities for bed and breakfasts in older homes, but few of them have direct ties to the American Revolution.

PART 3
THE FINAL BLOW: THE REVOLUTION IN THE SOUTH

6

A New Strategy: Georgia and South Carolina

OVERVIEW

The entry of France into the Revolutionary War as an American ally changed everything for the British. Instead of an internal squabble with a wayward set of colonies, the conflict had now become a war with another world superpower and an old enemy. The war was now a world war, fought on land and sea all over the globe and requiring vastly more resources than previously anticipated.

The new global strategy required a new strategy for America as well. The British would need to maintain control of as much of their American territory as they could while relying on fewer resources. Fortunately for the crown, there was one untapped asset that had been thus far mostly ignored.

In the estimation of British officials both in London and America, it was felt that the vast majority of Americans did not support the Revolution. Most of the people in America, from every indication they had, wanted to remain loyal to Britain. After all, they had enjoyed immense benefits as British subjects and had grown to be the wealthiest region on earth. Why would they possibly want to leave the king's good graces?

Actually, there were plenty of indications both before and after the

Opposite: The monument at Kettle Creek Battlefield, Georgia.

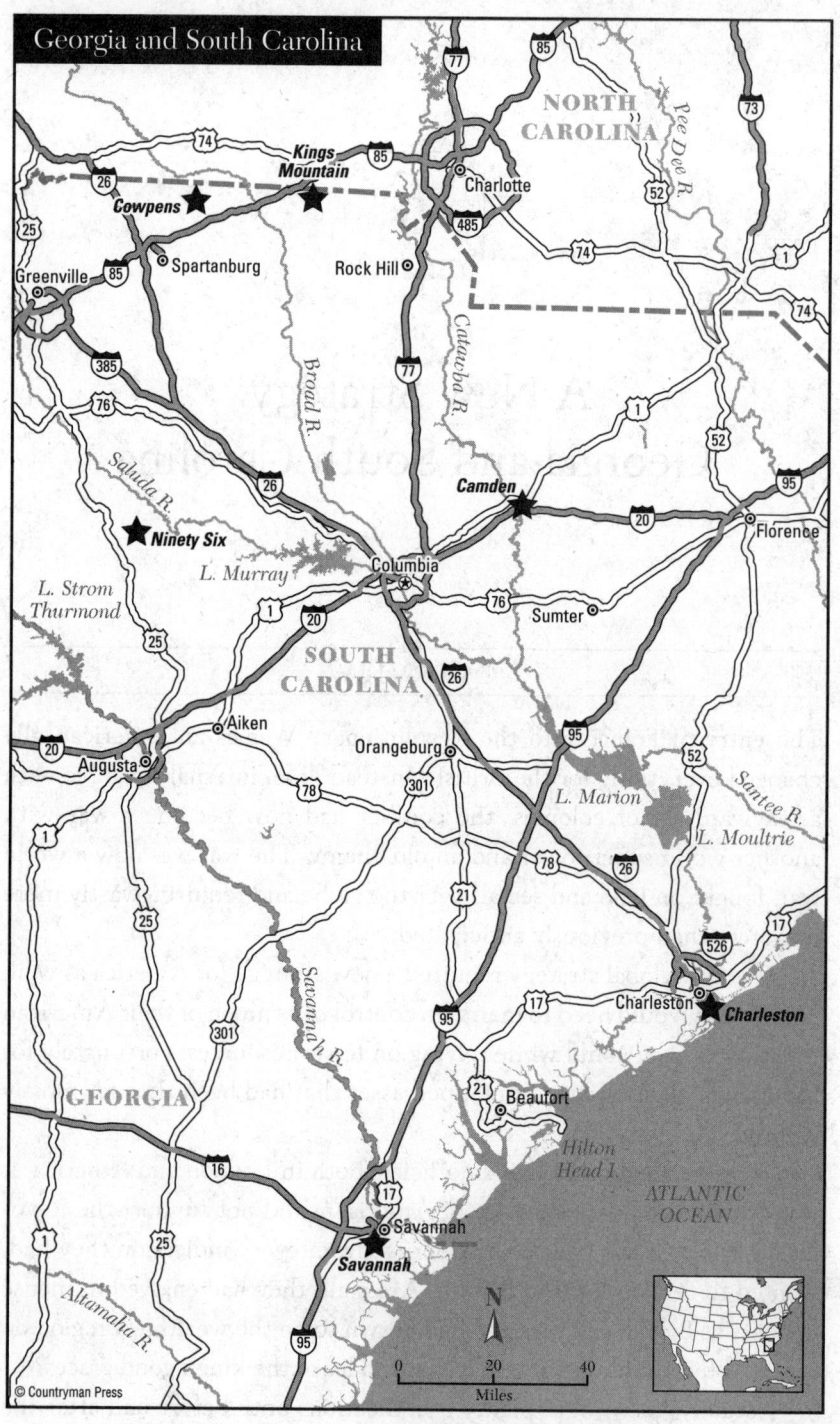

French alliance with America that this was not the case. The various governors of the colonies had made repeated attempts to gather their Loyalist "majorities" in forming militias and generally suppressing revolutionary activities. And while they were always able to muster up some support, for the most part, these efforts mostly went unheeded by the populace. A good portion of the people of the American colonies did indeed feel their freedoms eroding, and while not everybody was necessarily willing to fight for those freedoms, very few were motivated enough to fight for Britain.

Before the recruitment of soldiers could begin, the British needed a foothold in the south. That was accomplished late in 1778 with the capture of Savannah and the subsequent occupation of Georgia. However, just like previous efforts, recruiting in the backcountry yielded disappointing results and quickly dried up to nothing when the new recruits suffered several overwhelming defeats.

The need for a new British strategy was emphasized in September 1779 when the Americans and their new French allies arrived outside of Savannah intent on taking it back. In one of the bloodiest battles of the entire war, the British held on to the city, with French and American forces fighting valiantly but in an uncoordinated fashion. The alliance would take patience and practice to yield benefits, but the cooperating forces at Savannah were a harbinger of what was to come.

While capturing Savannah was an important step for the British, everyone knew that the real prize was Charleston. The center of commerce in the south and a very wealthy city, its capture, in the eyes of the British, would allow them to assert dominance in the south. After the British besieged and captured Charleston in 1780, they created outposts at Augusta, Georgia, and the towns of Ninety Six and Camden in South Carolina in order to gain control of the countryside. But this was not a European war, where the conquering of cities and capitals often meant the end of a conflict. The war shifted from one of large armies in the field to a brutal guerrilla war, fought by small bands of partisans, and the British would never have enough resources or support in order to truly conquer the south.

Meanwhile, the Continental Army and American militia were going through their own troubles. A large American force had surrendered at

Charleston, and new troops had to be sent from the north and recruited from the backcountry to fight for the American cause. General Horatio Gates, hero of the Battle of Saratoga, was sent to command the new army. But a devastating American defeat at Camden nearly destroyed the new army as well, and Gates was sent back north in humiliation.

However, in late 1780, just as things were looking bleak for the Americans, a monumental turn of events occurred. British threats against settlers west of the Appalachian Mountains, intended to sow fear and compliance, had the opposite effect, and militia gathered from what is now Tennessee, North Carolina, South Carolina, and Virginia in order to confront the British efforts. These Overmountain Men caught up with the British at Kings Mountain and gained a stunning victory, inflicting a knockout blow to British recruiting in the south.

British General Charles Cornwallis, in command of the southern theater, now sought to destroy what remained of the American army in the south. Now commanded by General Nathanael Greene, the Americans divided their forces, with General Daniel Morgan threatening the British in the west. Cornwallis dispatched his most feared weapon, Colonel Banastre Tarleton, to catch and destroy Morgan. But another lopsided American victory at the Battle of Cowpens kept the American momentum going and further drove the British to what would eventually be their end.

The story of the American Revolution in the south does not get the recognition of the actions in the north around Boston or Philadelphia. However, the large battles and the small, brutal guerrilla actions here proved to be some of the most dramatic of the entire war. This chapter will take you through the early part of the war in the south in Georgia and South Carolina.

PEOPLE TO KNOW

CASIMIR PULASKI—One of many foreign fighters to aid the American cause, Count Casimir Pulaski stands out among his peers mostly for his short and tragic career. Today, Pulaski is regarded as both an American and a Polish hero of the revolution.

Pulaski began his military career fighting the Russians in Poland, but was soon forced to flee, first to Turkey and then to Paris. It was here that he met American commissioners to France, Benjamin Franklin and Silas Deane, who sent him to America with their recommendations for a command. Congress made him a general, and Washington gave him the job of commander in chief of cavalry. He held this position for only a short time. Pulaski then organized an independent cavalry command known as the American Legion, more commonly known as Pulaski's Legion. The legion rode south as British strategy shifted south, and Pulaski quickly impressed with his courage (and possibly his recklessness). The height of Pulaski's fame came when he was mortally wounded at Savannah, where he led a futile charge against the British lines. Remembered for his dash, Pulaski was the epitome of the cavalryman.

BANASTRE TARLETON—If the American Revolution produced any one true villain, it was undoubtedly Banastre Tarleton. One of the British army's most effective fighters, Tarleton had a reputation for both skill and cruelty.

Tarleton came from a very wealthy family, and his place in the British army was purchased for him, as was common at the time. The war in America broke out shortly after he joined, and he was soon on his way to serve there as a volunteer. In 1776, Tarleton's unit scored a major coup when they captured American General Charles Lee in New Jersey—for which, as would become his trademark, he took full credit. However, it was not until he moved to the southern theater that he began to make his mark. Tarleton led his cavalry and light troops in several impressive victories, and with each of those victories came accusations of mistreatment of prisoners and killing American soldiers who were in the act of surrendering. Before long, Tarleton was both hated and feared throughout the south. It was not until his defeat at the Battle of Cowpens that the myth of Tarleton's invincibility was shattered, though he continued to lead his men effectively until the end of the war. Tarleton continued to serve and was eventually named a general in the British army. He died in 1833.

FRANCIS MARION—The war in South Carolina was one of small, partisan actions featuring stealthy and fast-moving bands of militia. And though there were several intrepid and important leaders of these men—Thomas Sumter and Andrew Pickens among them—none were as successful as the "Swamp Fox," Francis Marion.

Francis Marion was a farmer and a leader of the militia, first serving in an action against the Cherokee in 1761, where his performance and leadership skills impressed his commanders. Marion continued to serve, including at Fort Moultrie in Charleston Harbor during the British attack in 1776 and in the assault of Savannah in 1779. Narrowly avoiding capture in Charleston when that city fell, Marion formed a small guerrilla band of militia that would gather, fight, and disperse quickly. Pursued relentlessly by the British, Marion was never caught; his actions were so secretive that to this day the location of his encampment at Snow's Island, South Carolina, is not exactly known. A small man known for his kindness as much as his tactical brilliance, much of the Francis Marion story has devolved into legend, and even Disney made a television series about his exploits. But there is a good bit of truth to that legend, and to this day Marion is a well-known personality of the south.

THINGS TO KNOW

This trip may take a little bit more planning than the others described in this book. While there are a few large sites and cities, many of these locations are in rural and somewhat isolated locations. But don't let that deter you from visiting. Even the smaller sites are often well-preserved and organized, usually by dedicated local efforts, and you'll find at least some interpretation at most of them. In addition, because many of the sites are unstaffed and open as long as the sun is up, you can extend your day to see more if you'd like. If you do need more help finding out about these battles, you can look to the staffs at Ninety Six National Historic Site, Cowpens National Battlefield, and Kings Mountain National Military Park for more information.

THE TRIP

This trip follows the major events in the southern theater, moving generally south to north through Georgia and South Carolina. In between, you'll cover a lot of beautiful country and will be taking smaller highways rather than the interstate. Take advantage of that and make some stops in the smaller cities and towns along your route, and be sure to tell the people you meet that you're there to see their local history.

You'll cover a lot of ground on this trip. Plan ahead and reserve somewhere to stay when possible, especially during the summer, as both Savannah and Charleston can get busy during the tourist season. For the most part, though, you should be able to find food and lodging in most areas; you just may need to drive an extra hour or two to get to them.

THE CAN'T-MISS SITES

Savannah

When the British decided on their new Southern Strategy, Savannah, Georgia, was selected as the first target. In addition to Georgia being the southernmost colony, the British had also seen some conflict between Georgians and the British capital of East Florida at St. Augustine; capturing the capital at Savannah would provide a buffer between Florida and the rest of the colonies. Savannah was by far the dominant port in Georgia, and controlling that key point would suffice to control the rest of the colony.

Savannah had been attacked prior to the Revolutionary War, but the stakes had not been nearly as high. In early 1776, the British army in Boston was still under siege and desperately needed food and other supplies, and naval vessels were sent up and down the coast to search for them. A small fleet began arriving outside Savannah in January with the intention of purchasing food, but the Patriots in the city were not about to aid them, and even arrested the royal governor of Georgia to prevent his cooperation with them. On March 3, a landing party took command of several boats' worth of rice, and after a failed negotiation, a firefight erupted. Though the British were able to gather some of the provisions they needed in what became known as the Battle of the Rice Boats, it was too late, as Boston would be evacuated on March 17.

By late 1778, Savannah became important to the British. General Henry Clinton, commander of all British forces in America, sent Lieutenant Colonel Archibald Campbell with 3,000 men from New York City to take Savannah. They arrived at Tybee Island outside of the Savannah River on December 23, 1778. Arriving only weeks before was American General Robert Howe, who had just been removed as commander of the Southern Department for the Continental Army due to a recent scandal involving a woman. Howe was still waiting for his replacement, and being an ardent Patriot, he did not want to lose any territory to the British in the transfer. Howe found the Savannah defenses, which had been erected for the Seven Years' War, which ended in 1763, to be in a virtually useless state. In fact, Howe, considered abandoning the city to the British rather than risk his men in a desperate encounter. But after holding a council of war on December 24, other officers present convinced him that they could defend Savannah successfully.

Campbell's forces landed at Girardeau's Plantation, two miles east of Savannah, early on the morning of December 30, wading ashore to find a large bluff overlooking their position. The bluff, known as Brewton's Hill, was commanding, and any American forces there could easily pre-

The reconstructed Spring Hill Redoubt outside the Savannah History Museum.

vent the British from gaining a toehold on land. It was suggested to Howe that the Americans do exactly that, but Howe, with only about 850 men at his disposal, had decided that he did not have the men to spare, and that he did not know whether the British would land there or another spot. When an advance British scouting party found the bluff held by only a handful of American infantry, they scattered them with a bayonet charge and captured the position in only a few minutes, securing the landing for the rest of the force.

As the British marched toward Savannah, Howe placed the Americans into a V-shaped line in the fields southeast of the city, as it was thought that there was no other way to approach the city. Campbell, however, had other ideas. He had gathered intelligence from a slave about a hidden trail through the marsh just west of the American line that would allow his forces to pass around their right flank undetected. Arriving before the American lines at about 2:00 PM, he posted the British forces behind a rise in the ground, hiding their presence from the Americans, then climbed a tree to view their position. Satisfied that the plan would work, he sent 350 light infantry, guided by the slave, down the secret path and waited.

The plan worked perfectly. The flanking party arrived at a barracks in the rear of the American line and charged out of the woods at the handful of men who had been posted there. As soon as they began firing, the main British line emerged from behind the ridge and advanced on the front of the American position. Suddenly finding themselves under attack from the front and their rear right flank, the Americans could not put up much of a defense and were quickly put to flight. While Howe and a number of others were able to escape, 83 Americans were killed and 11 wounded, with another 453 captured, over half the force. British casualties were a light 7 killed and 17 wounded. The city of Savannah was now in British hands.

Over the course of the next eight months, Savannah served as a base for the British while they attempted to recruit Loyalists from Georgia and South Carolina, making expeditions to Augusta, Georgia, and Charleston, South Carolina. In the meantime, the Americans, without enough manpower to dislodge the British from the city, bided their time until they could receive some support. Finally, in June 1779, word came

SITE DETAILS

Battlefield Park—Savannah's Battlefield Park, just outside of the Savannah History Museum, is the only part of the 1779 battlefield that is preserved today. The park is on the site of the Spring Hill Redoubt, and there is a reconstructed redoubt here so that you can see for yourself what it may have looked like. Also on the grounds is a memorable set of paving stones—800 of them, representing the approximate number of men in one of the five French or American assault columns. The stones are arranged in a column, so if you look at them from the redoubt you may get an idea of the size of the battle. Finally, there is also a memorial and a raised berm at the actual site of the Spring Hill Redoubt. Along with all of these, there is plenty of interpretation, with signs, memorials, and markers scattered throughout the park. Coupled with the history museum, the park is an excellent place to learn about the battle. *Battlefield Park, intersection of Martin Luther King Jr. Blvd. and Louisville Rd., Savannah, GA 31401. GPS: 32.075677, -81.099220. Accessible daily.*

Savannah History Museum—The Savannah History Museum is one of several museums and historic sites operated by the Coastal Heritage Society. The museum has comprehensive displays of the city's history, and the section on the Revolutionary War is extensive, covering all the battles that took place in Savannah and their legacy, including a separate exhibit on the Pulaski Monument. Housed in the former Central Georgia Railway Passenger Depot, this museum makes for a great but not overwhelming visit. *Savannah History Museum, 303 Martin Luther King Jr. Blvd., Savannah, GA 31401; 912-651-6825; chsgeorgia.org/SHM. GPS: 32.075879, -81.099097. Open daily.*

Hutchinson Island View—On Savannah's riverwalk is an interpretive sign discussing the history of the city through the American Revolution, including the Battle of the Rice Boats. Across the water from the sign is Hutchinson Island, where the boats were taken from the Americans. *Historic Marker—Savannah in the American Revolution, on walking path along River St. just east of intersection with East Upper Factors Walk, Richmond, VA, 23219. GPS: 32.081752, -81.090534. Accessible daily.*

Haitian Monument—One of the French units with comte d'Estaing in 1778 was a regiment of Black volunteers from Santo Domingo, Les Chasseurs Volontaires de Saint Domingue. This was the largest all-Black unit that fought in the American Revolution. An impressive monument to their service was raised in 2007. *Haitian Monument, Franklin Square, intersection of Montgomery St. and West Bryan St., Savannah, GA 31401. GPS: 37.534794, -77.445442. Accessible daily.*

Nathanael Greene Monument—American General Nathanael Greene, one of the Revolutionary War's best generals, settled in Georgia after the war was over. Regrettably, he did not live a long life, dying in 1786. A memorial was built to Greene in Savannah, with the general's remains placed under the grand monument in the middle of Johnson Square. *Nathanael Greene Monument, Johnson Square, intersection of Bull St. and West Bryan St., Savannah, GA 31401. GPS: 32.079925, -81.091584. Accessible daily.*

William Jasper Monument—The story of Sergeant William Jasper begins in Charleston, South Carolina, during the battle at Fort Moultrie, where he braved heavy fire to rescue the flag after it had been shot down. Becoming a local hero, Jasper continued to serve, taking part in the assault on Savannah. As his unit approached the British lines, the color bearer was again shot down, and Jasper immediately went again to rescue the flag. He was mortally wounded in the action, forever sealing his legacy. The Jasper Monument memorializes his actions here and in Charleston. *William Jasper Monument, Madison Square, intersection of Bull St. and West Harris St., Savannah, GA 31401. GPS: 32.073676, -81.093950. Accessible daily.*

Casimir Pulaski Monument—It is not known for certain whether the body buried here is that of General Pulaski; he was thought to have died while en route to Charleston and had his body buried at sea. But when the monument was dedicated in 1855, a body alleged to be Pulaski's and generally fitting his attributes was buried here. Later genetic tests proved inconclusive. In any case, the monument to his memory stands somewhat near where he fell. *Casimir Pulaski Monument, Monterey Square, intersection of Bull St. and East Taylor St., Savannah, GA 31401. GPS: 32.073676, -81.093950. Accessible daily.*

continued on next page

> **Savannah Barracks Site**—A historical marker denotes the site of the American barracks during the 1778 British assault on Savannah. It was at these barracks that the British emerged after using the hidden trail around the American right and rear. *Historical marker—Revolutionary War Barracks and Fortifications, intersection of Bull St. and Liberty St., Savannah, GA 31401. GPS: 32.074545, -81.093461. Accessible daily.*

that a French fleet, commanded by comte d'Estaing, would be arriving to support the Americans near the end of summer. From a military standpoint, the American alliance with France had gotten off to a rocky start with the failed assault on Newport, Rhode Island; both the Americans and the French were hoping that success at Savannah would solidify their relationship.

The French fleet arrived outside of Savannah on September 1, 1779, and preparations to liberate the city were immediately underway. Initially intending to stay only eight days, d'Estaing's ships suffered severe damage in a storm the next night and were forced to stay longer, to the delight of the Americans. The French spent several days offloading troops, artillery, and supplies before breaking camp and heading inland toward Savannah, arriving September 15. The next day, d'Estaing sent a message into the British camp asking for surrender, and after some back and forth, the British commander General Augustine Prevost asked for 24 hours to consider the offer, which d'Estaing granted. It was a ruse; Prevost knew that 800 men from his South Carolina expedition were about to enter the city, but he needed to stall for them to arrive. When they did arrive, Prevost refused the surrender request, much to the chagrin of the French, who had seen the reinforcements arrive.

With their initial plan foiled, the French began to initiate siege warfare to capture Savannah. French troops began to dig approach trenches to creep closer to the British lines beginning the night of September 22. By October 3 the French siege artillery, 41 pieces in all, had been placed in proper batteries, and a heavy bombardment of the city began. However, it was evident that the bombardment was having little effect on the British defenses while causing much damage to the town. D'Estaing, who badly wanted to get his ships out of the region while it was still hurricane season, called a council of war on October 7. When his engineers told him it would be another 10 days before the trenches were able to breach the British lines, d'Estaing declared that it was too long. Instead of continuing the siege, the combined French and American forces would assault the British works.

The British defenses were vastly improved in the days between the arrival of the French and the beginning of the bombardment. Five lines of defense had been organized in front of the city, consisting of a wide open area cleared for fire, a thick line of abatis (felled trees whose branches had been sharpened), a number of redoubts, or earthen fortresses, an additional defensive line or earthworks, and a reserve force placed inside the city that could assist at any point needed. D'Estaing's attack plan was focused on one redoubt in particular, atop Spring Hill, near the right or westernmost end of the British line. A force of 4,000 French troops would march in three columns to assault the Spring Hill Redoubt and the batteries on either side, while the 1,500 Americans would focus on an adjacent redoubt to the left. The Americans would also be supported by the American Legion, a group of 200 horsemen and light infantry commanded by Polish General Casimir Pulaski.

The assault was to begin at 4:00 AM on October 9, 1779, but things became confused from the very beginning. D'Estaing reorganized his forces just before the battle, meaning that men were now fighting for new commanders they did not know well. Those French forces were also supposed to rendezvous with their American counterparts several hours before the launch time but were instead several hours late. By the time day began to break around 5:30 AM, the French were still not in position. It was not long before the British discovered the allied forces making their formations and sounded the alarm. D'Estaing, rather than wait for all of his troops to be in position, made a decision to begin the assault immediately and sent the first French column toward the British defenses.

It was a disaster. The plan of attack had called for all five columns to move simultaneously, but only one of the five was ready when d'Estaing began his attack. Each of the five columns consequently entered the battle one at a time, meaning that the British only needed to focus their fire on a single column rather than five. Firing on the attackers with musketry and grapeshot from their artillery, the British tore into the French attackers as they came on. Still, the French kept coming, and the fighting in and around the Spring Hill Redoubt was incredibly intense, with much of it hand to hand and with the bayonet. The Americans, who entered the fight after the French, were largely pushed into the swamps to the left as a result of the heavy fighting, making little progress toward their objective. The American Legion attempted a charge to break through the British line but faltered when Pulaski was mortally wounded and carried from the field. When d'Estaing was wounded for a second time and also had to be carried away, the French finally called a retreat and ended the fighting.

The Battle of Savannah had lasted only an hour, but it was one of the bloodiest of the American Revolution. Official casualty returns from the French list 151 killed and 370 wounded, and for the Americans 56 killed and 178 wounded. All of these numbers are thought to be lower than what actually occurred. The British, in contrast, only lost 16 killed and 39 wounded. The day after the battle, the French began gathering their troops and supplies, and they were back at sea by October 20, while the Americans headed to Charleston. Savannah would remain in British control until evacuated in July 1782.

Charleston

While Boston, Philadelphia, and New York could each lay some claim to its importance in the north, there was no arguing which city was supreme south of Pennsylvania. In terms of population, commerce, and wealth, Charleston, South Carolina, was the undisputed key city of the southern colonies.

Unlike the north, with its heavy focus on manufactured goods, the southern American colonies were almost entirely concerned with agriculture. As such, there was not as much need or desire for densely populated large cities. Charleston, too, was certainly not as large as the northern cities, but it had an excellent natural harbor that made it a natural trade center. As goods flowed into the city from throughout the south, its merchants became flush with wealth produced from cash crops, such as rice, indigo, and tobacco, as well as from the slave trade. In fact, the argument could be made that Charleston was America's wealthiest city.

Charleston was like other American cities in one way: It was heavily sympathetic to the Patriot cause. The city's merchants were just as affected by Parliament's acts restricting trade and were quick to protest. Between its importance as a trade center and its resistance to the crown's efforts to raise revenue, once war finally broke out, Charleston became an obvious target. So, when the fighting did come south at various times throughout the war, Charleston was often the center of attention.

Early in the war, with most attention focused on Boston and Canada, an opportunity arose for the British to gain a strong foothold in Charleston. British General Henry Clinton had sailed with 2,000 troops to aid the British colonial governor of North Carolina, arriving in March 1776 only to find that he was too late to help, since forces loyal to the crown had been decisively defeated a few weeks earlier at Moores Creek. Clinton, who was expecting naval support, now had discretion to use his men as he saw fit. After first considering an action in Virginia, he ultimately decided that a move on Charleston would make the biggest splash. Intelligence reports had informed him that an American fort at Sullivan's Island, a barrier island outside Charleston Harbor, was being built but was not finished. The new fort (later known as Fort Moultrie) would command the entrance to the harbor, making British access to the city very difficult; it was critical that the fort be destroyed before it was completed and fully effective.

The British arrived outside Charleston Harbor on June 4, 1776, sending the city into a frenzy. Building further defenses and finishing the fort became a priority, and every able-bodied man was pressed into this service. Things improved with the arrival of the American commander, General Charles Lee, on June 8. Lee, considered at the time to be one of America's most valuable and experienced officers, was tireless in his efforts to correct deficiencies and improve the city's state of defense. Notably, though, he did not like what was being called Fort Sullivan, nor did he like its position. Lee first urged that the fort be abandoned, but when he met strong resistance from South Carolina's American governor, he relented. But he insisted on creating an escape route to the mainland,

The Old Exchange was the scene of many of Charleston's most historic moments.

either via a floating bridge or boats. Short on resources, the escape route was never created. But the fort's commander, Colonel William Moultrie, had profound faith in his fort, insisting that it would hold.

While the Americans improved their defenses, the British designed their plan of attack. Troops would be landed on Long Island, to the north of Sullivan Island; informed that troops could walk from one island to the other at low tide, the men would cross what was known as the Breach and then attack the fort. Meanwhile, nine British ships, under Commodore Peter Parker, would bombard the fort with their guns. The ships were split into three divisions. The two biggest ships, the 50-gun HMS *Bristol* and HMS *Experiment*, would assault the fort directly on its southeast side. Two other ships, equipped with mortars, would fire on the fort from a distance. The last three ships would attack the unfinished western side of the fort, firing into the rear of the defenders and driving them from their works.

The British plan had two overriding complications. The first was that

SITE DETAILS

Fort Sumter and Fort Moultrie National Historical Park—The site of Fort Moultrie served as an American fortification from the years before the American Revolution all the way through World War II. This unit of the National Park system preserves that site, though most of what you'll find today consists of more modern fortifications built over the original. However, the exhibits in the visitor center as well as the grounds around the fort interpret the 1776 attack on Fort Moultrie vividly, presenting a complete picture of the British attack and its significance. The park contains a second visitor center in the city of Charleston that provides boat rides to Fort Sumter, the place where America's Civil War began. Together, the two sites provide an excellent overview of the extent of Charleston's defenses and the difficulties the harbor presented for attackers. Try to visit them both if you can. *Fort Sumter and Fort Moultrie National Historical Park—Fort Moultrie Unit, 1214 Middle St., Sullivan's Island, SC 29482; 843-883-3123; www.nps.gov/fosu. GPS: 32.760140, -79.857683. Open daily.*

Thomson Park—The aborted attack at the Breach during the British assault on Fort Moultrie in 1776 is preserved at Thomson Park on Sullivan's Island. Interpretive signs overlooking the Breach explain what the British intent was and tell the larger story of the battle on Sullivan's Island. *Thomson Park, near intersection of Jasper Blvd. and Middle St., Sullivan's Island, SC 29482. GPS: 32.774724, -79.814885. Accessible daily.*

Marion Square—Now a beautiful public square, Marion Square is the site of the center of the American lines as well as some of the British approach trenches during the 1880 siege of Charleston. The only artifact of the battle itself on the site is a remnant of the Horn Work, the central fortification on the American line at the city gates. The Horn Work was constructed using tabby, a strong cement made from oyster shells, which is why some of it still stands today; much of the rest of the work is just below the ground beneath the square. In 2024, the American Battlefield Trust and the South Carolina Battleground Preservation Trust placed bronze interpretive markers in the ground on the square outlining

continued on next page

the Horn Work and interpreting the battle, adding to what was already the best place to see the Charleston battlefield. *Marion Square, intersection of Calhoun St. and King St., Charleston, SC 29403. GPS: 32.786729, -79.936332. Accessible daily.*

Powder Magazine—The Charleston Powder Magazine was built in 1713 and was used during the Revolutionary War. Today the magazine is an outstanding museum exploring Charleston's colonial period and the city's role in the American Revolution. Though small, the museum contains artifacts, interactive exhibits, and models that will help you visualize what life was like before and during the British occupation. *The Powder Magazine Museum, 79 Cumberland St., Charleston, SC 29401; 843-722-9350; www.powder magazinemuseum.org. GPS: 32.779574, -79.930135. Open Tues.–Sun.*

The Exchange Building—Established as a customs house in 1771, the Exchange Building saw a number of South Carolina's most important moments during the Revolutionary period, including its vote for independence in 1776 and the ratification of the United States Constitution in 1788. When the British occupied the city in 1780, the dungeon of the building was turned into a prison. The site was also, as a merchant exchange, the scene of slave auctions. Today, in addition to being an artifact of the old city, the Exchange Building serves as a museum focusing on Charleston's colonial history. You can explore the upper portion of the building on a self-guided tour, then take a 25-minute guided tour of the dungeon. Still well preserved, the Exchange Building offers a diverse picture of colonial Charleston. *The Old Exchange and Provost Dungeon, 122 East Bay St., Charleston, SC 29401; 888-763-0448; www.oldexchange.org. GPS: 32.776868, -79.926982. Open daily.*

Ashley River Road—The final British approach to Charleston before crossing the Ashley River was along Ashley River Road. Drayton Hall, a large plantation, was the site where the British crossed the river to establish their presence on the Charlestown Peninsula. Touring Drayton Hall is a different experience than most plantations; rather than focus on the elaborate furnishings, the decision was made to focus on restoring the house and telling the stories of those who lived here, from the original Drayton family to the African slaves who worked the plantation. The story of the plantation during the American Revolution is told here as well. *Drayton Hall, 3380 Ashley River Rd., Charleston, SC 29414; 843-769-2600; draytonhall.org. GPS: 32.864983, -80.082328. Open daily.*

Charles Pinckney National Historic Site—Charles Pinckney was a member of one of South Carolina's prominent plantation families. During the war he served as a lieutenant in the Charles Towne Militia and took part in the attack on Savannah in 1779; when Charlestown fell, Pinckney was confined for some time on a British prison ship. After the war, he served in Congress and became outspoken for the need to create a new constitution; he was named a delegate to the Constitutional Convention. Pinckney went on to serve as governor and in other distinguished positions, though he was also a fierce fighter for the preservation of slavery in the South. Charles Pinckney National Historic Site preserves part of one of his rice and indigo plantations and tells the stories of not only the Pinckneys but also of the enslaved people who toiled here. The site shows an introductory film, has exhibits and artifacts about plantation life, and features trails around the large grounds. *Charles Pinckney National Historic Site, 1254 Long Point Rd., Mt. Pleasant, SC 29464; 843-577-0242; www.nps.gov/chpi. GPS: 32.846982, -79.823384. Grounds open Wed.–Sun.; visitor center and house open Fri.–Sun.*

Paul Pritchard Shipyard—South Carolina, like other states, developed its own navy when the Revolutionary War broke out. The state's primary shipyard was owned by Paul Pritchard, and it went on to develop several vessels for the state. Remnants of the site are still there today, but it is on private property; a historical marker near the site explains its significance. *Historical marker—Hobcaw Shipyards, near intersection of East Hobcaw Dr. and Muirhead Rd., Mt. Pleasant, SC 29464. GPS: 32.816439, -79.883530. Accessible daily.*

The Breach, site of the aborted British attack on Fort Moultrie.

Charleston Harbor was not easy to navigate and required a great deal of sailing skill to avoid grounding a ship on its sandbars. The second was that the navy had to wait until the winds allowed the ships to move next to the fort and begin firing. That day did not come until June 28, 1776, giving the Americans plenty of time to improve the fort. At 11:00 AM, the first division of British ships anchored only 400 yards from Fort Sullivan and began unleashing repeated broadsides against its facade. Much to everyone's astonishment, this heavy firing at close range did very little damage. The walls of the fort were made of palmetto logs, backed by 16 feet of earth; the palmetto logs were spongy, and rather than splintering like most wood, they simply absorbed the shock of the British cannonballs. The American gunners in the fort, on the other hand, had very easy targets right in front of them, and they tore into the British ships, focusing their fire on *Bristol* and *Experiment*. The mortars of the second division also proved ineffective, as the bombs mostly fell in the sand and mud around the fort, wounding very few of its defenders. The third division of ships, fully focused on the heavy fire coming from the fort, strayed too far from their designated path, and all three of the ships ran aground on a bar, putting them out of the fight. As for the land attack, Clinton's information had been incorrect; the Breach was mostly unfordable, and his men were forced to turn back, never entering the fray.

After nearly 10 hours of firing from Fort Sullivan, the British ships had finally had enough and pulled away to safety, eventually sailing to New York to aid in the invasion of Long Island. The fort had withstood the heavy beating it received, and the Americans suffered only 12 killed and 26 wounded. The two large British ships, however, had suffered severe damage and had lost 64 killed and 141 wounded. One of the ships that had run aground, HMS *Acteon*, never freed itself, and her crew set her on fire to prevent her capture. It was a decisive American victory.

Charleston was approached again several years later when American forces under General Benjamin Lincoln, the new commander of the Southern Army, decided to move to Augusta to better consolidate the Patriot hold on Georgia's backcountry. Lincoln left 1,200 men under Colonel Moultrie to hold South Carolina during his small campaign. The British army holding Savannah was running desperately short on supplies and saw an opportunity in Lincoln's absence: They would conduct a massive foraging expedition into South Carolina, and if the opportunity presented itself, would threaten Charleston.

The British, under General Augustine Prevost, crossed the Savannah River into South Carolina in late April 1779 and began moving north, gathering supplies and feeding off the land. Moultrie immediately alerted Lincoln as to the British movements and pulled his men back toward Charleston, but Lincoln seemed unconcerned. Moultrie's force, mostly made up of South Carolina militia, began to dry up as men left to protect their homes and families, eventually shrinking to 600 men by the time they finally got to Charleston. Moultrie entered Charleston on May 9, just behind the American Legion, a force that consisted of 120 cavalry and light infantry under General Casimir Pulaski, a Polish officer in the Continental Army.

On May 11, 1779, Prevost crossed the Ashley River onto the neck of land that led to Charleston. Leaving 1,200 men at the river landing, he moved 900 men toward the city, where they were met by Pulaski's legion in front of the city. A short, sharp fight followed, with the British eventually driving the smaller American force off. Now positioned in front of the lines but with no hope of conquering the city with their tiny force, the British decided to see if they could essentially trick the Americans into giving up the city. Remarkably, the American governor of South Carolina, John Rutledge, almost did just that. Rutledge, vastly overestimating the British force while underestimating the American numbers, wanted to avoid the destruction of the city, and asked the British the next day about the terms of a surrender. When the British replied that only an unconditional surrender would prevent their assaulting the city, the governor responded with a vague and confusing proposal that South Carolina become neutral for the duration of the war. The offer was refused, and while the Americans prepared to fight it out, the British simply slipped away. The Americans awoke on May 13 to find the British gone, headed back to Savannah with the food and supplies they had gathered.

After the capture of Savannah, the British moved to try to settle the matter of Charleston once and for all. A large flotilla of British ships under the command of British General Henry Clinton left New York Harbor the day after Christmas 1779 and slowly made their way down the Atlantic Coast. Scattered by constant storms, the ships only began to gather outside Savannah near the end of January 1780, with the last ships coming in over the next six weeks. As they waited, the British planned their campaign for Charleston, deciding to land on Simmons Island, 30 miles south of the city, then approach from the south. The British ships made their landing on February 11, 1780.

The Americans were aware of the British landing almost immediately, but though they sent some small forces out of the city to meet them, for the most part the Americans did not interfere with the activities of the British. This pattern continued, with the American offering very little resistance as the British crept ever closer to Charleston, establishing points along the way at Stono Ferry and Drayton Hall Plantation for supplies. In the meantime, the British fleet gathered outside Charleston Harbor, preparing to cross the shallow bar and make their entrance; though there were ships of the Continental Navy sent specifically to guard the harbor, the American admiral was unwilling to put up a defense. On both land and sea, the Americans mostly watched and waited.

Charleston sits at the end of a peninsula formed by the Ashley River to the south and the Cooper River to the north. To capture the city, the British would not only have to control the peninsula but also the waterways to ensure that supplies and reinforcements could not arrive via the rivers. On March 28, they accomplished the first of these when they crossed the Ashley River and established their presence on Charlestown Neck, the narrow spit of land between the rivers. The British then marched up to within 800 yards of the American defenses in front of Charleston and began to gather their army of what would eventually be over 12,000 men. On the night of April 1, they began to dig their first approach trench and initiated the siege of Charleston.

Inside the city, General Benjamin Lincoln, commander of all American forces in the south, was having trouble deciding what to do. He was in command of only about 4,500 men, a mix of both Continental Army soldiers and militia. Lincoln was also fighting the civilian authorities in Charleston, who had their own ideas about whether the Americans should fight or flee. The Charleston garrison received reinforcements on April 7, a Continental brigade of 900 men, but as the British tightened their grip on the city it became clear that a decision would have to be made. Unfortunately for the Americans, before they made that decision, a British force routed an American force across the Cooper River on April 13, closing the lines of communication to the city. Evacuation was no longer an option; the Americans would have to fight it out or surrender.

Meanwhile, British trenches steadily began to approach the American defensive works, which consisted of a substantial fortress known as the Horn Work and several redoubts, fronted by several wide ditches, including one filled with water, and abatis (felled trees with sharpened branches facing the enemy). The Americans kept up a fire on the British soldiers as they dug, and casualties were constant but usually did little to stop the digging. In addition to the fighting on the front lines, the British initiated a bombardment of Charleston, sending mortar shells into the city, killing civilians and setting homes on fire. Clinton did not want to destroy the city, and mortar fire would often slacken in order to allow citizens to put out fires as they broke out. But to those living in Charleston, the shelling must have been horrific.

On May 6, the British trenches crept close enough to drain the water from the ditch fronting the American works. From there, it was only a matter of time before the Americans would either have to surrender or be assaulted, a prospect which neither side wanted to entertain. Clinton, knowing that a French fleet arriving to save the city was a possibility, tried to get the Americans to surrender quickly. Finally, on May 11, Lincoln and his generals, along with the civilian leaders, agreed that the time had come. On May 12, 1780, the Americans at Charleston marched out of the city and laid down their arms; they were refused the dignity of flying their colors or playing a march, as often happened during these events. The result for the Americans was catastrophic. Though only 89 had been killed and 140 wounded over the course of the siege, 5,611 American soldiers were captured.

The capture of the army at Charleston was the largest British victory in the American Revolution, and Charleston would become the base of

The remnants of the Horn Work, center of the American defenses at Charleston.

operations for the new British Southern Strategy. Clinton immediately left for New York City once the city fell, giving command in the south to General Charles Cornwallis. Before he left, however, he committed one grave error. Though captured soldiers from the Continental Army were imprisoned by the British, Clinton had first agreed to parole the militia to return to their homes, with the understanding that they would not fight against the British again unless they were exchanged for British prisoners. Clinton then changed his mind, pardoned those militia, and demanded that they enlist to fight for the British. Many, from the lowest citizens up to the highest American commanders, saw this as a double cross. Far from swelling the British ranks as intended, Clinton's order generally served to push South Carolina's citizens toward fighting for the American cause. Charleston would nonetheless remain in British hands until evacuated in December 1782.

Ninety Six

The crossroads town of Ninety Six, though relatively small, was a major gathering point of the South Carolina backcountry. So named because it was ninety-six miles from the Cherokee town of Keowee on the road from Charleston, Ninety Six was also on the road to Augusta, Georgia, and therefore a natural trade center around which a community could form. When the American Revolution began, the town was a place where both Loyalists and Patriots could try to gather support for their cause, and so controlling Ninety Six became an objective for both sides.

The first hint of trouble in Ninety Six occurred early in the war. In July 1775, a cache of weapons was deposited at Ninety Six, and Patriots flooded the town to safeguard it. Loyalists saw this as a threat, and over the next few months tensions grew. Finally, on November 18, 1775, a collection of 600 Patriots were forced to barricade themselves within a makeshift stockade when a gathering of 1,400 Loyalists attacked them at Ninety Six. The fighting was sporadic but lasted for three days before the two sides came to an agreement that allowed the Patriots to keep the stockpile. Two men were killed and 14 were wounded. The battle at Ninety Six between Loyalists and Patriots—all Americans—signaled that the fighting in the backcountry would be fierce and personal.

Relative peace came over the Carolina backcountry for the next few years as the Revolutionary War played itself out in the northern colonies. That changed in 1780 when Charleston was captured by the British. The new Southern Strategy relied on recruiting Loyalist support in the backcountry, so after the city fell, British forces attempted to consolidate their gains and take possession of the countryside. Ninety Six, along with Augusta, Georgia and Camden, South Carolina, were immediately occupied and established as depots and recruitment centers for British operations. The British initially claimed victory, thinking that they had conquered South Carolina, but their efforts to gather support for the crown fell flat, because most of the people of the backcountry were driven to the American cause.

The commander of the British garrison at Ninety Six, Colonel John Cruger, was another American, a New York Loyalist. Cruger did not like the relatively open nature of the town and decided to build a fortification next to it. The Star Fort—built mostly by local slaves—was a strong work, with massive earthen walls, abatis (felled trees with their branches sharpened), and a deep ditch, and the star shape of the fort allowed

A reconstructed tower, used to fire into the British fort at Ninety Six.

> **SITE DETAILS**
>
> **Ninety Six National Historic Site**—Ninety Six National Historic Site preserves the location of this critical backcountry town. The visitor center has exhibits and a short film that highlight the founding and emergence of the town as well as all of the Revolutionary War activity that happened here. The Star Fort is in excellent condition, and you can walk into and around the remnants of the earthworks; the trail around the fort follows the outlines of the siege works dug by Greene's Continentals. A partial reconstruction of the original stockade around the town is also here. Though the town is now gone, you can still walk around the area on the many trails that are part of the historic site, including the original roads that crossed at Ninety Six, which are now just depressions in the ground after centuries of use. Plenty of signs are here to help you interpret what was once here at Ninety Six and what happened. Ninety Six National Historic Site may be a bit isolated but is well worth the trip for the unique stories it has to tell. *Ninety Six National Historic Site, 1103 Highway 248, Ninety Six, SC 29666; 864-543-4068; www.nps.gov/nisi. GPS: 34.146992, -82.024062. Grounds open daily; visitor center open Wed.–Sun.*

defenders to fire in any direction. There was also a covered way, a tall ditch that ran between the town and the fort to preserve communication.

Cruger's preparations—and his 550 men, also made of Loyalists—would be put to the test. On May 21, 1781, American Patriot General Nathanael Greene approached Ninety Six with 1,000 men. Observing the strength of the Star Fort, Greene settled on a siege and put Polish engineer Thaddeus Kosciuszko to work. After cutting off the British water supply, Kosciuszko directed the Americans to dig approach trenches, creeping ever closer to the fort. By June 10, the Americans were in musket range and began to harass the defenders constantly. A 30-foot tower was also built, allowing American marksmen to fire down into the fort. However, just as the Americans completed their siege works, word came that 2,000 British reinforcements were on their way to Ninety Six. With no more time available, Greene was left with two choices: abandon the siege and leave Ninety Six or attack the Star Fort. Greene chose to attack.

At noon on July 18, 1781, an advance force of 50 men moved through the American trenches and leapt onto the British works with the intention of clearing some of the obstructions the British had placed and creating a pathway for the main attacking force. The men, armed with axes for chopping through the abatis and long hooks for removing sandbags the British had placed atop the fort, ran into the ditch and began to do their work. But Cruger launched a bold attack from inside the fort into the ditch, repulsing the forward party after hand-to-hand fighting. The assault had failed, and Greene was forced to leave Ninety Six in the hands of the British.

Despite the defeat of the Americans, Ninety Six did not remain in British hands for very long. The writing had been on the wall for some time: the British Southern Strategy was failing, and holding the Carolina backcountry would take tens of thousands of soldiers. In July 1781, Cruger was ordered to abandon the fort and burn the town to the ground, then return to the British base at Charleston. For Ninety Six, the war was over.

Camden

Following the capture of Charleston, the Continental Army was left without an army or a leader in the south. General Benjamin Lincoln was a prisoner (on parole) and the Continental regiments that were in Charleston were the only units in the entire region. Seeing that the British strategy was clearly shifting south, Congress elected to send both soldiers and a new general to take command there. George Washington had asked Congress to give command to General Nathanael Greene, but Congress had other ideas. The position instead went to the hero of Saratoga, General Horatio Gates.

On the face of it, Gates was perhaps a natural choice. He was in overall command for the Americans' incredible victory at Saratoga, and he had been an officer in the British army before the American Revolution. But his actual command experience was somewhat lacking. Gates had seen combat but had not actually commanded troops on the battlefield. Even during the battles at Saratoga, Gates had remained far from the actual fighting, commanding from far behind the lines; those on the battlefield remembered the exploits and bravery of Generals Benedict Arnold and Daniel Morgan, not Gates. But Gates had nurtured relationships with those in Congress, so when the call came he was a natural choice for the politicians.

Washington chose some of his best and most battle-hardened troops to move south, the Maryland and Delaware lines. They were commanded, at least until Gates arrived, by General Jean, Baron de Kalb, a Bavarian officer who had traveled to America with Lafayette. The men left their encampment at Morristown, New Jersey, on April 16, 1780, and marched south, reaching Buffalo Ford on the Deep River in North Carolina in early July. Forced to forage along the way, the troops were weakened with hunger and decided to wait for Gates, their new commander, while they scoured the countryside for food.

Gates arrived on July 25, 1780, and almost immediately upon his arrival started to make things worse for the Continentals. He dismissed the issue of the troops' hunger, saying that a large amount of rations was

The remnants of the Wagon Road, site of the Battle of Camden.

SITE DETAILS

Camden Battlefield—The establishment of the Camden Battlefield and Long Leaf Pine Preserve was a victory in terms of both historic preservation and interpretation. Established in 2016, the park preserves the core of the battlefield, and restoration efforts have returned the landscape back to what it originally was, ensuring the visitor has an accurate picture of the fight. Multiple trails cross the park, with plenty of interpretive signs and maps that explain the battle. The park itself is a nice retreat, and unless you visit during an event or peak time you will be guaranteed a beautiful, peaceful walk through the pines. If you have questions about the battle or what you're looking at, you can visit Historic Camden for more information. *Camden Battlefield and Long Leaf Pine Reserve, 1698 Flat Rock Rd., Camden, SC 29020; 803-432-9841; www.historiccamden.org. GPS: 34.357617, -80.610504. Open daily.*

Historic Camden—Historic Camden preserves the site of the original town that the British garrisoned. Focused on Camden's colonial and Revolutionary War history, the site contains a number of historic buildings, including the recon-

on the way. (It was not.) Gates then set the army on a direct course for Camden, South Carolina, one of the British strongholds in the Carolina backcountry along with Ninety Six and Augusta. He had been advised by de Kalb and his other officers that a westward, more circular route would not only keep him close to Camden, but also provide food and a route of retreat into the more friendly Carolina backcountry. If Gates listened to this advice at all, he dismissed it immediately, instead relying on intelligence that the British had only 700 men at Camden and that it could easily be taken. In the meantime, further promises of food and supplies went mostly empty; in fact, the troops were given molasses for a ration, causing severe diarrhea among the men and leaving them in an even worse state than before. All along, the new Southern Army trudged

structed Kershaw House, where Cornwallis made his headquarters while in Camden. One of the seven redoubts that surrounded the town has also been re-created, as has a portion of the stockade wall that surrounded the town. Living history interpreters can be found throughout the site, and there is an excellent museum on site as well that tells the story of Camden's history. *Historic Camden, 222 Broad St., Camden, SC 29020; 803-432-9841; www.historiccamden.org. GPS: 34.233511, -80.605652. Open Tues.–Sat.*

Hobkirk Hill—Though much of the battlefield at Hobkirk Hill has been developed, it is well interpreted and worth investing a little of your time. Several pieces of parkland have been created that will allow you to view the terrain and picture the battle, and plenty of signs along the way will point out features and monuments and tell the story of the battle. You can start at Monument Square and try to make your way around, or, better yet, get a brochure from Historic Camden or from the Camden Archives and Museum to help you get from one site to another. Preservation efforts continue here, so look for more to come. *Hobkirk Hill—Monument Square/Camden Archives and Museum, 1314 Broad St., Camden, SC 29020; 803-425-6050; camdenschistory.com. GPS: 34.251127, -80.607391. Grounds accessible daily; museum open Mon.–Sat.*

toward Camden, hoping to take possession of the small garrison there before it could be reinforced.

By the time Gates had decided to assault Camden, the British garrison was no longer as small as he had thought. On August 9, word reached General Cornwallis in Charleston that the Americans were approaching Camden. Cornwallis, itching for field duty after taking care of administrative duties, left for Camden the next day, quickly pulling together a force of over 2,200 troops. Within a week, Cornwallis was at Camden and ready to fight.

By coincidence, both Gates and Cornwallis, now only 15 miles from each other, decided on a night march. At 2:00 AM on the morning of August 16, 1780, in the pitch-black darkness north of Camden, cavalry

A reconstructed redoubt at Historic Camden in South Carolina.

from each army stumbled upon each other. After a brief clash, the two groups retired back to their armies, each having captured a few of the others' forces and thus having gathered some intelligence. It was now known to both sides that the Americans had approximately 3,700 troops while the British fielded 2,239. Gates, in complete shock, held a council of war immediately and consulted his generals, who decided to fight it out.

Each side quickly made out their battle plans, with both deciding on an assault at first light. Both sides followed a European custom in placing their most honored troops on the right. What this meant for the Americans, though, was that Gates's least experienced troops—2,800 completely inexperienced militia from North Carolina and Virginia—would be facing the best troops in Cornwallis's command. In fact, though the Americans outnumbered the British, that British force was made up almost completely of experienced soldiers, while the majority of the Americans had never seen combat.

Facing each other along the Wagon Road from Camden to the Waxhaws, the armies lined up and faced each other as soon as the day began to break. Gates remained far behind his lines, so far, in fact, that he could not see what was going on or react to the events on the battlefield, and instead relied on his staff to convey information. The Americans opened the action, sending a small group forward to harass the British line. But once that British line began to move forward, the militia on the American left simply threw down their arms and ran, in many cases without even firing a shot. The sight of British Regulars, in resplendent uniforms and advancing steadily as one with fixed bayonets was simply too much.

While a complete panic ensued on the American left, the American right, made up of experienced Continental soldiers, held their own, repulsing several British assaults. However, rather than pursue the fleeing militiamen, the British line simply turned to their left and began to attack the Continentals' flank. Shortly afterward, British cavalry under Banastre Tarleton circled around the Americans left on the field and attacked them from the rear. Now surrounded, the Americans fought fiercely, but many were forced to flee or surrender.

The battle lasted for a full hour, mostly because of the firmness of the Continentals. But the result, decided early in the fight, was definitive and represents possibly the worst American battlefield defeat of the entire Revolutionary War. While the British lost 68 killed and 256 wounded, the Americans suffered 250 killed and up to 800 wounded and captured. Baron de Kalb was mortally wounded. As for Gates, he fled with his militia and even went ahead of them, not stopping until he reached Hillsborough, North Carolina, three days later. He would never command an army in the field again.

Less than a year later, the American Southern Army, newly committed to reconquering the south, approached Camden again, this time with 1,500 men, mostly Continental soldiers, under General Nathanael Greene. Greene approached Camden from the north and took a position on Hobkirk Hill, about a mile and a half north of the town. Camden was then garrisoned with 900 British soldiers under Lieutenant Colonel Francis Rawdon. Rawdon, though, decided not to wait for Greene but instead to attack him where he was.

Rawdon moved his force through thick woods to Hobkirk's Hill on April 25, 1781, in an attempt to surprise the Americans. First contact

The Americans attacked the British north of Camden at Hobkirk Hill.

was at 10:00 AM, but the Americans responded quickly and formed a line. Greene attempted to advance and flank both sides of the British line, but after Rawdon countered by extending his own line, the Americans fell into confusion in the woods and fell back first to the hill, then another 3 miles to the site of the original Camden battlefield. The British held Hobkirk's Hill but withdrew back into their Camden defenses.

Though the British were victorious at Hobkirk's Hill, they would not remain in Camden for long. Like the other fortified town of Ninety Six, Camden was now in an exposed condition as Cornwallis had by this time moved the bulk of his forces into Virginia. On May 10, Rawdon abandoned Camden and moved his men to Charleston, leaving the town to the Americans.

Kings Mountain

The story of the Battle of Kings Mountain and the events leading up to it is one of the more remarkable of the American Revolution. In fact, it can be said that Kings Mountain was perhaps the turning point in the Revolutionary War.

A key element of the British Southern Strategy was to harness what was perceived as significant support for the king in the southern colonies. To that end, British Major Patrick Ferguson was charged with recruiting in the Carolina backcountry. From the outset, he ran into many challenges, but Ferguson was able to cobble together what was available into several regiments of Loyalist militia, keeping many of them in camp with him as he continued to recruit.

As Ferguson moved around the countryside looking for support, he also attempted to deter support for the American cause. It was for this reason that he sent a message to American militia Colonel Isaac Shelby in early September 1780. The message was verbal, sent through a relative of Shelby's whom Ferguson had freed just for this purpose, and it was brief: If Shelby and his men would not stop resisting British arms, Fergu-

The Kings Mountain Centennial Monument.

son would "march over the mountains, hang their leaders, and lay their country waste with fire and sword."

Isaac Shelby, however, was not one to be intimidated, nor was his counterpart, Colonel John Sevier, who led his own militia. Shelby and Sevier were of the Overmountain Men, the fiercely independent people who had forced their way west over the Appalachian Mountains into Cherokee territory and carved their living out of the wilderness. Through necessity, the Overmountain Men had become fighters of great renown as they defended their homesteads against Native American attacks and other dangers. Shelby immediately tracked Sevier down and told him of the message, and it was quickly agreed that they would gather their men and send word out to the surrounding countryside that there was an imminent threat.

While Shelby and Sevier were from the region now known as East Tennessee, they gathered support from other locations. First was a call-out to Colonel Charles McDowell's militia in North Carolina, then to Colonel William Campbell's militia in Virginia. Others followed, and more would join along the way. A rendezvous was set for September 25, 1780, at Sycamore Shoals, and the party made their way across the mountains to try to surprise Major Patrick Ferguson.

The Overmountain Men traveled to Quaker Meadows in North Carolina on September 30, joining with two other bands of militia under Colonel Benjamin Cleveland and Major Joseph Winston. From there, the group attempted to track down Ferguson's camp, moving quickly but having to rely on secondhand reports. An additional complication soon presented itself when two of Sevier's men were found to have deserted. It was suspected that they would try to alert Ferguson of the force's approach, and those suspicions were proven correct. Ferguson found out about the march of the Overmountain Men on September 30.

After searching for several days, the Patriot force was becoming weaker. They had supplied themselves, and food was beginning to run out; their horses were also beginning to suffer, with many of them crossing the rugged terrain unshod. Then, on October 6, while en route to Cowpens, South Carolina, word came in through several sources that Ferguson was nearby. Ferguson had requested reinforcements from General Charles Cornwallis, who was in nearby Charlotte, North Carolina, at the time. After hearing no response, Ferguson began to ready his 1,125

SITE DETAILS

Kings Mountain National Military Park—The entire battlefield of Kings Mountain is preserved within Kings Mountain National Military Park. The visitor center contains a short film and exhibits about the people involved and the events leading up to the battle, and a light map display shows how the battle played out on the mountain. From there, you can take a winding path around the battlefield that slowly makes its way to the top; it's not steep, but there are benches along the way just in case. Along the way, you'll find memorials and interpretive signs at key points on the battlefield, ending at the burial site of Major Patrick Ferguson. The woods you'll be walking through on your way up the mountain look very much as they did in 1780, though the top of the mountain was cleared of trees at the time. Between the excellent visitor center, the pristine nature of the battlefield, and the story behind it, Kings Mountain is perhaps one of the best preserved and interpreted battlefields in the country. *Kings Mountain National Military Park, 2625 Park Rd., Blacksburg, SC 29702; 864-936-7921; www.nps.gov/kimo. GPS: 35.140948, -81.376348. Grounds open daily; visitor center open Wed.–Sun.*

---

men for battle and chose a position atop Kings Mountain in South Carolina to camp. The Overmountain Men quickly established the position of the camp and readied themselves for a fight.

On October 7, 1780, the men silently approached the camp in two columns and made their way around the short hilltop. The ground was wet with rain, rendering their footsteps silent, and the area was heavily wooded, concealing their presence from the Loyalist camp. At about 3:00 PM, the Overmountain Men rushed up the hill on every side, completely surprising Ferguson's men. The Patriots worked their way from tree to tree, using their rifles with deadly accuracy. Ferguson was able to organize three bayonet charges down the hillside to push the Overmountain Men back, but each time they returned. By 3:30, the Patriots had reached the clearing on the hilltop, and Ferguson was killed by a concentrated blast of rifle fire. The Loyalists then tried to surrender, but the fighting continued, and in many cases the Patriots were giving no quarter, shouting to avenge John Buford's massacre at the earlier battle at Waxhaws. It was only after a second surrender attempt that the leaders of the Overmountain Men began to control their men and put a stop to the violence.

Overall, 157 of Ferguson's Tory force had been killed at Kings Mountain, with another 163 badly wounded, and 698 of them taken prisoner. These prisoners were forced to march their way west. Not all would make it, as they were severely harassed, brutalized, and even killed along the way. As for the Overmountain Men, 28 were killed and 62 wounded. With the exception of Patrick Ferguson, all the combatants were Americans. The victory at Kings Mountain absolutely crushed British recruiting efforts for the rest of the war. It also provided a critical morale builder for American forces, who had broken a string of defeats at Charleston, Waxhaws, and Camden. The momentum now turned in favor of the Americans, and it would stay that way through the end of the Revolution.

Cowpens

On December 2, 1780, the new commander of the Southern Army arrived at Charlotte, North Carolina. This time, the new commander was chosen by George Washington, and not by Congress as the previous commanders had been. Nathaniel Greene, one of Washington's most trusted and capable generals, would take over for Horatio Gates. Though the transfer of command was probably awkward, it was done tactfully and civilly, and Gates rode north to an uncertain future while Greene immediately began gathering information about his new assignment.

The very day after Greene arrived, another accomplished American general rode into Charlotte. Daniel Morgan, who had been laid up at his farm in Virginia for over a year recovering from sciatica, had been called back to service by Gates, his old ally from Saratoga. Greene, knowing Morgan's impeccable reputation as a leader and a fighter, welcomed him with open arms and immediately gave him a command, and before long, a mission.

British General Charles Cornwallis was at the army's winter quarters in Winnsboro, South Carolina, and it was apparent that he was preparing for a strike into North Carolina when the opportunity presented itself.

Greene and Morgan would try to prevent that opportunity from coming about. After careful study of South Carolina's rivers and fords and an extensive gathering of intelligence about them, Greene decided to do something a bit unorthodox. He would divide his forces, with Greene holding down the army's main camp on the Pee Dee River, north of Cornwallis and thereby blocking any movement to the north. Meanwhile, Morgan would take a large force and move west of the Catawba River, taking charge of the militia in that area and threatening Cornwallis's left flank. Morgan would move about the country as he saw fit while staying close enough to Greene should they need to unite for battle.

Cornwallis was aware of the Americans' movements but did not know their intentions. He did realize, however, that he could not leave his base while Morgan remained a threat to the west. When he received false intelligence that Morgan was about to attack the critical outpost at Ninety Six, Cornwallis decided that it was time to strike. He summoned his most valuable strike force, the British Legion, commanded by perhaps the most feared and most hated man in the entire South: Colonel

The Green River Road, site of the critical Battle of Cowpens.

THE ROUTE OF THE PATRIOT MILITIA TO KINGS MOUNTAIN

Just as remarkable as the Patriot victory at Kings Mountain is the journey the American militia took to get there. Though not all of those who fought at Kings Mountain were from the back of the mountains, the group of nearly 2,000 have all become known as the Overmountain Men, and their toughness, especially in the face of a direct threat posed by the king's army, has become legend. Today, the Overmountain Victory National Historic Trail follows the routes that the three groups of militia used to reach Kings Mountain and their great victory. Not only is it an inspiring journey, it's also a beautiful one that will take you over and through the Blue Ridge Mountains, so take your time. *Overmountain Victory National Historic Trail; www.nps.gov/ovvi.*

ABINGDON MUSTER GROUNDS—Responding to the call, 200 men under Colonel William Campbell assembled at the Abingdon Muster Grounds before making their way to join the other Overmountain Men under Shelby and Sevier at Sycamore Shoals. The men then proceeded along Wolf Creek toward Sycamore Shoals, gathering men along the way.

The muster grounds, which is at the trailhead of the Overmountain Victory National Historic Trail, covers several acres where the men gathered and then set off for Sycamore Shoals. The site is accessible during daylight hours, but you'll also want to visit the excellent visitor center, the most thorough of several along the trail. Interactive exhibits cover the march and the Battle of Kings Mountain, as well as the war's effect on the Overmountain Men, women, African Americans, and Native Americans. *Abingdon Muster Grounds, 702 Colonial Rd., Abingdon, VA, 24210. GPS: 36.704027, -81.994262. Open daily.*

SYCAMORE SHOALS—September 25, 1780, was the designated muster date for the Overmountain Men, and the location was Sycamore Shoals in what is now Tennessee. Approximately 800 men under Shelby, Sevier, Campbell, and Colonel Charles McDowell gathered near Fort Watauga, many of them having brought their families. After gathering supplies and preparing equipment for the journey, the men left the others behind and set out on September 26.

Sycamore Shoals State Park, besides preserving where the Overmountain Men gathered, also contains a faithful reconstruction of Fort Watauga, which was attacked by the Cherokee in 1776. (The original site of the fort was not here.) The visitor center contains exhibits about the early Watauga settlement, the war with the Cherokee, and the journey of the Overmountain Men; a 15-minute film covers this history in impressive detail. The park also contains a small walkable section of the original route. *Sycamore Shoals State Park, 1651 West Elk Ave., Elizabethton, TN 37643; 423-543-5808; www.tnstateparks.com/parks/sycamore-shoals. GPS: 36.343415, -82.250926. Open daily.*

GILLESPIE GAP—Over three days, the Overmountain Men reached and then ascended the western side of the Appalachian Mountains, leaving modern-day Tennessee and entering North Carolina. On September 29, 1780, the group passed through Gillespie Gap, which marked the beginning of their descent into the Catawba Valley.

Outside the Museum of North Carolina Minerals, operated by the National Park Service, is a memorial to the passage of the Overmountain Men through Gillespie Gap, as well as action with the Cherokee that occurred earlier. Within the museum

continued on next page

itself is information about the trail, as well as some fascinating exhibits related to the unique geology of the Blue Ridge Mountains. If you feel like mixing a little natural history into your trip, this is the place. *Museum of North Carolina Minerals, 79 Parkway Maintenance Road, Spruce Pine, NC 28777; 828-765-2761. GPS: 35.854249, -82.051448. Open daily.*

QUAKER MEADOWS—The Overmountain Men reached the base of the Blue Ridge and headed for Quaker Meadows, where another contingent of militia from North Carolina was set to meet them. These men arrived on September 30, 1780, expanding the force to 1,100. That evening, under a large oak tree, the officers met to come up with a plan to use their combined forces to bag General Ferguson and the British.

The area where the Overmountain Men camped, the mansion at Quaker Meadows, has been preserved, though the existing mansion (also open for tours) postdates the march by several decades. The Council Oak, under which the decisive plans for catching the British were agreed upon, is now gone, but its former location has been memorialized. *Quaker Meadows—McDowell House, 119 St Marys Church Rd., Morganton, NC 28655; 828-437-4104; www.historic burke.org/the-mcdowell-house. GPS: 35.720449, -81.757486. Site accessible daily, house open Sundays April through October. Quaker Meadows—Council Oak, intersection of North Green St. and Bost Rd., Morganton, NC 28655. GPS: 35.754001, -81.71678. Accessible daily.*

BEDFORD HILL—Moving south from Quaker Meadows, the swelled band of militia stopped at Bedford Hill to camp, then were held there an additional day by rain. If there was a point where the Overmountain Men were going to break, this could have been it—cold and rainy weather, no tents, hunger, idleness, and an inability to protect the families they had left behind a week ago. On October 3, 1780, before heading to Ferguson's suspected location at Gilbert Town, all the men were given the opportunity to back out. Not one did.

There is currently no interpretation at Bedford Hill, though it isn't difficult to see the hilly open ground where the Overmountain Men camped. It is all private property, so look from the comfort of your vehicle. *Bedford Hill, intersection of US-64 and NC-226, Cane Creek, NC 28167. GPS: 35.582047, -81.845635. Private property.*

GILBERT TOWN—Upon reaching Gilbert Town October 4, 1780, the Patriots learned that Ferguson—who had been warned by the two suspected deserters from the American expedition—had left his camp here and headed toward Charlotte and Cornwallis's army. The Overmountain Men changed course and moved north, making their way to Cowpens on October 6. Now with a strength of nearly 2,000 due to the arrival of a contingent from South Carolina, the Overmountain Men marched to their destiny at Kings Mountain on October 7.

The site of Gilbert Town contains several historical highway markers, and there are plans to further interpret the area where the Overmountain Men camped. The open fields here mark the site where the men camped both to and from Kings Mountain. *Gilbert Town, on Rock Rd. 0.1 mile north of Old Gilbert Town Rd., Rutherfordton, NC 28139. GPS: 35.40531, -81.942397. Sign accessible daily.*

BIGGERSTAFF OLD FIELDS—Leaving Kings Mountain the day after the battle, the Overmountain Men stopped at Biggerstaff Old Fields on the evening of October 14. A number of their prisoners had been accused of atrocities before the battle, and 32

continued on next page

> of them were sentenced to hang. Nine of the executions were carried out before officers put a stop to them. The next morning the group continued on, dissolving along the way and heading for their homes.
>
> The site of the Biggerstaff Hanging Tree has now been developed into a nice waypoint along the Overmountain Victory National Historic Trail. Though the precise location of the original tree is not known with certainty, several possibilities are suggested as part of the existing interpretation. More development is planned, including more permanent parking and additional interpretation. *Biggerstaff Old Fields, on Whitesides Rd. 0.3 mile east of Engineer Rd., Bostic, NC 28018. GPS: 35.438269, -81.826837. Site accessible daily.*

Banastre Tarleton. Tarleton had a reputation for ruthlessness and dogged pursuit, and tracking down Morgan and bringing him to battle was a mission made for those qualities. Tarleton was given command of additional infantry and moved into the field with 1,100 men on January 2, 1781, determined to eliminate Morgan as a threat.

The movements of both Morgan's and Tarleton's forces were severely complicated by heavy rains and the flooding of the rivers in the area, with most of them being impassable for some time. Over the next several weeks, however, Tarleton zeroed in on Morgan's force, moving his men and horses by exhausting forced marches in order to catch up with him. When he began to come close, Morgan was alerted to his presence. He alerted Greene of his situation, but by this time Tarleton was too close to hope for any reinforcement. Morgan had little choice but to fight. He chose Cowpens as his grounds, a well-known location where cattle from the backcountry was gathered before being moved east to market.

As the Americans awaited Tarleton's arrival, Daniel Morgan came up

Top: Abingdon Muster Grounds, one of the gathering places of the militia before the Battle of Kings Mountain.
Bottom: A monument to the Overmountain Men at Gillespie Gap.

The reconstructed Fort Watauga at Sycamore Shoals State Park in Elizabethton, Tennessee.

with a battle plan that would prove ingenious. Of his 1,000 men, some were Continental troops or were experienced fighters, while others were inexperienced militia. Over the course of the war, time and again it was shown that these militia would often not be able to stand their ground against a British bayonet charge. Morgan knew this and decided to use his militia in the very front line. The militia was directed to fire only twice when the British advanced, then move off the field. Behind the militia line would be another line of those steady Continental soldiers. On both flanks, regiments of riflemen would take aim at the approaching British from a distance and serve as skirmishers. Cavalry would also be kept at the ready to support the militia as they came off the field. It was a completely original plan from an undoubtedly original field commander.

On the early morning of January 17, 1781, Tarleton and his exhausted troopers arrived at Cowpens. Morgan's line was already set and was ready to fight, so Tarleton, always eager, leapt into the action. The British advanced at about 7:00 AM. The riflemen peppered their ranks, but the

> **SITE DETAILS**
>
> **Cowpens National Battlefield**—The entire battlefield at Cowpens is preserved at Cowpens National Battlefield. It's a relatively small park, but this helps the scene to be more easily experienced and interpreted. The visitor center contains an excellent overview and short film about the battle and the events leading up to it as well as its consequences. From there, you can take a 1-mile loop trail around the battlefield. The field is relatively open with only sporadic trees, just as it was at the time of the battle, and it is easy to see the entire area. There are interpretive signs and memorials along the way to help you understand how everything happened in this short but critical fight. You can experience the entire park within a relatively short time while taking a nice easy hike, making Cowpens a great visit. *Cowpens National Battlefield, 338 New Pleasant Rd., Gaffney, SC 29341; 864-461-2828; www.nps.gov/cowp. GPS: 35.141689, -81.815918. Grounds open daily; visitor center open Wed.–Sun.*

British line steadily advanced. The militia held their fire until the British were only 50 yards away, then delivered two steady fires as they had been directed. The British were weakened, but the line kept moving as the American militia began to move off the field. The British saw what they expected to see, the Americans running from another bayonet charge in disorder, and Tarleton ordered his cavalry in to rout them. But the Americans were not running. The American cavalry swooped in to protect them, surrounding the British horses and driving them off.

The British assault line remained in motion and approached the second line, Morgan's Continentals. This line would not be moving. They delivered a heavy and devastating fire into the attackers, who could no longer withstand the pressure. Now boxed in by riflemen on both sides, the British line broke and scurried for the rear. Meanwhile, the militia, who had gathered behind the second line, moved out to the American right to counter a flanking movement, stopping the line and then starting their own bayonet charge. Tarleton ordered one more charge by his British Legion, but they were again met by American cavalry, and though the fight was fierce the British were again sent rearward.

Within an hour, the battle was over. The Americans had won a stunning and decisive victory. The British had lost 110 killed and 200 wounded, plus an additional 529 captured. The Americans had only 12 men killed and another 60 wounded. The one-sided battle at Cowpens would prove to be a huge morale booster not just in the south but throughout the colonies.

OTHER SITES IN THE CAROLINAS

CHEROKEE FORD—Tory recruits from the Carolinas attempting to cross the Savannah River and join British Regulars in Augusta ran into a lightly manned blockhouse at Cherokee Ford across the Savannah River. The Loyalists demanded its surrender but were refused, and they attempted to bypass the force and cross at Vann's Creek the next day, February 11,

A monument to the battle at Cherokee Ford.

THE RACE TO THE DAN

After the Battle of Cowpens, General Daniel Morgan knew that his unit of the Southern Army was in danger. Though they had scored a great victory, it was clear that General Charles Cornwallis would seek to destroy him while he was separated from the force under General Nathaniel Greene. Morgan immediately set out to reunite with Greene and help him in bringing the army to safety.

While Cornwallis desperately sought the Americans, Morgan and Greene were able to reunite at Guildford Courthouse in North Carolina. The danger had not passed, however, and the army was in no condition to fight after their rapid movements. It was clear that if the army could move north of the Dan River, they would be safe. But the flooded Dan, just to their north, had only a few viable crossings. Greene, however, had a plan. Having done an extensive investigation of the rivers in the area, Greene decided to gather as many boats as he could find to cross the river at Dix's Ferry in Virginia. Further, he would send a diversionary force under General Otho Holland Williams toward the existing crossings to throw Cornwallis off the scent.

The plan worked perfectly. Cornwallis assumed that the Americans would use the crossings and readily followed the diversion while the Americans went in a different direction. By the time Cornwallis realized his mistake, Williams had changed direction and was racing for the crossing the Americans had used. Williams brought his men across the river just before the British pulled into view, helplessly stranded on the south side of the Dan.

A historical highway marker has been placed near the site of Dix's Ferry in Danville. In South Boston, Virginia, where the

continued on next page

main body of Greene's army crossed, several monuments near the river commemorate the end of the race. Visitors driving north across the Dan River will be greeted by a cannon memorial placed by the Daughters of the American Revolution; an interpretive sign lies just a bit farther up the street. Closer to the crossing site, in a public park, you will find a permanent memorial to Greene's great feat. *Historic highway marker—Virginia Department of Historic Resources U-39 (Dix's Ferry), on US 58 at intersection with VA 729, Danville, VA 24540. GPS: 36.580715, -79.340646. DAR Memorial, intersection of Main St. and Broad St., South Boston, VA 24592. GPS: 36.694911, -78.900645. Interpretive sign—Retreat to the Dan, intersection of Broad St. and Wren St., South Boston, VA 24592. Crossing of the Dan memorial, 0.1 mile south of intersection of Seymour Dr. and Ferry St., South Boston, VA 24592. GPS: 36.696143, -78.899624. GPS: 36.694159, -78.903855. Sites accessible daily.*

1779. Though the outnumbered Patriot militia was forced to withdraw, the action slowed the Tory militia at a key time, only three days before the Battle of Kettle Creek.

The site of Cherokee Ford is now underneath Richard B. Russell Lake, created by the damming of the Savannah River. There is a monument near the ford site within Richard B. Russell State Park that describes the action and even gives the precise location of the fight, underwater though it may be. The monument is in the parking lot of a beach area, so take advantage if you are able. *Cherokee Ford Monument, Richard B. Russell State Park, on Christian Rd. 0.4 mile south of Russell State Park Dr., Elberton, GA 30635; 706-213-2045; gastateparks.org/RichardBRussell. GPS: 34.162371, -82.744529. Open daily.*

KETTLE CREEK—After crossing the Savannah River, the Loyalist force headed for Augusta camped along Kettle Creek. Aside from posting some pickets, the Tory band did little to protect their campsite. On February 14, 1779, American militia attacked from three sides, focusing on the high ground at the center of the camp. After a two-hour fight, the far-outnumbered Patriots drove the Tories out, with the Loyalists taking about 150 casualties and losing their commander. As it happened, the Tories' efforts had been for naught; the British had evacuated Augusta that same day.

The Kettle Creek Battlefield Association has done a tremendous job of making sure this important American battlefield is not forgotten, and it is now an affiliated area of the National Park Service. The War Hill site, which holds several monuments and a small graveyard, serves as the center point. From here, you can choose from several interpreted trails that crisscross the battlefield. The association isn't done yet, but this is already a great place to visit. *Kettle Creek Battlefield, on War Hill Rd. 1.2 miles west of Court Ground Rd., Washington, GA 30673; kettlecreekbattlefield.com. GPS: 33.690959, -82.885908. Site accessible daily.*

AUGUSTA—Augusta, Georgia, was the westernmost point in the British line of frontier posts stretching across the Carolinas. From posts such as Augusta, the British attempted to control the backcountry. The first British occupation of Augusta occurred on January 31, 1779, with few shots being fired. Most of the local inhabitants, instead of flocking to the Loyalist side, either went with the Patriots or signed a false oath to the king to protect their homes and families. After seeing their efforts wasted, the British left only a few weeks later, on February 14, 1779. They returned to the city in May 1780 after the fall of Charleston and made Augusta an important outpost along with Camden and Ninety Six. One year later, however, a Patriot force under General Andrew Pickens and Colonel Henry "Light Horse Harry" Lee arrived at Augusta to retake the city. Meanwhile, General Nathaniel Greene did the same at Ninety Six. At that time, Augusta's defenses consisted of one outwork, Fort Grierson, and a primary fortification, Fort Cornwallis, within the city. Fort Grierson was the first to fall, and the Americans soon built a so-called Mayham Tower, which was a tall wooden structure with artillery on top to fire down into Fort Cornwallis. The British held out until June 5, 1781, when they finally surrendered.

Downtown Augusta is undergoing a revitalization, and though a focus on its history isn't part of the plan, it sure makes the city a nice place to visit. You will still find history here, mostly in the form of historic markers, with several at the former site of Fort Cornwallis as well as others, that tell the story of the assaults on and occupation of Augusta. A stone monument is behind St. Paul's Church, site of Fort Cornwallis, commemorating the siege at an access stairway for the Augusta Riverwalk. Perhaps most impressive, though, is the Signers' Monument, which not only memorializes the three Georgians who signed the Declaration of Independence but also marks the burial site of two of them, Lyman Hall and George Walton. (The body of the third signer, Button Gwinnett, has never been found.) *Georgia Historical Commission—Fort Grierson, in parking lot on 11th St. at intersection with Reynolds St., Augusta, GA. GPS: 33.478835, -81.970182. The Mayham Tower, intersection of 8th St. and Reynolds St., 30901. GPS: 33.476725, -81.964527. St. Paul's Church, 605 Reynolds St., Augusta, GA 30901. GPS: 33.475692, -81.960958. Signers' Monument, inter-*

The site of Fort Cornwallis, the main fortification in Augusta, Georgia.

section of Greene St. and Monument St., Augusta, GA 30901. GPS: 33.471691, -81.961687. Sites accessible daily.

BRIER CREEK—After evacuating Augusta in early 1779, the British headed back toward Savannah. The Americans followed, now accompanied by some Continental officers, and this force settled along Brier Creek. The camp blocked the British supply line to farmers in the Georgia backcountry, and the British decided to dislodge them. On March 3, 1779, after having sent a decoy from their camp in New Ebenezer, the British approached the Briar Creek camp from the northwest. Through no small amount of negligence, the camp was not prepared for an attack, and though the position itself was a strong one, the rear and flanks of the camp were virtually unguarded. The Patriots did attempt to form a line quickly, but many of the men had not even been issued ammunition before the British appeared. The fight was a quick one, with the disorganized American position causing a gap in the line that the British quickly exploited with a bayonet charge, sending most of them to flight. Though a group of Continental soldiers from Georgia desperately tried to hold the field, they were eventually surrounded and forced to surrender. The Americans lost about 150 killed and 227 captured compared to the British 5 killed and 11 wounded.

A small, easily accessible piece of the Brier Creek battlefield has been set aside as a public park with interpretation about 1 mile from the actual battle site. Further development is coming, however, that will make this a great visit. The site, within Tuckahoe Wildlife Management Area, will soon have several trails with interpretation as well as an area set aside for larger groups to gather. The precise location of the battlefield was only confirmed several years ago, and the excitement that the find generated promises to turn into bigger things. *Brier Creek Battlefield, on Brannens Bridge Rd. 1.2 miles south of Old River Rd., Sylvania, GA 30467; briercreekbattlefield.org. GPS: 32.810880, -81.484078. Accessible daily.*

NEW EBENEZER—Founded in the 1730s, New Ebenezer became a center for silk along the Savannah River. It was a useful strategic position, too, and when the British came after the occupation of Savannah, New

Ebenezer soon became a base and supply center. Fortifying the town, the British built redoubts and took over the church and other buildings for supply houses, stables, and other functions until they finally left in 1782.

Remains of many of the old British redoubts built during the Revolution remain today, though they are all on private property. Still very much alive in New Ebenezer is the Jerusalem Lutheran Church, the oldest continuously operating Lutheran parish in the nation. Both the church itself and the cemetery predate the American Revolution, and historic markers are at both sites. *New Ebenezer, 2980 Ebenezer Rd., Rincon, GA 31326. GPS: 32.376371, -81.181259. Site accessible daily.*

FORT MORRIS—Sunbury, Georgia, was one of the sparsely populated colony's largest and most important port towns. Fortifications were first built here to defend against pirates and the Spanish, and when the American Revolution rolled around, those fortifications grew. The British threatened Fort Sunbury, now known as Fort Morris, on November 25, 1776, but Colonel John McIntosh disregarded the threat and simply said, "Come and take it!" The British backed off without a fight, but they returned on January 9, 1779, after the fall of Savannah. This time, Fort Morris could not hold out, and Sunbury remained in British hands for the duration of the war.

The historic significance of Sunbury and Fort Morris is captured at Fort Morris State Historic Site. Though the town of Sunbury above ground is mostly gone, continuing archaeological investigations, many enlisting local citizens, have revealed much of the history that occurred here. The excellent museum tells the story not only of the British invasions of the Revolution but also the town's rise and fall as one of Georgia's most important ports. Though mostly reconstructed, Fort Morris itself can be explored through a self-guided tour even when the museum is not open. There is also a very nice view of the water and some nice nature trails. *Fort Morris State Historic Site, 2559 Fort Morris Blvd., Midway, GA 31320; 912-884-5999; gastateparks.org/FortMorris. GPS: 31.759761, -81.289916. Open daily; museum open Thurs.–Sat.*

SHELDON CHURCH—On his way to Charleston in July 1779, British General Augustine Prevost was harassed by American militia along the

The entrance to Fort Morris at Sunbury, Georgia.

way. Sheldon Church, which had earlier been headquarters for American General Benjamin Lincoln, became a legitimate military target, and the British burned the church as they passed.

The ruins of Sheldon Church still exist, and they are striking. The drive to beautiful Beaufort should take you near them, and it's worth a stop to see the graceful columns standing defiantly among the live oaks and Spanish moss in the quiet churchyard. Though the ruins you see are from the Civil War, it is not difficult to picture them during the Revolution. *Sheldon Church, on Old Sheldon Church Road 0.5 mile south of Prescott Rd., Yemassee, SC 29945. GPS: 32.618599, -80.780611. Site accessible daily.*

FORT LYTTELTON—Beaufort was a prosperous and valuable port, and Fort Lyttleton had been built during the French and Indian War to protect it from an attack by sea. In 1779, not long after the British capture of Savannah, Beaufort and Fort Lyttleton became a target; the Amer-

The ruins of the twice-burned Sheldon Church in Yemassee, South Carolina.

ican defenders abandoned the fort on February 2, 1779, as the British approached, since it could not be defended from the landward side.

What little remains above ground of Fort Lyttleton is now on private property, and it is very little, mostly built into some existing homes along the water in Beaufort. One very tiny piece of the old tabby fort (tabby is a concrete made from oyster shells) is still visible at the far end of a driveway between two houses, and though visible from the road, it takes a sharp eye and can only be seen at a distance. *Fort Lyttelton, on Spanish Point Dr. 0.1 mile north of Fort Lyttleton Rd., Beaufort, SC 29902. GPS: 32.408775, -80.678850. Private property.*

STONO FERRY—Following his short-lived siege of Charleston, British General Augustine Prevost withdrew toward Savannah, continuing his forage operations along the way. In the process, the British set up a fortified camp at Stono Ferry on the Stono River west of Charleston. Protected by three redoubts and abatis but with their back to the river, the British remained here for almost a month while American forces under General Benjamin Lincoln approached. The Americans finally attacked on June 20, 1779, and though they initially pushed the British back into their works, they could not press their advantage and eventually withdrew. The Americans lost 34 killed and 112 wounded, while the British suffered 26 killed and 103 wounded.

The Stono Ferry battlefield remains frustratingly inaccessible, but efforts are underway to change that, as some of the land has now been preserved for the public. While some of the redoubts still exist, they are currently on private property. A golf course is on part of the original battlefield, but an attempt to "relocate" a redoubt that was destroyed for the course resulted only in an inauthentic earthwork in an incorrect location. A public park will take you down to the Stono River near the ferry site, but the battlefield sits just next door behind a wooden fence. *Stono Ferry, Old Wide Awake Park, end of Trexler Ave. 0.4 mile south of NC-62, Hollywood, SC 29449. GPS: 32.748755, -80.164931. Open daily.*

DORCHESTER—Once one of South Carolina's most prominent settlements, the town of Dorchester became a point of occupation when the British came in 1779. Dorchester's tabby fort, as well as its place along the Ashley River, made it an important point during the colonial period, but it wasn't long after the Revolution that Dorchester, like many other towns, became obsolete and faded into history.

Colonial Dorchester State Historic Site preserves what remains of the once-bustling town, including its old fort, the best-preserved tabby fortification in the United States. A walking tour through the site effectively makes Dorchester appear before your eyes, even though the site seems at first glance to be only a peaceful meadow. Most of the town is now underground, and archaeological exploration continues to uncover the mysteries of this very important place. *Colonial Dorchester State Historic Site, 300 State Park Rd., Summerville, SC 29485; 843-873-1740; southcarolinaparks.com/colonial-dorchester. GPS: 32.952534, -80.173231. Open daily.*

Ruins at Colonial Dorchester State Historic Site.

EUTAW SPRINGS—Nathaniel Greene's Southern Army of the United States emerged from a much-needed rest to attack a British encampment at Eutaw Springs on September 8, 1781. An organized American advance, with the British forming a defensive line across River Road to receive the Americans, turned into a hard-fought, hand-to-hand melee that went on for two hours. After American militia in the front line was finally pushed back after repeated British musketry volleys, a second line of Continental Army veterans was able to move forward and take their place, eventually pushing the British line rearward and causing its collapse. However, American success was stalled when the soldiers made their way into the British camp, causing them to forget the fight and become more preoccupied with the abandoned tents, food, and liquor. The British eventually regained the field, and after Major John Majoribanks charged and captured some American artillery, the Americans retreated in disorder. Majoribanks was mortally wounded, but the Americans left 251 dead on the field to the British 85.

The battlefield at Eutaw Springs is preserved as a public park.

The Eutaw Springs Battlefield Park sits at the location of the British camp, so eagerly ransacked by the American soldiers after the battle. Also within the park is the grave of Major Majoribanks. The battle occurred west of this site, with River Road serving as the axis for both the American and British battle lines. Additional sites along this road have been preserved by the American Battlefield Trust, so expect more interpretation and development of these locations to better tell the story of Eutaw Springs. *Eutaw Springs Battlefield Park, 12933 Old Number Six Highway, Eutawville, SC 29048. GPS: 33.407268, -80.298578. Site accessible daily.*

FORT WATSON/SANTEE INDIAN MOUND—Santee Indian Mound, built on the site of an Indian village between the years 1200 and 1450, provided the British a good point of high ground for an outpost in the Carolina backcountry, and they built a small fort atop it. Isolated after the British retreated to Wilmington, North Carolina, the British garrison here found themselves besieged on April 15, 1781, by the Swamp Fox,

Brigadier General Francis Marion, and Lieutenant Colonel Henry "Light Horse Harry" Lee. Over the next several days, the Americans built a tower tall enough to enable infantry to fire down into the fort. The British surrendered on April 23 when the tower became operational.

The large, ancient Santee Indian Mound is still intact, now sitting alongside artificial Lake Marion. A wooden staircase will take you to a viewing platform atop the mound, demonstrating why the British found it such an ideal position—and how impressive the Patriots' tower must have been. You will find additional interpretation at the site, as well as several monuments related to the fighting at Fort Watson. The site is well protected within the Bluff Unit of Santee National Wildlife Refuge. *Santee Indian Mound and Fort Watson, Santee National Wildlife Refuge, on Fort Watson Rd. 1.0 mile past entrance, Summerton, SC 29148; 803-478-2217; www.fws.gov/refuge/santee/. GPS: 33.539009, -80.436475. Open daily.*

BELLEVILLE PLANTATION—Belleville Plantation, caught in the middle between British posts and the backcountry and low country, became a

Santee Indian Mound was converted into the British Fort Watson.

fortified British post soon after the occupation of Charleston. British efforts to lure in supporters of the crown emanated from the plantation, but like at other locations, the efforts here proved futile.

What is left of Belleville Plantation, if anything, is inaccessible. The likely site of the plantation is now on private property, as are several British earthworks that allegedly still remain. Still, there is nothing to visit today, and the closest one can come is a small cemetery nearby that likely contains the remains of a few of the slaves who once worked the site. *Belleville Plantation, west of US 601 South of Congaree River, Fort Motte, SC 29135. GPS: 37.595753, -77.359286. Private property.*

SNOW'S ISLAND—Francis Marion, better known as the Swamp Fox, was one of the most irritating thorns in the side of the British in the Carolina backcountry. During the winter of 1780–1781, Marion made his camp on Snow's Island, a large land mass formed by the Pee Dee and Lynches Rivers and Clark Creek. Surrounded by thick forest and friendly Whig residents, Snow's Island provided an ideal hideout. Though the camp was raided in March 1781, Marion and his band of partisans were never captured. To this day, the exact location of the camp of the elusive Swamp Fox remains unknown.

Several historical highway markers surround the Snow's Island area today. Just as it was during the Revolution, however, there's not much of Francis Marion to see these days. It is easy to see, however, how these lush backwoods would make a perfect hiding spot. *Historical highway marker 34-16—Daughters of the American Revolution (Marion's Camp at Snow's Island), intersection of US 378 and Dunham Bluff Rd., Gresham, NC. GPS: 33.866417, -79.334214; Interpretive sign—Snow's Island, Den of the Swamp Fox, on Dunham Bluff Road at Pee Dee River, 0.5 mile south of Toms Camp Rd., Gresham, NC 29546. GPS: 33.842879, -79.341353. Interpretive sign—Witherspoon Ferry: Francis Marion Takes Command, on Odell Venters Landing 0.1 mile from NC-41, Johnsonville, SC 29555. GPS: 33.838990, -79.448336. Signs accessible daily.*

PEGUES PLACE—The exchange of some prisoners, particularly officers, was a somewhat common occurrence during the American Revolution. However, a general cartel—a negotiated exchange of large numbers of prisoners from both sides—proved elusive. Both sides, for military, political, and other reasons, found cause to avoid the general exchange of prisoners, believing it would harm their own efforts in the war. In the South, however, far from the two political centers of New York and Philadelphia, the British and Americans found a way to make a cartel of prisoners happen. It happened at the plantation at Pegues Place, on the state line between North Carolina and South Carolina, with representatives for Generals Nathaniel Greene and Lord Cornwallis coming to an agreement on May 3, 1781. It was the only general cartel of prisoners until the war ended in 1783.

Pegues Place is a private home today and cannot be visited. There is a historical highway marker approximately 1 mile east of the home. *Historical highway marker—Marlboro County Historic Preservation Commission (Pegues Place/Revolutionary Cartel), at intersection of US 1 and Pegues Dr., Wallace, SC 29596. GPS: 34.799931, -79.889518. Sign accessible daily.*

WAXHAWS—Immediately upon capturing Charleston, the British fanned out into the Carolina countryside to take control of the backcountry. One of their most effective weapons soon proved to be Banastre Tarleton's British Legion. Tarleton's light troops soon gained a reputation for efficiency, dependability, and brutality, and their ruthlessness became permanently cemented in the story of the southern war at a place called Waxhaws, north of Camden. American Colonel Abraham Buford had been active to the north of Camden, a critical backcountry post, and Tarleton was dispatched to catch him. Upon learning that he was 20 miles behind, Tarleton dispatched a rider to Buford asking for his surrender, which Buford refused but only after preparing his infantry for battle. Tarleton rode hard and caught up with the Americans later that afternoon, May 29, 1780. Tarleton formed his cavalry for a charge that broke the Continental line and effectively ended the battle. The massacre, however, had just begun. Though the Americans had produced a white flag in surrender, Tarleton's British Legion proceeded to bayonet and further decimate their foes for another 15 minutes, killing 113 and severely wounding another 150. (The British had lost 5 killed and 12 wounded.) The lack of mercy given Buford's command was shocking, even in a southern war that had already been extremely brutal. For the

A mass grave for American soldiers, casualties of Buford's Massacre at Waxhaws.

rest of the war, the cry of "Tarleton's Quarter" would be heard from American soldiers on every battlefield, thus continuing the bloodshed.

The site of Buford's Massacre is still an open field, and a large part of the site has been preserved by the American Battlefield Trust. Across the road from the main scene of the action lies a mass grave of the Americans who died at Waxhaws, along with several memorials and interpretive signs that tell the story of the battle. Always accessible and in a remote location, one can quietly reflect on the tragedy that took place here. Simple but powerful, don't be surprised if this is one of those locations that hits you right in the gut. *Waxhaws Battlefield, 262 Rocky River Rd., Lancaster, SC 29720. GPS: 34.741883, -80.625827. Open daily.*

HANGING ROCK—Soon after taking Charleston, the British chose Hanging Rock as one of their remote outposts. On August 6, 1780, General Thomas Sumter led 800 North and South Carolina militia against the 500 or so Loyalists stationed there. The British were soon routed, but the Patriots, upon taking the British positions, fell prey to the temptation of looting the enemy camp. An attempt by the British to retake their camp proved futile, and the Americans, with 12 killed and 41 wounded, claimed victory over the Loyalists, who suffered over 250 casualties. However, the objective of capturing and holding the camp proved to be too much for Sumter's band, one of whom—future general and president of the United States Andrew Jackson—had just witnessed his first battle.

Various parts of the battlefield at Hanging Rock have been preserved by the American Battlefield Trust, the state of South Carolina as part of Andrew Jackson State Park, and the Katawba Valley Land Trust. There is a memorial on the field, and getting to it requires a short hike and a little bit of climbing down a hillside, but the beauty of the place makes it worth the effort. You can park your car at the trailhead, then walk the well-marked path to a large rock formation; the monument is at the base of the rocks. *Hanging Rock Battlefield, trailhead on Hanging Rock Rd. 0.8 mile east of SR S-29-15, Kershaw, SC 29067. GPS: 34.566319, -80.659503. Open daily.*

The massive stones at the Hanging Rock battlefield.

FISHING CREEK—Banastre Tarleton and his British Legion were in hard pursuit of the "Carolina Gamecock," Thomas Sumter, after he had raided a British supply train. Though the British caught up with Sumter, they were separated by the Catawba River. The two parties paralleled each other for 8 miles before coming to Fishing Creek on August 18, 1780. The Patriots, feeling secure, began to relax, but the British found a nearby crossing and pounced on the camp. Completely surprised, the Americans scattered, but only after suffering 150 killed and wounded and losing over 300 prisoners to Tarleton's force, which numbered only 160 men.

The core of the Fishing Creek battlefield is now covered by Fishing Creek Lake. There is a low stone monument along the highway marking the action; the creek itself is just to the west of the highway. *Fishing Creek Monument, on US 21 0.2 mile south of Poorboy Rd., Great Falls, SC 29055. GPS: 34.635067, -80.904154. Monument accessible daily.*

LAND'S FORD—An important crossing of the Catawba River, Land's Ford was a critical point for both armies. Before and after many of the critical engagements in the immediate area—including Kings Mountain and Hanging Rock—the two armies mustered, encamped, and crossed here at Land's Ford.

Landsford Canal State Park preserves the site of Land's Ford, though over the years it's been obscured by the water. But the landscape is still the same as when the two sides camped on it long ago. There is no interpretation about the ford within the park, but a historical highway marker not far from the entrance to the park provides some context. *Landsford Canal State Park, 2051 Park Dr., Catawba, SC 29704; 803-789-5800; southcarolinaparks.com/landsford-canal. GPS: 34.785113, -80.895245. Open daily. Chester County Historical Society—Landsford Canal / Landsford Canal in the Revolution, intersection of Landsford Rd. and Catawba River Rd., Catawba, SC 29704. GPS: 34.794435, -80.920433. Sign accessible daily.*

HILL'S IRONWORKS—Colonel William Hill's Ironworks, while producing ammunition and artillery, was also a longstanding maker of farm equipment and other critical supplies for both Tories and Loyalists alike. Hill also provided a gristmill and sawmill, making him indispensable to both sides. As a military target, however, it was burned by the British on July 11, 1780. The British, under Captain Christian Huck of Tarleton's British Legion, not only burned the ironworks but also the homes of the Hill family and others, killing a young boy along the way. The next day, Patriots gathered to encounter the Tories, attacking them and killing 35, including Huck. Huck's Defeat, a product of the destruction of Hill's Ironworks, proved that trained Tory Regulars could be defeated by Patriot militia.

Hill's Ironworks, once massive, now have only a couple of historic markers to remember them. One is a historical highway marker, while the other, a stone memorial, offers more information on the Hill family and their service. Also noted on the memorial is that the famous Confederate General Daniel Harvey Hill, grandson of the man who operated the works, was born on the estate. *Hill's Ironworks marker and memorial, on Hands Mill Highway at intersection with Old Clay Hill Rd., York, SC 29745. GPS: 35.048497, -81.098704. Signs accessible daily.*

COWAN'S FORD—After the battle at Cowpens, the American army rapidly moved north to avoid a battle with General Charles Cornwallis, who was in close pursuit. A small force was left at Cowan's Ford in North Carolina to contest a crossing by the British, but the Americans under General William Lee Davidson were surprised when the British showed up and pushed rapidly across the swollen Catawba River. Davidson was killed in the action, but his men provided enough of a delay that Cornwallis would not catch up to the retreating American army.

Cowan's Ford itself is inaccessible, but it can be viewed, and there is plenty around that memorializes the battle. The old ford is now at the base of the dam forming Lake Norman. There is an overlook near the base of the dam that presents a nice view of the valley as well as some interpretive signage. Just a bit farther down the road, memorials to Davidson can be found that tell his story and that of the fight at Cowan's Ford. *Cowan's Ford Overlook, pull off area on NC 73 0.9 mile east of Club Dr., Stanley, NC 28164. GPS: 35.428272, -80.959899. General William Lee Davidson monuments, southwest corner of intersection of NC 73 and McGuire Nuclear Station Rd., Huntersville, NC 28078. GPS: 35.427415, -80.940963. Sites accessible daily.*

RAMSOUR'S MILL—In June 1780, a month after the fall of Charleston, British efforts began to gather what they assumed were many Loyalists in the Carolinas to fight for the crown. About 1,300 of these new recruits gathered at Ramsour's Mill, and Whigs in Charlotte, only 35 miles away, sent a force of 400 men to disperse them. An early morning surprise attack on June 20 led to a disorganized but fierce two-hour, hand-to-hand fight. When the dust had settled, the Whigs had control of the high ground while the larger force of Tory militia had fled. The Whig victory at Ramsour's Mill proved a severe blow to Loyalist recruiting in the Carolina backcountry.

Though several school structures are on the site of the fight at Ramsour's Mill, locals have done a great job of making sure that what happened here is remembered. The mill site itself is preserved as a public park, and the graves of the Patriot leaders are proudly memorialized. A mass grave is also on the school grounds, as well as a smaller memorial park and interpretive signs. *Ramsour's Mill Battlefield Park, parking at Battleground Elementary School, 301 Jeb Seagle Dr., Lincolnton, NC 28092. GPS: 35.477845, -81.262794. Ramsour's Mill Park, on Jeb Seagle*

Monuments dot the battlefield at Ramsour's Mill in Lincolnton, North Carolina.

Dr. 0.2 mile west of Linwood Dr., Lincolnton, NC 28092. GPS: 35.476911, -81.265920. *Patriot Captains' Gravesite, 0.1 mile west of Linwood Dr., Lincolnton, NC 28092. GPS: 35.477203, -81.263996. Open daily.*

BLACKSTOCK'S PLANTATION—British Lieutenant Colonel Banastre Tarleton had been attempting to suppress Patriot militia, and the "Carolina Gamecock," Thomas Sumter was one of his primary targets. Tracking down Sumter's band of 1,000 Patriots at Blackstock's Plantation on November 20, 1780, Tarleton, clearly outnumbered, chose to attack anyway. Sumter had chosen his position well, deploying on high ground in full view of Tarleton's dragoons but with picked marksmen on the flanks. The British advanced into a heavy fire and could not drive Sumter's men off their hill. The British took more casualties than the Americans, but the Americans lost Sumter, who was severely wounded. The battle at Blackstock's Plantation proved that the vaunted British, and Tarleton in particular, could be defeated in battle.

The Blackstock's battlefield is preserved, protected, and interpreted by nearby Musgrove Mill State Park. A one-way road will take you to a hilltop that overlooks the scene of the fighting and contains a monument and interpretive sign. There is also a nature trail on the property. If the gate is closed, a short hike from the parking area will take you to the hilltop. *Blackstock's Battlefield, on Monument Rd. 1.6 miles north of Blackstock Rd., Enoree, SC 29335. GPS: 34.679520, -81.811921. Open daily.*

MUSGROVE MILL—After learning that a group of Loyalists was on their way to join Major Patrick Ferguson's militia, Joseph McDowell led a force of 200 Patriots to attack their camp at Musgrove Mill. However, after a grueling all-night march, McDowell arrived at the camp to find that the Tories had just been reinforced and were now 500 strong, 200 of whom were British Regulars. Forced to confront them after being discovered, on August 18, 1780, the Patriots lured the British toward a strong, concealed position. The British took the bait, and though they weathered a devastating first volley and fought fiercely, their line was eventually broken and they fell back in confusion. The British took 223 casualties to the Americans' 11. The bold attack by the Patriot militia further hurt Tory recruiting in the backcountry.

Musgrove Mill State Park protects both the battlefield and the site of the British camp along the Enoree River. Walking trails with interpretive signs will take you through both locations, though you'll probably want to drive from one trail to the other. The site also has an interpretive center near the old Musgrove House, with exhibits and a helpful light map presentation that describes the action that day. As a nice bonus, the battlefield trail will take you past the very pretty Horseshoe Falls. *Musgrove Mill State Park, 398 State Park Rd., Clinton, SC 29305; 864-938-0100; southcarolinaparks.com/musgrove-mill. GPS: 34.587831, -81.851822. Open daily.*

CHISWELL LEAD MINES—In 1756, British officer John Chiswell discovered lead deposits in western Virginia that were eventually controlled by the state. Ideally located far to the west of the action, the lead mines produced ammunition for the Continental Army throughout the war. In 1780, the mines were sold to Moses and Stephen Austin; Austin's son, Stephen Jr., would go on to become one of the founders of the Republic of Texas.

Some of the Chiswell lead mining operations are preserved within New River Trail State Park, though there is no interpretation of the mine's operation during the American Revolution. (The historic shot tower, used to make ammunition, postdates the war.) There is a historical marker in the town of Fort Chiswell that discusses the origins of the mine and its relation to the Revolution. *Historical highway marker—Virginia Department of Historic Resources: K-39 (Lead Mines), on US 52 just south of Chapman Rd., Fort Chiswell, VA, 24360. GPS: 36.944360, -80.947827. Sign accessible daily. New River Trail State Park, 116 Orphanage Dr., Max Meadows, VA 24360; 276-699-6778; www.dcr.virginia.gov/state-parks/new-river-trail. GPS: 36.522000, -80.522033. Open daily.*

THE WARS WITH THE CHEROKEE

Through much of the war, Patriot settlers in the western Carolinas, Georgia, and what is now Tennessee found themselves fighting on two fronts: the British and their Loyalist allies and the Cherokee tribes to the west. The Cherokee, constantly on the defense against further encroachment by white settlers, took the offensive in 1776. While the response of the backwoods settlers did much to quiet these actions, the Cherokee were a constant threat. Not only did raids threaten the settlers of the backwoods, they also sometimes prevented these men and women from taking part in the larger Revolution along the coast.

The Cherokee Nation still has a strong presence in the disputed lands, and there is plenty to experience in the Carolina backcountry and beyond. Some of the landmark actions and sites associated with the period during the war are noted here, as well as additional resources that can help you understand the role of this conflict within the wider context of the Revolution.

MUSEUM OF THE CHEROKEE PEOPLE—The best place to learn about the Cherokee Wars, as well as the culture of the people who fought them, is the Museum of the Cherokee People. The museum takes you from the early days of the Cherokee and tells their story through today, with thought-provoking exhibits about major historical events, day-to-day life, and the achievements of the Cherokee. The museum underwent a major renovation to its main exhibit space beginning in late 2023, and the high quality of the museum as well as its history—dating back to 1948—virtually guarantees something great to come. *Museum of the Cherokee People, 589 Tsali Blvd., Cherokee, NC 28719; 828-497-3481; motcp .org. GPS: 35.485218, -83.316449. Open daily.*

NIKWASI (NEQUASSE)—Nikwasi was one of the oldest towns of the Cherokee and a cultural and spiritual center. On September 10, 1776, Americans seeking retaliation during the Cherokee War of 1776 burned Nikwasi to the ground. The Cherokee almost immediately rebuilt the town.

The Nikwasi Mound, center of the original village and location of the village townhouse and sacred fire, still stands. The mound now belongs to a nonprofit, and there are hopes of developing a history center around it. For now, there is an interpretive sign at the mound that tells its history. *Nikwasi Mound, intersection of E Main St. and Nikwasi Ln., Franklin, NC 28734. GPS: 35.184831, -83.373519. Site accessible daily.*

CHEROKEE MIDDLE TOWNS—The Cherokee Middle Towns were located in western North Carolina. Militia from North Carolina conducted a punitive expedition after the Cherokee attacked the western settlements and burned numerous towns over the summer of 1776.

One of the primary towns, Cowee, was one of those destroyed during the Revolution. There is a viewing platform with interpretive signs at its location. *Cowee Mound, on Bryson City Rd. 0.4 mile east of Cody Rd., Franklin, NC 28734. GPS: 35.266449, -83.421901. Site accessible daily.*

RING FIGHT (TAMASSEE)—A forage party under Andrew Pickens was surrounded near the Cherokee town of Tamassee on August 12, 1776. Facing greatly superior numbers, Pickens arranged his men in two circles for defense, and they were able to hold off the attackers until reinforcements arrived. After the so-called Ring Fight was finished, the Americans destroyed the abandoned town.

continued on next page

Historical markers indicate the location of both the town of Tamassee and the Ring Fight. The first is a historical highway marker about the town, while the second is a small boulder with a plaque noting the area of the battle. *Historical marker—Tamassee Town, intersection of Tamassee Knob Rd. and State Road SR-37-375, Tamassee, SC 29686. GPS: 34.883084, -83.048495. Historical marker—Commemorating the Ring Fight, on State Road SR-37-375 0.1 mile north of Tamassee Knob Rd., Tamassee, SC 29686. GPS: 34.884551, -83.047553. Sites accessible daily.*

CHEROKEE LOWER TOWNS (OCONEE)—The Cherokee Lower Towns were located in western South Carolina and Georgia. A punitive expedition in August 1776 led to the destruction of many of the towns, particularly in what is now Oconee County in South Carolina.

The site of Oconee, one of the primary Lower Towns, has a historical highway marker noting its significance. *Historical highway marker—Oconee Town, on Oconee Station Rd. 0.5 mile south of White Cut Rd., Walhalla, SC 29691. GPS: 34.840540, -83.066372. Sign accessible daily.*

CATHEY'S FORT—This fort was one of the muster points for white settlers who would invade the Cherokee Towns in the Cherokee War of 1776. Cathey's Fort was one of several forts along the frontier, including Old Fort, and they were often the subject of Cherokee raids in retaliation for settlers illegally crossing the Blue Ridge Mountains and encroaching on Cherokee lands.

The general site of Cathey's Fort is marked by a historic highway marker placed 1 mile to the west; the site is inaccessible today. The Old Fort Monument is a large stone arrowhead in the town of Old Fort, North Carolina. The monument marks what was supposed to be the dividing line agreed upon between the British and the Cherokee at the site of the frontier post, Old Fort. Interpretive signs tell the story of the Cherokee and pioneer life on the frontier. *North Carolina Archives and Highway Departments—N-26 (Cathey's Fort), intersection of US 221 and NC 226, Marion, NC 28752. GPS: 35.797886, -82.032314. Sign accessible daily. Old Fort Monument, intersection of West Main St. and Catawba Ave., Old Fort, NC 28762. GPS: 35.629092, -82.181446. Sign accessible daily.*

LONG ISLAND FLATS AND EATON'S STATION—In one of the early actions of the Cherokee War of 1776, the Cherokee leader Dragging Canoe and his party of warriors led a raid into the Overmountain region in what is now Tennessee. Local militia, hearing of the raid, gathered at Eaton's Station and fortified it to wait for the arrival of the Cherokee. On July 20, the Cherokee attacked, but having lost the element of surprise did not inflict major damage. Dragging Canoe was severely wounded in the action.

Several historical markers in Kingsport interpret the importance of Long Island of the Holston, and the Battle of Long Island Flats. The battle itself occurred in what is now downtown Kingsport, between the South Fork of the Holston River and the high ground to the east of it. As for Eaton's Station, its exact location is not known. *Historical highway marker—Battle of Island Flats— First Skirmish, intersection of Memorial Blvd. and East Center St., Kingsport, TN 37664. GPS: 36.531380, -82.514019. Historical highway marker—Battle of Island Flats, intersection of Memorial Blvd. and Jessee St., Kingsport, TN 37664. GPS: 36.531311, -82.518483. Signs accessible daily.*

continued on next page

CHICKAMAUGA INDIAN TOWNS—In late 1776, Dragging Canoe was essentially forced out of the Cherokee Towns, as most of the Cherokee were ready to make peace with the Americans. Those Cherokee who were still hostile to the American cause followed Dragging Canoe to what became known as the Chickamauga Indian Towns, near present-day Chattanooga, Tennessee. In April 1779, after the Chickamauga Cherokee left to raid backcountry settlements in Georgia and South Carolina, a large force of Americans traveled to the Chickamauga Towns and destroyed them.

One of the battles between the Patriots and Dragging Canoe occurred atop Lookout Mountain in Chattanooga. There is a historical marker at the site telling about the Chickamauga Cherokee and the battle. There is plenty of other history atop the mountain (not to mention a wonderful view), so plan to spend some time here. *American Revolutionary War Battle—Lookout Mountain, intersection of Scenic Highway 148 and Cravens Terrace, Chattanooga, TN 37350. GPS: 35.018759, -85.338529. Sign accessible daily.*

WHERE TO STAY IN GEORGIA AND SOUTH CAROLINA

Savannah and Charleston have numerous options for lodging. For the other major sites, even though some of them are remote, you'll find that the cities of Augusta, Georgia, Columbia, South Carolina, and Charlotte, North Carolina, are not too far of a drive from any of them. If you do stray into the more remote areas, though, you'll want to have a general idea of where you're going to stop and search out some places to stay. If you wish, you'll also find numerous places to camp out, including the wonderful Congaree National Park. One other note: The food in this part of the country is amazing, from Southern cuisine to seafood, so eat up!

Top: The Museum of the Cherokee People in Cherokee, North Carolina.
Bottom: A view of the battlefield at Musgrove Mill State Park.

7

War and Remembrance: North Carolina, Virginia, and Washington, DC

OVERVIEW

The sites described in this chapter cover the first major fighting in the south—the Battle of Moores Creek in 1776—and the effective end of the Revolutionary War, decided by the American victories at Guilford Courthouse and Yorktown in 1781. These sites also include great opportunities to consider how we remember the American Revolution today in the form of some of the historic homes of the Founding Fathers and the monuments and memorials in Washington, DC.

After the Battle of Cowpens and the ensuing Race to the Dan River, the commander of the British army in the south, General Charles Cornwallis, made a fateful decision. Instead of returning to his base in South Carolina—which he was ordered to protect at all costs—he instead chose to move the war north. Even though he had just lost a significant portion of his army, Cornwallis speculated that he could anticipate more support than he had found in South Carolina. Others had thought this before him, and as demonstrated at the Battle of Moores Creek, a resounding

Opposite: A statue of Nathan Hale, one of the numerous monuments to the American Revolution in Washington, DC.

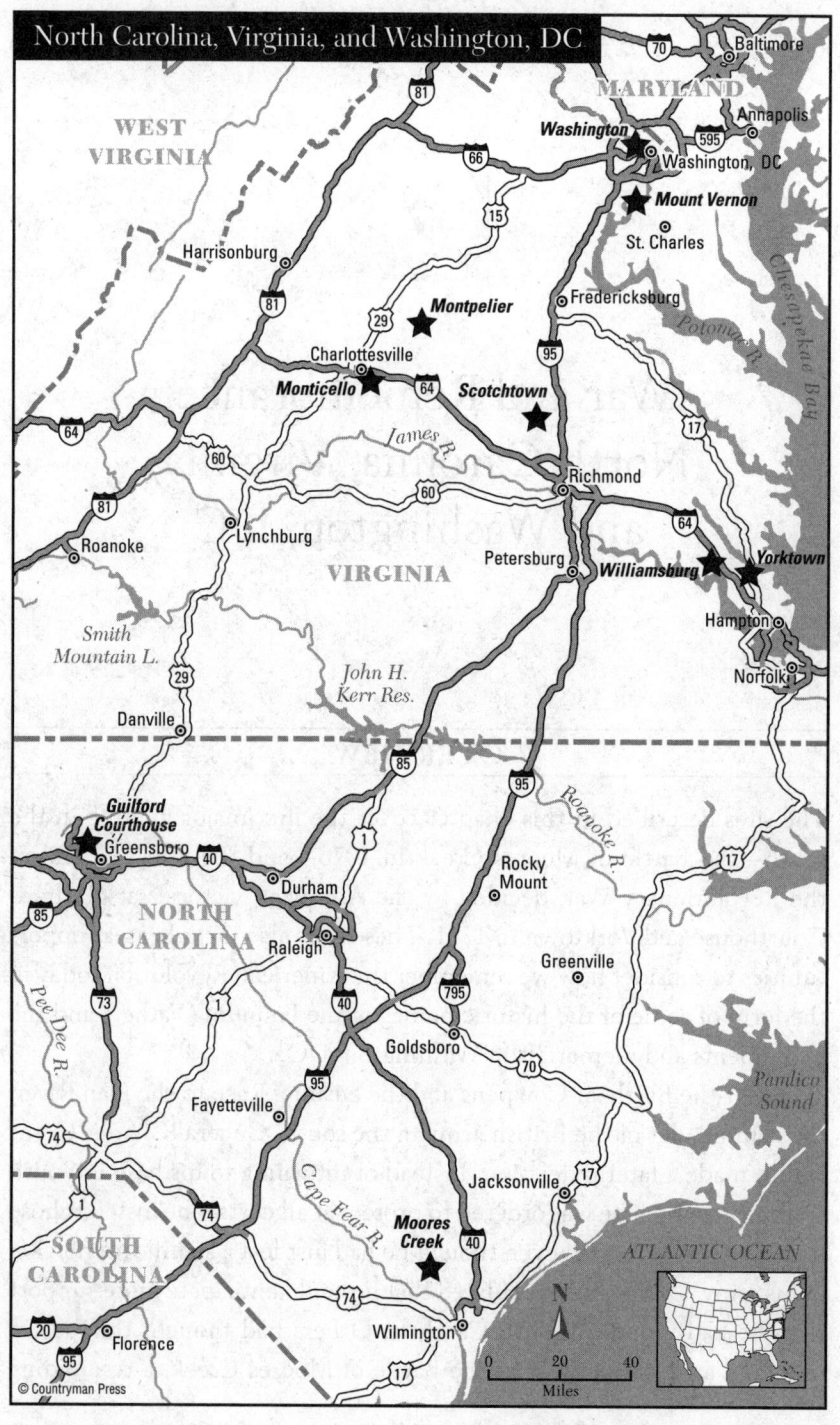

victory for the American militia, they were wrong; there would be as little support for the British cause in North Carolina and Virginia as there was in South Carolina. But he strongly felt that making Virginia the "seat of war" was the best chance to end the conflict. So he made his base in Wilmington, North Carolina, and prepared for his next movement.

Thanks to the new American commander in the south, Cornwallis would not have to wait long. After winning the Race to the Dan River, General Nathaniel Greene recrossed the river and began harassing the British, goading them into a fight. Greene was able to choose his ground, and though the Americans left the battlefield to the British at the Battle of Guilford Courthouse, near Greensboro, North Carolina, the British had taken terrible losses. But Cornwallis, convinced that taking the war to Virginia was the right move and eager to join another British force there, continued north.

Cornwallis's main concern was finding a strong supply base from which his army could be supplied, and he ultimately chose Yorktown, Virginia, for its deep water port and access to the Chesapeake Bay. However, other events were already conspiring against him. The allied American and French armies, looking for opportunities, learned of the approach of a French fleet to the Chesapeake. With hard marching from their base in New York, perfect timing, and some luck, the allies were able to trap the British between the French Navy and the combined American and French armies at Yorktown. Cornwallis was forced to surrender his force of 7,000 men, a blow that proved to be the end of British efforts to keep the American colonies.

After the Revolutionary War was over, it did not take long for Americans to begin to memorialize the men who created and fought for the United States. Rightly proud of their tremendous accomplishments, Americans began erecting statues and monuments to them, and their stories—some accurate, some not—became American history. Over time, however, some of the questions that came out of the American Revolution became too big to ignore. If these men were dedicated to the proposition that all men are created equal, then why did so many of them own slaves? Were these men as truly great as we portray them to be? And did women have no part in the Revolution? Fortunately, the incredible living history site at Williamsburg, Virginia, and the historic homes of four of our most important Founding Fathers—George Washington, Thomas Jefferson, James Madison, and Patrick Henry—are doing a great job of beginning to address these inconsistencies. Though you may not find a definitive answer—it's complicated—you will come away with a better knowledge of what the Founding Fathers faced in their time and how they thought about these issues. They will give you a lot to think about when you visit Washington, DC, which contains numerous memorials to the well-known and the obscure who helped make America as we know it today.

This chapter will take you through the sites and events of the American Revolution in the Upper South—North Carolina, Virginia, Washington, DC, and even Maryland. You will not only see how the Revolutionary War ended, but you will also get a good chance to consider how we remember the American Revolution today.

PEOPLE TO KNOW

NATHANAEL GREENE—Second only to George Washington, Nathanael Greene was America's most important general during the Revolutionary War. Though a lesser-known name, Greene's maneuvers in the southern theater (the central theater of military operations in the latter half of the war) ultimately induced the British to move toward Yorktown and their ultimate defeat.

Greene's beginnings did not point to a military life. Growing up in Rhode Island as a Quaker, he worked at the family iron forge into his 20s, but in 1774 helped to raise a group of militia. Remarkably, he was not elected an officer. But Greene stuck it out as a private and proved himself enough that only a year later, when Rhode Island began to raise their own regiments to fight in the Revolution, Greene was made a brigadier general of militia, and shortly afterward held the same rank in the Continental Army. Greene performed admirably, not only in command of troops but also in organization and logistics. Though Greene's inexperience led to the fall of Fort Washington on Manhattan, his battlefield command shortly afterward at Trenton made him one of Washington's most reliable generals. Greene was disappointed when Washington asked him to take over the Quartermaster Department, but he was a natural for the job and completely overhauled the system, dramatically improving the flow of food and supplies to the army. Greene was returned to field command in October 1780 when he took over command of the southern theater, where he proved to have great insight into British movements and strategy. After the war ended, Greene unfortunately fell into financial troubles and eventually left Rhode Island to settle on an estate near Savannah given to him by the state of Georgia. There, at the age of only 44, Greene died of sunstroke.

CHARLES CORNWALLIS—Though he was not the highest-ranking British general of the Revolutionary War, General Charles Cornwallis is probably the most readily remembered today. It was Cornwallis whose movements led to the British surrender at Yorktown and ultimately the loss of America for the British Empire.

Cornwallis came from a wealthy English family and got his start as an officer in the military at the age of 17. He had several positions and commands on the European continent before taking a seat in the House of Lords as Earl Cornwallis. Though he opposed the oppressive British policies in America, when King George III asked him to serve in America in 1775, he accepted without hesitation. Cornwallis sailed for America the next year, first heading for Charleston, South Carolina, but ultimately ending up in New York City, where he took a conspicuous part in the British victories at Long Island and Fort Washington. His fortunes soon turned, however, as he was caught off guard when George Washington attacked the British at Trenton and Princeton. Cornwallis was a major part of General William Howe's victory at the Battle of Brandywine, and led the successful counterattack during the Battle of Germantown. Cornwallis returned to Charleston under new Commander in Chief Henry Clinton, and he stayed in the south as his second in command, where he ultimately disobeyed Clinton's orders to stay near Charleston and eventually moved to Yorktown, where he was forced to surrender his entire army. Cornwallis went on to have a distinguished career, serving as commander in chief and governor general of Ireland and in India, where he died in 1805.

COMTE DE ROCHAMBEAU—Jean Baptiste Donatien de Vimeur, comte de Rochambeau, was the commander of French forces in America. It was Rochambeau's partnership with George Washington that ultimately led to victory during the American Revolution.

Rochambeau, born into a prominent French family, entered the military at a young age and made the most of his career, fighting in numerous commands in Europe. His reputation was well established when he was asked to take command of the French forces in America, which had gotten off to a rocky but promising start. Rochambeau arrived at Newport, Rhode Island, in 1780, and after some difficulties met with Washington to plan strategy. Though he could see some problems with Washington's plans, Rochambeau, as well as his entire staff, was impressed with Washington, and the two went on to cooperate on all facets of the war. When the opportunity at Yorktown presented itself, it was Rochambeau who proposed cooperating with the French fleet arriving outside the Chesapeake and trapping the British forces. After the war, Rochambeau returned to France, where he became caught up in the French Revolution and almost faced the guillotine but was spared. Rochambeau died in 1807.

THINGS TO KNOW

The primary sites noted in this chapter are all well developed. Though there's a good distance between them, there's plenty to see in between. Only three of them—Moores Creek, Guilford Courthouse, and Yorktown—are battlefields, while the rest are either historic homes or memorials to the American Revolution. But even if battlefields are your thing, be sure to visit these other sites, as they offer deep insight into how we remember the Revolution today.

You'll want to set aside some time for the sites in this chapter, not only because of the distance you'll travel but also because of the time you may want to spend at them. Williamsburg, Monticello, and Mount Vernon, in particular, will be sites that you may find yourself wanting to spend multiple days at, and there's so much to see in Washington, DC, that you are guaranteed to need additional time. Don't shortchange your visits to any of these rewarding sites.

THE TRIP

This trip starts near Wilmington, North Carolina, and ends in Washington, DC, and visiting the smaller sites may even take you into Maryland. That's a fair amount of driving time, but if you plan your route ahead of time, you should be able to cover multiple sites in one day—particularly on the Virginia Peninsula, where Yorktown and Williamsburg are located, and in central Virginia, where you'll find several of the historic homes. There's a lot of other history in this area, particularly when it comes to early America and the Civil War, so do a little research before you go and scope out other sites you may want to see.

Because of its historical legacy, Virginia makes a popular summer trip for families looking to explore American history. If you're making your trip during the summer, you should be able to find plenty of places to stay, but if you want to stay in a nicer hotel or want to spend less, you'll want to make your plans and reservations ahead of time.

THE CAN'T-MISS SITES

Moores Creek

Josiah Martin, royal governor of North Carolina, was facing the same challenges as the other colonial governors in America. His legislature, like all the other colonial legislatures, was heavily dominated by Whigs, and when the Americans began actively resisting Parliament's acts, he found himself mostly powerless. Martin, however, was absolutely convinced that the people of his colony—unlike the rabble-rousers in the northern colonies—were still loyal to King George III, and if given the chance would rally to his side. Therefore, after the fighting began in early 1775, Martin aggressively lobbied the secretary of state for the colonies for the capability to raise a small force of Loyalists to put down the rebels and end American resistance in North Carolina.

Much to his delight, Martin's plan was not only approved but supplemented. The British government also largely held to the belief that most of the colonists in America were still loyal to the crown, and that they would suppress the Patriot activities if just given the resources and the chance. Martin could not only expect the arms he was asking for, but he would also be given 2,000 regular British troops to assist. Estimating that he could count on more than 20,000 Loyalists to rise up, Martin felt more confident than ever that North Carolina would soon return to its natural state.

Martin's estimates were perhaps wildly optimistic, but not completely unfounded. In the Carolinas, the populated region along the coast was certainly mostly allied to the Patriot cause, as they tended to be the most dependent on trade and commerce and thus most affected by British taxes and restrictions. The region past the Appalachian Mountains, too, was also heavily sympathetic to the Americans, since British restrictions on westward settlement and what were seen as policies favoring Native Americans were frowned upon. That left the Piedmont, the vast farming area in between, where most colonists felt largely unaffected by the British acts. It was here, according to Martin's agents, that he could expect Loyalists to come to his aid and liberate North Carolina. In addition, a somewhat large group of Scottish Highlanders who had immigrated to America resided in the Piedmont and could be counted on to support the government. Finally, the Regulators, a vigilante group that largely sided with the crown, could be counted on to fight.

In January 1776, with the expectation that British Regulars would arrive in Wilmington in mid to late February, Martin issued a proclamation that all citizens rise to the occasion and side with the crown or be considered traitors. A meeting of Loyalist leaders was arranged for February 5, 1776, in the town of Cross Creek, North Carolina, to bring all available forces together. The results were largely disappointing for the British. The Highlanders could only summon about 600 to 700 men, and although the Regulators and other Tories promised to gather another 4,500, they were able to muster only about 800. After finally running out of hope, the Loyalist group, under the command of newly appointed General Donald MacDonald, set out on February 18 for Wilmington to meet the British Regulars.

Patriot leaders had been watching developments in Cross Creek. As MacDonald's force moved southeast along the Cape Fear River toward Wilmington, two American forces attempted to block their path. The first was a regiment of soldiers of the Continental Army under Colonel James Moore, which was able to stand in the Tories' path at Rock-

The battlefield at Moores Creek in Currie, North Carolina.

fish Creek on February 19. MacDonald managed to slip around them, however. A second Patriot group, 800 militia commanded by Colonel Richard Caswell, marched to confront MacDonald. After MacDonald bypassed Caswell in much the same manner at Corbett's Ferry on February 25, Caswell, along with 250 men dispatched by Moore, met at Moores Creek Bridge the next day to try again to engage MacDonald.

When MacDonald's men came to Moores Creek Bridge on February 26, they used a ruse, under a white flag, to get into the American camp to view their defenses. MacDonald learned that Caswell had built his defenses on the west side of the creek, with his back to the water and no line of retreat. Seeing an opportunity, MacDonald elected to attack early the next morning. Unfortunately for his men, what he did not know was that the Americans had also built earthworks on the east side of the creek.

The Tories left camp at 1:00 AM on February 27, 1776, and arrived at the bridge just before daylight. MacDonald found, to his surprise, that the Americans were gone. Caswell had realized his mistake and had pulled all the Americans to the east side of the creek. In addition, the Americans had pulled up the planks to the bridge, making it very difficult to cross. After some deliberation, it was decided that the attack would go on anyway. The Highlanders would lead the charge, using their traditional broadswords to attack the Americans.

Just as the Highlanders were about to attack, they were detected by American pickets, who alerted the rest of the camp. The Scotsmen began to make their way slowly across the bridge rails, which they found had been greased by the Americans. After finally making their way to the other side, they charged the earthworks, swords in hand. The Americans held their fire until they were well within range, then unleashed a volley that tore through the Highlanders, stopping them in their tracks. Subsequent fire sent them reeling back toward the bridge. The other Loyalists, whose ranks had already been decimated by desertion along the march, immediately began to flee in every way possible, and the Tory force quickly disintegrated, with many of them either captured or arrested in the following weeks.

The fight was very brief, with some estimates putting it as perhaps under three minutes. But it was decisive. The Highlanders had lost at least 30 killed, with another 20 or so missing and possibly having been killed and fallen into the creek. The Americans had lost one, killed during the pursuit after the firefight, and one wounded. Recruiting for the Americans skyrocketed, resulting in approximately 8,000 additional fighting men in North Carolina. As for the British Regulars who were expected, they finally arrived off the coast on March 12, too late to make any difference. Moores Creek was the first significant American victory of the Revolutionary War and solidified the Patriot hold on North Carolina for years.

Guilford Courthouse

After losing the Race to the Dan River following the Battle of Cowpens in February 1781, the British army of General Charles Cornwallis turned south to rest and refit at the town of Hillsborough, North Carolina. At least, that is what they had hoped to do. A poor supply situation led to an increasingly hungry army, and as had happened previously, recruiting

SITE DETAILS

Moores Creek National Battlefield—Moores Creek National Battlefield preserves all of this small but important site. The visitor center includes a short introductory film as well as a museum that relates the battle to the larger revolution. You can then take a short, self-guided walking tour of the battlefield; A brochure is available at the visitor center to guide you through it, as well as plenty of interpretive signs along the way. A number of monuments placed along the trail over the years provide additional context about the battle's legacy. *Moores Creek National Battlefield, 40 Patriots Hall Dr., Currie, NC 28435; 910-283-5591; www.nps.gov/mocr. GPS: 34.457034, -78.106476. Grounds accessible daily; visitor center open Tues.–Sat.*

efforts provided little in terms of restoring the army's strength. Cornwallis, whose army had been reduced to 1,900 men, was now far from his base at Charleston, South Carolina, which he had been commanded to protect at all costs. He desperately needed to justify his actions with a victory.

The Americans, on the other hand, were safely camped north of the flooded Dan River and took advantage of their situation. Resting his army, General Nathaniel Greene received both fresh troops and supplies that brought his army to 4,400 men. Greene knew that Cornwallis had been weakened, and within a few weeks the time to fight again had come. The Americans again crept closer to the British army to monitor their actions and put themselves in a position to strike a blow.

After several days of maneuver for each army, Greene selected his battleground. He chose Guilford Courthouse, the same ground where his force had reunited with General Daniel Morgan after Cowpens. Greene was confident that the British would be more than eager to attack him at this advantageous location, and he was right. When Cornwallis discovered the American location, he set his men on a 12-mile march the next day, March 15, 1781, with little rest and no breakfast, to confront them.

The Americans had plenty of time to prepare. The battle plan would be very similar to that of the American victory at Cowpens. There would be three lines, with the front line, again, consisting of green militia at the edge of a small field. These North Carolina militiamen would be asked to fire only two volleys to slow the British down, then retire. A second line would also be militia, with this force from Virginia posted in the woods 350 yards behind the first line. Greene's Continental Army troops from Delaware and Maryland would make the third line, posted in another clearing at the edge of a depressed area, meaning that the British would need to climb to attack them. Riflemen and cavalry would be posted on both flanks of the first line to support them and provide assistance where needed.

The British reached the clearing in front of the American first line at about 1:00 PM and immediately deployed, with no stop to rest from their long march. Still, they came on like the professional soldiers that they were, making a tight formation and steadily but forcefully approaching the Americans. The militia waited until they were within 150 yards,

The American second line at Guilford Courthouse.

SITE DETAILS

Guilford Courthouse National Military Park—The relatively intact battlefield at Guilford Courthouse is preserved at Guilford Courthouse National Military Park. At the visitor center, you can view a film that summarizes the action, and exhibits put the battle into the larger context of the war. From here, you can use the park's tour road to see the battlefield, and an audio guide is available on the park service's app to help you interpret the site. Other than memorials, markers, and interpretive signs, the landscape is little changed. You can also hike the compact battlefield to get a better idea of the terrain. Tours of the battlefield are also provided frequently, and they are perhaps your best bet for understanding what happened here. *Guilford Courthouse National Military Park, 2332 New Garden Rd., Greensboro, NC 27410; 336-288-1776; www.nps.gov/guco. GPS: 36.131312, -79.846694. Grounds open daily; visitor center open Wed.–Sun.*

then fired their two volleys. Unlike at Cowpens, though, these militia left the field in some disorder and did not redeploy to the rear; they simply went home, right in the middle of the fight. The British, staggered but still moving, advanced into the woods after them.

The second American line provided a bit more resistance than the first, though they, too, did not hold on long. However, the British became disordered moving through the woods, and by the time they reached the second clearing they were advancing in a piecemeal fashion. When the first British soldiers arrived at the clearing and saw the Continentals across the field, they immediately charged the position, running into the depression and beginning to move up the other side. This time, the Americans held their fire until they were only 50 yards away, then delivered a withering volley that sent the British backward. A second charge was made and repulsed in the same way. Finally, on the third try, the British gained some steam, and the fighting between the two lines became desperate and hand to hand. Cornwallis, seeing that his troops were taking a terrible beating, ordered his artillery to fire grapeshot directly into the melee to separate the two groups, killing British and American alike. It was a desperate move, but it served to calm the battlefield.

In the meantime, Greene had noticed that a gap had formed in his line where some of the Maryland troops had been driven back. It is possible that had Greene charged, he could have won the day, but he also could have lost his army, something that was not an option. So he cautiously but prudently withdrew his troops from the field, ending the battle. The British, as he suspected, were too badly beaten and exhausted to pursue.

In the technical sense, the British were the victors at Guilford Courthouse. They had driven the Americans from the field and held it. In reality, though, like the battle at Bunker Hill, it was a victory that they could little afford. British losses were 93 killed, with another 413 wounded and 26 missing, while the Americans suffered 70 killed and 185 wounded. Furthermore, strategically, Cornwallis had won nothing, as the Americans simply marched off and lived to fight another day. The British would retreat to Wilmington, North Carolina, where they would again try to resupply and recruit, while the Americans, now in control of the vast majority of the state, would move south to harass British efforts in South Carolina.

Yorktown

As the British army recovered in Wilmington in March and April of 1781, General Charles Cornwallis weighed his options. He was reasonably certain that the British strongholds in South Carolina were strong enough to hold against anything the Americans could bring against them, and he did not see a need to go back. In North Carolina, his army had found little support from the locals and even less in the way of food and other supplies, so staying there was not viable. His eyes turned to nearby Virginia, where he strongly felt that a British presence could make an impact on the war, separating north from south. Further, his vision of British possession of Chesapeake Bay coincided with that of his commander in New York, General Henry Clinton, who had been wanting to establish a presence there for years. Also in Virginia were reinforcements, as Clinton had sent a force of 3,800 men there to support Cornwallis. So the general got his men moving north, crossing into Virginia on April 25,

1781, and joining with the other British force in Petersburg on May 20. Cornwallis now had 7,000 soldiers under his command.

To the north, encamped in a wide circle around New York City, the American and French armies were trying to decide what to do with their combined forces. American General George Washington, having lost New York City in 1776, was intent on taking it back, but the French commander, comte de Rochambeau, was not convinced. One thing that they agreed on, however, was the need for French naval support. As long as the British controlled the American shoreline, they would be able to move up and down the coast as they pleased, while a French naval presence would not only prevent those movements but also disrupt or even prevent the flow of supplies to the British, who had to rely on overseas shipping.

Meanwhile, Cornwallis and Clinton, who had barely communicated for months, were bickering about what to do. Clinton finally directed Cornwallis to establish a post in either Portsmouth, Virginia, near the mouth of Chesapeake Bay, or at the town of Yorktown (or York) on the

The reconstructed Redoubt 10 at Yorktown Battlefield, Colonial National Historical Park.

SITE DETAILS

Yorktown Battlefield, Colonial National Historical Park—The Yorktown Unit of Colonial National Historical Park is a sprawling complex that encompasses much of the Yorktown siege lines. Some of the siege works have been reconstructed—many were lost over time, and even reused and reconfigured during the Civil War battle here—but the scene is still impressive and will give you an idea of the size of the operation. You'll start at the visitor center, where you can view a short film on the siege; inquire about ranger programs, as tours of the battlefield are given frequently. From there, you can tour the battlefield by car, visiting the American, French, and British siege works and batteries, as well as view the field where the British surrender took place. The Moore House, where the surrender was negotiated, is also available to visit. The village of Yorktown is just a short walk away from the visitor center, so be sure to go into town and do some shopping or grab a bite to eat while you're there. *Yorktown Battlefield, Colonial National Historical Park, 1000 Colonial Pkwy., Yorktown, VA 23690; 757-898-2410; www.nps.gov/york. GPS: 37.230104, -76.507174. Open daily.*

American Revolution Museum at Yorktown—The American Revolution Museum at Yorktown opened in 1976 and recently underwent a complete transformation, with a new museum building and complete overhaul of the site. The museum is excellent, covering the entire period of the American Revolution, and includes a 180-degree surround screen film on the siege of Yorktown. The exhibits are state of the art and are thought-provoking to boot, with many impressive artifacts. After you're done with the museum, you can wander outside to the living history area, which features a Continen-

York River. After investigating Portsmouth but finding that it could not be easily defended, Cornwallis reluctantly chose Yorktown, which provided a deep-water port where he could easily be supplied by British ships. With his army continuously being harassed by a force of 4,000 Americans under the Marquis de Lafayette and Major General Baron

tal Army encampment as well as a colonial-era farm. The site is operated by the Jamestown-Yorktown Foundation, which also operates the nearby Jamestown Settlement, and you can buy a combination ticket and experience both. *American Revolution Museum at Yorktown, 200 Water St., Yorktown, VA 23690; 757-253-4838; www.jyfmuseums.org. GPS: 37.239625, -76.518545. Open daily.*

Custom House—The Custom House was built to accommodate the many imports that came in through Yorktown, as it was a major deepwater port. During the siege, the Custom House housed British soldiers, and afterward the French took shelter there. Today, the Custom House is maintained by the local chapter of the Daughters of the Revolution and has a small museum that tells the tale of the building and its role during the siege. *Custom House, 410 Main St., Yorktown, VA 23690. GPS: 37.234902, -76.507719. Open Sun., June through October.*

Washington-Rochambeau Revolutionary Route National Historic Trail—Stretching over nine states from Massachusetts to Virginia, the Washington-Rochambeau Revolutionary Route traces the movement of the French and American armies along their journey from the northern colonies around New York City to the Yorktown battlefield in Virginia. With stops along the way including the smallest campsites to National Park Units, the locations on the trail, as well as its length, demonstrate just what an incredible and arduous journey it was. You can find more information about the trail at the National Park Service's website or at any of the many staffed sites along the route, including at its terminus at Yorktown. *Washington-Rochambeau Revolutionary Route National Historic Trail, multiple sites; 610-783-1006; www.nps.gov/waro. Trail accessible daily.*

Friedrich von Steuben, Cornwallis moved his men to Yorktown on August 1 and began to build fortifications.

On August 14, 1781, the allied commanders received word that their efforts to recruit French naval cooperation had paid off. The Admiral comte de Grasse, who had sailed for the Caribbean in March with 20 large warships, had heard the requests and announced that he would be sailing for Chesapeake Bay, with an estimated date of arrival of about September 1. The electrifying news changed everything. Plans were quickly made for the combined American and French forces to march south to Virginia and trap the British army at Yorktown. In addition, the French naval force at Newport, Rhode Island, under the Admiral comte de Barras sailed south to support de Grasse as well as haul the heavy French siege artillery. The armies began to move on August 18, marching all the way to Maryland, where they boarded boats and made the rest of their journey on the water.

De Grasse arrived at the Virginia Capes outside the Chesapeake on August 30. Only a few days later, a British squadron under Rear Admiral Thomas Graves arrived, and the navies met each other in the Battle of the Capes from September 5–8. The French drove the British off, consolidating control of the Chesapeake. Cornwallis, soon finding his position surrounded by French ships, had received word from Clinton that he would be reinforced, so he remained in Yorktown.

Washington and Rochambeau arrived in Williamsburg, Virginia, on September 14. Over the next 10 days, the combined French and American armies, supported by marines from the French fleets, swelled the allied force to 16,500 men. Establishing their camps around the British position at Yorktown on September 28, with the French on the left and the Americans on the right, the construction of siege parallels began on October 6. The British, who had constructed a series of batteries and redoubts around the town, abandoned their outer lines and consolidated their position, preparing themselves for a siege, all the while hoping that they would receive the reinforcements they would need to break out.

The first artillery batteries began bombarding the British works on October 8, sending cannonballs and mortar shells into the town through day and night, causing terrible damage to the British works and the town and killing hundreds of men. All the while, the Americans and French kept digging, beginning another siege parallel on October 11. However, two British redoubts—known as Redoubts 9 and 10—were in the path of the projected works and would have to be assaulted. On the night of October 14, the French assaulted Redoubt 9 while the Americans, under the command of Colonel Alexander Hamilton, assaulted Redoubt 10.

Though the fighting was heavy and hand to hand, the two redoubts were taken fairly quickly. There was now nothing to stop the allied forces from continuing to creep closer to the British works.

The British attempted a breakout across the York River at Gloucester Point, but poor planning and bad weather prevented the effort from gaining any advantage. Cornwallis, now seeing that his situation was impossible, decided that enough was enough. On October 17, a drummer boy appeared atop the British earthworks beating a parley, and an officer under a flag of truce brought the message that the British were ready to discuss terms of surrender. The firing stopped, and the two sides met the next day to negotiate the terms at the nearby Moore House. Pointedly, the surrender terms were the same as the British gave the Americans at Charleston the year before: Their colors would be cased instead of unfurled, and their musicians would play a British or German march rather than a traditional defiant march of their foe, a deep humiliation for Cornwallis and his army.

The next day, October 19, 1781, the British army marched out of their

An American encampment at the American Revolution Museum at Yorktown.

works along a road lined by the French and American armies. Cornwallis was not among them, claiming that he was ill, so the troops were led by British General Charles O'Hara. O'Hara tried to surrender to Rochambeau, who denied his sword and directed him toward Washington. Washington, for his part, deferred to General Benjamin Lincoln, who had been forced to surrender his garrison at Charleston. After some ceremony, the British soldiers marched forward and grounded their arms, then were marched to prisoner of war camps in Maryland, Virginia, and Pennsylvania.

Over the course of the siege, the British had lost 156 men killed and 326 wounded, while they surrendered an astounding 7,157 men. For the second time in four years, almost to the day, the British had lost an army in America. The American victory at Saratoga had brought the French into the war as American allies. Here at Yorktown, under a combined force of American and French soldiers and sailors, it would bring about the end of the Revolutionary War.

Williamsburg

The peninsula between the James and York Rivers in Virginia has seen more than its share of history, from the English settlement at Jamestown through the Civil War and beyond. It should come as no surprise, then, that the central city of Williamsburg, Virginia, factored into the American Revolution as well.

Williamsburg was a planned city, founded in 1699 when the Virginia settlers decided to move the capital inland from its original Jamestown location. Before long, the city, named after King William III, was booming as not just the political but also the economic, social, and religious capital of Virginia. The College of William & Mary was founded, and impressive buildings were built for both the Virginia legislature (the House of Burgesses) and the governor, whose new palace was to reflect Virginia's prominent place in the colonies.

In 1715, a powder magazine was built in Richmond for the storage of public gunpowder and armaments. On April 21, 1775, that magazine became the center of controversy when Virginia Governor John Dunmore had British soldiers slip into the magazine overnight and empty it of its contents. Only two days after a similar incident sparked the Revolutionary War at Concord, Massachusetts, the Gunpowder Incident sig-

The reconstructed Royal Palace at Williamsburg, Virginia.

nificantly moved the citizens and legislature of Virginia toward a war footing. Though the citizens, led by Patrick Henry, did accept a payment for the gunpowder, the event was enough to further organize Virginia militia all over the state and strengthen their resolve.

When the capital of Virginia was moved to Richmond during the Revolutionary War in 1780, Williamsburg slipped into being a much quieter town. Over the years, many of the original buildings remained, which led to an amazing development. In the 1920s, a movement was begun to preserve and even reconstruct the old Virginia capital as it was during the colonial period, and John D. Rockefeller Jr., son of the pioneering industrialist and one of the wealthiest men in America, soon got wind of the plan. Rockefeller, a philanthropist and a devoted proponent of historical preservation, provided much of the funding, and over the next few decades the core of what would become Colonial Williamsburg began to arise. Still conducting research and teaching about America's early history, Colonial Williamsburg continues to grow and is now one of America's most visited historic sites.

SITE DETAILS

Colonial Williamsburg—The experience at Colonial Williamsburg is unique. Among the hundreds of buildings in the old colonial capital, 89 are original from the colonial period, so stepping into the site is truly immersive. But these aren't just the run-of-the-mill blacksmith shops and other artisans seen at most living history sites. Among the buildings that can be found here are the Governor's Palace, the Virginia Capitol Building, and the original Powder Magazine that was the center of so much controversy in 1775. Totaling 301 acres, it is the world's largest living history museum, and costumed interpreters can be found throughout the park to help you maximize your experience. The number of programs and interactive experiences at Colonial Williamsburg are staggering, and virtually everyone will find something that piques their interest. Restaurants and shops abound, too, as well as lodging options. Between Williamsburg, Yorktown, and nearby Jamestown, there is much to see and do in the area, but be sure you don't shortchange your visit here—set aside at least a day, perhaps more, and plan ahead. *Colonial Williamsburg, 101 Visitor Center Dr., Williamsburg, VA 23185; 888-965-7254; www.colonialwilliamsburg.org. GPS: 37.278672, -76.700479. Open daily.*

Historic Plantations of the Founding Fathers

The legacy of America's Founding Fathers is a difficult subject. Without their courageous stand against British tyranny, the United States of America would not have become the beacon of freedom for the world that it has served as since the American Revolution. However, it can't be denied that the freedom they fought for was not as far-reaching as it may have seemed at the time. The legacy of slavery that still haunts our nation today is an obvious and deep contradiction to the proposition that all men are created equal.

There is perhaps no better place to consider the ideals of the American Revolution and the horrors of slavery than at the Virginia plantation homes of some of the men who created America. At all these sites, you will find not only an appreciation and celebration of their accomplishments, but also an investigation of how they wrestled with the question of slavery and in all cases came up on the wrong side of history. These American giants—brave, flawed, ahead of their time, products of their time, and undoubtedly privileged and wealthy—are inseparable from the story of America.

SCOTCHTOWN: HOME OF PATRICK HENRY—Patrick Henry was one of the American Revolution's most outspoken firebrands. Henry was a member of the House of Burgesses, was named a delegate to the First Continental Congress, and became the first governor of Virginia. Known as the Orator of the Revolution, it was during the height of the revolutionary years, from 1771 to 1778, that Henry lived here at his plantation known as Scotchtown.

Scotchtown, purchased from John Payne, father of Dolley Madison, was one of the largest homes in Virginia at the time. Henry was a slaveholder from the time he turned 18 through the rest of his life, though it is

The Patrick Henry home at Scotchtown, Beaverdam, Virginia.

SITE DETAILS

Patrick Henry's Scotchtown—Scotchtown is maintained today by Preservation Virginia. Though the grounds are open throughout the year, tours are more limited, and you will want to view the home. It has been restored to the period of Henry's residence, and unlike many other plantation homes of the period that you may tour, the house is relatively sparsely furnished—as Henry would have preferred it. As such, the tour heavily focuses on Patrick Henry's life during his time here, and not the house itself. There are also a number of excellent exhibits about Henry's life and legacy, including a thorough examination of slavery at Scotchtown and Henry's views and contradictions on the subject. *Patrick Henry's Scotchtown, 16120 Chiswell Ln., Beaverdam, VA 23015; 804-227-3500; preservation virginia.org/historic-sites/patrick-henrys-scotchtown. GPS: 37.844095, -77.587391. Grounds open daily; guided tours of home available Fri.–Sun., March through December.*

obvious that he saw the irony of preaching "Liberty or Death" and being a slaveowner. Scotchtown was used as a tobacco farm and had an iron foundry as well, all of which—along with the care of the home—used slave labor. Henry stated on many occasions that it was wrong and hoped for an eventual end to the institution, but he could not bring himself to free his own slaves. In response to the letter of an abolitionist who wrote a number of prominent politicians asking them to free their slaves as he had done, Henry responded, "I am drawn along by the general inconvenience of living without them. I will not, I cannot justify it." (Henry was the only one of those politicians who offered a response.)

MONTICELLO: HOME OF THOMAS JEFFERSON—Perhaps no Founding Father is as much of a lightning rod as Thomas Jefferson. Jefferson was undoubtedly one of America's most important figures, if for no other reason than that he authored our Declaration of Independence. But his relationship with slavery, and in particular with enslaved Sally Hemings, has made his legacy extremely controversial. It begs for further exploration, and there is no better place to explore Jefferson than his longtime plantation home, Monticello.

Construction on the home at Monticello began in 1769, and throughout Jefferson's life the house was constantly being renovated, redesigned, and rebuilt to Jefferson's designs. Jefferson remained in the home until his death in 1826, though because of his heavy debts it was sold shortly afterward. Monticello was a large estate, and the home, farms, and gardens required an enormous amount of slave labor to maintain; at any given time, Monticello would have as many as 130 slaves. In fact, throughout his lifetime, Jefferson would own over 600 slaves, with about 400 at Monticello and another 200 at his other properties. Jefferson, like others of his time, believed that slavery was an evil, but one that he relied on heavily to maintain his way of life. The author of the Declaration of Independence, who stated that "all men are created equal," was heavily influenced by the views of his time, particularly the paternalistic racism of the European Enlightenment.

Monticello, center of Thomas Jefferson's estate in Charlottesville, Virginia.

SITE DETAILS

Monticello—A visit to Monticello is guaranteed to be an interesting and thought-provoking experience. The large complex of course includes the home, which is an architectural masterpiece and is filled with interesting quirks of Jefferson's making. But the site also includes exhibits on numerous subjects as well as an excellent and thorough museum in the visitor center. The tours offered at Monticello are remarkable and numerous and include several unflinching explorations of slavery and the enslaved at the plantation, as well as architecture, archaeology, women, the gardens, and many other subjects; seasonal specialty tours and private tours are also available, as well as tours designed for children. Jefferson's grave and family cemetery are also here and worth a visit, and the site also includes dining and shopping opportunities. One can easily spend an entire day here, and it's the kind of site that rewards repeat visits. A World Heritage site, Monticello is a must-see. *Monticello, 1050 Monticello Loop, Charlottesville, VA 22902; 434-984-980; www.monticello.org. GPS: 38.005527, -78.456118. Open daily.*

MONTPELIER: HOME OF JAMES MADISON—James Madison was one of our younger Founding Fathers, and he made his mark primarily in the new state of Virginia before serving in the Continental Congress beginning in 1780. However, Madison's position as Father of the Constitution makes him one of our most important early Americans. Madison quickly gained a reputation as a bright thinker with a gift for diplomacy, and his construction of the government in the Virginia Plan, his part in writing the Federalist Papers, and his authorship of the Bill of Rights secured his place as a giant of history even before he became our fourth president.

Madison grew up at Montpelier and lived there until his death in 1836. He and his wife Dolley inherited the estate, along with over 100 slaves, upon his father's death in 1801. (Interestingly, Dolley Payne Madison's father, a Quaker, had freed his own slaves after the American Revolution.) Madison saw slavery as an evil and a great danger to the young nation, calling it "the most oppressive dominion ever exercised by man over man." He was an early proponent of the colonization movement, which would have sent freed slaves back to Africa. Though in his will he requested that Dolley not sell any slaves without their consent, Madison did not free any of his slaves.

MOUNT VERNON: HOME OF GEORGE WASHINGTON—George Washington is perhaps our most important American. He led the Continental Army to victory during the American Revolution, declined the opportunity to become a king, and formed many of the traditions of government during the nation's first presidency. By all contemporary accounts, he was a remarkable man, and without him it is difficult to imagine even the existence of the United States of America. Of course, Washington was also the wealthiest man in America, and as such he relied on slavery to operate his extensive plantation at Mount Vernon.

Slave cabins at Montpelier, home of James Madison in Montpelier Station, Virginia.

SITE DETAILS

James Madison's Montpelier—In the last few decades, Montpelier has undergone extensive restoration and renovation, and the result is a great user experience. The home will be the highlight of your visit, and the comprehensive one-hour tour covers the Madisons, their legacy, and the enslaved people who labored at the property. Additional exhibits dive deeply into Madison's construction of the Constitution and his views on slavery. The grounds are also open and are included in your tour ticket; there's a lot to see, as the outbuildings hold further exhibits and the trails take you to other parts of the property, including Madison's gravesite. For those interested in archaeology, Montpelier even offers interactive programs that allow visitors to assist with the ongoing investigations on the site. If you're in the area to see Jefferson's Monticello, set aside extra time to see Madison's Montpelier—it is absolutely worth it. *James Madison's Montpelier, 11350 Constitution Highway, Montpelier Station, VA 22957; 540-672-2728; www.montpelier.org. GPS: 38.218782, -78.172062. Open daily May through October, Thurs.–Sun., November through April.*

The first iteration of Mount Vernon was built by Washington's father in 1734, and Washington began overseeing operations on the plantation 20 years later in 1754. Mount Vernon remained his home through the rest of his life, except for when he was off fighting the war. Hundreds of enslaved persons labored in the home and on the property during Washington's lifetime, numbering 317 at the time of his death in 1799. Washington began to see slavery as contrary to the ideals of the American Revolution during the war; in private correspondence, he supported a legislative solution for ending slavery, but for the most part he did not take a public position on it. In his will, Washington stipulated that his slaves should be freed upon the death of his wife, Martha. In reality, though, this only meant freedom for about half the slaves at Mount Vernon, since the rest belonged to Martha. Washington clearly saw slavery as

A memorial marks the site of the slave cemetery at Mount Vernon, home of George Washington.

a dangerous issue for the new nation, but like his contemporaries could not conquer the issue himself.

Washington

The District of Columbia and the city of Washington were not established until 1790, when Congress chose a permanent capital during George Washington's presidency. However, the nation's founding and the American Revolution loom large in the city's monuments, parks, and buildings. There is a lot to see and do in Washington, and it's a trip that every American should make at least once during their lifetime. The sites listed here can all be seen when visiting our nation's capital.

WASHINGTON MONUMENT—The tallest building in the world upon its completion, the Washington Monument honors the hero of the American Revolution and our first president. Standing 555 feet tall, construction

SITE DETAILS

Mount Vernon—Located just outside of Washington, DC, Mount Vernon provides a complete exploration of the Father of the Country. The home, of course, will be central to your visit, and short tours are available that will show you Washington's impressive house. But there is much more to see here. Tours and programs are available for many topics, and every outbuilding at Mount Vernon is dedicated to further exhibits and living history, demonstrating what plantation life was like during Washington's time here for both the Washingtons and the enslaved. A farm, gristmill, and working distillery round out the property. The museums dedicated to Washington's life and legacy are extremely thorough and offer some choice artifacts, including those found during Mount Vernon's ongoing archaeological excavations. You'll also find Washington's burial site on the property, as well as a slave cemetery. Mount Vernon also has restaurants and shopping, which becomes very convenient when you get here and realize that one could easily spend an entire day exploring the plantation. Set aside at least a half day for this one. *Mount Vernon, 3200 Mount Vernon Memorial Highway, Mount Vernon, VA 22121;703-780-2000; www.mountvernon.org. GPS: 38.710859, -77.086633. Open daily.*

first began in 1848 as a private venture, but stalled from 1854 to 1876 due to political wrangling and lack of funds. Congress picked up the work in 1876 and the monument was completed in 1884. Today, you can of course view the monument from the outside (in fact, you can't miss it), but to get to the top you will need a timed ticket, which you can get either online (recommended) or same day at the Washington Monument Lodge on 15th Street. *Washington Monument, National Mall near intersection of 15th St. and Madison Dr. NW, Washington, DC 20004; 202-426-6841; www.nps.gov/wamo. GPS: 38.889462, -77.035220. Open daily.*

JEFFERSON MEMORIAL—Dedicated in 1943, the Jefferson Memorial design was influenced heavily by Jefferson's own designs for his home,

Monticello, and his rotunda at the University of Virginia. In the center is a 19-foot-tall statue of Jefferson, holding the Declaration of Independence and surrounded by some of his quotations. The monument is accessible 24 hours a day, and National Park Service staff are generally there until 10:00 PM to answer questions. The monument is beautiful, as is its setting next to the Tidal Basin, but be sure to visit the small museum in the base of the monument. *Thomas Jefferson Memorial, on East Basin Dr. SW near intersection with Ohio Dr. SW, Washington, DC 20242; 202-426-6841; www.nps.gov/thje. GPS: 38.881399, -77.036534. Open daily.*

GEORGE MASON MEMORIAL—The memorial to another Founding Father, George Mason, whose writings heavily inspired Thomas Jefferson, is fittingly located next to the Jefferson Memorial. Consisting of a small statue within a beautiful garden, the monument, dedicated in 2002, was designed to reflect the simple preferences Mason had during his life. Several quotations of Mason, as well as a couple from Jefferson

The Thomas Jefferson Memorial on the Tidal Basin in Washington, DC.

The small but effective George Mason Memorial in Washington, DC.

and the Marquis de Lafayette noting Mason's importance, round out the memorial. *George Mason Memorial, intersection of East Basin Dr. SW and Ohio Dr. SW, Washington, DC 20024; 202-426-6841; www.nps.gov/nama/planyourvisit/george-mason-memorial.htm. GPS: 38.879581, -77.039197. Open daily.*

CONSTITUTION GARDENS AND SIGNERS MEMORIAL—In 1976, a 50-acre public park was created on the National Mall to memorialize the men who signed the United States Constitution. In 1984, an additional memorial to those who signed the Declaration of Independence was added. The park is an oasis within its urban setting, with lush plant and animal life and a lovely design. If you're looking for a place to escape the crowds for a little while, this is a perfect spot. *Constitution Gardens, intersection of Constitution Ave. NW and 17th St. NW, Washington, DC 20004; 202-426-6841; www.nps.gov/coga. GPS: 38.891315, -77.042872. Open daily.*

LAFAYETTE SQUARE—Just north of the White House is Lafayette Square, named for the Marquis de Lafayette and dedicated during his return visit to the United States in 1824. Because of its proximity to the White House, the park has been and still is the site of frequent protests and demonstrations. You will find a statue of Lafayette and other revolutionary heroes here, though the largest statue in the center of the square is of Andrew Jackson. *Lafayette Square, intersection of Pennsylvania Ave. NW and 16th St. NW, Washington, DC 20001. GPS: 38.899502, -77.036576. Accessible daily.*

NATIONAL ARCHIVES MUSEUM—While the National Archives is a treasure trove of American history, the vast majority of visitors are there to see the exhibits in the rotunda—the Declaration of Independence, the United States Constitution, and the Bill of Rights. You are likely to see other famous documents in the rotunda—the Magna Carta, perhaps, or a draft of the Emancipation Proclamation—but if you have time, tour the museum, which has plenty of fascinating and often-rotating exhibits. While you don't need a ticket to visit the archives, you would do well to reserve a timed ticket online to ensure your spot and avoid waiting

The quiet Constitution Gardens and Signers Memorial in Washington, DC.

in what is often a long line. *National Archives Museum, 701 Constitution Ave. NW, Washington, DC 20408; visit.archives.gov. GPS: 38.892257, -77.022973. Open daily.*

NATIONAL PORTRAIT GALLERY—Many of the most famous portraits of the American Revolution—and America, for that matter—are housed in the National Portrait Gallery. You will find many of these in the sections dedicated to Early America and the Early Republic, as well as the presidential section, but you are likely to find yourself roaming the other halls as well. Part of the Smithsonian Institution, the National Portrait Gallery can be a quick and easy visit, but like the Smithsonian's other museums, it's easy to get lost in what you're looking at. *National Portrait Gallery, intersection of 8th St. NW and G St. NW, Washington, DC 20001; npg.si.edu. GPS: 38.897389, -77.023008. Open daily.*

The National Portrait Gallery in Washington, DC.

SMITHSONIAN NATIONAL MUSEUM OF AMERICAN HISTORY—If you're a history buff, the Smithsonian National Museum of American History has plenty to keep you busy. An entire section is dedicated to the American Revolution, and you will find related material scattered throughout the museum. *Smithsonian National Museum of American History, 1300 Constitution Ave. NW, Washington, DC 20560; americanhistory.si.edu. GPS: 38.891587, -77.030065. Open daily.*

REVOLUTIONARY WAR STATUES—The National Park Service, as stewards of the National Mall and surrounding areas, are the caretakers of 15 statues of figures from the American Revolution scattered throughout Washington. The statues were dedicated at different times from 1860 all the way through 2007, and though many garner little attention today, they are part of the Revolution's legacy. All of these statues are accessible daily (some more easily than others).

- John Barry (one of the fathers of the American Navy)—*in Franklin Square, intersection of I St. NW and 14th St. NW; GPS: 38.901926, -77.031713*

- Edmund Burke (member of British Parliament who supported American rights)—*in Burke Park, intersection of L St. NW and 12th St. NW; GPS: 38.903887, -77.027443*

- Benjamin Franklin—*in front of Old Post Office, 1100 Pennsylvania Ave NW; GPS: 38.894653, -77.027852*

- Bernardo de Gálvez—*in Bernardo de Gálvez Memorial Park, intersection of Virginia Ave. NW and E St. NW; GPS: 38.895686, -77.048536*

- Nathaniel Greene—*Stanton Park, intersection of C St. NE and 5th St. NE; GPS: 38.893583, -76.999515*

- Nathan Hale—*in front of U.S. Attorney General Building, intersec-*

tion of Constitution Ave. NW and 9th St. NW ; GPS: 38.892271, -77.024348

- John Paul Jones—*on National Mall, intersection of 17th St. SW and Independence Ave. SW; GPS: 38.888213, -77.039496*

- Thaddeus Kosciuszko—*in northeast corner of Lafayette Square, intersection of H St. NW and Madison Place NW; GPS: 38.900016, -77.035397*

- Marquis de Lafayette—*in southeast corner of Lafayette Square, intersection of Pennsylvania Ave. NW and Madison Place NW; GPS: 38.899028, -77.035368*

- Casimir Pulaski—*in Freedom Plaza, intersection of Pennsylvania Ave. NW and 13th St. NW; GPS: 38.895899, -77.029966*

- Comte Jean de Rochambeau—*in southwest corner of Lafayette Square, intersection of Pennsylvania Ave. NW and Jackson Place NW; GPS: 38.898999, -77.037723*

- Friedrich Wilhelm von Steuben—*in northwest corner of Lafayette Square, intersection of H St. NW and Jackson Place NW; GPS: 38.900020, -77.037719*

- Artemas Ward (took command of the early American army before Washington arrived)—*in Ward Circle Park, intersection of Nebraska St. NW and Massachusetts Ave. NW; GPS: 38.937923, -77.085907 (use extreme caution when visiting this site!)*

- George Washington—*Washington Circle, intersection of K St. NW and 23rd St. NW; GPS: 38.902529, -77.050153*

- John Witherspoon (member of Congress and signer of the Declaration of Independence) —*in Witherspoon Park, intersection of 18th St. NW and N St. NW; GPS: 38.907164, -77.041778*

THE LINDENS—One of the more curious historic homes in the country, The Lindens was built in 1754 for a wealthy merchant in Massachusetts. British Thomas Gage, commander in chief of British forces in North America, stayed here for several months. In 1934, on the verge of destruction, the home was dismantled and moved by rail to Washington, DC, where it was reconstructed. The home is privately owned today and is not open for tours. *The Lindens, 2401 Kalorama Rd., Washington, DC 20001. GPS: 38.918010, -77.053494. Private property.*

OTHER SITES IN THE UPPER SOUTH

JOHN BURGWIN HOUSE—In 1768, Wilmington's jail building burnt down, and when it was decided to rebuild the jail outside of the city, local magistrate John Burgwin purchased the property and made the strong stone ruins the foundation of his new home. When the Revolution came about, Burgwin leased the home to others, and when the British occupied Wilmington, the home was used as a headquarters. It was once thought that the home was the headquarters of Lord Cornwallis himself, but this is now in doubt; it is almost certain, however, that with what was once a commanding view of the river and town, the British commander spent some of his time here.

The Burgwin-Wright House and Gardens is open for tours. The guided tour focuses on the period just before and after the Revolution, and the building has been carefully restored. Even parts of the former jail have been put on exhibit, with a view of the prison's former dungeon available from the gift shop and museum. The gardens and exterior of the home are available for self-guided touring. *Burgwin-Wright House and Gardens, 224 Market St., Wilmington, NC, 28401; 910-762-0570; www.burgwinwrighthouse.com. GPS: 34.235293, -77.946260. Open for tours Mon.–Sat.*

WILMINGTON—Following the British defeat at Cowpens and coming up short in the Race to the Dan River, Cornwallis needed to rest and resupply his army. Wilmington was the natural choice based on its proximity and excellent harbor. The British did not have an easy stay in Wilmington, however, as the army was harassed by Whig partisans

The Burgwin-Wright House in Wilmington, North Carolina.

throughout their stay. These engagements took place in a wide circle around the city, and though none of them were large or had immediate consequences, they further wore down an army that was already feeling the toll of combat.

In addition to the Burgwin-Wright House above, a memorial downtown commemorates where North Carolina's stamp master, appointed by the British government to collect taxes on printed paper, was forced to resign. As far as the fighting around Wilmington, however, the only site with any type of memorial is at the former site of Heron's Bridge, a key passage north of the city that was eventually burned by the British. A historic highway marker is at the spot. *Stamp master historic markers, on Market St. at intersections with Water St. and Front St., Wilmington, NC 28401. GPS: 34.235267, -77.949664. Historic highway marker—North Carolina Department of Conservation and Development D-22 (Early Drawbridge), on US 117 0.1 mile north of Old Bridgeside Road,*

Castle Hayne, NC 28429. GPS: 34.362366, -77.898404. Sites accessible daily.

TRYON PALACE AND NORTH CAROLINA HISTORY CENTER—Governor William Tryon's palace, finished in 1770, was truly a palace. In the tense times of colonial dissent, its over-the-top luxury was often pointed to as a sign of the crown's excess while taxing the common man. While Tryon spared no expense in building it, he stayed here for only one year before leaving to become governor of New York. A few years later his successor in North Carolina, Governor Josiah Martin, was forced to flee the colony. The building served as North Carolina's capital for several years before burning to the ground in 1798.

A faithful reconstruction of Tryon Palace and its grounds has been recovered from what had become part of New Bern's cityscape. The palace, part of a larger system of museums and historical sites that covers New Bern's extensive history, is the crown jewel of the collection. Guided tours are frequent, and the gardens, stables, kitchen, and servant's quarters, as well as an unimpeded view of the Trent River, help keep the visitor grounded in the colonial period. Just across the street is the North Carolina History Center, which interprets New Bern's place in the American Revolution with a broader view. Your ticket, purchased from the New Bern Historical Society across from the palace, will cover both. *Tryon Palace and North Carolina History Center, 529 South Front St., New Bern, NC, 28562; 800-767-1560; www.tryonpalace.org. GPS: 35.107086, -77.044405. Open daily.*

SOMERSET PLACE STATE HISTORIC SITE—Somerset Place, one of the south's largest plantations, started producing crops in 1785, between the end of the American Revolution and the Constitutional Convention, and remained active through the end of the Civil War in 1865. As such, it provides a unique window into the story of slavery in the United States of America. The swampy area required hundreds of laborers to clear land and dig canals, and over 850 enslaved persons worked the plantation over its lifetime.

Somerset Place's mission as a historic site is to show plantation life as it truly was, not the sometimes-romanticized version we may have once seen in the movies. The authentic lives of the plantation owners and their families, overseers, enslaved persons, and the dozens of other people required to keep such a large operation running are all accounted for here. The diverse output of the plantation is also portrayed, from cash crops to food to lumber. Somerset Place is only a small portion of what it once was, but its stark portrayal of the slave economy helps us remember the primary issue that the new nation could not solve. *Somerset Place State Historic Site, 2572 Lake Shore Road, Creswell, NC 27928; 252-797-4560; historicsites.nc.gov/all-sites/somerset-place. GPS: 35.789549, -76.403772. Open Tues.–Sat.*

PENELOPE BARKER HOUSE—Though the Boston Tea Party of December 1773 gets the most attention, other similar tea protests broke out across the colonies. Perhaps the most unique of these was the Edenton Tea Party. Organized in October 1774, a group of 51 women, led by Penelope Barker, signed a petition resolving not to purchase or use British goods, including tea. The women of Edenton received attention both in the colonies and in London, where the group's resolves were printed in the newspapers.

Today the Penelope Barker House serves as a visitor center for Edenton and is open to the public. Along with information about the town, you will find excellent interpretation of the Edenton Tea Party and a beautiful view of Albemarle Sound from the second-story porch. A short walk will take you to the site of the Elisabeth King House, where you will find a fitting monument—an inverted cannon with an iron tea kettle on top. *Penelope Barker House, 505 South Broad St., Edenton, NC, 27932; 252-482-7800; ehcnc.org/836-2/the-barker-house. GPS: 36.056281, -76.609490. Open Wed.–Mon. Edenton Tea Party Monument, southwest of intersection of East King St. and Court St. West, Edenton, NC, 27932. GPS: 36.057523, -76.608224. Accessible daily.*

TAYLOR'S MILL—James Lee built a gristmill complex in 1762 on a 200-acre tract in rural North Carolina. Early in the Revolutionary War, his mills were contracted by the state to provide meal to the Continental Army.

The site of Taylor's Mill is on private property, and there are no mark-

The view of Albemarle Sound from the Penelope Barker House in Edenton, North Carolina.

ers to denote the former location. The original mill was built over in 1784 and was continually built over until the last mill was washed away in the 1980s, so there's little left above ground. *Taylor's Mill, intersection of Taylors Mill Rd. and Drivers Rd., Zebulon, NC 27597. GPS: 35.777222, -78.240000. Private property.*

SMITH'S FERRY—Smith's Ferry was a well-known crossing of the Cape Fear River, and when it was time to rally Loyalist men to the British cause, it was a natural rendezvous point. After the Loyalists had mustered, they marched to their devastating defeat at Moores Creek. As the Loyalist force scattered, much of the group made their way back to Smith's Ferry in order to recross the Cape Fear River; subsequently, Patriot forces followed them here and scooped up hundreds of prisoners of war.

A historical highway marker for the plantation Oak Grove has been placed near the site of Smith's Ferry, but it commemorates the Smith family's mansion, not the ferry site itself. The site is on private property, but if you look to the west, you will see the area of the ferry and the old town of Smithfield that rose around it. *Historical highway marker, North Carolina Archives and Highway Departments (Oak Grove), on Burnett Road 0.4 mile south of West Thornton Rd., Dunn, NC 28334. GPS: 35.249243, -78.681025. Sign accessible daily.*

HOUSE IN THE HORSESHOE STATE HISTORIC SITE—In 1770, only a few years before war broke out, Philip Alston built a fine house in a looping bend of the Deep River. When the fighting came to North Carolina, Alston established himself as a colonel. As his band camped around his home, they were attacked by a Tory unit led by David Fanning. Though surprised, the Loyalists were able to throw back several charges from within the shelter of the house. After four hours of fighting, it was Mrs. Alston's dramatic emergence on the front porch that finally brought a calm to the field and caused the parties to cease fire and separate.

The House in the Horseshoe is remarkably well-preserved as a North

The Alston House, centerpiece of the battle at House in the Horseshoe State Historic Site.

Carolina State Historic Site. Guided tours of the home present the story of the Alston family and the firefight that occurred around the home; a number of the original bullet holes are still on proud display. The site also has a small museum, and the spacious grounds and view of the river provide a great place for a picnic. *House in the Horseshoe State Historic Site, 288 Alston House Rd., Sanford, NC 27330; 910-947-2051; historic sites.nc.gov/all-sites/house-horseshoe. GPS: 35.467066, -79.383002. Open Tues.–Sat.*

BUFFALO FORD—An excellent crossing point of the Deep River, Buffalo Ford changed hands several times during the American Revolution. The Continental Army also camped at Buffalo Ford, and it was here that General Horatio Gates rendezvoused with the Southern Army and took command.

No markers exist at Buffalo Ford, but you are able to see what is roughly the ford area from the highway. As you cross the Deep River, the ford is on the north side, only a few hundred feet from the bridge. *Buffalo Ford, on Hinshaw Town Road 0.3 mile west of NC-22, Randolph County, NC 27316. GPS: 35.672498, -79.627300. Accessible daily.*

BELL'S MILL—The gristmill on the Deep River owned by William and Martha Bell was a natural crossing and muster point, and it was used by both sides during the American Revolution. The British stopped at Bell's Mill both before and after Guilford Courthouse, with Cornwallis taking the Bells' home as his headquarters while his weary troops rested. Legend has it that Mrs. Bell, her husband away with the Continental Army, forced Cornwallis to agree to spare the mill in exchange for its use; other stories say that "Light Horse" Harry Lee, chasing the British after the fight, received directions to the next British camp from the Bell family.

What little is left of Bell's Mill is now underwater, covered by Randleman Reservoir. There are no markers or memorials near the site, though you will find a memorial to Mrs. Bell's bravery at Guilford Courthouse National Military Park. As you cross the reservoir on the interstate, the mill would have been close to the north shore, west of the bridge. *Bell's Mill, under Randleman Reservoir, west of Interstate 73, Randleman, NC 27317. GPS: 35.846965, -79.831400. Site inaccessible.*

A view of Alamance Battleground State Historic Site from the visitor center.

ALAMANCE BATTLEGROUND STATE HISTORIC SITE—The complications of the Carolinas' backcountry politics manifested themselves far before the Revolution began. Responding to what they perceived to be unfair treatment at the hands of colonial officials, men in the remote regions of North Carolina gathered and formed a vigilante group known as the Regulators. The activities of the Regulators varied from righteous to exploitative, but in all cases they were clearly operating outside of the law. In response, Governor William Tryon called out the North Carolina militia, and the two sides met at Alamance on May 16, 1771. After both sides initially refused orders to fire shots at their neighbors, a firefight finally broke out, with the militia quickly crushing the small rebellion. Though sometimes referred to as the first battle of the Revolution, it should be noted that the men that fought at Alamance would later join both Whig and Tory forces.

The battlefield at Alamance is now a North Carolina State Historic

Site. Much of the field has been preserved, and the visitor center contains exhibits and an excellent film that tells the stories of the Regulators and the militia. Guided tours of the battlefield are also provided three times daily, and if you're not able to walk the grounds, most of the battlefield can be viewed with interpretation from the visitor center. *Alamance Battleground State Historic Site, 5803 NC-62 South, Burlington, NC 27215; 336-227-4785; historicsites.nc.gov/all-sites/alamance-battleground. GPS: 36.009797, -79.519452. Open Tues.–Sat.*

PYLE'S DEFEAT—On February 25, 1781, "Light Horse" Harry Lee, chasing after British menace Banastre Tarleton, thought he had caught up with Tarleton's troopers, but found he had instead come across a Loyalist unit commanded by Colonel John Pyle. Lee's fighting force wore green jackets, similar to those worn by British dragoons, and Pyle's men calmly approached Lee's men, also misidentifying that they were hostile to Tarleton. Lee decided to try to keep up the charade, and the two columns formed side by side. Accounts vary on what happened next, but what is known is that Lee's Patriots pounced on the Loyalists, killing over 90 of them, many of them brutally and reportedly with cries of "Tarleton's Quarter" and "Remember Buford." Pyle's Massacre, as Pyle's Defeat also came to be known, served to suppress what little Loyalist support was left in the backcountry, slowing British recruitment to a halt.

A memorial to the action that took place here is easily accessible, and though there isn't much interpretation, it accurately marks the site of Pyle's Defeat. The gravel road alongside the monument is essentially the same road that the two troops of cavalry were traveling along, and the rural area makes it easy to picture the short and bloody fight that occurred. *Pyle's Defeat Monument, intersection of Anthony Road and Old Trail Road, Burlington, NC 27215. GPS: 36.049996, -79.450369. Site accessible daily.*

TROUBLESOME CREEK IRONWORKS—By the time Nathaniel Greene's army encamped at the old Troublesome Creek Ironworks in 1781, the facility was already somewhat of a ruin. What attracted Greene, rather than the site's ability to produce iron, was its value as a defensive posi-

A marker denotes the site of Pyle's Defeat in Burlington, North Carolina.

tion. The army would return to the site on their way to the battle at Guilford Courthouse.

A historic marker commemorates the Troublesome Creek Ironworks and its role in the revolution. The marker is at an intersection; driving north about 1.3 miles will take you to a bridge over Troublesome Creek and the original location of the site, now owned by the Rockingham Historical Society. *Historic highway marker—North Carolina Department of Conservation and Development J-16 (Troublesome Iron Works), intersection of US 158 and Monroeton Rd., Reidsville, NC 27320. GPS: 36.289987, -79.734352. Sign accessible daily.*

HALIFAX—On April 12, 1776, before the Continental Congress and every other colony, the North Carolina Provincial Congress did something truly revolutionary. Meeting in Halifax, the Congress voted to approve the Halifax Resolves, a declaration of independence for the state. This remarkable action empowered North Carolina's delegates to the Continental Congress to vote for the independence of America from Great Britain, making North Carolina the first colony to formally vote for separation from the crown. If you wonder how important that date is to North Carolinians, look no further than their state flag, where the date of the Halifax Resolves is proudly emblazoned.

Historic Halifax State Historic Site commemorates more than just the Halifax Resolves; the site includes a historic tavern and jail, and there is Underground Railroad history here, too. But it's the Resolves that take center stage, and the best place to learn about them is in the excellent museum at the visitor center. There is also a short film that covers the Halifax Resolves and other parts of the town's varied history. A walking trail will take you to the other sites. *Historic Halifax State Historic Site, 25 St. David St., Halifax, NC 22839; 252-583-7191; historicsites.nc.gov/all-sites/historic-halifax. GPS: 36.330035, -77.589448. Open Tues.–Sat.*

RED HILL—PATRICK HENRY NATIONAL MEMORIAL—In 1794, after a storied political career, the volatile Patrick Henry finally decided to settle down and retire. Heading west for the countryside, Henry found the isolated plantation at Red Hill and purchased it. Henry happily continued his law practice here until his death in 1799, just as he was gearing up for another campaign for office.

Red Hill now serves as the Patrick Henry National Memorial. Most of the plantation burned down in 1919, including Henry's home, but the building he used as his law office is original. The home and other buildings have been reconstructed and are open for tours. Henry is also buried here with his second wife, Dorothea, and other members of the Henry family. The visitor center also contains exhibits covering Henry's life. *Red Hill—Patrick Henry National Memorial, 1250 Red Hill Rd., Brookneal, VA 24528; 800-514-7463; www.redhill.org. GPS: 37.033067, -78.897984. Open daily.*

POPLAR FOREST—After Thomas Jefferson left the presidency in 1809, he remained a highly sought-after figure in American politics. Though he could hardly retire in the traditional sense, Jefferson did create a retreat away from Monticello, the peaceful Poplar Forest. Jefferson spent most of his later years between these two grand homes. When needing to escape the constant business at Monticello, Poplar Forest was his choice for leisure, continued scientific exploration, and family time.

Slightly less accessible than its counterpart Monticello, Poplar Forest still stands and is lovingly cared for. Only recently preserved, restoration is ongoing, and new discoveries about the home are still being uncovered. You'll recognize Jefferson's stylistic presence immediately, both inside and outside the home and on the grounds. The history of enslaved persons at Poplar Forest has also been carefully researched and is presented with care. Though the scale is smaller than what you'll find at Monticello, you'll also have a much more intimate experience, and the story is told just as well. *Poplar Forest, 1542 Bateman Bridge Rd., Forest, VA, 24551; 434-525-1806; www.poplarforest.org. GPS: 37.358138, -77.267441. Open daily.*

PETERSBURG AND BLANDFORD CHURCH AND CEMETERY—Before Cornwallis approached Virginia, another British force was sent to set the stage for his invasion. That expedition was led by British Major General

Thomas Jefferson's getaway estate at Poplar Forest, Forest, Virginia.

William Phillips, though the Americans were certainly more interested in another commander present, Brigadier General Benedict Arnold. Petersburg, part of a primary communication line, was an obvious target. Landing to the east at City Point the day before, the British approached Petersburg on April 25, 1781, and steadily pushed back an American defense led by Major General Baron Friedrich von Steuben. Though the British took the city, von Steuben put up a respectable stand, eventually retreating north across the Appomattox River with his force intact.

The best way to follow the Battle of Petersburg today is through the several historical markers erected throughout the city. Though Petersburg thoroughly embraces its extensive Civil War history, it hasn't ignored the other parts of its often-overlapping heritage, and pieces of the landscape that dictated the battle can still be discerned. You'll find the first marker east of town and will finish just to the west. Blandford Church, located in the old town area of Petersburg where the fight started, still stands. And if you have the time to take the tour of the

Interpretive signs and historic markers tell the story of the Revolutionary War battle at Petersburg, Virginia.

chapel, it's worth it. British General Phillips, who was ill during the fight and died soon after, is buried on the grounds around the chapel, though the gravestone doesn't mark his unknown location. *Blandford Church, 111 Rochell Lane, Petersburg, VA 23803; 804-733-2396. GPS: 37.226593, -77.388027. Grounds open daily, tours Thurs.–Sun. Historical highway markers—Virginia Department of Historic Resources: QA-21 (British Line of Attack), intersection of East Washington St. and Puddledock Rd., GPS 37.239013, -77.374037; QA-23 (First Line of Defense), intersection of East St. and East Bank St., GPS 37.234729, -77.390082; QA-20 (Artillery Position), intersection of East Washington St. and South Little Church St., GPS 37.230185, -77.393456; QA-24 (Flanking Movement), on Graham Rd. 0.1 mile east of Jefferson Place, GPS 37.218105, -77.393231; QA-22 (East Hill) and QA-25 (Second Line of Defense), intersection of North Madison St. and 5th St., GPS 37.230996, -77.397621, Petersburg, VA 23803. Interpretive sign (The Battle at the Bridge), on Joseph Jenkins Roberts St. 0.2 mile north of 3rd St., Petersburg, VA 23803. GPS: 37.235351, -77.402777. Signs accessible daily.*

ST. JOHN'S EPISCOPAL CHURCH—Less than one month before the Revolutionary War opened in Lexington and Concord, far to the south, delegates gathered at St. John's Church in Richmond, Virginia, to discuss the actions of the British Parliament. On March 23, 1775, in a room full of future revolutionaries, one man—already known as a bit of a radical—stood up to make his convictions clear. Proposing that the colony of Virginia form a militia and prepare to defend itself, Patrick Henry boldly stated the words now known by all Americans, "I know not what course others may take; but as for me, give me liberty or give me death!" The words were just as inspiring then as they are now, and his motion was enthusiastically adopted by the convention.

Not everything is known about the happenings of that day—exactly where Patrick Henry stood, for example, or where Washington or Jefferson sat—but visiting St. John's Church is still enough to send a chill up your spine. The docents are extremely knowledgeable about both the event and the church's history, and they will help you separate fact from speculation. The church's museum also provides a great amount of detail. If possible, attend one of the reenactments of Henry's speech, faithfully performed by devoted historians. If that's not enough, you'll find the grave of George Wythe, one of the American Revolution's most influential thinkers and a signer of the Declaration of Independence, in the churchyard. *St. John's Episcopal Church, 2401 East Broad St., Richmond, VA, 23223; 877-915-1775; www.historicstjohnschurch.org. GPS: 37.531765, -77.415528. Open Thurs.–Mon.*

JOHN MARSHALL HOUSE—If one is going to speak about the birth of the United States of America, then John Marshall must be part of the conversation. In 1775, a 19-year-old Marshall helped fight off the British at the Battle of Great Bridge, and he went on to fight with his fellow Virginians in the Continental Army. It was after the war, however, that Marshall made his mark. Fighting for the ratification of a new constitution to replace the weak Articles of Confederation, Marshall entered politics, serving in Congress and eventually as secretary of state for John Adams. After several others turned down the position, Adams nomi-

Patrick Henry's famous speech is still regularly recited at St. John's Episcopal Church in Richmond, Virginia.

nated Marshall as chief justice of the Supreme Court in 1801, forever changing the American justice system. Initially the weakest branch of government, Marshall firmly established the power of the judicial system through landmark decisions and an unwavering faith in the rule of law. It is no overstatement that John Marshall had almost as much impact on the United States as we know it today as any other person in its history.

The John Marshall House, where this giant of American jurisprudence lived from 1790 through his death, is now owned by Preservation Virginia, and tours of the grand home are available most of the year. The focus is understandably on Marshall's life while on the Supreme Court, but the guides know their subject and can help you with any questions. Marshall was also a slaveholder, and the stories of those enslaved persons are also told. Rotating exhibits focusing on American justice are also featured in the Justice Gallery, and the grounds contain part of what was Marshall's garden. (Fittingly, his home is next to the site of his former law office and is now a state courthouse.) *John Marshall House, 818 East Marshall St., Richmond, VA, 23219; 804-648-7998; preservationvirginia.org/historic-sites/john-marshall-house/. GPS: 37.541868, -77.433191. Open Thurs.–Sun., March–December.*

WESTOVER PLANTATION—Since 1735, Westover Plantation has been a mainstay on the James River in Virginia. Home to the Byrd family for generations, it was the widow of the third generation, Mrs. Mary Willing Byrd, who is of interest during the American Revolution. The Byrds were thought to lean to the Loyalist side, and Mrs. Byrd's mother was a Shippen—a cousin to Peggy Shippen, wife of Benedict Arnold. When Arnold invaded Virginia in January 1781, it was at Westover that his army landed. Arnold accumulated a wealth of plunder during his time here, including numerous slaves, and almost no one was compensated for their losses—except for Mary Byrd, who was found not only in possession of some of her own confiscated goods but those of other local citizens as well. Byrd's dealings with Arnold led to her being ostracized for the remainder of her days.

Westover Plantation is still privately owned, but it is open for tours. One can roam the grounds any day of the year for a small, voluntary donation, and there's a lot to see. Besides the large manor house, the view of the James River is beautiful, and interpretive signs are tastefully located throughout the property. The family cemetery and gardens, which feature the grave of William Byrd II, founder of Richmond, are also accessible. Although open only by appointment or on limited public occasions, the interior of the home can be toured as well. *Westover Plantation, 7000 Westover Rd., Charles City, VA 23030; 804-829-2882; historicwestover.com. GPS: 37.312529, -77.154555. Grounds open daily; home open by appointment.*

CHICKAHOMINY SHIPYARD—Before the establishment of the United States Navy, each colony was responsible for creating their own navy, no matter how large or small. One of Virginia's primary construction sites was a shipyard on the Chickahominy River established in 1776. When the British came in 1781, the shipyard was an important target and was burned.

Very little remains of the Chickahominy Shipyard today. Though it's probable that some archaeological resources still exist, the site of the shipyard now sits both within a new housing development and in the Chickahominy River itself. *Chickahominy Shipyard, on Uncles Neck Rd. approximately 1 mile south of Forge Rd., Toano, VA 23168. GPS: 37.359317, -76.872554. Private property.*

GREEN SPRING—Before the arrival of Washington and the French to York on the Virginia Peninsula, the Marquis de Lafayette had been tasked with shadowing Lord Cornwallis's British army, staying close enough to harass but far enough to maintain safety. Cornwallis, knowing exactly what the young general was doing, devised a trap as he was about to lead his army over the James River. It would be expected that Cornwallis would leave some troops to guard his rear, and he was confident that Lafayette and his fellow general, the aggressive Anthony Wayne, would not be able to resist attacking them. He was right. On July 6, 1781, Wayne charged into the British force with 900 men and soon found himself being surrounded by 5,000 concealed British and Hessian soldiers. Realizing the mistake just in time, the Americans withdrew and escaped with most of their force intact.

The site of the battlefield is private property, but it can be viewed from a parking area across the road that contains interpretive signs and markers that explain the action clearly. In addition, the site of the Church on the Main, which marked the British right flank, is now a public park. The site contains archaeological information on the church, which almost certainly served as a field hospital and saw some of the soldiers of both sides buried in the area. There is also the grave of an unknown Patriot soldier, discovered here and buried only in 2016 with the moving epitaph, "Thou that Passest by, Tell them that Here I Died for INDEPENDENCE." *Green Springs Battlefield, on Greensprings Rd. 0.2 mile south of Mott Lane, Williamsburg, VA 23185. GPS: 37.234916, -76.784981. Church on the Main, on Sir Gilbert Loop near intersection with Prince Trevor Dr., Williamsburg, VA 23185. GPS: 37.237320, -76.775073. Sites accessible daily.*

GREAT BRIDGE—Lord Dunmore, Governor of Virginia, opted to flee to Norfolk, a heavily Loyalist city, when the majority Whig House of Burgesses began asserting its power. Trying desperately to hold on to his colony, Dunmore issued a proclamation calling for enslaved men to join his ranks and receive emancipation for their service to the crown, which only served to rally Patriots to the cause against them. The governor decided to fortify a key crossing of the Elizabeth River at Great Bridge to protect his stronghold in Norfolk, building a small fortification and manning the works with 400 men, including his recently recruited African Americans. Patriot militia gathered across from the British, and Dunmore launched a surprise attack across the bridge on December 9, 1775. The assault was repulsed heavily, and the British were driven back to their fortifications. The Patriots continued to pour rifle fire into the British fort but wisely decided not to cross the bridge. Dunmore's force retreated to Norfolk, then evacuated the city after additional American forces began to gather.

Exciting things have been happening at the Great Bridge Battlefield. An area of the battlefield has been protected and turned into a public park. Interpretive signs explain the fight and how it fit into the modern landscape, vividly describing elements like the British fortification that are no longer present. A reproduction of the bridge itself has also been created. The personal stories of those who fought here on both sides have not been neglected, particularly the stories of "Lord Dunmore's Ethiopian Regiment." Finally, an interpretive center has been opened to provide even greater insight into this important battle. *Great Bridge Battlefield, 1775 Historic Way, Chesapeake, VA 23320; 757-482-4480; gbbattlefield.org. GPS: 36.722107, -76.239353. Open daily.*

NORFOLK—After his defeat at Great Bridge, Lord Dunmore, realizing that he could not maintain his foothold on Virginia soil, evacuated the Loyalists from the city on December 14, 1775. Over the next few weeks, Americans occupied the town and often took potshots at the nearby British ships. Finally, after providing some warnings to evacuate women and children, the British began a cannonade of Norfolk and set fire to the docks. The fire spread quickly, burning most of the town to the ground.

Several locations in Norfolk did survive the blaze after the British bombing, but the only one that remains today is St. Paul's Church, built in 1739. Not only does the church have memorials and interpretive signs chronicling its survival of the bombardment, but one of the British cannonballs remains visibly stuck in the brickwork high on the south wall. The Revolutionary era Fort Norfolk is long gone, but the fort built shortly afterward for the War of 1812 is in the same location and is open for self-guided touring throughout the year, as well as more in-depth touring on summer Sundays. The site is maintained by the US Army Corps of Engineers and you'll need to go through their security gate, but they are happy to welcome visitors to the fort. In modern downtown Norfolk, the Hampton Roads Naval Museum celebrates "The Navy's Capital," and though there is little that is specific to this attack on Norfolk, there is an exhibit on the American Revolution and Norfolk's role in it. Other exhibits in this outstanding museum span the region's remarkable naval history, including the famous Battle of the Ironclads during the Civil War, which happened on the waters just outside. The huge battleship USS *Wisconsin* is also here and is available for tours; you'll need to park in one of the nearby garages. *Fort Norfolk, 810 Front St., Norfolk, VA 23510; www.nao.usace.army.mil/About/Visit-Fort-Norfolk/. GPS: 36.856329, -76.305619. Open daily. St. Paul's Episcopal Church, 201 St. Paul's Blvd., Norfolk, VA 23510. GPS: 36.847379, -76.285913. Accessible Daily. Hampton Roads Naval Museum, One Waterside Dr., Norfolk, VA*

23510; 757-322-2989; www.history.navy.mil/content/history/museums/ hrnm.html. GPS: 36.847233, -76.293790. Open Tues.–Sun.

KEMP'S LANDING—The first sizable action that took place in the greater Norfolk area was on November 16, 1775. It happened at Kemp's Landing, a port town on the Elizabeth River, when Dunmore's Regulars pushed a small group of Patriot militia out of the town and away from its strategic crossing of the river. One of the Patriot militiamen was killed in the action, and the British occupied the town with ease.

Near the center of the battle is Pleasant Hall, still standing but with an uncertain future. Pleasant Hall served as Dunmore's headquarters during the fight, which occurred just outside its doors. A monument on the grounds commemorates the action. At the moment, the building, which had been maintained by a local Baptist Church, is up for sale. Preservationists are trying to preserve Pleasant Hall, and not only for its significance in the Battle of Kemp's Landing. It is thought that the first public reading of the Declaration of Independence came from the Hall's steps, and a grand ball was held here at the war's end. Hopes remain that the building will be turned into something more publicly accessible and that can proudly tell Kempsville's ties to the revolution. *Kemp's Landing—Pleasant Hall, intersection of Singleton Way and Overland Rd., Virginia Beach, VA 23462. GPS: 36.827507, -76.162439. Site accessible daily.*

CHESAPEAKE CAPES—Without question, one of the most important battles of the American Revolution was the Battle of the Capes. The battle was a prelude to the final siege at Yorktown, and without it there would not have been a Yorktown at all. While the French and American armies debated on what to do with the British army in New York City, a large French fleet, headed by the Admiral comte de Grasse, headed for Chesapeake Bay per General Rochambeau's orders. Arriving on August 30, the French beat a British fleet led by Admiral Thomas Graves to the Chesapeake Capes by only a few days. On September 5, 1781, the two sides met and began sailing southeast, paralleling each other. The larger French fleet not only got the better of the British but pulled them away from the Chesapeake, with the French not turning back until September

9 and the British heading back to New York. The French Navy had guaranteed control of Chesapeake Bay, preventing any relief from reaching Lord Cornwallis's force trapped at Yorktown. An additional naval battle had occurred here on March 16, 1781, essentially ending in a stalemate that prevented the French from aiding the Marquis de Lafayette in his efforts in Virginia.

The Cape Henry Memorial unit of Colonial National Historical Park memorializes the actions of the French Navy in the Chesapeake, and interpretive signs tell the story of the action in detail. A statue of Admiral comte de Grasse also stands here. On the same ground, you will find the Cape Henry Memorial Cross, a granite representation of the wooden cross planted here in 1607 by English colonists when they first landed on Virginia soil. The unit stands within Fort Story Military Reservation, so visitors will need to park at Gate 6 where they can board a shuttle to the grounds. (Those with a military ID or other proper identification may be able to pass the gate.) There is also a great exhibit on the Battle of the Capes at the Hampton Roads Naval Museum. *Cape Henry Memorial Unit—Colonial National Historical Park, Fort Story Gate 6 near intersection of Shore Dr. and Atlantic Ave., Virginia Beach, VA 23459; 757-462-8423; www.nps.gov/came. GPS: 36.921887, -76.043330. Open daily.*

GWYNN'S ISLAND AND CRICKET HILL—Seeking a place to reestablish control in Virginia, former Governor Lord Dunmore landed on Gwynn's Island at the mouth of the Piankatank River. Arriving on May 26, 1776, after months of horrible conditions aboard ship, the British soldiers and Loyalists spread out across the island only to find it lacking food and fresh water. Virginia forces took notice, gathering on the mainland only 200 yards away from the island and building earthworks that came to be known as Fort Cricket Hill. Finally, on July 9, Patriot artillery arrived that would turn the tide, opening on the British works and naval vessels in the narrow waterway. Dunmore immediately evacuated the island, with parts of his fleet heading for New York and Florida. Though few were killed in action, those dead and dying of illness, scattered about the island, may have numbered up to 500, the majority of those being the enslaved persons who had escaped to their freedom after Dunmore's proclamation the previous November.

A view from Cricket Hill across the water to Gwynn's Island.

Only a small remnant of Fort Cricket Hill remains today, but it has been preserved and is well marked, along the shore adjacent to the parking area for a local marina. The Gwynn's Island Museum has considerable information about the battle, as well as artifacts that have been gathered from the island over the years, dioramas illustrating the fight, and a map of the action believed to have been drawn by none other than Thomas Jefferson. The museum is also famous worldwide for some of the Ice Age relics found both on the island and far offshore. *Fort Cricket Hill, 249 Mill Point Rd., Hudgins, VA 23076. GPS: 37.487297, -76.30739. Site accessible daily. Gwynn's Island Museum, 1775 Old Ferry Rd., Gwynn, VA 23066; 804-725-5022; www.gwynnsislandmuseum.org. GPS: 37.503584, -76.293026. Open Fri.–Sun., April through October, and by appointment.*

POINT OF FORK—At the confluence of the James and Fluvanna Rivers is Point of Fork. This fork was a strategic point that allowed the American army to easily distribute what little supplies they had while keeping those supplies out of reach of the British. Or so they thought. When Lord Cornwallis invaded Virginia, Point of Fork was an obvious target, and he sent a cavalry detachment, Colonel John Graves Simcoe's Rangers, to capture it. Major General Baron Friedrich von Steuben, having retreated here after being driven out of Petersburg, held Point of Fork as long as he could, but abandoned it upon learning of Simcoe's approach.

What had been the armory at Point of Fork is now private property. A historical marker nearby points out the land, but it is overgrown and difficult to see much of the site. There are apparently some ruins at the site, but nothing accessible to the public. *Historical highway markers— Virginia Conservation and Development Commission GA-32 (Point of Fork), on VA-6 0.5 mile west of Andrew St., Columbia, VA 23038. GPS: 37.762511, -78.180419. Sign accessible daily.*

HUNTER'S IRON WORKS—Hunter's Iron Works, founded in the 1750s, became one of the suppliers to the American cause. A fully integrated facility, the works produced weapons and equipment from blast furnace to finished product. Considered a potential target, the state of Virginia provided the vitally important site with a military guard.

A historical highway marker has been placed north of the site of Hunter's Iron Works. Most of the site, running along the Rappahannock River, has been developed and has subsequently been lost. Though some archaeological remnants of the old works still exist, none are accessible. *Historical highway marker—Virginia Department of Historic Resources: E-116 (Hunter's Iron Works), intersection of Warrenton Rd. and Olde Forge Rd., Fredericksburg, VA 22405. GPS: 38.336961, -77.485542. Sign accessible daily.*

FREDERICKSBURG GUN MANUFACTORY—Operating only for the length of the war, the Fredericksburg Gun Manufactory supplied weapons to the Continental Army and the Virginia militia throughout the conflict. The factory was operated by Fielding Lewis, brother-in-law to George Washington.

The site of the Fredericksburg Gun Manufactory is remembered today only by a couple of historical markers, near the site of a former school building. The same site also saw encampments during the Civil War and the Spanish-American War. *Historical highway marker—Virginia Department of Historic Resources: N-7 (Fredericksburg Gun Manufactory), on grounds of 823 Gunnery Rd., Fredericksburg, VA 22401. GPS: 38.293233, -77.458983. Sign accessible daily.*

GEORGE WASHINGTON'S FERRY FARM—When George Washington was six years old, his family moved to their Ferry Farm plantation along the Rappahannock River. Though the family would occasionally move between their landholdings, Ferry Farm is where Washington grew into manhood, inheriting the plantation at age 11 when his father died. (His older brother received the coveted land at Mount Vernon.) In 1774, Washington's mother sold the plantation to Dr. Hugh Mercer—the same Hugh Mercer who became one of Washington's generals and was killed at the Battle of Princeton.

Exciting archaeological work at Ferry Farm has revealed some treasures, and such work continues to be a focus of the site. In 2008, the location of the Washington home was discovered, and an interpretive reconstruction of the house has been developed to give visitors a sense of life at Ferry Farm. Tours of the property are also available, which you can download. The visitor center contains a working archaeological laboratory with observation windows and exhibits that will keep kids interested. A combination ticket to the local Kenmore Mansion, built by Washington's sister, can also be purchased. The site also has features dating to a Union Civil War encampment here before and after the pivotal battle of Fredericksburg. *George Washington's Ferry Farm, 268 Kings Highway, Fredericksburg, VA, 22405; 540-370-0732; kenmore.org/visit-george-washingtons-ferry-farm. GPS: 38.293911, -77.447884. Open daily March through December.*

GEORGE WASHINGTON BIRTHPLACE NATIONAL MONUMENT—The Washington family established a plantation on Popes Creek in Virginia in 1718. After decades of hard work (by the family and by their slaves and indentured servants), the Washingtons came to be known as one of Virginia's most prominent families. The plantation's legacy, of course, was destined to be far more important. George Washington, the third son of father Augustine, was born here in 1732. Washington's time here was short, but the site has been a shrine to the Father of Our Country since the American Revolution.

George Washington Birthplace National Monument preserves the land where Augustine Washington's plantation sat. Though very little remains of the original plantation (the existing house is a reconstruction), the foundation of the home where Washington was born is clearly marked outside. Not only has the site been an archaeological treasure trove, it is also a working farm and presents a wonderful picture of the difficulties of plantation life in the 18th century. The visitor center contains a museum highlighting the history of the Washington family, including a film on the plantation and its operation. The scenery at Popes Creek, just off the Potomac River, is also splendid. *George Washington Birthplace National Monument, 1732 Popes Creek Rd., Colonial Beach, VA 22443; 804-224-1732; www.nps.gov/gewa. GPS: 38.183756, -76.920197. Park open Wed.–Sun.*

KEDGES STRAITS—Though most fighting ended with the British surrender at Yorktown, the two nations were still at war. On November 30, 1782, a small force of the Maryland Navy caught a British raiding party inside Chesapeake Bay. In a short battle at Kedges Straits known as the Battle of the Barges, the British took an early advantage and drove the American barges off. Meanwhile, across the ocean, the drafting of the peace treaty that would end the war began in Paris.

The Battle of Kedges Straits occurred in the narrow waterway between Smith Island and South Marsh Island in Chesapeake Bay. Taking the ferry out to the Smith Island Cultural Center will be your best bet for both learning about the fight and seeing the water where the action occurred. *Smith Island Cultural Center, 20846 Caleb Jones Rd, Ewell, MD 21824; 410-425-3351; smithisland.org. GPS: 37.995379, -76.033467. Center open daily, May through October. Site accessible daily.*

CHAPEL POINT—The Port Tobacco River in Maryland was controlled by the British, but citizens in the area were staunch Patriots. The British landed occasionally, including at Chapel Point, to harass local landowners, but that did not stop residents in the area from finding a way to ship food to the Continental Army, notably during its siege of Yorktown in 1781.

Chapel Point State Park preserves the natural beauty of the area, though you won't find any historic interpretation. Just outside the park, though, is the Point's namesake, St. Ignatius Catholic Church, founded in 1641. The church building dates to just after the war (1785), but St. Thomas Manor, still used, was built in 1741. Interpretive signs about the church and its relationship to the revolution can be found outside. Behind the church, you will have a nice hilltop view of Chapel Point and the Port Tobacco River. *St. Ignatius Catholic Church / St. Thomas Manor, 8855 Chapel Point Rd., Port Tobacco, MD 20677. GPS: 38.465502, -77.023666. Accessible daily.*

PORT TOBACCO—Port Tobacco, Maryland, was once a prominent Maryland commercial center, and during the Revolution it saw much activity. Perhaps the most significant was when one of the French army's units passed through on their long march from Newport, Rhode Island, to Yorktown, Virginia, to play their part in Cornwallis's surrender.

Preservation efforts at Port Tobacco are ongoing, and continuing archaeological excavations make a strong case for them. Items of interest from colonial and Revolutionary periods have been found throughout the old town site, which is preserved as the Port Tobacco Town Square. Several original buildings still stand and are open for tours, and the former courthouse also serves as a museum detailing the history that has been unearthed here. *Port Tobacco Historic Village, 8190 Port Tobacco Rd., Port Tobacco, MD 20677; 301-392-3418. GPS: 38.511673, -77.019246. Open for tours Sat.–Sun., April through December. Site accessible daily.*

THOMAS STONE NATIONAL HISTORIC SITE—Only 56 men signed the Declaration of Independence, and though not all their names are of the household variety, all of them were equals in pledging their lives, their fortunes, and their sacred honor. Thomas Stone is one of those lesser-known names, but a look at his life paints a good picture of the more typical Founding Father. A wealthy man, mostly through inheritance and marriage, Stone was a hard-working lawyer who made a name for himself in the Maryland legislature and was chosen to represent the state at the Continental Congress. Initially resisting war, Stone eventually saw the writing on the wall and voted for independence from Great Britain. After signing the Declaration of Independence, Stone preferred to stay closer to home to be with his family and his ailing wife, Margaret, whom he loved dearly. When she died in 1784, Stone followed by only a few months.

Thomas Stone National Historic Site preserves the home and legacy of Stone and his family. A large plantation house but no mansion, the home is open for guided tours, where visitors can learn the entire story of how Stone went from being a prominent, wealthy plantation owner to a committed rebel. Stone is also here in the family cemetery, and the walk through the plantation grounds past the burial grounds is a quiet and pleasant one. The visitor center contains further exhibits regarding the history of the property and a film on Stone's life. *Thomas Stone National Historic Site, 6655 Rose Hill Rd., Port Tobacco, MD 20677; 804-224-1732; www.nps.gov/thst. GPS: 38.532539, -77.035820. Open Sat.–Sun., April through December.*

KINGSTON—Known for its architectural significance, Kingston, built before 1730, was part of a much larger plantation that surrounded the

The home and surrounding fields at Thomas Stone National Historic Site in Port Tobacco, Maryland.

grand home. David Crauford inherited the plantation and in 1774 was elected to the Maryland General Assembly. A proponent of liberty, Crauford was active in supplying the Continental Army, and it was his warehouse at Kingston that stored some of Maryland's official state records.

Kingston remains in private hands and is well-preserved but is rarely opened up to the public. A historic highway marker is outside the home that details Washington's stays in Upper Marlboro, but he did not stay at Kingston. *Kingston, 5415 Old Crain Highway, Upper Marlboro, MD 20772. GPS: 38.814523, -76.755459. Private property.*

WOODYARD PLANTATION—One of the wealthy Darnall family's holdings in Prince George County, the mansion at Woodyard Plantation was one of the largest homes in Maryland. The grounds at the plantation were used by a local industrialist, Stephen West, to manufacture arms, clothing, and other supplies for the Continental Army.

Woodyard Plantation and its associated manufacturing area is now considered an archaeological site. Though a few small tracts have been preserved, it is surrounded by an apartment complex and a very busy road. No interpretation exists at the site. *Woodyard Plantation Site, near intersection of Woodyard Circle and Halslip Way, Upper Marlboro, MD 20772. GPS: 38.786045, -76.841922. Site inaccessible.*

GUNSTON HALL—George Mason, unfortunately one of our lesser-known Founding Fathers, was one of the most prolific and influential early revolutionaries. Conspicuously active as early as the Stamp Act protests, Mason's writings, which included the Fairfax Resolves (a guide for resisting British tyranny) and the Virginia Declaration of Rights, heavily influenced fellow Virginian Thomas Jefferson as well as the French in their own revolution. Mason built Gunston Hall in 1759 and resided here until his death in 1792.

Gunston Hall is maintained by the National Society of the Colonial Dames of America. The mansion and gardens are constantly being updated and improved, and continuing investigation throughout the grounds has produced numerous archaeological finds. In addition to tour-

Gunston Hall, plantation home of Founding Father George Mason.

ing the mansion, the visitor center contains exhibits, and the grounds, only a small portion of the family's original landholdings, have several outbuildings, a great view of the Potomac, and the family cemetery, where Mason lies at rest today. *Gunston Hall, 10709 Gunston Rd., Mason Neck, VA 22079; 703-550-9220; www.gunstonhall.org. GPS: 38.666078, -77.162733. Open daily.*

OLD PRESBYTERIAN MEETING HOUSE—The 1775 Presbyterian Meeting House in Alexandria was the site of George Washington's memorial service in 1779. Though this building was largely destroyed by fire in 1835, it was rebuilt on the original foundation. Perhaps more interesting for today's visitor is the cemetery behind the meeting house. Along the north fence lies the Tomb of the Unknown Soldier of the Revolution, possibly the first of its kind in the nation. Also buried in the cemetery is Doctor James Craik, Washington's close friend and physician at the time of his death. The original cemetery for the meeting house is just behind the main church building. *Old Presbyterian Meeting House, 323 South Fairfax St., Alexandria, VA 22314; 703-549-6670; www.opmh.org/history/. GPS: 38.801570, -77.043359. Site accessible daily.*

WHERE TO STAY IN THE UPPER SOUTH

This chapter covers a good deal of ground, but you'll never be very far from numerous lodging options. Though some of the sites are a little bit remote, larger cities on your route include Wilmington, Raleigh-Durham, and Greensboro, North Carolina, followed by Richmond and Charlottesville, Virginia, and Washington, DC. All of these places provide numerous options for food and lodging, and you won't have any trouble finding a place to stay.

PART 4

THE SHOT HEARD 'ROUND THE WORLD: THE WIDE-RANGING WAR

8

The American Revolution on the Frontier

OVERVIEW

When we think of the American Revolution, we often think of the 13 colonies. However, the American expansion into the west had already begun long before the Revolutionary War, and they were not left unaffected. This chapter covers those sites stretching west to what at that time was the American frontier.

After the French and Indian War, which ended in 1763, Britain held virtually all the territory east of the Mississippi River, with the Spanish to the west of it. The British army had outposts at the major geographical points of this region, including the Mackinac Straits, Detroit, and on the Mississippi and Wabash Rivers, mostly to control the fur trade and maintain relations with the various Native American tribes that resided there. There was also the substantial bastion at Fort Pitt, located in what today is Pittsburgh, Pennsylvania, which served as a gateway to the west and a link between the colonies and the frontier. These outposts were linked by waterways and a series of trails, but between them lay vast stretches of wilderness populated only by Native Americans.

As the colonies grew in population, it was not long before Americans began to look to settle westward from the Atlantic coast. The col-

Opposite: The site of Fort Randolph at Point Pleasant, West Virginia.

onists were soon encroaching on what was then Native American soil, leading to disputes and conflict. In an effort to appease the tribes, the British issued the Proclamation of 1763, which forbade American settlement west of the Appalachian Mountains. The colonists' reaction to this restriction was anger, and the movement west only increased, leading to more violence but also to more established settlements.

When the American Revolution broke out, the British leveraged their relationship with the Native Americans, portraying themselves as protectors of their land and legacy. This led to many of the tribes falling to the British side during the war. Native American attacks on settlements were often guided by the British, and the tribes were only too eager to wage war on their new enemies. The conflict between Native Americans and colonists on the frontier was brutal and often cruel, lasting long after the British surrendered at Yorktown.

Early in 1779, British dominance in the west was turned on its head when a military expedition led by George Rogers Clark took Forts Kaskaskia and Vincennes. Though relatively small outposts in remote locations, the amount of territory controlled by the British army was suddenly reduced to a great degree. The Americans would hold this territory through the rest of the war, and when a peace settlement came in 1783, they could claim virtually all of the land south of Canada, laying the groundwork for the growth of the American nation—and further encroachment onto Native American land, leading to another century of conflict.

This chapter will take you through the story of the Revolution west of the Appalachians, all the way to and even past what was then the American frontier.

PEOPLE TO KNOW

GEORGE ROGERS CLARK—When it comes to the American Revolution in the west, no name looms larger than George Rogers Clark, the "Conqueror of the Old Northwest." Clark's exploits, notably the capture of Fort Vincennes, struck a major blow to British efforts to hold on to territory west of the Appalachians.

Clark was born in Virginia and began work as a surveyor. His curious nature led him to undertake excursions into the west, exploring the Ohio and Kentucky Rivers and other points west. Clark's military career began with Lord Dunmore's War, a conflict between Virginia and the Shawnee, in 1774. When the American Revolution began, the adventurous Clark, only 23 years old, proposed taking the British posts on the Mississippi and Wabash Rivers in preparation for seizing the stronghold of Detroit. Though Detroit never fell, Clark's conquests in the region released any British claim to the frontier. After the war, Clark continued to be active on the frontier, though at age 35 he fell out of favor with the government and lost a means to support himself. Clark started a gristmill on the Ohio River in 1803, the same year his brother, William, joined Meriwether Lewis in their famous expedition westward. George Rogers Clark remained active until he suffered a stroke and lost his leg, dying in Louisville in 1809.

DANIEL BOONE—When one thinks of America's pioneers, the name Daniel Boone is sure to be the first to come up. The famous frontiersman was the source of much legend, but his true exploits are impressive on their own.

Daniel Boone was born near Reading, Pennsylvania, in 1734 and moved to North Carolina with his family at the age of 16. Inspired by tales of the west, Boone began his exploration of Kentucky in 1769, for several years documenting what lay west of the famous Cumberland Gap. In 1775, he formed the settlement of Boonesborough with about 30 men; on a return trip with his family, he blazed what became known as the Wilderness Road, a future path westward for thousands after him. Of course, Boone's activities over the Appalachians were illegal under the British Proclamation of 1763 forbidding the settlement of the west. Boone was captured by the Shawnee and brought to the British in Detroit in 1778, but he managed to escape to Kentucky and warned the inhabitants there of British plans to attack their settlements. After the Revolutionary War, Boone lost much of the land he had settled due to defective claims, though Congress intervened and restored some of it. Daniel Boone eventually moved in with his son in St. Louis, dying there in 1820; though there is some dispute about his burial place, his gravesite overlooks a beautiful vista at Frankfort, Kentucky.

THINGS TO KNOW

While most of the sites described in this chapter may be smaller in the context of the larger American Revolution, many of them are very well developed and well worth your time. With only a few exceptions, states and local communities have for the most part done a fantastic job of interpreting their history and have created some very interesting and unique experiences. Many of these sites are staffed, too, so if you have questions about the ones that are not, they can usually help you with interpretation. In addition, you'll generally be traveling through some very pretty country, making for an ideal road trip.

THE TRIP

This chapter is broken into three sections, each of which you can consider its own road trip. For the Far West road trip, the sites are a little bit farther apart, but they are related in theme and context and overlap each other in history. The sites on the other two trips are close together, and you should be able to see all of them in just a few days.

Though many of these sites are remote, you should find plenty of options for food and lodging with a little planning. In all cases, you won't have too far of a drive to reach a larger city if you're particular about where you stay or what you eat. But don't dismiss your options in those smaller regions, as some of the things you'll discover are going to be very good and very memorable.

THE FRONTIER SITES

The Far West

Though beyond what was considered the American frontier at the time, the Revolutionary War stretched as far west as the Mississippi River. While settlements from the 13 colonies had just begun to stretch into what is now Kentucky and Ohio, the British held the territory all the way to the Mississippi River since the end of the French and Indian War in 1763. From this region, they were able to direct their Native American allies to attack the western American settlements in the Kentucky and

Ohio regions. Additionally, after the French and Spanish allied themselves with the Americans, the far west came further into play, as west of the Mississippi was Spanish territory, and much of the territory east of the river still held a heavily French influence. The daring raid of George Rogers Clark into the western territory, immensely important in securing the west for the United States, is only part of the story in a region that stretches from northern Michigan all the way to Missouri. Though many of these sites are remote, they are well worth the journey and will help round out your understanding of the American Revolution.

FORT MICHILIMACKINAC—Established by the French in 1715, Fort Michilimackinac was established at the meeting of the waters of Lake Michigan and Lake Huron and soon became a critical post for the fur trade. Following the French and Indian War, the fort was transferred to the British, who used the fort to recruit Native Americans of the Ojibwa, Odawa, and Menominee tribes to the British cause once the Revolutionary War broke out. In 1780, the British thought the fort too difficult

Archaeological investigations are conducted every summer at Fort Michilimackinac.

to defend in its existing position, and the garrison moved to Mackinac Island, burning Fort Michilimackinac to the ground.

Fort Michilimackinac has been rebuilt as Colonial Michilimackinac and is now a Michigan state park. There are exhibits, museums, and films that relate the fort's history as well as the histories of the people who lived and labored here, including the French, British, Native Americans, and enslaved persons. Living history exhibits show what life at the fort was like, and if you're lucky, you may even get to fire one of the cannons during a demonstration. Ongoing archaeological investigations continue to reveal more about the fort every year, and there is a museum devoted to just that subject. There is plenty to do for kids here, and the site also provides an excellent view of the famous Mackinac Bridge. *Colonial Michilimackinac, 102 West Straits Ave., Mackinaw City, MI 49701; www.mackinacparks.com/attraction/colonial-michilimackinac. GPS: 45.786842, -84.732039. Open May through mid-October and for special events.*

The barracks building at Fort Mackinac.

FORT MACKINAC—After abandoning Fort Michilimackinac, the British built Fort Mackinac on Mackinac Island, which is located within the straits between Lake Michigan and Lake Huron in 1780. Though the post saw no action, they held the post until 1796, long after the Treaty of Paris that ended the war was signed. The fort saw the beginning of the War of 1812 and remained in service until 1895, when the island was included as part of one of America's first national parks, a designation that was removed in later years.

Fort Mackinac has been reconfigured over the years, but it still has some original elements, including its stone ramparts, south sally port, and officer's quarters. The fort is a state park today and can be toured. It contains many exhibits, though most have to do with the fort's time under the American flag. Living history reenactors are also here who show military life during the fort's use. To get to the island, you will need to take a ferry, and no cars are allowed on the island, but there are plenty of restaurants and shops here to make the trip worth it. *Fort Mackinac, 7127 Huron Rd., Mackinac Island, MI 49757; 906-847-3328; www.mackinacparks.com/attraction/fort-mackinac. GPS: 45.851998, -84.617595. Open May through mid-October and for special events.*

FORT DETROIT—Claimed from the French after the French and Indian War, Fort Detroit was one of the primary British bases in the west. From here, the British maintained relations with the Native Americans and coordinated raids into the area that is now Ohio, Indiana, Illinois, and Kentucky during the Revolutionary War. Like other western fortifications, the handover of the fort to the Americans occurred long after the American Revolution was over.

Today, the site of Fort Detroit has been swallowed by the city of Detroit. Initially known as Fort Pontchartrain under the French, the fort has two historical markers on the site noting its other names—Fort Detroit, Fort Shelby, and Fort Lernoult. Though the fort is gone, you can visit the excellent museum of the Detroit Historical Society, which has an exhibit on the fort, complete with a large model of it. *Historical marker—Fort Pontchartrain, intersection of Washington Blvd. and Jefferson Ave., Detroit, MI 48226. GPS: 42.327532, -83.047982. Historical marker—Fort Lernoult, intersection of Shelby St. and Fort St., Detroit, MI 48226. GPS: 42.329957, -83.048707. Markers accessible daily. Detroit Historical Society, 5401 Woodward Ave., Detroit, MI 48202; 313-833-1805; www.detroithistorical.org. GPS: 42.359255, -83.067667. Open Wed.–Sun.*

FORT ST. JOSEPH—Fort St. Joseph was founded in 1691 by the French to serve the fur trade as well as protect local Native Americans from the constant threat of the Iroquois. Like other French forts east of the Mississippi River, the fort shifted to British control after the French and Indian War, though the fort was abandoned by the British from 1763 to 1775 after a massacre occurred there during Pontiac's War. On February 12, 1781, Fort St. Joseph was surprised by a raid originating from Spanish-held St. Louis, over 500 miles away; the invaders took control from the bewildered inhabitants, raised the Spanish flag, and looted the fort, then left after a single day of occupation.

A boulder and historical marker are at the site of Fort St. Joseph today, and archaeological investigations are continually being performed at the location. You can also visit the outstanding Fort St. Joseph Museum operated by the Niles History Center, which has findings from those investigations as well as a complete history of the fort. The museum also has an amazing collection of drawings from the famous Lakota chief Sitting Bull. *Fort St. Joseph Museum, 0508 East Main St., Niles, MI 49120; 269-845-4054; www.nilesmi.org/departments_and_divisions/niles_history_center/fort_st_joseph_museum.php. GPS: 41.829752, -86.253555. Open Wed.–Sat. Historical marker—Fort St. Joseph, intersection of Fort St. and Bond St., Niles, MI 49120. GPS: 41.812925, -86.260727. Site accessible daily.*

ST. LOUIS—After the French and Indian War, the Mississippi River marked the boundary between the British in the east and the Spanish in the west. Many of the former French who had lived east of the Mississippi moved to Spanish territory, including the settlement of St. Louis. In 1780, after both the French and Spanish entered the Revolutionary War on the side of America, the British sent 900 Indian allies against St. Louis, a village of 700 at the time with only about 300 fighting men. The

A large boulder marks the site of Fort St. Joseph in Niles, Michigan.

village had built a stone tower called Fort San Carlos to defend against attack, and although they held off the far superior force, 21 of them were killed and 71 were captured.

Fort San Carlos stood at approximately 4th Street and Walnut Street; you will find a historical marker nearby. To learn more about the battle, visit Gateway Arch National Park, which consists of the famous arch, the Old Courthouse, and a museum that contains information about the history of St. Louis, in addition to the exhibits on westward expansion. (If you're going to ride the tram to the top of the arch, too—and you should—be sure to get tickets ahead of time at the park's website.) *Historical marker—Fort San Carlos, intersection of South Broadway and Walnut St., St. Louis, MO 63102. GPS: 38.624710, -90.190521. Site accessible daily. Gateway Arch National Park, 11 North 4th St., St. Louis, MO 63102; 314-655-1600; www.nps.gov/jeff. GPS: 38.625117, -90.186970. Open daily.*

KASKASKIA–CAHOKIA TRAIL—The trail between the late 17th-century French settlements at Kaskaskia and Cahokia was actually used for thousands of years by the local Native Americans. During the American Revolution, George Rogers Clark, after his capture of Kaskaskia, sent a detachment north to Cahokia to take possession of that post on July 6, 1778.

The Kaskaskia–Cahokia Trail is now an Illinois historic and scenic route and features historic attractions and markers along its 60-mile length, and you'll also find magnificent views of the Mississippi River along the way. At Cahokia, you'll find the Cahokia Courthouse, which dates back to 1740. Today, along with its visitor center, you'll find exhibits that include information about the town's Revolutionary War period. *Cahokia Courthouse, 107 Elm St., Cahokia Heights, IL 62206; 618-332-1782; dnrhistoric.illinois.gov/experience/sites/site.cahokia-courthouse.html. GPS: 38.571028, -90.192033. Open Thurs.–Sat.*

KASKASKIA—Having been the victim of a number of Native American raids on the settlements in Kentucky (then part of the state of Virginia), Virginia authorities, spearheaded by George Rogers Clark, decided to strike at the source of these raids. Having received approval from Governor Patrick Henry, Clark led a force of 175 men to occupy the British settlement of Kaskaskia along the Mississippi River. Though the settlement was British in name, the inhabitants were mostly left over from the French period, and they welcomed Clark with open arms when he and his men entered the village on July 4, 1778.

The Kaskaskia Bell State Memorial preserves the "Liberty Bell of the West," a bell given to the inhabitants by French King Louis XV in 1741 and rung when Clark arrived to liberate the village. There are also historical markers and interpretive signs that relate the story of Clark and Kaskaskia. *Kaskaskia Bell State Memorial, 1st St., Kaskaskia Island, Kaskaskia, IL 62233; 618-859-3741; dnrhistoric.illinois.gov/experience/sites/site.kaskaskia-bell-memorial.html. GPS: 37.921664, -89.914513. Open daily.*

VINCENNES—Soon after the occupation of Kaskaskia, George Rogers Clark got word that British Lieutenant Governor Henry Hamilton was at Fort Sackville in Vincennes. Hamilton's policies of directing Native American raids toward the Kentucky settlements drove Clark's mission,

The Liberty Bell of the West is displayed at Kaskaskia Bell State Memorial in Illinois.

so he immediately set out for Vincennes from Kaskaskia. Braving freezing cold temperatures and a flooded landscape, Clark and his 170 men traveled only 18 days before arriving in Vincennes on February 23, 1779. Clark surrounded the fort and demanded its surrender, but while negotiations were still ongoing, a Native American raiding party returned from a raid and were captured by the Americans. To demonstrate what awaited the inhabitants of the fort if they did not surrender immediately, and in retaliation for the raids, five of the Native Americans were slaughtered with tomahawks in full view of the British soldiers. The gruesome display had its desired effect, and Fort Sackville surrendered on February 25. Clark's successes yielded great fruit when the British surrendered the entire frontier to the Americans when the Revolutionary War ended in 1783.

George Rogers Clark National Historical Park, situated along the Wabash River, preserves the site of Vincennes and Fort Sackville, though the exact location of the fort is not known. There is an impressive and

Inside the monument at George Rogers Clark National Historical Park in Vincennes, Indiana.

beautiful memorial to Clark that contains a large statue and several murals of his exploits. The visitor center contains excellent exhibits and a film on Clark's western campaign and its importance. The site is somewhat remotely located, but it's worth the trip. *George Rogers Clark National Historical Park, 401 South 2nd St., Vincennes, IN 47591; 812-882-1776; www.nps.gov/gero. GPS: 38.677956, -87.536675. Open daily.*

Kentucky and West Virginia

At the beginning of the American Revolution, the land that we now know as Kentucky and West Virginia—as well as a number of other states—was considered part of the Virginia colony. Though the British had restricted settlement west of the Appalachian Mountains by the British, the wave of white settlement did not stop, and in the years before the war, pioneers such as Daniel Boone made their way over the mountains and into Kentucky, forming settlements and fortified outposts at key points in the region. An uneasy peace with the Native Americans in the region was destroyed by the Revolution when Native Americans largely allied with the British and conducted raids on these settlements, usually with the encouragement and sometimes the participation of the British. The early history of white settlement is inextricably tied to the American Revolution, and these small but fierce battles had a critical impact on the continued western expansion of the United States.

FORT BOONESBOROUGH—Kentucky's second settlement, Boonesborough was founded in April 1775 by a group of Virginia pioneers. Built for defense, the fort was the recipient of several Native American attacks, some of these on behalf of the British during the American Revolution. The largest of these occurred in February 1778, when British soldiers, along with 400 Native American warriors of various tribes, besieged the fort for nine days. The Kentuckians were eventually able to drive the attackers off.

Fort Boonesborough State Park was established in 1965 at the site of the original Boonesborough. There is a reconstruction of the fort, and though twice the size of the original, the spirit of the people of Boonesborough is captured, with living history interpreters and demonstrations scattered throughout, along with museum exhibits. In addition, recent archaeological investigations have revealed the actual location of the original Fort Boonesborough on the property, and you will find monuments and interpretive signs at that location, including some on Boonesborough during the American Revolution. *Fort Boonesborough State Park, 4375 Boonesborough Rd., Richmond, KY 40475; 859-527-3131; parks.ky.gov/parks/find-a-park/fort-boonesborough-state-park-7811. GPS: 37.896093, -84.266862. Fort open Wed.–Sun, April through October.*

LOGAN'S FORT—In 1775, Benjamin Logan built a fort in Kentucky to guard against Native American raids. Known alternately as Logan's Fort or Logan's Station, the settlement was the target of a Native American raid in 1777. Shawnee warriors besieged the fort for two weeks, and two settlers were killed, before reinforcements arrived.

Logan's Fort has been reconstructed and can be visited at any time, though you may want to wait for a living history event. If not, you can download a self-guided tour brochure that will take you through the property. *Logan's Fort, 500 Martin Luther King St., Stanford, KY 40484; visitlincolnky.com/2023/10/16/history-of-logans-fort. GPS: 37.530860, -84.677452. Site accessible daily.*

FORT HARROD—The settlement of Fort Harrod was founded by pioneer James Harrod in 1774, and in 1775 the defensive structure was built. Beginning in March 1777, Shawnee warriors, prompted by their British allies, began regularly attacking the fort and did so for almost a year. The fort was never conquered.

Old Fort Harrod State Park is a reconstruction of the original with living history demonstrations and a museum. Also on the grounds are monuments and memorials to Kentucky's first settlement. The original fort was on the site of the present parking lot. In addition, the raid and settlement is the subject of a major reenactment every year. *Old Fort Harrod State Park, 100 South College St., Harrodsburg, KY 40330; 859-734-3314; parks.ky.gov/explore/old-fort-harrod-state-park-7823. GPS: 37.761854, -84.845894.*

Old Fort Harrod State Park in Harrodsburg, Kentucky.

Grounds open daily; fort and museum open Thurs.–Fri., January through February and Wed.–Sun., March through November.

BRYAN'S STATION—Fortified in 1779, Bryan's Station was founded by four brothers who had camped on the site several years earlier. In August 1782, the fort was besieged by 400 British and Native American attackers, and the settlers were almost out of water when the women and girls of the fort bravely went to the spring to refill their buckets, returning without incident. The fort was assaulted later that day, but the attackers were driven off.

There is a memorial at the site of the spring at Bryan's Station, but it is on private property. A historic marker at the site can be viewed from the road. *Historic marker—Bryan's Station, on Bryan Station Rd. 0.1 mile west of intersection with Briar Hill Rd., Lexington, KY 40516. GPS: 38.075955, -84.415410. Site accessible daily.*

RUDDELL'S STATION—In 1780, a British raiding party of over 1,000 British soldiers, Tories, and Native Americans under the command of Colonel Henry Byrd left Fort Detroit for the Kentucky territory. On June 24, the force, armed with artillery that would have quickly destroyed the fort, asked for and received the surrender of Ruddell's Station. However, after the surrender, the Native Americans rushed the fort, killing some and taking others prisoner. Byrd then moved on to nearby Martin's Station.

A historic marker is near the site of Ruddell's Station, though it is 2 miles away from the original site of the fort. More information on the raid can be found at the Hopewell Museum. *Historic Marker—Ruddell's Station, on unnamed Road 0.2 mile south of intersection with Lair Rd., Cynthania, KY 41031. GPS: 38.339977, -84.281230. Sign accessible daily. Hopewell Museum, 800 Pleasant St., Paris, KY 40361; 859-987-7274; www.hopewellmuseum.org. GPS: 38.208969, -84.251313. Open Wed.–Sat., February through December and by appointment.*

MARTIN'S STATION—After accepting the surrender of Russell's Station, British Colonel Henry Byrd led his men against the settlement at Martin's Station, where they again received a quick surrender after promising protection for the inhabitants from the Native Americans. That promise went unheeded, and the Native Americans in Byrd's party divided up the property in the station and took most of the settlers as prisoners. The prisoners were marched to Fort Detroit, with many of those who survived the march being scattered among Native American settlements.

The Hopewell Museum in Paris, Kentucky, has a great display on local history and has information on the 1780 raid. A historical highway marker is also near the original site of Martin's Station. *Hopewell Museum, 800 Pleasant St., Paris, KY 40361; 859-987-7274; www.hopewellmuseum.org. GPS: 38.208969, -84.251313. Open Wed.–Sat., February through December and by appointment. Historical marker—Martin's Station, on Cynthania Rd. 0.2 mile north of Brentsville Rd., Paris, KY 40361. GPS: 38.241281, -84.283193. Sign accessible daily.*

BLUE LICKS STATE BATTLEFIELD—A raiding party of British rangers as well as over 1,000 Native Americans under Captain William Caldwell came into Kentucky in August 1782 to attack the frontier settlements. After they unsuccessfully laid siege to Bryan's Station but then escaped, militia leaders in the area, including Colonel John Todd and Lieutenant Colonels Stephen Trigg and Daniel Boone decided to pursue the British force. On August 19, they caught up with them at Blue Licks, and the group began to realize that they were far outnumbered and that the British and Native Americans had taken up a commanding position. However, Major Hugh McGary challenged the leaders as they debated what to do, saying "All who are not cowards, follow me!" In a very short fight, the Americans were routed, and Todd and Trigg were killed, as was Boone's son Israel. Eighty of the American militia were killed—nearly 7 percent of the male population of Kentucky.

The battlefield at Blue Licks, discovered definitively only in 2008, is the centerpiece of Blue Licks Battlefield State Resort Park. The main part of the battlefield is preserved, and monuments and historical markers are on the site. For a better interpretation of the battle, though, visit the impressive museum first, where you will find a timeline showing how the fighting progressed, a model of the landscape, and artifacts from archaeological investigations. The museum also houses an impressive fossil collection, as animals and people have known the salt at Blue Licks for thousands of years. The park also has a resort, with a hotel, restaurant, and swimming pools, plus hiking trails and boating. The site is a bit remote, but if those other activities interest you, it can make for a great stay. *Blue Licks Battlefield State Resort Park, 10299 Maysville Rd., Carlisle, KY 40311; 859-289-5507; parks.ky.gov/explore/blue-licks-battlefield-state-resort-park-7782. GPS: 38.429283, -83.992110. Open Wed.–Sun., mid-March through October.*

FORT RANDOLPH—On October 10, 1774, in what some have referred to as the first battle of the American Revolution (though really part of Lord Dunmore's War), Shawnee warriors, led by Chief Cornstalk, attacked Fort Randolph at Point Pleasant in what is now West Virginia. Approximately 1,200 Shawnee and 800 militiamen fought in the day-long battle, and over 230 Native Americans were killed along with 50 of the Virginia militia. After the fight, Cornstalk made peace with the Virginians, but this was not enough to protect him. In 1777, Cornstalk went to Fort Randolph to

The powder magazine at Fort Randolph was converted into a mass grave after the battle.

warn the Americans about British overtures to the Shawnee, but he was murdered by soldiers who had family killed in Cornstalk's previous raids.

A reconstruction of Fort Randolph has been built, and though it lies some distance from the original, it's a great visit, with living history demonstrations and plenty of interpretation, including the fort's history. At the site of the original fort, you will find monuments and memorials to the fort and its history at the small but lovely Tu-Endie-Wei State Park. This includes the powder magazine, where a number of the militiamen were buried after the 1774 battle, and the gravesite of Cornstalk. You'll also have a beautiful view of the confluence of the Ohio and Kanawha Rivers, and the murals along the levee here are impressive. *Fort Randolph, Krodel Park, on Lighthouse Lane 0.2 mile from intersection with WV-62, Point Pleasant, WV 25550; fortrandolph.weebly.com. GPS: 38.837621, -82.122428. Open Sat.–Sun., Memorial Day through Labor Day, Fri. in June and July, and for special events. Tu-Endie-Wei State Park, 1 Main St., Point Pleasant, WV 25550; 304-675-0869; wvstateparks.com/park/tu-endie-wei-state-park. GPS: 38.839844, -82.140673. Open daily.*

The Ohio Country and the Pennsylvania Frontier

Less heavily settled than Kentucky, the Ohio Country was disputed territory, even among Americans, as it was claimed by both Pennsylvania and Virginia. When the Revolutionary War broke out, much of western Pennsylvania was still in the process of being settled by Americans, with the mighty Fort Pitt serving as the westernmost bastion. Just as in other parts of the American frontier, encroachment on Native American lands were the cause of a great deal of conflict, and these conflicts came to a head when many of the tribes came in on the side of the British. Raids and retaliation were frequent and brutal and often more closely resembled murder than warfare. The Ohio Country lies at the heart of many of the wars with Native Americans both before and after the Revolutionary War, and the American victory—as well as the ongoing push westward—contributed a great deal to the history of the continent.

FORT ROBERDEAU—In April 1778, Fort Roberdeau was built on the Pennsylvania frontier to guard a critical lead mining operation for the Continental Army as well as protect settlers against attacks from the British and Native Americans. Unfortunately for the Patriots, the mining operation was less than successful, and the fort was all but abandoned by 1780.

A reconstruction of Fort Roberdeau, along with many of its internal structures, was built for the 1976 bicentennial and is still an active historic site today. The fort reflects its unusual original construction of horizontal stockade logs, rather than vertical, which was not possible due to the shallow bedrock. The fort has a small museum with some artifacts and dioramas showing the fort's surrounding countryside, and the grounds around the fort feature hiking trails and a picnic area. *Fort Roberdeau, 383 Fort Roberdeau Rd., Altoona, PA 16601; 814-946-0048; fortroberdeau.org. GPS: 40.582487, -78.274037. Grounds open daily; fort open May through October.*

HANNASTOWN—Hannastown (also known as Hanna's Town) was founded in 1773 and quickly grew to be a significant settlement west of the Allegheny Mountains. The town made history on May 16, 1775, when the Hanna's Town Resolves were adopted, asserting the citizens' right to protect themselves from British tyranny. Hannastown was attacked by the Seneca tribe, as well as some British, on July 13, 1782, and was burned to the ground.

The Westmoreland History Education Center was recently opened at Historic Hanna's Town and features exhibits on the history of the settlement. You will also find reconstructions of the fort that was built here, as well as Hanna's Tavern. An hour-long tour will take you through all of it. *Historic Hanna's Town, 809 Forbes Trail Rd., Greensburg, PA 15601; 724-836-1800; westmorelandhistory.org/hannas-town. GPS: 40.344328, -79.507683. Open for tours Sat.–Sun. in May and October; Wed.–Sun., June through August; Fri.–Sun. in September; grounds open daily.*

FORT PITT—The French built Fort Duquesne at the confluence of the Susquehanna and Monongahela Rivers but destroyed and abandoned it during the French and Indian War. The British subsequently built the substantial Fort Pitt on the site. During the Revolutionary War, the Americans held the fort and made it the headquarters for their western operations, launching and supplying expeditions into the wilderness to the west. George Rogers Clark, in his efforts to raid British outposts to the west, used Fort Pitt as his launching point.

Point State Park preserves the site of Forts Pitt and Duquesne. The only remaining portion of the fort is the blockhouse from 1764, which contains a small museum and gift shop. The Fort Pitt Museum is housed in one of the fort's reconstructed bastions and contains plenty of interesting exhibits on the history of this critical point. Walking around the point, you will also find the outline of old Fort Duquesne, as well as plenty of monuments and memorials. You'll also have great views of the rivers and the Pittsburgh skyline. *Point State Park, 601 Commonwealth Place, Pittsburgh, PA 15222; 412-565-2850; www.dcnr.pa.gov/StateParks/Find APark/PointStatePark/pages/default.aspx. GPS: 40.441159, -80.006990. Open daily.*

FORT HENRY—Fort Henry was built in 1774 by Wheeling settlers seeking protection from Native American attacks. The fort was attacked twice during the American Revolution. The first attack was in September 1777 by the Wyandotte, Mingo, and Shawnee tribes, during which Major Samuel McCullough made a famous and daring escape, riding his horse over a steep cliff to get back to the fort. Fort Henry was then besieged from September 11–13, 1782, during which settler Betty Zane braved gunfire to fetch gunpowder from a building outside the fort, saving the inhabitants.

Several markers around Wheeling, West Virginia, denote the former site of Fort Henry and the events that happened there. Three of these are downtown along the Ohio River, with one of them along the river being more comprehensive. A monument is also at the site of McCullough's Leap. *Interpretive sign—Fort Henry, on walkway just north of Heritage Port, Wheeling, WV 26003. GPS: 40.069297, -80.724998. Historic Marker— Fort Henry, on side street west of Main St. and north of 11th St., Wheeling, WV 26003. GPS: 40.069602, -80.724498. Historic Marker—Siege of Fort Henry, on 11th St. walkway just off Main St., Wheeling, WV 26003. GPS: 40.068925, -80.723779. Historic Marker—McCulloch's Leap, intersection of US-40 and Mount Wood Rd., Wheeling, WV 26003. GPS: 40.079407, -80.722711. Sites accessible daily.*

GNADENHÜTTEN—A successful Moravian missionary entered the Ohio country in 1772 from Western Pennsylvania and began to work to convert Native Americans to Christianity. The Moravian town of Gnadenhütten was founded in October of that year, but the Mohican inhabitants were forcibly relocated by the British in 1781 after being suspected of aiding the Americans. After the group was on the verge of starvation in their new location, a portion of them were permitted by the British to return to the town to harvest some of the crops they had left behind. Unfortunately, Americans mistook them for a hostile band who had recently struck settlements in Pennsylvania and were sentenced to death. On March 8, 1782, the men were piled into one cabin and women and children into another. The pacifist Native Americans were then led out of the cabins a few at a time and then brutally and cruelly murdered with knives, clubs, tomahawks, and other implements in one of the more horrific actions of the Revolutionary War. The bodies were then piled back into the cabins and then burned.

The site of the Moravian town and the massacre is memorialized

A monument to the slain and a reconstructed cabin at Gnadenhütten Park in Ohio.

at Gnadenhütten Park. In addition to reconstructed versions of two buildings on the original foundations, the park contains a good museum that tells the history of the town and the massacre. The burial site of the massacred Native Americans is also here, as is a large monument to their memory. It's a simple site, but not one you're likely to forget. *Gnadenhütten Historical Society Museum and Park, 352 South Cherry St., Gnadenhütten, OH 44629; 330-432-3049; sites.google.com/view/gnaden huttenmuseumandpark/home. GPS: 40.353872, -81.434056. Grounds accessible daily; museum open Wed.–Sun.*

GOSCHACHGUNK AND LICHTENAU—The capital of the Delaware Nation, Goschachgunk, and the Moravian town of Lichtenau were situated near each other. On March 9, 1777, in the council house at Goschachgunk, the Delaware had promised to remain neutral in the Revolutionary War. However, in April 1781, 300 militia led by Colonel Daniel Broadhead raided the towns to avenge other Native American raids. In what became known as Broadhead's Massacre, 16 Delaware warriors, as well as a chief, were captured and murdered before the two towns were burnt to the ground.

Two historic markers are in the town of Coshocton, formerly Goschachgunk, that memorialize the Delaware and the action here. One is at the location of the council house, while the other marks the site of Broadhead's Massacre. *Historic Marker—Delaware Nation Council House, intersection of Main St. and North 2nd St., Coshocton, OH 43812. GPS: 40.273755, -81.868976. Historic Marker—Broadhead's Massacre, on Chestnut St. between North 16th and North 17th Sts., Coshocton, OH 43812. GPS: 40.275881, -81.844311. Sites accessible daily.*

FORT LAURENS—General George Washington wanted to extend a line of American forts into the Ohio Country, and in 1778 Captain Lachlan McIntosh conducted an expedition to site some of these forts. Fort Laurens, built in December 1778, was intended to be a base for an attack on Fort Detroit, as well as to deter Native American attacks on settlers. Several British and Native American attacks were led on and around Fort Laurens, including a lengthy but unsuccessful siege that lasted from

February 22 to March 20, 1779. Later that summer, after realizing that Fort Laurens was too far from Detroit to be useful, Washington ordered the fort abandoned.

The Fort Laurens Museum is situated within the site of the original fort and contains exhibits on Ohio's only Revolutionary War fort and its brief history. The fort walls are outlined on the ground outside so you can get an idea of where it was (though part of it was destroyed by a canal), and interpretive signs provide a virtual tour of the fort and where things were located. Also on the grounds is the Tomb of the Unknown Patriot, which houses the body of a soldier who died at the fort. Some short hiking trails are on the grounds, too, making this a nice place to stop for a while. *Fort Laurens Museum, 11067 Fort Laurens Rd., Bolivar, OH 44697; 330-874-2059; www.fortlaurensmuseum.org. GPS: 40.639867, -81.456521. Open Sat.–Sun. in May, Wed.–Sun., June through August, and Fri.–Sun. in September.*

CRAWFORD'S DEFEAT—In May 1782, Colonel William Crawford led 500 men on an expedition into what is now northwest Ohio to destroy Native American villages and deter them from attacking pioneer settlements. The British, anticipating their movements, organized Native American resistance, and the two forces fought from June 4–6. The Americans were routed, and though many were able to escape, a sizeable number of them were captured and executed, including Crawford, possibly in retaliation for the Gnadenhütten Massacre. Crawford was tortured for two hours before being burned at the stake.

A number of memorials in the area of what is now Upper Sandusky, Ohio, mark the scenes of Crawford's Defeat. Several are located at the various sites of the running battle, including the Battle Island and Olentangy memorials. There are also markers at the site of Crawford's capture as well as his execution, which provide a bit more information about the expedition. *Colonel Crawford Memorial Park, intersection of Ohio Rte. 199 and County Rd. 29, Carey, OH 43316. GPS: 40.919741, -83.346310. Colonel Crawford Burning Site, in Ritchey Cemetery on Country Road 300 0.2 mile north of intersection with County Rd. 29, Carey, OH 43316. GPS: 40.923833, -83.328935. Battle Island, on Tarhe Trail 0.1 mile southwest of Township Highway 121, Upper Sandusky, OH 43351. GPS: 40.861819, -83.267641. Olentangy Battle, on Ohio Rte. 19 0.2 mile east of intersection with Parcher Rd., Bucyrus, OH 44820. GPS: 40.770093, -82.896107. Crawford Capture Site (To the Memory of Colonel Wm. Crawford), on Leesville Rd. 0.2 mile east of Wood St., Crestline, OH 44827. GPS: 40.797468, -82.781736. Sites accessible daily.*

PIQUA—The large Shawnee town of Piqua, or Peckuwe, was a target of an expedition into the Ohio country led by George Rogers Clark from what is now Kentucky. On August 8, 1780, Clark crossed the Mad River and was discovered by the Shawnee, who put up a fierce fight in front of the village, which included a small stockade. The Shawnee eventually took shelter in the stockade but were forced out when Clark brought up a small cannon and bombarded the structure. Though most of the Shawnee were able to escape, Clark destroyed the village. One of the Shawnee

A reconstructed Woodland Indian Village at George Rogers Clark Park, site of the Piqua battlefield in Springfield, Ohio.

witnesses to the battle was the very young Tecumseh, who was born at Peckuwe and would go on to be a major figure in American history.

A good portion of the battlefield at Piqua has been preserved. Much of it is protected by George Rogers Clark Park, which in addition to having several memorials dedicated to the participants of the battle and to Tecumseh has a reconstruction of the stockade and Woodland Indian Village. Hiking, canoeing, and fishing are also available. For interpretation, you can visit the nearby Davidson Interpretive Center, also still on the battlefield. The interpretive center not only has great exhibits about the battle, but you can also walk outside and view the battlefield with the help of interpretive signs. *George Rogers Clark Park, 930 South Tecumseh Rd., Springfield, OH 45502; 937-328-7275; ntprd.org/george-rogers-clark-park. GPS: 39.908956, -83.910176. Open daily. Davison Interpretive Center, 5638 Lower Valley Pike, Springfield, OH 45502; 937-882-6000; ntprd.org/davidson-interpretive-center. GPS: 39.905170, -83.917448. Open Tues.–Fri.*

WHERE TO STAY IN THE WEST

Many of these sites are remote, so while on the one hand you may not find many immediate options for lodging, chances are good that those that are available will have plenty of room for you. If you're looking for larger cities, several sites in the far west are somewhat clustered around St. Louis. Lexington is a natural base for seeing the sites in Kentucky. In the Ohio Country, a drive from Pittsburgh will be relatively easy in most cases, or you could even stay in Wheeling, West Virginia, if you'd like to be closer.

9

The World War

OVERVIEW

With the entry of France and Spain into the American Revolution, what had been an internal struggle within the British Empire became a much larger world war. At the time, all three nations were major powers, and all three had empires that stretched all over the globe.

Of course, French and Spanish support of the American effort for independence began long before either country declared war on the British. Covert shipments of arms, supplies, and cash had been flowing into America for several years while the countries watched closely to see if the Americans really had a chance at victory. After the American triumph at Saratoga, the French and Spanish saw the new war as an opportunity to gain or regain territory that had been reshuffled among the nations after the Seven Years' War (also known as the French and Indian War) less than 20 years before, not to mention another chance to make trouble for their old enemies, the British.

For Great Britain, the entrance of France and Spain meant that resources that could have been focused on the conflict in America now had to be spread thin to protect British colonies and commerce all over the world. From Florida to India to South America, British subjects and

Opposite: The vast gardens at Versailles, palace of King Louis XVI of France.

interests had to be protected, all while still trying to regain control of the 13 American colonies.

It is difficult to understate the importance of the French and Spanish alliance with the new United States. Without that intervention, it is not clear at all that America would have emerged a new nation. While many Americans aren't even aware that there was an alliance, even fewer realize the truly global nature of the war that emerged. This chapter will take you to a few of the sites that played a part in the world war that was the American Revolution.

PEOPLE TO KNOW

KING GEORGE III OF GREAT BRITAIN—King George III of Great Britain and Ireland often takes the blame for losing America. The truth is certainly more complicated, and the actions of the British Parliament certainly had a lot to do with it. But without a doubt, George III supported the policies that led to separation and played a large role in America seeking its independence.

George William Frederick was born in 1738. He seems to have been a slow learner at a young age, but when his grandfather George II died in 1760, he was ready to take the throne at the young age of 22. George took an active part in the negotiations that produced the Treaty of Paris of 1763 ending the French and Indian War (Seven Years' War), which led to the imposition of new and heavy taxes in an effort to recoup the expenses of that war. The leaders he chose to push through these new taxes, particularly Prime Minister Lord North, proved to be out of touch and unable to actually enforce those taxes in the face of American opposition. Still, George pursued the policy all the way up to and through the American Revolution until it was far too late. He finally relented to the opposition in 1782 when he authorized peace negotiations to begin. Throughout most of his reign, George exhibited signs of mental illness, but his reign lasted until his death in 1820, though for the last nine years of his rule his son, to be King George IV, was regent.

KING LOUIS XVI OF FRANCE—The young King Louis XVI of France was only 21 years old when the American Revolution broke out. Normally very savvy in politics, the French king did not foresee that his ushering in the era of revolution would lead to his own downfall.

Born in 1754, Louis was the grandson of King Louis XV and took the throne at the age of 20, the same year he married Marie Antoinette, an Archduchess of Austria. Upon his taking the throne, France almost immediately began to run into financial troubles that would plague his reign throughout. Despite his being a king, the ideals of the American Revolution astoundingly appealed to Louis, and even with his country's sizeable debts, he agreed to send arms and supplies to America once the war broke out, then allied with them after the British surrender at Saratoga. The American victory in 1783 was much celebrated in France, and that inspiration, coupled with the many troubles France faced, quickly led to the events of the French Revolution. Louis and Marie were forced to leave Versailles for Paris in 1789, and after being caught trying to escape in 1791, they were arrested, tried, and executed by the guillotine in 1793.

BERNARDO DE GÁLVEZ—A truly unsung hero of the American Revolution, Bernardo de Gálvez is a name little known to most Americans. However, his triumphs in Louisiana and along the Gulf Coast directly led to those areas becoming part of a growing America.

Born in 1746, Gálvez was born into a prominent family, and he served in the Spanish military at a very young age, fighting in Portugal and in New Spain against the Apache tribe. In 1776, he was named governor of Louisiana, arriving in New Orleans the following year. Anticipating that Spain would eventually enter the American Revolutionary War, he actively planned to undermine British interests in the region, specifically in the colony of West Florida. Fully prepared when Spain declared its alliance with the United States, Gálvez immediately took decisive military action, and in a matter of just two years took Baton Rouge, Mobile, and Pensacola, completely ousting the British. Spain gained both East Florida and West Florida in the Treaty of Paris that ended the war in 1783, and those territories would eventually be sold to the United States. Shortly after the war, Gálvez became viceroy of New Spain, and he died in Mexico at the age of 40.

SITES AROUND THE WORLD

The Gulf Coast and West Florida

A large amount of territory changed hands in the outcome of the French and Indian War (1754 to 1763). Much of what was French Louisiana west of the Mississippi River now fell into Spanish control. Meanwhile, the Spanish holdings in Florida were ceded to the British, who separated the territory into East Florida and West Florida. When the Spanish and French sided with the Americans less than 20 years later during the Revolutionary War, these great powers again found themselves battling over this same territory. The fighting in what would become Arkansas and along the Gulf Coast would involve almost no American troops, but as part of the wider world war they became extremely important, especially when it came time to decide once again who would control what territory. The efforts of the Spanish in West Florida, under the leadership of Governor Bernardo de Gálvez, made a huge impact on the war and later on the expansion of the United States of America.

ARKANSAS POST—Spanish territory since the Treaty of Paris in 1763, this confluence of the Arkansas and White Rivers was once an important strategic point. The Spanish built Fort Carlos III here. After Spain entered the Revolutionary War, this fort became the focal point of a larger British strike. On April 17, 1783, the British attacked the fort, but before they could settle into a siege position the Spanish conducted a sortie, sending the mostly partisan force fleeing and leaving the post unharmed.

It's hard to believe that this remote corner of America holds so many stories, but from Hernando de Soto and the Spanish to the Civil War, Arkansas Post holds hundreds of years of America's history. The visitor center contains a short but comprehensive film covering all these periods, and exhibits inside and outside the center in the old town include much information about the 1783 attack on the Spanish fort. Several miles of excellent trails take you through a beautiful bayou landscape with alligator sightings aplenty. *Arkansas Post National Memorial, 1741 Old Post Rd., Gillett, AR 72055; 870-548-2207; www.nps.gov/arpo. GPS: 34.026611, -91.343207. Open daily.*

BATON ROUGE AND FORT BUTE—Once word came that the Spanish had entered the war against the British, Governor of Spanish Louisiana Bernardo de Gálvez wasted no time and immediately organized an expedition to capture British strongholds in West Florida, which stretched to the Mississippi River. The Spanish left New Orleans on August 27, 1779, for the dilapidated Fort Bute, which they attacked on September 7. The undermanned fort, a holdover from the French and Indian War, was taken easily, and Gálvez moved north to Baton Rouge and British Fort New Richmond, commanded by British Lieutenant Colonel Alexander Dickson. Gálvez arrived on September 12 and, after beginning siege works, began to fire on the fort on September 21. After only a few hours, Dickson saw the writing on the wall and surrendered Baton Rouge and Fort Panmure at Natchez. The lower Mississippi River was now completely under Spanish control.

There are plenty of memorials and pieces of art that highlight Gálvez's victory at Baton Rouge. Near Louisiana's Old State Capitol is Galvez Plaza, where you'll find *Marcha de Gálvez*, a relief depicting Gálvez's

A memorial to the Spanish victory at Baton Rouge, Louisiana.

campaigns, and a sculpture of Oliver Pollock, an American representative from Congress in New Orleans who led several American troops into the battle and financed much of the operation. Just across the street is a historic marker noting the position of one of the Spanish batteries. A bit farther north will bring you to the site of Fort San Carlos, with several interpretive signs describing the siege. Finally, atop a ceremonial Native American mound near the Old Arsenal is a full memorial to the Spanish victory. As for Fort Bute, south of the city, nothing remains; the site has been obscured by a levee of the Mississippi River. *Galvez Plaza, intersection of North Blvd. and St. Philip St., Baton Rouge, LA 70802. GPS: 30.446888, -91.188465. Historic marker—Spanish Battery Site, near intersection of Lafayette St. and North Blvd., Baton Rouge, LA 70802. GPS: 30.447306, -91.189396. Fort San Carlos, in A.Z. Young Park east of intersection of North 3rd St. and Spanish Town Rd., Baton Rouge, LA 70802. GPS: 30.454656, -91.189243. Battle of Baton Rouge Memorial, on north side of Veterans Memorial Park just south of Capitol Lake Drive, Baton Rouge, LA 70802. GPS: 30.458379, -91.184957. Sites accessible daily. Fort Bute, on LA-327 1.5 miles south of intersection with Nicholson Dr., Sunshine, LA 70780. GPS: 30.323620, -91.135678. No site.*

NEW ORLEANS—The capital of Spanish Louisiana, New Orleans, was already a well-established city when the Revolutionary War broke out. Ceded to the Spanish after the French and Indian War in 1763, New Orleans was where all Spanish operations during the American Revolution originated. It would remain under Spanish rule until transferred to the United States as part of the Louisiana Purchase.

New Orleans's famous Cabildo, where the Louisiana Purchase was signed, is now part of the state museum system. Besides being a historic treasure in itself, the Cabildo includes a thorough history of the region under Native American, French, Spanish, and American rule, doing a good job of untangling the sometimes-complicated timeline. The colonial period and New Orleans's role during the revolution is given plenty of attention. Just down the street, you will also find plaques marking the homes of Spanish Governor Bernardo de Gálvez and Revolutionary financier Oliver Pollock. *The Cabildo, 701 Chartres St., New Orleans, LA 70116; 800-568-6968; louisianastatemuseum.org/museum/cabildo. GPS:*

The Cabildo in New Orleans now houses one of Louisiana's state museums.

29.957555, -90.063750. Open Tues.–Sun. Plaque—Bosque House (home of Bernardo de Galvez), intersection of Chartres St. and Wilkinson St., New Orleans, LA 70130. GPS: 29.957042, -90.064250. Plaque—Homesite of Oliver Pollock, across from 532 Chartres St., New Orleans, LA 70130. GPS: 29.956365, -90.064853. Plaques accessible daily.

MOBILE AND FORT CONDÉ—Soon after consolidating Spanish positions along the Mississippi River, Governor of Spanish Louisiana Bernardo do Gálvez next set his eyes on the British city of Mobile. A force of 7,500 Spanish troops and militia set sail for Mobile from New Orleans in January 1780, arriving on February 25 and approaching the British stronghold of Fort Charlotte. Formerly known as Fort Condé when held by the French during the French and Indian War, the fort was not in good condition at the time of the assault, but the British were able to hold the fort through several days of artillery bombardment. British commander Captain Elias Durnford finally surrendered on March 14 after the walls of Fort Charlotte were breached. This left the British with only one remaining foothold in West Florida—the stronghold at Pensacola.

Fort Condé still stands in Mobile, though it is not the original structure. It was reconstructed for the US bicentennial in 1976 and serves as a living history museum. Along with the historically accurate reconstruction of the fort, including a detailed museum about its history, visitors will find lots of kid-friendly diversions, including a shooting gallery, escape room, and interactive exhibits. Just across the street are the last remaining brick ruins of the original fort and a large memorial to the French, British, Spanish, and Americans who make up Mobile's colorful history. Finally, the Mobile Museum of History, on an adjacent corner, contains further information and artifacts; the museum operates Fort Condé as well, and your admission to one will get you into the other. *Colonial Fort Condé, 150 South Royal St., Mobile, AL 36602; 251-544-5480; www.historymuseumofmobile.com/colonial-fort-conde. GPS: 30.689075, -88.039882. Open daily. History Museum of Mobile, 111 South Royal St., Mobile, AL 36602; 251-208-7569; www.historymuseumofmobile*

Only a small portion of the original Fort Condé still exists at Mobile, Alabama.

.com. GPS: 30.689544, -88.039895. Open daily. Ruins of the Second Fort Condé, on Church St. just east of intersection with South Royal St., Mobile, AL 36602. GPS: 30.689161, -88.040364. Site accessible daily.

MOBILE VILLAGE—Seeing their influence waning in West Florida, the British launched an attack on The Village, a Spanish fortification on the east side of Mobile Bay, on January 7, 1781. The British held a large numerical advantage, but the Spanish were able to hold the fort after a fierce day of fighting.

A historical highway marker has been placed near the site of The Village. The site itself is mostly inaccessible, overgrown or developed, and all on private property. *Historical highway marker—Sons of the Revolution (Revolutionary War Battlefield and Burial Ground at Spanish Fort), 29750 Larry Lee Cawyer Dr., Spanish Fort, AL 36527. GPS: 30.658932, -87.911711. Sign accessible daily.*

PENSACOLA—In late 1780, Governor of Spanish Louisiana Bernardo de Gálvez finally began his long-awaited attempt to capture the British capital of West Florida at Pensacola. A hurricane led to further delays, however, and after a detour to Havana, the Spanish finally landed outside Pensacola on March 9, 1781. The combined Spanish and French forces involved numbered thousands of soldiers and sailors, dwarfing the British contingent of less than 2,000 soldiers and Native Americans. The main British fortification of Fort George was an earthen fortification, with two extended earthworks known as the Prince of Wales Redoubt and the Queen's Redoubt. Siege operations began in late March, creeping closer to the British works and gradually weakening them. Things came to a head on May 8, when a lucky shot struck the magazine at the Queen's Redoubt, causing a huge explosion and killing scores of British soldiers. The Spanish took advantage of the confusion and stormed the redoubt, taking it after a brutal fight. From this new position, Spanish artillery could now bombard Fort George at close range. After suffering heavy damage, the British surrendered on May 10. Within just a year and a half, the Spanish army, under the leadership of Gálvez, had conquered all of West Florida.

Pensacola's Colonial Archaeological Trail and the work that has come with it reveals much of the Spanish capture of Pensacola and the British period preceding it. Remnants of the Fort of Pensacola / Fort San Miguel have been exposed and have plenty of interpretation to help the visitor understand Pensacola's British and Spanish stories. A small section of Fort George has been partially rebuilt as a city park and serves as a memorial to the siege. A historic marker can also be found at the site of the Queen's Redoubt, site of the critical explosion that ended British rule in West Florida; it was renamed Fort San Bernardo after the Spanish took it. Finally, in 2018, the grand Bernardo de Gálvez Monument was unveiled at the entrance to downtown Pensacola, memorializing his important contributions to American history. *Colonial Archaeological Trail, download brochure from historicpensacola.org/plan-your-visit/ museums-properties/colonial-archaeological-trail. Fort George Park, intersection of North Palafox St. and La Rua St., Pensacola, FL 32501. GPS: 30.418517, -87.216774. Historical marker—Fort San Bernardo, intersection of North Spring St. and West Brainerd St., Pensacola, FL 32501. GPS: 30.424594, -87.221012. Bernardo de Gálvez Monument, intersection of North Palafox St. and Wright St., Pensacola, FL 32501. GPS: 30.416510, -87.216226. Sites accessible daily.*

East Florida

East Florida, a British colony since the end of the French and Indian War, was a sparsely populated territory that remained loyal to the crown when the American Revolution broke out. Though the major population centers of St. Augustine and Savannah were some distance apart, that did not stop fighting from breaking out along the Georgia-Florida border. The Americans made no fewer than three efforts to attack or capture St. Augustine (though none actually reached the city), and both sides occasionally made raids into the other colony. The action in East Florida and southern Georgia was not highly consequential to the outcome of the American Revolution; however, the amazing history in this region is worth exploring, and finding what is related to the Revolutionary War will take you to some extraordinary sites.

ST. AUGUSTINE AND FORT ST. MARK—The capital of British East Florida, St. Augustine was a center of British governance not only for the colony but as a waypoint between the rebellious states to the north and

The Castillo de San Marcos, also known as British Fort St. Mark, overlooks the water at St. Augustine, Florida.

the Caribbean. Not only did St. Augustine possess the great Fort St. Mark (known as the Castillo de San Marcos under Spanish rule), but it also had a fortification that protected the old city's inhabitants and the crown's administrative buildings. Over the course of the Revolution, St. Augustine would serve both as a center for military operations and as a prison, notably for three signers of the Declaration of Independence, Thomas Heyward, Arthur Middleton, and Edward Rutledge Jr.

Remarkably preserved, Castillo de San Marcos National Monument focuses primarily on the Spanish period, but there is plenty of interpretation of the British occupation as well, including the fort's role as center of military operations for East Florida. Set aside a couple of hours to explore the fort; the National Park Service has done a great job of interpretation here. As for the city of St. Augustine, which has plenty to see, parts of the old fortifications still exist as ruins, and a rebuilt redoubt just outside the old city gates demonstrates how the landscape was used in its defense. Finally, though the British State House no longer stands, Government House (also known as Governor's House), which was home of the colony's governors during the British and Spanish periods, is still here; just outside, the Plaza de la Constitución has several memorials related to the American Revolution. Parking is at a premium, but the city is very walkable, and several accessible tourist buses run through. *Castillo de San Marcos National Monument, 1 South Castillo Dr., St. Augustine, FL 32084; 904-829-6506; www.nps.gov/casa. GPS: 29.897140, -81.312754. Open daily. Santo Domingo Redoubt, intersection of Orange St. and Cordova St., St. Augustine, FL 32084. GPS: 29.897768, -81.314989. Accessible daily. Governor's House Cultural Center and Museum, 48 King St., St. Augustine, FL 32084. GPS: 29.892383, -81.312954. Open daily.*

FORT MOSE—Spanish and English squabbling over Florida started long before the American Revolution. One source of consternation between the two powers was a proclamation by the Spanish government that

An observation platform at the site of Fort Mose.

slaves in British territory could escape to Florida and be freed if they would fight for the Spanish king and convert to Catholicism. Those brave enough to survive the perilous journey formed the settlement that came to be known as Fort Mose, just north of the old city of St. Augustine. Meant to be a first line of defense, the inhabitants of Fort Mose were put to the test when the English attacked in 1740. The victorious freedmen and the Spanish rebuilt the community, the first free Black settlement in what would become the United States.

Fort Mose Historic State Park is just north of St. Augustine and contains an excellent museum that tells the story of Fort Mose and the Spanish period. The site of the fort itself is now somewhat submerged, but the interpretation of the site and its remarkable story makes it worth a visit. Plans for a reconstructed fortification are in the works, and living history activities are frequent. *Fort Mose Historic State Park, 15 Fort Mose Trail, St. Augustine, FL 32084; 904-823-2232; www.floridastateparks.org/parks-and-trails/fort-mose-historic-state-park. GPS: 29.929013, -81.325292. Grounds open daily; museum open Thurs.–Mon.*

THOMAS CREEK—A group of Continental soldiers and Georgia militia under the command of Lieutenant Colonel Samuel Elbert moved south from Georgia to attempt to capture St. Augustine. The Georgia militia, only 165 strong and advancing separately from the Continentals, ran into an ambush by British soldiers, Loyalists, and Native Americans on May 17, 1777, at the mouth of Thomas Creek. Only 41 of the militia escaped, and they promptly turned for home, ending the expedition.

A historical marker is located at Seaton Creek Historic Preserve, thought to be the site of the Battle of Thomas Creek. The marker is just off the parking area at a trailhead. Another historic marker tells the story of the battle, though it's a bit removed from where the fight probably took place. *Seaton Creek Historic Preserve, 2145 Gold Star Family Pkwy., Jacksonville, FL 32218; 904-630-2489; www.timucuanparks.org/parks/seaton-creek-historic-preserve. GPS: 30.521091, -81.669239. Open daily. Historic marker—Battle of Thomas Creek, on US-23 0.2 mile south of intersection with Ratliff Rd., Callahan, FL 32011. GPS: 30.506972, -81.792416. Accessible daily.*

ALLIGATOR CREEK BRIDGE—American cavalry under Colonel Elijah Clarke, on another expedition to invade Florida, ran into a strong British position at Alligator Creek Bridge on June 30, 1778. The British Regulars and Loyalists held and were able to drive the Americans off. The Americans suffered 13 casualties while the British lost 9.

A historical marker is at the approximate site of the Alligator Creek Bridge, though it is not certain that the battle occurred here. *Historical marker—Skirmish of American Revolution, on South Kings Rd. 0.1 mile north of intersection with Brandies Ave., Callahan, FL 32011. GPS: 30.566783, -81.833583. Site accessible daily.*

FORT TONYN—A British outpost on the Georgia-Florida border, Fort Tonyn was located on the Kings Ferry Road, the main road between Charleston and St. Augustine. The post was abandoned when the Americans invaded Florida in 1778 on their way to the Battle of Alligator Creek Bridge.

A historical marker at Kings Ferry denotes the site of Fort Tonyn as 1 mile east of the ferry along the St. Mary's River. *Historical marker—Kings Ferry, at Kings Ferry Boat Ramp on Bill Johnson Rd., 0.1 mile north of intersection with Kings Ferry Rd., Hilliard, FL 32046. GPS: 30.786311, -81.840251. Site accessible daily.*

CAPTURE OF HMS *HINCHINBROOK* AND SLOOP *REBECCA*—During the Revolutionary War, each colony had its own small navy, and Georgia was no exception. On April 19, 1778, three galleys of the Georgia Navy followed three British ships—the brigantine HMS *Hinchinbrook*, sloop *Rebecca*, and a watering brig—into the Frederica River and attacked them. The British ships grounded in the shallow river and were all captured.

A wonderful spot from which you can view the section of the Frederica River where the action took place is Fort Frederica National Monument. The site preserves the remnants of an old British colonial town and fort abandoned long before the American Revolution. Archaeological work is continually exposing more of the town, and the interpretation of what used to be a sizeable settlement is wonderful. There is no interpretation of the naval battle here, but you will get a better idea of the hostile relationship between the British in Georgia and the Spanish in nearby

Florida. Just down the road from Fort Frederica National Monument, you will find a historical marker that tells the story of the battle. *Fort Frederica National Monument, 6515 Frederica Rd., St. Simons Island, GA 31522; 912-638-3639; www.nps.gov/fofr. GPS: 31.222321, -81.386952. Grounds open daily; visitor center open Wed.–Sun. Historical marker—The Georgia Navy, on Frederica Rd. 0.3 mile north of intersection with Stevens Rd., St. Simons Island, GA 31522. GPS: 31.222532, -81.386748. Sign accessible daily.*

France

The entry of France into the Revolutionary War was critically important to the American cause. A great deal of work, however, went into making the alliance official. Years of political maneuvering by the American ambassadors in Paris—including Benjamin Franklin, Thomas Jefferson, John Adams, and John Jay, among others—were necessary to obtain French recognition of the new nation. In addition, before that recognition came, the ambassadors, as well as Pierre-Augustin Caron de Beaumarchais, go-between between the Americans and the French court at Versailles, were busy arranging secret shipments of arms and other supplies to support the war effort. There are several places in Paris where you can still see reminders of this world-changing alliance—just another reason to visit one of the world's most beautiful cities.

HOTEL D'YORK, PARIS—The negotiation and ratification of the Treaty of Paris, which ended not only the American Revolution but all the fighting in what had become a world war, took months of hard work by delegates from the United Kingdom, France, Spain, and the newly born United States of America. When the agreement had finally been hammered out, the British and Americans affixed their signatures here, at the Hotel d'York (the French would sign at Versailles).

Privately owned but still standing, the former Hotel d'York cannot be visited. The treaty was signed in a room on the second floor. There is, however, a plaque in French on the face of the building, that reads "In this building, formerly the Hotel d'York, on September 3, 1783, David Hartley, in the name of the King of England, Benjamin Franklin, John Jay, John Adams, in the name of the United States of America, signed the definitive peace treaty recognizing the United States." *Hotel D'York, 56 Rue Jacob, 75006 Paris, France. GPS: 48.856257, 2.331953. Private property; plaque accessible daily.*

HOTEL DE VALENTINOIS, PARIS—Benjamin Franklin, a larger-than-life personality in America, France, and England, stayed at this appropriately sized home during most of his time in Paris. At the time it was part of the town of Passy but is now within the 16th Arrondissement of Paris, not far from the Eiffel Tower across the Seine.

The Hotel de Valentinois may be gone, but Franklin's presence in France is still strong. A large stone design high on the corner of the existing building marks Franklin's time here as well as his influence on the French. *Hotel de Valentinois site, northwest corner of Rue Raynouard and Rue Singer, 75016 Paris, France. GPS: 48.854870, 2.279488. Stone accessible daily.*

HOTEL DES AMBASSADEURS DE HOLLANDE, PARIS—Pierre Augustin Caron de Beaumarchais, the tireless advocate of the American cause to the court of Louis XVI and go-between for his king and the Spanish court of Carlos III, worked from here at the Hotel des Ambassadeurs de Hollande. Beaumarchais was instrumental not only in eventually gaining France's recognition of America, but also getting much-needed weapons, uniforms, and other supplies to the fledgling Patriots early in the war. The "business" located here, Roderigue Hortalez and Company, was a front that allowed Beaumarchais to covertly get those supplies to America.

The Hotel des Ambassadeurs de Hollande still stands and is known today as the Hôtel Amelot de Bisseuil. Its history goes far beyond just the American Revolution, and it is worth the short walk from Notre Dame or the Bastille to go and have a look. There is an interpretive sign posted on the front of the building. *Hotel des Ambassadeurs de Hollande, 47 Rue Vieille-du-Temple, 75004 Paris, France. GPS: 48.858214, 2.358133. Private property; outside accessible daily.*

PICPUS CEMETERY, PARIS—After the American Revolution, the Marquis de Lafayette went home to France, and though he was eventually swept up in a far bloodier uprising, the French Revolution, he survived the turmoil and remained a hero on both sides of the Atlantic. He is buried at the Cimetière de Picpus in Paris, along with over 1,000 victims of the guillotine from the terrible days of the Reign of Terror.

The private cemetery is open most days, but only for very limited times; check the hours before you go. Lafayette's grave is hard to miss—it is covered by numerous tributes, both French and American, in a corner of the cemetery. *Cimetière de Picpus, 35 Rue de Picpus, 75012 Paris, France. GPS: 48.843975, 2.400709. Open Mon.–Sat.*

VERSAILLES—The magnificent palace built by King Louis XIV is also the place where King Louis XVI heard petitions for the American cause. It is also where the Treaty of Paris was signed by the French, ending the war in America.

Versailles is an amazing spectacle, and the size of both the palace itself and the surrounding gardens is staggering. A number of tours, either guided or by self-guided audio, are available and will take you through

The massive palace at Versailles, France, home to King Louis XVI.

both. Versailles is a short and easy train ride from Paris, and the trip is well worth it; plan to spend the day, if you're able, since there is so much to see. *Palace of Versailles, Place d'Armes, 78000 Versailles, France; 33 1 3083 7800; en.chateauversailles.fr. GPS: 48.804273, 2.122329. Closed Mondays.*

SPAIN AND GIBRALTAR

King Carlos III of Spain did not wholeheartedly support the American efforts at independence; after all, the design of the entire business was to overthrow a fellow king. However, Spain was allied with France, and the opportunity to try to regain some of the territory they had lost in the French and Indian War and other conflicts—Menorca, Gibraltar, and Florida among them—proved too great to stand idly by. Spain began to covertly supply the American war effort as early as 1775, and when they formally entered the conflict in 1779, they did so with all their might. Though the French are often thought of as our most important ally of the American Revolution, one cannot discount the support in men and matériel provided by Spain.

ROYAL PALACE OF MADRID—From his palace in the Spanish capital of Madrid, King Carlos III, despite his misgivings, saw obvious opportunities for his country in supporting the Americans in their war against Great Britain. Carlos was the first Spanish king to inhabit the palace, which was built under his predecessor, Philip V, and his influence on the style and ornamentation of the building is massive.

The Palacio Real de Madrid still stands and is one of the premier attractions in a truly great city. Self-guided audio tours of the palace are available in English, and tours of the Royal Armory, Royal Kitchen, Royal Gardens, and special exhibits can also be taken. Tours are generally focused on Carlos III's legacy, which is tangible throughout the immense palace. Before you go, make sure you set aside enough time for a full visit, and be sure to check the schedule—the palace is still used for official functions and occasionally closes for them. *Royal Palace of Madrid, Calle de Bailén, 28071 Madrid, Spain; 0034 902 044 454; www.patrimonionacional.es/en/visita/royal-palace-madrid. GPS: 40.416603, -3.714430. Open daily.*

The impressive Royal Palace in Madrid, Spain.

ROYAL PALACE OF ARANJUEZ—On April 12, 1779, France and Spain entered a treaty to mutually support one another and the Americans in their efforts at independence. Signed at the remote Spanish palace of Aranjuez, the treaty would lead to Spain declaring war on Great Britain two months later.

While smaller than its counterpart in Madrid, the palace at Aranjuez is impressive, and its semi-remote location hints at why Carlos III liked to escape here. You won't find anything here about the 1779 Treaty of Aranjuez, but there is lots of great history here just the same. Tours of the palace are available in English via audio guide. The town of Aranjuez contains several other gardens and museums that you can see on the same ticket, and the short train ride from Madrid makes it quite accessible. It is worth spending a full day here. Like the Palacio Real de Madrid, this is still one of Spain's official palaces, so check the schedule for special events. *Royal Palace of Aranjuez, Plaza de Parejas, 28300 Aranjuez, Spain; 0034 902 044 454; entradas.patrimonionacional.es/en-*

The Spanish Royal Palace of Aranjuez was where the Spanish entered the war for American independence.

GB/informacion-recinto/4/palacio-aranjuez. GPS: 40.036419, -3.609385. Closed Mondays.

CASTLE OF SAN FELIPE, MENORCA—Possession of the island of Menorca was disputed for many years, and the small isle was the object of several contests between the Spanish, French, and British, with the British taking possession after the French and Indian War. In 1781, the Spanish laid siege to the Castle of San Felipe, the main fortification on the island, and remained for five months until the British finally surrendered on February 5, 1782. After conquering the island, the Spanish destroyed most of the fort.

The Castle of San Felipe falls under the care of Military Consortium Menorca, which also has a museum on the island. Though the castle was destroyed after the Revolutionary War, parts of it were incorporated into the existing defenses, and there is plenty left to see of the British occupation and the island's recapture by the Spanish, particularly underground. The fortress is only open for tours by appointment, so be sure to plan ahead. *Castle of San Felipe, 07720 Sant Felip, El Castell, Menorca, Spain; 0034 971 362 100; www.consorciomilitarmenorca.com/en/que-hacer-en-menorca/visit-philips-castle-menorca. GPS: 39.867339, 4.303025. Availability limited; call ahead for tours.*

GIBRALTAR—Great Britain has held the outpost of Gibraltar since 1704. When Spain declared war on the British during the American Revolution, they almost immediately shifted their attention to regaining the critical strategic point. In June 1779, the Spanish, later joined by the French, began a long siege of Gibraltar. The siege was lengthened several times when the British were able to resupply themselves. Growing weary of waiting and seeing that their blockade was not effective, the Spanish and French launched a massive assault of the British works by over 60,000 soldiers and sailors on September 13, 1782. The largest battle of the Revolutionary War, it was a massive failure, and the siege continued until it was lifted on February 7, 1783. During the three and a half years of the siege, the British lost about 1,300 casualties while the Spanish and French lost over 6,000.

The famous Rock of Gibraltar is far from the only thing to see in this territory of less than 3 square miles. Still an active British military installation, great pride is taken in Gibraltar's military legacy, and the Great Siege is its centerpiece. The impressive siege tunnels are in excellent shape and contain a wealth of information, while the City Under Siege Exhibition focuses on the civilian side of the British holdout. Other fortifications across Gibraltar dating back centuries were also part of the great action, and memorials to the British army and navy can be found throughout the territory. The tunnels and the exhibition can be accessed through the Upper Rock Nature Reserve. (And watch out for the monkeys; try, if you can, to enjoy them from a distance.) *Great Siege Tunnels, Gibraltar; 350 2007 1633; www.visitgibraltar.gi. GPS: 36.144685, -5.347991.Open daily.*

GREAT BRITAIN

The ties between the United States of America and the United Kingdom may have been strained during the Revolutionary War, but today they have never been stronger. It's also never been easier to visit the UK, as reasonable flights from America to London abound. Great Britain offers millennia of fascinating history, from Stonehenge to the Romans and including, of course, many links to the American Revolution. Still the "mother country," much of British history is still tied to that of early America, and of course the origins of the Revolution—the acts and taxes that proved so disruptive to the growth of America—came from King George III and the British Parliament. Whether it's a short trip to London or a grand excursion to the countryside, there's plenty to see in the United Kingdom tied to the American Revolution.

BENJAMIN FRANKLIN HOUSE, LONDON—Benjamin Franklin was an international celebrity before he was a Founding Father. Besides being a renowned scientist and one of America's foremost thinkers, he served as a representative of Pennsylvania's interests in London and de facto agent to Parliament for all the colonies. Franklin's influence was considerable, and his presence in London during the implementation of the taxation measures that led to rebellion helped to raise considerable political support for the colonies. Much of Franklin's life from 1757 through 1775 was spent in London.

London's Benjamin Franklin House is the only home of Franklin's that still stands. Tours of the house are highly experiential, with costumed interpretation and multimedia effects. Tickets are required. If you can't make the historical tour but would still like to see the building, you can also book an architectural tour of the home on Mondays. *Benjamin Franklin House, 36 Craven St., London WC2N 5NF, UK; 0207 839 2006; benjaminfranklinhouse.org. GPS: 51.507609, -0.124947. Historical tours Sat.–Sun.; architectural tours Fri.*

PALACE OF WESTMINSTER, LONDON—The Palace of Westminster has been home to the two houses of Parliament since their existence. It was here that Prime Minister Lord North and the rest of Parliament made the fateful decisions that pushed America over the edge and on the road to revolution. Over the years Westminster has survived its own revolts and revolutions, not to mention a few fires along the way (including a major one in 1834, which required most of it to be rebuilt).

You can take either a 90-minute guided tour of Parliament or a self-guided audio tour if you'd like to go at your own pace. The tours cover not only the building and its outstanding history but also how Parliament works. If you'd like to see that for yourself, you may also view a session of the House of Commons or the House of Lords from the visitor's gallery. *Palace of Westminster, London, England SW1A OAA; www.parliament.uk/visiting. GPS: 51.500294, -0.125260. Guided and audio tours on Sat. throughout the year; when Parliament is in recess, audio tours are Mon.–Sat. and guided tours are Tues.–Sat.*

ST. GEORGE'S CHAPEL, WINDSOR—Windsor Castle, a significant part of English royal history since William the Conqueror, was one of the favorite palaces of George III and his queen, Charlotte. When George died in 1826, he was buried in St. George's Chapel at Windsor alongside other kings and queens of England.

To say there's a lot to see at Windsor Castle is an understatement. Still an official royal household, there are numerous tours that will show you

Westminster, home to the British Parliament in London.

different aspects of royal life throughout the massive castle and the surrounding grounds. One of the tours available is of St. George's Chapel. Here you will find 10 rulers of England laid to rest, including George III; if the chapel looks familiar, it's because you may have seen it before—its most recent headline event was the wedding of HRH Prince Harry and Meghan Markle. Parking around the castle is tough; take the train into town if you're able. Also, be sure to book your tickets in advance, and check the schedule—as a working castle, royal events are frequent and sometimes planned on short notice. *Windsor Castle, Windsor SL4 1NJ, UK; www.rct.uk/visit/windsor-castle. GPS: 51.482792, -0.606849. Castle open Thurs.–Mon., chapel open Mon. and Thurs.–Sat.*

WHITEHAVEN—On April 23, 1778, John Paul Jones and men from the USS *Ranger* rowed ashore at the important British port of Whitehaven to destroy a large number of ships that were docked there. Jones and his men were able to capture the small fortress in the harbor, but the mission to destroy the boats was a complete failure. However, the broader mission was accomplished, as the United States Navy's bold landing on British soil started a panic along the entire coast.

If you visit the harbor at Whitehaven today, you'll find a number of statues around the marina depicting the Jones raid. You can also visit The Beacon, a local historical museum that will fill in the details of the famous raid. *The Beacon Museum, West Strand, Whitehaven, Cumbria CA28 7LY; 01946 592302; www.thebeacon-whitehaven.co.uk. GPS: 54.548767, -3.594517. Open Tues.–Sun.*

FLAMBOROUGH HEAD—On September 23, 1779, a small group of American and French ships led by Captain John Paul Jones in the *Bonhomme Richard* took on two British ships escorting a convoy of merchant ships off Flamborough Head on the Yorkshire coast. A fierce battle erupted between the *Bonhomme Richard* and HMS *Serapis*, and after officials on the British ship questioned whether the Americans were ready to surrender, Jones allegedly replied, "I have not yet begun to fight!" The legendary utterance was followed by several more hours of fighting, after which *Bonhomme Richard* emerged victorious (but just barely, as the ship had taken so much damage that it sank two days later).

Scarborough Castle at Flamborough Head covers over 3,000 years of history at this site, and though much of it is in ruins, what is left tells its stories well. A museum is on site where you can learn about the American victory that happened off the castle's waters, but you will want to make sure you have time to see the Roman signal tower and take in the beautiful views. *Scarborough Castle, Castle Road, Scarborough, North Yorkshire, YO11 1HY, UK; 0370 333 1181; www.english-heritage.org.uk/visit/places/scarborough-castle. GPS: 54.287080, -0.390972. Open weekends and most weekdays throughout year; see website for more information.*

Other Global Sites

Once the American Revolution became a global war, the conflict spread to several far-flung and surprising places. All of the European countries involved—the United Kingdom, France, and Spain—had colonies and interests all around the world, and the war became another opportunity to shuffle the possession of those territories. Here are a few of the more significant sites outside of the United States and Europe.

BRITISH ROYAL DOCKYARD, HALIFAX, NOVA SCOTIA, CANADA— Halifax, Nova Scotia, was home to the British Navy's primary naval base in the North Atlantic, and many of the actions against the United States originated from that port. In addition, Halifax became a destination for many of the Loyalists who fled the United States, either as a waypoint or a permanent home.

Halifax has a rich maritime history, and you can learn about all of it at the Maritime Museum of the Atlantic. The museum is located right in the waterfront district and contains exhibits on the British Royal Dockyard, the city's links to the Titanic, and the great Halifax Explosion of 1917. *Maritime Museum of the Atlantic, 1675 Lower Water St., Halifax, NS B3J 1S3; 902-424-7490; maritimemuseum.novascotia.ca. GPS: 44.647537, -63.570391. Open daily, May through October; closed Mon. November through April.*

FORTRESS OF EL CASTILLO, NICARAGUA—In an effort to sever the Spanish colonies in Central America in half, British forces sailed up the San Juan River in modern-day Nicaragua. On April 29, 1780, a force led by British captain and future legend Horatio Nelson led an attack against the Spanish at the Castle of the Immaculate Conception on Lake Nicaragua, taking the fortress. The expedition failed, however, when thousands of the British fell victim to Yellow Fever, and the force that was left turned back.

The town of El Castillo and Inmaculada Concepción Castle are accessible only by water. Day tours with transportation to the old fortress are available through several tour operators from the city of San Carlos. The site contains the remarkably intact fortress along with a small museum outlining its history. This part of Nicaragua, renowned for its beauty, is seldom visited, so plan far ahead. *Fortress of El Castillo, Rio San Juan, El Castillo, Nicaragua; 2583 0301; vianica.com/attraction/9/fortress-of-el-castillo. GPS: 11.019207, -84.396631. Open daily.*

CUDDALORE, INDIA—The Indian port of Cuddalore on the Bay of Bengal, controlled by the French, was the subject of a British siege in 1783. Shortly after it began, British and French fleets met off the shore of Cuddalore on June 23, resulting in a French victory that allowed the besieged garrison to receive reinforcements and supplies. However, on June 29, less than a week later, news arrived that a preliminary peace deal had been reached in Paris. The hostilities stopped, and the last great military action of the American Revolution was over.

The ruins of the Fortress of Cuddalore, also known as Fort St. David, can be visited in the port of Cuddalore today. Though there is no interpretation, you can visit the Cuddalore Government Museum, which presents the rich history of the city. *Fort St. David, on Tourist Banglow Rd., PQQJ+F28, Devanampattinam, Cuddalore, Tamil Nadu 607001, India; cuddalore.nic.in/tourist-place/fort-st-david. Accessible daily. Cuddalore Government Museum, QQ48+55R, Rajambal Nagar, Manjakuppam, Cuddalore, Tamil Nadu 607001, India; 04142-231232; govtmuseumchennai.org/district-museum/cuddalore. GPS: 11.738852, 79.780099. Contact museum for hours.*

ACKNOWLEDGMENTS

The historic sites of the American Revolution are scattered across many states and even countries. All of them, large and small, are treasures, and they all require care and constant attention. Whether they are preserved by the National Park Service or are represented only by a simple stone monument or historic marker, someone made an effort on behalf of all of us to make sure that our history was not forgotten. So to all the people over centuries who have found the time, energy, money, and other resources required to make America's history part of the landscape, thank you.

The sites noted in this book that are staffed are done so by people who live and breathe our history. Their extraordinary work, much of it done on a volunteer basis, makes visiting these sites the wonderful experiences that they are. It would be impossible to list the names of all the people who assisted me by gathering information, providing tours, and answering innumerable questions. Thank you to all of them, and you can thank them, too, by visiting.

The historic sites and monuments administered by the National Park Service are always outstanding, and the staff at each of them have always been willing to go out of their way to help me find the answers I needed. The interpretation of America's complicated history has become an increasingly tricky subject, yet they have generally found a way to provide insightful, representative, and most important, truthful analysis. These public servants deserve a hearty thank you from all of us.

The American Battlefield Protection Program produced the reports that are responsible for the idea behind this book and my previous book *The Complete Civil War Road Trip Guide*. This time I made a special effort to visit the ABPP's office at the Department of the Interior in Washington, DC, and the staff there could not have been more helpful. Thanks to them for their efforts, as well as all of the people who worked on their behalf to create their report to Congress.

The American Battlefield Trust works tirelessly to preserve the land on which America's history unfolded. They have been a great resource and an inspiration since I began visiting historic sites many years ago. Thank you to the American Battlefield Trust and all its staff who have expanded the organization's mission over the years and who do so much to preserve, protect, and teach our history.

The support provided by the Countryman Press over my years of writing has been amazing. The patience and understanding they have shown with this book, in particular, has been humbling. To my first editor, Kermit Hummel, and my new editors, James Jayo and Emma Peters, as well as other members of the Countryman team—Devorah Backman, Mike van Mantgem, Jessica Murphy, and more—thank you so much for care, your persistence, and your faith in me.

Finally, to my wife, Charlotte, thank you for everything. Your patience in putting up with the travel (both with and without me), the piles of books, papers and maps, and the countless conversations about this book kept me going throughout. I love you very much.

BIBLIOGRAPHY

EXCEPT FOR THE FEW critical examples listed here, much of the information presented in this book was gleaned from interpretive signs, faded highway markers, pamphlets, brochures, wandering exploration, and, most important, the many wonderful volunteers who keep the sites listed in this book on the map. Each battlefield and historical site in the book lists contact, site, and/or location information, and each of them should be considered references.

The following were used as sources:

Barefoot, Daniel W. *Touring North Carolina's Revolutionary War Sites*. Winston-Salem, North Carolina: John F. Blair, 1998.

Berleth, Richard. *Bloody Mohawk: The French and Indian War & American Revolution on New York's Frontier*. Delmar, New York: Black Dome Press, 2009.

Boatner III, Mark M. *Encyclopedia of the American Revolution*. Mechanicsburg, Pennsylvania: Stackpole Books, 1991.

Bobrick, Benson. *Angel in the Whirlwind: The Triumph of the American Revolution*. New York: Simon & Schuster, 1997.

Buchanan, John. *The Road to Guilford Courthouse: The American Revolution in the Carolinas*. New York: John Wiley & Sons, 1997.

De Hass, Wills. *History of the Early Settlement and Indian Wars of Western Virginia: Embracing an Account of the Various Expeditions in the West, Previous to 1795; also, Biographical Sketches*. Burbank, California: Creative Media Partners, 2022.

Desjardin, Thomas A. *Through a Howling Wilderness: Benedict Arnold's March to Quebec, 1775.* New York: St. Martin's Griffin, 2006.

Doddridge, Joseph. *Notes on the Settlement Indian Wars of the Western Parts of Virginia and Pennsylvania.* Albany, New York: J. Munsell, 1876.

Ellis, Joseph J. *Founding Brothers: The Revolutionary Generation.* New York: Alfred A. Knopf, 2001.

Ferling, John. *Almost a Miracle: The American Victory in the War of Independence.* New York: Oxford University Press, 2007.

Ferreiro, Larrie D. *Brothers at Arms: American Independence and the Men of France and Spain Who Saved It.* New York: Alfred P. Knopf, 2016.

Ferris, Robert G., and Charleton, James H. *The Signers of the Constitution.* Arlington, Virginia: Interpretive Publications, 1982.

Ferris, Robert G., and Morris, Richard E. *The Signers of the Declaration of Independence.* Arlington, Virginia: Interpretive Publications, 1982.

Fischer, David Hackett. *Paul Revere's Ride.* New York: Oxford University Press, 1994.

Fischer, David Hackett. *Washington's Crossing.* New York: Oxford University Press, 2004.

Fleming, Thomas. *Washington's Secret War: The Hidden History of Valley Forge.* New York: HarperCollins, 2005.

Flexner, James Thomas. *Washington: The Indispensable Man.* New York: Back Bay Books, 1994.

Foulke, Patricia, and Foulke, Robert. *A Visitor's Guide to Colonial & Revolutionary New England, Second Edition.* Woodstock, Vermont: Countryman Press, 2012.

Foulke, Patricia, and Foulke, Robert. *A Visitor's Guide to the Colonial & Revolutionary South.* Woodstock, Vermont: Countryman Press, 2009.

Greene, Jerome A. *The Guns of Independence: The Siege of Yorktown, 1781.* New York: Savas Beatie, 2005.

Hammon, Neal O., and Taylor, Richard. *Virginia's Western War, 1775–1786.* Mechanicsburg, Pennsylvania: Stackpole Books, 2002.

Houghton, Raymond C. *A Revolutionary War Road Trip on NY Route 5.* Delmar, New York: Cyber Haus, 2005.

Houghton, Raymond C. *A Revolutionary War Road Trip on US Route 20.* Delmar, New York: Cyber Haus, 2005.

Houghton, Raymond C. *A Revolutionary War Road Trip on US Route 60.* Delmar, New York: Cyber Haus, 2006.

Jones, Randell. *A Guide to the Overmountain Victory National Historic Trail* (2nd ed.). Winston-Salem, North Carolina: Daniel Boone Footsteps, 2016.

Kennedy, Frances H. *The American Revolution: A Historical Guidebook.* New York: Oxford University Press, 2014.

Ketchum, Richard M. *Decisive Day: The Battle for Bunker Hill*. New York: Doubleday, 1974.

Ketchum, Richard M. *Saratoga: Turning Point of America's Revolutionary War*. New York: Henry Holt and Company, 1997.

Ketchum, Richard M. *Victory at Yorktown: The Campaign That Won the Revolution*. New York: Henry Holt and Company, 2004.

Langguth, A. J. *Patriots: The Men Who Started the American Revolution*. New York: Simon & Schuster, 1988.

Lender, Mark Edward, and Stone, Gary Wheeler. *Fatal Sunday: George Washington, the Monmouth Campaign, and the Politics of Battle*. Norman: University of Oklahoma Press, 2016.

Logusz, Michael O. *With Musket & Tomahawk: The Saratoga Campaign and the Wilderness War of 1777*. Havertown, Pennsylvania: Casemate Publishers, 2010.

Logusz, Michael O. *With Musket & Tomahawk, Volume II: The Mohawk Valley Campaign in the Wilderness War of 1777*. Havertown, Pennsylvania: Casemate Publishers, 2012.

Maier, Pauline. *American Scripture: Making the Declaration of Independence*. New York: Vintage Books, 1997.

Maier, Pauline. *From Resistance to Revolution: Colonial Radicals and the Development of American Opposition to Britain, 1765–1776*. New York: A.A. Knopf, 1972.

Martin, Joseph Plumb. *The Adventures of a Revolutionary Soldier: A Narrative of Some of the Adventures, Dangers, and Sufferings of a Revolutionary Soldier Interspersed with Anecdotes of Incidents That Occurred Within His Own Observation*. London: Endeavor Press, 2016.

McCullough, David. *1776*. New York: Simon & Schuster, 2005.

McCullough, David. *John Adams*. New York: Simon & Schuster, 2001.

McGuire, Thomas J. *The Philadelphia Campaign, Volume I: Brandywine and the Fall of Philadelphia*. Mechanicsburg, Pennsylvania: Stackpole Books, 2006.

McGuire, Thomas J. *The Philadelphia Campaign, Volume II: Germantown and the Roads to Valley Forge*. Mechanicsburg, Pennsylvania: Stackpole Books, 2007.

Nebenzahl, Kenneth (Editor). *Rand McNally Atlas of the American Revolution*. Chicago: Rand McNally & Company, 1974.

Nelson, James L. *Benedict Arnold's Navy: The Ragtag Fleet that Lost the Battle of Lake Champlain but Won the American Revolution*. New York: McGraw Hill, 2006.

Nelson, James L. *George Washington's Great Gamble and the Sea Battle That Won the American Revolution*. New York: McGraw Hill, 2010.

Parker, Jr., John C. *Parker's Guide to the Revolutionary War in South Carolina, Second Edition*. West Conshohocken, Pennsylvania: Infinity Publishing, 2013.

Paine, Thomas. *Common Sense*. New York: Barnes & Noble, 1995.

Report to Congress on the Historic Preservation of Revolutionary War and War of 1812 Sites in the United States. Prepared for the United States Senate Committee on Energy and Natural Resources and the United States House of Representatives Committee on Resources. Washington, DC: National Park Service, American Battlefield Protection Program, September 2007.

Savas, Theodore P., and Dameron, J. David. *A Guide to the Battles of the American Revolution*. New York: Savas Beatie, 2013.

Schecter, Barnet. *The Battle for New York: The City at the Heart of the American Revolution*. New York: Walker & Company, 2002.

Shively, Julie. *The Ideals Guide to Places of the American Revolution*. Nashville, Tennessee: Ideals Publications, 2001.

Stokesbury, James L. *A Short History of the American Revolution*. New York: Quill, 1991.

Symonds, Craig. *A Battlefield Atlas of the American Revolution*. Baltimore, Maryland: The Nautical and Aviation Publishing Company of America, 1986.

Wilson, David K. *The Southern Strategy: Britain's Conquest of South Carolina and Georgia, 1775–1780*. Columbia: University of South Carolina Press, 2005.

Wood, Gordon S. *The American Revolution: A History*. New York: Modern Library, 2002.

Wood, Gordon S. *The Radicalism of the American Revolution*. New York: A. A. Knopf, 1992.

INDEX

―❖―

Page numbers in *italics* refer to illustrations.

A

Abigail Adams Historical Society, 32
Abingdon Muster Grounds, 386, *391*
Abraham Van Gaasbeek/Senate House, 258–59, *259*
Acland, John, 155
Adams, Abigail (née Smith), 8, 30–33, *33*
Adams, Charles Francis, 34
Adams, John, 8–9, 31–33; Adams National Historic Park, 30–34, *30*; Bentley Manor and, 274; Christ Church and, 299; France and, 531; Hotel d'York and, 531; Thomas Jefferson and, 289; Second Continental Congress and, 292
Adams, John Quincy, 9, 31, 46
Adams, Samuel, 6–7; Faneuil Hall and, 13, *16*; Hancock-Clarke House and, 25; Lexington and, 22; Old Granary Burying Ground and, *15*; Old South Meeting House and, 11–12, 14; taxation and, 5

Adams National Historic Park, 30–34, *30*
African Burial Ground National Monument, 247–48
Alamance Battleground State Historic Site, 466–67, *466*
Alexander, William. *See* Stirling
Allen, Ethan: Archibald Campbell and, 61; Battle of Longue-Pointe and, 116; Crown Point and, 164; Ethan Allen Homestead and Monument and, 133–34; Fort Ticonderoga and, 95, 101, 142
Alligator Creek Bridge, 530
Alston, Philip, 464–65, *464*
Altar to Liberty, 209, *210*
American Independence Museum, 66
American Revolution Museum at Yorktown, 438–39, *441*
American Soldiers' Burial Site, 113
Amherst, Jeffrey, 171

Andre, John, 266, 267
Andrew Jackson State Park, 410
Annapolis Convention, 331
Apthorp, East, 55–56
Aquidneck Island (Rhode Island), 37–38, 52
Arkansas Post, 520
Armstrong, John, Germantown and, 306
Arnold, Benedict, 94–96; Arnold Trail to Quebec, 101–10; Battle of the Cedars and, 129; Château Ramezay and, 118; Compo Hill and, 252–53; Crown Point and, 164; Fort Chambly and, 130–31; Fort Stanwix and, 159; Fort Ticonderoga and, 95, 142; Lake Champlain and, 120; Mabie's Tavern and, 266; New London and, 76–77; Petersburg and, 471; Quebec City and, 94–95, 110–15; Ridgefield and, 252; Saratoga and, 140, 153–56; Skenesborough and, 165; Smyth House and, 169; West Point and, 260; Westover Plantation and, 474
Articles of Confederation, 293, 334, 473
Ashley River Road, 364–65
Augusta, 107, 349, 355, 397–99
Austin, Stephen, Jr., 415

B

Balcarres, Alexander, 156
Baltimore American (newspaper), 328–29
Baltimore American Newspaper Office, 328–29
Baltimore Washington Monument, 329–30, *330*
Barren Hill, 184, 344
Barrett, James, 23, 24, *27*
Barry, John, 457

Bartlett, William, 63
Barton, William, 85
Baton Rouge, 519, 521, *521*
Bates, Sarah, 251
Battle Hill, 209
Battle Island memorial, 513
Battle of Alligator Creek Bridge, 530
Battle of Barren Hill, 184
Battle of Brandywine, 286, 294–305, *295*; Cornwallis and, 427; Dilworthtown Inn and, 337–38; Ephrata Cloister and, 336; Strode's Mill and, 337
Battle of Brooklyn, 205–9, *207*, *210*, *217*, *218*
Battle of Bunker Hill, 31, 45, 66
Battle of Connecticut Farms, 274
Battle of Cowpens, 97, 350, 351, *385*, 423
Battle of Fort Anne, *136*, 167
Battle of Fort Moultrie, 352, 357, 361, 363, 366
Battle of Freeman's Farm, 154–55
Battle of Germantown, *306*, 307, 341–42, 427
Battle of Great Bridge, 473
Battle of Johnstown, 186
Battle of Kedges Straits, 483
Battle of Kemp's Landing, 478
Battle of Kings Mountain, 380–84, 386, *391*
Battle of Klock's Field, 189–90
Battle of Long Island Flats, 419
Battle of Moores Creek, 423
Battle of Nantasket Road, 54
Battle of Oriskany, 184, 187
Battle of Penobscot Bay, 99–103
Battle of Petersburg, 471
Battle of Plattsburgh Bay, 124, 166
Battle of Princeton, 228, 232, 281
Battle of Red Bank, 316, 318, 319
Battle of Rhode Island, 37–45, 50–52, 79, 85
Battle of Saratoga, 55, 97, 350

Battle of September 6, 1775, National Historic Site of Canada, 132
Battle of South Mountain, 333
Battle of the Barges, 483
Battle of the Capes, 440, 478–79
Battle of the Cedars, 128–29
Battle of the Ironclads, 477
Battle of the Rice Boats, 353, 356
Battle of the Short Hills, 278
Battle of Thomas Creek, 529
Battle of Trenton, 61, 228–29, 281
Battle of Trois-Rivières, 128
Battle of Valcour Island. *See* Valcour Island
Battle Pass, 208–9
Battlefield Park (Savannah), 356
battlefields, xiii
Baum, Friedrich, 149–51
Baylor, George, 268–69
Beacon Hill, 70
Beaumarchais, Pierre Augustin Caron de, 531–32
Beavertail Lighthouse, 48, *52*
Beavertail State Park, 48
Bedford Green, 255
Bedford Hill, 388–89
Bell, William and Martha, 465
Belleville Plantation, 406–7
Bell's Mill, 465
Belvoir, 329–30
Benjamin Cooper House, 318
Bennington, 148–51, *150*, 169; Bennington Battle Monument, 152; Bennington Battlefield State Historic Site, 152; British defeat at, 139; Crown Point Military Road and, 172; Stark and, 172
Bentley / Conference House, 273–74, *275*
Bernardo de Gálvez Monument, 526
Betsy Ross House, 299
Beverly, 63–64
Bigfoot, 166
Biggerstaff Old Fields, 389–90

Bill of Rights, 51, 448, 455–56
Billerica Town Common, 60
Bird, Mark, 339
Black Rock Fort, 69–70, *71*
Blackstock's Plantation, 414
Blandford Church and Cemetery, 470–71
Block Island, 78
Bloody Run, 51
Blue Licks State Battlefield, 506
Blue Mountain Valley (supply ship), 279
Boardman, Offin, 65
"bog iron," 74
Bogart's Tavern, 280
Bonhomme Richard (ship), 540
Boone, Daniel, 493, 502, 506
Boone, Israel, 506
Bordley, John, 328
Boston: Dorchester Heights and, 17–18, 19, *19*; evacuation of, 6; siege of, cannon and, 164
Boston Common, 10–11, *11*, 12
Boston Light, 47, 54
Boston Massacre in 1770, *2*, 5; John Adams and, 9; Old South Meeting House and, 12; Paul Revere and, 8; site of, 13
Boston National Historical Park (Bunker Hill Unit), 10, 13, 31
Boston Tea Party, 5, 12–17, *18*, 81
Bowling Green, 245
Braddock, Edward, 202
Bradford, William, 84
Bradford Meeting House, 64–65
Brandywine Village, 321–22
Brant, Joseph: Fort Alden and, 193; Fort Stanwix and, 158; German Flatts and, 186–87; Newtown and, 181; Oneida Castle, 183; Oriskany and, 160–63
Brant, Molly, 160–61, 192
Brattle, William, 56, 58
Brewton's Hill, 354–55
Breymann, Heinrich, 151, 156

Brier Creek, 399
Brinckerhoff, John, 258
Bristol Waterfront, 83–84
British Navy Yard, 179–80
British Royal Dockyard, 541
Broadhead, Daniel, 512
Brophy Park, 54
Bryan's Station, 505–6
Buckman Tavern, 25, *27*
Buffalo Ford, 375, 465
Buford, Abraham, 384, 408–9
Buford's Massacre, 384, 408–9
Bull-Mawdsley House, 43
Bunker Hill, 6, 16–17, 28–31, *28*;
    Exeter and, 66; HMS *Somerset* and,
    89; Joshua Loring House and, 45
Burgoyne, John, 140–41; Bennington
    and, 148–51; endgame strategy and,
    137–39; Fort George and, 167; Fort
    Stanwix and, 160; Fort Ticonderoga
    and, 143–46; Montreal and, 117–
    18; Daniel Morgan and, 97; Rever-
    end Apthorp House and, 55–56;
    Saratoga and, 139, 151–56, 265;
    Skenesborough and, 165; Smyth
    House and, 169; Valcour Island and
    Lake Champlain, 118–23
Burgwin, John, house of, 459, *460*
Burial Hill Cemetery, 239, *240*
Burke, Edmund, 457
Burr, Aaron, 46, 270–71
Bushnell, David, 211
Butler, John, 181, 282
Butler, Walter, 186, 191–93
Butts Hill Fort, 38, 51
Byrd, Henry, 505–6
Byrd, Mary Willing, 474
Byrd, William, 475

C

Cabildo, 522, *523*
Cabot, John, 63–64
Caldwell, William, 506
Cambridge (slave), 60
Cambridge, 45, 55, *56*, 57
Camden, 140, 349, 350, 372, 374–80,
    375, *378*, 397
Camp Hill, 54
Camp Putnam, 55
Camp Reading Cantonment, 253–54
Camp Security, 335
Campbell, Archibald, 61, 354–60
Campbell, William, 382, 386, 387
Canada, 541
Canajoharie District, 190–91
Cape Henry Memorial Cross, 479
Cape Henry Memorial unit, 479
Capt. John Mawdsley House, 43
Captain John Moore House, 60
Carleton (British schooner), 122
Carleton, Christopher, 123
Carleton, Guy: DeWint House and,
    267; Lake Champlain and,
    122–23; Longueuil and, 129–30;
    Montreal and, 115–17; Quebec
    and, 93, 110, 111
Carlos III, 532, 534, 535
Carpenter's Hall, 291, 297
Carroll, Charles, Montreal and, 117
Casimir Pulaski Monument, 357
Castillo de San Marcos, 527-28, *527*
Castle of the Immaculate Conception,
    542
Castle of San Felipe, Menorca,
    536–37
Castle William, 47, 243
casualties, xvi
Caswell, Richard, 431–32
Catamount Tavern, 169
Cathey's Fort, 418–19
Caubert, Jean, 113
Cedars, The, 128–29
Chace-Cory House, 86
Champlain, Samuel de, 93, 131
Chapel Point, 483–84
Chappaqua Meeting House, 256
Charging Bull (statue), 245

INDEX ★ 553

Charles Pinckney National Historic Site, 365
Charleston, 349–50, 360–71
Chase, Salmon, 117, 173
Chasseurs Volontaires de Saint Domingue, Les, 357
Chastellux, Francois Jean de, 43
Château Ramezay, *116*, 118
Chatterton's Hill, 216
Cherokee Ford, 394–96, *394*
Cherokees: Cherokee Lower Towns (Oconee), 418; Cherokee Middle Towns, 417; Cherokee War of 1776, 417–19; Museum of the Cherokee People and, 416, *421*; Ninety Six, 371–74; Sycamore Shoals and, 387; wars with, 416
Cherry Valley, 176, 180, 193–94, *194*
Chesapeake Capes, 478–79
Chew, Benjamin, *306*, 307–8
Chew House, *306*
Chickahominy Shipyard, 475
Chickamauga Indian Towns, 420
Chiswell, John, 415
Chiswell Lead Mines, 415
Christ Church, 299
Christiana, 324
Church of St. Andrew, 273
Church on the Main, 476
Churchill, Elijah, 239
Churchill, Winston, 124
City Tavern, 298
Clark, George Rogers, 492–93; far west and, 495; Fort Pitt and, 510; Kaskaskia and, 500; Kaskaskia-Cahokia Trail and, 500; Piqua and, 514–15; Vincennes and, 500–502, *502*
Clark, William, 493
Clarke, Elijah, 530
Clarke, Jonas, 25
Clarke, Thomas, *231*, 233
Clarke Street Meeting House, 41
Cleveland, Benjamin, 382

Clinton, Henry: Battle of Brooklyn and, 206–7; Battle Pass and, 208; Charleston and, 361–371; Clinton-Sullivan Campaign, 176; forts Clinton and Montgomery and, 265–66; Monmouth and, 312–14; New London and, 76; Newport and, 37–45; St. James Church and, 241; Savanah and, 353–60; Stony Point and, 222; Thomas Smith House and, 319–20; Verplanck's Point and, 257; Yorktown, 436–42
Clinton, James, 181
Clinton-Sullivan Campaign, 176
Cliveden, 307–8
Cobble Hill Fort, 209
Colburn, Reuben, 106–8
Colburn House, *105*, 106, 107
Colonel Gilbert House, 89
Colonial Archaeological Trail (Pensacola), 525–26
Colonial National Historic Park, *437*, 479
Committees of Safety, 6, 75, 280
Compo Hill, 252–53
Conanicut Battery, 48, *53*
Concord, 18–27, *23*, 60, 61, 69
Concord Bridge, 23, *23*
Congress (galley), 121, 122
Constitution Gardens, 454, *455*
Constitution of the United States, 294, 296, 298–299, 448, 450
Continental Congress, First: Canada and, 94; Carpenter's Hall and, 291, 297; Christ Church and, 299; City Tavern and, 298; Silas Deane and 71; Mary Katherine Goddard and, 328; Halifax Resolves and, 468–69; Richard Howe and, 274; Samuel Huntington and, 76; New York and, 199; North Carolina and, 469; Philadelphia and, 5, 285, 291, 297; York Courthouse and, 334

Continental Congress, Second: Christ Church and, 299; City Tavern and, 298; Declaration of Independence and, 292; Fraunces Tavern and, 244; Hancock and, 7; Independence Hall and, 296; John Jay and, 255; Jefferson and, 289; Philadelphia and, 285; Washington and, 202
Continental Navy, 37, 78, 125, 339, 368
Conway, Thomas, 306
Conway Cabal scandal, 140
Cooch's Bridge, 295, 324–25, *325*
Cooper's Ferry, 318
Corbin, Margaret, 221
Cornstalk (Chief), 507–8
Cornwall Furnace, 338
Cornwallis, Charles, 427–28; Bell's Mill and, 465; Brandywine and, 300–305; Camden and, 377–80; Cowpens and, 384–94; Dan and, 395–96; Fort Washington and, 220; Green Spring and, 475; Guilford Courthouse and, 432–36; Kings Mountain and, 382; Monmouth and, 313–14; Old Stone House and, 208; Point of Fork and, 481; Princeton and, 230–31; prisoners and, cartel of, 408; St. James Church and, 241; southern theater and, 350; Trenton and, 225–30; Virginia and, 423–25; Wilmington and, 459–60; Yorktown, 425, 436–42, 479
Councils of Safety, 75
Coventry Forge, 340
Cowan's Ford, 412
"cowboys," 254
Cowpens, 384–94, *385*
Craik, James, 487
Crauford, David, 486
Crawford, William, 513
Crawford's Defeat, 513

Crown Point, 164–65, *164*
Crown Point Road, 171–72
Crown Point State Historic Site, 165
Cruger, John, 372–74
Cuddalore, India, 542
Culper Spy Ring, 240–41
Custom House (Yorktown), 439
Custom House Maritime Museum (Newburyport), 65

D

Dan River, 395–96, 423, 425, 433
Danbury, *198*, 252
Dandridge, Martha, 202
Darnall family, 486
Dartmouth College, 68, 173
Davidson, William Lee, 412
Dawes, Joseph, 21–22
Dawesfield, 342–43
de Grasse, François Joseph Paul, 439–40, 478–79
de Kalb, (Baron de, Jean), 375–76, 379
Deane, Silas, 71–72, 290, 351
Deane House, 72
Dearborn, Henry, 154–56
Declaration of Independence, 292; Floyd and, 238; Benjamin Franklin and, 288; Mary Katherine Goddard and, 328–29; Independence Hall and, 296; Samuel Huntington and, 76; Thomas Jefferson and, 289, 292, 297; National Archives Museum and, 455–56; New Hampshire Colonial State House and, 67; Pleasant Hall and, 478; Signers Memorial and, 454
Deer Island, 54, 179
Defence (privateer brigantine), 102
Defender's Park, 70–71
Delancey Hall, 254
Denyse's Ferry, *205*, 206, 208
d'Estaing, (Jean Baptiste Charles Henri Hector), 37–45, 357–60

Detroit, 491, 493
DeWint House, 267, *267*
Dickinson, John, 323
Dickson, Alexander, 521
Dilworthtown Inn, 337–38
Dr. Jabez Campfield House, 237
Donop, Car von, 316–17
Donop, Kurt von, 320
Dorchester, 403–4, *404*
Dorchester Heights, 16, 17–18, 19, 29, 142
Dragging Canoe, 419, 420
Dunmore, John (Lord Dunmore), 442, 476–79, 493
Durfee, Joseph, 88–89
Durham Village, 280, *281*
Durham Village Mill and Furnace, 280
Durnford, Elias, 523–24

E

East Florida, 519, 526–27
East India Company, Tea Act and, 11
Easton Furnace, 90–91
Eaton's Station, 419
Ecker, Wolfert, 259–60
Edenton Tea Party, 462
Edmonston House, 263
Edmund Fowle House, 57
El Castillo, 541–42
Elbert, Samuel, 529
Elijah West's Tavern, 170–71, *170*
Elizabethtown, 274
Ellison, John, 262
Emancipation Proclamation, 455–56
Enos, Roger, 108
Ephrata Cloister, 336–37, *336*
Erskine, Robert, 268
Ethan Allen Homestead and Monument, 133–34, *133*
Eustis, William, 46–47
Eutaw Springs, 404–5, *405*
Evergreens Cemetery, The, 209

Exchange Building, the, 364
Exeter, 65–66
Exeter Powder House, 66

F

Fairfax Resolves (Mason), 486
Falmouth, 123
Faneuil Hall, 13, *16*
Fanning, David, 464
far west, the, 494–95
Federal Hall, 245–46
Fells Point Shipyards, 328
Ferguson, Patrick, 381–84, 389, 414–15
Ferry Farm, 482
First Continental Congress: Canada and, 94; Carpenter's Hall and, 291, 297; Christ Church and, 299; City Tavern and, 298; Silas Deane and 71; Mary Katherine Goddard and, 328; Halifax Resolves and, 468–69; Richard Howe and, 274; Samuel Huntington and, 76; New York and, 199; North Carolina and, 469; Philadelphia and, 5, 285, 291, 297; York Courthouse and, 334
1st Rhode Island Regiment, 37–38, 51, 79
First State National Historical Park, 322–23
first victory, 69
Fishing Creek, 411
Fishkill Supply Depot, 257–58, 263
Fitch Tavern, 60
Flamborough Head, 540–41
Floyd, William, 238
Folsom Tavern, 66
Forage War, 235
Ford, Theodosia, 235
Forster, George, 129
Fort Adams, 48–49
Fort Alden, 193
Fort Anne, *136*, 167

Fort at No. 4, 171–72, *173*
Fort Barton, 51–52
Fort Boonesborough, 503
Fort Bute, 521–22
Fort Carlos III, 520
Fort Chambly, 130–131, *130*
Fort Charlotte, 523–24
Fort Clinton, 260–66
Fort Condé, 523–24, *524*
Fort Constitution, 68–69
Fort Cornwallis, 397–98, *398*
Fort Cricket Hill, 479–80, *480*
Fort Crown Point, 122, 142, 164–65
Fort Dayton, 186–87
Fort Detroit, 497, 506
Fort Detroit, Fort Laurens and, 512
Fort Duquesne, 202, 509–10
Fort Edward, 148, 167, 169
Fort Foster, 123–27
Fort Frederica National Monument, 530–31
Fort Frederick, 334
Fort George, 100, 103, *104*, 167–68, 525–26
Fort Golgotha, 239–40s
Fort Grierson, 397
Fort Griswold, 76–78, *77*
Fort Haldimand, 179–80
Fort Hamilton, 49, 208
Fort Harrod, 504, *504*
Fort Henry, 510
Fort Herkimer, 186–87
Fort Hill, 343
Fort Independence, 47
Fort Jay, 243
Fort Kaskaskia, 492
Fort Klock, 189–90
Fort Laurens, 512–13
Fort Lee, 201, 269–70, *270*; Fort Washington and, 221; Salem and, 62–63; Steuben House and, 269
Fort Lennox, 133
Fort Lyttleton, 401–2
Fort Machias, 127–28

Fort Mackinac, *496*, 497
Fort Mercer, 305, 315–16
Fort Michilimackinac, 495–96, *495*
Fort Mifflin, 305, 316–18, *317*
Fort Montgomery, 223, 260–66, *265*
Fort Morris, 400, *401*
Fort Mose, 528–29, *528*
Fort Moultrie, 357, 361, 363, *366*
Fort Nathan Hale, 69–70
Fort New Richmond, 521
Fort Niagara, 176–78, *177*, 180, 182
Fort Nonsense, *234*, 236
Fort Number Two, 62
Fort O'Brien, 127–28
Fort Ontario, 137, 156, 158, 178–79, *178*
Fort Panmure, 521
Fort Pickering, 62–63
Fort Pitt, 491, 508, 509–10
Fort Plain, 141, 190–91, *191*
Fort Putnam, 55, 241
Fort Randolph, *490*, 507–8, *507*
Fort Roberdeau, 508–9
Fort Sackville, 500–501
Fort Saint-Jean, *92*, 115–16, 119–20, 130–32
Fort Salem, 170
Fort Salonga, 239
Fort San Bernardo, 526
Fort San Carlos, 499, 522
Fort San Miguel, 526
Fort Schlosser, 174
Fort Schuyler. *See* Fort Stanwix
Fort Sewall, 61–62, *62*
Fort St. David, 542
Fort St. George, 238
Fort St. Joseph, 498, *499*
Fort St. Mark, 526–28, *527*
Fort Stamford, 251
Fort Stanwix (Fort Schuyler), 156–60, *158*; Fort Stanwix National Monument, 161; Fort Stanwix National Memorial, 141; St. Leger's expedition and, 139, 178; Tryon County Militia and, 187

INDEX ★ 557

Fort Story Military Reservation, 479
Fort Strong, 54
Fort Sullivan, 361, 366–67
Fort Sumter and Fort Moultrie National Historical Park, 363
Fort Sunbury, 400
Fort Ticonderoga, 141–47, *142, 144*; Arnold and, 95-96, 122; British assault on 138; naval superiority and, race for, 120; Skenesborough and, 165
Fort Tonyn, 530
Fort Trumbull, 76–77
Fort Tryon, 221
Fort Vincennes, 492
Fort Wadsworth, 272, *273*
Fort Washington, 219–21, *220*
Fort Washington State Park, 343
Fort Watauga, 387, *392*
Fort Watson, 405–6
Fort William and Mary, 69
Fort William Henry, 168
Fortress of El Castillo, 541–42
Forty Fort, 282–83
Fosterfields Living Historical Farm, 237
France, 347, 531
Francis, Ebenezer, 147–48
Franco-American alliance, 37–45
Franklin (American privateer), 54
Franklin, Benjamin, 288; Benjamin Franklin House and, 538; Benjamin Franklin Museum, 297; Benjamin Franklin National Memorial and, 301, *304*; Bentley Manor and, 274; Christ Church Burial Ground, 299; France and, 71, 531; Franklin Court and, 297; Hotel de Valentinois and, 532; Hotel d'York and, 531; "Join, or Die," 20–21; Montreal and, 117; Pulaski and, 351; Second Continental Congress and, 292; statue of, 457
Franklin Court, 297

Fraser, Simon, 143–44, 147, 154–56
Fraunces Tavern, 243–45, *244*
Fredericksburg Gun Manufactory, 481–82
Freeman, John, 154–57
Freemasons, 66–67
French Soldiers and Sailors Monument, 332
Friends Meeting House, 85, 319
Fulton Ferry Landing, 209

G

Gabreil Daveis Tavern, 318
Gage, Thomas: Bunker Hill and, 16, 29–30; Burgoyne and, 140; The Lindens and, 459; Provincial Powder House and, 58
Gálvez, Bernardo de, 519; Bernardo de Gálvez Monument, 526; Fort Bute and, 521–22; "Marcha de Gálvez," 521; Mobile and, 523; Pensacola and, 525–26; statue of, 457; West Florida and, 520
Gansevoort, Peter, 158
Gaspee Affair, 81–82, *81*
Gates, Horatio, 139–40; Buffalo Ford and, 465; Camden and, 350, 374–80; Edmonston House and, 263; General Gates House and, 335; John Ellison House and, 262–63; Monmouth and, 312; Saratoga and, 153–56; Trinity Church cemetery and, 245
Gateway Arch National Park, 499
General Grant National Memorial, 213
General James Mitchell Varnum House, 79
George Emlen House, 343
George Mason Memorial, 453–54, *454*
George III, 245, 518, 539, 540
Germain, George, 118–23, 137
German Flatts, 186–87
Germantown, 286, 305–8, *306*, 427

Gibraltar, 534, 537
Gilbert, Thomas, 89
Gilbert Town, 389
Gibraltar of the North. *See* Fort Ticonderoga
Gillespie Gap, 387–88, *391*
Gilman, Nicholas, Jr., 65–66
Gloucester, 64
Glover, John, 63, 215
Glover's Rock, 215
Glover's Wharf, 63
Gnadenhütten, 511–12, *511*
Goddard, Katherine, 328–29
Golden Plough Tavern, 335
Gomez-Ecker Mill House, 259–60
Goschachgunk and Lichtenau, 512
Governor John Wentworth House, 68
Governors Island, 201, 206, 242–43, *243*
Graff House, 297–98
grave of unknown Patriot soldier, 475
Graves, Thomas, 440, 478–79
Great Bridge, 145, 473, 476–77
Great Britain, 537–41
Great Carrying Place 107–9
Green End Fortifications, 50, *53*
Green Mountain Boys, 101; Battle of Longue-Pointe and, 116; Bennington and, 151; Crown Point and, 164; Fort Ticonderoga and, 142; Green Mountain Tavern and, 169; Hubbardton and, 147; Longueuil and, 129–30
Green Mountain Tavern, 169
Green Spring, 475–76
Green-Wood Cemetery, 209
Greene, Nathanael, 426–27; Bogart's Tavern and, 280; Brandywine and, 301; Bunker Hill and, 30; Camden and, 379–80; Cowpens and, 384–94; Dan and, 395–96; Eutaw Springs and, 404; Fort Washington and, 219–21; Germantown and, 306–8; Guilford Courthouse and, 425, 433–36; Hale-Byrnes House and, 324; homestead of, 79–80; John Tillinghast House, 43; Joshua Loring House and, 45; Nathanael Greene Monument and, 357; New Brunswick and, 277; Ninety Six, 373–74; Pegues Place and, 408; statue of, 457; Trenton and, 226–30; Troublesome Creek Ironworks and, 467–68; Valley Forge and, 310; west and, 350; Yorktown and, 425
Greenfield Hall, 319
Grey, Charles, 86–88, 268, 340–41
Grubb, Peter, 338
Grubb, Samuel, 338
Guilford Courthouse, 423–25, 432–36, *434*
Gulf Coast, 520
Gunpowder Falls State Park, 326
Gunpowder Incident, 442–43
Gunston Hall, 486–87, *487*
Gwynn's Island and Cricket Hill, 479–80, *480*

H

Haddonfield, 319
Haitian Monument, 357
Hale, Nathan, 74–75s, *422*, 457–58
Hale-Byrnes House, 324
Halifax, 468–69, 541
Hall, Lyman, 398
Hamilton, Alexander: Fishkill Supply Depot and, 257; Hamilton Grange National Memorial, 248–49, *249*; Morristown and, 235; Princeton and, 232; Ringwood Manor and, 268; Schuyler-Hamilton House and, 237; Trinity Church Cemetery and, 245; Van Wyck Homestead and, 257; Weehawken and, 270–71, *271*; Yorktown and, 440–41
Hamilton, Henry, 500–501

Hamilton, James, Saratoga and, 154
Hampton National Historical Site, 327, *327*
Hampton Roads Naval Museum, 477, 479
Hancock, John, 7, 9; Hancock-Clarke House and, 25; Lexington and, 20, 22; Old Granary Burying Ground and, 15; Old State House and, 13; taxation and, 5
Hancock, William, 320
Hancock House, 320–21, *321*
Hancock-Clarke House, 25
Hanging Rock, 409–10, *410*, 411
Hannah (schooner), 63
Hannastown, 509
harbor cruises, 54
Harbor Defense Museum, *207*, 208
Hard Winter, 235–36
Harlem Heights, 213, *217*
Harrod, James, 504
Hartley, David, Hotel d'York and, 531
Hasbrouck House, 262, *264*
Hemings, Sally, 447
Henry, Dorothea, 469
Henry, Patrick, 443; home of, 445–446, *445*; Kaskaskia and, 500; on liberty, 472; Patrick Henry National Memorial and, 469; St. John's Episcopal Church and, *473*
Heritage Park, 50
Herkimer, Nicholas, 160–63, 186–87, *187*
Hessians, 230; Albany and, 137; Battle of Hubbardton and, 147–48; Battle of Rhode Island and, 38; Bennington and, 150–51; Fort Mercer and, 316; Fort Ticonderoga and, 144; Fort Tryon and, 221; Fort Washington and, 219–20; Germantown and, 306, 307; Hessian Barracks, 332–33; Mount Holly and, 320; Portsmouth Meeting House and, 85; Saratoga and, 154–55; Trenton and, 226–27; White Plains and, 216
Heyward, Thomas, 527
Hill, Daniel Harvey, 412
Hill, William, 411–12
Hillman Hospital House, 318–19
Hill's Ironworks, 411–12
HMS *Acteon*, 367
HMS *Bristol*, 362, 366
HMS *Eagle*, 211
HMS *Experiment*, 362, 366
HMS *Falcon*, 64
HMS *Glasgow*, 78
HMS *Hinchinbrook*, 530–31
HMS *Serapis*, 540
HMS *Somerset*, 89–90, *90*
Hobkirk Hill, 377, 379–80, *380*
Hope Furnace, 80–81
Hopewell Museum, 505–6
Hopewell Village and Furnace, 338–39
Horn Work, 363–64, 369, *370*
Hôtel Amelot de Bisseuil, 532
Hotel de Valentinois, Paris, 532
Hotel des Ambassadeurs de Hollande, Paris, 532
Hotel d'York, Paris, 531–32
House in the Horseshoe State Historic Site, 464–65
Howe, George, 203
Howe, Richard, 38, 203, 211, 273–74
Howe, Robert, 354–60
Howe, William, 203; Battle of Brooklyn and, 205–7; Boston and, evacuation of, 18; Brandywine and, 286, 294–305; Bunker Hill and, 16–18, 29; endgame strategy and, 137–39; Fort Washington and, 219–21; Kip's Bay, 211–12; Monmouth and, 312; Oak Tree Engagement and, 278; Pell's Point and, 214–15; Philadelphia and, 286–87, 293; Trenton and, 225–30; White Plains and, 215–16; Whitemarsh and, 343; St. James Church and, 241

Hubbardton, *146*, 147–49
Huck, Christian, 412
Hunter, William, 39
Hunter House, 39
Hunter's Iron Works, 481
Huntington, Samuel, 76
Huntington Homestead Museum, 76
Hutchinson Island View, 356

I

Independence Hall, *292*, *293*, 296
Independence National Historic Park, 296
India, 542
Indian King Tavern, 319
Inflexible (schooner), 120
Intolerable Acts in 1774, 5
iron industry, Pennsylvania and, 338
Iron Works Hill, 320
Iroquois: Fort Chambly National Historic Site and, 131; Fort Dayton and, 187; Fort Niagara and, 176; Fort St. Joseph and, 498; Fort Stanwix and, 158–60; Iroquois Confederacy, 184; Newtown and, 180; Onondaga Creek, 181–83; Sharon Springs and, 194–95; Skä-noñh—Great Law of Peace Center, 182–83, *182*; William Johnson and, 192
Isaac Royall House, 58
Isle aux Noix, 121, 131, 132–33

J

Jackson, Andrew, 410, 455
Jacob Arnold House, 236
Jacob Purdy House, 216
Jacobus Vanderveer House, 276–77
Jarvis, Leonard, 87
Jason Russell House, 26
Jay, John, 255, 531
Jefferson, Thomas, 288–89; Jefferson Memorial, 452–53, *453*; France and, 531; Graff House and, 297–98; Gwynn's Island Museum and, 480; George Mason and, 486; Monticello and, 446–48; Poplar Forest and, 469–70; Second Continental Congress and, 292
Jenkin's Fort, 282
Jersey (prison ship), 241
Jerusalem Lutheran Church, 400
Jerusalem Mill, 326
Jewish home, oldest in North America, 259
John Bannister House, 42–43, *44*
John Brinckerhoff House, 258
John Burgwin House, 459, *460*
John Cabot House, 63
John Dickinson Plantation, 323
John Ellison House, 262–63
John Jay Homestead State Historic Site, 255
John Marshall House, 473–74
John Tillinghast House, 43
Johnson, John, 189–90
Johnson, William, 160, 192–93
Johnson Ferry House, 228
Johnson Hall, 192–93, *192*
Johnston, Augustus, 42
Johnstown, 191–92
"Join, or Die," 20–21
Jones, John Paul, 332, 458, 540
Joseph Purdy Homestead, 254
Joseph Webb House, 71
Joshua Loring House, 45
Journal of the American Revolution, xi–xii

K

Kanowarohare. *See* Oneida Castle
Kaskaskia, 500, *501*
Kaskaskia-Cahokia Trail, 500
Kedges Straits, 483
Keeler Tavern, 252–53

Kemp's Landing, 478
Kenmore Mansion, 482
Kentucky, 502–3
Kettle Creek, 347, 396–97
Keys, Francis Scott, 330
King Park, 49
King Philip's War, 84
King's Ferry, 257
Kings Mountain, 350, 380–84, *381*, 386, 389, *391*
Kingston, 258–59, 279, 485–86
Kip's Bay, 211–12, *217*
Klock's Field, 189–90
Knox, Henry: Boston artillery and, 142; Cliveden and, 308; Dorchester Heights and, 17–18; Jacobus Vanderveer House and, 277; John Ellison House and, 262; Ogden Farm and, 237; Trenton and, 226–30
Knyphausen, Wilhelm von, 219–20, 300
Kosciuszko, Thaddeus, 300; John Tillinghast House and, 43; Ninety Six, 373; Saratoga and, 153; statue of, 458; West Point and, 260

L

La Salle, 176
Ladd-Gilman House, 66
Lafayette, Marie-Joseph Paul Yves Roch Gilbert du Motier, Marquis de La Fayette, 289–90; Barren Hill and, 344; battle of Rhode Island and, 38; Belvoir and, 330, *330*; Durfee and, 88–89; George Mason Memorial and, 454; Green Spring and, 475; Hale-Byrnes House and, 324; John Tillinghast House and, 43; Lafayette Square, 455, 458; Lafayette-Durfee House, 88–89; Picpus Cemetery and, 532–33; Shirley-Eustis House and, 46; statue of, 458; Tiverton Four Corners, 86; Van Wyck Homestead and, 257; Vernon House and, 42; Yorktown and, 438–39
Lake Champlain, 117–23, *126*
Lake Champlain Maritime Museum, 125
Lake Champlain Navy Memorial, 124–25
Lake George Battlefield Park, 168
Lamson, Samuel, 59
Lancaster County Courthouse, 335–36
Landlord Fay's Tavern, 169
Land's Ford, 411
Learned, Ebenezer, 156
Ledyard, William, 77
Lee (schooner), 64
Lee, Arthur, 71
Lee, Charles, 85, 313–15, 351, 361
Lee, Ezra, 211
Lee, Henry "Light Horse Harry:" Augusta, 397; Bell's Mill and, 465; Paulus Hook and, 272; Pyle's Defeat and, 467; Santee Indian Mound and, 406
Lee, James, 462–63
Lee, Richard Henry, 292
Lefferts Homestead, 208–9
Lehigh Hill, 51
"Letters from a Pennsylvania Farmer" (Dickinson), 323
Leutze, Emanuel, 228
Lewis, Fielding, 481
Lewis, Meriwether, 493
Lewiston Portage Landing, 175–76
Lexington, 6, 16, 18–27, *22*; Ephraim Parker, 61; Portsmouth Alarm and, 69; Samuel Lamson and, 59; Weston Twon Common and, 59
Liberty Bell, *293*, 296–97
"Liberty Bell of the West," 500, *501*
lighthouses: Beavertail Lighthouse, 48, *52*; Boston Light, 47; cruise and, 54; Poplar Point, 79; Portsmouth, 69; Sandy Hook 279

Lincoln, Benjamin: Camden and, 374; Charleston and, 367–71; Saratoga and, 153–55; Sheldon Church and, 401; Stono Ferry and, 403; Yorktown and, 442
Lindens, The, 459
Livingston, Robert, 292
Livingston, William, 245
Logan, Benjamin, 503
Logan, Jonathan, 275–76
Logan's Fort, 503
Lone Sailor (statue), 125, *126*
Long Island Flats, 419
Longfellow, Henry Wadsworth, 8, 14, 26, 57
Longueuil, 129–30
Lord Dunmore's war, 493
Louis XVI, 518–19
Lovell, Solomon, 100
Lucas-Johnston House, 42
Ludington, Sybil, 252
Luzerne County Historical Society Museum, 282

M

Mabie's Tavern, 266
MacDonald, Donald, 430–31
Mackinac Straits, 491
Madison, Dolley, 32, 445, 448–49
Madison, James, 448–50
Magna Carta, National Archives Museum and, 455–56
Majoribanks, John, 404–5
Marblehead, 61
Marcha de Gálvez (sculpture), 521
Marion, Francis "Swamp Fox," 351–52, 405–7
Marion Square, 363
Marshall, John, 473–74
Martha's Vineyard, 88
Martin, Josiah, 429, 461
Martin's Station, 505–6

Maryland Journal, and Baltimore Advertiser (newspaper), 328
Maryland School for the Deaf, 332
Maryland State House, 330–31, *331*
Mason, George, 453–54, 486–87
Masons, 66–67
Massachusetts Colonial State House, 12–13, *15*
Massasoit (Chief), 84
Mawhood, Charles, 320, 231–32
Mayflower (ship), 33, 36
Mayham Tower, 397
McConkey's Ferry Inn, 226, 228
McCrea, Jane, 152, 168
McCullough Samuel, 510
McDowell, Charles, 382, 387
McDowell, Joseph, 414–15
McGary, Hugh, 506
McIntosh, John, 400
McIntosh, Lachlan, 512
McLean, Francis, 100
Memorial to the 56 Signers of the Declaration of Independence, 454, *455*
Menominee, 495
Menorca, 536–37
Mercer, Hugh, 231, 273, 482
Mercer Oak, 233
Merchants and Drovers Tavern, 278–79
Metacomet (Philip), 84
Metuchen Meeting House (Oak Tree), 278
Miantonomi Fortifications, 50
Middlebrook Cantonment, 276
Middleton, Arthur, 527
Mifflin, Thomas, 56
Military Road from Fort Edward to Lake George, 168
Mill Hill Park, 229
Miller, Nathan 84
Mills, Robert, 329
Minerva, statue of, 209
Mingo tribe, 510

Minute Man National Historical Park, 24
minutemen, 20; Buckman Tavern and, 25; Concord, 26; Fitch Tavern and, 60; Provincial Powder House and, 58; Weston Town Common and, 59
Mobile, 523–24
Mobile Museum of History, 524
Mobile Village, 525
Mohawk Valley, 156–61, 164; Walter Bennet and, 191; Brant and, 183, 186; Canajoharie District and, 190; Fort Dayton and, 187; Fort Plain Museum and, 190–91, *191*; John Johnson and, 188; Johnson Hall and, 192–93; Johnstown and, 191; Klock and, 189; John Ross and, 191; Steuben and, 185; things to know, 141; Marinus Willett and, 191, 195
Mohawks, 160–63, 186, 192. *See also* Joseph Brant
Monmouth, 235, 287, 290, 311–15, *313*
Monroe, James, 228
Montgomery, Richard: Château Ramezay and, 118; Fort Chambly and, 130; Montgomery Burial Place, 113; Montgomery House Site, 113; Montreal and, 115–17; Quebec and, 95, 112–15
Monticello, 446–48, *447*
Montour, Esther "Queen Esther," 282
Montpelier, 448–50, *449*, 450
Montreal, 95, 105, 115–19, 135
Montresor's Island, 214
Moore, James, 430
Moore, John, 60
Moore House, 438, 441
Moores Creek, 361, 429–33, *431*
Morgan, Daniel, 96–97; Camden and, 375; Cowpens and, 350, 384–94; Dan and, 395–96; Guilford

Courthouse and, 433; Quebec, 107, 115; Saratoga and, 154–56
Morris, James, 342–43
Morris, Roger, 213
Morris-Jumel Mansion, 213
Morristown, 232–36, *234*
Moultrie, William, 362, 367
Mount Defiance, 143–45, *144*
Mount Holly, 320
Mount Hope Farm, 84
Mount Independence, 143–45, *146*
Mount Vernon, 202, 449–52, *451*
Munroe Tavern, 25–26
Murray, Mary Lindley, 212
Musée du Fort, 113
Museum of Newport History at the Brick Market, 40
Museum of the American Revolution, 298, *302*
Musgrove Mill, 414–15, *421*
Mystic Seaport Museum, 33–36, *35*

N

Nancy (ordnance brig), 64
Nantasket Road, 54
Nassau Hall, 232–33
Nathan Hale Homestead, 74–75
Nathan Tufts Park, 59
Nathanael Greene Homestead, 79–80
Nathanael Greene Monument, 357
National Archives Museum, 455–56
National Constitution Center, 298–99, *302*
National Portrait Gallery, 456, *456*
National Purple Heat Hall of Honor, 262
Native American perspective, 141
"Navy's Capital, The," 477
Nelson, Horatio, 542
New Bedford / Fair Haven / Fort Phoenix, 86–88, *87*
New Bridge, 269

New Brunswick, 277
New Castle, 66, 69
New Castle Court House Museum, 322–23
New Ebenezer, 399–400
New Hampshire, 67
New Haven, 69–71, *70*
New London, 76-77
New Orleans, 521–23
New River Trail State Park, 415
New Windsor Cantonment, 261–62, *264*
New York, where to stay, 283
Newburgh Addresses, 261, 263
Newburgh Docks, 263
Newburyport, 65
Newport, 37–45, 48–49
Newport Jazz Festival, 48–49
Newtown, 180–81, *180*, 281
Niagara Portage Road, 175–76
Nicaragua, 541–42
Nikwasi (Nequasse), 417
Ninety Six, 371–74, *372*, 397
Noddle's Island, Fort Strong and, 54
Norfolk, 477–78
North (Prime Minister Lord), 538
North Battery, 49–50
North Carolina History Center, 461
North Salem Town Hall, 254
Northampton Iron Works, 326–27
Northup, Solomon, 169
Nova Scotia, 541
numbers, names, and terms, a note on, xvi
Nutt, Anna, 339
Nutting, Wallace, 72

O

Oak Grove, 463–64
Oak Tree Engagement, 278
Oak Tree Pond Historic Park, 278
O'Brien, Jeremiah, 127
Odawa, 495

Odell House, 251
Ogden Farm, 237
O'Hara, Charles, 442
Ohio Country, The, 508, 511–15
Ojibwa, 495
Old Barracks Museum, 229
Old Cambridge and Cambridge Common Encampment, 55, *56*
Old Constitution House State Historic Site, *170*, 171
Old Exchange, *362*, 364
Old Fort, 418–19
Old Fort Western, 106–7, *108*
Old Granary Burying Ground, 7, *15*
"Old Ironsides," 61–62
Old Mastic House, 238
Old New-Gate Prison & Copper Mine, 73–74, *73*
Old North Church, 14, 21
Old Presbyterian Meeting House, 487
Old '76 House, The, 266
Old South Meeting House, 11, 12
Old Stone Chimney, 175
Old Stone Fort Museum Complex, 188
Old Stone House, 208
Old Tappan, 268
Olentangy memorial, 513
Oliver Hazard Perry House, 40
Olmsted, Frederick Lay, 329
"100 Best American Revolution Books of All Time, The," xi–xii
Oneida, the, 183, 184, 186
Oneida Carrying Place, 157
Oneida Castle, 183
"one life to lose," 74
Onondaga Creek, 181–83
Oriskany, 139, 160–63, *162*, 184, 187
Otis, James, taxation and, 5
Overing, Nicholas, 85
Overing Farm, 85
Overmountain Men, 350; Biggerstaff Old Fields, 389–90; Gilbert Town and, 389; Gillespie Gap, 387–88,

391; Kings Mountain and, 382–84, 386; Sycamore Shoals and, 387
Overmountain Victory National Historic Trail, 386, 390

P

Paine, Thomas, 201
Palace of Westminster, London, 538–39
Palatine Church, 190
Paoli, 268, *284*, 305, 306, 340–41, *342*
Paoli Massacre, 268, *284*, 306
Parker, Ephraim, 60–61
Parker, Peter, 362
Parker's Revenge, 24
Parker Tavern, 60–61
Patrick Henry National Memorial, 469
Patrick Smyth House, 169
Patriots Park, 51
Paul Pritchard Shipyard, 365
Paul Revere House, 14
Paulus Hook, 272
Payne, John, Scotchtown and, 445
Pegues Place, 407–8
Pell's Point, 214–15, *218*
Penelope Barker House, 462, *463*
Penn, William, 299, *323*
Pennsylvania Frontier, 508
Penobscot Bay, 99–100
Penobscot Bay Expedition, 99–101, 102
Penobscot Marine Museum, 102
Penobscot Narrows Bridge Observatory, 103
Penobscot River, *99*
Penobscot River Overlook, 102
Pensacola, 525–26
Percy, Hugh, Fort Washington and, 219–20
Perry, Oliver Hazard, 40
Peter Wentz Homestead, 341–42
Petersburg, 470–71, *471*
Phelps, John, 74

Philadelphia, 291–94, *292*, 344
Philadelphia (gondola), 122, 125, *126*
Philip (Metacomet), 84
Philipse Manor Hall, 249–50, *250*
Phillips, William, 471–72
Pickens, Andrew, 352, 397, 417–18
Picpus Cemetery, Paris, 532–33
Pigot, Robert, 37
Pinckney, Charles, 365
Piqua, 514–15, *514*
Piscataway, 277
Pittston Fort, 282
Plantation No. 4, 172
plantations, 444–51
Pleasant Hall, 478
Pluckemin Artillery Cantonment, 276–77
Point of Fork, 480–81
Point Pleasant, *490*
Pollock, Oliver, 522
Ponkiesburg Fort, 209
Pontiac's War, 498
Pooles Island, 328
Poor, Enoch, 155
Poor Richard's Almanack (Franklin), 288
Poplar Forest, 469–70, *470*
Poplar Point, 79
Poplar Point Lighthouse, 79
Port Tobacco, 484
Portsmouth Alarm, 69
Portsmouth Friends Meetinghouse and Parsonage, 84–85
Potts, Isaac, 309
"powder alarms," 18, 58
Powder Magazine, 364
Prescott, Richard, 42–43, *44*, 85
Prescott, Samuel, 22
Prescott, William, *28*, 29, 31
Prescott Farm, 85
Pres-de-Ville Barricade Site, 112
Prevost, Augustine, 358, 367, 402–3
Prince of Wales Redoubt, 525
Princeton, 228, 230–33, *231*, 233

Princeton Battle Monument Historic Site, 233
Princeton Battlefield State Park, 233
Principio Furnace, 325–26
prison camp, 334–35
Prison Ship Martyrs' Monument, 241–42, *242*
Pritchard, Paul, 365
Privateer Trail, The, 64
privateering: Benedict Arnold and, 76–77; Beverly and, 63–65; Offin Boardman and, 65; Fells Point and, 328; Martha's Vineyard and, 88; New London Harbor and, 76; Newburyport and, 65; Westport Point and, 86
Proclamation of 1763, 492, *493*
Provincial Congress, 57, 65, 244, 468
Provincial Powder House, 18, 56, 58–59, *59*, 68
Pulaski, Casimir, 350–51; Charleston and, 367; Pulaski Monument, 356, *357*; Savannah and, 359–60; statue of, 458
Purdy, Joseph, 254
Purple Heart, 66, 239, 262
Putnam, Israel, 55, 242, 253–54
Pyle, John, 467
Pyle's Defeat, 467, *468*

Q

Quaker Hill, 38, 51, 85
Quaker Meadows, 382, 388
Quebec City, 95–96, 105–6, 110–19, *111*, 128, 134–35
Queen Esther, 282
Queen's Rangers, 240
Queen's Redoubt, 525–26

R

Rahway (Spanktown), 278–79
Rall, Johann Gottlieb, 225–30
Ralston Gristmill, 275–76

Ramsour's Mill, 413, *413*
Rawdon, Francis, 379–80
Raynham Hall, 239–41
Reading, Parker Tavern and, 61
Rebecca (sloop), 530–31
Red Bank Battlefield Park, 316, *316*
Red Hill, 469
Regulators, 430, 466–67
Report to Congress on the Historic Preservation of Revolutionary War and War of 1812 Sites in the United States, xii
Revere, Paul, 7–8; Hancock-Clarke House and, 25; Massachusetts Colonial State House and, 13; Minute Man National Historic Park and, 24; Old Granary Burying Ground and, *15*; Paul Revere House and, 14; Penobscot Bay Expedition and, 100; Portsmouth and, 69; ride of, 21–22; *Somerset* and, 89
Reverend Apthorp House, 55–956
Revolutionary War and War of 1812 Historic Preservation Study Act of 1996, xiii
Revolutionary War Office, 75–76
Revolutionary War Statues, 457
Rhode Island Colonial State House, 40–41
Ridgefield, 252–53
Ridgely, Charles, 326–27
Riedesel (Friedrich Adolph), 144, 147–48, 154
Ring Fight (Tamassee), 417–18
Ringwood Manor and Iron Works, 268
Rivington's Print Shop, 246–47
Rochambeau (Jean Baptiste Donatien de Vimeur, comte de Rochambeau), 428; Bedford Green and, 255; Belvoir, 329; Chesapeake Capes and, 478–79; Joseph Webb house and, 72; Newport and, 45; North Salem Town Hall and, 254;

Odell House and, 251; Charles O'Hara and, 442; Rochambeau Monument, 49; statue of, 458; Vernon House and, 42; Washington-Rochambeau Revolutionary Route National Historic Trail, 439; Waterman Tavern and, 80; Williamsburg and, 440; Yorktown and, 437
Rockefeller, John D., Jr., 443
Rockingham State Historic Site, 279
Roderigue Hortalez and Company, 532
Roger Williams National Memorial, 82–83
Ross, Betsy, 299
Ross, John, 186, 191–92, 329
Roxbury High Fort, 45–46, *46*
Roxbury Line, 45
Royal Palace of Aranjuez, 535, *536*
Royal Palace of Madrid, 534, *535*
Royal Savage (schooner), 121–22
Royall, Isaac, 58, 84
Ruddell's Station, 505
Rush-Bagot Treaty, 177
Russell, Jason, 26
Rutledge, Edward, Jr., 274, 527
Rutledge, John, 368

S

Sag Harbor Village, 236–37
Salem, 62–63
Salem County Militia, 320
Saltonstall, Dudley, 100–101
Samptown, 278
Sandy Hook Lighthouse, 279
Santee Indian Mound, 405, *406*
Saratoga, 151–56, *153*; American victory at, 139; Arnold and, 96; Bennington and, 172; Burgoyne and, 139; Fort Stanwix and, 160; Forts Clinton and Montgomery and, 260; Franco-American alliance and, 37, 442, 517, 519; Horatio Gates and, 139–40, 374; Morgan and, 97; Peter Wentz Homestead and, 342; Saratoga National Historical Park, 141, 157; Schuyler Flatts and, 174; things to know, 141
Sasquatch capital, 166
Sault-au-Matelot Barricade Site, 112
Savannah, 353–60
Savannah Barracks Site, 358
Savannah History Museum, *354*, 356
Scarborough Castle, 541
Schoharie Lower Fort, 188, *189*
Schoharie Middle Fort, 188
Schuyler, Elizabeth, 237
Schuyler, Hon Yost, 159–60
Schuyler, Philip: Bennington and, 148–51; Canada, invasion of, 95; Fort Dayton and, 187; Fort Stanwix and, 159; Fort Ticonderoga and, 143; Patrick Smyth House and, 169; Philip Schuyler house and, 157; Quebec and, 105–6; Saratoga, 140, 152–53; Valcour Island and Lake Champlain and, 118–23
Schuyler Flatts, 173–74
Schuyler-Hamilton House, 237
Scituate, 81
Scotchtown, 445–46, *445*
Scottish Highlanders, 430, 432
Seaton Creek Historic Preserve, 529
Second Continental Congress: Christ Church and, 299; City Tavern and, 298; Declaration of Independence and, 292; Fraunces Tavern and, 244; Hancock and, 7; Independence Hall and, 296; John Jay and, 255; Jefferson and, 289; Philadelphia and, 285; Washington and, 202
Seneca tribe, 282, 509
Seven Years' War (French and Indian War), 3, 89, 354, 517–18
Sevier, John, 382–84, 386, 387
Shako:wi Cultural Center, 141, 183

Sharon Springs, 194–95
Shawnee: Fort Harrod and, 504; Fort Henry and, 510; Fort Randolph and, 507–8; Logan's Fort and, 503; Lord Dunmore's War and, 493; Piqua and, 514–15
Shelby, Isaac, 381–84, 386, 387
Sheldon Church, 400–401, *402*
Sherman, Richard, 292
Shippen, Peggy, 474
Shirley, William, 46
Shirley-Eustis House, 46–47
"shot heard 'round the world, the," 24, 26, 60
Signers' Hall, 299
Signers Memorial, 454, *455*
Signers' Monument, 398
Silliman, Gold Selleck, 252
Simcoe, John Grave, 481
Simcoe, Robert Graves, 240
Sitting Bull, 498
Skä-noñh—Great Law of Peace Center, 141, 182–83, *182*
Skene, Philip, 119–20
Skenesborough, 120, 144, 147, 165–67, *166*
Smallwood, William, 306
Smith's Ferry, 463
Smithsonian National Museum of American History, 457
Smyth, Patrick, 169
Snow's Island, 407
Somerset Place State Historic Site, 461–62
Sons of Liberty: Concord and, 20–21; French Soldiers and Sailors Monument and, 332; Lexington and, 20–21; Portsmouth Alarm and, 69; Provincial Powder House and, 58; Paul Revere and, 8
Spain, 534–37; American Revolution and, 517; Florida and, 519; Fort Carlos III and, 520; Treaty of Paris and, 531

Speaker's Corner, 12
Spell Hall, 80
Split Rock, 215
Spring Hill Redoubt, *354*, 356, 359–60
Springfield, 274
St. Augustine, 526–30
St. Clair, Arthur, 143–44, 147, 263
St. George's Chapel, 539–40
St. Ignatius Catholic Church, 484
St. James Church, 241
St. John's Episcopal Church, 472–73, *473*
St. John's First Nations, 57
St. Leger, Barry, 137, 139, 156–60, 178–79
St. Louis, 498–99
St. Mark's Cemetery, 256
St. Thomas Manor, 484
Stafford Hollow Furnaces, 74
Stage Fort Park, 64
Stamp Act, 5–6, 31, 42, 67
Star Fort, 372–74
Stark, John: Benington and, 149–52; Crown Point Military Road and, 171; Fort at No. 4 and, 172; Isaac Royall House and, 58; Mount Hope Farm and, 84
"Star-Spangled Banner, The" (Keys), 330
state constitution, first, 65
Stavers, John, 66–67
Stavers' Tavern, 66–67
Stephens, Adam, 303
Steuben (Friedrich Wilhelm), 310, 311; John Tillinghast House and, 43; Petersburg and, 471; Point of Fork and, 481; statue of, 458; Steuben House, 269; Steuben Memorial State Historic Site, 185–86, *185*; Yorktown and, 438–39
Stirling (William Alexander): Battle Hill and, 209; Battle of Brooklyn and, 207; Battle of Connecticut Farms and, 274; Brandywine and,

303; Green-Wood Cemetery and, 209; Newtown and, 281; Trinity Church Cemetery and, 245
Stone, Thomas, 484–85
Stone Arabia, 188–89
Stono Ferry, 368, 402–3
Stony Point, 222–24, *222*, 257
Stoughtonham Furnace, 91
Strawberry Banke Museum, 67, *68*
Strode's Mill, 337
Sugar Act, 5–7
Sullivan, John: Battle of Germantown and, 306; Battle of Rhode Island and, 37–38; Brandywine and, 303; Fort Chambly and, 131; Hale-Byrnes House and, 324; Mount Hope Farm and, 84; Newtown and, 180–81; Sullivan-Clinton Campaign, 176, 181; Trenton and, 226–30; Trois-Rivières and, 128
Sumter, Thomas "Carolina Gamecock," 409–11, 414
Sycamore Shoals, 382, 386, 387, *392*
synagogue, Touro Synagogue, 41, *41*

T

Tarleton, Banastre, 351; Battle of Cowpens and, 350; Blackstock's Plantation and, 414; Camden and, 379, 390; Cowpens and, 392–94; Fishing Creek and, 411; Hill's Ironworks and, 412; Pyle's Defeat and, 467; Waxhaws and, 408–9
Tatnall, Joseph, 322
taxation, 3–5
Taylor's Mill, 462–63
Tea Act, 6, 11, 14
Tecumseh, Piqua and, 515
Thaddeus Kosciuszko National Memorial, 300
3rd Continental Light Dragoons, 268–69
Thomas, John, 128, 131

Thomas Clarke House, *231*, 233
Thomas Creek, 529
Thomas Smith House, 319–20
Thomas Stone National Historic Site, 484–85, *485*
Thompson, William, 128, 131
Thompson-Neely House, 228
Thomson Park, 363
Thunderer (radeau), 120
Tiverton Four Corners, 86
Todd, John, 506
tolerance, 82
Tomb of the Unknown Patriot, 513
Tomb of the Unknown Soldier of the Revolution (Alexandria), 487
Tomb of the Unknown Soldier of the Revolution (Philadelphia) 300–301, *304*
Touro Synagogue, 41, *44*
town names, xvi
Townsend, Robert, 240–41
Townsend, Samuel, 239–40
Townshend Acts, 323
Tracy, Nathaniel, 65
treaty, first US, 57
Treaty of Paris: Franklin and, 288; George William Frederick and, 518; Hotel d'York and, 531; John Jay and, 255; Maryland State House and, 330–31; Rockingham State Historic Site and, 279; Spain and, 519, 520; Versailles and, 533
Trenton, 201, 224–32, *225*, *227*; Greene and, 426–27; Marblehead and, 61; Trenton Battle Monument Historic Site, 229
Trigg, Stephen, 506
Trinity Church Cemetery, 213, 245
Trois-Rivières, 128, 131
Troublesome Creek Ironworks, 467–68
Trumbull, John, 251
Trumbull, Jonathan, 75–76
Tryon, William, 69–70, 252, 461, 466
Tryon County Militia, 159, 187

Tryon Palace, 461
Tuckahoe Wildlife Management Area, 399
Tu-Endie-Wei State Park, 508
Turkey Hill, 38
Turn: Washington's Spies (TV series), 241
Turtle (submersible), 211
Twelve Years a Slave (Northup), 169

U

United States Constitution, 7, 66, 364, 454–55
United States Naval Academy Museum, 331–32
United States Navy: John Adams and, 33; birthplace of, 165–67; Fort O'Brien and, 127; Lake Champlain Navy Memorial and, 124; Penobscot Bay Expedition and, 99; privateering and, 63; Whitehaven and, 540
USS *Constitution*, 61–62
USS *Ranger*, 540
USS *Ticonderoga*, 166
USS *Wisconsin*, 477

V

Valcour Island, 95, 117–25, *119*, 143
valentine, first, 240
Valley Forge, 287, 309–12, *310*; Baren Hill and, 344; Monmouth and, 314; the Oneida and, 184; Strode's Mill and, 337
Van Gaasbeek, Abraham, 258–59
Van Schaick, Goose, 181–83
Van Wyck Homestead, 257–58
Vanderbilts, 39
Vanderveer, Jacobus, 276–77
Varnum, James Mitchell, 79
Vernon, William, 42

Vernon House, 42
Verplanck's Point, 257
Verrazano-Narrows Bridge, *205*
Versailles, *516*, 519, 531, 533–34, *533*
Vincennes, 492, 500–502
Von Donop, Car von, 316–17
Von Donop, Kurt von, 320

W

Wallace House, 276
Walnut Street Prison, 300–301
Walton, George, 398
Wampanoag tribe, 84
Wanton, Joseph, 39
Ward, Artemas, 458
Warner, Seth: Bennington and, 151; Crown Point and, 164; Hubbardton and, 147; Longueuil and, 129–30
Warwick Furnace, 339–40, *341*
Washington (galley), 122
Washington, Augustine, 482–83
Washington, George, 202–3; John Andre and, 267; Badge of Military Merit and, 239; Baltimore Washington Monument and, 329–30, *330*; Battle of Brooklyn and, 206–10; Battle of the Short Hills and, 278; John Berrien and, 279; birthplace of, 482–83; Brandywine Village, 322; Brinckerhoff House and, 258; Christ Church and, 299; Cobble Hill Fort, 209; commission, resignation of, 330; Continental Army, farewell address to, 279; Culper Spy Ring and, 240–41; DeWint House and, 267; Durham boat and, 280; Falmouth and, 123; Federal Hall and, 245–46, *246*; Ferry Farm, 482; first white house and, 294, 297; Fishkill Supply Depot and, 257;

Fort Washington and, 219–21; Fraunces Tavern, 244; George Emlen House and, 343; George Washington Birthplace National Monument, 482–83; Germantown and, 286, 305–6; *Hannah* and, 63; Hasbrouck House and, 262; Iroquois and, 180; Jacob Purdy House and, 216; Joseph Webb and, 71–72; Henry Knox and, 17; Longfellow House and, 57; Maryland State House and, 330, *331*; Monmouth and, 314; Morristown and, 234; Mount Vernon and, 449–51; New Hampshire Colonial State House and, 67; New Windsor Cantonment, 261–62; New York City and, 199; Newburgh Addresses and, 261; Newtown and, 180, 281; Oak Tree Engagement and, 278; Odell House and, 251; Ohio and, 512; Old Presbyterian Meeting House and, 487; Oneida and, 184; Peter Wentz Homestead and, 341–42; Philadelphia and, 294, 297; Princeton and, 230–32; Purple Heart and, 66; Quebec and, 94, 105; religious freedom and, 41; Ringwood Manor and, 268; Rochambeau and, 428; Philip Schuyler and, 105; statue of, 301, 458; Treaty of Paris and, 279; Trenton and, 224–30; Valley Forge and, 309–11; Van Wyck Homestead and, 257; Wallace House and, 276; West Point and, 260; Wilmington and, 321–22; Yorktown and, 437
Washington Crossing Historic Park, 228
Washington Crossing State Park, *225*, 228
Washington Crossing the Delaware (Leutze), 228
Washington, DC, 451–59
Washington Monument (Washington, DC), 451–52
Washington Monument (Baltimore), 329, *330*
Washington Monument Maryland State Park, 333–34, *333*
Washington Square (New York), 248
Washington Square (Philadelphia), 301, 304
Washington-Rochambeau Revolutionary Route National Historic Trail, 439
Waterman Tavern and Encampment, 80
Waxhaws, 408–9, *409*
Wayne, "Mad" Anthony: Brandywine and, 301, 322; Germantown and, 306–8; Green Spring and, 475; Hale-Byrnes House and, 324; Monmouth and, 313; Paoli and, 340; Stony Point and, 223, 257
Webb, Joseph, 71–72
Webb Deane Stevens Museum, 72
Weehawken, 270–71
Wentworth, John, 68–69
Wentz, Peter, 341–42
Wentz, Rosanna, 341–42
West, Stephen, 486
West Canada Creek, 186, 191
West Florida, 519–26
West Hartford Cantonment, 72
West Point Fortifications, 260
West Virginia, 502–3, 507, 510, 515
Westminster, 141, 203, 266, 538, *539*
Westmoreland History Education Center, 509
Weston Town Common, 59–60
Westover Plantation, 474–75
Westport Point, 86
whaling, 35, 86–87, 236
White Plains, 215–16, *217*, *218*
Whitehall. *See* Skenesborough

Whitehaven, 540
Whitemarsh (Chestnut Hill), 343
"whites of their eyes," 29
Wickford, 79
Wilhelm, Friedrich (Baron von Steuben), 185–86, *185*, 310, 311
Wilkes-Barre Fort, 282
Willet, Marinus, 186, 191–92, 194–95
William Brattle House, 56, 58
William Floyd Estate, 238
William Jasper Monument, 357
William Pitt Tavern, 66–67
Williams, Otho Holland, 395–96
Williams, Roger, 82–83
Williamsburg, 425, 440, 442–44, *443*
Wilmington: Brandywine and, 295, 321–22; Cornwallis and, 425, 436; Fort Watson and, 405; Guilford Courthouse and, 436; John Burgwin House and, 459–60; Moore's Creek and, 430
Winston, Joseph, 382
Winter Island Park, 63
Witherspoon, John, statue of, 458

Woodyard Plantation, 486
Wooster, David, 117–18, 130–31, 252–53
Wyandotte tribe, 510
Wyman, Isaac, 173
Wyman Tavern, 173
Wyoming Valley, 176, 180, 181, 282–83
Wythe, George, 473

Y

York County History Center's Colonial Complex, 335
York Courthouse, 334–35
Yorktown, 72, 423, 425, 436–42, *437*, *441*, 478
Yorktown Campaign, 72
Young, Joseph, 256

Z

Zabriskie, Jan, 269
Zane, Betty, 510